METHODS OF INTERREGIONAL A
REGIONAL ANALYSIS

For Barclay G. Jones
and
Benjamin H. Stevens

Methods of Interregional and Regional Analysis

WALTER ISARD
IWAN J. AZIS
MATTHEW P. DRENNAN
RONALD E. MILLER
SIDNEY SALTZMAN
ERIK THORBECKE

Ashgate

Aldershot • Brookfield USA • Singapore • Sydney

Published by
Ashgate Publishing Limited
Gower House
Croft Road
Aldershot
Hants GU11 3HR
England

Ashgate Publishing Company
Old Post Road
Brookfield
Vermont 05036
USA

British Library Cataloguing in Publication Data
Methods of interregional and regional analysis
   1.Regionalism
   I.Isard, Walter
   304.2'3

Library of Congress Catalog Card Number: 98-071955

Printed and bound in Great Britain by
MPG Books Ltd, Bodmin, Cornwall

Contents

References 240

6. Gravity and spatial interaction models **243**

6.0 Introduction 243
6.1 A simple probability point of view 244
6.2 Definition and measurement of mass 250
6.3 Definitions and measures of distance 253
6.4 Functional forms for spatial separation 253
6.5 Constrained gravity (spatial interaction) models 257
6.6 Calibration, tests and applications of spatial interaction models 263
    6.6.1 The use of OLS (ordinary least squares) to test the effect of distance, cooperation and hostility upon trade of nations 264
    6.6.2 The use of maximum likelihood in a policy oriented application with particular attention to characteristics of origins, destinations and types of distance (separation) measures 269
6.7 Conclusion 272
Endnotes 273
References 277

7. Social accounting matrices and social accounting analysis **281**

7.0 Introduction 281
7.1 The overall conceptual framework 283
7.2 Classification and disaggregation of accounts 293
    7.2.1 Production activities cum commodities 294
    7.2.2 Institutions 294
    7.2.3 Factors of production 296
7.3 Data requirements in the construction of a SAM 298
7.4 SAM multiplier analysis and extensions 300
    7.4.1 Unconstrained multipliers 300
    7.4.2 Constrained multipliers 306
    7.4.3 Structural path analysis and transmission of economic influence within the SAM framework 308
    7.4.4 SAM as the foundation of computable general equilibrium models 316
7.5 Studies and applications based on the SAM 317

Figures and tables

About the authors

Walter Isard, Professor Emeritus of Economics and Regional Science,
Cornell University

Iwan J. Azis, Visiting Professor of Regional Science, Cornell University and
Professor of Economics, University of Indonesia

Matthew P. Drennan, Professor of City and Regional Planning,
Cornell University

Ronald E. Miller, Professor Emeritus of Regional Science,
University of Pennsylvania

Sidney Saltzman, Professor of Regional Science and Planning,
Cornell University

Erik Thorbecke, H. Edward Babcock Professor of Economics and Food
Economics, Cornell University

Acknowledgments

In writing this book the authors wish to thank many scholars for recommendations on topics to be covered, suggestions for significant developments and writings in the field, and for critical but helpful comments. At the risk of failing to name all those to whom we are indebted, we note: Suarev Dev Bhatta, David E. Boyce, Steven B. Caldwell, A. Stewart Fotheringham, Eduardo Haddad, Geoffrey J. D. Hewings, Barclay G. Jones, Maureen Kilkenny, Jose Lobo, Joseph Mathews, Suahasil Nazara, Atsuyuki Okabe, David A. Plane, Adam Rose, Luis Santiago, Ashish Sen, Tony E. Smith, Benjamin H. Stevens, Michael Wegener and Masakazu Watanuki.

Extensive and careful typing was provided by Helena M. Wood and Gail A. Canterbury. In addition we were recipients of very fine technical typesetting by Henning Pape-Santos and excellent artwork by Helena M. Wood.

This book is dedicated to Barclay G. Jones and Benjamin H. Stevens. In their lifetimes, each has had an historic influence on the development of regional science. At Cornell University, Barclay G. Jones founded and nurtured over the years, graduate study in the field of regional science and organized its faculty. He effected a productive marriage of planning analysis and regional science and the many students he has had continue to pass on the fruits of this marriage throughout the world.

Benjamin H. Stevens contributed immensely to the development at the University of Pennsylvania of the regional science department in the early years when it confronted many difficulties. Of immeasurable value was his warmth and enthusiasm, and the stimulation and inspiration he provided graduate students and the faculty.

Preface

It has been 38 years since the 1960 book, *Methods of Regional Analysis: An Introduction to Regional Science*, was published. The writing of this book was motivated by the need to pull together at one place the diverse regional theories, hypotheses, concepts, techniques and tools existing in the social sciences, most of which were at an elementary/primitive level. Admittedly, at that time and earlier, except in sociology, regional analysis was close to the bottom rung in most areas of study. It was hoped that through discussions at the annual meetings of the newly formed Regional Science Association and the writing of a Methods book that the strengths of the diverse unconnected theories, concepts, techniques and tools could be joined. Thereby it was anticipated that a deeper understanding of regional phenomena could be achieved, and that there would evolve analytical methods of greater significance for coping with regional problems.

The book that resulted turned out to be successful in a number of respects, it being christened by some early graduate students as the 'bible' of regional science. Its very success contributed to the great advance of regional science scholarship. As a result the 1960 book has become obsolete as a text for incoming graduate students in regional science and related areas such as planning analysis and quantitative geography.

Recognition of this obsolesce led faculty at Cornell in 1995 to address the problem of the lack of teaching materials for incoming graduate students. They reached the decision that a new up-to-date methods text should be written. In their desire to have input from interested regional scholars from around the world they organized Thursday night sessions at the annual North American Regional Science Association meetings. Those in attendance were informed of the progress in writing of the text and were encouraged to point out shortcomings and gaps in the coverage of relevant materials and to make suggestions for the further development of the text and changes in emphasis and topics. A number of fruitful recommendations were received which have been incorporated in the finished product.

This 1998 book contrasts with the 1960 one. The latter was able to cover most if not all of the advanced material current in regional science and related fields. This 1998 one cannot do so today since over the years regional science has advanced to the stage where it can be said to be comparable in quality and depth of analysis to the best of the social sciences. Consequently, it is now impossible to cover in a single text all the advanced materials in the field, let alone cover these materials in less than at least three years of intense graduate study. Hence, a text for the first year of such study can only provide a coverage that is comprehensive and yet of sufficient depth to pave the way for advanced research.

The orientation of the 1998 book also differs from that of 1960. While the 1960 book fully recognized the need for interregional analysis, it tended to concentrate on single region problems and effective attacks on them. This book places greater weight on interregional analysis (as is indicated in the title), and on greater understanding of the functioning of a system of regions, whether within a nation, or a global or continental community at one extreme or a small region comprising a set of urban communities at the other. Moreover, the relative importance assigned to the several methods has changed. Analysis of population (growth and decline) has been deemphasized and migration analysis has come to be explored by several methods of analysis — econometrics, gravity and spatial interaction models, and microsimulation to name three — thus finding a split home among them. In contrast, nonlinear programming models and general equilibrium analysis (in 1960 a purely conceptual framework) have come to the fore as a result of the computer revolution; and microsimulation, an intensive consumer of computer time, is seething at the bit. On the other hand, the comparative cost approach (for location problems of industry and service trades), input-output, and social accounting analysis (SAM) have held their own and gravity-type models have flourished, all having potential for further development as a result of the blossoming of GIS (geographic information systems), the comprehensive data base that replaces the meager data sets of the 1950s. Finally, the primitive statistical studies of the 1950s have been replaced by the rigorous approaches of Econometrics, the more advanced procedures of spatial econometrics still being beyond the scope of a first year graduate course.

At times, in the writing of this book, the editor may have been too harsh on economists. In the 1956 book on *Location and Space Economy* he criticized economists for dwelling in a wonderland of no dimensions. Recently, in part because of Paul Krugman's writings, there has come to be in some economic studies and models a recognition of the role of space, distance and transport costs. But by and large these elements continue to be ignored, given inadequate attention, or given improper treatment. In trade theory particularly there continues to be much too much reliance on the findings on the Heckscher-Ohlin model and variants of it which are proper for a no dimension world, but decidedly fallacious for a real world. One cannot help but reach the conclusion that given the fact that regional scientists have certainly caught up with economists in handling sophisticated techniques of analysis, except perhaps the highly mathematical, highly abstract and clearly highly unrealistic ones, I look forward to regional scientists forging ahead of economists, who seem to have great difficulty in shedding themselves of obsolete, traditional thinking particularly when it facilitates the use of more advanced mathematics.

Finally, along with economists and other social scientists, we still confront the problem of inadequate treatment of intertemporal and dynamic analysis. Great opportunities exist for developing this type of analysis, as well as innumerable fruitful studies based on the fusion of regional science methods discussed in the last chapter. Hopefully, this can be achieved with at least some inclusion of conflict management analysis. As we conclude in that chapter, 'There is plenty of work to do.' I encourage the incoming graduate student and young research scholar to go at it.

One last comment. In developing this text, the editor must apologize for not recognizing all the important developments in regional science that should be brought to the attention of the incoming graduate student. In the intervening years too much good scholarship has been conducted for a single mind to keep track of. Perhaps soon some energetic scholar will step forward to develop an index of regional science literature.

Walter Isard
March 1998

1. The setting and introduction

Walter Isard

Formally speaking, regional science as a field of study is, at the time of writing, almost a half-century old. It dates from December 1954, the time when the Regional Science Association was organized. At that time many scholars from diverse fields of study were conducting regional studies. There was, however, little similarity in their approaches, tools and analytical methods. This was most obvious when these scholars would come together at the annual meetings of the American Economic Association and others. Yet, it was realized by most of these scholars, if not all, that much could be gained from sharing and transforming knowledge about the approaches and tools frequently employed in each field of study. This situation prompted the formation of the Regional Science Association. As stated in its constitution, the 'main objective shall be to foster exchange of ideas and promote studies focusing on the region and utilizing tools, methods and theoretical frameworks designed for regional analysis, as well as concepts, procedures and analytical techniques of the various social and other sciences.' And indeed the first volume of its *Papers and Proceedings* has contributions by geographers, city planners, sociologists, political scientists and economists, several of whom had background and substantial training in mathematics and engineering.

From the start and still today, the field of Regional Science has been and is interdisciplinary. The first book which attempted to bring together the diverse analytical techniques was *Methods of Regional Analysis* (Isard et al., 1960). After an introduction on the setting and contents, the book began with a chapter on *population projection*, largely in those days a concern of sociologists and demographers. It was followed by a chapter on *migration estimation*, again a major concern of sociologists and demographers, but also of some real interest to city planners and economists. The next chapter was on *regional income estimation and social accounting*, a central interest of economists. Then came one on *interregional flow analysis and balance of payments*, the former topic being pioneered by geographers, and the latter, involving money flows, reflecting a deep interest of economists. The sixth chapter was on *regional cycle and multiplier analysis*, once more a concern largely of economists; however, its appendix on *economic base and central place theory* was an area deeply rooted in geographic thought, and one of major interest to city planners. The ensuing chapter on *industrial location analysis and related measures* embraced topics of interest to economists, regional planners and geographers; the considerable discussion of relevant measures was informally a 'mini-GIS' (Geographic Information System), a forerunner of the current widespread development and use of GIS. The appendices of this chapter considered topics pioneered by sociologists, such as factor analysis.

The next three chapters covered application of models stemming from a conceptual mathematical formulation of an advanced economy — the Walrasian general equilibrium system. The first of these was on *interregional and regional input-output techniques* developed by mathematically trained scholars coming into the field of economics. The development of these techniques was greatly encouraged by urban planners who were struggling to incorporate in their design of cities a sound economic base. The second was *industrial complex analysis*, an approach stimulated in the post–World War II era by the need and widespread desire to offer lagging or undeveloped regions a way to spark their development, to identify a sound core of economic activities that could lead them out of their poverty. The third was on *regional and interregional linear programming*, a technique once again developed by mathematically trained scholars who shifted to economics but also by operations researchers; it was a technique that was eagerly embraced by central planners for it allowed them explicitly to place at the center of a study an objective (in the form of an objective function). Balancing these three chapters was the next-to-last one on *gravity and potential models*. Although these models grew out of thinking by physicists and others, they were pioneered and extensively probed by the geographer Warntz and his colleagues, these models being scoffed at by economists, and inadequately appreciated by the vast majority of geographers. They found first application by urban and transportation planners for forecasting meaningful and likely traffic patterns. The final chapter was on *channels of syntheses*, ways in which the several methods could be fruitfully fused, a number of which have been achieved in the years subsequent to the book's publication. We will have occasion to note some of these achievements in the chapters of this new book.

The years since the formation of the Regional Science Association have seen a revolution in the use of computers for analytical purposes. For regional scientists this has led to a much greater interest in lines of analysis that can exploit the new computer capability, which is continuously mounting. Hence, while the range of topics and problems scrutinized by regional scientists has been greatly extended, these scholars have been able to and have probed more deeply into the forces at play in any given situation. This has resulted in a shift in emphasis and attention given to subjects as regional analysts have successfully probed problem areas overlapping other fields of investigation. Particular subjects, such as estimation of population numbers, migration and regional income, *per se*, have become less important while the causal interconnection or interrelationship of forces leading to change (such as in population numbers, migration and regional income) have become examined more intensely. Thus we start with a subject whose analysis enables us to attain deep anchorage in causal or interconnectedness analysis, namely forces affecting change in employment (jobs). For example, analysis of forces leading to change in jobs clearly has direct implications for change in population, migration and regional income, and also all the phenomena associated with such magnitudes.

The title of chapter 2 (the first analytical chapter) is *Location analysis for industry and service trades: comparative cost and other approaches*. There, basic industry location principles are discussed as well as applications of the standard comparative cost approach. There, too, the driving force of the service trades in creating jobs (hardly present in the 1950s) is fully appreciated and location principles are extended to cover them. Also, the chapter recognizes that a successful effort at probing more deeply into the forces at play — at understanding more fully causal connections — requires an extensive expansion of conceptually relevant information systems; hence, this chapter also discusses the basic features of a GIS.

Since the 1950s the one technique that has perhaps been most extensively exploited and developed in regional science is *Regional and interregional input-output analysis*. The basics as well as a number of important developments in this approach are discussed in chapter 3.

Chapter 4 is on *Regional and spatial econometric analysis*. In the 1950s, this type of research activity — of vigorously testing hypotheses, making statistically significant forecasts and carefully examining them — was not extensively engaged in by regional scientists, but it has become basic to regional study. The term econometrics is misleading since formal testing and careful examination of forecasts is an activity fundamental to all science. In chapter 4, the presentation of the relevant basic elements of econometrics has been organized having in mind the needs of regional science graduate students and researchers who have not been formally trained in this area.

Another major development in regional science research stemming from the revolutionary advance in computer technology has been the potential to employ effectively nonlinear functions — to conduct research that goes well beyond the classical input-output, linear programming investigations of the 1950s and 1960s. Programming (linear and nonlinear) is discussed in chapter 5. So also are industrial complex and urban complex analyses, since they (as well as analysis of other types of complexes essential to regional and urban development planning) involve major nonlinearities and can be viewed as nonlinear programming.

Chapter 6 concerns *Gravity and spatial interaction models.* Tremendous progress has been scored by regional scientists developing and applying the models: geographers are increasingly employing them in their respective spatial and macroeconomic (e.g., international trade) studies, and economists are just starting to. This chapter examines the theoretical foundations of these models, illustrates and cites some of their latest applications.

Chapter 7 on *Social accounting matrices and social accounting analysis* develops in a thorough manner the motivation, rationale and key aspects of this approach. With our greater capacity for storing and treating data, social accounts (especially when they are constructed to embody intraindustry and in time financial accounts) should soon come to be an integral part of any comprehensive regional and interregional study. This should be especially so, once their structure is basically redefined, along lines to be suggested in chapters 8 and 9 — redefined to be causally embedded and more directly oriented to the needs of regional and interregional analysis and policy formulation.

The following chapter is on *Applied general interregional equilibrium (AGIE) models.* As discussed in connection with programming, the computer revolution with the ability to handle nonlinear relationships has enabled economists to develop applied general equilibrium (AGE) for nations, primarily to evaluate the impact of policies. However, in doing so, economists have typically considered a wonderland of no dimension; they have not taken into account distance, transport inputs and costs, and space. Accordingly this chapter aims to include these key elements, and, *at the very beginning.* Necessarily, it starts from scratch with very simple situations in order to end up with the scaffolding (the identification of the basic structural elements and their interconnectedness) for a comprehensive AGIE model. Although a number of significant initial contributions have already been made by regional scientists and drawn upon in this chapter, it remains for graduate students and others to conduct the truly creative research to fill out the scaffolding, to realize a full-blown comprehensive interregional model of a space economy ready for application.

The next-to-last chapter is on microsimulation. This probabilistic approach to simulating behavior based on extensive sampling and other sources of data requires highly intensive computer use. As a consequence, it has had relatively little opportunity to develop on a widespread basis. However, recognition of its great potential for adding depth to behavioral studies in attacking difficult urban-regional problems and formulating spatial/interregional policies coupled with continuing major advances in computer capabilities should lead to its much greater employment in regional science analysis.

The final chapter is on diverse syntheses of regional science methods. It is in such syntheses, in the integration and fusion of methods, that great progress in regional science will be scored. We have described only some of the many possible combinations of regional science methods that can be fruitfully investigated. The exact combination or fusion of these methods in attacking a problem must of course depend on the inclination of the researcher and data availability. We have also suggested that it would be desirable for regional scientists researching conflict-laden problems — as clearly is the case for most if not all environmental problems whose spatial aspect cannot be ignored — to introduce one or more conflict management procedures into their investigation. We have illustrated how a researcher might do so in a transportation conflict problem employing a priorities-determining method.

2. Location analysis for industry and service trades: comparative cost and other approaches

Walter Isard

2.0 Introduction

We begin this book with a brief chapter on relevant factors for the location of industry and service trades. We could of course begin with another question basic to regional development. However, many regional scientists who have come from developing areas, or ones facing decline or stagnation, or ones simply opting for growth place priority on the location of a new industry or service trades in their region. Such new economic activity would provide jobs and generate new income that could lead to significant multiplier effects. While these regional scientists may be concerned that the new industry or set of services may lead to more pollution, intensify transportation problems, and negatively impact the ecosystem, without such new economic activity and jobs, they reason, the region may be unable to move forward. They may say: let's pay attention to environmental degradation, transport congestion, ecosystem disturbance after we identify what the new industry or service trades can be, making sure that the new economic activity will be sound for the region both in the short- and long-run. Hence, we are inclined in this book to start with the analysis of relevant location factors — an analysis which of course is pertinent to the more general question: what industries and service trades and how much of each is economically efficient for a given region?

When we consider in sufficient detail the set of factors relevant in its choice of a location, each industry or set of service trades (hereafter designated a *service complex*) is unique. However, broadly speaking there are some basic factors that generally affect decisions on industry and service activity location. One is access to and costs of inputs, whether raw materials, intermediate (partially finished goods), diverse services and others (capital, labor, energy), both at a given location and elsewhere. A second is access and delivery cost to the markets, again both at a given location and elsewhere. Historically, however, the general concept of access has been given only secondary attention by location analysts. They have been primarily concerned with specific cost factors in the location of basic industry such as iron and steel, glass, cement, textiles, oil refineries and petrochemicals. By and large, the service trades, requiring relatively few inputs from each other, were found to be located where the industry and households (then markets) were. Today, this is not the case, as we shall discuss below. However, we choose to start with location factors for basic industries since location analysts have been concerned with such for so many decades and have been successful in developing useful principles and analytical methods. These principles and methods now have significant applicability for the much more recent high-technology industry and service trade developments.

2.1 Industry location principles and the comparative cost approach

There exists an extensive literature on location theory.[1] Much of this is abstract and for the most part does not bear directly on the problems with which regional analysts and planners are concerned today. However, this literature has led to at least one basic general procedure which is exceedingly useful, namely the comparative cost technique, which also has roots in international trade theory.

A comparative cost study typically proceeds for any given industry on the basis of an established or anticipated pattern of markets and a given geographic distribution of raw materials and other productive factors used in the industry. The objective of the study is to determine in what region or regions the industry could achieve the lowest total cost of producing and delivering its product to the market. If the analyst is concerned with the industrial growth prospects of a particular region, one or more such comparative cost studies is rather essential.

The initial justification for a comparative cost study may be the discovery of a rich resource in a region of concern, or a change in technology that makes an existing mineral deposit potentially exploitable, or the opening of new markets as a result of political changes, or the construction of a port facility or a major transport link that drastically reduces delivered cost of raw materials to the region or cost of shipping a finished product to the market, or a growth of the region's market that enables local production to realize significant scale economies, or change in consumer tastes, or new financial sources able to provide needed capital, or any of many other possible developments.

Given the many possible situations that can justify a comparative cost study, we turn to procedures for conducting one. The most direct way to pursue a comparative cost study to assess the feasibility of locating an industry in a given region would be to secure enough information to calculate the total production costs the industry would incur in the given region and in each of the regions in which it currently exists or which are potential low-cost locations. The region or regions with the lowest total of production and transport costs to a given market would be the most desirable location for producing for that market. Since the difference in total cost from region to region is the important magnitude, it is clear that the regional comparative cost study need consider only the production and transport cost elements which actually differ from region to region. Those elements that do not vary regionally in amount may be ignored; they give rise to no regional advantage or disadvantage. For example, if as a result of extensive unionization labor costs in production are the same in all regions of a nation, and if the location of an activity must be confined to sites within the nation, then it is not necessary to calculate what labor costs are (assuming productivity is the same in each region) no matter how high these costs. In practice, consideration of only locational cost differentials is sufficient, and it can lead to considerable saving of research time since many items of production cost for many industries do not exhibit systematic or significant regional variation.

Observe also that in considering an element of production cost which does vary regionally, it is often possible to estimate the amount of its difference between regions without knowledge of its absolute regional levels. For example, take two similar plants, one in New York City, the other in a coal town near Pittsburgh. Each consumes ten tons of coal a day, the cost of coal in New York City tending to exceed the cost of coal in the coal town by the cost of transporting coal from the coal town to New York City. If it is known that the transport rate is $3 per ton, the daily coal cost of the New York plant would exceed by $30 the daily coal cost of the other plant. However, this method of computing a regional cost differential can be used only if the relevant productive factor input is (or would be) the same in each region, both in type and quantity. Thus, if the New York plant used only eight tons of coal a day as compared to ten in the other plant, the analyst would need to know the price or cost of coal in at least one of the sites as well as its transport cost in order to compute the daily coal cost differential. Also, if one of the plants adopted a production process that used electricity rather than coal, the analyst would need to know the absolute cost of both electricity and coal in order to calculate the energy (fuel and power) cost differential between the two plants.

2.1.1 Locational analysis for the iron and steel industry

To point up the key role of locational cost differentials and the use of diverse location principles, we examine location factors in the iron and steel industry. Historically, when ten tons of coal, two-to-three tons of ore and some limestone were required to produce one ton of finished product, the iron works were located at the coal site. By far the dominant locational cost differential was associated with transport cost, and when transport rates on coal, ore and finished product were not significantly different, it was most efficient to transport the two-to-three tons of ore to the coal site and the one ton of finished product from the coal site to the market than to ship ten tons of coal either to the ore site or the market.[2] This would be so even if the ore site and the market were to coincide. This outcome illustrates the principle that weight loss in production tends to pull location toward the site of a material undergoing weight loss, and, in the above case, to the coal site since coal incurred the dominant weight loss. For why transport that part of the raw material that is not usable? A companion principle is that the use of a ubiquitous material is associated with little if any locational force. For example, early in the 20th century relatively pure water was present practically everywhere. There was no reason for transporting water to a potential location when water was there available for direct use?

Other locational principles, useful for providing insights in the conduct of a comparative cost study become evident as we set down in a basic table relevant locational cost differentials for iron and steel production. To do so, consider the effort in 1951 of the Boston Federal Reserve Bank to establish an integrated iron and steel works in New England, a time when New England was a declining region in the United States. In the United States, the iron and steel industry was highly unionized at that time, and although labor was the largest cost item in iron and steel production, its cost was generally expected to be the same no matter where an iron and steel works located in the United States. Hence, labor costs was not a relevant locational factor, even though it was fully recognized that the realized average productivity of labor in any works to be constructed would depend on the quality of management. Also, every major iron and steel company which was being urged and/or lured to construct an integrated iron and steel works in New England had unimpeded access to the New York money market so that capital costs would be practically the same regardless of where any new works would be situated. Tax factors were of importance, but given the unpredictable behavior of local and state authorities regarding levels of taxation in the long-run (at least for 40 years in the future), major steel companies could not be expected to (and did not) pay much attention to political authorities offering tax concessions — authorities who at best could control only short-run tax levels. Finally, costs of controlling environmental pollution were not relevant for decision makers, for in 1951 the emerging environmental problems were given scarce attention if any. Hence, at that time the key locational cost differentials are evident from the data of Table 2-1. This table illustrates the competitive situation for serving the Boston market.

Table 2-1 Transportation costs on ore and coal required per net ton of steel and on finished product for selected actual and hypothetical producing locations serving Boston

| | Transportation Costs on: | | | |
Location	Ore	Coal	Finished Product	Total
Fall River	3.68	5.63	4.60	13.91
New London	3.68	5.42	6.80	15.90
Pittsburgh	5.55	1.56	15.20	22.31
Cleveland	3.16	3.85	15.20	22.21
Sparrows Point	3.68	4.26	12.40	20.34
Buffalo	3.16	4.27	12.60	20.03
Bethlehem	5.56	5.06	10.60	21.22
Trenton	3.68	4.65	10.40	18.73

Source: Isard and Cumberland (1950).

To serve the Boston market, two New England locations, Fall River, Massachusetts and New London, Connecticut, were identified as good locations, both having solid bedrock conditions and other necessary features such as port facilities. Costs at these locations were to be compared to costs at existing iron and steel locations (Pittsburgh, Cleveland, Sparrows Point, Buffalo, and Bethlehem) and costs at the best available alternative new location for iron and steel production. In the case of the New England study, the best alternative new location was judged to be Trenton, New Jersey. (A basic principle in comparative cost analysis is to compare the location of an operation under investigation with not only existing locations of that operation, but also non-existing ones that are the best alternative new locations.)

First, for each production site the best source of iron ore was determined to estimate for that site the transport cost on ore required per ton steel. Since different sources of ore were or would be used by the several sites under consideration, and since the ores were of different quality, different amounts of them would be required per ton steel. Also, different amounts of coking coal would be required for smelting. The transport costs on the required ore were adjusted to take into account these differences, as well as differences in costs at the mine for ore and coal. The adjusted transport costs on ore are recorded in column 1 of Table 2-1. The differences among them, reflecting primarily differences in transport costs, are taken to be *locational cost differentials* (advantages or disadvantages) in access to ore.

The second column in Table 2-1 records for each site estimated transport costs on required coal per ton steel from that site's best source of coal. The differences among the sites are then taken to represent locational cost differentials on coal. The third column records for each producing site the estimated transport cost per ton steel to the given market at Boston. The differences represent locational cost differentials on access to the market.

The final column of Table 2-1 sums the three dominant locational cost differentials just noted. It indicates that both Fall River and New London, as eligible New England locations, have decided advantage over other locations in serving the Boston market, and in particular with reference to transport cost. Since differences in other costs did not exist, were minor, or were unpredictable, one might conclude from the above data that a New England location for an integrated iron and steel works would be economically justifiable — an operation that might be designated as transport-oriented.

However, there are other factors that do not bear directly on location. One that is universally important is scale economies. Typically, the unit costs of a production operation falls as output increases (a situation of scale economies), and at a later point rises with further increases (a situation of scale diseconomies). It turned out that when the annual magnitudes of steel consumption were estimated for the Boston, Worcester, Providence, New Haven markets and other markets in New England, the total was not sufficient to attain the full scale economies that an optimal size of an integrated iron and steel would require. Nor was the total large enough when (1) increased by the magnitude of the markets in other regions which a New England location could capture and (2) decreased by the amount of the New England market which non-New England steel works might serve. Hence, in the minds of the major iron and steel companies full scale economies would not be attainable by a New England integrated works. No company was able to be induced to construct such a works in New England. It turned out that the Trenton location, advantageous for serving the New England markets (were no works constructed in New England) and having decided transport cost advantages over other production sites for serving the Greater New York–Philadelphia region, did have effective access to large markets (estimated to total 9 to 11 million tons annually). These markets were also growing. Thus it was concluded that they would allow an integrated works to achieve full scale economies. Such a works was actually constructed near Trenton. See data on Trenton, page 96.

Up until the middle of the 20th century, the iron and steel industry was characterized as *transport oriented* — locational cost differentials on transportation dominated those on other factors. At first, as already remarked, iron and steel production was oriented to coal sites. However, by the mid 20th century technological progress had drastically reduced coal requirements per ton steel. As a consequence steel's orientation had shifted to markets (often denoted as *market orientation*) when the markets were of sufficient size. The rationale for the shift in orientation can be easily seen by comparing the advantage of a Pittsburgh location (a coal site) whose transport cost on coal per ton steel was only $1.56 (see Table 2-1) over a Fall River location whose transport cost on coal per ton steel was $5.63 — a disadvantage for Fall River of $4.07. However, transport cost of finished product to the market (Boston) from Pittsburgh was $22.31 but only $13.91 from Fall River, an advantage of $8.40 for Fall River that significantly overrides its coal disadvantage.[3]

A properly constructed comparative cost study, however, has relevance primarily for the short-run. It depicts a situation at a given point of time. Where heavy investments are involved which take several decades to write off, as with an integrated iron and steel works, it becomes necessary to project future as well as current locational cost differentials — an extremely difficult, if not an almost impossible task. The importance of this task, however, is boldly illustrated by the recent history of the iron and steel industry. As already noted, in the early 1950's when comparative cost studies were conducted on the location of iron and steel works, for which times the data of Table 2-1 pertain, the iron and steel industry was so highly unionized that labor costs, differentials among regions (locations) in the United States were considered to be negligible if not zero. At that time, too, very few, if any, analysts would have taken seriously the possibility of large steel imports from Japan, South Korea and other non-European producers. It was not anticipated that Japan or South Korea would be able to master the technology, acquire the necessary capital and manage an integrated works. Yet such did transpire. Japanese and later South Korean works were able to outcompete the existing market-oriented plants in the U.S. primarily because of extremely low labor costs. In effect, steel industry changed from being market- or transport-oriented to being labor-oriented. A recent study of the feasibility of a North Korean integrated iron and steel works, to be discussed below, boldly illustrates this point. [It is of interest to note that in the early 19th century, the textile industry was oriented to water power sites. Since water power, an indispensable input in textiles production, was immobile, the textile industry had to locate at water power sites. (This illustrates an obvious, but basic location principle. When an immobile but indispensable input is required in production, production must locate at the source of the input.) However, once electric power became generally available, the industry was free to relocate at cheap labor locations, the labor cost differential becoming the dominant one.]

2.1.2 Analysis of the aluminum industry, and energy and other location factors

Another interesting case of locational dynamics is provided by the aluminum industry. In the post-World War II years when the demand for aluminum products rose sharply, new locations for large-scale production of aluminum were required. To understand the location decisions that were being taken in the United States a comparative cost study was undertaken. From the standpoint of transport costs alone, the best locations at that time within the United States for serving several of its major markets were the markets themselves. Yet little, if any, new aluminum production capacity was constructed at these markets. Clearly there was some locational influence at work stronger than that exerted by regional transport cost differentials. It proved to be the influence of regional differences in the cost of electric power. To illustrate this point, a location in the New York

City area, a major market center, was compared with a location in the Pacific Northwest, a region possessing cheap hydroelectric power. Table 2-2 compares regional transport costs alone.[4]

Table 2-2 Regional transportation costs (1955): aluminum production for New York market

Item	Location at:	
	New York	Pacific Northwest
Transport costs per pound pig aluminum		
a. On raw materials	0.458¢	1.312¢
b. On pig aluminum	0.000¢	0.950¢
Total	0.548¢	2.262¢
Net transport cost advantage of New York: 1.714		

Now consider the influence of the power cost differential. The production of 1 pound of pig aluminum required approximately 9 kilowatt-hours of electric power. This means that a difference of 1.91 mills (1.714 cents divided by 9) per kilowatt-hour in the cost of electric power would be enough to offset completely the net transport cost advantage of the New York location. Actually, power rates in the Pacific Northwest ranged from 2.5 to 3.5 mills per kilowatt-hour whereas in the New York area rates were approximately 8 mills per kilowatt-hour. Thus, any advantage that New York possessed on transport cost account was clearly overshadowed by its disadvantage on power cost account.

Other regional cost differentials in the production of aluminum were relatively slight. As a result, the aluminum industry was expected to be located and grow in a cheap-power region, and it did grow substantially at low-cost power sites in the Pacific Northwest. This region's annual production capacity grew from about 200,000 tons in 1947 to 1,600,000 in 1983.

However, the post-World War II era witnessed a major growth of the Pacific Northwest economy, in part stimulated by the expansion of aluminum capacity there that was significant for expansion of the aircraft industry. As a consequence, the demand by households and industry for electric power increased tremendously, causing power rates for aluminum producers to increase from 3 mills per kilowatt-hour under contract in

1979 to 26.8 mills under contract in 1984 (U.S. Bureau of the Mines, 1985). Thus the original regional attraction of exceedingly low power rates has disappeared. Practically all new aluminum facilities for meeting the increasing demand for this metal are arising at cheap power sites outside of Pacific Northwest. Gradual reduction in this region's capacity and even more in the operating rates of its plants is occurring and can be expected to continue as the production facilities age, become high cost and in time obsolete.

At this point we have illustrated sufficiently the comparative cost approach from the standpoint of quantifiable locational cost differentials whether with regard to transportation, labor, energy, raw material, land or capital costs, or taxation, pollution charges (or abatement expenditures) and other outlay items. However, there are two location factors exceedingly difficult to quantify. One is agglomeration economies sometimes designated as spatial juxtaposition, localization, or urbanization economies, and often viewed as externalities. Localization economies arise for example when several like plants or other production units locate near each other to: (1) take advantage of together purchasing inputs in volume (large lots) and thus at lower prices rather than separately purchasing inputs in higher-cost small lots; (2) obtain cost savings by sharing a common repair or other facility when no one plant requires its services more than occasionally; (3) present the variegated features of their outputs in a joint display that is more attractive to buyers needing to compare offerings and designs, or to customers immersed in or who simply enjoy comparison shopping, or (4) reduce costs or increase their sales in a number of other ways.

Urbanization economies realized by a plant or firm are positive externalities that in general depend on the size or overall total activity (economic, social and political) of the city or metropolitan region or other cluster of diverse enterprises in which a production unit is located. These economies are generated, among other factors, by (1) the availability of a larger and more diverse set of trucking or forwarding services; (2) more extensive library, consulting and other information storing and generating facilities; (3) direct access to a larger and more specialized pool of skilled labor and top quality management; (4) a greater variety of and more attractive entertainment and cultural facilities and like fringe elements that eases the unit's problem in securing and holding on to a productive labor force; and (5) more advanced and sophisticated infrastructure. These are economies generally available to any unit, independent of the presence of like production units.

While the presence of agglomeration economies may be crucial for any particular location decision, their measurement is an extremely difficult task, and frankly speaking, has not as yet been satisfactorily performed by analysts. Thus they are rarely, if ever, able to be included in a comparative cost table; they can only be broadly recognized, and subjectively taken into account by a decision maker.

We should add here that localization, urbanization and other agglomeration economies are extremely important for the growth of underdeveloped regions which can offer only one specific location advantage, say cheap labor or low-cost energy. For firms to locate in any of these regions to exploit this advantage, these firms must be able to obtain there a set of one or more essential (complementary) inputs, inclusive of infrastructure services. Such, however, can be economically provided at a low or reasonable cost only if there is an agglomeration of like or other activities than can provide an aggregate demand sufficient to supply these inputs and services, such as shipping and transportation, at reasonable or low costs. When this occurs, agglomeration strengthens the pull of that specific location advantage.

Except for special circumstances, the second major type of location factor yet to be satisfactorily quantified and evaluated in a comparative cost table are environmental conditions and regulations. These comprise the costs (and benefits) of a unit's operation arising from the need to control the generation of pollution and avoid the ecological damage it can cause — costs (and benefits) not only to the unit, but to the community, region and nation to which the unit belongs, as well as to other parts of the globe. In certain circumstances, the unit may confront a cost difference between sites A and B in complying with the different pollution regulations in force at these sites. Differences in regulations can result in differences in capital and operating costs of pollution control equipment (such as scrubbers), or abatement processes that convert undesirable emissions such as hydrogen sulphide into valuable sulphur as a product. But such quantification does not capture the important indirect costs from ill effects on the health of the population and labor force of an area, and local or world-wide ecological damage.

Today, a comparative cost table takes on a somewhat more extensive and comprehensive form than one a half-century ago. To illustrate this point, we draw upon a very recent, detailed study by Hyung-Seog Lee. This study was conducted during the period 1995–97 before the financial collapse of the late 90s in South Korea and neighboring Asian countries. It was motivated by the desire to evaluate industrial development possibilities for North Korea should political conditions change in both North and South Korea to permit extensive and gainful economic cooperation. (North Korea is rich in mineral resources while South Korea is relatively poor.) At that time, the outlook for such change in political conditions was bleak. Currently (early 1998), the severe food shortage in North Korea and new South Korean leadership have increased the probability of such change.

Despite these changes in the financial and political state of affairs, the relevant up-to-date factors for location analysis in the steel industry have not yet changed. One is the size of the market. In 1995 it was estimated by South Korean Development Institute that South Korea's annual demand for steel would grow by 15 million tons by 2004, and Lee anticipated that were North Korean costs low enough, a North Korean steel works could penetrate markets in Japan, Taiwan and Western United States. (While it was recognized that growth in parts of these markets may also be potentially served by an integrated works in another underdeveloped region of the world, such as the Philippines, prospects for growth of the markets just noted suggest that they can easily absorb the output of more than one works.) Lee noted that already South Korean locations in the Pusan area have been able to compete profitably for these markets based on significantly lower labor costs — lower costs which have outweighed higher transport and other costs in assembling the necessary raw materials and in producing and delivering product to these markets. Hence for these markets, expansion of capacity at an existing South Korean production site (Pohang or Kwangyang) or establishment of a new works at the best possible South Korean location (say Kunsan) can be said to constitute a most competitive alternative to the construction of iron and steel works in the North Korea Chungjin area.

Before presenting Lee's comparative cost table, a few preliminary remarks are in order. North Korea possesses numerous iron ore deposits. A number of them in the Western part of this country are of high quality (50-60% iron content), but they are of insufficient magnitude to provide an adequate long-run ore supply for a large integrated works. A huge deposit of iron ore (estimated at 1.3 billion tons) exists in the Eastern part of North Korea in the Chungjin area. However, this ore is of low quality (30-37% iron content) and requires upgrading (beneficiation) for use. Large deposits of bituminous coal exist in North Korea, but the coal is not of coking quality. Hence, as with South Korea, coke or bituminous coal for coking will need to be imported for a North Korean works.

With regard to transportation, Chungjin is the major port of North Korea, and has potential for significant expansion. Its Eastern shore location is excellent for reaching population and industrial concentrations in South Korea, Japan, Taiwan and Western United States. It also is a leading urban area of North Korea and would be a natural location for expansion of steel fabricating (steel consuming) activities were a modern iron and steel works constructed there. Given the extensive Musan ore deposits nearby, a Chungjin area location is clearly the best in North Korea for an integrated works.[5] Hence in the comparative cost table which follows and which is based on 1994 data. Lee examined the Chungjin area in competition with an existing South Korean location, Kwangyang, and an alternative, presumably efficient new South Korean location, Kunsan.

The first row of Table 2-3 relates to the cost of ore. For North Korea it was estimated conservatively at $5 per ton steel, being based on the 1994 cost of upgrading the low grade U.S.A. Mesabi ore to a 65% level,

Table 2-3 Comparative costs per ton steel (1994) for selected locations re: South Korea and Japan markets

		Production Site		
		North Korea (Chungjin)	South Korea (Kunsan)	South Korea (Kwangyang)
Ore	(1)	51	49	49
Coal	(2)	39	37	37
Scrap	(3)	53	50	48
Labor	(4)	35	80	80
Environmental Costs in Excess of Chonguin's	(5)	0	++	+++
Total Production Cost	(6)	178	216++	214+++
Transport Cost to South Korea Market	(7)	23	5	5
Locationally Sensitive Costs re: South Korea Market	(8)	201	221++	219+++
Transport Cost to Japan Market	(9)	28	28	28
Locationally Sensitive Costs re: Japan Market	(10)	206	244++	242++++

recalculated to take into account the much lower cost of North Korean labor. The cost of ore at Kwangyang for imported ore as reported by POSCO, the South Korean steel company, is $49, which Lee also took to be the cost of ore at Kunsan.

The second row is on the cost of coal for coking purposes. It is $37 for the South Korean sites based on data from POSCO, and is set at $39 for Chungjin to allow for higher transport cost to cover the greater shipment distance that would be involved. The third row is on costs of scrap. The cost for Kwangyang is reported to be $48. The costs at Kunsan and Chungjin are set higher to reflect less access to scrap generating sources.

The fourth row lists labor costs at the three locations, those for South Korea being set at 1994 levels. The labor costs for North Korea are based on one possible conservative set of reasonable assumptions, namely that North Korean labor will be one-half as productive as South Korean and that the North Korean wage per hour will be less than one-quarter of the South Korean.

Next, Lee tried to take into account overall environmental costs. As already remarked, at this time it is impossible to do so on any objective basis. However, one can indicate that the environmental costs from the pollution generated by an iron and steel works is likely to be highest at a site such as Kwangyang. This site was becoming heavily polluted; it was attracting much basic industry that will intensify its pollution problem and require much more pollution control and abatement. Chungjin is a site much less polluted and is likely to remain so for at least a number of years. Thus in the fifth row Lee employed the symbol +++ to indicate that a new steel works at Kwangyang will incur much greater pollution control costs than one at Chungjin. He assumed that the Kunsan works would need to expend considerably more funds than Chungjin on pollution control, land developments and maintenance of the ecosystem. Thus he used the symbol ++ to indicate this.

The total of the production costs listed in the first four rows plus the differential on pollution control costs is indicated in row 6. However, there is one more significant cost that must be taken into account, namely shipping cost to the market. Row 7 records estimated transport cost to the South Korean markets. This cost when added to the production costs of column 6 yields the resulting total of locational sensitive costs in serving the growing South Korean market (row 8). (Other costs, set at $161 by POSCO are taken to be roughly the same for all three sites.) Clearly the North Korea location has a significant advantage over a South Korean one, primarily because of both its significantly lower labor and environmental-type costs.

As already noted, the North Korean location with its cheap labor and environmental advantages can also compete in world markets. Consider the Japanese market, access to which is approximately the same for all three Korean sites; Lee took the cost to be $28 (see row 9). Hence Chungjin's production cost advantage remains unchanged (row 10). Likewise, for serving other major world markets, such as Western United States, access to which is roughly equivalent for all three Korean sites.

In brief, the comparative cost Table 2-3 suggests the economic feasibility of a North Korean works when compared with South Korean locations — locations which have been indicated to be advantageous compared to those in such major industrialized regions as Japan, Taiwan and Western United States. Lee also conducted a further study designed to compare the Chungjin location with what he considered to be the best competitive location that might develop in Northeast China (Isard and Lee, 1996). Once again he found the Chungjin location to be definitely superior economically speaking. However, it must be borne in mind that other non-locationally sensitive factors such as management, political stability and work ethic can affect the profitability of any site that is from a locational standpoint economically sound. While in the minds of many, the location of a modern iron and steel development in North Korea may be highly questionable, this case study clearly points up the new iron and steel location strategy, a strategy that has important implications for less developed countries. Labor costs and environmental-type costs are now key primary factors. While transport costs remain an important location factor, the iron and steel industry is no longer transport-oriented as it was in the 1950s.

2.2 Service trades location principles

Essentially, the same basic principles governing industry location apply to the location of service trades — principles based on: (1) access to sources of inputs (raw materials, intermediate goods, services and others); (2) access to markets; and (3) scale of operations of a production unit and agglomeration economies. Typically, however, access to raw materials and intermediate goods are of much less importance in the location of service trades, and access to markets much more; scale, localization, and urbanization economies remain of major if not overwhelming importance.

Since access to markets is such a critical factor, it becomes essential to distinguish between key characteristics of markets and in particular to take into account the spatial extent of the market.

Historically, the dominant type of service trade that existed was that which served a local population such as: (1) a general store and a one-room school in a village or small community; (2) retail shops for food, clothing and dry goods, repair services, a funeral parlor, a pub and an elementary school in a small town; (3) a department store, a newspaper, a secondary school, and speciality shops in an urban area; (4) a hospital complex, a college, a major newspaper and central city businesses in a metropolitan region; and so forth, all consistent with central place theory of the early and mid-20th century. By and large all these activities served a population in a restricted area, the size of the area's population governing the scale economies achievable by any economic activity. Thus a hospital complex with all its specialized services could not be justified for a small community, town or urban area since the demand for the diverse medical services by the populations of these units would not be sufficient to justify the economic operation of each service. Likewise for a hospital in a small town, or the location of a doctor in a very small village. Moreover, in those days when mass transit facilities were generally available and automobile use not excessive (a quick drive downtown with easy parking was generally available), an establishment's choice of a central location in a town, urban or metropolitan area would maximize the population's access to it and hence demand for its services. Thus, concentrations of services in the centers of towns and urban and metropolitan areas occurred.

Since the mid-20th century, advance of technology, economic growth and other factors have drastically changed the location pattern of service trades — both the old and the new ones that have sprouted. Major growth in the use of automobiles has resulted in congestion in central cities of major metropolitan regions. With the subsequent construction of circumferential and other highways to ease congestion, it has become possible for the traditional service trades to be offered at non-central city locations provided a population large enough to generate sufficient demand had access to them. Thus suburban-type regional shopping centers, malls and other similar site developments emerged.

Equally, if not more important, has been the appearance of new service trades, especially in the affluent and highly developed countries extensively exploiting recent technological innovations. These new trades have come directly to service business as well as population, to meet demands of businesses as well as those of populations. Moreover, for many of these trades the access to markets in general has become greatly extended. This has partly resulted from the advance in telecommunications and other technology which has greatly reduced the cost of transport of high-value products and transmission of information. These trades are thus able to serve the demands of not only the local area but also much larger areas — the nation, continental regions and the globe. Thus many service establishments have come to seek a site that has optimal access to all these markets; and since a national market, a major region market or a global market is much larger in magnitude than that of a local area (especially when direct demands of businesses dominate those of any local population), access to other businesses is much more important in the location decision than access to population. Yet, many of these service trades, especially business services, are interconnected. They use as inputs each other's services. Hence a number of them come to agglomerate in clusters (business-services complexes), and frequently a new business service-oriented enterprise seeks location in such a cluster.

In general, service trade clusters form for the same reasons as do industries. However, the concrete nature of the economic factors are quite different. For the new business trades, face-to-face and similar type of interactions are much more important. This may be so because the service involved in a transaction is not a well-defined standard (codefiable) item. It may be that in one or more aspects of a transaction that a process, at times painful, of working out the details of what is to be delivered is required at a meeting of the key transactors. Or the transaction (e.g., a contract) may be so complex as to require a set of conferences involving exchange of views on workable provisions. Or the exact service to be provided may be uncertain because of weather conditions, availability at the right time of high-skilled operators, fluctuations of spot market prices and foreign exchange and interest rates, etc. Under any of these conditions, spur of the moment meeting of the involved parties is required to reinterpret or redefine the conditions of a contract. Or because of contingencies that are foreseen in advance and recognized in a contract, the transactors must be available at any instant to discuss and actually agree upon what contingency has been realized.

All these elements require face-to-face interactions — the potential to meet, negotiate, renegotiate, and clear up unexpected problems at a moment's notice. Hence, the cost of geographic distance between key transactors (the suppliers and the consumers) rises sharply when there exists uncodefiability, complexity, uncertainty, need for interpretation of contingencies, let alone need for quick perception of changing business conditions, learning and other cognitive-type activity. Thus, many service trades tend to aggregate in clusters to avoid this geographic distance cost, despite today's dramatic reductions in the cost of information transmission and cost of delivering (transporting) a service.

To sum up, the analysis of the location of service trades falls back upon the same general principles of accessibility to sources of inputs and markets, scale of operations, and agglomeration economies and diseconomies as does the location of industry (manufacturing) and other economic activities. Location cost differentials (inclusive of transport and transmission cost differentials) will: (1) in some cases justify location of service trades of different scales at isolated or undeveloped sites (regions), say because of cheap labor cost in providing a highly standardized service for markets of different sizes and configurations; (2) in other cases lead to small-to-medium-to-large clusters of different services having different kinds and levels of interconnections; and (3) in a relatively few cases to tremendous concentrations of highly interconnected and specialized services such as characterize the few truly global financial centers.

2.3 Spatial and location measures[6]

2.3.1 The location quotient

The discussion in the previous sections has concentrated on analysis that is especially relevant when a region has already identified an industry or service trade that it wishes to consider for location (or expansion) in its area, especially when the region has a particular resource (such as cheap labor or low-cost energy) attractive for that industry. Often, however, a region, concerned with growth or how to offset a decline in employment with new economic activity, may not be able to identify right off one or more industries that should be considered for development. Its analysts may then want information on: (1) what industry the region has and does not have, (2) the extent to which each industry is under- or over-represented in the region compared say to the nation — or as some analysts might state, in what industries does the region have less than its fair share and in which ones, more than its fair share); (3) the extent to which the region's imports of goods and services can be reduced by production within its area (that is how much import substitution might be possible); and (4) the extent to which the output of its export industries (often viewed as points of strength) can be justifiably expanded for export trade enhancement.

To help provide background information on one or more of these interrelated questions, a tool often employed is the *location quotient*. This quotient is a device for making comparisons. For example, suppose one wishes to compare for a given region J its percentage share of its nation's employment in activity i with its share of the nation's total employment, where, we let

E_i^J = employment in activity i in a given region J.

E_i = employment in activity i in the nation.

E^J = total employment in region R.

E = total employment in the nation.

We construct the ratio

$$\frac{E_i^J/E_i}{E^J/E} \text{ or the equivalent } \frac{E_i^J/E^J}{E_i/E},$$

which is defined as the location quotient. Note that the second ratio represents the percentage of the region's total employment in activity i compared to that for the nation.

Because of its simplicity the location quotient is a useful device in the early exploratory stages of research. However, as a tool for analysis it must be used cautiously to avoid misleading results. For example, consider the use of the location quotient to identify the export and import industries of a region. Often when the location quotient is less than unity, an analyst infers that the region imports the output of industry i, and when more than unity, that the region exports that output. This can easily be a wrong inference for a number of reasons.

First, tastes and expenditure patterns (propensities to consume) of households of the same type and income differ among regions. In a very warm region little fuel is required by households; in a very cold one, significant amounts. *Ceteris paribus*, this means that in the fuel-manufacturing industry a location quotient of unity or less for the warm region could be consistent with major exports of fuel oil; and a quotient of unity or more for the cold region could be consistent with major imports of fuel oil.

Second, income levels of households differ among regions. The Northeast in the U.S. consumes per household many more men's suits than does the Southeast. Thus, a location quotient well in excess of unity in the

Northeast for the men's suits manufacturing industry can be consistent with major net imports of men's suits; and a location quotient below unity in the Southeast can be consistent with major net exports.

Finally, production practices (including labor productivity) and perhaps most important, industrial 'mixes' vary considerably among regions. In the past, the location quotient for the power industry in the Pacific Northwest exceeded unity because of the relatively high concentration there of intensive power-consuming activities. Yet the region as a whole did not export major blocks of power, as an unqualified use of the location quotient might be taken to imply.

In sum, the location quotient when used alone can be a meaningless coefficient. Yet, it can be of value when used in conjunction with other tools and techniques of analysis to be discussed in later chapters — techniques which fully recognize and incorporate in their framework nonlinear production and consumption functions and regional differences in tastes, income levels and distributions, production practices, and industrial mixes.

In his/her construction of a location quotient the analyst may find it desirable to use a different base (denominator) than total employment. If he/she is interested in the spatial concentration of industry i, he/she may use for the base a measure of geographic area (in terms of square miles) to see which regions are overrepresented and which underrepresented in terms of this base. Or if he/she is interested in a service-type economic activity, say hospitals, he/she may use total population as base, to provide an indication of how well (on average) the constituents of the region are served relative to those of the nation. Or he/she may use as base, total income, or employment in another industry j (to make comparisons), or other magnitude.

2.3.2 The coefficient of localization

In addition to the location quotient, the *coefficient of localization* has been employed on a number of occasions. To construct it: (1) for each region of the nation calculate its percentage share of national employment in industry i and its percentage share of total national employment, (2) for each region take the difference between the two percentages, (3) compute the sum over all regions of either the plus differences, or negative ones, and divide by 100. See Table 2.4 where the plus differences add to 20, and thus yield a coefficient of 0.2. The higher the resulting coefficient of localization, the greater the concentration. As with the location quotient, here, too, the analyst may wish to use a base other than a region's total employment. If he/she were to use as base employment in a second industry or area or total population, he/she would derive what has often been designated a *coefficient of geographic association.*

Table 2-4 Data for computation of coefficient of localization

	Regions			
Item	*A*	*B*	*C*	*D*
1. Percent of national total employment of industry *i* in region	20	30	35	15
2. Percent of total United States manufacturing employment in region	15	20	30	35
Difference (row 1–row 2)	+5	+10	+5	–20
(Location quotient)	(1.33	1.5	1.17	0.43)

2.3.3 The localization curve

The information on the relative concentration of industry *i* in the nation may be helpful to the analyst, perhaps in suggesting the scale of output that efficient operations requires. Other useful information can be provided by a *localization curve.* To construct such a curve: (1) calculate for each region of the nation the location quotient for industry *i* as in Table 2-4; (2) order these location quotients by size, starting with the highest; (3) plot on a graph a first point representing for the region (region B) with the highest location quotient the percentage share of its employment in industry *i* (as measured along the vertical axis) and its percentage share of total national employment (as measured along the horizontal); (4) add the percentage shares of the region having the second largest quotient to those of the first to obtain a second point; and (5) keep on cumulating percentages of the regions and plotting points until 100% of employment in industry *i* and of total national employment is reached. Connecting these points starting with the origin as a point yields the localization curve. (See Figure 2.1 based on the location quotients of Table 2-4.) Thus, the analyst can note his/her region's position in the ordering of location quotients and compare its location quotient with others by observing the steepness (slopes) of the several linear segments of the curve. He/she may also construct on the same graph localization curves for other industries, or aggregates of industries,

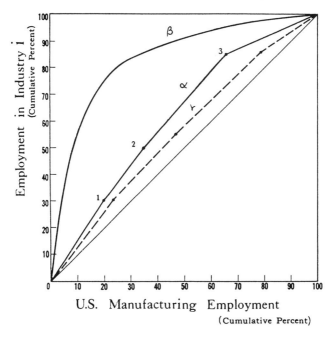

U.S. Manufacturing Employment
(Cumulative Percent)

Figure 2.1   The localization curve

and make comparisons with them. Even more, on the same graph he/she may plot the above percentages for one or more previous years to observe first the redistribution among the regions that is occurring with respect to industry i as well as any change in the location quotient for his/her region and change in the relative position of the region's location quotient.

Moreover, the analyst may find it informative to calculate a *coefficient of redistribution* for industry i by (1) obtaining for each region the difference between its location quotient in the current year and that in a previous base year and (2) summing over the regions either the positive or the negative differences. Even more useful might be calculations for a series of years to provide a better historical perspective.

In addition to the location quotient, the coefficient of localization and localization curve, a number of other ratios, coefficients, curves and the like (such as indices) have been employed in the location and associated urban and regional literature. They comprise: shift ratios; shift-share measures; regional purchase coefficients; coefficients of spatial variation, specialization, scatter and urbanization; indices of diversification, specialization, dissimilarity, segregation and diversification; and urbanization and related curves, a number of which have been usefully mapped, better to point up contrasts among regions. Also, there are in the older location literature labor and similar coefficients. The labor coefficient, as Weber employed it, is the average ratio of the labor cost per unit of product to the 'locational weight' of that unit, where locational weight is the sum of the required weights of localized raw materials plus product.

Thus far we have suggested for exploratory purposes the use of various quotients, coefficients and related measures and concepts which have been discussed. However, like most techniques, they are subject to major limitations. One of the most glaring shortcomings of any quotient, coefficient, index or graphic representation which is based on the deviation between, or ratio of, two percentage distributions is that the results obtained will generally differ, depending on the degree of areal subdivision. The location quotient will generally differ according to which definition of his/her region an analyst uses. And clearly this would be so for the corresponding coefficient of localization. For example, the coefficient of localization of an industry's workers compared to total manufacturing workers would almost certainly be higher if the nation were broken down by counties (as regions) rather than by states. Furthermore, the degree of variation in the value of the quotient or coefficient under such conditions would differ for different industries. Thus, two industries might have virtually the same coefficient of localization if states were the unit of subdivision but substantially different ones if counties were. This reduces the usefulness of interindustry comparison based on the location quotient, the coefficient of localization and similar devices.

A second major difficulty of the location quotient, the coefficient of localization and related concepts reflects the tendency of any such measure to vary considerably, depending on the choice of base. Localization, centralization, redistribution, etc. are necessarily expressed relative to a base magnitude — there is no unique, best base. Thus, if a large portion of a country's total industry is concentrated in a relatively few metropolitan areas, a specific industry also heavily concentrated in these same areas will quite likely show low location quotients and low coefficient of localization when they are computed with total industry employment or output as a base. If the coefficient were computed with geographic area as a base, the value would be considerably higher — and so would by and large the location quotients.

A third major difficulty of the location quotient, the coefficient of localization and related coefficients, indices, graphic curves concerns the identification of the specific industry category or set of industrial categories (or income classes, occupational groups, urban population, city size, etc.) that is appropriate. Thus far we have assumed that the specific industry or set of categories is predetermined. However, if we are concerned with the proper use of a region's resources, say perhaps its cheap labor, it may not be appropriate to consider just the broad category of say textiles (e.g., the U.S. two-digit SIC group 22) and calculate the region's location quotient for that category. Much more useful would be the location quotient for say a 5-digit SIC category, namely knit sport shirts. Or more broadly speaking, if we are concerned with diversifying the industrial structure of our region and wish to select a few industries that appear suitable for development in our region (or in each of the set of regions in an underdeveloped nation), we may judge that there ought to be constructed a complete set of location quotients, coefficients of localization, localization curves and so forth. Unfortunately, the values of the quotients, coefficients, ratios, etc., obtained will be very much dependent on the fineness of the industrial classification employed. A gross industrial classification, such as a two-digit one, for example, would tend to yield low coefficients of localization, etc., just as large geographic divisions do. In contrast, a fine industrial classification, such as a four- or five-digit one, would tend to yield high coefficients, just as small areal subdivisions do. Further, the pattern of change in quotients, coefficients, etc. over time may be very much a function of the degree of industrial disaggregation.

The limitations and defects discussed to this point are technical. They are direct consequences of the method by which the coefficients, ratios, and curves are defined or derived and data and regions classified. A more serious and fundamental limitation to the use of quotients, coefficients, ratios, indices, curves, etc. is that they are of little help in identifying cause and effect relationships. They are essentially mechanical devices with which empirical facts can be processed to reveal certain statistical tendencies or regularities. And even when they are accompanied by maps which help establish past trends and patterns of change, they are not able to explain or identify the economic and other forces which interact to produce these outcome tendencies and regularities. As a consequence, the current general trends and patterns revealed by the various curves and coefficients cannot be assumed to apply automatically to future development or, by analogy, to individual industry and regional situations. However, this is not to deny that the various coefficients are valuable to the regional analyst as an aid in ordering and classifying his empirical data and in helping to decide which avenues of further research are likely to be fruitful.

2.4 Geographic information systems (GIS)

At this point, it is useful to discuss the role in regional science of Geographic Information Systems, hitherto designated GIS. In one way the location quotients, coefficients of localization, localization curves and related measures and concepts represented a mini-GIS in the era before the computer revolution. However, for the regional analysts of the early 1940s and policy-makers associated with the National Resources Planning Board in the United States, these measures and associated data constituted an advanced GIS. Now, with the revolutionary developments in computational capabilities GIS can provide an unending set of data and measures for locational as well as other spatial analyses. Specifically, GIS can not only help extend and store attribute data for sites, census tracts, counties, states and other specific geographic spaces — such as industry employment, population and its age–sex composition, and location quotients. It also can compute and store internally spatial data such as characteristics of points (coordinates), lines (lengths), and polygons (area, boundaries and center). Hence, we need to reexamine the potentialities of GIS for comparative cost and other methods to be discussed in this book.

Following Anselin and Getis (1992) we view GIS as involving interaction between four basic functions. (See Figure 2.2.) A first function is characterization of reality by a set of data and measures (an input function). Thus, data on the location of different industries would be an input, as would the set of measures constituting location quotients, coefficients of localization, etc.

The second function of a GIS would be storage of the resulting quotients, coefficients and other measures and values — storage by location, spatial arrangement (topology) or in terms of other characteristics. This function is of obvious value for an analyst or policy-maker requiring data at any given point of time. A third function is analysis — a function which breaks into four parts. The first is *selection or sampling* of observational units from the data base, together with the choice of the proper scale of measurement. For example, in the case of location quotients, an analyst might judge that in the United States quotients by counties in the United States rather than by states are more appropriate for the problem being attacked. Further, he/she may not wish to examine the quotients for each of the 3000 counties, but only a sample of them. Accordingly he/she must designate the number of units to be studied, the need for representation by region and/or size of area, and so forth.

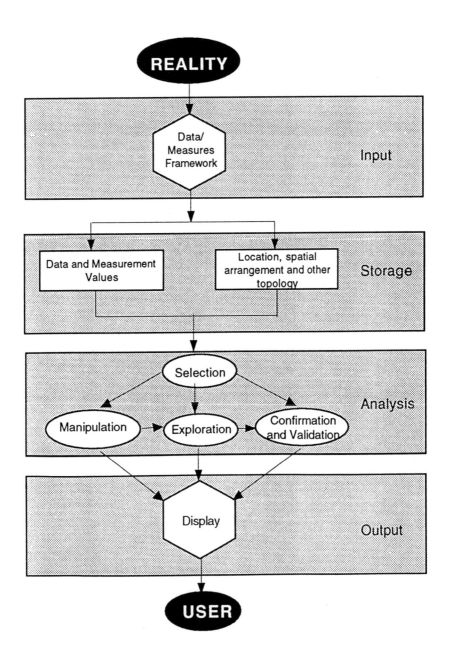

Figure 2.2 GIS structure (after Anselin and Getis, 1992, Fig. 1)

The three other parts of the function are manipulation, exploration and confirmation (validation). A typical *manipulation* might be the construction of a localization curve for a complete set of location quotients. This manipulation might be designed to indicate the extent of differences among states, and the overall concentration in the location of the item being examined. A typical *exploration* might be the construction of localization curves for key years in the past. The purpose might be to see how the concentration of an industry by the selected areal unit (e.g., state or county) has been changing, if at all. A typical *confirmation* or *non-confirmation* might be of an hypothesis that the concentration of the industry has been steadily increasing over time. However, when it comes to making a decision regarding the expansion of the industry in any given area, then comparative cost analysis built upon the base of the existing GIS would require regional science theory and advanced analysis. Such would be necessary to identify the key locational cost and revenue differentials for decision making, as discussed in the previous sections.

We can also illustrate this GIS process with regard to the location of a shopping center (a services complex). A first element in the data framework might be the identification of each area that might be served by a new shopping center. Next might be the determination of the population of each such area, and its per capita income. Then information on age–sex ratio and family composition of the population of each area might be essential since purchases by type and magnitude would vary by such attributes.

A next step in the use of a GIS might involve sampling the population of each area. There identification of each area that has desirable attributes must be made as well as a decision on the size of the sample and degree of stratification by age–sex ratio and family type. Among others, a key question might be asked of each person or family: if a new shopping center were located one (two, three or four) miles or five (ten, fifteen or twenty-five minutes) travel time from your residence, what percent of your expenditures on each of several specified goods and services would be made at that center?

Finally, once all the data were in, and extrapolated over time to take into account obvious changes (like aging of the population and expected settlement of new population) in each sampled area, it would be necessary to consider the impact upon each of these areas of the new road construction that would be required. Here a regional science type transportation model would need to be employed, ultimately to yield expected sales, revenues, costs and profits of each area, and thereby to reach a final decision on location.

The above two examples illustrate how GIS can and should be developed to furnish basic information for a location decision. In similar fashion GIS can provide basic information for the many decisions and policies regarding problems that can be usefully attacked by regional science methods to be discussed in subsequent chapters.

At this point, it is in order to remark generally about the way in which the GIS phases and various regional science methods complement each other and interconnect. The storage (stored data) phase will often need to be supplemented, at times extensively, for attacking a particular problem. This will be necessary if an appropriate selection of relevant aspects, scale of analysis, aggregation, clustering propensities, and sampling of elements or units is to be obtained for a regional science analysis. In the GIS data manipulation phase, construction of new indices, complicated ratios, curves, graphic presentations, and use of new concepts (as often is the case in identifying the relevant definition of distance, space and spatial associations) may be required as well as different smoothing processes and data disaggregation, partitioning and elimination for the application of regional science methods.

In subsequent exploratory analysis which looks for suggested patterns and arrangements, spatial or not, the overlap of GIS and regional science starts to become significant. Does spatial concentration seem to be decreasing? Has a new spacing or spatial arrangement been emerging in the last decade? Is an as yet unidentified force impacting the locational configuration? These are questions that are common to both GIS and regional science. They and other speculative-type inquiries and insights lead to the GIS confirmatory or validation phase and regional science investigations where there is need to employ techniques and ways to test hypotheses, establish confidence limits and other statistical techniques embracing in particular spatially oriented ones such as spatial autocorrelation.

In brief, GIS can and should provide the critical information for regional science analysis that employs those methods discussed in this book as well as others. Needless to say, there is no clear demarcation between GIS analysis and regional science methods. There is and can be much overlap. However, generally speaking and in the minds of many scholars, the GIS framework by and large emphasizes empirically oriented research whereas, as is evident in the chapters to follow, regional science methods by and large focus on theoretical (causally) oriented investigations.

2.5 Concluding remarks

This chapter has been concerned with the comparative cost procedure for evaluating the economic feasibility of the location of any particular industry or service trade in a given region. It focuses on one type of optimizing behavior, namely cost minimization. It has had a widespread and fruitful application and promises to continue to be one of the most powerful tools in the kit of the regional scientist. Yet this approach in its traditional framework pertains to partial equilibrium only. That is, it looks at behavior within a single industry, assuming as given the structure of all other industries as well as demand and prices. Therefore, as already noted, sound regional analysis requires that the traditional comparative cost approach be supplemented with more general techniques capable of cutting through the restrictive bounds of single-industry analysis. This supplementation will be pursued in the subsequent chapters dealing with interregional and regional input-output techniques, econometrics, programming, industrial complex analyses, gravity models, social accounting, and applied general interregional equilibrium analysis. Additionally, factors outside the economic sphere must be weighed in forming locational decisions.

Surrounding the comparative cost approach are a number of measures relating to industrial location and regional distributions — location quotients, coefficients of localization, localization curves, shift ratios, indexes of specialization, and many others. They are essentially designed to describe and summarize systems of industrial locations, spatial patterns of population and subpopulations, and locations of other relevant items and phenomena. They are valuable for portraying the 'what' of systems as they are or have been. They permit a view of the internal structure of regions along several dimensions. They permit the comparison of a given region's structure with the structure of other regions and, where justifiable, with the system as a whole or other fictitious norms. Moreover, they permit identification of changes over time in the structure of industry, the region and the system. Thus, in a very important way they supplement approaches such as comparative cost analysis and various other methods of analysis to be discussed in subsequent chapters. These methods require, both for implementation and testing, structural knowledge in the form of factual materials on the outcome of the interplay of underlying forces, both currently and in the past. However, such supplementation is not of an analytical nature. For example, although comparative cost analysis can suggest changes to be expected in coefficients of localization, shift ratios, specialization curves, etc., the converse cannot be stated. True, a high coefficient of localization for a particular industry may reflect a major cost differential or scale economy factor, but of itself it tells nothing of what the causal factor is, how important it is in relation to others, and to what extent this factor is expected to persist.

However, in the chapters to follow we shall see how these quotients coefficients, curves, indices, etc. do play an essential role along with the basic comparative cost approach in the study of regional development and the formulation of appropriate regional policy.

Finally, we have cursorily discussed basic elements of a GIS (Geographic Information System). While the several spatial and location measures (location quotients, etc.) discussed in this chapter have in essence been a GIS for location analysts in the early 40s, and while all of them belong to a modern GIS, as yet GIS has not been sufficiently and comprehensively developed for use in location studies and for most of the studies discussed in later chapters. Nonetheless, in the revolutionary computer age that is rapidly unfolding, GIS will come to be a major, if not indispensable, input into all regional science research.

Endnotes

1   For older literature on location theory, the reader is referred to von Thünen (1826), Launhardt (1882, 1885), Weber (1929), Palander (1935), Lösch (1954), Dean (1938), Hoover (1937), Dunn (1954), Greenhut (1956), Isard (1956). There is an elementary statement on location theory in Hoover (1948). For more recent literature, much of which has become abstract and advanced, the reader is referred to Beckmann and Thisse (1986), Chatterji and Kuenne (1990), and to recent articles such as McCann (1993) in issues of the *Journal of Regional Science, Regional Science and Urban Economics* and other journals and publications cited therein.

2   Or to an intermediate site within the locational triangle formed by connecting with straight lines the coal, ore and market sites.

3   This transport cost advantage of Fall River results from the much higher transport rates charged on steel compared to coal, reflecting the practice of transport companies of charging 'what the traffic can bear.' However, if 5 tons of coal were required per ton steel, as was the case

in the mid-19th century, Pittsburgh's advantage on coal would greatly outweigh its disadvantage on access to the Boston market.

4   These transport cost figures are taken from Isard and Whitney (1952), Tables XXII, XXIII, pp. 125, 127.

5   Political factors are also relatively favorable for a Chungjin area works. Close by, to the North, is the recently established Sunbong Free Trade Zone, and to the East and North is the Tumen River Development Area in whose development planning North Korea participates along with Russia, China and Mongolia.

6   For an extended discussion of items covered in this section and other related ones, see Isard et al. (1960) chapters 5 and 7.

References

Airov, Joseph. 1959. *The Location of the Synthetic Fiber Industry: A Study in Regional Analysis.* New York: John Wiley.

Alexander, J. W. 1958. 'Location of Manufacturing: Methods of Measurement,' *Annals of the Association of American Geographers*, 48.

Anselin, Luc, and Arthur Getis. 1992. 'Spatial Statistical Analysis and Geographical Information Systems,' *Annals of Regional Science*, 26, 19–23.

Bachi, Roberto. 1957. *Statistical Analysis of Geographical Series.* Jerusalem: Kaplan School, Hebrew University and Israel Central Bureau of Statistics.

Beckmann, Martin, and Jacques-Francois Thisse. 1986. 'The Location of Production Activities,' in P. Nijkamp, *Handbook of Regional Economics.* Amsterdam: North Holland, pp. 21–95.

Chatterji, Manas, and Robert E. Kuenne. 1990. *New Frontiers in Regional Science.* London: Macmillan.

Creamer, Daniel. 1943. 'Shifts of Manufacturing Industries,' in *Industrial Location and National Resources.* Washington, D.C.: U.S. National Resources Planning Board.

Cumberland, John. 1951. *The Locational Structure of the East Coast Steel Industry with Emphasis on the Feasibility of an Integrated New England Steel Mill.* Doctoral dissertation, Harvard University, Cambridge, Mass.

Dean, William H., Jr. 1938. *The Theory of the Geographic Location of Economic Activities.* Doctoral dissertation, Harvard University. Selections published, Ann Arbor, Mich.: Edward Brothers, Inc.

Duncan, Otis, R. P. Cuzzort, and Beverly Duncan. 1960. *Statistical Geography.* Glencoe, Ill.: The Free Press.

Dunn, Edgar S. 1954. *The Location of Agricultural Production.* Gainesville, Fla.: University of Florida.

Florence, P. Sargant. 1948. *Investment, Location, and Size of Plant.* Cambridge, England: University Press.

Florence, P. Sargant, W. G. Fritz, and R. C. Gilles. 1943. 'Measures of Industrial Distribution,' in *Industrial Location and National Resources.* Washington, D.C.: U.S. National Resources Planning Board, ch. 5.

Greenhut, Melvin L. 1956. *Plant Location in Theory and Practice.* Chapel Hill, N.C.: University of North Carolina Press.

Hagood, M. J., and Daniel O. Price. 1952. *Statistics for Sociologists.* New York: Henry Holt.

Hoover, Edgar M. 1937. *Location Theory and the Shoe and Leather Industries.* Cambridge, Mass.: Harvard University Press.

Hoover, Edgar M. 1948. *Location of Economic Activity.* New York: McGraw-Hill.

Hoover, Edgar M., and Joseph L. Fisher. 1949. 'Research in Regional Economic Growth,' *Problems in the Study of Economic Growth.* New York: Universities-National Bureau Committee on Economic Research, National Bureau of Economic Research.

Hurter, A. P., and J. S. Martinich. 1989. *Facility Location and the Theory of Production.* Boston: Kluwer.

Isard, Walter. 1948. 'Some Locational Factors in the Iron and Steel Industry Since the Early Nineteenth Century,' *Journal of Political Economy*, 56.

Isard, Walter. 1956. *Location and Space-Economy.* New York: John Wiley.

Isard, Walter, and William M. Capron. 1949. 'The Future Locational Pattern of Iron and Steel Production in the United States,' *Journal of Political Economy*, 57.

Isard, Walter, and John Cumberland. 1950. 'New England as a Possible Location for an Integrated Iron and Steel Works,' *Economic Geography*, 26.

Isard, Walter, and Hyung-Seog Lee. 1996. 'Economic Cooperation Between the Koreas: A Yessable Proposition,' *Peace Economics, Peace Science and Public Policy*, 4, Summer.

Isard, Walter, and Eugene W. Schooler. 1955. *Location Factors in the Petrochemical Industry*. Washington, D.C.: Office of Technical Services, U.S. Department of Commerce.

Isard, Walter, and Vincent H. Whitney. 1952. *Atomic Power, an Economic and Social Analysis*. New York: McGraw-Hill.

Krutilla, John V. 1952. *The Structure of Costs and Regional Advantage in Primary Aluminum Production*. Doctoral dissertation, Harvard University, Cambridge, Mass.

Lee, Hyung-Seog. 1997. *A Comparative Cost Analysis for an Integrated Steelworks for North Korea*. Doctoral dissertation, Cornell University.

Lindsay, John Robert. 1954. *The Location of Oil Refining in the United States*. Doctoral dissertation, Harvard University, Cambridge, Mass.

Lindsay, John Robert. 1956. 'Regional Advantage in Oil Refining,' *Papers and Proceedings of the Regional Science Association*, 2.

Lösch, August. 1954. *The Economics of Location*. New Haven, Conn.: Yale University Press.

McCann, Philip. 1993. 'The Logistic-Cost Location-Production Problem,' *Journal of Regional Science*, 33, 503–16.

Palander, Tord. 1935. *Beiträge zur Standortstheorie*. Uppsala, Sweden: Almqvist & Wiksells Boktryckeri-A.-B.

Schooler, Eugene W. 1954. *Regional Advantage in the Production of Chemicals from Petroleum and Natural Gas*. Doctoral dissertation, Harvard University, Cambridge, Mass.

Sternlieb, George, and James W. Hughes. 1988. *America's New Market Geography*. New Brunswick, N.J.: Center for Urban Policy Research, Rutgers University.

Thompson, Wilbur R. 1957. 'The Coefficient of Localization: An Appraisal,' *Southern Economic Journal*, 23.

Thünen, Johann Heinrich von. 1826. *Der isolierte Staat in Beziehung auf Landwirtschaft und Nationalökonomie*. Hamburg, Germany.

Weber, Alfred. 1929. *Theory of the Location of Industry*, translated by C. Friedrich. Chicago: University of Chicago Press.

3. Regional and interregional input-output analysis

Ronald E. Miller

3.0 Introduction

In the previous chapters we were concerned with regional growth and in particular the factors governing the location of basic industries and service trades in a given region of interest, among others, to a researcher, businessman, or policy maker.

We paid much attention to the steel industry, which has been so basic to the past economic growth of England, France, Germany, the United States, and more recently of Japan and South Korea, and whose development promises to be critical to further growth of lesser industrialized countries such as North Korea and China. But in conducting our comparative cost analysis, we needed to have beforehand estimates of: (a) size of the *existing* market (e.g., 9–11 million tons annually in the case of the 1953 Trenton steel works study for the Greater New York-Philadelphia Industrial Region) and/or (b) the *growth* of the market (e.g., the 15 million tons growth over the period 1994–2004 in South Korea's consumption of steel for the North Korean steel works study). To do the best possible job in estimating the size of the market, we in turn need to estimate the consumption of each steel fabricating and other steel consuming sectors, such as the automotive, shipbuilding, machinery, and construction sectors, among others, in the North Korean study. But such sectors must expand to enable a new steel works to operate; for example the automotive sector will need to supply: (a) new trucks for shipping the steel that is produced, (b) additional automobiles for the better-paid new steel workers, and (c) additional busses for transporting lesser-paid workers to the plant, etc. To provide these new demands for its product, the automotive sector will need to consume more steel (designated an indirect demand for steel). And so will most if not every other steel fabricating sector. But the increase in indirect demand does not stop here. The new income that will be earned in the steel and steel fabricating sectors will lead to demands of workers for new housing (which will cause the construction industry to expand still further and require still more additional steel), new power-driven equipment (which will cause the machinery sector to expand still further and require still more additional steel), more electricity (which will cause the electricity-producing sector to increase its demand for steel), and so forth. Thus, there result many rounds of indirect demand effects which can come to be a significant addition to the direct demand for steel.

While not perfect in many respects, the input-output framework does enable an analyst to arrive at a much more accurate estimate of what will be the relevant demand for steel once the steel works and related stimulated industry is in operation. This identification of indirect demands is one of the several tasks that make the input-output framework indispensable for effective regional science research. At the same time, by making explicit the interconnections of the many sectors of an economy with each other, it provides a very useful detailed statistical snapshot of an economy for any given base year. And as already implied in the above discussion, it is extremely useful in analyzing the impact of a change in any sector on the output of others.

The input-output framework of analysis was developed by Wassily Leontief in the late 1920s and early 1930s.[1] Because of its use of mathematics (mathematics, however, which is fairly simple) and relative complexity for the social scientist in those times, it was largely ignored. It came into preeminence during World War II in the United States when it was of critical importance to avoid bottlenecks in military production, particularly those that arise from large unexpected indirect demands.

In the beginning, input-output analysis was designed for application at a national level; subsequent developments have extended it to both the sub-national (regional) and supra-national (global) level. While our ultimate concern in this chapter will be with input-output at the regional (and interregional) level, some of the basic fundamentals are most easily described if the regional aspect is ignored. This will be done from time to time.

The basic framework is set out in Section 3.1, which moves from input-output accounts to an input-output model and then to illustrations of the diverse kinds of analysis that are possible with that model. The focus is on the economy of a single region. Sections 3.2 and 3.3 explore some of the input-output structures that have been developed to capture the ways in which two or more regions are connected economically. In Section 3.4 we examine some of the ways in which real-world input-output studies have dealt with the issue of data (un)availability. The final section indicates the kinds of connections that input-output accounts and models have with other techniques of regional analysis. Additional refinements and details are contained in four appendices. Throughout the chapter it will be assumed that you are familiar with the fundamentals of matrix notation and matrix algebra. These materials are reviewed in a brief Mathematical Appendix at the end of this chapter.

3.1 A single region

3.1.1 The statistical framework: input-output accounts

We imagine that the economic activity of a region can be associated with a number, say n, of producing 'sectors.' These can be thought of as 'industries' and might include resource-based activities (such as agriculture, forestry and mining), manufacturing (such as automobile, household appliance, computer or iron and steel production), and services (examples are finance, insurance, real estate, medical, private hospitals and schools, lodging and entertainment). For the present, we make the simplifying assumption that each of the sectors in the region produces a single, unique product. Input-output *accounts* attempt to capture the interconnections of an economy by recording, for a given period (say one year), the economic *transactions* that occur in the economy. These transactions can be viewed from the point of view of either the *selling* sector in the region or the *buying* sector in the region.

a. Accounting for transactions[2] The sales of a product by the sector that produced it may be to a sector where it will be used as an input to a production process (as in the case of electricity bought by an automobile manufacturer) or as a good to be consumed as a final product, for example, by households (electricity used for home lighting or television), by local, state or federal government (electricity to light an office building) or exported to users outside the region (New England electricity exported to Canada). There is also a 'middle ground' between an input bought for production, where it is used up in the manufacturing process (eggs bought by a bakery to make bread) and for final use (eggs bought by a consumer for tonight's dinner). Consider a stove (product of the 'electrical machinery' sector) that is bought by the bakery. A stove is certainly needed in the bread-making process, but it is not immediately used up. It may serve to replace a worn-out stove or to add to the current number of stoves, increasing the productive capacity of the bakery. In either case, it is a 'capital account' transaction (replacement capital in the first case, an addition to capital stock in the second); the others (eggs, electricity) are 'current account' items. The input-output data that are of most interest to us in this chapter are current account transactions. Sales of stoves to all industrial sectors would appear lumped together as sales from electrical machinery to 'investment.'[3]

In what follows

z_{ij} = the monetary value of sales from sector i to sector j over some period (often a recent year, the *base-year* data)

f_i = the value of sales of sector i goods to final consumers (households, exports, investment, and all levels of government are the major components of this 'final demand' category), and

x_i = the total value of goods produced by sector i in the region during the year (sector i's *gross output*).

Then

$$x_i = z_{i1} + z_{i2} + ... + z_{in} + f_i \qquad (3\text{-}1)$$

There is one of these equations for each sector ($i = 1, ..., n$).[4]

Alternatively, we might record the *purchases* that each sector in the region made in the base year in order to engage in production. These required inputs would generally be of two kinds: (1) those that come from some (usually not all) of the producing — sometimes called 'processing' — sectors (the electricity bought by the automobile sector), including possibly several types of services, and (2) inputs from what are known as the 'value added' or 'payments' sectors. These inputs would include payments to factors of production — labor (wages and salaries), land (rents), capital (interest and depreciation charges) — as well as direct and indirect taxes (considered to be payments for government services) and profits. Also, a sector will probably need imported goods.

Using the same notation as above, and letting

va_j = sector j's payments for value added items and

m_j = sector j's total imports (of all goods),

then a complete accounting of sector j's total outlays which is necessarily the same as sector j's total output, would be

$$x_j = z_{1j} + z_{2j} + ... + z_{nj} + va_j + m_j \tag{3-2}$$

There is one of these equations for each sector ($j = 1, ..., n$).

This double-entry kind of bookkeeping scheme is illustrated in Table 3-1. Each of the first n rows indicates the distribution of a sector's *output*, each of the first n columns shows the distribution of a sector's *input*; hence the name input-output accounts. In Table 3-1, the *interindustry* transactions are recorded in the upper left (dark box); this is where the economic connections among producing sectors are captured. This is known as an input-output *transactions* table, or matrix, often denoted in the input-output literature by $\mathbf{Z}$.

Table 3-1 Input-output accounts

	Interindustry Sales (Z)			Sales to Final Demand (f)				Total Sales (x)
	z_{11} z_{12}	$\cdots$	z_{1n}	c_1	i_1	g_1	e_1	x_1
	z_{21} z_{22}	$\cdots$	z_{2n}	c_2	i_2	g_2	e_2	x_2
	z_{n1} z_{n2}	$\cdots$	z_{nn}	c_n	i_n	g_n	e_n	x_n
Value Added	ℓ_1 ℓ_2 $\cdots$ ℓ_n ov_1 ov_2 $\cdots$ ov_n			Transactions between the payments sectors (including imports) and final demand				L OV
Imports	m_1 m_2 $\cdots$ m_n							M
Total Outlays (x)	x_1 x_2 $\cdots$ x_n			C	I	G	E	

Sector i's sales of output to final demand are represented in the rows in the box to the right of the transactions table; they are broken down into

c_i = personal consumption expenditures
i_i = purchases of i goods as investments
g_i = government purchases, and
e_i = exports.

Often in regional accounts, the government term is disaggregated into sales to state and local government, sg_i, and sales to the federal government, fg_i; so $g_i = sg_i + fg_i$. Also, exports are often distinguished between those to the rest of the country, er_i, and foreign exports, ef_i; so $e_i = er_i + ef_i$. And the total of all the elements in row i represents sector i's total sales or gross output, x_i.

Sector j's purchases of inputs from value added sectors are recorded in columns in the box below the transactions table. These include

ℓ_j = payments for labor services
ov_j = payments for all other value added items, and
m_j = payments for imported inputs.

Often in regional accounts imports, like exports, are broken down to those from the rest of the country, mr_j, and foreign imports, mf_j; so $m_j = mr_j + mf_j$. In a complete accounting scheme like this, the total value of all outlays (inputs) in column j will be the same as the total value all sales (outputs) in row j.

b. Connections to macroeconomic measures   The connection between the kind of information in Table 3-1 and more macroeconomic national or regional accounts is straightforward. Let C (personal consumption), I (investment), G (Government) and E (exports) denote *totals* of all elements in each of the four standard final demand columns. Also, let L, OV and M be *totals* across the two value added rows and the imports row.[5] Then

$$\sum_{i=1}^{n} x_i + L + OV + M$$

is the total value of all economic activity in the economy found as the sum of all row sums in Table 3-1. Also,

$$\sum_{j=1}^{n} x_j + C + I + G + E$$

is the total value of all economic activity found as the sum of all column sums in Table 3-1. These two ways of adding up everything must give the same result. And since $\sum_{i=1}^{n} x_i = \sum_{j=1}^{n} x_j$ (both are total gross outputs summed over all n sectors), then

$$C + I + G + (E - M) = L + OV = VA$$

where va_j (value added in sector j) is just $\ell_j + ov_j$ (sector j's expenditures on labor and on all other value added items). At the national level, the left-hand side is a measure of gross domestic product, and the right-hand side is national income (total factor payments); for regional accounts, the associated concepts are gross regional product and regional income.

c. Numerical example: Washington state transactions We use aggregated 1988 data for Washington State here and later to illustrate the basic input-output concepts. Transactions for an eight-sector version of the Washington economy are shown in Table 3-2.[6]

In Washington, aerospace is a very important sector (a great deal of Boeing aircraft production is located in the state), and both food products and forestry products are also very developed. This is reflected in the fact that these three sectors are displayed separately in the table; much of the remaining interindustry structure is aggregated into several other 'umbrella' sectors, such as 'Other Manufacturing and Construction.' Regional tables are often constructed in this way, so that the prominent sectors in the regional economy are portrayed in more explicit detail. Obviously, with such broadly defined sectors, the assumption of a single unique product as the output of each sector is less tenable. Nonetheless, this level of sectoral detail serves to illustrate general principles.

It is important to understand how expenses on transportation and on wholesale and/or retail trade are usually accounted for in an input-output transactions table. Consider plywood in the Washington economy (an output of sector 3, forest products) that is bought for housing construction purposes by a developer (sector 5, other manufacturing and construction) and by a home-owner to build a dog house (personal consumption in final demand). The flow of this product begins at the plywood manufacturer (a mill in sector 3) and ends at either the developer's site (sector 5) or the consumer's home (final demand). Assume that the developer deals directly with the mill whereas the home-owner buys from a lumber yard. Between origin and destination there will be transportation services for which a charge is imposed (probably trucking in this case) to move the plywood from the mill to either the developer's site or to a wholesaler or retailer (the lumber yard), which, in turn, provides a service (wholesale or retail trade, 'merchandising') for which another charge is imposed. A buyer, then, usually pays a *purchaser's price* that includes (a) the *producer's price* [f.o.b. (free on board) price], (b) a transportation charge (margin) and (c) unless the buyer deals directly with the producer, a wholesale and/or retail trade charge (margin). [The items in (a) and (b) constitute what is known as the c.i.f. price (cost, insurance and freight).]

If an input-output transactions table were to record all of the plywood purchasers' payments as going to trade (sector 7) and/or transportation (in

Table 3-2 Washington transactions, 1988 (billions of dollars)

	Agriculture, Forestry, Mining	Food Products	Forest Products	Aerospace	Other Manuf. and Construction	Transport., Communicat., Utilities	Trade	Other Services
1 AGRICULTURE, FORESTRY, MINING	464.0	1244.5	770.5	1.6	144.8	75.2	49.9	15.8
2 FOOD PRODUCTS	124.7	345.4	9.7	0.0	4.6	23.2	775.6	45.2
3 FOREST PRODUCTS	23.6	164.0	2224.9	21.0	592.7	22.0	213.5	60.3
4 AEROSPACE	0.0	0.0	0.0	206.9	25.6	24.3	0.0	0.0
5 OTHER MANUFACTURING AND CONSTRUCTION	259.9	355.9	489.5	163.8	2554.5	811.0	850.1	1771.4
6 TRANSPORTATION, COMMUNICATIONS, UTILITIES	135.0	213.5	653.4	131.2	1055.7	1583.8	1073.4	1248.5
7 TRADE	121.0	295.0	308.7	54.1	1309.6	214.9	781.7	567.4
8 OTHER SERVICES	87.3	201.6	227.1	512.3	1258.1	636.3	2141.6	5017.9
LABOR INCOME	1445.2	594.5	1254.1	3415.0	7197.4	4448.5	8556.5	13874.1
OTHER VALUE ADDED	1330.5	1282.6	1949.2	339.4	5087.1	4595.1	6561.0	6676.5
IMPORTS (FROM REST OF U.S.)	384.9	1479.1	902.1	8185.0	8966.6	1539.4	1853.9	1977.1
IMPORTS (FOREIGN)	62.8	120.7	214.8	1178.2	1943.6	682.5	326.3	137.0
TOTAL PURCHASES	4438.9	6296.8	9004.1	14208.5	30140.3	14656.2	23183.5	31391.2

FINAL DEMAND SECTORS

	Personal Consumption	State and Local Government	Investment	Federal Government	Exports (to Rest of U.S.)	Exports (Foreign)	Total Sales
1 AGRICULTURE, FORESTRY, MINING	259.9	21.0	247.9	9.1	698.1	436.5	4438.9
2 FOOD PRODUCTS	1393.5	94.5	30.2	133.7	2774.8	541.7	6296.8
3 FOREST PRODUCTS	61.9	32.1	5.6	30.5	2997.4	2554.6	9004.1
4 AEROSPACE	0.0	0.0	45.0	2411.7	4883.0	6612.0	14208.5
5 OTHER MANUFACTURING AND CONSTRUCTION	1506.0	2317.3	7308.4	2038.1	7350.2	2364.2	30140.3
6 TRANSPORTATION, COMMUNICATIONS, UTILITIES	3447.1	383.1	94.2	145.2	3723.8	768.3	14656.2
7 TRADE	12995.3	157.6	427.7	83.2	4204.3	1663.1	23183.5
8 OTHER SERVICES	13641.1	1002.8	71.0	215.4	6136.7	242.0	31391.2
LABOR INCOME	0.0	5698.8	0.0	2514.5	0.0	0.0	48998.6
OTHER VALUE ADDED	6804.1	879.0	0.0	747.8	0.0	0.0	36252.3
IMPORTS (FROM REST OF U.S.)	13623.4	1334.4	1408.0	0.0	0.0	0.0	41653.9
IMPORTS (FOREIGN)	1339.1	44.0	440.0	0.0	0.0	0.0	6489.0
TOTAL	55071.4	11964.5	10078.0	8329.2	32768.3	15182.4	267713.3

Note: Sales to final demand sectors, and total sales by row are recorded below the transactions matrix.

sector 6) and then most of the transportation sector's purchases as coming from the sectors whose outputs were being moved (like the plywood from sector 3), the fact that plywood is used as an input by developers and households would get lost. It would appear that most, if not all, plywood was 'used' as an input by the transportation sector and that households' major consumption 'good' was trade. So the usual convention is to show the value of the plywood in *producers'* prices in the construction and household columns, while transportation and trade charges (reflected in *purchasers'* costs) are recorded as 'sales' from the transportation and trade sector rows, respectively, to the construction and household columns.

3.1.2 Technical coefficients and the input-output model

To move from the information in an input-output transactions table to an input-output *model* of the regional economy, we need to define what Leontief called technical coefficients of production (or direct input coefficients). Take an observed z_{ij} in the transactions table and divide it by x_j, the output of the sector that bought the input. These coefficients are usually denoted by a_{ij}, so

$$a_{ij} = z_{ij}/x_j \qquad (3\text{-}3)$$

They indicate the value of input i used in making a dollar's worth of output j. If we arrange all of these in a table of n rows and columns, we have a technical coefficients or direct input coefficients matrix (also known as a direct requirements matrix):

$$\mathbf{A} = \begin{bmatrix} a_{11} & a_{12} & \cdots & a_{1n} \\ \vdots & \vdots & \vdots & \vdots \\ a_{n1} & a_{n2} & \cdots & a_{nn} \end{bmatrix} \qquad (3\text{-}4)$$

In a regional context, this is more properly called an *intraregional* direct input coefficients matrix. Often the name is compressed to regional direct inputs (or requirements) matrix, sometimes denoted **R**, with elements r_{ij}. Irrespective of the name, the important fact is that it records the inputs of regionally supplied inputs per dollar of regionally produced output.

Notice that the sum down column j is the total amount that sector j spent on inputs from all regional sectors per dollar's worth of its output.[7] At a national level, Leontief suggested that the information in each column is very much a kind of 'recipe' for production in that sector — for each dollar's worth of its output, sector j bought $\$a_{1j}$ of sector 1's output, $\$a_{2j}$ from sector 2, ..., and $\$a_{nj}$ from sector n. Value added and foreign imports used in production are not included in the **A** matrix. At the regional level, this 'recipe' view may be a bit misleading — many necessary sectoral inputs may be imported from outside the region.[8]

These direct input coefficients are, at this point, just a reexpression of base year facts. In an input-output model, they are used in the following way: if one were to predict that x_j next year was going to be \$1000, then the necessary inputs to that production would be calculated as a_{1j} x \$1000 from sector 1, a_{2j} x \$1000 from sector 2, ..., and a_{nj} x \$1000 from sector n. If, instead, x_j was predicted to be \$50,000, then the input-output model requires that the value of inputs purchased from each sector i would be a_{ij} x \$50,000. The assumption is that these coefficients of production are fixed and independent of the level of output of each of the sectors. Twice the output requires twice the inputs; ten times the output requires ten times the inputs; etc. There are no economies of scale in production in any of the sectors in this input-output model — one of the weaknesses of the input-output method.[9]

Once a complete set of base-year coefficients has been calculated, each of the z_{ij} terms in (3-1) can be rewritten [from the definition in (3-3)] as $z_{ij} = a_{ij}x_j$, so (3-1) can be expressed as

$$x_i = a_{i1}x_1 + a_{i2}x_2 + ... + a_{in}x_n + f_i \tag{3-5}$$

There is one linear equation like this for each of the n sectors, just as there were n original equations in (3-1).

All of this information can be nicely summarized using matrix notation. Let the n gross outputs be arranged in an n-element column vector, $\mathbf{x} = \begin{bmatrix} x_1 \\ x_2 \\ \vdots \\ x_n \end{bmatrix}$ and let the n final demand figures be similarly arranged in an n-element column vector, $\mathbf{f} = \begin{bmatrix} f_1 \\ f_2 \\ \vdots \\ f_n \end{bmatrix}$.

Using notations and operations from matrix algebra (these are reviewed in the Mathematical Appendix), compact representations of the n equations in (3-1) and (3-5) are

$$\mathbf{x} = \mathbf{Zi} + \mathbf{f} \tag{3-6}$$

and

$$\mathbf{x} = \mathbf{Ax} + \mathbf{f} \tag{3-7}$$

where **i** is an n-element column vector of 1s. Using an $(n \times n)$ identity

matrix, $\mathbf{I} = \begin{bmatrix} 1 & 0 & \dots & 0 \\ 0 & 1 & \dots & 0 \\ \vdots & \vdots & & \vdots \\ 0 & 0 & \dots & 1 \end{bmatrix}$, and rearranging,

$$\mathbf{Ix} - \mathbf{Ax} = \mathbf{f}$$

or

$$(\mathbf{I} - \mathbf{A})\mathbf{x} = \mathbf{f} \tag{3-8}$$

For later reference, it is worth noting that the process of creating the **A** matrix whose elements are given in (3-3) can be expressed compactly as[10]

$$\mathbf{A} = \mathbf{Z}\,(\hat{\mathbf{x}})^{-1} \tag{3-9}$$

This representation also allows straightforward derivation of (3-7) from (3-6).[11]

a. Numerical example: direct input coefficients for Washington state Table 3-3 is the eight-sector **A** matrix for Washington, representing direct inputs of Washington-made products per dollar's worth of output of the Washington sectors. It is found by dividing each of the first eight entries in column 1 of Table 3-2 by $x_1 = \$4438.9$, each of the first eight entries in column 2 by $x_2 = \$6296.8$, ..., etc.[12]

Table 3-3 Washington state direct requirements matrix

	1	2	3	4	5	6	7	8
1	.1045	.1976	.0856	.0001	.0048	.0051	.0022	.0005
2	.0281	.0549	.0011	.0000	.0002	.0016	.0335	.0014
3	.0053	.0260	.2471	.0015	.0197	.0015	.0092	.0019
4	.0000	.0000	.0000	.0146	.0008	.0017	.0000	.0000
5	.0586	.0565	.0544	.0115	.0848	.0553	.0367	.0564
6	.0304	.0339	.0726	.0092	.0350	.1081	.0463	.0398
7	.0273	.0468	.0343	.0038	.0435	.0147	.0337	.0181
8	.0197	.0320	.0252	.0361	.0417	.0434	.0924	.1599

3.1.3 Input-output analysis

One of the most popular uses of an input-output model for economic *analysis* is to assess the economic impact of some 'external' shock to the economy. This could be, for example, a new foreign order for the product of one of the sectors in the economy, an anticipated decrease in consumer spending on a particular sector's product (for example, because of a government imposed luxury tax) or on the output of all sectors (for example, because of an increase in federal income tax rates). These are changes in elements of the final demand part of the model. In addition, the economic impacts of new plant openings (or of plant closings) can be examined in an input-output framework.

a. Economic impacts The expressions in (3-7) and (3-8) are just rearrangements of the base-year facts, **x**, **f** and **Z**, using the definition in (3-9) that transforms the elements of **Z** into **A**. The next step, to a model for economic analysis, is straightforward. Assume that, in the absence of 'new' information, the snapshot of the economy that is recorded in the direct requirements matrix, **A**, remains valid for a period beyond the base year. Suppose that a forecast is made of final demand elements for the coming year, based for example on anticipated federal tax policy changes (meaning either more or less spendable income for households, depending on the tax change) and perhaps also on announced foreign orders for one or more export products (such as Boeing airliners). This means that there is a new set of final demand numbers, **f***.

A typical illustration of input-output *impact analysis* is to use (3-8) to assess the effect on the economy in question of the new final demands. So **f*** and **A** are known, and we want to find the new gross outputs in each sector of the economy, **x***, that are required to satisfy the new demand. From (3-8),

$$(\mathbf{I} - \mathbf{A})\mathbf{x}^* = \mathbf{f}^* \tag{3-10}$$

Since final demands are the driving force in this input-output framework, this version of the model is said to be 'demand driven;' alternatively this is said to be a 'demand side' input-output model.[13] Just to be clear about the structure of this problem, here is a three-sector version of (3-7), with three known new final demands (the f_j^*'s). We are looking for three unknown new outputs, the x_j^*'s.

$$x_1^* = a_{11}x_1^* + a_{12}x_2^* + a_{13}x_3^* + f_1^*$$

$$x_2^* = a_{21}x_1^* + a_{22}x_2^* + a_{23}x_3^* + f_2^*$$

$$x_3^* = a_{31}x_1^* + a_{32}x_2^* + a_{33}x_3^* + f_3^*$$

By putting all terms except the f^*'s on the left-hand side, these equations become,

$$(1 - a_{11})x_1^* - a_{12}x_2^* - a_{13}x_3^* = f_1^*$$

$$- a_{21}x_1^* + (1 - a_{22})x_2^* - a_{23}x_3^* = f_2^* \tag{3-11}$$

$$- a_{31}x_1^* - a_{32}x_2^* + (1 - a_{33})x_3^* = f_3^*$$

This is (3-8) written out for this illustration. The a_{ij}'s and the f_i^*'s are known; the x_i^*'s are to be determined. This is a set of three *linear equations* with three unknowns. Solution of a set of linear equations as in (3-8) and (3-11) employs $(\mathbf{I} - \mathbf{A})^{-1}$, the inverse of $(\mathbf{I} - \mathbf{A})$.[14] Here,

$$\mathbf{x}^* = (\mathbf{I} - \mathbf{A})^{-1}\mathbf{f}^* \tag{3-12}$$

The inverse matrix on the right is known as the *Leontief Inverse*. It serves to transform the elements in $\mathbf{f}^*$ into necessary outputs throughout the economy in question, $\mathbf{x}^*$. It is also known as the *total requirements matrix* or as the *direct and indirect requirements matrix*. In the input-output literature, $(\mathbf{I} - \mathbf{A})^{-1}$ is often denoted by $\mathbf{B}$, so (3-12) can alternatively be expressed as

$$\mathbf{x}^* = \mathbf{Bf}^* \tag{3-12'}$$

The connection between the mathematics of the solution as in (3-12) and the concept of direct and indirect economic effects is provided by a mathematical series expression. In ordinary algebra, $1/(1 - a)$ or $(1 - a)^{-1}$ is known to be expressible as $(1 - a)^{-1} \cong 1 + a + a^2 + a^3 + \ldots + a^k$ provided $0 \le a \le 1$. The sum on the right becomes more accurate as k becomes large.[15] There is a similar kind of result in matrix algebra, for a square matrix $\mathbf{A}$ in which all elements are nonnegative and less than one, and in which all column sums are less than one. The direct requirements matrix in an input-output model satisfies these conditions. This result, known as the *power series expansion* of $(\mathbf{I} - \mathbf{A})^{-1}$, is

$$(\mathbf{I} - \mathbf{A})^{-1} \cong \mathbf{I} + \mathbf{A} + \mathbf{A}^2 + \mathbf{A}^3 + \ldots + \mathbf{A}^k \tag{3-13}$$

This looks exactly like the result for $(1 - a)^{-1}$, except that now the '1' is replaced by its matrix equivalent, an identity matrix, $\mathbf{I}$, and the single number 'a' is replaced by a matrix, $\mathbf{A}$.[16]

The point of this mathematical observation on the power series approximation to the Leontief inverse is that it provides an economic interpretation of the elements in the inverse. Instead of finding $\mathbf{x}^*$ as $(\mathbf{I} - \mathbf{A})^{-1}\mathbf{f}^*$, as in (3-12), we could use (3-13), so that,

$$\mathbf{x}^* \cong (\mathbf{I} + \mathbf{A} + \mathbf{A}^2 + \mathbf{A}^3 + \dots + \mathbf{A}^k)\mathbf{f}^* =$$
$$\mathbf{f}^* + \mathbf{A}\mathbf{f}^* + \mathbf{A}^2\mathbf{f}^* + \mathbf{A}^3\mathbf{f}^* + \dots + \mathbf{A}^k\mathbf{f}^* \qquad (3\text{-}14)$$

The first term on the right is just $\mathbf{f}^*$. This obviously captures the *initial effects* of the new final demand on each of the sectors in the economy. It says that the new outputs must certainly be as large as the new final demands. The next term is $\mathbf{A}\mathbf{f}^*$; it records the fact that in making the new outputs for $\mathbf{f}^*$, a set of direct inputs of the sort $a_{ij}f_j^*$ are needed. Suppose $a_{ij} = 0.2$ and $f_j^* = \$100$; the *direct effect* on sector i will be that sector j has to buy $a_{ij}f_j^* = \$20$ of i's goods as inputs to production to satisfy $f_j^* = \$100$. The next term, $\mathbf{A}^2\mathbf{f}^*$, will contain terms like $a_{ki}a_{ij}f_j^*$. Suppose $a_{ki} = 0.05$ — sector i uses $\$0.05$ of sector k's product as an input for each dollar of sector i production. Since we have just seen that i's output must increase by $\$20$ to satisfy demands on it from sector j, this means that sector k's output must increase by $\$1.00$ $[a_{ki}a_{ij}f_j^* = (0.05)(0.20)(\$100)]$. This is an *indirect effect* of f_j^* on sector k through sector i. Each succeeding term in (3-14) captures another 'layer' of interconnection. In $\mathbf{A}^3\mathbf{f}^*$ there will be terms like $a_{gk}a_{ki}a_{ij}f_j^*$ in which the output effect on sector g is transmitted from f_j^* via *two* intermediate sectors, i and k. And so forth for the terms containing $\mathbf{A}$ to higher and higher powers. This illustrates why the Leontief inverse is known as the matrix of direct and indirect requirements. (Actually, it is *initial*, direct and indirect requirements; often $\mathbf{f}^*$ and $\mathbf{A}\mathbf{f}^*$ are lumped together and called 'direct' effects.)

It is important to recognize that we can just as well use the structure in (3-8) and (3-10) to find *changes* in $\mathbf{x}$ ($\Delta\mathbf{x}$) due to changes in $\mathbf{f}$ ($\Delta\mathbf{f}$). In this form,[17]

$$\Delta\mathbf{x} = (\mathbf{I} - \mathbf{A})^{-1}\Delta\mathbf{f} \qquad (3\text{-}15)$$

Notice also that one or more elements in $\Delta\mathbf{f}$ may be negative as well as positive (and zero, if no change is projected for one or more sectors). For example, a relaxation of tariffs on agricultural goods might lead to increased exports from agriculture (a positive element in the agriculture row of $\Delta\mathbf{f}$) while an increase in those tariffs could well lead to a decrease in agricultural exports (a negative element in the agriculture row of $\Delta\mathbf{f}$).

b. Numerical example: economic impacts in Washington state The Leontief inverse that captures direct and indirect connections for the Washington State economy is shown in Table 3-4. Suppose that a foreign airline places a new order with Boeing in Washington State for $250 million worth of commercial airliners. What might be the economic impact of this order on the state's economy? A response to this question is easily found using the input-output framework. Since it is the impact of this single exogenous change in export final demands for airliners that we wish to assess, we formulate a Δf in which the new airliner demand appears in row 4 (the aerospace sector) and all other elements are zero, namely,[18]

$$\Delta f = \begin{bmatrix} 0 \\ 0 \\ 0 \\ 250 \\ 0 \\ 0 \\ 0 \\ 0 \end{bmatrix}$$

Table 3-4 Washington state total requirements matrix

	1	2	3	4	5	6	7	8
1	1.1264	.2408	.1306	.0007	.0098	.0081	.0131	.0027
2	.0350	1.0678	.0078	.0003	.0026	.0030	.0377	.0030
3	.0120	.0422	1.3332	.0027	.0299	.0048	.0161	.0057
4	.0002	.0002	.0003	1.0148	.0010	.0020	.0002	.0002
5	.0818	.0941	.1016	.0169	1.1044	.0742	.0575	.0794
6	.0477	.0622	.1230	.0138	.0519	1.1289	.0651	.0587
7	.0390	.0664	.0589	.0060	.0531	.0222	1.0435	.0273
8	.0389	.0628	.0613	.0459	.0647	.0650	.1232	1.2006

Using the $(I - A)^{-1}$ matrix in Table 3-4 and the model in 'Δ-form' [as in (3-15)] in conjunction with this Δf, we have (remember that the units here are millions of dollars)

$$\Delta\mathbf{x} = (\mathbf{I} - \mathbf{A})^{-1}\Delta\mathbf{f} = \begin{bmatrix} .1662 \\ .0823 \\ .6668 \\ 253.7037 \\ 4.2258 \\ 3.4441 \\ 1.4888 \\ 11.4666 \end{bmatrix}$$

The economic impact has been quantified, in terms of values of output needed from each of the sectors in the Washington economy to support delivery of \$250 million worth of commercial airliners for export. In terms of *changes in gross outputs* (and now not in millions), $\Delta x_1 =$ \$166,200, $\Delta x_2 =$ \$82,300, ..., $\Delta x_7 =$ \$1,488,800 and $\Delta x_8 =$ \$11,466,600.[19] Notice that there is no 'time' element here. This is not necessarily the impact next week or next month or next quarter. It represents what the total value of output from each sector will have to have been by the time that the \$250 million airplane order is completely filled by Boeing.

c. Closure with respect to households One criticism of this use of the input-output model is that it tends to *underestimate* economic impacts because it omits the interaction between households' spendable income (particularly wages and salaries) that results directly or indirectly from economic activity and the consequent household spending on consumer goods. This is because households are *exogenous* in the model; payment for labor services is included in value added and consumer spending is included in final demand. Both are outside the transactions matrix.

One way to overcome this criticism is to treat households as another economically connected 'production' sector, adding one more row and column to the $\mathbf{Z}$ and $\mathbf{A}$ matrices; households become the $(n + 1)$-st sector, selling the 'product' labor services and buying consumer goods. Denote the transactions and direct inputs matrices with $(n + 1)$ rows and columns by $\overline{\mathbf{Z}}$ and $\overline{\mathbf{A}}$. Elements in the $(n + 1)$-st row of $\overline{\mathbf{Z}}$, $z_{n+1,j}$, represent payments by sector j for labor inputs during the base year. Elements in the $(n + 1)$-st column of $\overline{\mathbf{Z}}$, $z_{i,n+1}$, record the value of household base year purchases of sector i goods. In the added row of the $\overline{\mathbf{A}}$ matrix, the coefficients are $a_{n+1,j} = z_{n+1,j}/x_j$; these are 'labor input coefficients.' In the added column in the $\overline{\mathbf{A}}$ matrix, the new coefficients will be $a_{i,n+1} = z_{i,n+1}/x_{n+1}$, where the denominator is some measure of the gross output of the household sector, which can be taken to be total household income.[20] These are 'household consumption coefficients.' There could also be an element in the bottom row and last column of the new $\overline{Z}$ and $\overline{A}$; the coefficient would be $a_{n+1,n+1}$ $= z_{n+1,n+1}/x_{n+1}$. The numerator in this case (bottom row and last column element of $\overline{Z}$) would represent expenditures by households during the base year on labor services (baby sitters, window washers, gardeners, maids), although it is often the case that all of these kinds of 'labor' inputs used by households are recorded as household purchases from one or more of the services sectors.[21]

In an input-output model that has been closed with respect to households in this way, the Leontief inverse (total requirements matrix) is found using $\overline{A}$, namely as $\overline{B} = (I - \overline{A})^{-1}$. It is common in the literature to speak of this matrix as capturing the direct, indirect and *induced* effects of new final demands. 'Induced' is the indication that the input-output model has been closed with respect to households.

d. Numerical example: a closed model for Washington state Tables 3-5 and 3-6 contain the $\overline{A}$ and $\overline{B}$ $[= (I - \overline{A})^{-1}]$ matrices for the Washington economy with households introduced into the endogenous part of the model as sector 9. To illustrate this kind of exercise, without going into the many subtleties regarding exactly how to get at a measure of disposable personal income in the state, we use total sales in the labor income row (Table 3-2) as x_9, so that, for example, the first coefficient in column 9 is $z_{19}/x_9 = \$259.9/\$48998.6 = 0.0053$. The accompanying Leontief inverse containing direct, indirect and induced requirements in the Washington economy is in Table 3-6.[22]

If we now use this input-output model with household activities endogenized to assess the impact of the foreign airline order of $250 million for Boeing commercial aircraft, the approach is exactly the same, except that now the vector of changes in final demands, $\Delta\overline{f}$, will have nine elements. There will still be 250 in the fourth position, so that $\Delta\overline{f}$ looks like

$$\Delta\overline{f} = \begin{bmatrix} 0 \\ 0 \\ 0 \\ 250 \\ 0 \\ 0 \\ 0 \\ 0 \\ 0 \end{bmatrix}$$

Table 3-5 Washington state direct requirements matrix (closed model)

	1	2	3	4	5	6	7	8	9
1	.1045	.1976	.0856	.0001	.0048	.0051	.0022	.0005	.0030
2	.0281	.0549	.0011	.0000	.0002	.0016	.0335	.0014	.0163
3	.0053	.0260	.2471	.0015	.0197	.0015	.0092	.0019	.0007
4	.0000	.0000	.0000	.0146	.0008	.0017	.0000	.0000	.0000
5	.0586	.0565	.0544	.0115	.0848	.0553	.0367	.0564	.0177
6	.0304	.0339	.0726	.0092	.0350	.1081	.0463	.0398	.0404
7	.0273	.0468	.0343	.0038	.0435	.0147	.0337	.0181	.1524
8	.0197	.0320	.0252	.0361	.0417	.0434	.0924	.1599	.1600
9	.3256	.0944	.1393	.2403	.2388	.3035	.3691	.4420	.0000

Table 3-6 Washington state total requirements matrix (closed model)

	1	2	3	4	5	6	7	8	9
1	1.1384	.2484	.1398	.0082	.0190	.0191	.0263	.0186	.0274
2	.0626	1.0854	.0292	.0177	.0237	.0283	.0681	.0395	.0630
3	.0186	.0464	1.3383	.0069	.0350	.0109	.0235	.0145	.0152
4	.0003	.0003	.0004	1.0149	.0012	.0021	.0004	.0004	.0004
5	.1345	.1278	.1425	.0501	1.1449	.1226	.1157	.1492	.1206
6	.1249	.1114	.1830	.0624	.1112	1.1998	.1505	.1611	.1766
7	.2307	.1885	.2077	.1265	.2001	.1981	1.2552	.2813	.4381
8	.2873	.2211	.2540	.2022	.2552	.2929	.3976	1.5297	.5679
9	.6614	.4215	.5133	.4162	.5074	.6069	.7307	.8763	1.5122

The bottom 0 represents the fact that there is no change in final demand for labor services. In this case, $\Delta\bar{\mathbf{x}}$ contains nine elements, where Δx_9 represents the impact on household earnings in Washington because of the airliner order. Now we find that

$$\Delta\bar{\mathbf{x}} = (\mathbf{I} - \bar{\mathbf{A}})^{-1}\Delta\bar{\mathbf{f}} = \begin{bmatrix} 2.0483 \\ 4.4185 \\ 1.7140 \\ 253.7313 \\ 12.5222 \\ 15.5981 \\ 31.6353 \\ 50.5405 \\ 104.0450 \end{bmatrix}$$

To make it easier to compare results from the open and the closed models, we put $\Delta\mathbf{x}$ (open model) and $\Delta\bar{\mathbf{x}}$ (closed model, except for the last element), side by side:

$\Delta\mathbf{x}$ (Open Model)

$\Delta\bar{\mathbf{x}}$ (Closed Model)
(Sectors 1 through 8)

$$\begin{bmatrix} .1662 \\ .0823 \\ .6668 \\ 253.7037 \\ 4.2258 \\ 3.4441 \\ 1.4888 \\ 11.4666 \end{bmatrix} \qquad \begin{bmatrix} 2.0483 \\ 4.4185 \\ 1.7140 \\ 253.7313 \\ 12.5222 \\ 15.5981 \\ 31.6353 \\ 50.5405 \end{bmatrix}$$

With the possible exception of sector 4 (aerospace), the differences are substantial; total output, summed over the eight original sectors in the Washington economy, is \$275.2443 million in the open model and \$372.2082 in the closed model. The difference is a measure of the importance of the labor income/consumer spending link in the regional economy, at least as it is reflected in the input-output model that is closed with respect to households.[23] In addition, in the closed model $\Delta x_9 =$ \$104,045,000 represents the direct and indirect effects of the airplane order on household income in the state.

e. Multipliers A multiplier in an input-output model is the ratio of the *total* effect, T, to the *initial* effect, N, of an exogenous change (such as a change in final demand for sector i, Δf_i); it is the amount by which the initial

effect is magnified (multiplied) to become a total effect. In input-output
terms, total effects may be found in an open model (direct and indirect
effects) or in a closed model (direct, indirect and induced effects).

There is not complete consistency in the input-output literature on the
labels to use to identify various multipliers; the basic ideas, however, are
fairly straightforward. The three main kinds of multipliers are *output*,
income and *employment*; at the regional level, *value added* multipliers may
also be of interest. Different names are often used, depending on what one
chooses to call the 'initial' effect.[24]

Output multipliers For the three-sector illustration in (3-11), the
general solution in (3-12′) looks like,

$$\mathbf{x}^* = \begin{bmatrix} b_{11} & b_{12} & b_{13} \\ b_{21} & b_{22} & b_{23} \\ b_{31} & b_{32} & b_{33} \end{bmatrix} \begin{bmatrix} f_1^* \\ f_2^* \\ f_3^* \end{bmatrix}$$

or, written out in full,

$$x_1^* = b_{11}f_1^* + b_{12}f_2^* + b_{13}f_3^*$$
$$x_2^* = b_{21}f_1^* + b_{22}f_2^* + b_{23}f_3^* \tag{3-16}$$
$$x_3^* = b_{31}f_1^* + b_{32}f_2^* + b_{33}f_3^*$$

Each b_{ij} translates a new final demand figure, f_j^*, into the output needed
from sector i (on the left) to satisfy that final demand, $b_{ij}f_j^*$. The right-
hand side of row i, $\sum_{j=1}^{3} b_{ij}f_j^*$, gives the total amount of sector i output
needed to satisfy *all* elements of new final demand — f_1^*, f_2^* and f_3^*; this
is just x_i^*.

Look, instead, down a column on the right-hand side of (3-16). For
column j, $b_{1j}f_j^*$ represents the output from sector 1 needed to satisfy f_j^*.
Similarly, $b_{2j}f_j^*$ and $b_{3j}f_j^*$ indicate what is needed from sectors 2 and 3,
respectively, to satisfy f_j^*. Then the *economy-wide impact* of f_j^* will be

$$b_{1j}f_j^* + b_{2j}f_j^* + b_{3j}f_j^* = \sum_{i=1}^{3} b_{ij}f_j^*$$

This just adds up the output from each of the sectors (all are in monetary
terms) to give a 'total output' figure that is required from all sectors
because of the new final demand for sector j, f_j^*.

Suppose $f_2^* = \$1.00$; then this economy-wide economic impact is just
$\sum_{i=1}^{3} b_{i2}$, the sum of elements in column 2 of **B**. In the input-output literature,

these column sums of $\mathbf{B}$ $[= (\mathbf{I} - \mathbf{A})^{-1}]$ are generally known as an 'output multipliers;' they represent how much each dollar of *final demand* for a particular sector (column) is blown up (multiplied) to an *economy-wide* output requirement. In fact, the entire matrix $\mathbf{B}$ is a matrix of *sector-specific* output multipliers, since each element, b_{ij}, translates final demand for a particular j into required output from a specific i.[25]

For an n-sector model, if the exogenous change is $\Delta f_j = \$1$; this induces an initial *output* effect, N, of $\Delta x_j = \$1$. [Sector j must certainly produce (at least) $\$1$ in new output to satisfy the new final demand of $\$1$ for its product. This corresponds to the $\mathbf{f}^*$ term in the power series in (3-14).]

The economy-wide response is the total effect, T, which is $\sum_{i=1}^{n} b_{ij}$. [This is the direct and indirect (but not induced) effect, since this model is not closed with respect to households.] So $T/N = \sum_{i=1}^{n} b_{ij}/\Delta x_j$; since $\Delta x_j = 1$, the denominator disappears, and the multiplier is just $\sum_{i=1}^{n} b_{ij}$. This is often denoted by O_j, so

$$O_j = \sum_{i=1}^{n} b_{ij} \tag{3-17}$$

Income multipliers Many analysts feel that such output multipliers are not very useful since they add up outputs over all sectors in the economy, treating a dollar's worth of output from sector 1 and from sector 3 (for example) as equally 'important.'[26] (Are a new dollar's worth of aircraft output and of construction or electricity output of equal value in an economy?) A more interesting measure of economic importance may be some indicator that reflects the *employment* effects associated with output in the various sectors; *income multipliers* provide one way to do just that.

Suppose we have the information that would be needed to construct a set of labor input coefficients for the economy [in particular, the first n coefficients for the $(n + 1)$-st row of $\overline{\mathbf{A}}$, the $a_{n+1,j}$'s]. In our $n = 3$ example, a_{43} would represent the value of labor inputs needed per dollar's worth of output of sector 3. Then, from the interpretation of, say, b_{32} as the value of *output* needed directly and indirectly from sector 3 for a dollar's worth of final demand for sector 2, we see that $a_{43}b_{32}$ gives the value of labor inputs to sector 3 that are embodied in the b_{32} dollars' worth of sector 3 output.

Therefore, if *each element* in column 2 of the Leontief inverse, b_{i2}, is *weighted* by the labor input coefficient for sector i (the sector that is selling to sector 2), a_{4i}, this column sum

$$a_{41}b_{12} + a_{42}b_{22} + a_{43}b_{32}$$

would represent employment (in terms of wages) throughout the economy needed in order to supply one dollar's worth of final demand for sector 2. Again, the initial effect is the dollar's worth of final demand. Each element in the output multiplier matrix, b_{ij}, is converted into an *income* multiplier by weighting each of the elements in row i of **B** by a_{4i}.

In an n-sector input-output model, this weighting produces an $(n \times n)$ matrix with elements $a_{n+1,i}b_{ij}$. Each of these is a *sector-specific income multiplier*, indicating the amount of wages and salaries that the sector on the left would have to pay per dollar's worth of final demand for the sector at the top.[27] The column sums of this *income multiplier matrix* are what are generally known as *income multipliers*. Using H_j to denote the (household) income multiplier for sector j in an n-sector model, we have

$$H_j = \sum_{i=1}^{n} a_{n+1,i}b_{ij} \tag{3-18}$$

As with output multipliers, the exogenous change is $\Delta f_j = \$1$ which translates into an initial *output* effect, N, of $\Delta x_j = \$1$, so the ratio T/N is just T.

A different kind of income multiplier is based on the initial *income* effect that results from the exogenous change $\Delta f_j = \$1$. With both O_j and H_j, above, the initial effect of that Δf_j was taken to be $\Delta x_j = \$1$. Suppose we look beyond that output change in sector j to the change in income paid to labor in sector j, $\Delta \ell_j$, to support $\Delta x_j = \$1$. Here $\Delta \ell_j = a_{n+1,j}$ (sector j's labor input coefficient). If we consider this to be the initial effect (an income effect, not an output effect) of $\Delta f_j = \$1$, this (different) multiplier would now be $\mathcal{H}_j = T/(\Delta \ell_j)$ so

$$\mathcal{H}_j = (\sum_{i=1}^{n} a_{n+1,i}b_{ij})/a_{n+1,j} = H_j/a_{n+1,j} \tag{3-19}$$

This version of an income multiplier would be appropriate in the following kind of situation. Suppose a new establishment in sector j were thinking of moving into a region and that the measure of the initial level of economic activity in that establishment was the size of its payroll, say \$400,000. This \$400,000 represents $\Delta \ell_j$, an initial change in the amount of labor payments in sector j. Then $\mathcal{H}_j$ times \$400,000 would be an indicator of the increase in income to be earned by workers in all sectors throughout the economy because of the in-movement of the new establishment. In the literature, this is often called a 'Type I' income multiplier. ('Type I' because the model is open with respect to households; we will see that the parallel concept with a closed model is called a 'Type II' income multiplier.)

Notice that Type I income multipliers can also be used to study the (negative) impacts of a plant closing in sector k, for example. In this case, $\Delta \ell_k$ would be negative, representing the *decrease* in payments by sector k for labor services, and $\mathcal{H}_k \times (\Delta \ell_k)$ would provide an estimate of the economy-wide wage loss.

A 'Type I income multiplier matrix' could be created by dividing each element in column j of the income multiplier matrix by $a_{n+1,j}$. Thus a typical element in this matrix would be $a_{n+1,i}b_{ij}/a_{n+1,j}$ [exactly the term after the summation sign in (3-19)]. This simply disaggregates the total effect in (3-19) into sector-specific Type I income multipliers — the amount of income earned by workers in the sector on the left per dollar's worth of wages and salaries in the sector at the top. In the case of a plant closing, this matrix would distribute the wage *losses* across sectors.

Employment multipliers Another approach to assessing employment impacts of alternative final demand scenarios is to weight the elements in **B** not by labor input coefficients in monetary terms but rather to use some physical measure of employment, such as an employment-to-output ratio for each sector.

For example, if we know that $x_j = \$1000$ in the base year and if we also know that employment in sector j, call it w_j (for 'workers') that year was 50 people, then a *physical* labor input coefficient for sector j might be denoted $e_j = w_j / x_j = 50/1000 = 0.05$ — this is workers per dollar of sector j's output.[28] Generally these kinds of physical labor input coefficients are expressed per \$1000, or \$100,000 or even \$ million of output, to keep them from being extremely small numbers (far to the right of the decimal point). If we have this kind of information for each sector, then by weighting each element in row i of **B** by e_i, a matrix of *sector-specific employment multipliers* is created.[29] Column sums of this matrix are known as *employment multipliers*.

Returning to the three-sector illustration,

$$e_1 b_{12} + e_2 b_{22} + e_3 b_{32}$$

would represent employment (in physical terms) throughout the economy needed to supply one dollar's worth of final demand for sector 2. Output multipliers are in this way converted into employment multipliers. Using E_j to denote the employment multiplier for sector j in an n-sector economy, we have

$$E_j = \sum_{i=1}^{n} e_i b_{ij} \qquad (3\text{-}20)$$

As with Type I income multipliers, a *Type I employment multiplier* might be useful in certain kinds of analysis. In this case, instead of considering the chain of repercussion as $\Delta f_j = \$1 \Rightarrow \Delta x_j = \$1 \Rightarrow \Delta \ell_j = a_{n+1,j}$, the dollar's worth of change in sector j output is translated into $\Delta w_j = e_j$; $\Delta x_j = \$1 \Rightarrow \Delta w_j = e_j$. This, then, becomes the initial effect, N. The Type I employment multiplier for sector j is $\mathcal{E}_j = T/(\Delta w_j)$, so

$$\mathcal{E}_j = (\sum_{i=1}^{n} e_i b_{ij})/e_j = E_j/e_j \qquad (3\text{-}21)$$

A multiplier like this would be appropriate in the same scenario as for the Type I income multiplier, only when the magnitude of the new enterprise in sector j was given in initial number of employees rather than dollars of payroll. For example, if the new factory planned on providing an initial 200 jobs, then $\mathcal{E}_j$ times this 200 would provide an estimate of the total number of jobs throughout the economy that would be generated by the in-movement of the factory. Similarly, the region-wide employment impact of a plant closing in sector k could be estimated using $\mathcal{E}_k$. If the plant closing puts 170 employees out of work, then $\mathcal{E}_k \times 170$ would be the input-output model estimate of the total impact in terms of lost jobs throughout the economy.

Again, a complete Type I employment multiplier matrix could be created; its i,j-th element would be $e_i b_{ij}/e_j$ [the element after the summation sign in (3-21)]. These represent sector-specific Type I employment multipliers — the employment needed in the sector on the left per employee in the sector at the top.[30]

f. Numerical example: multipliers in the Washington state model

Output multipliers in the Washington economy Output multipliers from the open model for the Washington State economy are the column sums of the direct and indirect requirements matrix in Table 3-4. Arranged as a row vector, O, we have

$$O = [1.3810 \quad 1.6365 \quad 1.8166 \quad 1.1010 \quad 1.3175 \quad 1.3082 \quad 1.3563 \quad 1.3776]$$

For aerospace (sector 4), we see that O_4 is 1.1010. As is to be expected, O_4 multiplies the final demand change in sector 4, \$250 (million) up to \$275.25 (million); this is (except for rounding) what we found as the economy-wide output effect from $\Delta\mathbf{x}$, $\sum_{i=1}^{n}\Delta x_i$.

It is important to emphasize that output multipliers, and indeed any of the other multipliers as well, indicate a total effect that is stimulated by *one dollar's* worth of demand for a sector's output. By themselves they do not provide much of a 'ranking' of sectors. They must be viewed in conjunction with the magnitudes of alternative final demand changes. The aerospace output multiplier (sector 4) is the smallest, which may seem peculiar, until we realize that an order for even one airplane from Boeing may represent anywhere from at least \$40 million (for a 737) to \$160 million (for a 747 or 777). (The estimate given by the aerospace output multiplier of the total economy-wide effect of the \$40 or \$160 million order would be \$44 million or \$176 million, respectively.) So, while the multiplier itself may seem small, the initial effect which it multiplies is likely to be large. On the other hand, sector 3 (forest products) has the largest output multiplier (1.8166) but a 'typical' export order for plywood might be, say, \$10 million; this would generate an economy-wide effect of \$18 million.

Income multipliers in the Washington economy A full income multiplier matrix for Washington would be created if elements in row i of the Leontief inverse for the open input-output model (Table 3-4) were weighted by the direct input coefficient a_{9i} from the closed model. This matrix is not shown in detail. Its column sums are the household income multipliers; here these are:

$$H = [.4373 \quad .2787 \quad .3394 \quad .2752 \quad .3355 \quad .4014 \quad .4832 \quad .5795]$$

Notice that the rankings of sectors in terms of the sizes of their income multipliers is different from that provided by the output multipliers. This simply reflects the fact of differing labor input requirements in the sectors. Using $H_4 = 0.2752$, we see that the input-output model would estimate an economy-wide *income* impact of some \$68.8 million in the region due to the airplane order. Expected income payments in each sector could be found by multiplying each of the elements in column 4 of a complete income multiplier matrix by \$250 million.

Here are the Type I income multipliers for Washington; these are the $\mathcal{H}_j$ = $H_j/a_{n+1,j}$ as in (3-19):

$\mathcal{H}$ = [1.3433 2.9524 2.4370 1.1451 1.4051 1.3223 1.3092 1.3112]

As an example of the kind of impact analysis that is possible with these multipliers, suppose a new food products establishment (sector 2) were planning to move into the state, with an expected initial payroll of $150,000. The state-wide impact in terms of new income created would be estimated at something like $442,860 ($150,000 x 2.9524, which is the Type I income multiplier for sector 2). This reflects the fact that in the base year data, each dollar of income paid to employees in sector 2 'supported' a total of $2.9524 in income payments by all sectors.

The $442,860 could be distributed across paying sectors if we used a complete Type I income multiplier matrix for Washington. This matrix is not shown, but the element in row 1 (agriculture, forestry and mining), column 2 (food products) is 0.8303, so of the total $442,860, something on the order of $124,593 ($150,000 x 0.8303) would be the wages and salaries expected to be paid by sector 1 because of the new food products establishment.

Employment multipliers in the Washington economy For the year in question, the employment to output ratios, e_i, in Washington are shown in the row vector EMP (in units of employees per million dollars worth of output)

EMP = [21.6236   4.7484   5.1643   6.2568   9.3071
                      9.7714   22.8070   26.3216]

These are used to weight the elements in each column of the direct and indirect requirements matrix in Table 3-4 to produce a matrix of employment multipliers in the open model. This matrix is not shown. Its column sums are employment multipliers. Here these are[31]

E = [27.7306   15.1477   14.8520   8.0143   14.0853
                       14.1657   28.7599   33.6415]

Again, the rankings differ from those provided by output multipliers. In the hypothetical illustration, the $250 million airplane order would be expected to support an economy-wide total of 2004 (= 8.0143 x $250 million) jobs. Expected employment in each of the Washington sectors could be found by multiplying each of the elements in column 4 of a complete employment multiplier matrix by $250 million.

Type I employment multipliers, $\mathcal{E}_j = E_j/e_j$ [as in (3-21)] for Washington are

$$\mathcal{E} = [1.2823 \quad 3.1900 \quad 2.8759 \quad 1.2809 \quad 1.5134$$
$$1.4497 \quad 1.2610 \quad 1.2781]$$

This information suggests that, for example, if a cutback of 20,000 employees ('downsizing') were planned by Boeing, through layoffs or retirement buyouts, over the course of the coming six months, the total impact of the state economy might be the loss of more like 25,600 jobs (20,000 x 1.2809, the Type I employment multiplier for aerospace).

Again, a complete Type I employment multiplier matrix would allow distribution of the employment loss across sectors. The table is not shown, but the element in row 6 (transportation, communications and utilities), column 4 (aerospace) is 0.0215; this means that of the 25,600 jobs lost, we would expect around 430 (20,000 x 0.0215) of those losses to occur in sector 6.

g. Multipliers in a closed model   Output, income, and employment multipliers can also be found using a model that is closed with respect to households. That means the elements of $\bar{\mathbf{B}}$ [$= (\mathbf{I} - \bar{\mathbf{A}})^{-1}$] rather than of $\mathbf{B}$ [$= (\mathbf{I} - \mathbf{A})^{-1}$] would constitute the fundamental data. Output multipliers are found as column sums of $\bar{\mathbf{B}}$, but excluding the new [$(n + 1)$-st] row. This is because the point is to continue to measure the aggregate output effect over the n original sectors.[32]

Similarly, there are exact parallels for income and employment multipliers from the closed model. Weighting row i of $\bar{\mathbf{B}}$ by $a_{n+1,i}$ or e_i would generate matrices of sector-specific multipliers, and then summing down the columns [again, usually excluding the $(n + 1)$-st row] would produce those multipliers in the closed model. There are also exact parallels to the Type I income and employment multipliers, now from the closed model; they are designated 'Type II' multipliers.[33] For output and employment, all of these multiplier options are summarized in Table 3-7.

h. Extensions to energy and environmental impacts

Energy impacts   A very basic kind of energy input-output analysis can be undertaken if one has a physical measure of energy use by each sector. Suppose that an additional row in a transactions matrix contains electricity use, for example, in millions of kilowatt-hours (kwh), by sector. (This is the kind of information that is directly available from meter readings at each establishment in a sector.) Let K_i be the kilowatt-hours of electricity used by all firms in sector i last year in the course of producing an amount

Table 3-7 Input-output multipliers

	Output Effects	Employment Effects	
Exogenous Change	$\Delta f_j = 1$	$\Delta f_j = i$	$\Delta w_j = e_j$ (Change in sector j's employment because of $\Delta x_j = 1$)
Initial Effect (N)	$\Delta x_j = 1$	$\Delta x_j = 1$	
Total Effect (T) In Open Model (Direct + Indirect)	$\displaystyle\sum_{i=1}^{n} b_{ij}$	$\displaystyle\sum_{i=1}^{n} e_i b_{ij}$	
Multiplier (T/N)	$O_j = \displaystyle\sum_{i=1}^{n} b_{ij}/\Delta x_j = \sum_{i=1}^{n} b_{ij}$	$E_j = \displaystyle\sum_{i=1}^{n} e_i b_{ij}/\Delta x_j$ $\;= \displaystyle\sum_{i=1}^{n} e_i b_{ij}$	$\mathcal{E}_j = \displaystyle\sum_{i=1}^{n} e_i b_{ij}/\Delta w_j$ $\;= \displaystyle\sum_{i=1}^{n} e_i b_{ij}/e_j = E_j/e_j$ (Type I employment multiplier)
In Closed Model (Direct + Indirect + Induced)	$\displaystyle\sum_{i=1}^{n} \bar{b}_{ij}$	$\displaystyle\sum_{i=1}^{n} e_i \bar{b}_{ij}$	
Multiplier (T/N)	$\bar{O}_j = \displaystyle\sum_{i=1}^{n} \bar{b}_{ij}/\Delta x_j = \sum_{i=1}^{n} \bar{b}_{ij}$	$\bar{E}_j = \displaystyle\sum_{i=1}^{n} e_i \bar{b}_{ij}/\Delta x_j$ $\;= \displaystyle\sum_{i=1}^{n} e_i \bar{b}_{ij}$	$\bar{\mathcal{E}}_j = \displaystyle\sum_{i=1}^{n} e_i \bar{b}_{ij}/\Delta w_j$ $\;= \displaystyle\sum_{i=1}^{n} e_i \bar{b}_{ij}/e_j = \bar{E}_j/e_j$ (Type II employment multiplier)

Note: w_j = sector j's total employment; $e_j = w_j/x_j$, employee to output ratio for sector j.

of output equal to x_i. Then $k_i = K_i/x_i$ represents kilowatt-hours that were needed per dollar of output in sector i.

These energy-use coefficients could be used in exactly the same way as, say, the employment-to-output coefficients. Multiplying each element in row i of the Leontief inverse, b_{ij}, by k_i converts an output from sector i into electricity used by i to make that output. The entire converted matrix might be called an 'energy multiplier' matrix, and the sum down column j would indicate the energy (electricity) required (in kwh) to satisfy a dollar's worth of final demand for sector j. Similar analyses could be made for other kinds of energy inputs to production — coal, gas, oil, etc.[34]

Environmental impacts Suppose, instead of energy consumption, we have a set of figures representing pollution (of a particular kind, and measured in physical units — tons of particulate, gallons of chemical waste, etc.) created by each sector last year; P_i tons by sector i, for example. Then $p_i = P_i/x_i$ is a 'pollution-generation coefficient' for sector i, and these coefficients can be used in exactly the same way to create a 'pollution multiplier matrix' out of $\mathbf{B} = (\mathbf{I} - \mathbf{A})^{-1}$, by weighting each b_{ij} in row i by p_i. And, as with energy impacts, similar kinds of analyses could be carried out for each kind of pollutant.[35]

i. Linkage measures It is often important, particularly in developing economies (whether nations or regions), to seek out policies that will attract new industries or stimulate the output of existing industries (for example, through tax incentives or export subsidies). For that reason, it makes sense to attempt to identify 'key' sectors — those sectors whose growth might be expected to bring particularly strong economic benefits to the region. Several measures of the 'importance' of a sector in an economy have been developed using input-output data.

Backward linkages One straightforward measure is expressed in terms of a sector's use of inputs from other sectors in the economy; it is given by column sums of the $\mathbf{A}$ matrix. For column j, this represents the total value of inputs from other sectors in the economy per dollar's worth of sector j's output. The larger this value, it might be argued, the more sector j 'depends' on others in the economy for its inputs, and therefore the more that economy might be expected to be stimulated by an increase in sector j's output. This is a sector's *direct backward linkage*;

$$\text{DBL}_j = \sum_{i=1}^{n} a_{ij} \qquad (3\text{-}22)$$

One drawback to this measure is that it accounts for *direct* effects only. The essence of the input-output approach is that it provides a way of measuring *direct plus indirect* effects, via the Leontief inverse. Therefore, a second measure of backward linkage is found in the output multipliers — the column sums of $(I - A)^{-1}$ and not just A. These are known as *total backward linkages*; for sector j

$$\text{TBL}_j = O_j = \sum_{i=1}^{n} b_{ij} \tag{3-23}$$

The larger this measure, the more sector j depends on other sectors in the economy, both directly and indirectly, and, again, the more that economy might be expected to be stimulated by increases in final demand for sector j and therefore by increases in sector j's output.[36]

Other linkages   Backward linkage measures are concerned with 'upstream' dependence — how much a sector relies on inputs flowing into it from other sectors in the local economy. An alternative kind of 'importance' is indicated by a measure of 'downstream' dependence, namely how much the outputs flowing out of a given sector serve as inputs to other sectors in the economy.

Forward linkage measures are designed to quantify this kind of dependence. They are presented, briefly, in Appendix 3.2, along with some measures of combined (backward and forward) linkage.

3.2   Two or more regions: the interregional input-output (IRIO) system

3.2.1   The statistical framework: interregional input-output accounts

An essential aspect of many-region input-output models is the measurement and modelling of the economic interconnections among the regions. In Section 3.1 we explored the character of an input-output model for a single economy in isolation, in the sense that imports from suppliers and exports to buyers outside the economy were treated as exogenous to the model. They were placed among the elements in the value added rows and final demand columns of the transactions accounts. It should be clear that the smaller the economy (nation, state, county, urban area, community), the larger the role that will be played by imports and exports in accounting for inputs to production (and consumption) and sales of outputs.

It should also be clear that in a single-region input-output model, there is no way of assessing the economic *spillover effects* in the system. For example, an order from a foreign airline for Boeing aircraft would lead to an increase in aerospace output in Washington State. This could generate increased purchases of electronic components from suppliers outside the state (in California, for example). These new demands for California exports (which are increases in an element of California's final demand vector) will generate an output effect (increase) in electronics and, directly and indirectly, in other sectors of the California economy. This is an *interregional spillover effect*, and in a model of Washington State alone, this stimulus to production outside the state simply is not captured. It could be argued that such 'external' stimuli need not be a part of the calculation, if one's interest is exclusively in Washington production caused by a new Washington final demand.

But there is more. Suppose that the stimulated production in California includes increased output of sectors that use imports from Washington as inputs to their production processes — for example, electronic components in California may use aluminum that is made in Washington. Thus the increased aerospace production in Washington leads to increased electronics output in California which, in turn, leads to more aluminum production in Washington. This is known as an *interregional feedback effect*. It too will be absent in a single-region model. Even if one's interest is only in the within-Washington effects of the new aircraft order, a single-region model will fail to capture this feedback from the state to itself, via the rest of the country.

If we want to create a *connected* regional input-output model, the simplest would probably contain the region of interest (say Washington State) and the rest of the national economy (the rest of the U.S.). But ideally, or at least in principle, one could have for the U.S., say, a connected 51-region model, where each state (plus the District of Columbia) was treated as an individual region. And there are many other possibilities for the level of spatial detail — a twelve-region model (Federal Reserve Bank Districts), a two-region model (east of the Mississippi, west of the Mississippi), etc. For illustration purposes, we explore a two-region IRIO model in this section.

In the single-region model, the basic accounting equation for a sector's output was given in (3-1); it is repeated below

$$x_i = z_{i1} + z_{i2} + \ldots + z_{in} + f_i$$

Suppose now that we designate the two regions in the two-region input-output model as L and M (just as we use i and j for sectors). Since the convention is to use *subscripts* for sectoral designation, we can use *superscripts* for spatial (regional) identification. In the IRIO model, an attempt is made to capture exactly the shipments of output from, say, sector i in region L, not only to sectors in region L (as well as to final demand in L) but also to all sectors in region M. (Sales from sector i in L to final demand in M will still be contained in the 'exports' component of region L's final demand.) Just as z_{ij} was used for transactions from i to j, we can use z_{ij}^{LM} to denote the value of a transaction from sector i in region L to sector j in region M; in the same spirit, z_{ij}^{LL} would represent a within-region transaction. [These latter were the kinds of transactions recorded in Equation (3-1), when there was only one region and so a spatial identifier was unnecessary.] We assume that there are n sectors in both region L and region M.[37]

With an ideal data set, one would be able to account for the sales of output of each sector i in region L as follows:

$$x_i^L = [z_{i1}^{LL} + z_{i2}^{LL} + \ldots + z_{in}^{LL}] + [z_{i1}^{LM} + z_{i2}^{LM} + \ldots + z_{in}^{LM}] + f_i^L \qquad (3\text{-}24)$$

The sum in the first set of brackets on the right-hand side accounts for interindustry sales within region L (*intra*regional interindustry sales). In the second set of brackets we find interindustry sales that cross the regional boundary; these are *inter*regional interindustry sales. These transactions would appear lumped together as part of the 'exports' component of final demand in the single-region model of Section 3.1. Finally, f_i^L is where all sales from sector i in region L to the remaining final demand components are recorded; notice that this will include sales to satisfy final demands in M — they will be part of the 'export' component of f_i^L. Instead, then, of just a single transactions matrix, Z, as in Table 3-1, we see that there is the (n x n) table of intraregional transactions, which we can denote Z^{LL}, and a second, reflecting the interregional flows from L to M, Z^{LM}. The elements in the first bracket in Equation (3-24) are from the i-th row of Z^{LL} and the elements in the second bracket of that equation are from the i-th row of Z^{LM}.

Just as we have explicitly accounted for the sales of output from sector i located in region L to the producing sectors in M (the interregional interindustry sales), we must also recognize that there will be interregional interindustry purchases — sectors in L may use in their production processes inputs bought from sectors in region M. This means that Equation (3-2) from Section 3.1 would be spatially disaggregated as

$$x_j^L = [z_{1j}^{LL} + z_{2j}^{LL} + \ldots + z_{nj}^{LL}] + [z_{1j}^{ML} + z_{2j}^{ML} + \ldots + z_{nj}^{ML}]$$

$$+ va_j^L + m_j^L \tag{3-25}$$

where z_{ij}^{ML} indicates the value of a transaction from sector i in region M to sector j in region L and m_j^L now represents imports to L except for interindustry inputs purchased from sectors in region M by sectors in L. The elements in the first set of brackets on the right-hand side are, again, intraregional transactions in L — in this case, the z_{ij}^{LL} come from the j-th column of $\mathbf{Z}^{LL}$. Elements in the second brackets in Equation (3-25) are from the j-th column of a new set of transactions, $\mathbf{Z}^{ML}$, in which region M is the origin of shipments and region L is the destination.

In a complete two-region IRIO system, economic activity of each of the sectors in both regions would be totally accounted for. This means that there would be equations just like (3-24) and (3-25) for each sector in region M. Here is a small example, for two regions with two sectors in each region (we have rearranged the information in the two equations for region M, putting interregional before intraregional transactions):

$$x_1^L = z_{11}^{LL} + z_{12}^{LL} + z_{11}^{LM} + z_{12}^{LM} + f_1^L$$

$$x_2^L = z_{21}^{LL} + z_{22}^{LL} + z_{21}^{LM} + z_{22}^{LM} + f_2^L$$

$$x_1^M = z_{11}^{ML} + z_{12}^{ML} + z_{11}^{MM} + z_{12}^{MM} + f_1^M \tag{3-26}$$

$$x_2^M = z_{21}^{ML} + z_{22}^{ML} + z_{21}^{MM} + z_{22}^{MM} + f_2^M$$

Arrange the transactions into two intraregional and two interregional matrices, where, for example

$$\mathbf{Z}^{LL} = \begin{bmatrix} z_{11}^{LL} & z_{12}^{LL} \\ z_{21}^{LL} & z_{22}^{LL} \end{bmatrix} \text{ and } \mathbf{Z}^{LM} = \begin{bmatrix} z_{11}^{LM} & z_{12}^{LM} \\ z_{21}^{LM} & z_{22}^{LM} \end{bmatrix}$$

and similarly for $\mathbf{Z}^{MM}$ and $\mathbf{Z}^{ML}$, and let the gross outputs and final demands be represented in the vectors

$$\mathbf{x}^L = \begin{bmatrix} x_1^L \\ x_2^L \end{bmatrix}, \mathbf{x}^M = \begin{bmatrix} x_1^M \\ x_2^M \end{bmatrix}, \mathbf{f}^L = \begin{bmatrix} f_1^L \\ f_2^L \end{bmatrix}, \mathbf{f}^M = \begin{bmatrix} f_1^M \\ f_2^M \end{bmatrix}$$

Then, using the **i** vector for row sums, (3-26) can be written as

$$\mathbf{x}^L = \mathbf{Z}^{LL}\mathbf{i} + \mathbf{Z}^{LM}\mathbf{i} + \mathbf{f}^L$$

$$\mathbf{x}^M = \mathbf{Z}^{ML}\mathbf{i} + \mathbf{Z}^{MM}\mathbf{i} + \mathbf{f}^M$$

(3-27)

Finally, more (partitioned) matrix notation makes possible an even simpler representation. Let

$$\mathbf{x} = \left[\begin{array}{c} \mathbf{x}^L \\ ---- \\ \mathbf{x}^M \end{array}\right], \mathbf{Z} = \left[\begin{array}{c|c} \mathbf{Z}^{LL} & \mathbf{Z}^{LM} \\ ------ & ------ \\ \mathbf{Z}^{ML} & \mathbf{Z}^{MM} \end{array}\right], \text{and } \mathbf{f} = \left[\begin{array}{c} \mathbf{f}^L \\ ---- \\ \mathbf{f}^M \end{array}\right]$$

Then the complete two-region IRIO model in (3-27) is representable (using a larger **i** vector) as

$$\mathbf{x} = \mathbf{Z}\mathbf{i} + \mathbf{f}$$

[Compare (3-6) in Section 3.1; it looks exactly the same, but now the interpretation of each of the matrices is more complex.]

The important observation to make about these data is that they require both spatial and sectoral information about the origin of an interindustry transaction and also about the destination. For several regions with many sectors each, that level of detail is not often available.[38]

3.2.2 Technical and trade coefficients in the IRIO model

Direct input coefficients for the IRIO model are formed in the same way as in the single-region model, as in (3-3) and (3-9). The important consideration to keep in mind is that a transaction is always divided by the output of the purchasing industry, which now will have a regional designation. Therefore,

$$a_{ij}^{LL} = z_{ij}^{LL}/x_j^L \text{ and } a_{ij}^{MM} = z_{ij}^{MM}/x_j^M$$

(3-28)

represent *intraregional* direct input coefficients in regions L and M, respectively — for example, a_{ij}^{LL} indicates the amount of input from sector i located in L that is used per dollar's worth of output of sector j, also located in L. Similarly,

$$a_{ij}^{LM} = z_{ij}^{LM}/x_j^M \text{ and } a_{ij}^{ML} = z_{ij}^{ML}/x_j^L$$

(3-29)

represent *interregional* direct input coefficients (sometimes called 'trade coefficients'). For example, a_{ij}^{LM} is the amount of input from sector i located in L that is needed per dollar's worth of output of sector j located in region M.

If it is possible to calculate all of these direct input coefficients, then the accounting equations can be rewritten, in the same spirit as was done in Section 3.1 for the single-region model. We do that here for our two-region, two-sector illustration in (3-26). [Compare (3-5), for sector i in the single-region model.]

$$x_1^L = a_{11}^{LL}x_1^L + a_{12}^{LL}x_2^L + a_{11}^{LM}x_1^M + a_{12}^{LM}x_2^M + f_1^L$$

$$x_2^L = a_{21}^{LL}x_1^L + a_{22}^{LL}x_2^L + a_{21}^{LM}x_1^M + a_{22}^{LM}x_2^M + f_2^L$$

$$x_1^M = a_{11}^{ML}x_1^L + a_{12}^{ML}x_2^L + a_{11}^{MM}x_1^M + a_{12}^{MM}x_2^M + f_1^M$$

$$x_2^M = a_{21}^{ML}x_1^L + a_{22}^{ML}x_2^L + a_{21}^{MM}x_1^M + a_{22}^{MM}x_2^M + f_2^M$$

As in (3-4) in Section 3.1, we can collect the two sets of intraregional direct input coefficients into (2 x 2) matrices

$$\mathbf{A}^{LL} = \begin{bmatrix} a_{11}^{LL} & a_{12}^{LL} \\ a_{21}^{LL} & a_{22}^{LL} \end{bmatrix} \text{ and } \mathbf{A}^{MM} = \begin{bmatrix} a_{11}^{MM} & a_{12}^{MM} \\ a_{21}^{MM} & a_{22}^{MM} \end{bmatrix} \tag{3-30}$$

and similarly for the trade coefficient matrices[39]

$$\mathbf{A}^{LM} = \begin{bmatrix} a_{11}^{LM} & a_{12}^{LM} \\ a_{21}^{LM} & a_{22}^{LM} \end{bmatrix} \text{ and } \mathbf{A}^{ML} = \begin{bmatrix} a_{11}^{ML} & a_{12}^{ML} \\ a_{21}^{ML} & a_{22}^{ML} \end{bmatrix} \tag{3-31}$$

Recalling the definitions of $\mathbf{x}^L$, $\mathbf{x}^M$, $\mathbf{f}^L$, $\mathbf{f}^M$ from above, the equations in (3-27) are

$$\mathbf{x}^L = \mathbf{A}^{LL}\mathbf{x}^L + \mathbf{A}^{LM}\mathbf{x}^M + \mathbf{f}^L$$
$$\mathbf{x}^M = \mathbf{A}^{ML}\mathbf{x}^L + \mathbf{A}^{MM}\mathbf{x}^M + \mathbf{f}^M \tag{3-32}$$

[compare (3-7)] and, finally, using partitioned matrices again

$$\mathbf{x} = \begin{bmatrix} \mathbf{x}^L \\ ---- \\ \mathbf{x}^M \end{bmatrix}, \mathbf{A} = \begin{bmatrix} \mathbf{A}^{LL} & | & \mathbf{A}^{LM} \\ ------ & | & ------ \\ \mathbf{A}^{ML} & | & \mathbf{A}^{MM} \end{bmatrix}, \text{ and } \mathbf{f} = \begin{bmatrix} \mathbf{f}^L \\ ---- \\ \mathbf{f}^M \end{bmatrix}$$

(3-32) can be (very) compactly represented as

$$\mathbf{x} = \mathbf{A}\mathbf{x} + \mathbf{f} \tag{3-33}$$

[again, compare (3-7)] from which

$$(\mathbf{I} - \mathbf{A})\mathbf{x} = \mathbf{f} \tag{3-34}$$

[which looks just like (3-8) but is much more complicated].

As in the single-region model, all of these representations are simply rearrangements of a set of base-year data, using the definitions (now) of both intraregional and interregional direct input coefficients.

3.2.3 Input-output analysis with the IRIO model

a. Economic impacts Again, as with the single-region case, we use this model structure for analysis by assuming that a base-year A matrix remains valid for subsequent years. Notice that this means unchanged technology *within* each of the regions as well as unchanged interregional commodity flow (trade) patterns *between* the regions. If we are given a forecast of a change in one or more elements in final demand *in either region*, so that we have a new final demand vector, $f^* = \begin{bmatrix} f^{L*} \\ \hline f^{M*} \end{bmatrix}$, this forecast is used to drive the model and generate the economic impacts, in terms of required new sectoral outputs *in each of the regions*, $x^* = \begin{bmatrix} x^{L*} \\ \hline x^{M*} \end{bmatrix}$, via $x^* = (I - A)^{-1}f^*$, just as in Section 3.1. The parallel, in terms of matrix representation, is exact. The data requirements, however, are vastly different.

Partitioning $(I - A)$ and using b_{ij}, as in Section 3.1, for elements of the Leontief inverse, we can denote $x^* = (I - A)^{-1}f^*$ as

$$\begin{bmatrix} x^{L*} \\ \hline x^{M*} \end{bmatrix} = \begin{bmatrix} (I - A^{LL}) & \vline & -A^{LM} \\ \hline -A^{ML} & \vline & (I - A^{MM}) \end{bmatrix}^{-1} \begin{bmatrix} f^{L*} \\ \hline f^{M*} \end{bmatrix}$$

or

$$\begin{bmatrix} x^{L*} \\ \hline x^{M*} \end{bmatrix} = \begin{bmatrix} B^{LL} & \vline & B^{LM} \\ \hline B^{ML} & \vline & B^{MM} \end{bmatrix} \begin{bmatrix} f^{L*} \\ \hline f^{M*} \end{bmatrix} \qquad (3\text{-}35)$$

Thus new final demands in either or both regions have impacts on gross outputs in both regions, namely

$$x^{L*} = B^{LL}f^{L*} + B^{LM}f^{M*}$$

$$x^{M*} = B^{ML}f^{L*} + B^{MM}f^{M*} \qquad (3\text{-}36)$$

Notice that the impacts are now distinguished both sectorally (as always in an input-output model) and spatially. Even if the only new element in f^* is a change in final demand for one sector in region L — so that f^{L*}

differs from $\mathbf{f}^L$ in one element only, while $\mathbf{f}^{M*} = \mathbf{f}^M$ — there may be impacts on outputs in both region L and region M, in $\mathbf{x}^{L*}$ and $\mathbf{x}^{M*}$, respectively.

b. Numerical example: Washington state and the rest of the U.S. in a two-region IRIO model The two tables in Appendix 3.3 contain direct inputs and total requirements matrices for a two-region model illustration with Washington State as region L and the rest of the U.S. as region M, using the same eight sector aggregation in both regions.[40] The matrix $\mathbf{A}^{LL}$ represents direct inputs of Washington products per dollar of Washington sector output. This is exactly the $\mathbf{A}$ matrix (open with respect to households) that was used for the Washington illustration in Section 3.1. The $\mathbf{A}^{MM}$ matrix is designed to represent U.S. technology.[41] Underlying the trade coefficients in $\mathbf{A}^{LM}$ and $\mathbf{A}^{ML}$ are transactions matrices that were created to reflect the known facts about Washington exports to and imports from the rest of the U.S. (Table 3-2).[42]

The contribution of a connected-region model is made clear if we explore again the impacts of a foreign airline order of \$250 million for Boeing aircraft. As before, we let this be $\Delta f_4^L = 250$; the other seven elements of $\Delta \mathbf{f}^L$ remain zero, as do all eight elements in $\Delta \mathbf{f}^M$. Thus for this story we have

$$[\Delta \mathbf{f}]' = [0 \ \ 0 \ \ 0 \ \ 250 \ \ 0 \ \ 0 \ \ 0 \ \ 0 \ \vdots \ 0 \ \ 0 \ \ 0 \ \ 0 \ \ 0 \ \ 0 \ \ 0 \ \ 0]$$

Following the structure in (3-35), only now with $\Delta \mathbf{f}$ and $\Delta \mathbf{x}$, we have,

$$\Delta \mathbf{x} = \begin{bmatrix} \Delta \mathbf{x}^L \\ ---- \\ \Delta \mathbf{x}^M \end{bmatrix} = \begin{bmatrix} \mathbf{B}^{LL} & | & \mathbf{B}^{LM} \\ ------- & | & ------- \\ \mathbf{B}^{ML} & | & \mathbf{B}^{MM} \end{bmatrix} \begin{bmatrix} \Delta \mathbf{f}^L \\ ---- \\ \Delta \mathbf{f}^M \end{bmatrix}$$

which for this example works out to be (in millions of dollars)

$$\Delta x(\text{IRIO}) = \begin{bmatrix} .2176 \\ .1448 \\ .8435 \\ 254.2194 \\ 4.5826 \\ 3.6449 \\ 1.6755 \\ 11.7867 \\ \text{-----------} \\ 6.9605 \\ 2.3048 \\ 5.8038 \\ 46.0336 \\ 75.4423 \\ 30.3863 \\ 10.3622 \\ 93.3727 \end{bmatrix}$$

Recall from the single-region illustration in Section 3.1 that the same \$250 million aircraft order generated a Washington impact of

$$\Delta x = \begin{bmatrix} .1662 \\ .0823 \\ .6668 \\ 253.7037 \\ 4.2258 \\ 3.4441 \\ 1.4888 \\ 11.4666 \end{bmatrix}$$

The output of each of the Washington sectors [the first eight elements in $\Delta x(\text{IRIO})$] is consistently larger than in the single-region model. Total Washington output across all sectors in the IRIO model is \$277.1 million; it was \$275.2 million in the single-region model. This difference can be viewed as one indicator of the size of the interregional feedback effect for the Washington economy, and we see that it was not large — total output was underestimated by less than one percent when the single-region model was used.[43]

These numerical results do not illustrate any universal truths about the importance of interregional feedbacks in interregional input-output models. They are valid only for the particular airline order story that we have used with the illustrative data for the two regions and their economic interconnections. It is true, however, that the smaller the elements in $\mathbf{A}^{LM}$ and/or $\mathbf{A}^{ML}$, the smaller will the interregional feedbacks be (and in this case, $\mathbf{A}^{LM}$ has elements that are very small). This makes economic sense; the less important interregional trade is to either region (or both), the smaller will be interregional spillovers and/or interregional feedbacks.[44]

In addition, of course, only with a connected-region model of this sort can spillover effects be quantified. Here the bottom half of the $\Delta\mathbf{x}$(IRIO) vector represents outputs from the eight sectors in the rest of the U.S. that would be called forth because of the new export order in Washington state. In this illustration, total output in the rest of the U.S. would be $270.7 million, nearly as much as the within-Washington impact.

c. Closure with respect to households As in the single-region case, it may be relevant to consider closing an IRIO model with respect to households. This could be done in either or in both regions. For region L alone this kind of closure would mean:

(a) Breaking out consumption of households in region L from the elements in $\mathbf{f}^L$ (a portion of each element, f_i^L, is sales from sector i in region L to households in L) in order to be able to create a household consumption coefficient column for spending on goods made in region L (to add to $\mathbf{A}^{LL}$).

(b) Identifying in the value added row for L ($\mathbf{va}^L$) that part of each element that represents inputs of labor from households located in region L. From this would come the labor input coefficients row to add to $\mathbf{A}^{LL}$.

Since $\mathbf{A}^{LL}$ now has $(n + 1)$ rows and columns, this means that $\mathbf{A}^{ML}$ must have $(n + 1)$ columns and $\mathbf{A}^{LM}$ must have $(n + 1)$ rows. This means, in turn

(c) Breaking out household consumption in region L from the elements in $\mathbf{f}^M$ (a portion of f_i^M is sales from sector i in region M to exports, and a part of those export sales may be to consumers in region L) to create a column of consumption coefficients for households in L on products of sectors in M (thus adding a column to $\mathbf{A}^{ML}$).

(d) Identifying what, if any, labor services from households in L were used as inputs to production in M (commuters, for example; these payments would be included in the imports row for region M). From this would come an additional row for $\mathbf{A}^{LM}$, representing cross-boundary labor input coefficients.

If, in addition, the model were to be closed to households in region M, the same kind of information would be required in order to add one row and one column to $\mathbf{A}^{MM}$, one row to $\mathbf{A}^{ML}$ and one column to $\mathbf{A}^{LM}$. The interpretation is similar, with 'L' and 'M' interchanged in the story in (a) through (d), above.

d. Multipliers

Output multipliers In terms of Leontief inverse elements, we now have double regional superscripts as well as double sectoral subscripts, but the interpretation remains the same. For example, an element in $\mathbf{B}^{MM}$ is b_{ij}^{MM}, representing the direct plus indirect effect on output of sector i in region M per dollar's worth of final demand for region M's sector j. Similarly, an element in $\mathbf{B}^{ML}$, b_{ij}^{ML}, indicates what the influence is on region M's sector i of a dollar's worth of final demand for region L's sector j. So, as would be expected, we now have spatially distinct multipliers — both *intra*regional output multipliers (in $\mathbf{B}^{LL}$ and $\mathbf{B}^{MM}$) and *inter*regional output multipliers (in $\mathbf{B}^{LM}$ and $\mathbf{B}^{ML}$).

Other multipliers In an IRIO model the same possibilities exist for converting elements in the Leontief inverse matrix into income (monetary) or employment (physical) multipliers. The procedure mirrors closely that in the single-region model.

For income multipliers, for instance, input coefficients reflecting use of labor located in region L are based on two distinct sets of labor input coefficients. From materials that would be needed for the closed model, intraregional labor input coefficients in region L ($z_{n+1,j}^{L\ L}/x_j^L = a_{n+1,j}^{L\ L}$) are the elements for the added row in $\mathbf{A}^{LL}$. They provide the weights for elements in each of the columns in $\mathbf{B}^{LL}$, converting outputs from each of the n sectors in L into within-region labor input requirements.

Similarly, the added row in $\mathbf{A}^{ML}$ (where $a_{n+1,j}^{M\ L} = z_{n+1,j}^{M\ L}/x_j^L$) provides weights for elements in $\mathbf{B}^{ML}$, in order to convert outputs from each of the n sectors in L into across-region labor input requirements, supplied by households in region M. Similar modifications of $\mathbf{B}^{MM}$ and $\mathbf{B}^{LM}$ capture within-region labor income effects in M and across-region labor income effects from M to L.[45]

e. Linkage measures No new principles are involved when we consider linkage measures that might be derived from the data in an IRIO model. However, as with multipliers, now there is a spatial as well as a sectoral dimension. We illustrate with the kinds of backward linkages that can be measured in an IRIO model. Extensions to other linkage measures would follow the logic of the aspatial measures in Appendix 3.2.

Within-region *direct backward linkages* would come from column sums of $\mathbf{A}^{LL}$ and $\mathbf{A}^{MM}$; across-region backward linkages are in the column sums of $\mathbf{A}^{ML}$ and $\mathbf{A}^{LM}$. For instance,

$$\text{DBL}_j^{LL} = \sum_{i=1}^{n} a_{ij}^{LL}$$

shows the dependence of region L's sector j on direct inputs from all sectors in L. Similarly,

$$\text{DBL}_j^{ML} = \sum_{i=1}^{n} a_{ij}^{ML}$$

is a measure of the dependence of region L's sector j on direct inputs from all sectors in region M. [Compare (3-22) in Section 3.1.] Measures for each of the sectors in region M, DBL_j^{MM} and DBL_j^{LM}, would be found from the elements in $\mathbf{A}^{MM}$ and $\mathbf{A}^{LM}$.

Within-region and between-region *total backward linkages* would again parallel those for the single-region case, now coming from column sums of $\mathbf{B}^{LL}$ and $\mathbf{B}^{ML}$, for region L, and from $\mathbf{B}^{MM}$ and $\mathbf{B}^{LM}$ for region M. [Compare (3-23) in Section 3.1.] Notice that a measure of *spatial linkage* could be generated from, say, DBL_j^{ML} by averaging over all j in L. That is

$$(1/n) \sum_{j=1}^{n} \text{DBL}_j^{ML}$$

is a number that indicates, on average, how much a sector in L relies, per dollar of its output, on inputs from all sectors in region M.[46]

3.3 Two or more regions: the multiregional input-output (MRIO) system

3.3.1 The statistical framework: multiregional input-output accounts

We have seen in Section 3.2 that the data required to link more than just a few regions in a true interregional input-output model could be enormous. For this reason, many-region IRIO models have seldom been implemented in practice. A model that is designed to overcome some of these data requirements, while retaining the spirit of the IRIO framework, has come to be known as the multiregional input-output model. The simplifying idea here is to make use of transactions data in which the sector of destination is ignored. In terms of IRIO kinds of transactions, z_{ij}^{LL} and z_{ij}^{LM}, this means that data are used in which the second subscript is suppressed. What is needed is information on shipments of goods between regions, z_i^{LM}, and within regions, z_i^{LL}. These kinds of shipments data are generally likely to be easier to acquire (for example, from the kind of commodity shipment data that are collected together in Censuses of Transportation).[47]

This can be illustrated again for the case of two regions with two sectors each. Suppose that for each sector in each region we have information on the intra- and interregional shipments of the outputs of those sectors. For sectors 1 and 2 in region L, this means just z_1^{LL} and z_1^{LM} (for sector 1) and z_2^{LL} and z_2^{LM} (for sector 2). Similarly, we would have z_1^{MM}, z_1^{ML}, z_2^{MM}, and z_2^{ML} for the outputs of the two sectors in M.

Arrange all of the information for good 1 in an origin-destination table

		Destination Region		
		L	M	
Origin Region	L	z_1^{LL}	z_1^{LM}	(3-37)
	M	z_1^{ML}	z_1^{MM}	

Column sums, s_1^L and s_1^M, record the total amount of good 1 in each of the two regions (ignoring imports from outside the two-region system). Dividing an element in a column by the column sum gives the *proportion* of good 1 in a destination region (column) that came from a particular origin region (row). For example, $t_1^{LL} = z_1^{LL}/s_1^L$ and $t_1^{ML} = z_1^{ML}/s_1^L$ indicate, respectively, the proportion of good 1 in region L that came from regions L and M. Thus the shipment data in (3-37) can be reexpressed in terms of these proportions, as

		Destination Region		
		L	M	
Origin Region	L	t_1^{LL}	t_1^{LM}	(3-38)
	M	t_1^{ML}	t_1^{MM}	

And an exactly similar table of coefficients can be generated for the output of sector 2.

The essential idea in the MRIO model is to assume that the sales of region L's sector 1 output to sectors in region M is put into a 'pool' of 1-goods, along with all the sector 1 output from region M. Suppose that, for good 1, region L delivered 40 percent of the total in the pool of good 1 in region M (that is, $t_1^{LM} = 0.4$), with the rest coming from within region M ($t_1^{MM} = 0.6$). Then for all users of good 1 in region M it is assumed that 40 percent of their supply of 1 as an input to production comes from L and 60 percent comes from M. And similarly for the use of each of the two goods in each of the regions.

Along with these kinds of trade coefficients, the MRIO model requires a technical coefficients matrix for each region. This means a set of production recipes that record total inputs of each good used by each sector in each region, irrespective of the regional source of those inputs. If $z_{ij}^{\cdot M}$ represents the total amount of good i used as an input to production by sector j in M, and x_j^M, as before, is total gross output of j in M, then $a_{ij}^{\cdot M} = z_{ij}^{\cdot M}/x_j^M$ represents the amount of i needed per dollar's worth of output of j in M, aggregated over all possible regions that might supply i. This is a true 'technical coefficient' in that it indicates a technological relationship between input of good i and the output of j in region M — like the value of eggs used per dollar's worth of bread baked in region M, wherever the eggs came from (except for foreign imports; see Section 3.4.2).

Continuing with the example above, with $t_1^{LM} = 0.4$ and $t_1^{MM} = 0.6$, suppose that the inputs of good 1 per dollar's worth of output of the two sectors in region M are $a_{11}^{\cdot M} = 0.25$ and $a_{12}^{\cdot M} = 0.30$. Then the MRIO model creates *estimates* of a_{11}^{MM} and a_{12}^{MM} and also of a_{11}^{LM} and a_{12}^{LM} as

$$a_{11}^{MM} \cong t_1^{MM}a_{11}^{\cdot M} = (0.6)(0.25) = 0.15 \text{ and}$$

$$a_{12}^{MM} \cong t_1^{MM}a_{12}^{\cdot M} = (0.6)(0.30) = 0.18$$

$$a_{11}^{LM} \cong t_1^{LM}a_{11}^{\cdot M} = (0.4)(0.25) = 0.10 \text{ and}$$

$$a_{12}^{LM} \cong t_1^{LM}a_{12}^{\cdot M} = (0.4)(0.30) = 0.12$$

The MRIO model structure is easily represented in matrix terms. For each region we need a technical coefficients matrix; in the two-region example, we can denote these by $\mathbf{A^{\cdot L}}$ and $\mathbf{A^{\cdot M}}$. Here

$$\mathbf{A^{\cdot L}} = \begin{bmatrix} a_{11}^{\cdot L} & a_{12}^{\cdot L} \\ a_{21}^{\cdot L} & a_{22}^{\cdot L} \end{bmatrix} \text{ and } \mathbf{A^{\cdot M}} = \begin{bmatrix} a_{11}^{\cdot M} & a_{12}^{\cdot M} \\ a_{21}^{\cdot M} & a_{22}^{\cdot M} \end{bmatrix}$$

Additionally, we need the trade coefficients information. Suppose that we arrange these in the following *diagonal* matrices each of which shows the coefficients for *all* goods for a specific origin-destination pair of regions:

$$\mathbf{T^{LL}} = \begin{bmatrix} t_1^{LL} & 0 \\ 0 & t_2^{LL} \end{bmatrix} \quad \mathbf{T^{LM}} = \begin{bmatrix} t_1^{LM} & 0 \\ 0 & t_2^{LM} \end{bmatrix}$$

$$\mathbf{T^{ML}} = \begin{bmatrix} t_1^{ML} & 0 \\ 0 & t_2^{ML} \end{bmatrix} \quad \mathbf{T^{MM}} = \begin{bmatrix} t_1^{MM} & 0 \\ 0 & t_2^{MM} \end{bmatrix}$$

Then the MRIO estimates of $\mathbf{A^{LL}}$, $\mathbf{A^{LM}}$, $\mathbf{A^{ML}}$, and $\mathbf{A^{MM}}$ in the IRIO structure are given by

$$\mathbf{A^{LL}} \cong \mathbf{T^{LL}A^{\bullet L}} = \begin{bmatrix} t_1^{LL} & 0 \\ 0 & t_2^{LL} \end{bmatrix}\begin{bmatrix} a_{11}^{\bullet L} & a_{12}^{\bullet L} \\ a_{21}^{\bullet L} & a_{22}^{\bullet L} \end{bmatrix} = \begin{bmatrix} t_1^{LL}a_{11}^{\bullet L} & t_1^{LL}a_{12}^{\bullet L} \\ t_2^{LL}a_{21}^{\bullet L} & t_2^{LL}a_{22}^{\bullet L} \end{bmatrix} \text{ and}$$

$$\mathbf{A^{LM}} \cong \mathbf{T^{LM}A^{\bullet M}} = \begin{bmatrix} t_1^{LM} & 0 \\ 0 & t_2^{LM} \end{bmatrix}\begin{bmatrix} a_{11}^{\bullet M} & a_{12}^{\bullet M} \\ a_{21}^{\bullet M} & a_{22}^{\bullet M} \end{bmatrix} = \begin{bmatrix} t_1^{LM}a_{11}^{\bullet M} & t_1^{LM}a_{12}^{\bullet M} \\ t_2^{LM}a_{21}^{\bullet M} & t_2^{LM}a_{22}^{\bullet M} \end{bmatrix} \quad (3\text{-}39)$$

$$\mathbf{A^{ML}} \cong \mathbf{T^{ML}A^{\bullet L}} = \begin{bmatrix} t_1^{ML} & 0 \\ 0 & t_2^{ML} \end{bmatrix}\begin{bmatrix} a_{11}^{\bullet L} & a_{12}^{\bullet L} \\ a_{21}^{\bullet L} & a_{22}^{\bullet L} \end{bmatrix} = \begin{bmatrix} t_1^{ML}a_{11}^{\bullet L} & t_1^{ML}a_{12}^{\bullet L} \\ t_2^{ML}a_{21}^{\bullet L} & t_2^{ML}a_{22}^{\bullet L} \end{bmatrix} \text{ and}$$

$$\mathbf{A^{MM}} \cong \mathbf{T^{MM}A^{\bullet M}} = \begin{bmatrix} t_1^{MM} & 0 \\ 0 & t_2^{MM} \end{bmatrix}\begin{bmatrix} a_{11}^{\bullet M} & a_{12}^{\bullet M} \\ a_{21}^{\bullet M} & a_{22}^{\bullet M} \end{bmatrix} = \begin{bmatrix} t_1^{MM}a_{11}^{\bullet M} & t_1^{MM}a_{12}^{\bullet M} \\ t_2^{MM}a_{21}^{\bullet M} & t_2^{MM}a_{22}^{\bullet M} \end{bmatrix} \quad (3\text{-}40)$$

[Compare (3-30) and (3-31) in Section 3.2.] Premultiplying the technical coefficients matrices by the appropriate diagonal trade coefficients matrix assures that those trade coefficients are applied uniformly across a given row of either $\mathbf{A^{\bullet L}}$ to $\mathbf{A^{\bullet M}}$.[48]

Since the trade coefficient information used in the MRIO model comes from origin-to-destination commodity shipment information, without specification of the buyer at the destination, it includes shipments not only for interindustry use but also to satisfy final demand (for example, household consumption) in the region of destination. Therefore in the MRIO model a 'final demand' term, such as $\mathbf{f^L}$, is viewed as also being satisfied from 'pools' of goods — that is, in part by purchases from suppliers in the region, $\mathbf{T^{LL}f^L}$ and in part by purchases from suppliers in region M, $\mathbf{T^{ML}f^L}$. And similarly for final demand in region M.

With more than two regions, the 'pool' for each good will contain (at least potentially) contributions from each of the regions. In the case of three regions (L, M and N), the 'Origin-Destination' matrices in (3-37) and (3-38) will have three rows and columns each, and there will be nine (3^2) diagonal trade coefficients matrices — $\mathbf{T^{LL}}$, $\mathbf{T^{LM}}$, $\mathbf{T^{LN}}$, $\mathbf{T^{ML}}$, ..., $\mathbf{T^{NN}}$ with which to adjust each region's technical coefficients matrix ($\mathbf{A^{\bullet L}}$, $\mathbf{A^{\bullet M}}$, $\mathbf{A^{\bullet N}}$) and final demand vector ($\mathbf{f^L}$, $\mathbf{f^M}$, $\mathbf{f^N}$).

The MRIO parallel to the fundamental equation set in the two-region IRIO model example in (3-32) can be written as

$$\mathbf{x^L} = \mathbf{T^{LL}A^{\bullet L}x^L} + \mathbf{T^{LM}A^{\bullet M}x^M} + \mathbf{T^{LL}f^L} + \mathbf{T^{LM}f^M}$$

$$\mathbf{x^M} = \mathbf{T^{ML}A^{\bullet L}x^L} + \mathbf{T^{MM}A^{\bullet M}x^M} + \mathbf{T^{ML}f^L} + \mathbf{T^{MM}f^M}$$

$$(3\text{-}41)$$

If we build larger **A** and **T** matrices as follows

$$\mathbf{A} = \begin{bmatrix} \mathbf{A}^{\bullet L} & | & 0 \\ ------ & | & ------ \\ 0 & | & \mathbf{A}^{\bullet M} \end{bmatrix} \text{ and } \mathbf{T} = \begin{bmatrix} \mathbf{T}^{LL} & | & \mathbf{T}^{LM} \\ ------ & | & ------ \\ \mathbf{T}^{ML} & | & \mathbf{T}^{MM} \end{bmatrix}$$

and use the same definitions of **x** and **f**, namely

$$\mathbf{x} = \begin{bmatrix} \mathbf{x}^L \\ ---- \\ \mathbf{x}^M \end{bmatrix} \text{ and } \mathbf{f} = \begin{bmatrix} \mathbf{f}^L \\ ---- \\ \mathbf{f}^M \end{bmatrix}$$

then the compact statement of the basic accounting relations in an MRIO model is seen to be

$$\mathbf{x} = \mathbf{TAx} + \mathbf{Tf} \tag{3-42}$$

[Compare (3-33) in the IRIO model.]

3.3.2 Input-output analysis with the MRIO model

a. Economic impacts Once the structure of the multiregional economy has been captured in a set of base-year data that lead to **A** and **T** matrices, the model is used in the same way as the IRIO model. That is, given a forecast of one or more elements in final demand in either or both regions, $\mathbf{f}^{L*}$ and $\mathbf{f}^{M*}$, these are used to generate new values of sectoral gross outputs in both

of the regions, $\mathbf{x}^* = \begin{bmatrix} \mathbf{x}^{L*} \\ ---- \\ \mathbf{x}^{M*} \end{bmatrix}$, via the rearrangement of $\mathbf{x} = \mathbf{TAx} + \mathbf{Tf}$ to

$$(\mathbf{I} - \mathbf{TA})\mathbf{x} = \mathbf{Tf} \tag{3-43}$$

[compare (3-34)], so that, given **f***,

$$\mathbf{x}^* = (\mathbf{I} - \mathbf{TA})^{-1}\mathbf{Tf}^*$$

b. Multipliers and linkages As in the IRIO example, various sectoral and spatial multipliers can be generated from elements in this model. Notice here that it is not just the inverse matrix, $(\mathbf{I} - \mathbf{TA})^{-1}$, that transforms new final demands, **f***, into new gross outputs, **x***. The product **Tf*** distributes new final demands in each region, $\mathbf{f}^{L*}$ and $\mathbf{f}^{M*}$, across supplying sectors in both region *L* and region *M*. Then premultiplication by $(\mathbf{I} - \mathbf{TA})^{-1}$ generates total sectoral output impacts in each of the regions. So column sums from $(\mathbf{I} - \mathbf{TA})^{-1}$ and $[(\mathbf{I} - \mathbf{TA})^{-1}\mathbf{T}]$ are alternative kinds of output multipliers in the MRIO model. They transform region-specific final demands after or before distribution to region-specific sectors, respectively. Similarly, income, employment or value added multipliers can be derived from weightings on the elements in one or the other inverse. Once the numbers are in place, in **A** and **T**, the approach, via the Leontief inverse, is the same. Similarly, linkages of various kinds can be found within the MRIO framework, adapting the general ideas from the IRIO case.

3.4 Constructing models from less than perfect data sets

Underpinning the single-region and connected-region models in Sections 3.1 through 3.3 is a set of input-output accounts. In the single-region case, if one knows the transactions among sectors in the region (**Z**) and regional gross outputs (**x**), then **A** and its associated Leontief inverse can be found. For the complete IRIO model, transactions must be broken down by both sector and region of origin and sector and region of destination (as in **Z**^{LL} and **Z**^{LM}, for example). The MRIO model relaxes the stringent IRIO requirements, relying instead on (a) transactions matrices for each region in which the region of origin of inputs is ignored (such as **Z**$^{\bullet L}$ and **Z**$^{\bullet M}$) and (b) intra- and interregional shipment matrices (for example, **T**^{LL} and **T**^{LM}) in which the sector of destination is ignored.

3.4.1 Survey-based tables

Under the most ideal conditions, detailed surveys of regional purchases, by sector, and of regional sales, by sector, can be undertaken. In fact, there is usually not enough time and/or money to allow this kind of data gathering. But even if it were possible, a problem of conflicting information virtually always arises. This is because, in sampling establishments in each of the sectors, the purchasing information about goods from sector i that is provided by firms in sector j (z_{ij}, from j's point of view) is very likely to differ from the sales information provided by sector i (z_{ij} from i's point of view). This kind of conflicting information may exist for many if not all of the n^2 elements in the transactions matrix for an n-sector regional economy, and therefore a *reconciliation* problem arises.[49] Of course, one could choose to work with sales information only (a 'rows-only' approach) or with purchases information only (a 'columns-only' approach), but usually one is faced with some of both and not enough of either.

3.4.2 Nonsurvey-based tables

In reality, it is virtually impossible to conduct such surveys frequently, if at all, for every region for which regional economic analyses are desired. At the very least, data are generally put together in semi-survey or partial survey approaches, in which survey-based information from, say, the most prominent or important sectors in a regional economy is combined with other kinds of estimates for the remainder of the table (either transactions or direct input coefficients). These estimates may sometimes come from 'expert opinion' or from information that already exists for the national economy or for a 'similar' region.

Using notation from the IRIO model, what is really needed for the single region model of Section 3.1 is $\mathbf{Z}^{LL}$ so that

$$\mathbf{x}^{L*} = (\mathbf{I} - \mathbf{A}^{LL})^{-1}\mathbf{f}^{L*}$$

This is (3-12) with the *intra*regional character of the direct input coefficients in the $\mathbf{A}$ matrix made clear. To generate these kinds of data through a survey, respondents must be able to distinguish regionally supplied inputs from imported inputs (for example, Boeing in Washington must be able to identify how much of its purchases of aluminum was supplied from within Washington and how much came from other states).

Often, less detailed data are the best that can be obtained [for example, transactions in terms of inputs, without identification of the origin of the inputs (these are the $\mathbf{Z}^{\bullet L}$ of the MRIO model)]. In conjunction with regional outputs, $\mathbf{x}^{L}$, a technical coefficients matrix, $\mathbf{A}^{\bullet L}$ with elements $a_{ij}^{\bullet L}$ (again, as in the MRIO model) could be found. How then might these data be translated into an estimate of $\mathbf{Z}^{LL}$ or $\mathbf{A}^{LL}$ for the single-region model? What is needed is an estimate of the kinds of elements that would be in $\mathbf{T}^{LL}$ in the MRIO model (but, for a single-region model, without the necessity of the between-region trade coefficients such as are in $\mathbf{T}^{LM}$, $\mathbf{T}^{LN}$, $\mathbf{T}^{ML}$ and so on). As a last resort, it is sometimes necessary to assume that the technology matrix for the region is the same as for the nation (the 'production recipe' for Coca Cola is the same whether it is made in Massachusetts or Texas). This is the most 'simplistic' approach to approximating $\mathbf{A}^{\bullet L}$; it still requires conversion to an *intra*regional direct requirements matrix, $\mathbf{A}^{LL}$.

Even a national table will not reflect 'true' production recipes to the extent that imported inputs are not accounted for. It is customary in constructing national tables to distinguish between 'competitive' and 'non-competitive' imports. For the U.S., the former, like grapes from Chile, have a domestically produced counterpart (grapes from California, for example). The latter, like coffee beans from Brazil, have no U.S.-produced equivalent product. If sector j uses both grapes and coffee beans as inputs, the value of Chilean grapes purchased would be recorded in the domestic 'grape' sector row, while the value of coffee beans appears as part of sector j's imports. So noncompetitive imports used for j's production are absent from the national recipes in the national direct inputs coefficients table. (See Hewings and Jensen, 1986, for further thoughts on this problem.)

a. Regional purchase coefficients If we know $\mathbf{x}^L$, $\mathbf{e}^L$ and $\mathbf{m}^L$ — which means each regional output, x_i^L, regional exports from each sector, e_i^L, and regional imports[50] of good i, m_i^L. — then construct the ratio

$$P_i^L = (x_i^L - e_i^L)/(x_i^L - e_i^L + m_i^L.) \tag{3-44}$$

The numerator is the amount of good i made in L that is available for use in L; the denominator is the total amount of good i in L. This is therefore an estimate of a kind of 'regional supply percentage' for sector i which could be used exactly like t_i^{LL} in Section 3.3 to modify elements in row i of $\mathbf{A}^{\bullet L}$ to generate an estimate of row i in $\mathbf{A}^{LL}$.

If a set of these percentages, p_i^L ($i = 1, ..., n$), is arranged in a diagonal matrix

$$\mathbf{P}^L = \begin{bmatrix} p_1^L & 0 & . & . & . & 0 \\ 0 & p_2^L & . & . & . & 0 \\ . & & . & & & . \\ . & & & . & & . \\ . & & & & . & . \\ 0 & 0 & . & . & . & p_n^L \end{bmatrix}$$

then $\mathbf{P}^L\mathbf{Z}^{\bullet L}$ is an estimate of $\mathbf{Z}^{LL}$ or $\mathbf{P}^L\mathbf{A}^{\bullet L}$ is an estimate of $\mathbf{A}^{LL}$. [$\mathbf{P}^L$ plays exactly the role of $\mathbf{T}^{LL}$ in the MRIO model in Section 3.3; $\mathbf{P}^L\mathbf{A}^{\bullet L}$ is the same kind of estimate of $\mathbf{A}^{LL}$ as was $\mathbf{T}^{LL}\mathbf{A}^{\bullet L}$ in (3-39) in that section.]

More sophisticated approaches than that in (3-44) to estimating these kinds of percentages, often called 'regional purchase coefficients' (often denoted by RPC_i^L), use regression techniques, in an attempt to relate the proportion of the total supply of good i originating in region L to independent variables which are measures of (or proxies for) relative (regional vs. national) wages, relative output levels, shipping distances (and other economic variables that influence delivered costs).[51]

b. Location quotient techniques Location quotients were introduced in Chapter 2 as one measure of a sector's concentration or 'importance' in a regional economy. Using $\Sigma \mathbf{x}^L$ for total region L gross output $(\sum_{j=1}^{n} x_j^L)$ and $\Sigma \mathbf{x}^{\text{nat}}$ for total national gross output $(\sum_{j=1}^{n} x_j^{\text{nat}})$, the location quotient for sector i in region L is defined as

$$LQ_i^L = (x_i^L / \Sigma \mathbf{x}^L) \div (x_i^{\text{nat}} / \Sigma \mathbf{x}^{\text{nat}})$$

The numerator, $x_i^L / \Sigma \mathbf{x}^L$, shows the proportion of total region L gross output that is accounted for by sector i's production in that region. The denominator, $(x_i^{\text{nat}} / \Sigma \mathbf{x}^{\text{nat}})$, shows this same proportion for sector i at the national level.[52]

Location quotients are often used to modify a set of national direct input coefficients, $\mathbf{A}^{\text{nat}}$, into an intraregional matrix, $\mathbf{A}^{LL}$. The assumption is that if a sector's location quotient is one or larger [the sector is as concentrated ($LQ^L = 1$) or more concentrated ($LQ^L > 1$) in the region], then that sector will be able to supply all inputs needed in the region. Conversely, if a sector's location quotient is less than one (relative non-concentration), then it is assumed that the location quotient itself represents the *proportion* of total regional interindustry input requirements that can be supplied from within the region. This is compactly expressed as[53]

$$a_{ij}^{LL} = \begin{cases} a_{ij}^{\text{nat}} & \text{if } LQ_i^L \geq 1 \text{ (for } j = 1, \ldots, n) \\ (LQ_i^L)a_{ij}^{\text{nat}} & \text{if } LQ_i^L < 1 \text{ (for } j = 1, \ldots, n) \end{cases}$$

Notice that when a sector's location quotient is less than 1, modification is uniform across an entire row of $\mathbf{A}^{\text{nat}}$; LQ_i^L is used in the same way as t_i^{LL} in the MRIO model or as regional purchase coefficients or regional supply percentages. In fact, in the location quotient approach, the simple RPCs and LQs are easily seen to be related as follows:

$$RPC_i^L = \begin{Bmatrix} 1 \\ LQ_i^L \end{Bmatrix} \text{ if } \begin{Bmatrix} LQ_i^L \geq 1 \\ LQ_i^L < 1 \end{Bmatrix}$$

c. The RAS approach A 'matrix balancing' technique for input-output data was developed at Cambridge University under the leadership of Sir Richard Stone.[54] It was used to 'update' tables, and it is still a popular approach to deal with the 'age' problem of input-output data; namely that even the best tables take time to produce, so in some sense they are out of date before they appear.[55] RAS has also often been used in real-world input-output applications to generate a regional table from data at the national level or from a different region.[56] The mechanics of the procedure are described in some detail in Appendix 3.4.

d. Numerical example: an estimate of Washington coefficients using location quotients and RAS   To illustrate these two regionalization techniques in practice, we use as $\mathbf{A}^{nat}$ the $\mathbf{A}^{MM}$ matrix from Section 3.2 (Appendix 3.3). We assume that $\mathbf{A}^{LL}$ from that section is the 'true' Washington state direct requirements matrix, against which we can compare the estimates provided by the location quotient and RAS approaches. (Recall that the elements in $\mathbf{A}^{LL}$ are the Washington regional coefficients in Table 3-3 of Section 3.1.)

For location quotients, we need the gross output vectors for the region and for the nation, $\mathbf{x}^L$ and $\mathbf{x}^{nat}$. These come from Table 3-2 and from national data that are behind $\mathbf{A}^{MM}$ in Appendix 3.2, respectively. Sectoral proportions of total gross output in Washington and in the U.S. (the numerator and denominator, respectively, of each sector's location quotient) are then easily found. The resulting location quotients turn out to be

$$\mathrm{LQ}^L = [.8382 \quad 1.0685 \quad 5.0303 \quad 2.4762 \quad .6656 \quad .7878 \quad 3.5816 \quad .7095]$$

and the estimates of regional purchase coefficients are therefore

$$\mathrm{RPC}^L = [0.8382 \quad 1 \quad 1 \quad 1 \quad 0.6656 \quad 0.7878 \quad 1 \quad 0.7095]$$

Using these regional purchase coefficients, we generate a location quotient estimate of $\mathbf{A}^{LL}$, denoted $\mathbf{A}^{LL}(\mathbf{LQ})$.[57] This and its accompanying Leontief inverse are shown in Table 3-8. Table 3-9 contains the estimates of Washington direct input coefficients and the total requirements matrix provided by the RAS procedure.

Assuming that we believe $\mathbf{A}^{LL}$ to be the 'true' matrix, the question is: how good are the approximations given by $\mathbf{A}^{LL}(\mathbf{LQ})$ and $\mathbf{A}^{LL}(\mathbf{RAS})$?[58] It is clear from comparison with $\mathbf{A}^{LL}$ in Table 3-3 that individual direct input coefficients in both $\mathbf{A}^{LL}(\mathbf{LQ})$ and $\mathbf{A}^{LL}(\mathbf{RAS})$ are often quite different. However, one could argue that the proof is in the using. In that case, it is really $(\mathbf{I} - \mathbf{A}^{LL})^{-1}$ (in Table 3-4) vs. $[\mathbf{I} - \mathbf{A}^{LL}(\mathbf{LQ})]^{-1}$ or $[\mathbf{I} - \mathbf{A}^{LL}(\mathbf{RAS})]^{-1}$, and their performance in an impact analysis, that should be compared.

To that end, we use the same impact scenario of a foreign airline order for \$250 million from the aerospace sector in Washington. Table 3-10 contains the three $\Delta\mathbf{x}$ vectors — $\Delta\mathbf{x}(\mathbf{LQ})$, $\Delta\mathbf{x}(\mathbf{RAS})$ and $\Delta\mathbf{x}$ (which is from Section 3.1) — transposed and rounded to two decimal places. The rows under $\Delta\mathbf{x}(\mathbf{LQ})$ and $\Delta\mathbf{x}(\mathbf{RAS})$ contain sector-by-sector percentage differences from $\Delta\mathbf{x}$.

Table 3-8 Location quotient estimates of A^{LL} and $(I - A^{LL})^{-1}$

$A^{LL}(LQ)$

	1	2	3	4	5	6	7	8
1	.1694	.1935	.0526	.0005	.0332	.0304	.0032	.0028
2	.0340	.1572	.0004	.0001	.0012	.0273	.0337	.0042
3	.0013	.0007	.2197	.0086	.0161	.0011	.0011	.0002
4	.0027	.0002	.0009	.1842	.0014	.0028	.0027	.0064
5	.0647	.0714	.1047	.1762	.1743	.0428	.0371	.0505
6	.0372	.0496	.0551	.0497	.0513	.0577	.0518	.0212
7	.0118	.0225	.0244	.0236	.0220	.0188	.0212	.0080
8	.1142	.0569	.0506	.0571	.0581	.1221	.1385	.1462

$[I - A^{LL}(LQ)]^{-1}$

	1	2	3	4	5	6	7	8
1	1.2245	.2903	.0953	.0184	.0560	.0523	.0206	.0104
2	.0534	1.2036	.0100	.0064	.0082	.0390	.0451	.0081
3	.0048	.0048	1.2859	.0196	.0258	.0033	.0032	.0022
4	.0060	.0030	.0034	1.2277	.0035	.0055	.0053	.0096
5	.1182	.1434	.1863	.2803	1.2322	.0765	.0682	.0787
6	.0636	.0884	.0947	.0872	.0756	1.0753	.0681	.0332
7	.0216	.0375	.0405	.0395	.0317	.0255	1.0276	.0126
8	.1887	.1480	.1227	.1241	.1096	.1733	.1874	1.1860
Σ	1.6809	1.9191	1.8388	1.8030	1.5425	1.4506	1.4254	1.3407

Table 3-9 RAS estimates of A^{LL} and $(I - A^{LL})^{-1}$

$A^{LL}(RAS)$

	1	2	3	4	5	6	7	8
1	.1033	.1566	.0347	.0001	.0181	.0207	.0026	.0032
2	.0141	.0865	.0002	.0000	.0004	.0127	.0180	.0033
3	.0017	.0012	.2936	.0031	.0179	.0015	.0018	.0006
4	.0005	.0000	.0002	.0104	.0002	.0006	.0007	.0023
5	.0387	.0568	.0677	.0306	.0934	.0287	.0287	.0567
6	.0351	.0622	.0561	.0136	.0434	.0610	.0632	.0376
7	.0166	.0423	.0372	.0097	.0279	.0298	.0388	.0211
8	.0638	.0422	.0306	.0093	.0291	.0764	.1000	.1532

$[I - A^{LL}(RAS)]^{-1}$

	1	2	3	4	5	6	7	8
1	1.1214	.1968	.0608	.0017	.0257	.0293	.0103	.0083
2	.0189	1.1005	.0042	.0006	.0026	.0166	.0225	.0058
3	.0044	.0050	1.4193	.0054	.0284	.0037	.0042	.0032
4	.0009	.0005	.0006	1.0106	.0005	.0010	.0011	.0029
5	.0579	.0880	.1188	.0366	1.1127	.0445	.0464	.0784
6	.0517	.0921	.1003	.0182	.0588	1.0763	.0803	.0544
7	.0258	.0594	.0644	.0124	.0369	.0384	1.0485	.0307
8	.0953	.0882	.0768	.0158	.0510	.1064	.1348	1.1933
Σ	1.3762	1.6306	1.8452	1.1013	1.3166	1.3160	1.3481	1.3769

Table 3-10   LQ and RAS approaches in action

Δx	= [0.17	0.08	0.67	253.70	4.23	3.44	1.49	11.47]
$\Delta x(LQ)$	= [4.59	1.59	4.89	306.93	70.06	21.79	9.87	31.02]
	[2600	1888	630	21	1556	533	562	170]
$\Delta x(RAS)$	= [0.42	0.15	1.36	252.64	9.15	4.56	3.11	3.95]
	[150	87	104	0	116	32	109	-66]

It is apparent in this illustration that location quotient based estimates of Washington technology were much less successful than those produced by the RAS technique. (That need not be surprising, since RAS requires three times as much region-specific data as does the location quotient procedure; see Appendix 3.4.) Total economy-wide output is $275.2443 million using the ('true') Washington table, $275.3363 million with RAS estimates and $450.7412 million using the location quotient estimates.

This single illustration should not be taken as a blanket condemnation of location quotient based approaches to modifying a national matrix to reflect regional practices nor as unqualified support for the RAS technique. However, the poor location quotient showing here reflects in part what is known as the 'product mix' problem. For example, 'Food Products' in Washington may be primarily apples and canned fish; in other states the goods produced in the food products sector will be vastly different (guava jelly, perhaps, in Florida; tomato soup in New Jersey). And the information in the *national* table, A^{nat}, is an 'average' of the food products sector activity in all of the states. In this illustration, the national recipes for sectors 2, 3, 4 and 7 were used as Washington recipes also, because for each of those sectors $LQ_i^L > 1$. This product-mix problem is diminished if the input-output model has more sectors; the more disaggregated the data, the more likely it is that 'national' and 'regional' sectors are matched. (If there were a 'Coca Cola' sector, its production recipe would be virtually the same wherever it was produced.)

In addition, since the RAS procedure requires, among others, the column sums of the (unknown) regional transactions matrix, this means that *by definition* the column sums of A^{LL} and $A(RAS)$ will be the same. This in turn means that the column sums of the first two terms in the power series approximations to $(I - A^{LL})^{-1}$, namely $I + A^{LL}$, and to $[I - A^{LL}(RAS)]^{-1} — I + A^{LL}(RAS)$ — will be identical. So RAS has a built-in tendency to get output multipliers right. Also, the RAS approach easily accommodates additional information, if one has it.

The figures in Table 3-10 only illustrate the kinds of results that one might expect from the LQ and RAS techniques in action. But in repeated experiments, it has generally been shown that (a) techniques that require more 'correct' information will do better than those requiring less and (b) within the RAS procedure, more sector specific information usually does not hurt and often leads to a much better estimate.

3.4.3 Hybrid tables

The use of the term 'hybrid' is meant to suggest that tables are constructed through a combination of techniques that include some survey and some nonsurvey elements. These are also sometimes known as 'semi-survey,' 'partial-survey' or 'mongrel' approaches. In a sense, this is also the character of the 'nonsurvey' methods just discussed. But hybrid approaches take a more formal and structured approach. An example is provided by the GRIT (Generation of Regional Input-output Tables) technique pioneered by Jensen, West and others (Jensen, Mandeville and Karunaratne, 1979).[59] Something like the following steps are involved:

(a) Updating the basic matrix (probably national);
(b) Regionalization of the matrix produced in (a);
(c) Possibly aggregating the matrix in (b) to reflect the (smaller) level of regional sectoral detail that it is reasonable to use;
(d) Insertion of 'superior' data into the matrix from (c).

The last step requires identification of 'critical' cells in the matrix in (c), for which superior data would be gathered. The trick is to decide what constitutes 'criticality' of a sector; some guidelines are obvious — if there is one clearly dominant sector in a region with very little other economic activity, then any information that is available (provided that it is 'reliable,' which is another issue) ought to be used. In a more mixed economy, criticality may be in the eye of the beholder. One approach, employed by Hewings and Romanos (1981), identified the five largest input and output coefficients for each sector in a national table; these coefficients were then adjusted by firms in the region in order to reflect regional production practices.[60]

3.4.4 Interregional connections

For the connected-region input-output models that were explored in Sections 3.2 and 3.3, much more than just single region tables are needed. In the IRIO version, estimates are needed of each interindustry transaction, z_{ij}^{LM}, for all regions and all sectors. In the MRIO approach, these are replaced by trade coefficients, t_i^{LM}, where the buying sector in region M is ignored.

In two-region models (Washington State and the Rest of the U.S., for example), once a specific regional purchase coefficient, RPC^L_j (= t^{LL}_j in MRIO terms), is estimated, then the associated t^{ML}_j is also known; it is just $(1 - t^{LL}_j)$. For that reason, there has been considerable work on estimation of the trade components of two-region ('biregional') input-output models.[61]

In general, with more than two regions, variations of gravity model approaches to interregional commodity flow estimation have been explored in some detail. In these methods, exchange of goods between two regions is related to the relative 'sizes' of the two regions and to the distance between them. But these subjects are beyond the scope of this chapter.[62]

3.4.5 Empirical implementation

A number of what have come to be called 'ready-made' regional input-output modelling systems have been developed for use by analysts who need to find answers to real-world questions for specific regions. The Australian GRIT system, noted above, is one such approach. [There is an associated system known as GRIMP — GRit IMpact Program (West, 1988).] In the U.S., among the most widely cited are:

RIMS (Regional Input-output Modeling System) from the Bureau of Economic Analysis (BEA) at the U.S. Department of Commerce (Cartwright, Beemiller and Gustely, 1981). [RIMS II is a more recent version (U.S. Department of Commerce, 1986).]

IMPLAN (IMpact analysis for PLANning) from the Forest Service, U.S. Department of Agriculture, in conjunction with Engineering-Economics Associates, Berkeley, California (Palmer, Siverts and Sullivan, 1985).

RSRI (Regional Science Research Institute), with a personal computer version PC-IO (Stevens, Treyz, Erlich and Brower, 1983).

ADOTMATR [which began as a program named MATRIX on a computer's 'A' drive, hence A.MATRIX; the current label emerged as a file name in which the '.' ('dot') could not be used and where the length limit was eight characters] (Lamphear and Konecny, 1986).

SCHAFFER (Schaffer and Davidson, 1985).

These systems employ a variety of regionalization techniques (some allow the user to choose from among several), including location quotients (several varieties), supply-demand pool and RAS.[63] Comparisons of the structure and the performance of these alternative approaches can be found in, among others, Brucker, Hastings and Latham (1987, 1990) and Sivitanidou and Polenske (1988).

3.5 Fusion of comparative cost and input-output: editorial remarks

As indicated in the introductory statement of this chapter, regional and interregional input-output is an indispensable tool for providing estimates of the size of the market that not only exists but will come to exist to absorb the output of a firm. Such estimates are required to evaluate the feasibility of a location for a new enterprise such as an integrated iron and steel works. Moreover, once an enterprise is located in a region, input-output is extremely valuable for estimating the impact of such a development. These relationships between the comparative cost and input-output methods have on a number of occasions led to their fruitful fusion in regional planning and development studies. We can anticipate that such fusion will be conducted increasingly in the future, particularly to yield a basic component of a more comprehensive synthesis of regional science and other methods which will be discussed in later chapters. A clear-cut illustration of the coordinated joining of just these two methods (without the incursion of other methods) is the 1952 study on the feasibility of the Trenton location for an integrated iron and steel works and its impact on the greater New York–Philadelphia region (Isard and Kuenne, 1953).

In chapter 2 we discussed the feasibility of a New England location for an integrated iron and steel works. The same procedure (set of steps) was performed to evaluate the Trenton location. The major difference in the relevant cost data for the two studies related to the cost of transporting the finished product to the market. The data in Table 3-11 on this cost indicate the great advantage of Trenton over existing New England locations. Additionally, it was estimated that the market for steel in this region was 9 million to 11 million tons annually, which together with penetration into other markets would justify the construction of a works that could realize full-scale economies. Bedrock conditions, potential transport capabilities and other factors proved to be favorable. Thus, a works with at least 3 million tons annual capacity was projected.

Before introducing the input-output analysis, it was necessary to project the location of new steel fabricating activities. The historical record, location theory, and the judgment of those business persons knowledgeable regarding steel and steel-fabricating activities all supported the hypothesis that considerable new steel-fabricating activities would develop in the region were a new steel works constructed. Hence it was necessary to project such development on the basis of experience in the steel/steel-fabrication sectors, theory and interviews. Once this was done, input

Table 3-11 Transportation costs on ore, coal, and finished
           products for selected producing locations serving
           New York City

(In dollars)

	Transportation Costs on:			
Location	Ore	Coal	Finished Products	Total
New London (hypothetical)	3.68	5.42	8.80	17.90
Pittsburgh	5.55	1.56	12.40	19.51
Cleveland	3.16	3.85	14.00	21.01
Sparrows Point	3.68	4.26	8.40	16.34
Buffalo	3.16	4.27	11.60	19.03
Bethlehem	5.56	5.06	5.80	16.42
Trenton	3.68	4.65	4.80	13.13

requirements of the projected steel works and steel-fabricating activities
were calculated using national input-output coefficients. (Regional
coefficients were not available.) These input requirements are listed in
column (1) of Table 3-12. This constitutes the Δf vector discussed in
section 3.1.3 above. The next step was to estimate the minimum
percentages of each input requirement to be produced in the region. These
are listed in column (2). They then yield the first-round expansions listed
in column (3). These first-round expansions lead to second-round input
requirements, which in turn lead to second-round expansions, and so forth.
(See section 3.1.3 on the round-by-round method.) The sum of rounds of
expansions plus extrapolations for subsequent rounds are recorded in
column (6). The overall total of new employees is listed by sector in
column (9).

For full details on all the above operations, see Isard and Kuenne
(1953). Again, to repeat, the above represents an outdated study but one
that is useful to illustrate how the two methods (comparative cost and
input-output) can be fused without the additional complexities and
improvements that subsequent studies have made and which will be
discussed in the ensuing chapters.

Table 3-12 Direct and indirect repercussions of new basic steel capacity

	Input requirements of initial steel and steel-fabricating activities (in $ thousand) (1)	Minimum percentage of input requirements to be produced in area (2)	First round expansions in area (in $ thousand) (3)	Second round expansions in area (in $ thousand) (4)	Third round expansions in area (in $ thousand) (5)	Sum of round expansions in area (in $ thousand) (6)	Total new employees corresponding to round expansions (7)	Total new employees in initial steel and steel-fabricating activities (8)	Over-all total of new employees (9)
1. Agriculture & fisheries	50.0	0	0.0	0.	0.	0.	0		0
2. Food & kindred products	294.6	60	176.8	17,660.	8,249.	42,492.	1,833		1,833
3. Tobacco manufactures	0.0	0	0.0	0.	0.	0.	0		0
4. Textile mill products	3,864.7	10	386.5	406.	39.	1,280.	142		142
5. Apparel	1,285.6	75	964.2	10,124.	3,461.	21,155.	2,302		2,302
6. Lumber & wood products	5,610.7	5	280.5	93.	36.	450.	64		64
7. Furniture & fixtures	1,753.4	33	578.6	802.	198.	2,000.	234		234
8. Paper & allied products	4,818.7	40	1,927.5	1,674.	1,297.	6,574.	426		426
9. Printing & publishing	425.5	90	383.0	5,929.	3,014.	14,617.	1,667		1,667
10. Chemicals	10,626.4	45	4,781.9	3,599.	1,630.	12,077.	601		601
11. Products of petroleum & coal	10,936.6	25	2,734.2	2,547.	1,118.	7,634.	228		228
12. Rubber products	8,381.5	15	1,257.2	355.	102.	1,879.	169		169
13. Leather & leather products	647.7	20	129.5	679.	194.	1,371.	150		150
14. Stone, clay, & glass products	9,031.7	15	1,354.8	441.	139.	2,083.	268		268
15. Iron & steel	121,170.5	50	60,585.3	13,566.	2,965.	78,335.	6,093	11,666	17,759
16. Nonferrous metals	33,997.4	20	6,799.5	1,667.	381.	9,063.	505		505
17. Plumbing & heating supplies	3,192.4	25	798.1	248.	50.	1,189.	118	3,640	3,758
18. Fabricated structural metal prod.	3,480.7	40	1,392.3	312.	33.	1,809.	151	1,420	1,571
19. Other fabricated metal products	31,770.9	40	12,708.4	2,146.	561.	16,121.	1,537	10,060	11,597
20. Agric'l, mining, & const. machinery	3,651.3	5	181.6	46.	11.	251.	22	707	729
21. Metal-working machinery	7,389.1	25	1,847.3	270.	43.	2,210.	289	2,705	2,994
22. Other machinery (except electric)	28,463.6	40	11,385.4	2,675.	551.	15,384.	1,486	28,607	30,093
23. Motors & generators	11,265.9	20	2,253.2	226.	42.	2,560.	301	10,392 (rows 23–24)	12,312 (rows 23–24)
24. Radios	4,562.2	30	1,368.7	428.	101.	2,026.	192		
25. Other electrical machinery	21,773.9	50	10,887.0	2,011.	432.	13,903.	389	8,770	9,159
26. Motor vehicles	50,530.8	10	5,053.1	742.	260.	6,421.	717	4,005	4,722
27. Other transportation equipment	2,605.5	20	521.1	276.	69.	958.	117		416
28. Professional & scientific equip.	3,221.4	50	1,610.7	801.	287.	3,123.	416		6,953
29. Miscellaneous manufacturing	5,116.8	60	3,070.1	2,888.	982.	8,418.	845	6,108	1,100
30. Coal, gas, & electric power	7,767.0	50	3,883.5	1,843.	2,693.	11,079.	1,100		3,308
31. Railroad transportation	13,575.8	75	10,181.9	6,010.	2,390.	21,532.	3,308		110
32. Ocean transportation	457.3	75	343.0	331.	170.	1,021.	110		2,394
33. Other transportation	4,179.4	95	3,970.4	8,422.	2,836.	19,694.	2,394		13,874
34. Trade	13,969.8	95	13,271.3	36,585.	11,855.	83,642.	13,874		
43. Undistributed	103,638.6	50	51,819.3	5,875.	6,019.	69,236.	7,208		7,208
44. Eating and drinking places	000.0	95	0.0	16,916.	3,903.	29,551.	3,705		3,705
45. Households	348,281.0	82	285,590.4	63,002.	80,894.	509,578.			
Totals	903,807.7		521,377.2	282,024.	164,400.	1,177,812.	70,089	88,680	158,769

Appendix 3.1 The commodity-industry approach in input-output models

A3.1.1 Introduction

Beginning with the U.S. 1972 input-output tables, U.S. data have been collected and presented in what is known as commodity-by-industry form. This accounting framework, largely due to Sir Richard Stone, has also been proposed by the United Nations as a standard for data gathering throughout the world. (Stone, 1961; Cambridge University, 1963; United Nations, 1968.) It has been a feature of Canadian input-output statistics since 1971 (Poole, 1995), and it is generally employed internationally. A major advantage of the approach is that it allows a distinction to be made between primary and secondary industrial output (by-products, secondary products, etc.) by relaxing the usual input-output assumption that each industry produces a single product.

The underlying observation is that *industries* use *commodities* to make *commodities*. It is commodities that are the inputs to industrial processes and that are used to satisfy final demands. An industry is defined by its primary product (commodity). If every commodity produced in an economy is primary to some industry then the number of commodities and the number of industries will be the same. In this brief introduction, we will assume that this is the case. (Since an industry is defined by its primary commodity, there cannot be fewer commodities than industries.)

A3.1.2 Commodity-industry accounts

The essentials of the commodity-industry accounts are contained in two matrices.

a. The use matrix   The interindustry transactions matrix, $\mathbf{Z} = [z_{ij}]$, in ordinary input-output accounts, is replaced by a *use* matrix, $\mathbf{U} = [u_{ij}]$, where u_{ij} is the value of purchases of *commodity i* by *industry j*. If we also have information on *commodity* sales to final demand, $\mathbf{e} = [e_i]$, and on *industry* purchases of value added items, $\mathbf{va} = [va_j]$, this information is arranged as in Table 3-1-1.

A kind of parallel to a direct input coefficient in the ordinary input-output accounts,

$$a_{ij} = z_{ij}/x_j \text{ or } \mathbf{A} = \mathbf{Z}(\hat{\mathbf{x}})^{-1}$$

Table 3-1-1 The use matrix (U) and other data for a two-commodity, two-industry hypothetical example (in dollars)

		Industry 1	Industry 2	Final Demand for Commodities (e)	Total Commodity Output (q)
Commodity	1	12	8	80	100
	2	10	7	83	100
Value Added		68	95		
Total Industry Inputs		90	110		

is then

$$b_{ij} = u_{ij}/x_j \text{ or } \mathbf{B} = \mathbf{U}(\hat{\mathbf{x}})^{-1}$$

so b_{ij} is the value of commodity *i* inputs per dollar's worth of industry *j* output. Rows of **B** represent commodities and columns represent industries; thus the 'commodity-by-industry' name.[64]

b. The make matrix The 'industries use commodities' part of 'industries use commodities to make commodities' is quantified in the use matrix. As might be expected, the matrix showing how industries make commodities is called the *make* matrix, usually denoted $\mathbf{V} = [v_{ij}]$, where v_{ij} shows the value of the output of *commodity j* made by *industry i*.[65] Table 3-1-2 provides an example.

Table 3-1-2 The make matrix (V) and other data for a two-commodity, two-industry hypothetical example (in dollars)

		Commodity 1	Commodity 2	Total Industry Output (x)
Industry	1	90	0	90
	2	10	100	110
Total Commodity Output (q')		100	100	

Table 3-1-3 shows one way of presenting all of the data in a commodity-industry framework.

Table 3-1-3 The complete set of commodity-by-industry data (in dollars)

		Commodities 1	2		Industries 1	2	Final Demand	Total Output
Commod-	1			U	$\begin{bmatrix}12 \\ 10\end{bmatrix}$	$\begin{bmatrix}8 \\ 7\end{bmatrix}$	e $\begin{bmatrix}80 \\ 83\end{bmatrix}$	q $\begin{bmatrix}100 \\ 100\end{bmatrix}$
ities	2							
Indus-	1	V $\begin{bmatrix}90 \\ 10\end{bmatrix}$	$\begin{bmatrix}0 \\ 100\end{bmatrix}$					x $\begin{bmatrix}90 \\ 110\end{bmatrix}$
tries	2							
Value Added					va [68	95]		163
Total Inputs		q′ [100	100]		x′ [90	110]	163	

A3.1.3 The commodity-industry model

In the commodity-industry framework, both total industry output ($x = [x_j]$) and total commodity output ($q = [q_j]$) are accounted for. In particular, industry outputs are row sums of the make matrix:

$$x = Vi \tag{3-1-1}$$

(where i, as usual, is a column vector of 1s of appropriate length), and commodity outputs are column sums of that matrix, $q = i'V$. Alternatively, from the illustration in Table 3-1-3,

$$q_1 = u_{11} + u_{12} + e_1 \text{ and } q_2 = u_{21} + u_{22} + e_2$$

In matrix terms, for a model of any size,

$$q = Ui + e \tag{3-1-2}$$

In the original input-output model accounts, it is straightforward to move from accounting for (industry) outputs

$$x = Ax + f \tag{3-1-3}$$

to the operational form of the model (driven by final demand for industry output)

$$x = (I - A)^{-1} f \tag{3-1-4}$$

The commodity-industry approach uses (3-1-2) in conjunction with the direct (commodity) input coefficients matrix, B, to generate a parallel to (3-1-3), namely

$$q = Bx + e \tag{3-1-5}$$

The problem is that it is impossible to go directly to an operational form, as in (3-1-4), because of the presence of both $\mathbf{q}$ (commodity output) and $\mathbf{x}$ (industry output) in (3-1-5).

The algebraic solution to this problem is to find an expression that transforms industry outputs to commodity outputs (or the other way around), so that either $\mathbf{x}$ can be replaced by a function of $\mathbf{q}$ or $\mathbf{q}$ can be replaced by an expression involving just $\mathbf{x}$. We illustrate just one such transformation.[66]

Define $d_{ij} = v_{ij}/q_j$, so that d_{ij} represents the fraction of commodity j's total output that was produced by industry i. In matrix terms,

$$\mathbf{D} = [d_{ij}] = \mathbf{V}(\hat{\mathbf{q}})^{-1} \tag{3-1-6}$$

This is known as the matrix of *commodity output proportions*. Using it, together with (3-1-1), we see that $\mathbf{D} = \mathbf{V}(\hat{\mathbf{q}})^{-1} \rightarrow \mathbf{D}\hat{\mathbf{q}} = \mathbf{V} \rightarrow \mathbf{D}\hat{\mathbf{q}}\mathbf{i} = \mathbf{V}\mathbf{i}$, so

$$\mathbf{Dq} = \mathbf{x} \tag{3-1-7}$$

so (3-1-5) can be expressed as

$$\mathbf{q} = \mathbf{B}(\mathbf{Dq}) + \mathbf{e} \tag{3-1-8}$$

from which

$$\mathbf{q} = (\mathbf{I} - \mathbf{BD})^{-1}\,\mathbf{e} \tag{3-1-9}$$

The inverse matrix on the right-hand side, $(\mathbf{I} - \mathbf{BD})^{-1}$, is called a *commodity-by-commodity total requirements matrix*, since it connects *commodity* final demand to *commodity* output. It thus plays the role of the Leontief inverse in the ordinary input-output model in (3-1-4). Notice now that the 'parallel' to the $\mathbf{A}$ matrix in that model is seen here to be the product $\mathbf{BD}$.

From (3-1-7), $\mathbf{q} = \mathbf{D}^{-1}\mathbf{x}$ (assuming that $\mathbf{D}$ is nonsingular), and a variation of this approach rewrites (3-1-5) as

$$\mathbf{D}^{-1}\mathbf{x} = \mathbf{Bx} + \mathbf{e}$$

or, multiplying both sides by $\mathbf{D}$ and rearranging,

$$\mathbf{x} = [(\mathbf{I} - \mathbf{DB})^{-1}\mathbf{D}]\mathbf{e}$$

Now *commodity* final demand is connected to *industry* output. Additionally, transformations of commodity final demand ($\mathbf{e}$) into industry final demand ($\mathbf{f}$) are easily derived, and thus two more possible operational models can be generated, making either $\mathbf{q}$ or $\mathbf{x}$ a function of $\mathbf{f}$, not $\mathbf{e}$. All these variants (and others) are covered in more advanced references.

Appendix 3.2 Additional linkage measures from input-output data

We explore very briefly some further measures of sectoral linkage based on data in input-output direct coefficients and total requirements matrices. To cover these in any detail would go beyond the intent of this chapter. However, these measures are used very much in the input-output literature, especially for developing economies, and they deserve at least passing reference.

A3.2.1 Forward linkage measures

A direct measure of a sector's 'downstream' or *forward* linkage cannot logically come from row sums of an $\mathbf{A}$ matrix, since each a_{ij} in a given row results from division of z_{ij} by a different total output. An alternative kind of coefficients matrix, often called a 'direct *output* coefficients' matrix (in contrast to the 'direct *input* coefficients' in $\mathbf{A}$) comes from dividing all elements in row i of the transactions table (Table 3-1) by x_i, the output of the *selling* sector; $\overrightarrow{a_{ij}} = z_{ij}/x_i$.[67] Each of these coefficients indicates the *proportion* of sector i's total output that was used by sector j as an input to production. In a complete $(n \times n)$ matrix of these output coefficients, $\overrightarrow{\mathbf{A}}$, the i-th row sum indicates the proportion of sector i's output that served as inputs to all sectors in the regional economy. These are known as direct forward linkages;

$$\text{DFL}_i = \sum_{j=1}^{n} \overrightarrow{a_{ij}} \tag{3-2-1}$$

The larger a sector's direct forward linkage, the more its output is used as an input to production in the economy. If one assumes that the distribution patterns reflected in $\overrightarrow{\mathbf{A}}$ remain fixed and that a doubling of sector i's output would result in a doubling of purchases from i by each sector that uses i goods as inputs, then the larger a sector's DFL, the more an increase in its production would stimulate the economy.

Again, using only direct output distribution information ignores the indirect linkages in an economy. Parallel to the *total backward linkage* measure, total forward linkages can be calculated as *row sums* of $\overrightarrow{\mathbf{B}} = (\mathbf{I} - \overrightarrow{\mathbf{A}})^{-1}$, the parallel to the Leontief inverse in the usual input-output model, so that[68]

$$\text{TFL}_i = \sum_{j=1}^{n} \overrightarrow{b_{ij}} \tag{3-2-2}$$

A3.2.2 Combined linkage measures

One way of presenting results on both backward and forward linkage is to normalize by dividing by the average of a particular measure over all sectors. For example, denote the normalized backward linkage as $TBL_j^* = TBL_j/[(1/n)\sum_{j=1}^{n}TBL_j]$. Then, if $TBL_j^* > 1$, sector j is considered to be more dependent than the average regional sector on inputs from sectors within the region; if $TBL_k^* < 1$, the opposite is true — sector k is less dependent than the average regional sector on regional inputs. Total forward linkages could be similarly normalized. Then a simple visual way of presenting results on both backward and forward linkages is to create a (2 x 2) table (as in Table 3-2-1) in which each sector can be located in one of the four quadrants. Those sectors that appear in the upper left can then be regarded as relatively most 'important' in the regional economy since they are above average on both backward and forward linkage measures.[69]

Table 3-2-1 Classification of backward and forward linkages

		Total Forward Linkage	
		High (TFL* > 1)	Low (TFL* ≤ 1)
Total Backward Linkage	High (TBL* > 1)		
	Low (TBL* ≤ 1)		

In addition, a number of other approaches have been developed for identification of relatively important sectors in an economy.[70] An illustration is provided by the notion of 'hypothetical extraction' which has generated a number of variants. The essential idea here is to inquire how different the outputs of sectors in the economy would be if some sector in that economy, say the *k*-th, did not exist. One approach is simply to remove the *k*-th row and column from the **A** matrix, in effect 'extracting' the sector from the economy. Then if one calculates the outputs of the other (*n* − 1) sectors when faced with a specified final demand in both the original model and in the model without sector *k*, the difference in these output vectors has been proposed as one measure of sector *k*'s importance in the economy.[71] Further details are beyond the scope of this chapter.

Appendix 3.3 Data for the two-region IRIO numerical example

Table 3-3-1 contains the four quadrants of the two-region IRIO model with L = Washington State and M = Rest of the U.S. Sources for the elements in each of the matrices are discussed in Section 3.2. In particular, $\mathbf{A}^{LM}$ and $\mathbf{A}^{ML}$ reflect information on Washington exports to and imports from the rest of the U.S. that was known only in the aggregate (one column and row) in Table 3-2.

The *average* values in each of the four **A** matrices are:

	L	M
L	.0361	.0008
M	.0241	.0632
Total	.0602	.0640

These reflect (a) Washington's relatively strong dependence on inputs from the rest of the U.S. (compare .0361 and .0241), (b) the relative independence of the rest of the U.S. from inputs supplied by Washington (compare .0632 and .0008). At the same time, total domestically supplied inputs are similar for both Washington and the rest of the U.S., consistent with the relatively developed status of the Washington economy.

Average values of output multipliers (column sums) in each of the four quadrants of the Leontief inverse (Table 3-3-2) are:

	L	M
L	1.4148	.0146
M	.4569	1.9403

As might be expected, the average intraregional multiplier is larger for the rest of the U.S. than for Washington. And, on average, a final demand change of $1 in Washington State generates $0.4569 in output in the rest of the U.S., whereas a final demand change of $1 in the rest of the U.S. leads to an increase in Washington output of just $0.0146.

Appendix 3.4 The RAS approach to updating or regionalization of input-output tables

In this appendix we explore the mechanics of the RAS approach, a procedure that is very often used in real-world input-output studies, either for updating a table that is out of date or for creating a set of input-output data for the economy in a particular region from data for a different region or for the nation. The procedure is essentially the same for both the updating and the regionalization problem; in this appendix we consider

Table 3-3-1　Direct input coefficients in the IRIO example

$$A = \begin{bmatrix} A^{LL} & A^{LM} \\ A^{ML} & A^{MM} \end{bmatrix}$$

A^{LL}

	1	2	3	4	5	6	7	8
1	.1045	.1976	.0856	.0001	.0048	.0051	.0022	.0005
2	.0281	.0549	.0011	.0000	.0002	.0016	.0335	.0014
3	.0053	.0260	.2471	.0015	.0197	.0015	.0092	.0019
4	.0000	.0000	.0000	.0146	.0009	.0017	.0367	.0000
5	.0586	.0565	.0544	.0115	.0848	.0553	.0463	.0564
6	.0304	.0339	.0726	.0092	.0350	.1081	.0337	.0398
7	.0273	.0469	.0343	.0038	.0435	.0147	.0337	.0181
8	.0197	.0320	.0252	.0361	.0417	.0434	.0924	.1599

A^{LM}

	1	2	3	4	5	6	7	8
1	.0005	.0005	.0001	.0000	.0001	.0001	.0000	.0000
2	.0008	.0035	.0000	.0000	.0000	.0006	.0008	.0001
3	.0001	.0000	.0000	.0004	.0007	.0000	.0002	.0003
4	.0002	.0000	.0010	.0100	.0001	.0002	.0003	.0004
5	.0004	.0007	.0006	.0006	.0006	.0006	.0006	.0005
6	.0004	.0006	.0004	.0006	.0007	.0006	.0006	.0002
7	.0004	.0007	.0004	.0008	.0007	.0006	.0007	.0003
8	.0009	.0004	.0004	.0004	.0004	.0009	.0010	.0011

A^{ML}

	1	2	3	4	5	6	7	8
1	.0331	.0719	.0165	.0005	.0062	.0023	.0007	.0001
2	.0089	.0605	.0002	.0000	.0002	.0007	.0105	.0003
3	.0017	.0137	.0476	.0106	.0221	.0007	.0000	.0004
4	.0000	.0000	.0000	.1444	.1330	.0008	.0029	.0000
5	.0185	.0297	.0105	.1226	.0386	.0251	.0116	.0128
6	.0096	.0178	.0140	.0622	.0495	.0354	.0146	.0090
7	.0086	.0246	.0066	.0215	.0067	.0067	.0106	.0041
8	.0062	.0168	.0049	.2142	.0473	.0334	.0291	.0362

A^{MM}

	1	2	3	4	5	6	7	8
1	.2021	.2308	.0628	.0006	.0396	.0362	.0039	.0033
2	.0340	.1572	.0001	.0001	.0012	.0273	.0337	.0042
3	.0014	.0007	.2198	.0086	.0161	.0011	.0011	.0002
4	.0027	.0073	.0009	.1842	.0014	.0028	.0027	.0064
5	.0972	.1073	.1573	.2647	.2618	.0643	.0558	.0759
6	.0472	.0629	.0699	.0631	.0651	.0732	.0658	.0270
7	.0118	.0225	.0244	.0236	.0220	.0188	.0213	.0080
8	.1610	.0802	.0714	.0805	.0819	.1721	.1952	.2060

Table 3-3-2　Leontief inverse elements in the IRIO example

$$B = \begin{bmatrix} (I - A^{LL}) & -A^{LM} \\ -A^{ML} & (I - A^{MM}) \end{bmatrix}^{-1} = \begin{bmatrix} B^{LL} & B^{LM} \\ B^{ML} & B^{MM} \end{bmatrix}$$

B^{LL}

	1	2	3	4	5	6	7	8
1	1.1266	.2411	.1308	.0009	.0100	.0082	.0132	.0028
2	.0352	1.0684	.0080	.0006	.0028	.0031	.0378	.0031
3	.0122	.0427	1.3343	.0034	.0307	.0049	.0163	.0058
4	.0002	.0003	.0004	1.0169	.0012	.0020	.0002	.0002
5	.0821	.0949	.1021	.0183	1.1052	.0745	.0577	.0796
6	.0479	.0627	.1234	.0146	.0524	1.1291	.0653	.0589
7	.0392	.0669	.0593	.0067	.0536	.0224	1.0437	.0275
8	.0392	.0635	.0617	.0472	.0654	.0653	.1235	1.2008

B^{LM}

	1	2	3	4	5	6	7	8
1	.0011	.0021	.0020	.0004	.0004	.0005	.0004	.0001
2	.0015	.0051	.0005	.0003	.0003	.0004	.0012	.0003
3	.0005	.0007	.0158	.0015	.0017	.0004	.0004	.0003
4	.0004	.0003	.0003	.0127	.0003	.0004	.0004	.0006
5	.0020	.0027	.0038	.0040	.0032	.0014	.0013	.0012
6	.0014	.0019	.0031	.0019	.0016	.0014	.0013	.0007
7	.0012	.0020	.0020	.0024	.0015	.0012	.0012	.0007
8	.0024	.0024	.0026	.0026	.0018	.0021	.0022	.0021

B^{ML}

	1	2	3	4	5	6	7	8
1	.0626	.1468	.0513	.0278	.0326	.0133	.0166	.0069
2	.0197	.0908	.0084	.0092	.0091	.0053	.0190	.0032
3	.0080	.0281	.0871	.0232	.0389	.0086	.0086	.0047
4	.0011	.0022	.0015	.1841	.0035	.0026	.0011	.0010
5	.0707	.1314	.0879	.3018	.2461	.0736	.0525	.0520
6	.0320	.0635	.0520	.1216	.0819	.0580	.0338	.0257
7	.0201	.0452	.0238	.0415	.0674	.0161	.0197	.0125
8	.0545	.1186	.0711	.3735	.1446	.0844	.0748	.0794

B^{MM}

	1	2	3	4	5	6	7	8
1	1.2881	.3720	.1302	.0376	.0820	.0715	.0314	.0184
2	.0582	1.2097	.0138	.0099	.0116	.0417	.0474	.0098
3	.0074	.0080	1.2903	.0246	.0298	.0050	.0047	.0038
4	.0076	.0047	.0048	1.2314	.0048	.0067	.0065	.0108
5	.2265	.2714	.3354	.4952	1.4095	.1470	.1320	.1479
6	.0981	.1323	.1391	.1343	.1154	1.1071	.9970	.0520
7	.0270	.0438	.0465	.0472	.0379	.0291	1.1309	.0158
8	.3202	.2668	.2212	.2314	.2011	.2825	.3007	1.2964

regionalization. Assume that we want to 'adjust' a national table (either $\mathbf{Z}^{nat}$ or $\mathbf{A}^{nat}$) to reflect within-region technology ($\mathbf{Z}^{LL}$ or $\mathbf{A}^{LL}$). (For a numerical illustration of this kind of matrix adjustment procedure in the context of gravity and spatial interaction models, see pp. 89–90,94.)

The RAS approach works on either transactions or direct input coefficients; for this illustration, we use the coefficients matrices. This means that we need to know $\mathbf{A}^{nat}$. The data for region L that are needed are: (a) regional gross outputs, $\mathbf{x}^L$, (b) total *intra*regional interindustry sales, by sector and (c) total *intra*regional interindustry purchases, by sector. The totals in (b) are the *row sums* of the intraregional transactions matrix, $\mathbf{Z}^{LL}$, arranged as a column vector.[72] Denote this vector of interindustry sales by $\mathbf{u}^L$, with elements u_j^L ($j = 1, ..., n$), each of which might be found as the difference between x_j^L [which is known, from (a)], and sector j's total sales to final demand, f_j^L. Similarly, the totals in (c) are the *column sums* of the unknown transactions matrix, arranged in a row vector. They might be estimated, for sector j, as the difference between x_j^L and sector j's total payments for value added, va_j^L, and imports, m_j^L. Let this vector of total interindustry purchases be denoted $\mathbf{v}^L$, with elements v_j^L ($j = 1, ..., n$).

In the absence of any further region-specific information, the initial assumption made is that $\mathbf{A}^{LL} = \mathbf{A}^{nat}$. How can this be checked against the regional facts — $\mathbf{x}^L$, $\mathbf{u}^L$ and $\mathbf{v}^L$? A straightforward test is to create the $\mathbf{Z}^{LL}$ matrix that would result from $\mathbf{A}^{nat}$ and $\mathbf{x}^L$ — namely $\mathbf{Z}^{LL(1)} = \mathbf{A}^{nat}(\hat{\mathbf{x}}^L)$. [The superscript (1) denotes that this is the first of what will be a series of estimates of the unknown $\mathbf{Z}^{LL}$, and we will drop the 'LL' superscript to simplify appearances.][73] For $\mathbf{A}^{nat}$ to be an acceptable representation of $\mathbf{A}^{LL}$, the row sums of $\mathbf{Z}^{(1)}$ must be equal to $\mathbf{u}^L$ and the column sums must be equal to $\mathbf{v}^L$.

Assume that this is not the case. For example, consider row i. Using the coefficients from $\mathbf{A}^{nat}$ we would obtain

$$z_{i1}^{(1)} + z_{i2}^{(1)} + \ldots + z_{in}^{(1)} = a_{i1}^{nat}x_1^L + a_{i2}^{nat}x_2^L + \ldots + a_{in}^{nat}x_n^L = u_i^{(1)}$$

Suppose that this row sum is too large. Since the x_j^L's are known, the only way to decrease $u_i^{(1)}$ is to decrease one or more of the $a_{i1}^{nat}, \ldots a_{in}^{nat}$ (the elements in row i of $\mathbf{A}^{nat}$).

The RAS approach reduces *each* of these coefficients by the same proportion. For example, suppose that $u_i^{(1)} = 500$ and $u_i^L = 250$. (The sum for row i that we got from the assumption $\mathbf{A}^{LL} = \mathbf{A}^{nat}$ is twice as large as what we know it must be.) A straightforward way to *force* equality between the row sum and u_i^L is to reduce each a_{ij}^{nat} in row i to one-half of its original value; that is, multiply each coefficient by $u_i^L/u_i^{(1)} = (250/500)$ — the sum that we want divided by the sum that we got. Denote this (first) modifier for row i as $r_i^{(1)}$.

Similarly, if the k-th row sum in $\mathbf{Z}^{(1)}$ is 300 and $u_k^L = 450$, then the correct (larger) value for $u_k^{(1)}$ could be forced by multiplying each element in row k of $\mathbf{A}^{nat}$ by $u_k^L/u_k^{(1)} = (450/300) = 1.5$; again, the ratio is what we want (450) divided by what we got (300). Denote this (first) row k modifier by $r_k^{(1)}$.

If each row in $\mathbf{A}^{nat}$ is 'corrected' in this way, we have a new (first) estimate of $\mathbf{A}^{LL}$; call it $\mathbf{A}^{(1)}$. A compact way of representing $\mathbf{A}^{(1)}$ is to arrange the *row modifiers*, $r_j^{(1)}$ ($j = 1, ..., n$), into a diagonal matrix, $\mathbf{R}^{(1)}$, so that

$$\mathbf{A}^{(1)} = \mathbf{R}^{(1)}\mathbf{A}^{nat} \qquad (3\text{-}4\text{-}1)$$

If we now create a second (and better) approximation to $\mathbf{Z}$ as $\mathbf{Z}^{(2)} = \mathbf{A}^{(1)}\hat{\mathbf{x}}^L$, we know that the row sums of this transactions matrix will equal $\mathbf{u}^L$. Our row modifiers, just applied, have seen to this. So then the question is, how well are the column sums of $\mathbf{Z}^{(2)}$, $v_j^{(2)}$, in correspondence with the known $\mathbf{v}^L$? The usual answer is, not very well. So now this new $\mathbf{A}$ matrix, $\mathbf{A}^{(1)}$, needs to be modified to force column-sum accountability. The procedure is the same as with row sums, except that it is now each *column* in the current estimate, $\mathbf{A}^{(1)}$, that must be changed. Again, the RAS procedure does this by multiplying each element in column j by the same modifier, and these are found in essentially the same way as those for the rows — what we want, v_j^L, divided by what we got, $v_j^{(2)}$. Let these column modifiers be denoted by $s_j^{(1)}$. [They come from $\mathbf{Z}^{(2)}$, but they are the *first* attempts at column modification; hence the superscript (1).] Arranging them in a diagonal matrix, $\mathbf{S}^{(1)}$, and multiplying $\mathbf{A}^{(1)}$ on the right [which modifies each element in the j-th *column* of $\mathbf{A}^{(1)}$ by $s_j^{(1)}$], gives $\mathbf{A}^{(2)} = \mathbf{A}^{(1)}\mathbf{S}^{(1)}$ which is, because of (3-4-1),

$$\mathbf{A}^{(2)} = \mathbf{R}^{(1)}\mathbf{A}^{nat}\mathbf{S}^{(1)} \qquad (3\text{-}4\text{-}2)$$

Now we know that the $\mathbf{v}^L$ column sums are met [from the just-performed column modifications of $\mathbf{A}^{(1)}$] but the row sum requirements on the transactions matrix may now be once again out of kilter. So we generate $\mathbf{Z}^{(3)} = \mathbf{A}^{(2)}\hat{\mathbf{x}}^L$, and the same kind of row-sum investigation proceeds again, this time on $\mathbf{Z}^{(3)}$. That will generate $\mathbf{A}^{(3)}$, as

$$\mathbf{A}^{(3)} = \mathbf{R}^{(2)}\mathbf{A}^{(2)} = \mathbf{R}^{(2)}\mathbf{R}^{(1)}\mathbf{A}^{nat}\mathbf{S}^{(1)} \qquad (3\text{-}4\text{-}3)$$

[using (3-4-2)]. This now must be investigated for column sum conformance. From this investigation, $\mathbf{A}^{(4)}$ will result. By now

$$A^{(4)} = A^{(3)}S^{(2)} = R^{(2)}R^{(1)}A^{nat}S^{(1)}S^{(2)} \qquad (3\text{-}4\text{-}4)$$

and so on. In general, this procedure converges to an acceptable level of conformability (with both u^L and v^L) after a 'reasonable' number of row and column modifications (often less than 20), although there are some exceptions. Eventually, then

$$A^{(2k)} = [R][A^{nat}][S] \qquad (3\text{-}4\text{-}5)$$

where

$$R = [R^{(k)}R^{(k-1)} \cdots R^{(2)}R^{(1)}] \text{ and } S = [S^{(1)}S^{(2)} \cdots S^{(k-1)}S^{(k)}]$$

(Both R and S are diagonal matrices, since they are products of diagonal matrices only.) Notice that the 'A' in the 'RAS' name represents the original direct coefficients matrix (the matrix that is being modified); the 'R' and 'S' stand for the series of sequential row and column modifications.[74]

The general ideas are exactly the same for the 'updating' problem. One has a matrix for a base year $[A(0)$ or $Z(0)]$ and is looking to estimate a coefficients matrix for a 'current' year, $A(1)$. In this case, current values of gross outputs, $x(1)$, interindustry sales, $u(1)$, and interindustry purchases, $v(1)$, are required, and the technique proceeds exactly as above.

This is an entirely mathematical technique. Some suggestions have been made regarding possible economic content of the RAS procedure (for example, in Stone, 1961), but not everyone finds them convincing. However, it turns out that a matrix generated in this way has a possibly interesting mathematical property. It is 'closest' to the original matrix $[A^{nat}$ or $A(0)]$ by a special measure of 'distance' between matrices.[75] It may be reasonable, in the absence of coefficient-specific information, to want to 'disturb' the old or national technology as little as possible while at the same time conforming to new or region-specific facts.

If one *does* have some specific knowledge about elements in A^{LL} (in the regionalization problem) or in $A(1)$ (in the updating problem), it can be incorporated into the RAS procedure. At the regional level, this kind of information might be from surveys of, say, the region's most important industry — either with respect to inputs (elements of a column in A) or outputs (elements of a row of A), or, indeed, both. Essentially, known coefficients are inserted into the A matrix, the associated row and column totals in Z, u and v, are adjusted (reduced), and the remaining (unknown) cells are found via RAS.

Endnotes

1   Professor Leontief was awarded the Nobel Prize for Economic Science in 1973 for his pioneering work in this area.

    The earliest detailed discussion of both a regional and an interregional input-output model is to be found in Isard et al. (1960). More recent treatments are in Miller and Blair (1985), Hewings (1985) and Hewings and Jensen (1986). Bulmer-Thomas (1982) provides an excellent and thorough overview of the input-output structure in general.

    There are two international journals that cover input-output topics. During the Eighth International Conference on Input-Output Techniques (Sapporo, Japan, 1986) it was determined to establish The International Input-Output Association and an affiliated journal, *Economic Systems Research.* Later the Pan Pacific Association of Input-Output Studies (Keio University, Tokyo, Japan) was founded and began publication of the *Journal of Applied Input-Output Analysis.*

2   With encouragement from the United Nations, many countries are using an alternative to the system that we are about to describe. It is known as commodity-industry accounting. One major advantage is that the assumption of a single product from each sector is relaxed. The commodity-industry system has been less generally embraced at the regional level. In any case, in this introductory exposition we ignore the added complications of the commodity-industry system. It is described in Appendix 3.1.

3   'Dynamic' input-output models are those that incorporate changes in capital stocks explicitly. Discussion of these models lies outside the scope of this introductory chapter. There is a brief treatment of the topic in Miller and Blair (1985, Section 9.5, pp. 340–351).

4   The first n terms on the right-hand side of (3-1) are known as *interindustry* sales (or *intermediate* sales). Since this may include a z_{ii} term (electricity bought by the electricity producing sector), there could be an *intra*industry sale too. Traditionally, this possibility is included in the term 'interindustry.'

5   There will also be transactions recorded in the intersections of the value added or imports rows and final demand columns. For example, the labor row, government column would include the value of

compensation paid to government employees; the other value added row, consumption column would include the value of households' income tax payments to the federal government. Without dealing with the specifics of all of these entries, we assume that they are included in the value added and imports row sums and in the final demand column sums.

6   I am grateful to Professor William B. Beyers, Department of Geography, University of Washington, Seattle, for providing the data from which this table was derived.

7   Row sums in an **A** matrix are meaningless since each a_{ij} in a row represents a transaction divided by a different denominator.

8   If a bakery in one region (state, for example) buys its eggs from chicken farmers across the river (which happens to be another state), then the *regional* production recipe for bakery goods would not include any eggs.

9   Economists characterize this as a requirement that production functions in all sectors be linear and homogeneous.

10 This is because (a) the 'hat' notation creates a diagonal matrix from a vector, (b) the inverse of a diagonal matrix contains reciprocals of the diagonal matrix elements and (c) postmultiplication by a diagonal matrix modifies columns of the matrix on the left uniformly. See the Mathematical Appendix for details.

11 Since $\mathbf{A} = \mathbf{Z}(\hat{\mathbf{x}})^{-1}$, $\mathbf{A}\hat{\mathbf{x}} = \mathbf{Z}$ and $\mathbf{A}\hat{\mathbf{x}}\mathbf{i} = \mathbf{Z}\mathbf{i}$. But the row sums of a diagonal matrix are just a column vector of the diagonal elements (in particular, $\hat{\mathbf{x}}\mathbf{i} = \mathbf{x}$) and so $\mathbf{A}\hat{\mathbf{x}}\mathbf{i} = \mathbf{A}\mathbf{x} = \mathbf{Z}\mathbf{i}$ and (3-7) follows directly from (3-6).

12 There does not seem to be any standard convention regarding the number of decimal places to keep in direct requirements matrices. To the extent that the original transactions table data (Table 3-2) are rounded to millions of dollars, it might seem that not too many places to the right of the decimal point could be justified in an **A** matrix, where the elements are the ratios of two of these transactions table elements. On the other hand, the interpretation of a_{ij} as dollars' worth of input of i per dollar's worth of output j, suggests that at least two decimal places are needed, so that $a_{ij} = .36$ (36 cents' worth of i per

dollar of *j*) would not be rounded to 40 cents. Most studies seem to use between three and six decimal places; following no particular convention, we use four throughout this chapter.

13 There is an alternative 'supply driven' or 'supply side' input-output model. We will use it only briefly in Appendix 3.2 when we explore several input-output linkage measures.

14 Again, the Mathematical Appendix explains the use of an inverse matrix in solving a set of linear equations.

15 For example, if $a = 0.2$, $(1 - a)^{-1} = 1.25$, exactly. Using the series approximation as far as $k = 4$ gives 1.2496, as far as $k = 6$, gives 1.249984, etc.

16 The (n x n) matrix $\mathbf{A}$ raised to a power, say $\mathbf{A}^2$, means the product of $\mathbf{A}$ times itself; $\mathbf{A}^3$ is the product of $\mathbf{A}$ and $\mathbf{A}^2$; etc.

17 To verify this, subtract (3-10) from (3-8),

$$(\mathbf{I} - \mathbf{A})(\mathbf{x}^* - \mathbf{x}) = \mathbf{f}^* - \mathbf{f} \text{ or } (\mathbf{x}^* - \mathbf{x}) = (\mathbf{I} - \mathbf{A})^{-1}(\mathbf{f}^* - \mathbf{f})$$

Let $\mathbf{f}^* - \mathbf{f} = \Delta\mathbf{f}$ and $\mathbf{x}^* - \mathbf{x} = \Delta\mathbf{x}$, so, substituting,

$$\Delta\mathbf{x} = (\mathbf{I} - \mathbf{A})^{-1}\Delta\mathbf{f}$$

18 Notice that since Δf_4 is expressed in millions of dollars, each of the resulting changes in sector outputs will also be in millions of dollars. If Δf_4 had been recorded in Δf as 250,000,000, then all resulting sectoral output changes would have been in dollars, not millions.

19 The power series approximation [(3-13) and (3-14)] could also be used. For this particular illustration, here is $\Delta\mathbf{x}$ (shown as a row vector, to save space) as approximated by $(\mathbf{I} + \mathbf{A} + \mathbf{A}^2 + \mathbf{A}^3)\Delta\mathbf{f}$, with percentage errors from the 'true' $\Delta\mathbf{x}$ in the text:
$$\Delta\mathbf{x} = [.1387 \ .0719 \ .6272 \ 253.7028 \ 4.1275 \ 3.3555 \ 1.4455 \ 11.3278]'$$
$$\% = \ \ [17 \quad 13 \quad 6 \quad 0 \qquad 2 \qquad 3 \qquad 3 \qquad 1]$$
If the series is carried out to $\mathbf{A}^6$, all errors are less than one percent.

20 It is not so easy to decide what should be included in household spendable income at a regional level. Income generated within the region will primarily be in the form of wages, salaries and proprietors' income, but if some employees in the region are daily commuters from elsewhere, then at least some of their consumption

spending occurs outside of the region in which they work. In addition, there are a number of 'external' sources of income for residents of a region — transfer income (federal social security and/or unemployment payments), interest and/or rents on assets held outside the region, dividends from stocks of companies headquartered outside the region, etc. So total wages and salaries earned by households in a region are, at best, just a proxy for disposable personal income.

21 This is a most elementary way in which to model the interaction between household income, household spending, and sectoral output in an input-output framework. Much more elaborate 'extended' input-output models include disaggregations of households as consumers (for example, by income level) and as providers of labor services (for example, by skill level or by labor category). This means that the added consumption coefficients column and labor inputs row vectors become matrices. Finally, input-output accounts are only one portion of a more extensive set of data contained in a *social accounting matrix* (SAM). Discussions of some of these topics will be found in Chapter 8, below.

22 All that differentiates $\bar{A}$ (Table 3-5) from A (Table 3-3) is the addition of a ninth row and column of new (household) coefficients, so the submatrix made up of the first eight rows and columns in $\bar{A}$ is the same as A. Notice, by contrast, that *all* elements in the upper left (8 x 8) submatrix in $(I - \bar{A})^{-1}$ (Table 3-6) differ from those in $(I - A)^{-1}$ (Table 3-4).

23 Most analysts feel that an open input-output model underestimates impacts and a closed input-output model probably overestimates impacts. In the context of the foreign airliner order example, it is assumed in the input-output framework that no sectors have capacity constraints so that all are able to expand production as much as is needed to satisfy demands for their products and that no part of any of the increased outputs in any of the sectors comes from, say, increased labor productivity. [This is a consequence of constant returns to scale–doubling output requires doubling inputs, including (in the closed model) labor.]

24 A somewhat different typology for multipliers has been suggested by Jensen and others; for example, in Jensen (1978), West and Jensen (1980) or Hewings and Jensen (1986). Once the underlying principles

are understood, one is free to choose (or even create) a specific multiplier that seems appropriate for the particular application under consideration.

25 If you are familiar with differential calculus, then you will recognize that the elements in **B** are partial derivatives. For example, from (3-16), $\partial x_2^*/\partial f_3^* = b_{23}$, and, in general, $\partial x_i^*/\partial f_j^* = b_{ij}$. In linear equations like these, (partial) derivatives are just the coefficients multiplying the f_j^*'s.

26 This does not mean that the individual elements in **B** are not of interest in translating final demands into *sector-specific* output requirements.

27 In matrix algebra terms, the matrix of income effects is generated as

$$<\text{LAB}>(\mathbf{I} - \mathbf{A})^{-1}$$

where LAB is the row vector of labor input coefficients, $a_{n+1,j}$, and <LAB> is the diagonal matrix formed from this vector.

28 Notice that since we are now using '*e*' to designate 'employment,' it is unnecessary to have an '*n* + 1' superscript, as we did originally when closing the model with respect to households using (monetary) labor input coefficients, $a_{n+1,j}$.

It is not at all obvious exactly how best to measure the amount of 'employment' in a given sector over a particular time period — for example, if there are both part-time and full-time employees. These issues have been considered extensively in the literature.

29 Again, in matrix algebra terms, given a vector of employment-to-output ratios, EMP = $[e_1, \ldots, e_n]$, then the matrix of employment effects is generated as

$$<\text{EMP}>(\mathbf{I} - \mathbf{A})^{-1}$$

where <EMP> is the diagonal matrix formed from this vector.

30 The elements in row *i* of a total requirements matrix could also be weighted by sector *i*'s 'value added coefficient,' v_i, defined as the ratio of value added to total gross output of sector *i*, va_i/x_i. This would produce a *value added multiplier matrix* whose column sums are known as *value added multipliers*. Since total value added in a region is a measure of gross regional product, this provides another potentially valuable index of each sector's contribution to a regional economy.

In a manner exactly parallel to the income and employment multiplier cases, a *Type I value added multiplier matrix* could be created; its column sums would be *Type I value added multipliers.*

31   These appear large because they are on a per million dollars' worth of final demand basis. Division of each figure by one million would put them on a completely comparable basis with the income and output multipliers, but all of the figures would need more decimal places — for example, 27.7306 would become .0000277306, which is tedious to read.

32   In some situations, it might be appropriate to sum all $n + 1$ elements in the columns of $\bar{\mathbf{B}}$. This would explicitly capture the direct plus indirect plus induced output needed from the household sector (as well as all others).

33   The 'II' serves to indicate that they are from the closed model. There are also 'Type III' and 'Type IV' multipliers. These are the same in spirit as the Type II multipliers, only they are associated with a model that is closed in more elaborate detail. Type III income multipliers (Miernyk et al., 1967) have been derived from a model in which labor income payments were distinguished between current residents or new residents in a region, and the current residents were divided into four income classes. In a model in which Type IV income multipliers (Madden and Batey, 1983) are derived, a distinction is made between the spending patterns of currently employed local residents and those that are currently unemployed. These kinds of distinctions are made because of the belief that current (and employed) residents of a region will spend each dollar of new income according to a set of *marginal* consumption coefficients while new residents (or, perhaps, newly reemployed residents) will distribute their purchases according to a set of *average* consumption coefficients. (The current resident may own a house; the new resident may have to buy one.)

34   This is the most elementary kind of 'energy input-output analysis.' As with the household sector, it is possible to create input-output models that are 'closed' with respect to (physical) energy use. See Miller and Blair (1985, Chapter 6, and references there cited) for much more detail.

35 Also as with energy analysis, this represents the most elementary approach to 'environmental input-output analysis.' See Miller and Blair (1985, Chapter 7 and references cited therein) for much more detail.

36 However, as we have seen, it is not just the size of a sector's output multiplier but also the (average) size of final demand for its output that is important. You can buy $100 worth of plywood but not of Boeing airplanes.

37 There is no reason why the number of sectors in region L must be the same as in region M, but assuming so simplifies the notation a bit.

38 The total number of transaction cells for r regions of n sectors each is n^2r^2. If one wanted to construct such a model for the 51 region U.S. economy (states plus D.C.) with, say, 50 sectors each, we are looking at just over 6.5 million possible transactions! Obviously, many of them would be zero (no shipments of pineapples from Maine to Nebraska), but even determining all of the zero-valued transactions would be quite a task.

39 As in (3-9) in section 3.1, these can be compactly summarized as, for example, $\mathbf{A}^{LL} = \mathbf{Z}^{LL}(\hat{\mathbf{x}}^L)^{-1}$, $\mathbf{A}^{LM} = \mathbf{Z}^{LM}(\hat{\mathbf{x}}^M)^{-1}$, etc.

40 These data are made available in case you are interested in seeing how the components of a two-region IRIO model might look in practice. They are put into Appendix 3.3 so as not to intrude too much on the discussion of this section.

41 It was produced by aggregating a larger set of U.S. data for 1988 that was provided by Dr. Janusz Szyrmer, Social Science Data Center, University of Pennsylvania.

42 This means that the row sums of $\mathbf{Z}^{LM}$ were equal to the figures in column 13 of Table 3-2 and the column sums of $\mathbf{Z}^{ML}$ were equal to the figures in row 11 of that table. Clearly, there are many possible arrangements of elements in $\mathbf{Z}^{LM}$ and $\mathbf{Z}^{ML}$ that will satisfy those column or row sum requirements, so there is nothing unique about the resulting trade coefficients in the tables of Appendix 3.3. They are used simply to indicate in general what a two-region IRIO model looks like and the kinds of results that such a model can produce.

43 The aggregate percentage difference was less than one percent because it was a *weighted* average, where the weights are the individual sector outputs. In that averaging process, the weight for sector 4, which had an almost zero percent difference, was much larger than any of the others.

Expressing the differences in output for each of the Washington sectors in the two models as a percentage of the output in the IRIO model, we find (rounded to no decimal places and displayed in a row, to save space)

[24 43 21 0 8 6 11 3]

So averages can be deceptive — for example, the output of sector 2 is around 43 percent less when interregional feedbacks are ignored whereas the output of sector 4 is virtually unaffected.

44 Notice that if $\mathbf{A}^{LM} = \mathbf{A}^{ML} = \mathbf{0}$, the 'IRIO' model in (3-32) collapses to two single-region models.

45 The same principles apply if one is concerned with employment multipliers measured in physical terms. To continue with a two-region example, there would now be four different sets of 'employment coefficients' (employment/output ratios) needed. Within-region effects would be captured using

$$e_j^{LL} = w_j^{LL}/x_j^L \text{ and } e_j^{MM} = w_j^{MM}/x_j^M$$

where the x's are as already defined and where w_j^{LL}, for example, indicates the number of region L workers employed by region L's sector j. Similarly, across-region effects would require

$$e_j^{ML} = w_j^{ML}/x_j^L \text{ and } e_j^{LM} = w_j^{LM}/x_j^M$$

where w_j^{LM} is a measure of the number of workers in region M's sector j that commute from L.

Value added multipliers in the IRIO model can be constructed similarly.

46 As with sectoral linkages, there are numerous additional measures of spatial linkage among regions that are based on the kinds of data in IRIO accounts. Miller and Blair (1988) and Blair and Miller (1990) contain many examples.

47 A complete reference to the MRIO model and its implementation with U.S. data can be found in Polenske (1980).

48 This and other properties of diagonal matrices are discussed in the Mathematical Appendix.

49 There is a good deal of published material describing how different analysts have addressed this issue in empirical applications. See also Miller and Blair (1985, Section 8-6, pp. 306–308).

50 Earlier, in Section 3.1, m_i was used to denote imports of all goods by sector i (as in Table 3-1). For that reason, we now use $m_{i\bullet}^L$ to denote region L imports (by all sectors and by final demand) of good i.

51 See Stevens, Treyz and Lahr (1989) for a discussion of RPC estimation procedures and comparisons with other approaches.

52 Location quotients are not always based on gross outputs as the measure of sector 'size.' Sectoral employment, wages and salaries paid or value added, for example, at the regional and national levels, are sometimes used.

53 There are many variations on the simple location quotient modifiers presented here. See, for example, Miller and Blair (1985, Section 8.5).

54 Early reports on the RAS approach appear in Cambridge University, Department of Applied Economics (1963) and Bacharach (1970).

55 How seriously out of date is another issue. To the extent that technology changes slowly in an economy, it may not matter that tables from the past (recent, we hope) are used for analysis for the future (near, we hope). But old tables will never be perfect for present or future analysis.
    There has certainly been extensive input substitution of, say, plastics for metal in automobile manufacture over time. While the year-to-year variation might not be so large, a ten-year-old table would probably reflect an input of metal to automobiles that is unrealistic ten years hence. Also, some kinds of technological change can be quite startling. There may simply be a new industry next year that was not around last year (silicone chips provide an example). So updating last year's table for present- or future-year analysis would completely fail to capture the presence of that industry in the economy.

56 The updating issue can be thought of as moving data across time; the regionalization problem is one of moving data across space. And of

course both can be done simultaneously — for example, generating a (new) regional table from (old) national data.

57 Creating a diagonal matrix from the RPC^L vector, the compact matrix algebra representation is $\mathbf{A}^{LL}(\mathbf{LQ}) = <RPC^L>\mathbf{A}^{nat}$.

58 There is a lot of discussion in the input-output literature about how to decide what a 'true' matrix is (even survey-based tables may be full of error) and how to measure the 'distance' between an estimate, like $\mathbf{A}^{LL}(\mathbf{LQ})$ and that 'true' matrix. Is element-by-element accuracy ('partitive' accuracy) or accuracy in use ('holistic' accuracy) the appropriate measure? In addition, should the comparison be between direct input coefficients matrices (the $\mathbf{A}$'s) or between their associated Leontief inverses [the $(\mathbf{I} - \mathbf{A})^{-1}$'s]? Jensen, who first used the terms 'partitive' and 'holistic,' has written often on these issues; for example, see Jensen(1980) or Hewings and Jensen (1986, Section 2.3).

59 See, for example, the discussion in Hewings and Jensen (1986) or in West (1990).

60 See Lahr (1993) for a discussion of these and related issues with numerous bibliographic references.

61 See, for example, Round (1983) (and other articles by Round that are cited there) and also Boomsma and Oosterhaven (1992).

62 Thorough accounts are given in Batten (1983) or in Batten and Boyce (1986). See also Chapter 7, below.

63 On the supply-demand pool approach, see Miller and Blair (1984, Section 8.5).

64 It should be clear from the context when $\mathbf{B}$ denotes these coefficients in a set of commodity-industry accounts and when (as earlier in the text) it is used for $(\mathbf{I} - \mathbf{A})^{-1}$.

65 In an economy in which there is no secondary production, the make matrix will be diagonal and all of the commodity-industry results reduce to the original Leontief industry-based approach.

66 There are a number of alternatives, but discussion of these is beyond the scope of this chapter. For more detail, see Miller and Blair (1985, Section 5-3).

67 The '→' reminds us that we are normalizing across rows in the **Z** matrix rather than down columns, as is done to generate direct input coefficients, a_{ij}. In matrix terms, $\overrightarrow{\mathbf{A}} = (\hat{\mathbf{x}})^{-1}\mathbf{Z}$.

68 In contrast to the 'demand driven' or 'demand side' input-output model in the text, a direct output coefficients matrix is the basis for a 'supply driven' or 'supply side' input-output framework. Early work with the supply-side input-output approach can be found in Ghosh (1958) and Augustinovics (1970). There has been considerable debate in the literature on the underlying economic rationale of the supply-side input-output *model*. Examples can be found in, among others, Oosterhaven (1988), Cella (1988) and Dietzenbacher (1989).

69 This two-way table is only a visual aid, but it has been used often in published studies. It seems to have originated with Chenery and Watanabe (1958); it also appears, for example, in Yotopoulos and Nugent (1973), Boucher (1976), Schultz (1977) and, in a spatial-linkage context, in Shao and Miller (1990). The basic idea is simply to identify sectors that score above average on both measures. One could also go further and divide each of the two measures into more than just two intervals ('high' and 'low').

70 Examples are to be found in Miller and Blair (1988), Batten and Martellato (1988), Mellar and Marfán (1981) or Dietzenbacher (1992). There are many empirical articles in which linkages (forward, backward and/or combined) are calculated for particular economies and conclusions suggested on which sectors are relatively 'key' for the economy in question.

71 The act of 'extracting' a sector from an **A** matrix is simple mathematically (physically remove the sector's row and column or, equivalently, set all elements in both row and column equal to zero), but what are the economic ramifications? For example, consider the extraction of sector k. With the removal of the k-th row in **A**, from where do the regional sectors get the inputs that formerly came from sector k? The usual *assumption* is that these inputs are replaced by imports of k goods. The removal of the k-th column in **A** is perhaps easier to fathom. Each of the remaining sectors in the region simply has one less regional sector as a potential user of its goods as inputs.

72 Of course, this matrix is not known. If it were, then, in conjunction with x^L, the intraregional matrix A^{LL} could be found immediately, as we have seen, as $A^{LL} = Z^{LL} (\hat{x}^L)^{-1}$.

73 If we were adjusting transactions rather than coefficients, the initial assumption would be that $Z^{LL} = Z^{nat}$. This is obviously unacceptable, because row and column sums of a national transactions matrix will surely always be larger than those for a regional matrix. The coefficients matrices, A^{LL} and A^{nat}, overcome this relative size problem because transactions are normalized (divided) by regional and national outputs, respectively.

The computational wrinkle introduced by working with coefficients matrices is that the regional *transactions matrix* must be generated at each step, since it is row and column sums of that matrix which are known at the regional level. From (3-9), given *any* A and x, the associated transactions matrix can be found as $Z = A\hat{x}$.

74 It is immaterial whether one starts with a column correction or, as in the illustration, a row correction. It seems that 'RAC' might have been a more appropriate acronym.

75 The distance is the 'information' measure. See Miller and Blair (1985, Appendix 8-1, pp. 309–310) or Bacharach (1970) for details.

References

Augustinovics, Maria. 1970. 'Methods of International and Intertemporal Comparison of Structure,' in *Input-Output Techniques*, Vol. 1 of *Contributions to Input-Output Analysis* (Anne P. Carter and Andrew Brody, eds.). Amsterdam: North-Holland, pp. 249–69.
Bacharach, Michael. 1970. *Biproportional Matrices and Input-Output Change*. Cambridge: Cambridge University Press.
Batten, David F. 1983. *Spatial Analysis of Interacting Economies*. Boston: Kluwer-Nijhoff.
Batten, David F., and David E. Boyce. 1986. 'Spatial Interaction, Transportation, and Interregional Commodity Flow Models,' Chapter 9 in *Handbook of Regional and Urban Economics*, *Volume I* (Peter Nijkamp, ed.). New York: Elsevier, pp. 357–406.
Batten, David F., and Dino Martellato. 1988. 'Modelling Interregional Trade within Input-Output Systems,' *Ricerche Economiche*, 42, 204–21.

Blair, Peter D., and Ronald E. Miller. 1990. 'Spatial Linkages in the U.S. Economy,' in *Dynamics and Conflict in Regional Structural Change, Essays in Honor of Walter Isard*, Vol. 2 (Manas Chatterji and Robert E. Kuenne, eds.). London: Macmillan, pp. 156–79.

Boomsma, Piet, and Jan Oosterhaven. 1992. 'A Double Entry Method for the Construction of Biregional Input-Output Tables,' *Journal of Regional Science*, 32, 269–84.

Boucher, Michel. 1976. 'Some Further Results on the Linkage Hypothesis,' *Quarterly Journal of Economics*, 90, 313–18.

Brucker, Sharon M., Steven E. Hastings, and William R. Latham III. 1987. 'Regional Input-Output Analysis: A Comparison of Five "Ready-Made" Model Systems,' *Review of Regional Studies*, 17, 1-16.

Brucker, Sharon M., Steven E. Hastings, and William R. Latham III. 1990. 'The Variation of Estimated Impacts from Five Regional Input-Output Models,' *International Regional Science Review*, 13, 119–139.

Bulmer-Thomas, Victor. 1982. *Input-Output Analysis in Developing Countries*. New York: John Wiley and Sons.

Cambridge University, Department of Applied Economics. 1963. *Input-Output Relationships, 1954-1966*. Vol. 3 of *A Programme for Growth*. London: Chapman and Hall.

Cartwright, Joseph V., R. M. Beemiller, and R. D. Gustely. 1981. *RIMS II. Regional Input-Output Modeling System: Estimation, Evaluation and Application of a Disaggregated Regional Impact Model*. Washington, D.C.: U.S. Department of Commerce, Bureau of Economic Analysis.

Cella, Guido. 1988. 'The Supply Side Approaches to Input-Output Analysis,' *Ricerche Economiche*, 42, 433–51.

Chenery, Hollis B., and Tsunehiko Watanabe. 1958. 'International Comparisons of the Structure of Production,' *Econometrica*, 26, 487–521.

Dietzenbacher, Erik. 1989, 'On the Relationship Between the Supply-Driven and the Demand-Driven Input-Output Model,' *Environment and Planning*, A., 21, 1533–39.

Dietzenbacher, Erik. 1992. 'The Measurement of Interindustry Linkages: Key Sectors in the Netherlands,' *Economic Modelling*, 9, 419–37.

Ghosh, A. 1958. 'Input-Output Approach in an Allocation System,' *Economica*, 25, 58–64.

Hewings, Geoffrey J. D. 1985. *Regional Input-Output Analysis*. Beverly Hills, Ca.: Sage Publications Inc.

Hewings, Geoffrey J. D., and Michael C. Romanos. 1981. 'Simulating Less Developed Regional Economies Under Conditions of Limited Information,' *Geographical Analysis*, 13, 373–90.

Hewings, Geoffrey J. D., and Rodney C. Jensen. 1986. 'Regional, Interregional and Multiregional Input-Output Analysis,' Chapter 8 in *Handbook of Regional and Urban Economics, Volume I* (Peter Nijkamp, ed.). New York: Elsevier, pp. 295–355.

Isard, Walter et al. 1960. 'Interregional and Regional Input-Output Techniques,' Chapter 8 in *Methods of Regional Analysis*. New York: John Wiley and Sons and The Technology Press of MIT, pp. 309–74.

Isard, Walter, and John H. Cumberland. 1950. 'New England as a Possible Location for an Integrated Iron and Steel Works,' *Economic Geography*, 26, 245–59.

Isard, Walter, and Robert E. Kuenne. 1953. 'The Impact of Steel upon the Greater New York–Philadelphia Industrial Region,' *Review of Economics and Statistics*, 35, 289–301.

Jensen, Rodney C. 1978. 'Some Accounting Procedures and Their Effects on Input-Output Multipliers,' *Annals of Regional Science*, 12, 21–38.

Jensen, Rodney C. 1980. 'The Concept of Accuracy in Regional Input-Output Models,' *International Regional Science Review*, 5, 139–54.

Lahr, Michael L. 1993. 'A Review of the Literature Supporting the Hybrid Approach to Constructing Regional Input-Output Models,' *Economic Systems Research*, 5, 277–93.

Lamphear, F. Charles, and Ronald T. Konecny. 1986. 'ADOTMATR,' Lincoln, Nebraska: Resource Economics and Management Analysis.

Madden, Moss, and Peter W. J. Batey. 1983. 'Linked Population and Economic Models: Some Methodological Issues in Forecasting, Analysis, and Policy Optimization,' *Journal of Regional Science*, 23, 141–64.

Meller, Patricio, and Manuel Marfán. 1981. 'Small and Large Industry: Employment Generation, Linkages and Key Sectors,' *Economic Development and Cultural Change*, 29, 263–74.

Miernyk, William H. et al. 1967. *Impact of the Space Program on a Local Economy: An Input-Output Analysis*. Morgantown, W.Va.: West Virginia University Library.

Miller, Ronald E., and Peter D. Blair. 1985. *Input-Output Analysis: Foundations and Extensions*. Englewood Cliffs, N. J.: Prentice-Hall.

Miller, Ronald E., and Peter D. Blair. 1988. 'Measuring Spatial Linkages,' *Ricerche Economiche*, 42, 31–54.

Oosterhaven, Jan. 1988. 'On the Plausibility of the Supply-Driven Input-Output Model,' *Journal of Regional Science*, 28, 203–17.

Palmer, Charles, Eric Siverts, and Joy Sullivan. 1985. 'IMPLAN Version 1.1: Analysis Guide,' Fort Collins, Colorado: U.S. Department of Agriculture, Forest Service, Land Management Planning Systems Section.

Polenske, Karen R. 1980. *The U.S. Multiregional Input-Output Accounts and Model.* Lexington, Mass.: Lexington Books (D. C. Heath and Co.).

Poole, Erik. 1995. 'A Concise Description of Statistics of Canada's Input-Output Models,' *Canadian Journal of Regional Science*, 18, 255–70.

Round, Jeffery I. 1983. 'Nonsurvey Techniques: A Critical Review of the Theory and the Evidence,' *International Regional Science Review*, 8, 189–212.

Schaffer, William A., and Laurance S. Davidson. 1985. 'Economic Impact of the Falcons on Atlanta: 1984,' Atlanta: The Atlanta Falcons.

Schultz, Siegfried. 1977. 'Approaches to Identifying Key Sectors Empirically by Means of Input-Output Analysis,' *Journal of Development Studies*, 14, 77–96.

Shao, Gang, and Ronald E. Miller. 1990. 'Demand-Side and Supply-Side Commodity-Industry Multiregional Input-Output Models and Spatial Linkages in the U.S. Regional Economy,' *Economic Systems Research*, 2, 385–405.

Sivitanidou, Rena M., and Karen R. Polenske. 1988. 'Assessing Regional Economic Impacts with Microcomputers,' *JAPA, Journal of the American Planning Association*, 54, 101–6.

Stevens, Benjamin H., George I. Treyz, David J. Ehrlich, and James R. Bower. 1983. 'A New Technique for the Construction of Non-Survey Regional Input-Output Models,' *International Regional Science Review*, 8, 271–286.

Stevens, Benjamin H., George I. Treyz, and Michael L. Lahr. 1989. 'On the Comparative Accuracy of RPC Estimating Techniques,' Chapter 18 in *Frontiers of Input-Output Analysis* (Ronald E. Miller, Karen R. Polenske, and Adam Z. Rose, eds.). New York: Oxford University Press, pp. 245–57.

Stone, Richard. 1961. *Input-Output and National Accounts.* Paris: Office of European Economic Cooperation.

United Nations, Department of Economic and Social Affairs. 1968. *A System of National Accounts.* Series F, No. 2, revision 3. New York: United Nations.

U.S. Department of Commerce. 1986. *Regional Multipliers: A User Handbook for the Regional Input-Output Modeling System (RIMS II).* Washington, D.C.: U.S. Government Printing Office.

West, Guy R. 1988. 'GRIMP. Input-Output Analysis Computer Program. Version 6.0. User's Reference Manual,' St. Lucia, Australia: Department of Economics.

West, Guy R. 1990. 'Regional Trade Estimation: A Hybrid Approach,' *International Regional Science Review*, 13, 103–18.

West, Guy R., and Rodney C. Jensen. 1980. 'Some Reflections on Input-Output Multipliers,' *Annals of Regional Science*, 14, 77-89.

Yotopoulos, Pan A., and Jeffrey B. Nugent. 1973. 'A Balanced-Growth Version of the Linkage Hypotheses: A Test,' *Quarterly Journal of Economics*, 87, 157–71.

Mathematical appendix. Elements of matrix algebra

1. Introduction

A matrix is a collection of elements arranged in a grid — a pattern of rows and columns. In all cases that will be of interest to the topics in this book, the elements will be numbers whose values either are known or are unknown and to be determined. Matrices are defined in this 'rectangular' way so that they can be used to represent systems of linear relations among variables.

The general case, then, will be a matrix with *m* rows and *n* columns. If $m = 2$ and $n = 3$, and using double subscript notation, a_{ij}, to denote the element in row *i* and column *j* of the matrix, we have

$$\mathbf{A} = \begin{bmatrix} a_{11} & a_{12} & a_{13} \\ a_{21} & a_{22} & a_{23} \end{bmatrix}$$

A particular example of such a matrix might be

$$\mathbf{M} = \begin{bmatrix} 2 & 1 & 3 \\ 4 & 6 & 12 \end{bmatrix}$$

These are said to be (2 x 3) [read '2 by 3'] matrices or matrices of *dimension* 2 by 3.

When $m = n$ the matrix is *square*. If $m = 1$ (a matrix with only one row) it is called a *row vector*; if $n = 1$ (a matrix with only one column) it is called a *column vector*.[1]

2. Matrix operations: addition and subtraction

2.1 Addition Addition of matrices, say $\mathbf{A} + \mathbf{B}$, is accomplished by the simple rule of adding elements *in corresponding positions*. This means $a_{ij} + b_{ij}$, for all *i* and *j*; and this, in turn, means that only matrices that have exactly the same dimensions can be added. Given $\mathbf{M}$, above, and if $\mathbf{N} = \begin{bmatrix} 1 & 2 & 3 \\ 3 & 2 & 1 \end{bmatrix}$, then their sum, $\mathbf{S} = \mathbf{M} + \mathbf{N}$, will be another (2 x 3) matrix

$$\mathbf{S} = \begin{bmatrix} 3 & 3 & 6 \\ 7 & 8 & 13 \end{bmatrix}$$

2.2 Subtraction Subtraction is defined in a completely parallel way, namely subtraction of elements *in corresponding positions*, so again only matrices of exactly the same dimensions can be subtracted. For example, the difference matrix, $\mathbf{D} = \mathbf{M} - \mathbf{N}$, will be another (2 x 3) matrix

$$\mathbf{D} = \begin{bmatrix} 1 & -1 & 0 \\ 1 & 4 & 11 \end{bmatrix}$$

2.3 Equality The notion of equality of two matrices is also very straightforward. Two matrices are equal if they have the same dimensions and if elements in corresponding positions are equal. So $\mathbf{A} = \mathbf{B}$ when $a_{ij} = b_{ij}$ for all i and j.

2.4 The null matrix A zero in ordinary algebra is the number which, when added to (or subtracted from) a number leaves the number unchanged. The parallel notion in matrix algebra is a *null matrix,* simply defined as a matrix containing only zeros. Suppose $\mathbf{0} = \begin{bmatrix} 0 & 0 & 0 \\ 0 & 0 & 0 \end{bmatrix}$, then it is obvious that $\mathbf{M} + \mathbf{0} = \mathbf{M} - \mathbf{0} = \mathbf{M}$.

3. Matrix operations: multiplication

3.1 Multiplication of a matrix by a number If a matrix is multiplied by a number (called a *scalar* in matrix algebra), each element in the matrix is simply multiplied by that number. For example, using the matrix $\mathbf{M}$ from above,

$$2\mathbf{M} = \begin{bmatrix} 4 & 2 & 6 \\ 8 & 12 & 24 \end{bmatrix}$$

3.2 Multiplication of a matrix by another matrix Multiplication of two matrices is defined in what appears at first to be a completely illogical way. But we will see that the reason for the definition is precisely because of the way in which matrix notation is used for systems of linear relations, especially linear equations. Using $\mathbf{M}$, again, and a (3 x 3) matrix $\mathbf{Q} = \begin{bmatrix} 2 & 0 & 4 \\ 1 & 1 & 2 \\ 3 & 4 & 5 \end{bmatrix}$, the product, $\mathbf{P} = \mathbf{MQ}$, is found as

$$\mathbf{P} = \begin{bmatrix} 2 & 1 & 3 \\ 4 & 6 & 12 \end{bmatrix} \begin{bmatrix} 2 & 0 & 4 \\ 1 & 1 & 2 \\ 3 & 4 & 5 \end{bmatrix} = \begin{bmatrix} 14 & 13 & 25 \\ 50 & 54 & 88 \end{bmatrix}$$

which comes from

$$\begin{bmatrix} (4+1+9) & (0+1+12) & (8+2+15) \\ (8+6+36) & (0+6+48) & (16+12+60) \end{bmatrix}$$

The rule is: for element p_{ij} in the product, go *across row i* in the matrix on the left (here **M**) and *down column j* in the matrix on the right (here **Q**), multiplying pairs of elements and summing. So, for p_{23} we find, from row 2 of **M** and column 3 of **Q**, $(4)(4) + (6)(2) + (12)(5) = (16 + 12 + 60)$ = 88. In general, then, for this example

$$p_{ij} = m_{i1}q_{1j} + m_{i2}q_{2j} + m_{i3}q_{3j} \quad (i = 1, 2; j = 1, 2, 3)$$

This definition for multiplication of matrices means that in order to be *conformable for multiplication*, the number of *columns* in the matrix on the left must be the same as the number of *rows* in the matrix on the right. Look again at p_{ij} above; for the three elements in (any) row i of **M** — m_{i1}, m_{i2} and m_{i3} — there need to be three 'corresponding' elements in (any) column j of **Q** — q_{1j}, q_{2j} and q_{3j}.

The definition of matrix multiplication also means that the product matrix, **P**, will have the same number of rows as **M** and the same number of columns as **Q**. In general,

$$\begin{matrix} \mathbf{P} & = & \mathbf{M} & \mathbf{Q} \\ (m \text{ x } n) & & (m \text{ x } r) & (r \text{ x } n) \end{matrix} \qquad \text{(A-1)}$$

The definition also means that, in general, order of multiplication makes a difference. In this example, the product the other way around, **QM**, cannot even be found, since there are three *columns* in **Q** but only two *rows* in **M**.[2] For this reason, there is language to describe the order of multiplication in a matrix product. For example, in **P = MQ**, **M** is said to *premultiply* **Q** (or to multiply **Q** on the left) and, equivalently, **Q** is said to *postmultiply* **M** (or to multiply **M** on the right).

3.3 The identity matrix   In ordinary algebra, 1 is known as the *identity element for multiplication*, which means that a number remains unchanged when multiplied by it. There is an analogous concept in matrix algebra. An *identity matrix* is one which leaves a matrix unchanged when the matrix is multiplied by it.

If we use $\mathbf{M} = \begin{bmatrix} 2 & 1 & 3 \\ 4 & 6 & 12 \end{bmatrix}$, by what matrix could **M** be *post*multiplied

so that it remained unchanged? Denote the unknown matrix by **I** (this is the standard notation for an identity matrix); we want **MI = M**. We know from the rule in (A-1) that **I** must be a (3 x 3) matrix; it needs three rows to be conformable to postmultiply **M** and three columns because the product, which will be **M** with dimensions (2 x 3), gets its second dimension from the number of columns in **I**. You might try letting **I** be a (3 x 3) matrix containing all 1s. It may seem logical but it is wrong. In fact, the only **I** for which **MI** = **M** will be $\mathbf{I} = \begin{bmatrix} 1 & 0 & 0 \\ 0 & 1 & 0 \\ 0 & 0 & 1 \end{bmatrix}$. You should try it, and also try other possibilities, to be convinced that only this matrix will do the job.

An identity matrix is always square and can be of any size to fulfill the conformability requirement for the particular multiplication operation. It has 1s along the *main diagonal*, from upper left to lower right, and 0s everywhere else. We could also find another identity matrix, **J**, by which to *pre*multiply **M** so that it remains unchanged, so that **JM** = **M**. You can easily check that in this case **J** will be the (2 x 2) matrix $\begin{bmatrix} 1 & 0 \\ 0 & 1 \end{bmatrix}$.

4. Representation of linear equation systems

Here are two linear equations in two unknowns, x_1 and x_2:

$$2x_1 + x_2 = 10$$
$$5x_1 + 3x_2 = 26 \tag{A-2}$$

Define **A** as a (2 x 2) matrix that contains the coefficients multiplying the x's in exactly the order in which they appear, so

$$\mathbf{A} = \begin{bmatrix} 2 & 1 \\ 5 & 3 \end{bmatrix}$$

Define a two-element *column vector*, **x**, containing the unknown xs, and another two-element column vector, **b**, containing the values on the right-hand sides of the equations, again exactly in the order in which they appear, namely

$$\mathbf{x} = \begin{bmatrix} x_1 \\ x_2 \end{bmatrix} \text{ and } \mathbf{b} = \begin{bmatrix} 10 \\ 26 \end{bmatrix}$$

Then, precisely because of the way in which matrix multiplication and matrix equality are defined, the equation system in (A-2) is compactly represented as

$$\mathbf{Ax} = \mathbf{b} \tag{A-3}$$

(You should be sure that you see exactly why this is true.)

In ordinary algebra, when we have an equation like $3x = 12$, we 'solve' this equation by dividing both sides by 3 — which is the same thing as multiplying both sides by ($\frac{1}{3}$), the reciprocal of 3. So, in more detail, we go from $3x = 12$ to $x = 4$ in the logical sequence $3x = 12 \Rightarrow (\frac{1}{3})3x = (\frac{1}{3})12$ [or $(3^{-1})(3x) = (3^{-1})(12)$] $\Rightarrow 1x = 4 \Rightarrow x = 4$. Of course in ordinary algebra the transition from $3x = 12$ to $x = 4$ is virtually immediate. The point here is to set the stage for a parallel approach to systems of linear equations, as in (A-2).

Given the representation in (A-3), it is clear that a way of 'solving' this system for the unknowns would be to 'divide' both sides by **A**, or, alternatively, multiply both sides by the 'reciprocal' of **A**; parallel to the notation for the reciprocal of a number, this is denoted A^{-1}. If we could find such a matrix, with the matrix property that $(A^{-1})(A) = I$, we would proceed in the same way, namely

$$Ax = b \Rightarrow (A^{-1})Ax = (A^{-1})b \Rightarrow Ix = (A^{-1})b \Rightarrow x = (A^{-1})b$$

and the values of the unknowns, in **x**, would be found as the matrix operation in which the vector **b** is premultiplied by the matrix A^{-1}. Usually in matrix algebra A^{-1} is called the *inverse* of **A**.

5. Matrix operations: division

In matrix algebra, 'division' by a matrix is represented by multiplication by the inverse.[3] Finding inverses is a rather tedious mathematical procedure, but modern computers can do it very, very quickly. Without going into details, it is worth noting that there are some matrices for which an inverse cannot be found. (This is similar to the problem with '0' in ordinary algebra; you cannot divide by 0, which means that the reciprocal of 0, $\frac{1}{0}$, is not defined.) A matrix that has no inverse is called *singular*. The matrix **A** from (A-2) is *nonsingular*; it has an inverse, namely

$$A = \begin{bmatrix} 2 & 1 \\ 5 & 3 \end{bmatrix} \text{ and } A^{-1} = \begin{bmatrix} 3 & -1 \\ -5 & 2 \end{bmatrix}$$

which you can easily check. Here is an example of a singular matrix: $C = \begin{bmatrix} 2 & 4 \\ 6 & 12 \end{bmatrix}$. There is no matrix by which **C** can be pre- or postmultiplied to generate a (2 x 2) identity matrix.[4]

Since we have found A^{-1} for the equations in (A-2), we realize that the solution is exactly

$$\mathbf{x} = \mathbf{A}^{-1}\mathbf{b} = \begin{bmatrix} 3 & -1 \\ -5 & 2 \end{bmatrix} \begin{bmatrix} 10 \\ 26 \end{bmatrix} = \begin{bmatrix} 4 \\ 2 \end{bmatrix}$$

and you can easily check that $x_1 = 4$ and $x_2 = 2$ are the (only) solutions to the two equations in (A-2).

6. Matrix operations: transposition

Transposition is a matrix operation for which there is no parallel in ordinary algebra. It will be used occasionally in the text. The *transpose* of an (m x n) matrix $\mathbf{M}$, denoted usually with a " " sign, creates an (n x m) matrix in which row i of $\mathbf{M}$ becomes column i of $\mathbf{M}'$. For our example,

$$\mathbf{M}' = \begin{bmatrix} 2 & 4 \\ 1 & 6 \\ 3 & 12 \end{bmatrix}$$

Notice that the transpose of an n-element column vector [with dimensions (1 x n)] is an n-element row vector [with dimensions (1 x n)].

7. Diagonal matrices

Identity matrices are examples of *diagonal matrices*. These are always square, with elements on the diagonal from upper left to lower right and zeros elsewhere. In general, an (n x n) diagonal matrix is

$$\mathbf{D} = \begin{bmatrix} d_1 & 0 & \ldots & 0 \\ \vdots & \vdots & \vdots & \vdots \\ 0 & 0 & \ldots & d_n \end{bmatrix} \qquad (A-4)$$

A useful notation device is available for creating a diagonal matrix out of a vector. Suppose $\mathbf{x} = \begin{bmatrix} x_1 \\ x_2 \\ x_3 \end{bmatrix}$; then the diagonal matrix with the elements of $\mathbf{x}$ strung out in order along its main diagonal is denoted by putting a 'hat' over the $\mathbf{x}$. (Sometimes '<' and '>' are used.) So

$$\hat{\mathbf{x}} = <\mathbf{x}> = \begin{bmatrix} x_1 & 0 & 0 \\ 0 & x_2 & 0 \\ 0 & 0 & x_3 \end{bmatrix}$$

One useful fact about diagonal matrices is that the inverse of a diagonal matrix is another diagonal matrix, each of whose elements is just the reciprocal of the original element. For $\hat{\mathbf{x}}$ this means

$$(\hat{\mathbf{x}})^{-1} = \begin{bmatrix} (1/x_1) & 0 & 0 \\ 0 & (1/x_2) & 0 \\ 0 & 0 & (1/x_3) \end{bmatrix}$$

You can easily check that $(\hat{\mathbf{x}})(\hat{\mathbf{x}})^{-1} = (\hat{\mathbf{x}})^{-1}(\hat{\mathbf{x}}) = \mathbf{I} = \begin{bmatrix} 1 & 0 & 0 \\ 0 & 1 & 0 \\ 0 & 0 & 1 \end{bmatrix}$.

When a diagonal matrix, $\mathbf{D}$, *post*multiplies another matrix, $\mathbf{M}$, the j-th element in the diagonal matrix, d_j, multiplies all of the elements in the j-th *column* of $\mathbf{M}$; when a diagonal matrix *pre*multiplies $\mathbf{M}$, d_j multiplies all of the elements in the j-th *row* of $\mathbf{M}$. For example,

$$\begin{bmatrix} 2 & 1 & 3 \\ 4 & 6 & 12 \end{bmatrix} \begin{bmatrix} d_1 & 0 & 0 \\ 0 & d_2 & 0 \\ 0 & 0 & d_3 \end{bmatrix} = \begin{bmatrix} 2d_1 & d_2 & 3d_3 \\ 4d_1 & 6d_2 & 12d_3 \end{bmatrix}$$

and

$$\begin{bmatrix} d_1 & 0 \\ 0 & d_2 \end{bmatrix} \begin{bmatrix} 2 & 1 & 3 \\ 4 & 6 & 12 \end{bmatrix} = \begin{bmatrix} 2d_1 & d_1 & 3d_1 \\ 4d_2 & 6d_2 & 12d_2 \end{bmatrix}$$

Putting the facts about inverses of diagonal matrices together with these observations about pre- and postmultiplication by a diagonal matrix, we see that postmultiplying $\mathbf{M}$ by $\mathbf{D}^{-1}$ will *divide* each element in column j of $\mathbf{M}$ by d_j; premultiplying $\mathbf{M}$ by $\mathbf{D}^{-1}$ will divide each element in row j of $\mathbf{M}$ by d_j.[5]

8. Summation vectors

If an (m x n) matrix, $\mathbf{M}$, is postmultiplied by an n-element column vector of 1s, the result will be an m-element column vector containing the *row sums* of $\mathbf{M}$; if $\mathbf{M}$ is premultiplied by an m-element row vector of 1s, the result will be an n-element row vector containing the *column sums* of $\mathbf{M}$. For example,

$$\begin{bmatrix} 2 & 1 & 3 \\ 4 & 6 & 12 \end{bmatrix} \begin{bmatrix} 1 \\ 1 \\ 1 \end{bmatrix} = \begin{bmatrix} 6 \\ 22 \end{bmatrix} \text{ and } \begin{bmatrix} 1 & 1 \end{bmatrix} \begin{bmatrix} 2 & 1 & 3 \\ 4 & 6 & 12 \end{bmatrix} = \begin{bmatrix} 6 & 7 & 15 \end{bmatrix}$$

Usually, a column vector of 1s is denoted by $\mathbf{i}$, and so a corresponding row vector is $\mathbf{i'}$. These are often called *summation vectors*; they are also known as *unity* vectors.[6]

9. Partitioned matrices

Sometimes it is useful to divide a matrix into *submatrices*, especially if there is some logical reason to distinguish some rows and columns from others.[7] This is known as *partitioning* the matrix; the submatrices are usually separated by dashed or dotted lines. For example, we might create four submatrices from a (4 x 4) matrix **A**

$$
A = \begin{bmatrix} a_{11} & a_{12} & | & a_{13} & a_{14} \\ a_{21} & a_{22} & | & a_{23} & a_{24} \\ \text{---} & \text{---} & | & \text{---} & \text{---} \\ a_{31} & a_{32} & | & a_{33} & a_{34} \\ a_{41} & a_{42} & | & a_{43} & a_{44} \end{bmatrix} = \begin{bmatrix} A_{11} & | & A_{12} \\ \text{---} & | & \text{---} \\ A_{21} & | & A_{22} \end{bmatrix}
$$

If matrices are partitioned so that submatrices are conformable for multiplication, then products of partitioned matrices can be found as products of their submatrices. For example, suppose that in conjunction with the (4 x 4) matrix **A** above we have

$$
x = \begin{bmatrix} x_1 \\ x_2 \\ \text{---} \\ x_3 \\ x_4 \end{bmatrix} = \begin{bmatrix} x_1 \\ \text{---} \\ x_2 \end{bmatrix}
$$

Then

$$
Ax = \begin{bmatrix} A_{11} & | & A_{12} \\ \text{---} & | & \text{---} \\ A_{21} & | & A_{22} \end{bmatrix} \begin{bmatrix} x_1 \\ \text{---} \\ x_2 \end{bmatrix} = \begin{bmatrix} A_{11}x_1 + A_{12}x_2 \\ \text{---} \\ A_{21}x_1 + A_{22}x_2 \end{bmatrix}
$$

Endnotes to mathematical appendix

1   The ultimate in shrinkage is when $m = n = 1$, a matrix of only one element. These will not be useful for the materials in this book.

2   Try to carry out the multiplication in the order **QM** and you can easily see where the trouble arises.

3   In this appendix, we will look at inverses only for square matrices. This means that if we are dealing with the coefficient matrix from an

equation system, as in (A-2) or (A-3), there are the same number of unknowns as equations in the system. There are more advanced concepts of 'pseudo' inverses for nonsquare matrices, but they are unnecessary for the material in this book.

4   It is usually important to understand what causes a matrix to be singular and, when it is the coefficient matrix from an equation system [as in (A-2) or (A-3)], what that singularity implies about the equations. This is covered in any matrix algebra text but is not needed for the material in this book.

5   This is of particular use in defining technical coefficients matrices in input-output models.

6   As compared with *unit vectors* which contain all zeros except for one 1 (hence they are columns or rows of an identity matrix and are also known as *identity vectors*).

7   A perfect example of this is in the expression of basic relationships in an interregional or multiregional input-output model.

4. Regional and spatial econometric analysis

Matthew P. Drennan and Sidney Saltzman

4.0 Introduction

In the last section of the previous chapter, we considered the fusion of comparative cost and input-output methods and, in particular, the determination of changes in the final demand vector, namely Δy, of an input-output framework. The careful reader may very well ask: How is the final demand vector determined? After all, it is basic to so many uses of input-output models. One way that has been and is still employed is with the use of econometric analysis, the topic considered in this chapter.

Econometric methods are among the most important general-purpose tools available for the analysis of regional phenomena. The regional science literature, and social science literature in general, are replete with a broad range of applications of these methods for modelling, understanding, and/or helping to find solutions to a wide range of socio-economic problems at both the micro and macro levels in our society. Applications that are often of general interest in regional science deal with a broad range of issues related to migration and population projections, the analysis of regional product, price and wage estimation, and demand and supply estimation, among others. In particular, the applications we consider in this chapter deal with the determinants of gross regional product, per capita income growth, the rank-size rule, regional trade, and regional production functions.

Econometric methods also can be used to broaden and enhance the usefulness of other regional science models including input-output, social accounting matrices, and applied general equilibrium models, among others (see chapter 9). Furthermore, econometric methods are used to model regional phenomena that other regional science methods are unable to handle, such as time dependent relationships among socio-economic variables. In addition, the careful analysis and examination of a data set and its resultant model may spark the development of a new theory to explain some regional phenomena. For such a new theory to be credible, it is necessary to test its validity on a different data set that was not used previously to develop the new theory.

Econometrics may be defined, very briefly, as the application of statistical methods to economic data, but that does not tell the full story of how econometric methods are used in the analysis of economic phenomena. An econometric analysis should begin with the formulation of a mathematical model that is grounded in economic theory. That model is then specified in a form that can be tested with data using appropriately selected techniques based on statistical theory. The results of testing the model are then analyzed in order to determine whether or not the underlying economic theory provides a satisfactory explanation of the empirical results. Unfortunately, this process is not implemented as cleanly as it is described here and there is much reformulation, respecification, reselection and retesting required in a typical econometric analysis.

In this chapter, we provide a brief and somewhat intuitive introduction to econometric analysis which focuses primarily on the selection process for deciding which statistical techniques are most appropriate in a given application. In addition, we provide some examples to illustrate these applications to real-world problems in a regional setting, and some discussion of the 'art' of econometric model building.

In addition to the more conventional models and types of applications of regression methods of interest to us here, we also examine other types of econometric models that have special relevance for regional analysis. These include brief introductions to the use of dummy variables, discrete choice models, pooled cross section and time series models, simultaneous equations models, and spatial econometric models. Where appropriate, applications are integrated with discussions of the statistical methodology and are used to illuminate some of the underlying statistical issues.

With the broad range of desk-top computers and econometric software available today, many different types of econometric methods are accessible for use in the analysis of real world data. Regional analysts and other users of econometric methods need to know the strengths as well as the shortcomings of the methodologies they employ. Analysts should use the correct or, at least, the most suitable methods, not only to maintain credibility and intellectual honesty but also to avoid inaccurate or wrong forecasts and/or policy decisions which may impose high unexpected costs.

The goals of this chapter, then, are (1) to provide readers with an overview and 'roadmap' of econometric methodologies and their applications at the regional level (we assume readers have had only a beginning one-semester course in statistical methods including an introduction to multiple regression), and (2) to motivate readers to undertake more advanced work in this subject which has great significance for regional science research and applications.

In the rest of this chapter, section 4.1 provides an introduction to the basic framework for the econometric analysis to be discussed later. Section 4.2 briefly introduces the underlying statistical theory including criteria for evaluating estimators, discusses the popular ordinary least squares (OLS) estimators and indicates some important alternative estimators. Section 4.3 considers some of the more important general estimation problems associated with econometric models, briefly introduces alternative estimating procedures when they exist, and discusses applications related to some of these issues.

Section 4.4 briefly considers some extensions of econometric models that are relevant to research and professional work in regional analysis: the use of dummy variables, discrete choice models, pooled time series and cross-section models, and simultaneous equations models. The following section (4.5) introduces spatial econometrics, an increasingly important area of application of econometric methods for regional analysis. Section 4.6 contains concluding remarks, an introduction to the 'art' of econometric model building and also introduces some practical problems of model implementation and use. Some editorial remarks are made in section 4.7 on the fusion of econometrics with methods discussed in the previous chapters.

The materials summarized in this chapter (including Figures 4.1 through 4.8) are drawn from and are discussed in much greater detail in a number of popular econometric texts including Greene (1993), Griffith, Hill and Judge (1993), Gujarati (1995), Johnston and DiNardo (1997), Kennedy (1992), Maddala (1992) and Pindyck and Rubinfeld (1991), among others. Since the basic information presented in this chapter is common to most all of these texts, additional detailed references are not provided in the remainder of this chapter in the interest of minimizing repetition. However, references to other sources are provided where appropriate.

4.1 Econometric models and their uses

A major reason econometric models are so ubiquitous in research and professional work is because they can be used in a variety of ways. First, with the use of formal statistical methods of analysis, it is possible to employ such models with appropriate data to test, in a rigorous manner, the validity of the theories they represent about real world phenomena. These formal methods make it possible to pose specific hypotheses and then accept or reject such hypotheses in a structured, formal testing process.

Second, such models are often used to forecast or predict values of their dependent variable under various conditions. For example, we are all familiar with predictions about the future values of national economic variables such as gross domestic product, the consumer price index, wage rates, etc., and their counterparts at regional levels. Governments, at federal, state and local levels, use econometric models to forecast revenues and expenditures. Also, many large businesses use econometric models to forecast their future sales. Migration and population projections are often made using econometric models.

A third use of econometric models is to predict the likely effects of policy decisions, a process which is sometimes referred to as 'policy analysis.' For example, we may want to know what is likely to happen to the national or a regional economy (e.g., changes in consumption, profits, tax revenues, etc.) if tax rates are raised or lowered by a specified amount. Similar questions are often asked regarding changes in interest rates, wage rates, and so forth. Many local, regional and federal governments use econometric models to forecast revenues and expenditures when evaluating alternative policies. These uses of econometric models try to provide answers to 'What if...?' questions.[1]

An econometric model may be used for all three of these types of applications. Examples are presented following a brief discussion of the basic structure of econometric models.

4.1.1 The basic structure

The basic model we deal with in this chapter is in the form of a linear multiple regression equation:

$$Y_i = \beta_0 + \beta_1 X_{1i} + \beta_2 X_{2i} + ... + \beta_k X_{ki} + \varepsilon_i \qquad \text{(for } i = 1, 2, ..., n) \qquad (4\text{-}1)$$

where Y is the dependent variable (or regressand), the Xs are the independent or explanatory variables (or regressors), the βs are the coefficients or parameters to be estimated, ε is a stochastic error or disturbance term, subscript k is the number of explanatory variables, subscript i represents the i-th sample or observation, and n is the sample size.[2] This estimation model is an abstract representation of the underlying theory or model that relates the dependent left hand side variable (Y) to the explanatory or independent variables (the Xs) on the right hand side of the equation. Using multiple regression techniques (see section 4.2), the parameters of the model (i.e., the βs) can be estimated and the model can then be written as:

$$\hat{Y}_i = \hat{\beta}_0 + \hat{\beta}_1 X_{1i} + \hat{\beta}_2 X_{2i} + ... + \hat{\beta}_k X_{ki} \qquad (4\text{-}2)$$

where $\hat{Y}$ is the estimated value of the dependent variable and the βs are the estimated values of the coefficients or parameters. These parameter estimates are calculated using the known values of the dependent and independent variables in the model. Once the values of the coefficients, $\hat{\beta}_j$ are known, the predicted value of the dependent variable $\hat{Y}_i$, can be calculated given a set of assumed or known values of the independent variables X_{ji} (see section 4.2.2).

Before discussing the important assumptions that are often made about these models and data in order that the statistical estimates of the parameters have desirable properties, we illustrate three possible applications.

4.1.2 Three typical applications

(1) Hypothesis testing In the following model, a time-series regression analysis is used to test the hypothesis that the New York–New Jersey (NY–NJ) metropolitan economy[3] is sensitive to both U.S. foreign trade in services and to economic growth in Europe. The dependent variable is the regional product originating in the producer services sector (financial services, legal services, and business services), one of the three traded goods and services or export sectors in the NY–NJ metropolitan economy model. Traditional export base theory identifies national demand as the primary determinant of an urban area's export sector. This model is somewhat novel, however, because it is hypothesized that demand for the output of that sector (PS$_t$) is not only national but also international. The econometric model is stated as follows:[4]

$$PS_t = \beta_0 + \beta_1 GNPEUR_t + \beta_2 USEXP_t + \beta_3 RCPI_{t-2} + \beta_4 UER_t + \varepsilon_t \qquad (4\text{-}3)$$

where

PS_t = Regional product (millions of U.S. 1987 dollars) in the producer services sector for the NY–NJ region in year t;

$GNPEUR_t$ = Gross national product of European members of OECD (Organization for Economic Cooperation and Development), in millions of U.S. 1987 dollars, in year t, which represents an international demand factor;

$USEXP_t$ = U.S. exports of producer services, in millions of U.S. 1987 dollars, in year t, which represents an international demand factor;

$RCPI_{t-2}$ = A ratio of the CPI (consumer price index) of the NY–NJ region to that of the U.S., lagged two years (year $t-2$), which represents the region's competitive cost position in the nation as a whole;

UER_t = U.S. unemployment rate, percent, in year t, which represents the impact of cyclical conditions in the national economy and is a proxy for national demand;

ε_t = a stochastic error term in year t.

The hypothesis is tested by using the estimated coefficients and their standard errors. If the partial regression coefficients on the two international variables, GNPEUR and USEXP, are positive and statistically significant, then the hypothesis that the region's economy is sensitive to international demand factors is supported. The coefficient on RCPI is expected to be negative because a higher inflation rate in the NY–NJ region than in the nation indicates an adverse or declining competitive position for the region's exports. The coefficient on UER is also expected to be negative because higher national unemployment indicates lower national demand. The model was estimated using data for the period 1963 through 1993 (see Table 4-1).

The results of the initial estimation of (4-3) showed the presence of serial correlation.[5] To eliminate this condition, the model was reestimated using the Cochrane Orcutt procedure, thus requiring the addition of the variables AR(1) and AR(2) (see section 4.3.4). The 't' statistic provides a measure of the statistical significance of each explanatory variable in the model. A very rough 'rule of thumb' sometimes used in preliminary analysis of the results of fitting a regression equation is that a t-value greater than approximately 2 indicates a statistically significant variable. The 'F' statistic, on the other hand, provides an indication of whether or not the model, as a whole (i.e., all of the explanatory variables, as a group), is statistically significant. The value of 419 for the F statistic indicates the model is highly statistically significant. The 'Adjusted R^2'

statistic is a measure of how much of the variation in the dependent variable, PS, is explained by the independent variables. In this case, the explanatory variables explain 98.8% of the variation in PS.

Table 4-1 Regression results for hypothesis test equation

Dependent Variable: PS_t	Coefficient	t-statistic
Intercept	118,678.0	5.8
$GNPEUR_t$	24.7	11.3
$USEXP_t$	0.337	4.4
$RCPI_{t-2}$	−87,338.0	−4.4
UER_t	−959.0	−2.0
AR(1)	0.612	2.4
AR(2)	−0.500	−2.2
n	31	
Adjusted R^2	0.988	
F statistic	419.0	

Note that the coefficient on GNPEUR is +24.7 and its t statistic is 11.3. The coefficient on the other international variable (USEXP) is also positive, +0.337, with a t statistic of 4.4. Thus the hypothesis that the region's economy is sensitive to international demand factors is (not surprisingly) supported.

(2) Policy analysis There are a variety of policy issues that could be evaluated using the above basic econometric model. In this section, we consider only one example in which the NY–NJ model is used as the starting point to try to understand how changes in the European economy would affect tax revenues in NYC with its resulting implications for policy.

For example, we can start the analysis by estimating what would be the effect upon the NY–NJ region's producer services' sector output of: (a) an economic slump in Europe, and (b) a drop in foreign demand for U.S. producer services? To answer this policy question, the model specified in (4-3) was estimated in natural log form in order to obtain estimates of relevant elasticities:[6]

$$\ln PS_t = \beta_0 + \beta_1 \ln GNPEUR_t + \beta_2 \ln USEXP_t$$
$$+ \beta_3 RCPI_{t-2} + \beta_4 \ln UER_t + \varepsilon_t \tag{4-4}$$

Table 4-2 presents the variables in this formulation of the basic model (4-4). All the variables have the prefix ln, indicating that they are natural logarithms of the variables defined above. The coefficient on lnGNPEUR, the natural log of European GNP, is +0.328. That indicates that a 1% increase in European GNP would raise the NY–NJ region's output in the producer services' sector by 0.328%. The coefficient of lnUSEXP, the natural log of U.S. exports of producer services, is +0.103 which indicates that a 1% increase in U.S. exports of producer services would raise the region's output of producer services by 0.103%.

Table 4-2 Regression results for policy analysis equation

Dependent Variable: $\ln PS_t$	Coefficient	t-statistic
Intercept	8.16	7.7
$\ln GNPEUR_t$	0.328	2.0
$\ln USEXP_t$	0.103	3.8
$\ln RCPI_{t-2}$	–0.310	–0.8
$\ln UER_t$	–0.126	–3.4
AR(1)	0.601	2.5
AR(2)	–0.284	–1.2
n	30	
Adjusted R^2	0.985	
F statistic	419.0	

If we assume that a recession in Europe reduces annual GNP there by 2.5% and cuts U.S. exports of producer services by 5.0%, what would be the combined effect upon the NY–NJ region's output of producer services? Using the elasticities calculated in Table 4-2, the combined effect is estimated as:

0.328(–2.5%) + 0.103(–5.0%) = –1.33%

So if PS = $110.7 billion in 1997, and we assume that the European recession occurs in 1998, then we calculate a fall of $1.5 billion [($110.7) x (0.0133)] in PS in 1998, *ceteris paribus*.[7]

One can go further in examining these impacts. The (marginal) multiplier (discussed in chapter 3) which links changes in the *region's* producer services' output to New York City's total output is +1.14, with a one year lag. Thus, the estimated change in NYC total output in 1998 is −$1.71 billion [(1.14) x (−$1.5)]. Still further, the marginal tax rate for New York City government taxes, excluding the property tax, which links changes in total city output to city taxes is +0.069.[8] And so the estimated impact of the reduction in total city output upon the city's tax revenues is −$0.118 billion [(0.069) x (−$1.71)].

Thus, the estimated effect upon the NYC government tax revenues due to the hypothetical fall in European GNP and fall in U.S. producer services exports is a drop of $118 million one year later. Knowledge of this financial impact could then influence the city government's budget plan. Discretionary expenditures, such as summer youth employment programs or retirement of debt before it is due, could be scaled back in advance to avoid a budget gap during which expenditures exceed revenues.

(3) Forecasting   The linear form of the above time-series equation estimating PS, the region's producer services output (shown in Table 4-1), can be used to forecast PS for 1998 and 1999. That, of course, requires having values for the four independent variables in the estimated equation in Table 4-1. The table below presents those values to be used in forecasting PS:

Year	$GNPEUR_t$	$RCPI_{t-2}$	UER_t	$USEXP_t$
1998	3570	1.0655	5.5	61.2
1999	3638	1.0655	5.3	64.6

Note that the values for $RCPI_{t-2}$ are for 1996 and 1997 because that variable is lagged two years. Substituting the above values of the variables into the equation estimated in Table 4-1 yields forecasts of PS:

1998 Forecast: PS = 118,678 + 24.7(3570) − 87,338(1.0655)
     − 959(5.5) +.337(61.2) = $108,544 millions (1987 $)

1999 Forecast: PS = 118,678 + 24.7(3638) − 87,338(1.0655)
     − 959(5.3) + .337(64.6) = $110,417 millions (1987 $)

The forecasts for 1998 and 1999 are called 'conditional' forecasts because they are conditional on the values used for the independent variables. If the forecast is made in 1997, presumably the value for $RCPI_{t-2}$ for 1996 may be known and, if so, it would be used in developing the forecast. Since the values of the other independent variables would be unknown in 1997, their values would have to be assumed or predicted (perhaps using similar regression equations).

In this section, we thus see how a single equation econometric model can be used for hypothesis testing, forecasting and policy analysis, although other econometric models that are built may be used for only one, two or all three purposes.

4.2 Some underlying statistical theory

Using multiple regression methods, the estimated econometric model (4-2) is obtained from the theoretical model (4-1). We now present a brief overview of some of the statistical theory underlying multiple regression. Section 4.2.1 outlines the criteria used to evaluate alternative estimators. Section 4.2.2 introduces the popular ordinary least squares (OLS) estimators of the coefficients of equation (4-1) and section 4.2.3 introduces the assumptions upon which these estimators are based. Section 4.2.4 briefly considers some other important estimators that are employed when the use of OLS is not appropriate.

4.2.1 Desirable properties of estimators

There are various related techniques or methods (called estimators) that could be used to estimate the coefficients or parameters of the hypothesized theoretical model (4-1) in order to obtain the estimated model (4-2). The question is how to decide which of the available estimators is the best one to use in any particular case. In order to answer this question, it is first necessary to establish the criteria that are used in evaluating alternative estimators. There is general agreement that the properties of *unbiasedness*, *efficiency*, *consistency* and, when appropriate, *minimum mean square error* are the basic desirable characteristics that estimators should possess. We now consider these criteria.

(1) Unbiasedness An unbiased estimator is one whose expected value is equal to the parameter being estimated, that is:

$$E(\hat{\beta}) = \beta \qquad\qquad\qquad (4\text{-}5)$$

where E is the expected value operator and $\hat{\beta}$ is the estimator of the parameter β. This property is illustrated in Figure 4.1, which shows typical probability density functions for both unbiased $\hat{\beta}$ and biased estimators $\hat{\beta}'$.

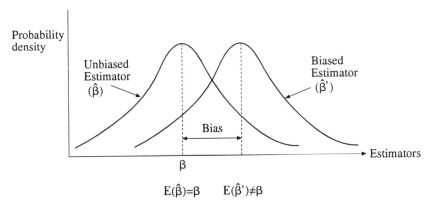

$$E(\hat{\beta})=\beta \qquad E(\hat{\beta}')\neq\beta$$

Figure 4.1 Illustration of unbiased and biased estimators

The amount of bias is defined as

$$\text{Bias} = E(\hat{\beta}') - \beta \qquad (4\text{-}6)$$

Clearly, if all other things are equal, unbiased estimators would be preferred to biased estimators. In a practical situation, it would be difficult to justify the use of a biased estimator (in preference to an unbiased estimator) unless the error (i.e., the amount of bias) and its associated variance could be demonstrated to be small (see (4) Minimum Mean Square Error below).

(2) Efficiency An efficient estimator, $\hat{\beta}$, of a parameter, β, is one whose variance (var) is less than that of all other estimators of that parameter for a given sample size, n, i.e.,

$$\text{var}(\hat{\beta}) < \text{var}(\hat{\beta}')$$

where $\hat{\beta}'$ is another estimator of the parameter, β. This situation is illustrated in Figure 4.2.

A measure of efficiency between these two estimators is given by

Efficiency of $\hat{\beta}$ compared to $\hat{\beta}' = [\text{var}(\hat{\beta}')/\text{var}(\hat{\beta})] \times 100\%$ (4-7)

There are at least two practical reasons for preferring estimators with minimum variance as compared to those with larger variances. First, for two different estimators with equal sample size, the more efficient estimator will provide sharper statistical decisions; that is, the probability of rejecting the null hypothesis[9] when it is false will increase. Second, to achieve equal variance for two different estimators, $\hat{\beta}$ and $\hat{\beta}'$, the required

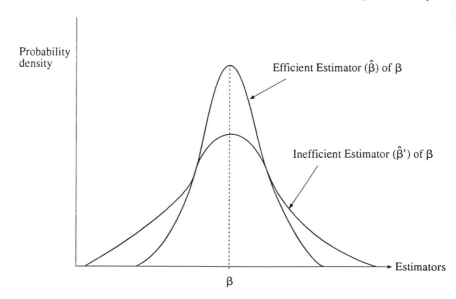

Figure 4.2 **Illustrations of an efficient estimator $(\hat{\beta})$ and inefficient estimator $(\hat{\beta}')$ of β**

sample size, n, of the more efficient estimator, $\hat{\beta}$, will be less than that required for the less efficient estimator, $\hat{\beta}'$, a desirable property.

As we shall see in section 4.2.3, ordinary least squares (OLS) estimators have the above desirable properties (i.e., unbiased, efficient) if the assumptions upon which they are based are true for the model and data set being analyzed. In such situations, we may say that an OLS estimator is BLUE. That is, OLS is the best (i.e., it has minimum variance and is, therefore, efficient), linear, unbiased estimator of all linear, unbiased estimators of the parameter under consideration.[10,11]

(3) Consistency Some estimators in econometrics have either one or both of the above desirable properties but only asymptotically, that is, only as the sample size, n, gets large. These estimators require the use of the consistency criteria for making judgments about their desirability.

A consistent estimator is one whose probability limit (plim)[12] approaches the true value of the estimator as the sample size gets large, i.e., $\text{plim}(\hat{\beta}) \to \beta$ as $n \to \infty$. In effect, the bias and variance both approach zero as the sample size gets large, i.e., bias $\to 0$ and $\text{var}(\hat{\beta}) \to 0$ as $n \to \infty$. A consistent estimator is illustrated in Figure 4.3, where, as n increases from n_1 to n_4, both the variance and the bias of the estimator, $\hat{\beta}$, decrease.

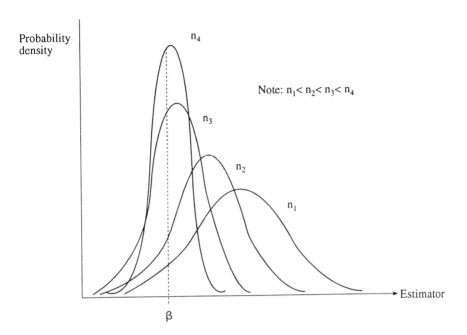

Figure 4.3 A consistent estimator $\hat{\beta}$ of β as n increases

In general, we prefer estimators that are both unbiased and efficient but, when these are not available, we may have to settle for estimators that are consistent.

(4) Minimum mean square error In comparing estimators, it is sometimes the case that one estimator may be unbiased (or with small bias) with a relatively large variance (estimator A in Figure 4.4) while the other estimator may have a relatively large bias with a relatively small variance (estimator B in Figure 4.4). In such circumstances, it may not be clear how to choose the one 'best' estimator — to minimize the bias or to minimize the variance.

A measure that often is used in such circumstances is the mean square error (MSE) between the true parameter and its estimate [i.e., minimize $E(\hat{\beta} - \beta)^2$].[13] When faced with this type of choice among alternative estimators, it is common practice to make the decision as to which estimator is best on the basis of the minimum MSE.

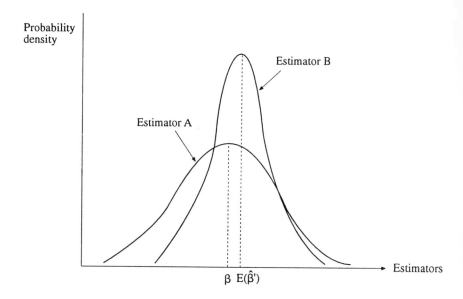

Figure 4.4   Estimators with different measures of bias and variance

4.2.2 Ordinary least squares (OLS) estimators

There are a wide variety of estimators available to calculate the values of the parameters of multiple regression equations (e.g., ordinary least squares, weighted least squares, maximum likelihood, generalized least squares, and two stage least squares, among others). Each is based on its own set of assumptions and each generates estimates that have their own properties with respect to those criteria outlined in section 4.2.1. However, the OLS estimator is usually considered to be the traditional estimator, it is the easiest to understand and employ, and is, by far, the most commonly used technique for econometric analysis.

The OLS method of estimating the coefficients of the regression equation (4-1) can be easily illustrated in the special case when the number of independent variables (X_i) is equal to one:

$$Y_i = \beta_o + \beta_l X_i + \varepsilon_i \tag{4-8}$$

This instance is illustrated in Figure 4.5 (below). The least squares method minimizes the sum of the squared deviations between the observed value of the dependent variable, Y_i, and its estimated value on the regression line,

$\hat{Y}_i$ [i.e., min $\Sigma(Y_i - \hat{Y}_i)^2 = \varepsilon_i^2$], where $i = 1, 2, ..., n$ and n is the number of observations (or data points). Although the coefficients (β_0, β_1) of the model are assumed to be unknown, fixed parameters, their estimators ($\hat{\beta}_0$, $\hat{\beta}_1$) are random variables which are assumed to have or, at least, to approach a bell shaped, normal distribution with mean $\mu_{\hat{\beta}} = E(\hat{\beta}) = \beta$.

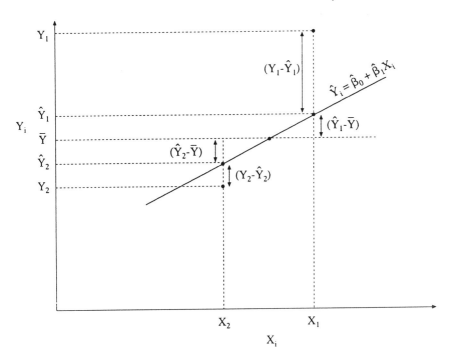

Figure 4.5 Squared deviations in graphical form

The equation for estimating the slope coefficient ($\hat{\beta}_1$) in the simple regression equation

$$\hat{Y}_i = \hat{\beta}_o + \hat{\beta}_1 X_i \qquad (4\text{-}9)$$

is given by[14]

$$\hat{\beta}_1 = \Sigma x_i y_i / \Sigma x_i^2 \qquad (4\text{-}10)$$

and the intercept term ($\hat{\beta}_0$) by

$$\hat{\beta}_0 = \overline{Y} - \hat{\beta}_1 \overline{X} \qquad (4\text{-}11)$$

where y_i and x_i are the deviations of the Y_i and X_i variables from their respective means $\overline{Y}$ and $\overline{X}$; that is,

$$y_i = (Y_i - \overline{Y}) \qquad\qquad x_i = (X_i - \overline{X})$$

and

$$\overline{Y} = \Sigma Y_i/n \qquad\qquad \overline{X} = \Sigma X_i/n$$

The equations for estimating the variance of the coefficient estimators $\hat{\beta}_0$ and $\hat{\beta}_1$ are:

$$\text{var}(\hat{\beta}_1) = \sigma^2/\Sigma x_i^2 \tag{4-12}$$

$$\text{var}(\hat{\beta}_0) = (\Sigma X_i^2/n\Sigma x_i^2)\sigma^2 \tag{4-13}$$

where $\sigma^2 = \Sigma\varepsilon_i^2/(n-2)$. The divisor $(n-2)$ is called the 'degrees of freedom' (i.e., the number of observations, n, minus the number of parameters being estimated — in this case, 2: β_0 and β_1).

The usual method for testing the statistical significance of an estimate, say $\hat{\beta}$, of either $\hat{\beta}_0$ or $\hat{\beta}_1$ is based on the 't' statistic which can be calculated as

$$t = \frac{\text{the estimate } (\hat{\beta}) - \text{the hypothesized value } (\beta)}{\text{the standard error of the estimate (i.e., } \sqrt{\text{var}\hat{\beta}})} \tag{4-14}$$

A common hypothesis is that $\beta = 0$, i.e., the explanatory variable X has no effect on the dependent variable Y. If the calculated t statistic is less than the critical value of t (call it t*), the difference between the values of $\hat{\beta}$ and β is assumed to be small enough to be due primarily to sampling error and the null hypothesis that $\beta = 0$ is the true value of the coefficient is not rejected. If, on the other hand, $t \geq t^*$, the null hypothesis is rejected. Critical values for t* can be obtained from tables in virtually any textbook on statistics or econometrics. A common rule-of-thumb assumes that $t^* = 2$ provides a useful first approximation in deciding whether or not an estimated coefficient value ($\hat{\beta}$) is statistically significant.

The t statistic can be used to test the statistical significance of each estimated coefficient individually in a regression equation. The statistical significance of the complete equation (as a single unit) can be tested using the F statistic, as follows:

$$F = (\text{RSS}/df_{RSS})/(\text{ESS}/df_{ESS}) \tag{4-15}$$

where RSS is the regression sum of squares (i.e., the sum of squares explained by the fitted regression line — for example, see Figure 4.5) which is equal to $\Sigma(\hat{Y}_i - \overline{Y})^2$ and ESS is the error or unexplained sum of squares which is equal to $\Sigma(Y_i - \hat{Y}_i)^2$. The term, df, stands for the degrees of freedom associated with RSS and ESS, respectively. If a calculated F statistic is greater than the critical F*, the null hypothesis that the model does not explain the behavior of the dependent variable is rejected. If F < F*, the null hypothesis is not rejected.

The assumptions upon which OLS estimators are based and the implications of their being violated are reviewed in the next section and in section 4.3.

4.2.3 Assumptions of OLS estimators

In order that OLS estimators have the desirable properties of being unbiased and efficient, there are a number of important assumptions about the data and the specified model that must be satisfied. These assumptions are noted here. We include in these assumptions some that often are not explicitly noted in the textbooks and are then presumed to hold implicitly (for example, the number of observations in a sample, n, must be greater than the number of independent variables in the model). Regression models that satisfy these assumptions are sometimes called classical linear regression models (CLRM). A more detailed explanation of how these assumptions may be violated in practice, how to test for such violations, alternative strategies for dealing with such violations when they occur, and illustrations of these problems in regional modelling applications are presented beginning in section 4.3.

(1) No specification error An important underlying assumption in using OLS to estimate the parameters of a regression model is that the model is specified correctly as to its functional form and included independent variables. This question occurs initially during the conceptual and/or theoretical phase of the modeling process (e.g., see section 4.6). However, there are practical methods that can sometimes be used to test whether or not this assumption is correct after the model's coefficients have been estimated (e.g., see section 4.3.1). If the model is not specified correctly, the OLS estimates of its coefficients may be biased (depending on the nature of the mis-specification) and alternative approaches to estimating the parameters may need to be taken.

The term 'linear' to describe equation (4-1) above refers to the structure of the model and the constraint either that it be linear in its parameters or that it can be transformed so that it is linear in its parameters. For example, consider the following regression model:

$$Y = \beta_0 + \beta_1 X_1 + \beta_2 X_2 + \beta_3 X_1 X_2 + \beta_4 X_2^2 + \varepsilon \qquad (4\text{-}16)$$

which is linear in the coefficients (the βs) and non-linear in the variables (X_1X_2 and X_2^2). Since this model is already linear in the parameters, a simple transformation of the variables would make it suitable for OLS estimation, as follows:

$$Y = \beta_0 + \beta_1 X_1 + \beta_2 X_2 + \beta_3 Z_1 + \beta_4 Z_2 + \varepsilon \tag{4-17}$$

where $Z_1 = X_1X_2$ and $Z_2 = X_2^2$.

Although the following model is not linear in the parameters (β_1 and β_2),

$$Y = \beta_0 X_1^{\beta_1} X_2^{\beta_2} e^\varepsilon \tag{4-18}$$

it can be transformed by taking natural logarithms, ln (i.e., logarithms to the base e and e = 2.718), of both sides giving

$$\ln Y = \ln\beta_0 + \beta_1\ln X_1 + \beta_2\ln X_2 + \varepsilon \tag{4-19}$$

which can be written (and its coefficients estimated) as

$$\ln Y = \beta_0^* + \beta_1\ln X_1 + \beta_2\ln X_2 + \varepsilon \tag{4-20}$$

where $\beta_0^* = \ln\beta_0$.

On the other hand, the model

$$Y = \beta_0 X_1^{\beta_1} X_2^{\beta_2} + \varepsilon \tag{4-21}$$

is an example of one which cannot be transformed to make it linear in its parameters because of the additive (rather than multiplicative) error term (ε).

(2) The error term has expected value of zero [E(ε_i) = 0] This assumption is straightforward and intuitively appealing. If it is not satisfied, the difference between the actual value of the error term and its expected value of zero will, in general, be absorbed by the intercept term $\hat{\beta}_0$ in the specified model (see section 4.3.2).

(3) The error term has constant variance [var(ε_i) = σ^2] The variance of the error term, ε_i, is fixed, i.e., it is the same for all values of the independent variable. If the variance of the error term is fixed, the condition is called homoskedasticity; if not, the condition is called heteroskedasticity. OLS estimators under homoskedasticity have the desirable properties of being unbiased and efficient (if the other assumptions also hold). However, the same does not hold true under conditions of heteroskedasticity, in which case the OLS estimators are unbiased but no longer efficient. Fortunately, there are alternative estimating procedures (weighted least squares) that are both unbiased and efficient as we shall see in section 4.3.3.

(4) The error term is statistically independent [$\text{cov}(\varepsilon_i\varepsilon_j) = 0$ for $i \neq j$] A basic assumption of the OLS method is that the error term, ε_i, is independently distributed. One of the conditions for this to exist is that there is no correlation between any two error terms, a situation that can be tested in an objective manner (see section 4.3.4).

(5) The independent variables are non-stochastic A basic assumption of OLS regression often specified in introductory materials is that the independent variables, X_j, are non-stochastic, i.e., they are fixed in repeated samples, and are independent of the error term, ε_i. This assumption is usually satisfied more easily in the laboratory sciences than in economics, regional science, planning, and related disciplines. However, it is possible to invoke a somewhat broader assumption that the X_js can be stochastic rather than fixed values with zero correlation between them and the error term, ε_i, [$\text{cov}(X_{ji}\varepsilon_i) = 0$ for $j = 1, 2,..., k$ explanatory variables] and still have an estimator with desirable properties (see section 4.3.5). The somewhat related assumption that there are no errors in measuring the values of the random variables (i.e., the Xs, Ys and Zs) in a model is also discussed in that section. Note that of the assumptions discussed in subsections (1) through (5), the first focuses on the structure of the specified model while the others focus primarily on the data used to estimate the parameters of the model if we can assume the model is specified correctly.

(6) Other assumptions Another assumption (somewhat related to (5)) is that there is no multicollinearity among the independent variables. Multicollinearity can be defined as the case when there is significant positive or negative correlation between two or more independent variables (the Xs). OLS estimators, in the absence of multicollinearity, are unbiased and efficient; with multicollinearity they are still BLUE but with increased variance. Although there are no foolproof methods for dealing with this condition, there are approaches that can be tried that often work to reduce the amount of collinearity in a data set. Also it is assumed that there are no errors in measuring the values of the random variables (i.e., the Xs, Ys and Zs) in a model. (See section 4.3.5.)

In addition to the above, there are other assumptions that are more or less implied when estimating the coefficients of econometric models. (We list them here but do not discuss them in the following section.) For example, if an assumption of normality concerning the distribution of the error term cannot be made, the Central Limit Theorem is often invoked in order to allow statistical significance tests of various characteristics of the estimated model. In addition, the number of observations must be larger than the number of variables in the model so that the estimators can be calculated. Furthermore, we assume also that the parameters of the model are constant over time.

As indicated earlier, the most desirable properties for an estimator to have are that it is unbiased and efficient (i.e., that it be BLUE). In general, if these assumptions are violated, the OLS estimators will be biased and/or inefficient and alternative strategies for parameter estimation should be used.

4.2.4 Other estimators

In spite of its popularity and ease of use, OLS estimators are not always the best estimators to use in a particular application. If all the assumptions upon which OLS estimation is based are not satisfied, there may be other estimators with more desirable properties (see section 4.3). In this section, we very briefly introduce some of the more important estimators, other than OLS, that are commonly used.

(1) Maximum likelihood estimator (MLE) Recall that OLS estimators of the coefficients and standard errors of a regression line are derived by minimizing the square of the deviations between the observed values of the dependent variable and those predicted by the fitted regression equation values. ML estimators, on the other hand, are derived by choosing estimators that maximize the probability of drawing the observed random sample from the population with unknown parameters. For example, Figure 4.6 shows three probability distributions, A, B, and C, and a random sample of observations (Z_i) on the horizontal axis. Of these three distributions, only B maximizes the probability that this observed sample would be drawn. In this case, distribution B is the MLE.

Thus, the ML estimators of the regression coefficients, β_j, are the respective values, $\hat{\beta}_j$, which maximize the probability that the observed random sample, Y_i, would be chosen from its population. In multiple regression, ML estimators are usually based on the assumption that the error term (ε_i) has a normal distribution, an assumption that is not required in deriving the OLS estimators of the regression coefficients. However, an assumption of normality is usually invoked in OLS in order to be able to make statistical inferences using the estimated regression coefficients.

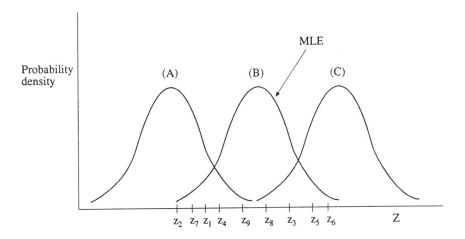

Figure 4.6 **The distribution (B) that maximizes the likelihood of drawing the indicated sample observations**

The MLEs of the regression coefficients β_j are BLUE (as are the OLS estimators) in the classical linear regression case but the MLE of the variance of the error term, while consistent, is biased when sample sizes are small. On the other hand, MLEs may exhibit more desirable properties than OLS estimators in certain cases where the OLS assumptions are violated. We consider this issue again in section 4.3. In general, MLEs of the regression coefficients are considered equivalent to OLS estimators, generalized least squares estimators, and weighted least squares estimators (see below) when the OLS assumptions are satisfied. In summary, MLEs are derived using a different approach and set of assumptions than do OLS estimators in the classical linear regression case and they are more difficult to derive.

(2) Generalized least squares (GLS) The term GLS describes an approach or process for obtaining estimators with desirable properties in some cases in which the classical regression assumptions are violated. In general, with GLS, the original variables in a model which do not satisfy the classical linear regression assumptions are transformed (so that these assumptions are satisfied) and appropriate methods are then applied to the transformed variables to provide estimators with more desirable properties than those obtained using OLS directly on the original variables. OLS estimation can be considered to be a special case of GLS estimation when the original variables satisfy the classical linear regression assumptions. Section 4.3

contains some illustrations of where GLS estimation should be used in econometric analysis.

(3) Weighted least squares (WLS) WLS estimation is a special case of GLS estimation. In WLS (for example, as used in models with data that are heteroskedastic), the transformation of the original variables is accomplished by weighting (or adjusting) the original X_{ji} and Y_i variables using the known or assumed values of the non-constant standard deviation of the error term. WLS is an accepted method of dealing with estimation problems when the assumption of constant variance of the error term is violated (see section 4.3.3).

(4) Instrumental variable estimation (IVE) Under certain conditions, it may be necessary to substitute a different variable for one of the explanatory variables specified in a regression model in order to avoid violating an assumption of OLS. In this situation, the substitute variable is called an instrumental variable. For example, OLS assumes that the explanatory variables (the Xs) in a regression equation are uncorrelated with the error term (ε). If this assumption is violated, it may be possible to substitute an instrumental variable (i.e., one that is highly correlated with the explanatory variable and is uncorrelated with the error term) and, thereby, satisfy the OLS assumptions (see section 4.4.4).

(5) Two-stage least squares (2SLS) In some applications, it is not always obvious which variables in a regression model are dependent and which are explanatory. A common example of this case is that of estimating a product's price and quantity that will clear the market. Since economic theory tells us that the price and quantity are often jointly determined, it is not possible to represent this situation in a single regression equation since the influences are assumed to flow from the explanatory independent variables on the right hand side of the equation to the dependent variable on the left hand side. In this example, the question arises as to which variable, price or quantity, is the dependent variable and which is the independent. The standard approach to this problem is to specify a model that contains a set of simultaneous regression equations rather than a single regression equation. For such a model, OLS estimators are biased and it is important to resort to more suitable estimation techniques such as 2SLS. This type of model and its estimation problems are introduced in section 4.4.4.

(6) Indirect least squares (ILS) Indirect least squares is a method of obtaining estimates of the coefficients of small simultaneous equations models. If the original simultaneous equations can be rewritten in what is called 'reduced form,' OLS can be safely used to estimate the coefficients of the reduced form equations. The coefficients of the original simultaneous equations model may then be obtained algebraicly under certain conditions. This procedure is called ILS (see section 4.4.4).

These are a few of the alternative estimators that have been developed to deal with situations that arise when assumptions underlying the use of OLS estimators are not satisfied. Much of the practice of econometric analysis is devoted to selecting the particular estimators that have the best properties given a specified model and data set.

4.3 Some problems of estimation

In this section we consider how to deal with violations of the assumptions noted in section 4.2.3. We consider each of these violations in turn.[15] Issues raised include: the nature of the assumption, tests to determine if the assumption has been violated, alternative estimating methods if the assumption is violated, and properties of the alternative estimating methods (i.e., efficiency, unbiasedness, etc.).

Up to this section, we have used the familiar $\wedge$ ('hat') and $'$ (prime) notation to indicate an estimator (or estimated value) of a parameter, for example, $\hat{\beta}$, $\hat{\beta}'$, $\hat{\delta}$. In this section, we introduce additional notation to indicate the specific type of estimator under discussion, for example, $\hat{\beta}^{OLS}$, $\hat{\beta}^{GLS}$, $\hat{\delta}^{OLS}$, etc.

4.3.1 Specification errors

We consider three ways in which an econometric model may be misspecified: an irrelevant or extraneous variable may be included in an otherwise correctly specified model; a theoretically correct explanatory variable may be omitted from a model; and/or it may be that the functional form of the theoretical model is incorrectly specified (e.g., a linear function rather than a log function). In this section, we review the results of using OLS under each of these three types of misspecification, indicate ways of checking for their presence and, where appropriate, suggest some alternative strategies for making improved estimates of the coefficients.

(1) Including an irrelevant variable We start with two alternative models. The first is assumed to be the true underlying equation that correctly models the economic phenomena of interest:

$$Y_i = \beta_0 + \beta_1 X_{1i} + \varepsilon_i \qquad (4\text{-}22)$$

where the terms are the same as those described earlier in this chapter.

The second model

$$Y_i = \beta_0^* + \beta_1^* X_{1i} + \beta_2^* X_{2i} + \varepsilon_i^* \qquad (4\text{-}23)$$

is the same as (4-22) except there is one additional term (X_2) that is extraneous in terms of explaining the economic phenomena under study.

This misspecification is the easiest one to treat. This is so because (a) the OLS estimators of each of the coefficients in the incorrectly specified model (4-23) are unbiased, consistent but inefficient estimators of the coefficients in the true, correctly specified model, and (b) the expected value of the estimator of the coefficient of the extraneous variable is zero, as we would anticipate.

These points are summarized in Table 4-3. The first column of that table specifies the two theoretical models. The second column lists the assumption violation, if any. The third column records the relevant estimators of each of the models. The subscript j in column 3 is an index representing the j-th coefficient (β_j) of the j-th variable (X_j) in the model where $j = 0$ (i.e., β_0) represents the intercept term. The fourth column lists the properties of the OLS estimators for both the correctly and incorrectly specified models. The fifth column indicates a way to test for the presence or absence of the assumption violation noted in column 2.

Although the OLS estimator of the variance of the error term $[(\text{var}(\hat{\varepsilon}_i^{*OLS})]$ in the misspecified model is also unbiased, the estimated variances of the coefficients $[\text{var}(\hat{\beta}_j^{*OLS})]$ in the misspecified model (i.e., the model with the extraneous variable) are generally biased toward the high side when compared with the estimates of the coefficients of the correctly specified model $[\text{var}(\hat{\beta}_j^{*OLS}) \geq \text{var}(\hat{\beta}_j^{OLS})]$. Since this may lead to incorrect results when testing the statistical significance of the estimates of the coefficients, there is some penalty associated with this type of error but it is not as serious as that associated with the other two types of specification errors (i.e., omitting a relevant variable or specifying an incorrect functional form) noted above and discussed in subsection (2) and (3) below.

Furthermore, the expected value of the coefficient of the included extraneous term in the model equals zero $[\text{E}(\hat{\beta}_2^{*OLS}) = 0]$. Thus, it should be

Table 4-3 Summary table for the addition of an irrelevant variable

(1) Theoretical Models	(2) OLS Assumption Violation	(3) Estimators	(4) Properties of OLS Estimator	(5) Test for Presence of Violation
True Model				
(I) $Y_i = \beta_0 + \beta_1 X_{1i} + \varepsilon_i$	None	$\hat\beta_j^{OLS}$ var($\hat\beta_j^{OLS}$) var($\hat\varepsilon_i^{OLS}$)	BLUE Unbiased Unbiased	
Incorrectly Specified Model				
(II) $Y_i = \beta_0^* + \beta_1^* X_{1i} + \beta_2^* X_{2i} + \varepsilon_i^*$	An irrelevant variable (X_2) has been added to the true model	$\left.\begin{array}{l}\hat\beta_0^{*OLS}\\ \hat\beta_1^{*OLS}\\ \hat\beta_2^{*OLS}\end{array}\right\}$ var($\hat\beta_j^{*OLS}$) var($\hat\varepsilon_i^{*OLS}$)	Unbiased, consistent, but inefficient Biased (upward) Unbiased	If the null hypothesis ($H_0: \beta_2 = 0$) is not rejected on the basis of a t-test, X_2 is judged to be an irrelevant variable

possible to determine whether or not an included variable in a model is extraneous by testing the statistical significance of its estimated coefficients, bearing in mind the caution noted above about the estimator's lack of efficiency. The 't' test of the null hypothesis (i.e., $\beta_2 = 0$) is represented in column (5). If the null hypothesis cannot be rejected, then model (II) is assumed to have been misspecified with the properties as indicated in column 4 of Table 4.3. An example which includes the addition of an irrelevant variable in a regression model is presented in sub-section (3) following a discussion of misspecification due to the omission of a relevant variable.

(2) Omitting a relevant variable   Omitting a variable that theory says should be included in a model has more serious implications than does the error of including an irrelevant explanatory variable. In general, including an irrelevant variable creates a situation where the OLS estimates are unbiased and inefficient; omitting a relevant variable gives rise to a situation where the estimators of both the coefficients and the variances can be biased.

Consider, for example, the following pair of models:

$$Y_i = \beta_0 + \beta_1 X_{1i} + \beta_2 X_{2i} + \varepsilon_i \qquad (4\text{-}24)$$

and

$$Y_i = \beta_0^* + \beta_1^* X_{1i} + \varepsilon_i^* \qquad (4\text{-}25)$$

where the terms are all as described in the previous section. In this case, we assume that (4-24) is the correct theoretical model and that (4-25) is the incorrectly specified model that is to be estimated. See columns (1) and (2) in Table 4-4.

As expected for the true model (I), the OLS estimators of the parameters are BLUE and those of the variances are unbiased (see columns 3 and 4). However, the expected values of the OLS estimators of the coefficients (β_j^*) of the variables included in the misspecified model (4-25) are biased and inconsistent (i.e., the bias in the estimates will not be eliminated by increasing the sample size). More specifically, if the omitted variable (X_2) is correlated with the included variable (X_1), then OLS estimates of the coefficients are biased and inconsistent (see columns (4) and (5) for model (II) in Table 4.4). Such correlation is usually the case when dealing with economic data. On the other hand, in the unlikely case that the omitted variable and the included variable are uncorrelated, the estimator for the intercept term is biased while the estimator for the slope

Table 4-4 Summary table for the omission of a relevant variable

(1) Theoretical Models	(2) OLS Assumption Violation	(3) Estimators	(4) Properties of OLS Estimator	(5) Comments	(6) Test for Presence of Violation
True Model					To determine if the model is correctly specified:
(I) $Y_i = \beta_0 + \beta_1 X_{1i} + \beta_2 X_{2i} + \varepsilon_i$	None	$\hat{\beta}_j^{OLS}$ var($\hat{\beta}_j^{OLS}$) var($\hat{\varepsilon}_i^{OLS}$)	BLUE Unbiased Unbiased		(1) Simple tests examine— a) R^2 b) t-test on $\hat{\beta}_j^{*OLS}$ c) residuals
Incorrectly Specified Model					(2) More advanced tests include:
(II) $Y_i = \beta_0^* + \beta_1^* X_{1i} + \varepsilon_i^*$	A relevant variable (X_2) has been omitted from the true model	$\hat{\beta}_j^{*OLS}$ var($\hat{\beta}_j^{*OLS}$) var($\hat{\varepsilon}_i^{*OLS}$)	Biased & inconsistent Biased (upward) Biased (upward)	The properties shown in column (4) are obtained if X_1 and X_2 are correlated (likely in practice)	a) Durbin–Watson b) Ramsey's RESET c) Wald's test d) Hausman's test e) Likelihood ratio test f) Lagrange multiplier test
		$\hat{\beta}_0^{*OLS}$ $\hat{\beta}_1^{*OLS}$ var($\hat{\beta}_j^{*OLS}$) var($\hat{\varepsilon}_i^{*OLS}$)	Biased Unbiased Biased (upward) Biased (upward)	The properties shown in column (4) are obtained if X_1 and X_2 are uncorrelated (not likely in practice)	

coefficient is unbiased (again, see columns (4) and (5)). In both cases (i.e., with correlated and with uncorrelated variables), the estimators for the variances of the coefficients and for the variances of the error terms are both biased upwards. Futhermore, the upward bias increases the probability of not rejecting the null hypothesis that each of the remaining coefficients are equal to zero when each may, in fact, not be true.

Column (6) in table 4.4 lists some of the available ways for testing a model to determine whether or not it is specified correctly. The first set of tests (examination of R^2, the t-tests on the estimated coefficients, and examination of the residuals) are relatively easy to perform but generally do not provide precise or sharp answers to the question. The second set of tests are more advanced and are listed here for completeness without being described further. Additional information about these tests can be found in most econometric texts (see References).

A regional economic example illustrating these alternative cases (omitting a relevant variable and including an irrelevant variable) is presented below. Bear in mind that there are no straightforward solutions to either of these estimation problems.

(3) Examples with (a) inclusion of an irrelevant variable and (b) omission of a relevant variable The guide to proper specification of an equation is theory combined with prior empirical work. For example, in the theory of regional economic growth, key determinants of growth in per capita personal income are growth in the average wage and increases in the rate of utilization of labor in the region. In a famous empirical analysis of regional growth in the United States, Perloff et al. (1960) established that increasing wages and an increasing ratio of employment to population (a measure of increasing utilization of labor) were major causes of growth in per capita personal income. They are both positively related to growth, of course. Omission of either one from a regional income growth equation for a developed economy like the United States would result in a specification error. Likewise, for a country of numerous regions, regional growth theory does not argue that the initial size of the economy affects subsequent growth. So inclusion of total employment, a superfluous variable, in a regional income growth equation would also result in a specification error.

The following three models have been estimated for all 269 metropolitan areas in the United States for the period 1979-89.[16]

$$\ln PCI_{89-79,i} = \alpha_0 + \alpha_1 \ln W_{89-79,i} + \alpha_2 \ln PCI_{79,i} + \varepsilon_i \qquad (4\text{-}26)$$

$$\ln PCI_{89-79,i} = \beta_0 + \beta_1 \ln W_{89-79,i} + \beta_2 \ln PCI_{79,i}$$
$$+ \beta_3 \ln(E/P)_{89-79,i} + \varepsilon_i \qquad (4\text{-}27)$$

$$\ln PCI_{89-79,i} = \gamma_0 + \gamma_1 \ln W_{89-79,i} + \gamma_2 \ln PCI_{79,i}$$
$$+ \gamma_3 \ln(E/P)_{89-79,i} + \gamma_4 \ln E_{79,i} + \varepsilon_i \qquad (4\text{-}28)$$

where the variables are:

$\ln PCI_{89-79,i}$ — log per capita personal income, 1989, minus log per capita personal income, 1979, for metropolitan area i;

$\ln W_{89-79,i}$ — log of average wage, 1989, minus log of average wage, 1979, for metropolitan area i;

$\ln PCI_{79,i}$ — log of per capita personal income at the beginning of the period, 1979, for metropolitan area i;

$\ln(E/P)_{89-79,i}$ — log of employment to population ratio, 1989, minus log of employment to population ratio, 1979, for metropolitan area i;

$\ln E_{79,i}$ — log of total employment, 1979, for metropolitan area i;

ε_i — separate error term for metropolitan area, i, for each model;

and the α, β, and γs are the coefficients to be estimated.

The estimation results for the three equations are listed in Table 4-5. In equation (4-26), the wage growth variable, $\ln W_{89-79,i}$, has the expected sign, positive, and is highly significant. The initial income variable, $\ln PCI_{79,i}$, is negative as expected and is also highly significant. The reason the expected sign is negative is that the neoclassical regional growth model hypothesizes that in an open economy, regional income tends to converge over time. Convergence implies that higher income regions have slower growth than lower income regions. So higher income at the beginning of the period would curb growth. Thus a negative coefficient on the initial income variable supports the convergence hypothesis.

Note that the positive coefficient on the wage growth variable is +0.949 in equation (4-26), and the adjusted R^2 is 0.749. In equation (4-27), which includes the key variable omitted from equation (4-26), namely $\ln(E/P)_{89-79,i}$, the adjusted R^2 rises to 0.836, and the coefficient on the wage growth variable, $\ln W_{89-79,i}$, drops considerably to +0.787. The coefficient on the growth of the employment to population ratio variable, $\ln(E/P)_{89-79,i}$, is +0.433 and is highly significant.

These results strongly suggest that equation (4-26) is misspecified, omitting a key explanatory variable, $\ln(E/P)_{89-79,i}$. The effect of that omission is to bias upward the coefficient on the wage growth variable, $\ln W_{89-79,i}$. Its coefficient drops from +0.949 in equation (4-26) to +0.787 in equation (4-27). The higher value in equation (4-26) indicates that the wage growth variable is picking up part of the positive effect of the omitted variable, $\ln(E/P)_{89-79,i}$.

Another form of specification error is the inclusion of a superfluous variable. The consequences are usually not so dire; that is, the coefficients are not biased but there may be some loss in statistical significance. For example, equation (4-28) has an added variable which is superfluous, namely the log of total employment at the beginning of the period, 1979 ($\ln E_{79,i}$). Note that the coefficients on the wage growth variable ($\ln W_{89-79,i}$) and on the employment to population growth variable [$\ln(E/P)_{89-79,i}$] hardly change and continue to be statistically significant from equation (4-27) to equation (4-28). But the initial per capita income variable, $\ln PCI_{79,i}$, which was just barely significant in equation (4-27) becomes insignificant in equation (4-28). Note also that the superfluous variable in equation (4-28), initial employment ($\ln E_{79,i}$), has a coefficient near zero (-0.004) and it is not statistically significant.

The changing values of the F statistic in Table 4-5 support this analysis. For example, the increase from equation (4-26) to equation (4-27) (i.e., from $F = 401$ to 457) reflects the addition of the correct variable,

Table 4-5 Specification error equations

Dependent Variable: $\ln PCI_{89-79,i}$

	Equation (4-26)		*Equation (4-27)*		*Equation (4-28)*	
	Coefficient	*t-stat*	*Coefficient*	*t-stat*	*Coefficient*	*t-stat*
Intercept	0.844	5.1	0.509	3.7	0.403	2.7
$\ln W_{i,89-79}$	0.949	27.6	0.787	25.5	0.805	24.8
$\ln PCI_{i,79}$	−0.072	−4.0	−0.031	−2.1	−0.015	−0.8
$\ln(E/P)_{i,89-79}$			0.433	12.0	0.439	12.1
$\ln E_{i,79}$					−0.004	−1.7
n	269		269		269	
Adjusted R^2	0.749		0.836		0.837	
F	401		457		346	

$\ln(E/P)_{89-79,i}$, to the equation. The decrease in the F statistic from 457 to 346 [in equations (4-27) and (4-28)] reflects the addition of a superfluous variable (lnE) with its resultant loss in degrees of freedom and little or no increase in the explanatory power of the equation.

(4) Nonlinearities in the model's functional form In addition to 'over specifiying' or 'under specifying' a model, it also is possible for the functional form of a model to be misspecified.[17] For example, assume we specify a linear model of the form

$$Y_i = \beta_o + \beta_1 X_{1i} + \varepsilon_i \tag{4-29}$$

when, in fact, the true underlying model is nonlinear, as follows:

$$Y_i = \beta_0^* + \beta_1^* X_{1i} + \beta_2^* X_{1i}^2 + \varepsilon_i^* \tag{4-30}$$

In this and similar cases, the model would be underspecified in that relevant variables (e.g., the power term of X_1) that should be included in it are omitted. Under these conditions, OLS estimators would, in general, be biased and inconsistent (see section 4.3.1 (2)).

Similarly, suppose the true model is equation (4-29) and we, by mistake, specify equation (4-30) as the true model. In this case, the true model would be overspecified and the situation would be the same as discussed in section 4.3.1 (1).

Even if the same variables are specified in both equations (i.e., the true model and the incorrectly specified model) but in different functional forms (e.g., linear vs. power function, log vs. log linear, etc.) the estimators of the incorrect model will provide incorrect results of the assumed theoretically correct model.[18]

On the other hand, if the variables in a theoretically correct model are specified in non-linear form and can be linearized, their coefficients can be estimated using OLS. In this situation, the OLS estimators are BLUE if all other OLS assumptions are satisfied. For example, assume the true model is of the form:

$$Y_i = \beta_0 + \beta_1 X_{1i} + \beta_2 X_{2i}^2 + \beta_3 \ln X_{3i} + \varepsilon_i \tag{4-31}$$

The variables can be linearly transformed and since the parameters of (4-31) are linear, OLS can be used as estimators (as follows):

$$Y_i = \beta_0 + \beta_1 X_{1i} + \beta_2 Z_{1i} + \beta_3 Z_{2i} + \varepsilon_i$$

where $Z_{1i} = X_{2i}^2$ and $Z_{2i} = \ln X_{3i}$.

(5) An example with a misspecified functional form The rank size rule[19] can be expressed as

$$G(X_i) = AX_i^{-b} \tag{4-32}$$

where $G(X_i)$ is the rank of urban area i based on population, and X_i is the population of urban area i. If $b = 1$, then $G(X_i) \times (X_i) = A$, i.e., the rank of urban area i multiplied by its population, X_i, is equal to a constant, A, which is the population of the largest urban area. To test the rank size rule, the above exponential equation (4-32) could be made linear in natural logs, i.e.,

$$\ln G(X_i) = \ln A - b \ln X_i \tag{4-33}$$

If we incorrectly specify the functional form as follows

$$G(X_i) = \gamma_0 + \gamma_1 X_i \tag{4-34}$$

and estimate that misspecified equation, we will get incorrect results. Both of these equations have been estimated for the 110 largest metropolitan areas in the United States for 1969. The results are presented in Table 4.6.[20]

Table 4-6 Misspecification of functional form

Dependent variable	Col. #1 Correctly Specified Equation (4-33) lnRANK		Col. #2 Incorrectly Specified Equation (4-34) RANK	
	Coefficient	*t-stat*	*Coefficient*	*t-stat*
Intercept	10.335	161	65.12	23
lnPOP	−1.0098	−104	−.00766	−7.0
n	110		110	
Adjusted R^2	0.990		0.303	
F	10,771		48	

Column 1 shows the estimated equation for the correct functional form. The estimated coefficient is −1.0098 with a t statistic of −104. The adjusted R^2 is .990. The extremely good fit plus the fact that the coefficient is virtually equal to −1.0 represents powerful support for the rank size rule for U.S. urban areas. Recall that the estimated value of 'A' equals the population of the largest urban area if the rank size rule holds true. The constant term of 10.335 is the log of A. So the estimated value of A is the antilog of 10.335, or 30,792; because the population variable is measured in thousands, the estimated population is 30,792,000 or about 31 million. That is about 50% larger than the 1969 population of the New York–Northeastern New Jersey metropolitan area, the largest urban area in the United States. So as is often the case, the econometric estimate of 'A' is in the ballpark but it is far from an exact correspondence with our theory.

Column 2 of Table 4-6 shows the estimated equation for the incorrect functional form. The same sample of 110 urban areas in 1969, and the same variables are used (rank and population) but they are in linear form. Note that the adjusted R^2 is only 0.303, indicating a very weak relationship. Clearly the relationship between rank and urban population in not captured by this linear equation. However, it is also interesting to note that the two t-values and the F-value for the incorrectly specified equation are statistically significant although they are much smaller than those for the correctly specified equation.

4.3.2 The expected value of the error term is not equal to zero

One of the violations of the classical linear regression assumptions introduced in section 4.2.3 is that the expected value of the error term is not zero (i.e., $E(\varepsilon_i) \neq 0$). In many, but certainly not all, econometric applications, the intercept term of a regression equation has little if any theoretical interest; it is used primarily to locate the origin of the regression equation. In most applications, the slope coefficients are the important parameters to be estimated. Nevertheless, it is important to understand the limitations imposed on the results of OLS estimation when this violation exists, especially if the model's intercept term (β_0) is presumed to be important conceptually and also because the OLS estimates of the slope coefficients, in certain cases, may not be BLUE.

In Case I of Table 4-7, we assume the original model has a non-zero intercept term (β_0) and the expected value of the error term (ε_i) is not equal to zero. Under these conditions, the OLS estimator ($\hat{\beta}_0^{OLS}$) provides biased estimates of the intercept term while the slope estimator ($\hat{\beta}_1^{OLS}$) is BLUE. Recognizing this assumption violation in the original model, it can be revised so that the intercept term now contains its original value (k_1) plus the non-zero expected value of the error term (k_2) as indicated in Table 4-7. The revised model then satisfies the (expected value of the error

Table 4-7 Summary table for expected value of the error term not equal to zero

(1) Theoretical Models	(2) OLS Assumption Violation	(3) Estimator	(4) Properties of OLS Estimator
CASE I			
Original Model			
$Y_i = \beta_0 + \beta_1 X_{1i} + \varepsilon_i$	$E(\varepsilon_i) \neq 0$	$\hat{\beta}_0^{OLS}$	Biased
where —		$\hat{\beta}_1^{OLS}$	BLUE
$\beta_0 = k_1 \neq 0$			
$E(\varepsilon_i) = k_2 \neq 0$			
Revised Model			
$Y_i = \beta_0^* + \beta_1 X_{1i} + \varepsilon_i^*$	None	$\hat{\beta}_0^{*OLS}$	BLUE
where —		$\hat{\beta}_1^{OLS}$	BLUE
$\beta_0^* = k_1 + k_2$			
$E(\varepsilon_i^*) = 0$[1]			
CASE II			
$Y_i = \beta_1 X_{1i} + \varepsilon_i$	$E(\varepsilon_i) \neq 0$	$\hat{\beta}_1^{OLS}$	Biased
(i.e., $\beta_0 = 0$)			
CASE III			
$Y_i = \beta_0 + \beta_1 X_{1i} + \varepsilon_i$	$E(\varepsilon_i) \neq 0$	$\hat{\beta}_0^{OLS}$	Biased
where		$\hat{\beta}_1^{OLS}$	Biased
Y_i values are restricted			

[1]On the other hand, if $E(\varepsilon_i) = k_{2i}$ (i.e., the constant term k_{2i} is not the same for all i but may change as i changes), the estimator $\hat{\beta}_j^{OLS}$ provides biased and inconsistent results.

term equals zero) assumption of the classical linear regression model and the OLS estimators of the coefficients are BLUE.

There are special cases, however, where the above generalizations do not hold. For example, in the case where theory suggests that the intercept term should be equal to zero, OLS estimates of a model without an intercept term will provide biased estimates of the slope coefficients (see Case II in Table 4-7).

Also, in models with limited dependent variables, (i.e., variables for which the range of values is constricted), the OLS estimates of all the coefficients are biased (see Case III in Table 4-7).

4.3.3 The variance of the error term is not constant

One of the conditions for the OLS estimator to be BLUE is that the variance of the error term is a fixed constant across all the observations in the data set being analyzed, i.e.,

$$E(\varepsilon_i^2) = \sigma^2 \tag{4-35}$$

If this condition holds, the data set is said to be *homoskedastic* (see Figure 4.7a), and the use of OLS is appropriate. On the other hand, if this is not the case and the variance changes with i,

$$E(\varepsilon_i^2) = \sigma_i^2 \tag{4-36}$$

the data set is said to be *heteroskedastic* (Figure 4.7b) and other estimating procedures are necessary.

Heteroskedasticity may arise under various conditions. At the regional level, for example, a time series analysis of an urban government's expenditures for services may show increasing variation as the urban government grows in size just as personal consumption expenditures of an initially poor region is anticipated to have greater variation once its population becomes affluent. Also, in a time series equation in which the dependent variable is the price of some raw material, there may be prolonged periods of volatility unrelated to the structure of the model. In such a case, the residuals for the sub-period of volatility would tend to be much larger in absolute terms and so the variance of the error term would be larger for that sub-period.

A similar situation may arise, for example, when dealing with cross-sectional data for analysis of the demand for health services at the regional level. There may be greater variation in demand for larger regions than for smaller ones. For another example, consider a cross-section equation in

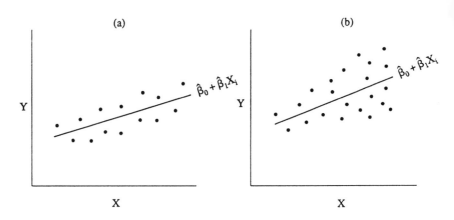

Figure 4.7   Illustrations of (a) homoskedasticity and (b) heteroskedasticity

which the dependent variable is a discretionary consumption item such as vacation expenditures. If the observations are individual households over a wide range of incomes, the residuals would tend to be small at the low end of the income range but very large at the high end of the income range. Thus the variance of the error term would not be constant, and heteroskedasticity would exist in the data set.

In the absence of prior information about the variance of the error term, there is no alternative except to test the data for constant variance. If the data set is homoskedastic and other OLS assumptions hold, OLS estimators of the coefficients are BLUE. On the other hand, if heteroskedasticity is present, the OLS estimators of the coefficients, although still unbiased, are no longer efficient; the variance of the OLS estimator is biased upward (see the top row of columns (3) and (4) in Table 4-8).

When this is the case, the use of a 'weighted least squares' estimator ($\hat{\beta}_j^{WLS}$) instead of OLS provides coefficient estimates with desirable statistical properties (i.e., unbiased and efficient) when the weights (i.e., σ_i) are known. See the second row of columns (3) and (4) in Table 4-8 for the case when σ_i^2 is known. Essentially, the method of weighted least squares compensates for the different values of the variance of the error term by weighting the influence of the variables by the inverse of their standard deviations. Thus, observations with larger variances receive less weight than observations with smaller variances in computing the total sum of squares.

Table 4-8 Summary table for heteroskedasticity

(1) Theoretical Model	(2) Assumption Violation	(3) Estimators	(4) Properties of Estimators	(5) Some Tests for Presence of Heteroskedasticity
$Y_i = \beta_0 + \beta_1 X_i + \varepsilon_i$ for $i = 1, 2, ..., n$	$E(\varepsilon_i^2) \neq \sigma^2$ (i.e., $E(\varepsilon_i^2) = \sigma_i^2$)	$\hat{\beta}_j^{OLS}$	Unbiased, consistent, inefficient.	(1) Observation
		$var(\hat{\beta}_j^{OLS})$	Biased	(2) White test
		If σ_i^2 is known: (unlikely in practice) $\hat{\beta}_j^{WLS}$	BLUE	(3) Goldfeld-Quandt test
		If σ_i^2 is unknown: (more likely in practice) Use White's heteroskedastic-consistent estimators procedure.		(4) Breusch-Pagan-Godfrey test
		$\hat{\beta}_j^{White}$	Unbiased	
		$var(\hat{\beta}_j^{White})$	Consistent	

The third row of columns (3) and (4) deal with heteroskedasticity when σ_i^2 is unknown, the situation more likely to arise in empirical work. Recall that under heteroskedasticity OLS provides unbiased estimates of the regression coefficients and biased estimates of their variances. However, consistent estimates of the variances can be obtained using White's procedure (see the third row of column 3) for heteroskedasticity. Thus, it is possible to obtain both unbiased estimates of the coefficients and consistent estimates of their variances.

White's approach can be used if there is no information available about the nature of the heteroskedasticity. On the other hand, if some information is available, it may be possible to transform the original model and data to a form in which heteroskedasticity may not exist (e.g., a log transformation). However, this approach usually implies that there is some information available about the nature of the heteroskedasticity which may not be likely in practice.

Column (5) in Table 4-8 identifies some procedures that are available for testing for the presence of heteroskedasticity. A somewhat obvious and intuitive way to check for the presence of heteroskedasticity is to examine a plot of the residuals (or their squares) after the model has been estimated using OLS. Variations on this observational approach (e.g., the Park test and the Glejer test) are also available. Other more reliable procedures for testing for the presence of heteroskedasticity are also available. Among these are the White test, the Goldfield-Quandt test, and the Breusch-Pagan-Godfrey test. Each of these methods provide a formal statistical test regarding the presence or absence of heteroskedasticity. Advantages, disadvantages, and procedures for these tests are discussed in most econometric texts.

(1) An example of heteroskedasticity One time-series equation in Drennan (1994) specifies that New York City's output of non-traded goods and services in the private sector (PX) is a function of city population lagged one year (POP_{t-1}), the U.S. unemployment rate ($UNEMPR_t$), and city output of traded goods and services two years earlier (CX_{t-2}).

$$PX_t = \beta_0 + \beta_1 POP_{t-1} + \beta_2 UNEMPR_t + \beta_3 CX_{t-2} + \varepsilon_t$$

That equation, estimated over the period 1961 to 1995, is shown in the first column of Table 4-9. Although the U.S. unemployment rate variable, UNEMPR, in that equation has the expected negative sign, the t statistic indicates that the regression coefficient is not significant at the .05 or the .10 level. That may be the result of heteroskedasticity. (Recall that OLS estimates of the variances are biased if the assumption of homoskedasticity is violated.)

Table 4-9 Heteroskedasticity equations

Dependent Variable: PX_t

	Before Correction		After Correction	
	Coefficient	t-stat	Coefficient	t-stat
Intercept	−17,925.	−2.7	−17,925.	−3.4
POP_{t-1}	4.288	6.3	4.288	8.1
$UNEMPR_t$	−161.	−1.4	−161.	−1.9
CX_{t-2}	0.061	4.0	0.061	3.9
n	35		35	
Adjusted R^2	0.760		0.760	
F	36.9		36.9	

To obtain better estimates of the variances, White's heteroskedastic-consistent procedure was applied. The corrected results are shown in the second column of Table 4-9. Note that the constant term and the three coefficients in the corrected equation are identical to those in the equation before correction since the estimates of the coefficients are unbiased. White's procedure provides consistent estimates of the standard errors. Three of the four standard errors are markedly lower after correction. As a result, the t statistics are markedly higher. In fact, the t statistic on UNEMPR moves from −1.4 in the equation before correction to −1.9 in the equation after correction. So the significance level of that variable improves, from 0.16 to 0.06. Thus the UNEMPR coefficient which was insignificant at the 0.10 level becomes significant at the 0.10 level in the equation after correction. The fact that the White procedure led to some reductions in standard errors argues that the equation before correction suffered from heteroskedasticity.[21]

4.3.4 Correlated error terms

Serial correlation or autocorrelation occurs when the error terms, ε_i, in a regression model are correlated with each other. That violates the OLS assumption that the

$$cov(\varepsilon_i \varepsilon_j) = 0 \quad \text{for } i \neq j. \tag{4-37}$$

Serial correlation can occur in time series models, and also in spatial econometric models where cross-sectional data may indicate serial correlation between adjacent regions. We discuss the first case in this section and leave the second case to section 4.5 on spatial econometrics.

In theory, we could be concerned with the presence of serial correlation for any non-equal values of i and j in equation (4-37). In practice, however, we are concerned primarily with the case where j lags i by only one or two units or, more usually, one or two time periods. This is often called first order or second order correlation. If serial correlation is present, we would expect to find that sequential values of the error terms, i and j, are related to each other in a positive or negative fashion as shown in Figure 4.8. Most economic data would likely generate positive rather than negative serial correlation.

Serial correlation may arise for a number of reasons. Economic data frequently exhibit serial correlation because the activities that the numbers represent often do not change by large amounts. For example, there is usually a consistency over time in the behavior of economic data such as payrolls, interest rates, prices, rents, income, sales, costs, etc.

Also, serial correlation may arise due to a model being misspecified. Recall that the error term in a regression equation is assumed to represent a random process. If a model is misspecified and an explanatory variable is, by mistake, not included in the model, the values of that variable will appear in the error term and may dominate its randomness thereby giving rise to serial correlation.

It is generally assumed that first-order correlated error terms in a regression model are generated by the following first-order autoregressive process (designated AR(1)):

$$\varepsilon_t = \rho \varepsilon_{t-1} + u_t \qquad\qquad (4\text{-}38)$$

where $-1 < \rho < 1$, and the usual assumptions of OLS apply (i.e., $E(u_t) = 0$, $\text{var}(u_t) = \sigma^2$, and $\text{cov}(u_t, u_{t+h}) = 0$ for $h \neq 0$). Rho (ρ), the slope coefficient of the error term (ε_t) on its immediate predecessor (ε_{t-1}), is sometimes called the first-order serial correlation coefficient or, alternatively, the coefficient of autocorrelation lag one, or the coefficient of autocovariance.

The second order autoregressive process (AR(2)) can be written as

$$\varepsilon_t = \rho_1 \varepsilon_{t-1} + \rho_2 \varepsilon_{t-2} + u_t \qquad\qquad (4\text{-}39)$$

In this case, error terms from $t-1$ and $t-2$ are assumed to impact the error term in t. Information about the rhos is important in order to obtain

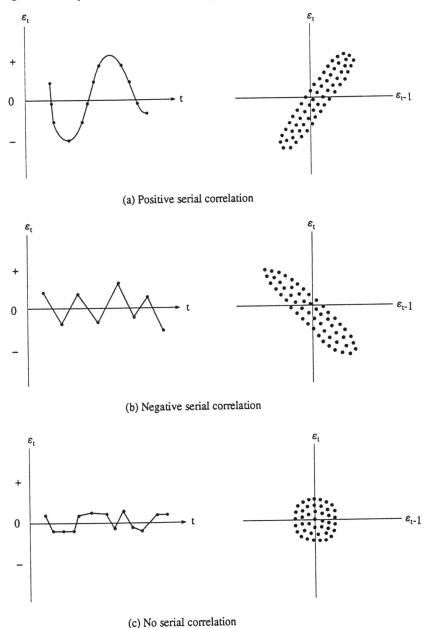

(a) Positive serial correlation

(b) Negative serial correlation

(c) No serial correlation

Figure 4.8 Examples of the presence and absence of serial correlation

estimators that have desirable properties (for example, see column 6 of Table 4-10).

Table 4-10 contains a summary of various conditions that exist when serial correlation is present in a regression model. The simplified bivariate theoretical model for time series data is presented in column (1) while the assumption violation under consideration is presented in column (2). The upper part of columns (3) and (4) indicate that the OLS estimator of the coefficients are, in the case of serial correlation, unbiased but are no longer minimum variance. On the other hand, OLS estimates of the variances are biased, usually downward. The use of generalized least squares provides estimates of the coefficients that are BLUE (see the lower part of columns (3) and (4)).

As noted in column (5), the presence of serial correlation may sometimes be determined by examining a plot of the residuals from a fitted regression model (see the example of a model with serial correlation which follows in subsection (1) below). More formal tests for the presence of serial correlation are also noted in column (5) of Table 4-10. The Durbin-Watson 'd' test is probably the most popular formal test and many econometric computer packages automatically provide values of the Durbin-Watson (DW) 'd' statistic in the standard output of their regression analysis.[22] Interpretation of the DW 'd' statistic can be understood most easily by reference to the following continuum:

(A)	(B)	(C)	(D)	(E)
Positive serial correlation present (+)	No decision possible(?)	No serial correlation present (None)	No decision possible(?)	Negative serial correlation present (−)

0	d_L	d_U	2	4−d_U	4−d_L	4

where the values for d-lower (d_L) and d-upper (d_U) are obtained from tables originally developed by Durbin and Watson (1951). The given values of d_L and d_U are dependent on the desired statistical level of significance (e.g., 0.01 or 0.05), the number of observations, and the number of explanatory variables in the model. For example, if the calculated DW 'd' statistic falls in the range between 0 and d_L [see (A) above], then positive serial correlation is present. If the calculated DW 'd' statistic falls between d_L and d_U [see (B) above], no decision is possible regarding the presence or absence of serial correlation. In a similar manner, boundaries are indicated for the decisions noted in categories (C), (D), and (E). An illustration of

Table 4-10 Summary table for serial correlation

(1) Theoretical Model	(2) Assumption Violation	(3) Estimator	(4) Properties of OLS Estimator	(5) Tests for Presence of Serial Correlation	(6) Corrections for Serial Correlation
$Y_t = \beta_0 + \beta_1 X_{1t} + \varepsilon_t$	$cov(\varepsilon_t \varepsilon_{t-1}) \neq 0$	$\hat{\beta}_J^{OLS}$ $var(\hat{\beta}_1^{OLS})$	Unbiased, consistent, inefficient. Biased	*Observational test:* 1) Graphical *Formal tests:* 1) Durbin-Watson 'd' test 2) Large-sample test 3) Breusch-Godfrey test 4) Geary test	*When ρ is known:* 1) Use OLS with transformed variables (i.e., GLS) which is also equivalent to MLE *When ρ is unknown:* 1) Cochrane-Orcutt procedure 2) Durbin's Two-stage procedure 3) Hildreth-Lu procedure
		$\hat{\beta}_1^{GLS}$ $var(\hat{\beta}^{GLS})$	BLUE Unbiased		

how the DW 'd' statistic is used in practice is given in the example of a model with serial correlation [see subsection (1) below].

The DW 'd' statistic provides a formal test of the null hypothesis that no positive or negative serial correlation is present in a regression model, i.e, $\rho = 0$. As noted in column (5) of Table 4-10 an alternative test of the same null hypothesis is available using a large sample test [test number 2 in column (5)]. These two tests deal with first order serial correlation. The Breusch-Godfrey test, on the other hand, provides a test of the null hypothesis that there is no serial correlation of first, second, or greater order. The Geary test is a non-parametric runs test (i.e., there is no assumption made about the shape of the underlying distribution) on the signs (plus or minus) of the residuals of an estimated regression model.

Column (6) of Table 4-10 deals with the question of what to do if serial correlation is present in a regression model. If the value of rho (ρ) is known, GLS (in which the variables are transformed using ρ) can be used to obtain BLUE estimates of the coefficients. On the other hand, if the value of ρ is not known, it is usually possible to use a two step procedure in which ρ is estimated first and then used in an estimated generalized least squares (EGLS) procedure to estimate the parameters of the model. Column (6) lists three such procedures — others are also available.

(1) Example of a model with serial correlation In Drennan's (1994) econometric model of the New York City economy, there are three traded goods and services sectors. The sum of those traded goods and services sectors' outputs is an explanatory variable, lagged two years, in the equation which determines output in the non-traded goods and services sector or local sector. That estimated equation is shown above in Table 4-9 (the example about heteroskedasticity). It is repeated below in Table 4-11 to illustrate serial correlation. Note that the Durbin-Watson statistic (DW) is 0.516. With 35 observations ($n = 35$), a 0.05 level of significance and three independent variables ($k = 3$), we use the Durbin-Watson table to find the lower limit, $d_L = 1.283$, and the upper limit, $d_U = 1.653$, in order to perform the test for serial correlation. Recall, that the outcome for this two-tailed test of the null hypothesis that there is no serial correlation depends upon where the calculated DW 'd' statistic falls on the continuum:

(+)	?	None	?	(−)
0 ↑ d_L	d_U	$4-d_U$	$4-d_L$	4
DW 'd'				
0.516 1.283	1.653	2.347	2.717	

Table 4-11 Serial correlation equations

Dependent Variable: PX_t

	Before Correction		*After Correction*	
	Coefficient	t-statistic	*Coefficient*	t-statistic
Intercept	−17,925.	−2.7	−14,331.	−1.7
POP_{t-1}	4.29	6.3	4.02	4.3
$UNEMPR_t$	−161.	−1.4	−212.	−2.2
CX_{t-2}	0.061	4.0	0.048	1.8
AR(1)			0.916	4.7
AR(2)			−0.199	−1.1
n	35		33	
Adjusted R^2	0.760		0.902	
F	36.9		60.2	
Durbin-Watson	0.516		1.918	

Our calculated DW 'd' of 0.516 falls in the positive autocorrelation range, indicating that the residuals are positively correlated with each other.

The residuals of that equation are plotted in Figure 4.9. The visual pattern of correlated or non-random residuals is quite striking. Clearly that equation should not be used for forecasting or analysis because positive serial correlation is present in the data set.

To correct for serial correlation, the Cochrane-Orcutt procedure was employed. A first order autoregressive scheme, i.e.,

$$\varepsilon_t = \rho_1 \varepsilon_{t-1} + u_t$$

was not sufficient for removing the positive autocorrelation, and so a second order autoregressive scheme, i.e.,

$$\varepsilon_t = \rho_1 \varepsilon_{t-1} + \rho_2 \varepsilon_{t-2} + u_t$$

was used. The second column of Table 4-11 is the corrected equation. Note that the DW 'd' statistic is 1.92, which is in the 'no serial correlation' range, and is close to the ideal DW 'd' value of 2.0. The residuals of the corrected equation are shown in Figure 4.10; they now appear to be more random.

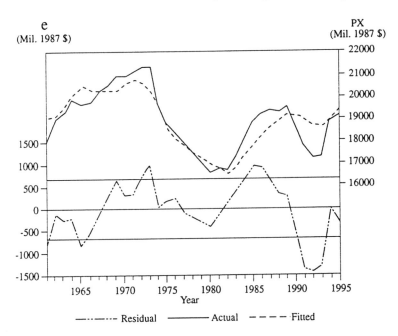

Figure 4.9   City product, local goods and services (PX) actual, fitted, and residual, 1961–1995 before correction

4.3.5 Stochastic explanatory variables, multicollinearity, and measurement errors

One of the assumptions of OLS is that the explanatory variables, X_j, in a regression equation are fixed in repeated samples, that is, they are non-stochastic. While this assumption may not be unreasonable in the laboratory sciences (e.g., physics, biology, etc.), it is usually not very realistic when dealing with data from economics (and the social sciences more generally) where data are generally assumed to be affected by random, stochastic processes or shocks (e.g., the unemployment rate, corporate profits, regional income, etc.). This more realistic assumption about the data available for econometric research in regional analysis may give rise to two somewhat related problems or assumptions: multicollinearity[23] and errors of measurement in the variables. The implications of these three conditions are discussed in this section.

(1) Stochastic explanatory variables independent of the error term The assumption of fixed (non-stochastic) explanatory variables arises from the

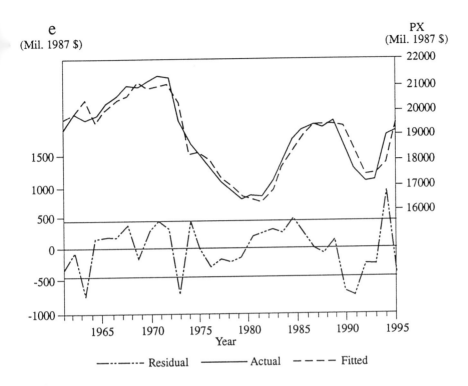

Figure 4.10 City product, local goods and services (PX) actual, fitted, and residual, 1962–1995 after correction

way the equation defining the OLS estimator of the slope coefficients of the classical linear of a regression model are derived. For illustrative purposes, consider the simple regression model (equation (4-6) rewritten) where the estimator $\hat{\beta}^{OLS}$ of β is defined as

$$\hat{\beta}^{OLS} = \Sigma x_i y_i / \Sigma x_i^2 \qquad (4\text{-}40)$$

where $x_i = (X_i - \bar{X})$ and $y_i = (Y_i - \bar{Y})$. If we assume the Xs are fixed, $\hat{\beta}^{OLS}$ is a linear combination of the Ys. Then, along with its other characteristics of unbiasedness and minimum variance, the OLS estimator, $\hat{\beta}^{OLS}$, is BLUE. Equation (4-40) is also the maximum likelihood (ML) estimator ($\hat{\beta}^{MLE}$) of β.[24]

The inconsistency between this assumption of OLS (i.e., non-stochastic independent variables) and the reality of social science data (i.e., stochastic variables) is usually resolved in practice by changing the nature of the assumption. Although the data are recognized generally as being stochastic, for the particular problem and data set at hand, it is assumed that the values of the independent variables are given. In effect, the estimated regression results are conditional on the data used for the analysis.

Regardless of whether the explanatory variables are considered to be fixed or stochastic, it is very important that they be independent of the error term (i.e., $cov(X_i \varepsilon_i) = 0$). If not, the OLS (and ML) estimators of β are biased. This issue is discussed further in section 4.4.4 on simultaneous equation systems.

(2) Multicollinearity Multicollinearity exists in a regression model when two or more explanatory variables (X_h, X_j) in that model with k explanatory variables are correlated with each other, i.e.,

$$cov(X_h, X_j) \neq 0 \qquad \text{for } h, j = 1, 2,...,k; \text{ and } h \neq j \qquad (4\text{-}41)$$

When this occurs,[25] the estimators of the coefficients are still unbiased but have increased variance. This can be seen easily by examining the estimator $var(\hat{\beta}^{OLS})$ for the two regressor model (i.e., $Y = \beta_0 + \beta_1 X_{1i} + \beta_2 X_{2i} + \varepsilon_i$):

$$var(\hat{\beta}_1^{OLS}) = \sigma^2 / [\Sigma x_{1i}(1 - r_{12}^2)]$$

$$var(\hat{\beta}_2^{OLS}) = \sigma^2 / [\Sigma x_{2i}(1 - r_{12}^2)] \qquad (4\text{-}42)$$

where the sample correlation coefficient, r_{12} (where $-1 \leq r_{12} \leq +1$) is a measure of the strength of the statistical relationship between X_1 and X_2.[26] If $r_{12}^2 = 0$, the $var(\hat{\beta}_j^{OLS})$ will be at a minimum. As r_{12}^2 increases (i.e., as the multicollinearity between X_1 and X_2 increases), the estimators $var(\hat{\beta}_1^{OLS})$ and $var(\hat{\beta}_2^{OLS})$ will therefore increase. Thus, the penalty associated with multicollinearity is that there is increased probability of not rejecting the two null hypotheses (i.e., $\beta_1 = 0$, $\beta_2 = 0$) when they are not true.

Unfortunately, there is no easy 'fix' for this problem as there is in the case of some other assumption violations. One might consider doing nothing about multicollinearity, in particular if the model is to be used primarily for forecasting purposes since the coefficient estimators are unbiased. Also, if the estimated 't' statistics are all large enough that the null hypothesis (i.e., $\beta_j = 0$) can be rejected, there may be no need to do anything about multicollinearity. A common approach to the problem sometimes is to drop one or more of the collinear variables but that may give rise to problems of misspecification. Another approach might be to combine the two or more highly correlated variables into some 'rational' index that is representative of the concepts or factors embodied by the collinear explanatory variables.

(3) Measurement errors Given the nature of economic and social data, it is easy to see that errors may occur in the measurement of the dependent variable, Y, and in the measurement of the independent variables, X_j. We consider each case separately.

Measurement errors in Y give rise to estimators of the coefficients that are unbiased. Although the estimators of their variances are also unbiased, they are no longer efficient when compared to estimators when the dependent variable is measured without errors.

Estimation problems are more serious when there are measurement errors in the independent explanatory variables. In this case, the OLS estimators are both biased and inconsistent. A possible solution to this problem is to try to find another variable (called an instrumental variable) that is error free, is highly correlated with the variable with measurement errors and is uncorrelated with the error term in the model (see sub-section (1) above). This may not be easy to do in empirical work.

4.4 Other relevant econometric models

This section provides brief introductions to four important extensions of the regression models discussed in the previous sections: (1) the use of dummy variables; (2) discrete choice models; (3) pooled time series and cross section models; and (4) simultaneous equations models. Although these are general purpose extensions with wide application, they are particularly relevant for regional analysis because they provide a means of incorporating some regional and/or spatial components of economic phenomena into econometric models.

4.4.1 The use of dummy variables

One implicit assumption in our explanation of the linear regression model has been that the independent variables are measured on a continuous scale. But, in fact, we may extend a model to include on the right-hand side of the equation nominal variables, i.e., variables that have no real number measure but rather represent categories such as region, state, city, nation, gender, political party, etc. Such categorical variables are called dummy variables and take on only one of two values, 0 or 1, in a regression equation. In this way, the applicability of regression models is extended.

In representing a nominal variable, the number of dummy variables required is one less than the number of categories which defines the

184 Methods of Interregional and Regional Analysis

nominal variable. These categories must be mutually exclusive and exhaustive. For example, if we define the variable 'region' as the eight Census regions of the United States, then we need to explicitly state seven dummy variables to represent the eight regions. For another example, the variable 'gender' has two categories, male and female, so we would need one dummy variable to represent gender in a regression equation.

To illustrate, let X be gender in a regression model where the observations are individuals. Define X_i as $= 1$ if the i'th person is female, otherwise $X_i = 0$. So the variable X_i has only two values, one and zero. It is arbitrary which one of the two categories is excluded, i.e., has a value of zero. In this example it is the category male. In estimating regression equations with dummy variables, it is crucial to have one excluded category. Otherwise the extra dummy variable is an exact linear transformation of the other dummy variables, leading to insoluble OLS equations.[27] The impact on the dependent variable of the dummy variable when its value is one is given by the estimated coefficient of the dummy variable. The impact when the dummy variable equals zero is absorbed into the intercept term of the estimated regression equation.

Aside from representing nominal variables, another use of dummy variables is for representing sub-periods in time series equations such as years of war time and peace-time, or years of regulation and deregulation. Also dummy variables can be used to test for the presence of seasonal patterns in time series equations in which the observations are quarters or months. The example below employs a dummy variable to represent a particular geographic region of the United States.

(1) Example using dummy variables Beginning in the late 1980s, there has been a revived interest in analyzing differences in economic growth rates across regions, states, nations, and even cities. That literature recognizes that growth, or decline, can be stimulated by temporal 'shocks.' One such shock was the sharp rise in oil and other energy prices in the decade of the 1970s. Equation (4-43) tests the hypothesis that economic growth among U.S. metropolitan areas in the decade of the 1970s was stronger in those areas located in the major energy producing states of Texas, Oklahoma, and Louisianna. The test depends on the use of a dummy variable, OIL. If a metropolitan area in the sample is located in one of those three states, then OIL is set equal to one. Otherwise, OIL is set equal to zero. If the regression coefficient on OIL is positive and statistically significant, then the hypothesis that location in the energy producing region added something to economic growth in the 1970s is supported.

Equation (4-43) is in log difference form. The dependent variable measures the growth of per capita personal income from 1969 to 1979 for all metropolitan areas in the U.S. with populations in 1969 of 250,000 or more ($n = 111$). The first independent variable, $\ln\Delta POP_i$, measures the growth or decline in utilization of labor over the decade in each metropolitan area. The second independent variable, $\ln\Delta ED_i$, measures the growth or decline in the level of human capital, represented by the share of the adult population with 16 or more years of education. The last independent variable is the dummy variable, OIL. The estimated equation is:

$$\ln\Delta PCI_i = 0.727 + 0.718\ln\Delta POP_i + 0.138\ln\Delta ED_i + 0.063 OIL_i \quad (4\text{-}43)$$
$$(24.1) \quad (8.2) \qquad\qquad (2.2) \qquad\qquad (4.2)$$

for which $n = 111$, the adjusted R^2 is 0.476 and the F statistic is 34.3, the t-statistics are in parentheses, and where

$\ln\Delta PCI_i$ = ln(per capita personal income, 1979) minus ln(per capita personal income, 1969) in metropolitan area i;

$\ln\Delta POP_i$ = ln((employment, 1979/population, 1979) × 100) minus ln((employment, 1969/population, 1969) × 100) in metropolitan area i;

$\ln\Delta ED_i$ = ln(% population with 16+ years education, 1980) minus ln(% population with 16+ years education, 1970) in metropolitan area i;

OIL_i = 1 if metropolitan area i is in Texas, Oklahoma, or Louisiana; 0 if not.

Note that the coefficient on the dummy variable, OIL, is positive and highly significant, with a t statistic of 4.2. Thus the results support the hypothesis that metropolitan areas in the energy producing region had stronger growth in the 1970s, *ceteris paribus*. But the addition to growth is not dramatic. The coefficient is +0.063, which is the amount added to the dependent variable when OIL = 1. That is about the same size as the standard deviation of the dependent variable, 0.0684. So the addition to growth may not be dramatic, but neither is it trivial.

4.4.2 Discrete choice models

In the previous section, we considered regression models in which one or more independent variables are of a discrete or qualitative nature (i.e., dummy variables with values 0 or 1) rather than variables with measurements on a continuous scale. In this section, we consider the use of these [0,1] values to characterize dependent rather than independent variables. As we shall see, this leads to the formulation of a model quite different than that discussed in the previous section.

Dichotomous [0,1] dependent variables are interpreted the same way as dichotomous independent variables in that they identify one of two possible states in which a sample element can exist. For example, an individual may choose to drive a car to work or take public transportation, an individual may choose to rent or buy a house, or perhaps to attend college A rather than college B, or to marry or stay single, or choose either one of two possible options in many other binary decision situations.

The right hand side independent variables in such models of discrete choice are, conceptually, no different than they are in more traditional regression models with dependent continuous random variables. As we shall see, the output from an estimated discrete choice model will be the probability that an individual with a given set of characteristics (as represented by the independent variables) will be in one or the other qualitative states under study. An example of such output would be the probability that a household head would either own or rent a home in a particular section of a city (the dependent variable) given different levels of income, wealth, education, age, gender, race, and number of children (the independent variables).

A popular way to represent the above phenomena in an econometric framework is to use the logit model which is based on the cumulative probability distribution of the logistic function.[28] This function is used to define the probability (P_i) that individual i will select one of two alternatives given particular values of X_j, as follows:

$$P_i = \frac{1}{1 + e^{-Z_i}} = \frac{1}{1 + (1/e^{Z_i})} \qquad (4\text{-}44)$$

where $Z_i = \beta_0 + \beta_1 X_{1i} + ... + \beta_k X_{ki} + \varepsilon_i$. (Note that as $Z_i \rightarrow -\infty$, then $P_i \rightarrow 0$; if $Z_i = 0$, then $P_i = 0.5$; and as $Z_i \rightarrow +\infty$, then $P_i \rightarrow 1.0$.)

By forming the 'odds ratio' of an event occurring (i.e., the ratio of the probability that event i will occur, P_i, to the probability that it won't occur, $1 - P_i$), it is possible to rewrite the above equation as:

$$\ln\left(\frac{P_i}{1 - P_i}\right) = \beta_0 + \beta_1 X_{1i} + ... + \beta_k X_{ki} + \varepsilon_i. \qquad (4\text{-}45)$$

The left hand side of the regression equation is the natural logarithm of the odds ratio that event i will occur.

If we have data on individuals only and cannot group the data in a meaningful way, maximum likelihood methods may be used to obtain estimates of the coefficients of the logit model (4.45). On the other hand, if the data can be grouped together so that we can obtain estimates of P_i for each group of individuals with the same (or similar) characteristics, weighted least squares may be used to obtain coefficient estimates.

Although the above discussion is limited to cases in which there are only binary outcomes, the use of more sophisticated discrete choice models can be applied to more complicated cases in which there are more than two possible outcomes of a decision. For example, there may be more than two choices available (e.g., drive alone, or ride in a car pool, a bus, or a train) when modeling travel demand. Or there may be more than two alternatives available when using discrete choice models to analyze land use in a city (e.g., whether a land parcel is used for apartments, retail shops, offices, or light manufacturing). Thus, there are a broad range of applications of discrete choice models that are of potential interest in regional analysis.

4.4.3 Pooled time-series and cross-section models

Sometimes one has cross-section or panel data for n individual units (e.g., households, firms, cities, regions, nations) and also has data for the same variables for T time periods for each of these individual units. If there are enough observations (i.e., individual units in the cross-section data set), we can estimate a single cross-section model of the following form:

$$Y_i = \beta_0 + \beta_1 X_{1i} + \beta_2 X_{2i} + ... + \beta_k X_{ki} + \varepsilon_i \qquad (4-46)$$

where the Y, βs, and Xs are as defined earlier and the subscript $i=1,2,..., n$ represents the individual units in the panel. Thus, we could estimate T different cross-section models (one for each time period), each with sample size n. In this case, the intercept term (β_0) and the slope coefficients ($\beta_1,...,\beta_k$) would be expected to be statistically the same (or different) across time periods, t, depending on the theory underlying the specification of the basic model.

In addition, if there are enough observations (i.e., time periods) we could estimate a time series model of the following form for each of the n individual units in the panel:

$$Y_t = \beta_0 + \beta_1 X_{1t} + \beta_2 X_{2t} + ... + \beta_k X_{kt} + \varepsilon_t \qquad (4-47)$$

where t represents the time periods $1,2,...,T$. In this case, there would be n equations, each with T observations. In this case also, the intercept term

(β_0) and the slope coefficients ($\beta_1,...,\beta_k$) would be expected to be statistically the same (or different) across panel members, again depending on the theory underlying the specification of the basic model.

If neither n or T is large, there may be problems in estimating the coefficients of the cross-section model and/or the time series model because of an insufficient number of degrees of freedom. In this case, and also more generally, it may be desirable to combine (or pool) the cross-section data and the time series data into one common data set and one model, as follows:

$$Y_{it} = \beta_0 + \beta_1 X_{1it} + \beta_2 X_{2it} +...+ \beta_k X_{kit} + \varepsilon_{it}$$
$$\text{for } i = 1, 2,..., n; \quad t = 1,2,...,T \tag{4-48}$$

with nT observations. In this case, we could obtain coefficient estimates that are more reliable and precise then either the cross-section or time-series models by themselves. For instance, if we were interested in estimating even a small model for the six New England states and we had ten years worth of annual data, we would not have much confidence in the estimates of the coefficients for either a cross-section model or for a time-series one; the number of both cross-section observations (6) and of time series observations (10) would be too small. If we pooled the data, we would have 60 observations which would provide much greater statistically reliable coefficient estimates. Of course, this model with such a pooled data set assumes a common set of coefficients (β_j for $j = 0, 1, 2,..., k$) across the states and over time.

In each of the above three cases, if we are willing to accept the standard assumptions that justify the use of OLS estimation (see section 4.2.3), we would obtain estimates of the coefficients that are BLUE. Recall that the OLS assumptions require that the disturbance term is independent, identically distributed with expected value equal to zero and with a constant variance. Using the pooled data set with equation (4-48) and OLS estimation, we must also assume that all the items in the panel for each of the time periods have a single common intercept term and common slope coefficients. That may be a very restrictive assumption and, as a result, we may not be willing to accept this model as being credible for the data set being analyzed.

The case in which the intercept term is not assumed to be common for all cross-section items nor for all time periods may be dealt with by adding dummy variables to (4-48) in the following manner:

$$Y_{it} = \beta_0 + \beta_1 X_{1it} +...+ \beta_k X_{kit} + \gamma_2 P_{2t} + \gamma_3 P_{3t} +...+ \gamma_n P_{nt}$$
$$+ \delta_2 S_{i2} + \delta_3 S_{i3} +...+ \delta_T S_{iT} + \varepsilon_{it} \tag{4-49}$$

where

P_{it} = 1 for the *i*-th item in the panel, $i = 2, 3,..., n$;
      0 otherwise;
S_{it} = 1 for the *t*-th period in the time series, $t = 2, 3,..., T$;
      0 otherwise.

This dummy variable model is sometimes called the covariance model. In addition to the k explanatory variables in (4-49), we now have $(n - 1)$ dummy variables (P_i) representing the individual panel members and $(T - 1)$ dummy variables (S_t) representing the time periods.[29] For each panel member, *i*, and time period, *t*, the value of the intercept term will be given by the coefficient of the respective dummy variable relative to the intercept term, β_0. That is, the estimated intercept term will include the values of the intercept term and the estimated values of the coefficients associated with the dummy variables P_{It} and S_{il} not included in (4-49). If the assumptions about the disturbance term, ε_{it}, in (4-49) satisfy the standard OLS specifications and *n* is not large relative to *T*, the use of OLS provides unbiased and consistent (but not efficient) estimates. When *T* is large, the OLS estimates are also efficient. A potential problem in this approach is a possible significant loss in degrees of freedom. For equation (4-49), there would be $nT - (k + 1) - (n - 1) - (T - 1)$ degrees of freedom involved. Consider the example noted above of a small model (say with *k = 4* explanatory variables) for the six New England states over a ten-year period. In this case the number of degrees of freedom available for statistical analysis would decrease from 55 (i.e., 60 − 5) with equation (4-48) to 41 (i.e., 60 − 5 − 5 − 9) with equation (4-49). The model's statistical power will likely be reduced by the decrease in the degrees of freedom.

When using panel or longitudinal data in which *n* is very large relative to *T*, the estimation problems become more complex and the discussion here provides only a very brief introduction to this topic [see, for example, Baltagi (1995), Hsiao (1986), Johnston and DiNardo (1997), and Judge et al. (1988)]. In this case, OLS estimates are no longer efficient (even asymptotically). An error components model with GLS, then, is often used as the basis for analyzing such a pooled data set. With this approach, the error term, ε_{it}, of equation (4-48) may be assumed to be composed of three separate components: a cross section error component (μ_i), a time series error component (v_t) and a combination error component (w_{it}), as follows:

$$\varepsilon_{it}, = \mu_i + v_t + w_{it} \tag{4-50}$$

The error components model assumes that the intercept terms, while basically random variables, are represented by their respective unknown mean intercept values ($\bar{\beta}$) and the individual specific error term (μ_i):

$$\beta_{0i} = \bar{\beta}_0 + \mu_i \tag{4-51}$$

(A similar interpretation can be applied to the time series component when appropriate.)

The variance of the overall error term, $\text{var}(\varepsilon_{it})$, is equal to the sum of the individual variances of the three error components,

$$\text{var}(\varepsilon_{it}) = \text{var}(\mu_i) + \text{var}(v_t) + \text{var}(w_{it}) \tag{4-52}$$

Generalized least squares estimators of the error components model are unbiased and consistent.

For the case when we are interested in measuring differences across individuals by estimates of their intercept terms, the structure of the error term would be

$$\varepsilon_{it} = \mu_i + w_{it} \tag{4-53}$$

in which the combination error component, w_{it}, is assumed to be independent of the explanatory variables, X_{it}.

Within the framework described by (4-52), two different types of models are identified in the literature: the fixed effects model and the random effects model.

In the fixed effects model, it is assumed that the $\text{var}(\mu_i) = \text{var}(v_t) = 0$ (that is, the error terms μ_i and v_t are both constant or fixed), and their values are incorporated in the intercept terms. Under these conditions, this model can be estimated using a method sometimes called the least-squares dummy variable (LSDV) method (analogous to the dummy variable model described above). In general, the fixed effects model would be used in cases where these assumptions are satisfied and there is no need to make inferences to a larger population.

In the random effects model, on the other hand, it is assumed that $\text{var}(\mu_i) \neq 0$ or $\text{var}(v_t) \neq 0$ and the error component is uncorrelated with the independent variables. In this case, although OLS is a consistent estimator of the coefficients, it is not efficient in comparison to the recommended feasible GLS method. However, if the individual error component, μ_i, is highly correlated with the independent variables, the GLS estimates of the slope coefficients are biased and it is suggested that the fixed effects model be used instead. In the random effects model, inferences may be made from the sample of observations used in the analysis to the larger population from which the sample was randomly drawn.[30]

(1) Example of pooling An application of pooling in regional analysis is illustrated in a recent study of Nazara (1997). The question under consideration is whether or not there is a difference in total factor productivity in the agricultural sector between the Eastern and Western regions of Indonesia. Data for the 26 provinces of Indonesia for the time period 1983-1993 were used in the analysis. The following form of the Cobb-Douglas production function was used:

$$Y_{it} = A_{it} \, K_{it}^{\beta_K} \, L_{it}^{\beta_L} \, H_{it}^{\beta_H} \tag{4-54}$$

where Y is agricultural output, A is assumed to represent total factor productivity, K is agricultural capital stock, L is agricultural labor, H is harvested area, each in province i in time t, the βs are the input elasticity coefficients associated with their respective subscripts, (K, L, H) and ε_{it} (below) is the error term. The above model was formulated as follows for estimation purposes:

$$\ln Y_{it} = \ln A_{it} + \beta_K \ln K_{it} + \beta_L \ln L_{it} + \beta_H \ln H_{it} + \varepsilon_{it} \tag{4-55}$$

where ln represents the natural logarithm. The estimated model is[31]

$$\ln Y = 8.861 + 0.067 \ln K + 0.205 \ln L + 0.078 \ln H \tag{4-56}$$
$$\quad (12.84) \quad (2.23) \quad (5.13) \quad (2.60)$$

where the numbers in parentheses are the t statistics, each of which is statistically significant at the 5% level. The adjusted R^2 is 0.995 and the F-statistic is 1,447 (highly significant).

The underlying assumption in this model is that the coefficients of the intercept terms vary over province and over time and the slope coefficients are fixed. When the model was estimated across the provinces of Indonesia the intercept terms (i.e., total factor productivity) for the Western Region provinces varied between 0.59 and 3.85 (with a mean of 1.62); for the Eastern Region provinces the variation was between 0.51 and 1.82 (with a mean of 0.82). Thus, it is clear there is a difference in total factor productivity across the two regions. Over the ten-year period covered by the data (1983 to 1993), the intercept term increased by about fifty percent (from 0.82 to 1.25).

4.4.4 Simultaneous equations models

Simultaneous equations models play a very important role in econometric analysis. Most national governments and large corporations have their own large scale (e.g., hundreds or more equations) multipurpose simultaneous equations models or subscribe to commercially available services with such models. In the last generation, the use of such models at the regional level has increased to the point that many states in the U.S. (and many sub-national regions in other countries) now have or have access to large scale econometric models for forecasting and/or policy analysis. Such simultaneous equations econometric models can be used also on a much smaller scale (i.e., models with fewer equations) to more accurately represent economic phenomena without making restrictive assumptions about a one-way flow of influence from the independent variables to the dependent variable in a single equation model.

Thus far, this chapter has considered regression models in which the dependent variable appears only on the left-hand side of the equation. This formulation of an econometric model works well in many situations and is perfectly satisfactory for obtaining reliable statistical results given that the appropriate assumptions (e.g., as outlined in section 4.2.3) are satisfied.

Nevertheless, there are certain cases where the assumptions about the left hand side (LHS) variables (i.e., which are dependent and endogenous) and the right hand side (RHS) variables (i.e., which usually are independent and exogenous) are not necessarily an accurate representation of the economic phenomena under study. For example, the quantity of a product sold (as a LHS variable) would very likely be determined by the price of the product and the values of other relevant variables as well on the RHS of the equation (e.g., the price of substitutes, cost, income, interest rates, etc.). However, in this case if we want the model to be comprehensive, we have to recognize that there often is also a reverse effect that flows from the quantity sold to the price of the product. In this latter case, the price of the product would be the dependent, endogenous variable while the number sold would be one of the independent, exogenous variables. Clearly, we are describing a situation in which the price and quantity demanded for a good are determined simultaneously. If we want to model this situation in a more comprehensive manner, we need to formulate a more complex (i.e., more than one equation) model in which the special characteristics of these interrelated phenomena are recognized explicitly.

Models that do this are called simultaneous equations models. An important characteristic of such models is that a particular variable (e.g., price) may appear as a dependent variable on the LHS of one equation and as an explanatory variable on the RHS of another equation. Other variables of interest may also be specified in a similar manner — i.e., as a dependent variable on the LHS of one equation and as an explanatory variable on the RHS of another equation. For such a simultaneous system of equations, which is usually a more accurate representation of some economic phenomena, the standard single equation estimating technique (OLS) is not appropriate. In general, OLS estimators applied to this type of model are biased and inconsistent. This is the case because the error terms in the simultaneous equations are no longer independent of the endogenous variables that appear on the RHS of these equations (see section 4.2.3).

Under certain conditions, it is possible to solve the system of simultaneous equations algebraically so that all the endogenous variables appear on the LHS of the equations (one equation for each endogenous variable) and one or more exogenous explanatory variables appear on the RHS of each equation — that is, to obtain what are designated 'reduced form' equations. In this case, the independence assumption of the error term and the explanatory variables is satisfied and OLS estimators are unbiased and consistent. If the model is to be used exclusively for forecasting purposes, the reduced form estimates may well be sufficient. It may be possible conceptually to transform the estimated results of these reduced form equations to those of the originally specified simultaneous equations system, the so called 'structural equations,' but that is usually not feasible in practice. However, it is the parameters of the structural equations that are often of primary interest to the researcher in order to understand the empirical relationships among the endogenous and exogenous variables in the economic system being studied. In such cases, alternative estimators such as, for example, two-stage least squares (2SLS) may be used. With this approach, forecasts can usually be obtained by simulation. Some of these issues are illustrated in the following example.

(1) Simple example with simultaneous equations Consider the following very simple model of a region's economy in three equations.

$$LGS_t = \alpha_0 + \alpha_1 TGS_t + \alpha_2 G_t + \varepsilon_{1t} \qquad (4\text{-}57)$$

$$Y_t = \beta_0 + \beta_1 TGS_t + \beta_2 GDP_t + \varepsilon_{2t} \qquad (4\text{-}58)$$

$$TGS_t = Y_t - (LGS_t + G_t) \qquad (4\text{-}59)$$

where the endogenous variables are:

LGS_t — Region's output of private local goods and services, millions of 1987 \$, in year t;

TGS_t — Region's output of private traded goods and services, millions of 1987 \$, in year t;

Y_t — Region's total output, millions of 1987 \$, in year t;

and the exogenous variables are:

GDP$_t$ — U.S. gross domestic product, billions of 1987 \$, in year *t;*

G$_t$ — Region's government expenditures, millions of 1987 \$, in year *t.*

Note that the first two equations are regressions with disturbance ε_{1t} and ε_{2t} while the third equation is deterministic, i.e., TGS$_t$, is a difference among the three RHS variables.

The model is in three linear equations with three unknowns, the endogenous variables LGS, TGS, and Y. Therefore, it can be solved simultaneously for those three variables. The model as expressed in the three equations above is called the structural model. The structural model should not be estimated by means of OLS because endogenous variables appear on the right-hand side of the equations. Using simple algebra (e.g., straightforward substitution), the three equations can be rewritten so that all endogenous variables appear only on the left hand sides of the equations, and exogenous variables appear on the right-hand side only. This yields the reduced form equations. Then the reduced form equations are estimated statistically using OLS. The estimated reduced form equations of the above structural equations for the period 1970–95 ($n = 26$) are presented below, with t statistics in parentheses:[32]

$$\text{LGS}_t = 50{,}726 + 11.8\text{GDP}_t - 1.27\text{G}_t \qquad \bar{R}^2 = .79 \quad (4\text{-}60)$$
$$(3.3) \qquad\quad (5.5) \qquad\quad (-1.7)$$

$$\text{TGS}_t = 21{,}670 + 28.6\text{GDP}_t + 2.03\text{G}_t \qquad \bar{R}^2 = .94 \quad (4\text{-}61)$$
$$(0.8) \qquad\quad (7.0) \qquad\quad (1.5)$$

$$\text{Y}_t = 72{,}396 + 40.4\text{GDP}_t + 1.76\text{G}_t \qquad \bar{R}^2 = .95 \quad (4\text{-}62)$$
$$(2.0) \qquad\quad (7.9) \qquad\quad (1.0)$$

As shown, only endogenous variables appear on the left-hand sides of the reduced form equations, and only exogenous variables appear on the right-hand sides. Thus, if the exogenous variables are known or can be forecast reliably, it is possible to obtain directly forecasts of the endogenous variables without resorting to the structural equations form of the basic simultaneous equations model.

Under certain conditions, it is possible to find algebraically the structural coefficients from the reduced form coefficients but that is not usually done in practice. The more common alternative strategy is to use an estimation method [such as two-stage least squares (2SLS)] which directly provides estimates of the structural coefficients which are consistent. The use of other more sophisticated estimators is also possible but is beyond the scope of this introductory chapter.

Here we have used two-stage least squares to estimate the coefficients of the structural model, shown below, with t statistics in parentheses:

$$LGS_t = 41,793 + 0.412TGS_t - 2.11G_t \qquad \bar{R}^2 = .74 \quad (4\text{-}63)$$
$$\qquad\quad (2.7) \qquad (5.0) \qquad (-2.2)$$

$$Y_t = 53,627 + 0.866TGS_t + 15.6GDP_t \qquad \bar{R}^2 = .99 \quad (4\text{-}64)$$
$$\qquad\quad (2.1) \qquad (2.2) \qquad (1.2)$$

Note that the coefficient on TGS in equation (4-63) is +0.412, indicating that a one million dollar increase in traded goods and services (TGS) adds $412,000 to the region's output of private local goods and services (LGS), which is a plausible estimate of the marginal multiplier.

Of course there are no estimated structural coefficients for equation (4-59) because it is an identity.

(2) Another example — the Klein interwar model A small simultaneous equations model of the U.S. economy by Klein (1950) is useful to illustrate a more realistic application of such models. The Klein interwar model, which covers the period 1921–1941, is formulated as three behavioral equations (for consumption, investment, and private wages) and three identities (income, profits, and net investments). The estimated model is as follows:

(1) $C = 16.79 + 0.800(W_P + W_G) + 0.02\Pi + 0.235\Pi_{-1}$ (4-65)

(2) $I = 17.78 + 0.231\Pi + 0.546\Pi_{-1} - 0.146K_{-1}$ (4-66)

(3) $W_P = 1.60 + 0.420(Y + T - W_G)$
$\qquad + 0.164(Y + T - W_G)_{-1} + 0.135t$ (4-67)

(4) $Y = C + I + G$ (4-68)

(5) $\Pi = Y - W_P - T$ (4-69)

(6) $K = K_{-1} + I$ (4-70)

where the six endogenous variables are:[33]

W_P = private wages   C = consumption   K = capital stock
Y = output   I = investment (net) Π = profits
the four exogenous variables are:
G = government nonwage expenditures   T = business taxes

W_G = public wages t = time

and the subscripts (-1) in equations (4-65), (4-66), (4-67) and (4-70) represent their respective variable lagged one time period (i.e., year).

This Klein model can be used also to illustrate an important linkage between econometric models and input-output models. The need for economic forecasts from an econometric model (or elsewhere) comes up frequently in input-output studies when the magnitude (the totals) of some basic final demand sectors such as total consumer expenditures (C) total investment (I), and net exports (E – M) need to be estimated. These estimates then are disaggregated by the use of appropriate coefficients. In turn, in certain cases, the estimates of the macromagnitudes in the Klein and other macromodels may profit from detailed information by industry provided by input-output models [for example, wages by industry to check the macromagnitude 'private' wages (W_P)].

4.5 Spatial econometrics

As you have learned, econometrics has to do with the specification, estimation and testing of statistical models for purposes of hypothesis testing, forecasting, and policy analysis. The use of econometrics in the field of regional science presents particular methodological problems which are related to the central organizing feature of regional science: space. The issue of spatial phenomena and the resulting methodological problems are not encountered in standard economic applications of econometrics. Hence, almost all econometric textbooks do not cover spatial econometrics. We introduce the basic ideas given the introductory character of this text. For a thorough treatment of the topic, see Anselin (1988a).

We turn to Anselin for the definition of spatial econometrics as '...those methods and techniques that, based on a formal representation of the structure of spatial dependence and spatial heterogeneity, provide the means to carry out the proper specification, estimation, hypothesis testing, and prediction for models in regional science' (Anselin, p. 10).

The key terms in that definition are spatial dependence and spatial heterogeneity. These characteristics of much spatial data create problems that are ignored in standard econometrics. We briefly consider each of those characteristics.

4.5.1 Spatial dependence

One of the assumptions of the OLS method is that the error terms are uncorrelated, i.e.,

$$cov(e_i e_j) = 0 \quad \text{for } i \neq j. \tag{4-71}$$

As we have seen (section 4.3.4 above), when that assumption is not true the errors or residuals exhibit serial correlation. In standard econometrics texts, it is usually stated or implicitly assumed that serial correlation is a problem which only occurs with time-series data and never with cross-section data. The Durbin-Watson test for serial correlation requires that the observations be in chronological order so that the errors are in a simple two-directional pattern: forward one period or back one period.

If serial correlation for cross section data is assumed away, then the order of the observations is irrelevant. But if there exists spatial dependence among the observations and the observations are in random order, the Durbin-Watson test will fail to reveal the serial correlation. For example, if a model includes residential land price as a variable and the observations are Census tracts in one metropolitan area, regional science theory indicates that land prices in contiguous tracts would tend to be positively correlated. That is, we have spatial dependence. Because the Census tracts cannot be ordered from left to right in one dimension as time periods can be ordered from earlier to later in chronological sequence, the Durbin-Watson test for serial correlation is not appropriate.

A test for spatial dependence is the Moran I statistic:

$$I = \frac{\displaystyle\sum_{j=1}^{n} \sum_{i=1}^{n} w_{ij} e_i e_j}{S_e^2 \displaystyle\sum_{j=1}^{n} \sum_{i=1}^{n} w_{ij}} \tag{4-72}$$

where w is a n by n matrix of spatial weights. The entry in cell i,j is 0 if spatial unit i and j are not contiguous, and 1 if they are contiguous. Alternatively, proximity can be expressed in terms of absolute distances. The entry in cell i,j is 0 if the geographic center of spatial unit i is more than k miles (meters, etc.) from the geographic center of spatial unit j. The entry in cell i,j is 1 if the distance from i to j is k miles (meters) or less. Note that the value of w in cell ii is 0. The e's are the residuals or error terms from some cross-section regression in which the n observations are spatial units and S_e^2 is the variance of the error term.

The distribution of I is normal and so it can be used to test the hypothesis that the residuals are spatially correlated.

4.5.2 Spatial heterogeneity

There are three forms of spatial heterogeneity which can cause problems in a regression model (Anselin and O'Loughlin (1990)). The first two arise from the fact that the structure of the model may not be fixed over space. If the parameters of the model are not constant for all i, where i designates spatial units of observation, but rather vary in some sytematic manner over space, then OLS applied to the entire sample is not appropriate. Similarly, if the parameters show structural instability with respect to space, say taking on two different values for two spatial subsets of the sample, then OLS is not appropriate. The identification and correction of these two problems of spatial heterogeneity are beyond the scope of this chapter but are found in Anselin (1988b).

The third form of spatial heterogeneity is that the variance of the error term (σ^2) is not constant but rather varies over space. That of course is the problem of heteroskedasticity, explained in Section 4.3.3 above.

For example, if the observations are counties of the United States and the dependent variable is average annual earnings, spatial heterogeneity will be present. That is because average earnings in metropolitan counties are considerably higher than in non-metropolitan counties. In states such as South Dakota and Minnesota, there are numerous non-metropolitan counties. In states such as New Jersey and California, there are almost no non-metropolitan counties. So in clusters of counties which comprise South Dakota and Minnesota, there would be much more variation in average earnings between the counties than between the counties in New Jersey or California. In other words, heteroskedasticity would be present and its source would be spatial proximity of observations, not temporal proximity of observations. One of the tests for heteroskedasticity may be used in such a case to determine if, in fact, heteroskedasticity is present. Further, if it is present and the variances, σ_i^2, are known, then the 'weighted least square' estimator ($\hat{\beta}_j^{WLS}$) is used instead of OLS. If these variances are not known, White's procedure is required (see 4.3.3).

4.6 The 'art' of econometric model building

The statistical *theory* underlying the structure and use of econometric methods is quite sophisticated, rigorous and comprehensive as indicated by the very extensive literature on these topics.[34] Unfortunately it is not possible to achieve these same high standards in the *practice* of econometrics. Nevertheless, the contributions made to the field of regional analysis by the use of econometric methods have been immeasurable.

Some reasons why problems exist in applying econometric methods are discussed in this section. First, any model (econometric or otherwise) is but an abstraction of reality, i.e., it is a representation of some real world phenomena, but it is not the real world phenomena that it is purported to represent. As such, a model is by definition, an incomplete representation of the real world. The best a researcher can hope for is that the model includes all the *important* components of the real world phenomena under study.

Second, in econometric model building, the 'true model' (the parameters of which are to be estimated) is unknown. Theory and prior empirical evidence provide guidelines for specifying a model correctly but, in the final analysis, we can never know with certainty what is the correct theoretical model even if we get good statistical results. For example, more than one model may fit the data with statistically acceptable outcomes. In addition, even if our hypothesized model contains all the correct explanatory variables, they may not be specified in their true functional form. For example, compare the two models of the rank-size rule in subsection 4.3.1 (5). Even though model 2 in Table 4-6 includes the theoretically correct variables, its functional form (linear) is incorrect. Nevertheless, the 't' and 'F' statistics indicate that the intercept term, the coefficient of the independent variable (POP), and the incorrectly specified linear model are all statistically significant even though the adjusted R^2 is low (.303) by conventional econometric standards. Given these results, a naive analyst might assume that the estimated linear rank-size rule model is, in fact, the correct model if he or she was not aware of the existing theory and its alternative log linear model.

Third, it has been said of economic phenomena that everything is related to everything else. If this is true at the national level, it is certainly also true at the urban and regional levels. The problem this poses is that it is exceedingly difficult then to specify a precisely correct model. At best, what we can hope for is to specify and estimate a credible empirical model that is a close approximation to the true, unknown model.

There are other problems as well in the empirical aspects of econometrics. For example, it is highly unlikely that all the assumptions about the model and the data underlying the use of the estimation techniques introduced previously have not been violated. In addition to those violations, there may be other sources of estimation problems: (1) the distribution of the error term is usually unknown; (2) the data needed to measure a phenomenon of interest may not be available and so proxy variables may need to be used, introducing unknown errors; (3) more than one violation of the assumptions may occur at the same time; (4) many of the available estimation techniques have desirable properties only for large sample sizes (e.g., they may only be consistent rather than BLUE) but, in practice, we often have available samples that may be quite limited in size giving rise to estimators with unknown properties.

Although larger sample sizes are generally considered desirable, under certain circumstances they may create their own difficulties. Increasing the sample size increases the probability of rejecting the null hypothesis which may be a problem if, in fact, the explanatory variable should not be in the model. On the other hand, the presence of multicollinearity decreases the probability of rejecting the null hypothesis. The advice offered by Hendry (1979) for building econometric models is to test, test, test but even here the advice has one recognizable drawback — it decreases the statistical level of confidence of the estimates.

It has been suggested that 'models are to be used, not believed,' an obvious overstatement designed to make a point.[35] Nevertheless, it should be clear by now that while models are to be used, one should do so with a questioning attitude.

A problem, of course, is how to operationalize such advice when doing empirical research. Wonnacott and Wonnacott (1990) suggest the following guidelines in which strong and weak theories and evidence are paired in order to provide a measure of credibility for the outcomes of an econometric analysis:

Theory	Evidence	Credibility
Strong	Strong	High
Strong	Weak	Some
Weak	Strong	Some
Weak	Weak	Little

Thus, if one specifies models based on good, sound theory and obtains highly significant and corroborating parameter estimates, then the model (theory) deserves a high level of credibility. On the other hand, if either the theory or the evidence is weak, the model's credibility will be also.

Finally, if the theory and evidence are both weak, the model's credibility will be very low.

The art of econometric model building then may be likened to picking one's way through a mine field in which one is trying to carry enough statistical and economic theory without some or all of it being blown away by the various mines (i.e., problems or errors as outlined in section 4.3 and in this section) that lie in one's path to credible model building. The best way for a novice to develop this capability is to study additional economic and statistical theory and to practice (with some skepticism) the art of econometric model building.

4.7 Fusion of econometrics and input-output: some editorial remarks

As suggested in the opening remarks of this chapter, there can exist in a number of studies a fruitful fusion of econometric and input-output methods. One way suggested was the use of econometric methods in forecasting final demand sectors. A demonstration of the fruitfulness of the resulting fusion is the Washington Projection and Simulation Model III (Conway, 1990). There, as depicted by Figure 4.11, the procedure was to start with coefficient changes of a base year input-output table (specifically, the 1982 Washington table noted in chapter 3). Next, the export sector of Washington state was projected given the projections of U.S. industrial requirements and the estimated extent to which the state could satisfy this U.S. demand. (At this point, one or more comparative cost studies could have been significant.) With the export sector (which has been the major driving force in the Washington economy during the 1980s) as a first final demand vector to be considered, the induced outputs of local industries could be and were calculated via the use of an input-output inverse. These outputs then were taken to be a *first set of internal demands.*

Industrial employment and earnings were determined from the above forecasts of outputs coupled with labor productivity and wage rate estimates. The latter were based on U.S. projections with appropriate adjustments regarding labor force participation and local unemployment rates. From industrial employment and earnings, population and personal income were forecast.

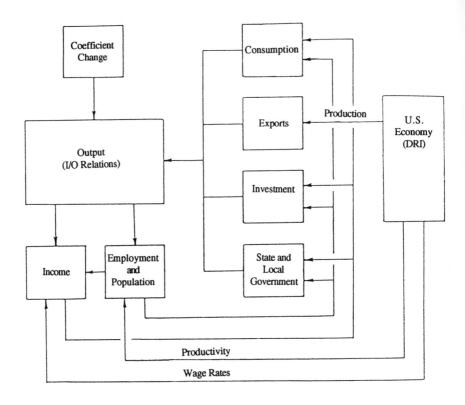

Figure 4.11 Washington projection and simulation model III

As Conway notes:

> Personal income and population in turn are important variables
> explaining the second tier of internal demands, the final demands of the
> consumption, investment, and state and local government sectors.
> Personal consumption expenditures are a function of per capita income,
> population, and the relative prices of goods and services; investment is a
> function of population and income as well as the stock of capital,
> interest rates, and the cost of construction; and state and local
> government spending is a function of school-aged population and
> federal highway funding, in addition to income and population (p. 143).

It is not necessary to go into any further details on this study to provide
information on how fusion of input-output and econometrics can generally
succeed. Figure 4.11 provides a suggestive overview. There are of course
numerous *specific* ways in which fusion or integration of these methods can

be accomplished, the particular way is in large part dependent on the availability of data, research resources, and goals of the research.

In closing these editorial remarks, it is important to bear in mind some gaps in this type of fusion. A major one is the fact that fusion, and in particular the excellent Conway study, is demand oriented. There is little of the supply side of production and pricing that is captured, and the effects of resource constraints are not fully taken into account even though comparative cost analysis may be employed in helping to determine the level of export activity. (See, for example, the comments of Beaumont, 1990.) To overcome these shortcomings, we turn to the methods to be considered in subsequent chapters. However, it should be noted that in Israilevich, Hewings, Sonis and Schindler (1997) movement in the direction of achieving a balance between supply and demand on certain commodity markets has been taken through annual adjustments of input coefficients. Also, it should be recognized that the approach of Conway in *coupling* via overlap of input-output and econometric methods is only one way of integrating these two methods. Other ways that exist involve *embedding* the input-output framework within econometrics and *linking* the two methods without overlap. See Rey (1997, 1998).

Endnotes

1. Note that not all economists believe that econometric models can be used to predict the effects of policy changes. See, for example, Lucas (1976), and Sargent and Lucas (1981) for critiques of this type of application.

2. In this chapter, we follow conventional notation found in many econometric and statistics textbooks. Capital Roman letters (e.g., X, Y, Z) represent random variables in their original form. Lower-case letters (e.g., x, y, z) represent either realizations of the values of the random variable X, Y, Z or the variables as deviations, usually from their mean (e.g., $x_i = X_i - \bar{X}$). The intended usage is clear from the text.

3. The region under discussion encompasses 27 metropolitan counties of the New York–Northeastern New Jersey Consolidated Metropolitan Statistical Area (CMSA), as defined by the U.S. Office of Management and Budget. It includes New York City (five counties), seven suburban

Methods of Interregional and Regional Analysis

counties in New York and fifteen suburban counties in northeastern New Jersey. The full model is presented in Drennan (1997).

4. The notation for the variable names in this and some subsequent examples have been changed somewhat from those used in the referenced sources in order to bypass some of the restrictions imposed by using computer printout and, hopefully, making the examples easier to read. The definitions and concepts involved remain unchanged.

5. In this case, the presence of serial correlation indicates that the error terms, ε_t, ε_{t-1} and ε_{t-2}, are correlated with each other. The presence of this condition may result in estimates of the coefficients (i.e., the βs) that do not have desirable properties. The presence of serial correlation in this example was indicated by a value of 0.52 for the Durbin-Watson statistic (a measure that is explained in section 4.3.4). After reestimation using a correction procedure, the D-W statistic was 2.07, indicating the absence of serial correlation.

6. Elasticity is defined as the percentage change in one variable given a one percent change in another variable. It can be shown that in a regression model in which the variables are all expressed in logarithmic terms, the estimated coefficients are measures of the elasticity between the dependent variable (in this case, PS) and each respective independent variable (e.g., GNPEUR).

7. This means that all other conditions are assumed to remain unchanged.

8. The marginal multiplier and marginal tax rate were estimated from ordinary least squares equations in Drennan's revised model of the NY–NJ region (1994, unpublished manuscript).

9. In econometric analysis, the null hypothesis usually specifies that the coefficient of interest is equal to zero (that is, $\beta_j = 0$) indicating there is no statistically significant relationship between the dependent variable, Y, and the independent variable, X_j. In such cases, the alternative hypothesis might be that $\beta_j \neq 0$ indicating there is a statistically significant relationship between Y and X_j. If, in fact, the null hypothesis is false and should be rejected (and, therefore, the alternative hypothesis should not be rejected), it is desirable that the probability of rejecting (or not accepting) the null hypothesis be as large as possible.

10. In this case, the term 'linear' refers to the fact that the OLS estimator of the regression coefficient is a linear combination of the sample observations on Y_i, the dependent variable in the regression equation. It does not refer to the functional form of the model being estimated. This is illustrated in equation (4-10) in the case of simple linear regression where the values of the independent variable, x_i, are assumed to be fixed (i.e., non-stochastic). The value of the slope coefficient, $\hat{\beta}_1$, is shown to be a linear combination (i.e., the ratios of the x_i and Σx_i^2) of the dependent variable, y_i.

11. This is sometimes referred to as the Gauss-Markov theorem. Its proof can be found in many textbooks on econometrics.

12. A probability limit can be defined as

$$\lim \text{Prob} \, (|\hat{\beta} - \beta| < \Phi) \rightarrow 1.\,0 \text{ as } n \rightarrow \infty$$

where Φ is an arbitrarily small positive number.

13. The MSE can be represented also as the sum of the variance and the square of the bias: MSE = variance + (bias)^2. It should be noted that at least one author (Kennedy, 1994) proposes additional criteria (e.g., highest R^2, computational ease and cost) in selecting desirable estimators.

14. Derivations of equations (4-10) through (4-13) can be found in many statistics and econometric texts.

15. Cases in which more than one violation occur at the same time are not considered in this introduction to econometric models.

16. These estimations were done for this chapter.

17. We limit our discussion here only to models that are linear in the parameters since consideration of more complex models is beyond the scope of this chapter.

18. Problems related to specification errors are more complicated than those outlined in this introductory section because, in fact, we often do not know the correct specification of the true model whose parameters we want to estimate. Some implications of this situation are discussed briefly in section 4.6.

19. See Isard (1960), pp. 55–60 and, also, Krugman (1996) for discussions of the rank size rule.

20. These estimates were done for this chapter.

21. The estimates using White's procedure may be higher or lower than those obtained using OLS.

22. The equation for computing the DW 'd' statistics is

$$d = \Sigma_{t=2}^{T}(\hat{\varepsilon}_t - \hat{\varepsilon}_{t-1})^2/\Sigma_{t=1}^{T}\hat{\varepsilon}_t^2$$

23. Multicollinearity occurs when two or more explanatory variables in a regression model are correlated with each other.

24. The maximum likelihood approach to deriving equation (4-40) is very different and more complicated than that taken in the OLS approach even though they both achieve the same final result, in this case (i.e., $\hat{\beta}$OLS = $\hat{\beta}$MLE = $\Sigma x_i y_i/\Sigma x_i^2$). Since the two approaches are different from each other, it is not unexpected that the underlying assumptions are different. The OLS assumptions are presented and analyzed in this section (4.3). The primary ML assumption is that the error term (ε_i) in the regression equation has a normal (bell shaped) curve.

25. For example, the covariance between X_1 and X_2 is defined as cov (X_1, X_2) = $E[(X_1 - E(X_1))(X_2 - E(X_2))]$ where E is the expected value operator. The unbiased estimator of this covariance is

$$c\hat{o}v (X_1, X_2) = [\Sigma(X_{1i} - \bar{X}_1)(X_{2i} - \bar{X}_2)]/(n - 1).$$

26. Note, $r_{12}^2 = [\Sigma(X_{1i} - \bar{X}_1)(X_{2i} - \bar{X}_2)]^2/\Sigma(X_{1i} - \bar{X}_1)^2\Sigma(X_{2i} - \bar{X}_2)^2$. Thus, as X_1 and X_2 move together (either positively or negatively), r_{12}^2 will tend to a value of 1; if they are statistically independent, r_{12}^2 will, in theory, be zero.

27. Recall that the explanatory variables, X_j, in a regression equation are assumed to be independent of each other. Although that requirement is not rigid, if the correlation between two independent explanatory variables is equal to +1.00, the OLS equations for the parameters cannot be solved. When one so-called independent variable is an exact linear transformation of another, by definition the correlation between them is equal to +1.00. This is what happens when there is no excluded category when a dummy variable is employed. To illustrate consider

the nominal variable 'gender.' Let $X_1 = 1$ if the person is female; otherwise $X_1 = 0$. Let $X_2 = 1$ if the person is male; otherwise $X_2 = 0$. Consider the following five observations on those two dummy variables.

Observation	X_1	X_2
1.	1	0
2.	1	0
3.	0	1
4.	1	0
5.	0	1

There is a linear equation which transforms X_1 into X_2,

$$X_2 = 1 - X_1$$

So X_1 and X_2 are absolutely not independent.

28. Two other approaches usually presented in introductory/intermediate textbooks are the linear probability model (LPM) and the probit model. The way the LPM is formulated may allow estimated probabilities to be above 1 or below 0, an obvious shortcoming of the model. The probit model (based on the cumulative normal distribution) is similar in its approach to the logit model but usually requires non-linear maximum likelihood estimation, a more difficult process than the estimation process used for the logit model.

29. Recall from section 4.4.1 that the use of one fewer dummy variables than there are different categories avoids the problem of perfect collinearity.

30. More complex models in which slope coefficients vary may be dealt with using appropriate pooled estimating methods.

31. These results were estimated using a data base that excluded Jakarta and Irian Jaya because they were considered to be outliers compared with the rest of the provinces. Jakarta was excluded because its agricultural sector is very small and Irian Jaya because of the very low level of its agricultural development. Actually, the results obtained from using the full data set (i.e., all provinces) were very close to those using the reduced data set.

32. This simple model was estimated specifically for this chapter.

33. Economic variables are measured in billions of 1934 dollars. K is a stock variable; the other economic variables are flows.

34. We have been able to consider only 'the tip of the iceberg' in this overview of the econometric methods. Interested readers are referred to recent popular textbooks on econometric methods for appropriate references to the current literature.

35. This advice is attributed to H. Theil (Wonnacott and Wonnacott, 1990, p. 324), an important contributor to the econometrics literature.

References

Anselin, Luc. 1988a. *Spatial Econometrics: Methods and Models.* Dordrecht: Kluwer Academic Publishers.

Anselin, Luc. 1988b. 'Model Validation in Spatial Econometrics: A Review and Evaluation of Alternative Approaches,' *International Regional Science Review*, 12.

Anselin, Luc, and John O'Loughlin. 1990. 'Spatial Econometric Analysis of International Conflict,' in Manas Chatterji and Robert E. Kuenne (eds.), *Dynamics and Conflict in Regional Structural Change.* London: Macmillan, pp. 325-345.

Baltagi, Badi. 1995. *Economic Analysis of Panel Data.* New York: John Wiley.

Beaumont, Paul M. 1990. 'Supply and Demand Interaction: Integrated Econometric and Input-Output Models,' *International Regional Science Review*, 13, 167–181.

Belsley, D. A., E. Kuh, and R. E. Welsh. 1980. *Regression Diagnostics: Identifying Influential Data and Sources of Collinearity.* New York: John Wiley.

Berndt, E. R. 1991. *The Practice of Econometrics: Classic and Contemporary.* Reading, Mass.: Addison-Wesley.

Chow, G. C. 1983. *Econometric Methods.* New York: McGraw-Hill.

Conway, Richard S. 1990. 'The Washington Projection and Simulation Model: A Regional Interindustry Econometric Model,' *International Regional Science Review*, 13, 141–165.

Dhrymes, P. J. 1978. *Introductory Economics.* New York: Springer-Verlag.

Dielman, T. E. 1991. *Regression Analysis for Business and Economics.* Boston: PWS-Kent.

Draper, N. R., and H. Smith. 1981. *Applied Regression Analysis*, 2nd ed. New York: John Wiley.

Drennan, M. P. 1985. *Modeling Metropolitan Economies for Forecasting and Policy Analysis*. New York: New York University Press.

Drennan, M. P. 1994. *Revised Econometric Model of New York–Northeastern New Jersey*, unpublished manuscript. Ithaca, N.Y.: Cornell University.

Drennan, M. P. 1997. 'The Performance of Metropolitan Area Industries,' Federal Reserve Bank of New York, *Economic Policy Review*, 3(1).

Durbin, J., and G. S. Watson. 1951. 'Testing for Serial Correlation in Least Squares Regression,' *Biometrika*, 38, 159–171.

Dutta, M. 1975. *Econometric Methods*. Cincinnati: South-Western Publishing.

Goldberger, A. S. 1991. *A Course in Econometrics*. Cambridge, Mass.: Harvard University Press.

Greene, W. H. 1993. *Econometric Analysis*. 2nd ed. New York: Macmillan.

Griffiths, W. E., R. C. Hill, and G. G. Judge. 1993. *Learning and Practicing Econometrics*. New York: John Wiley.

Gujarati, D. N. 1995. *Basic Econometrics*, 3rd ed. New York: McGraw-Hill.

Hamilton, J. D. 1994. *Time Series Analysis*. Princeton: Princeton University Press.

Harvey, A. C. 1990. *The Econometric Analysis of Time Series*, 2nd ed. Cambridge, Mass.: MIT Press.

Intriligator, M. D., R. Bodkin, and C. Hsiao. 1996. *Econometric Models, Techniques, and Applications*, 2nd ed. Englewood Cliffs, N.J.: Prentice Hall.

Isard, Walter. 1956. *Location and Space Economy*. New York: John Wiley, 55–60.

Israilevich, P. R., G. J. D. Hewings, M. Sonis, and G. R. Schindler. 1997. 'Forecasting Structural Change with a Regional Econometric Input-Output Model,' *Journal of Regional Science*, 37, 1–27.

Johnston, J., and J. DiNardo. 1997. *Econometric Methods*, 4th ed. New York: McGraw-Hill.

Judge, G. G., C. R. Hill, W. E. Griffiths, H. Lütkepohl, and T.-C. Lee. 1988. *Introduction to the Theory and Practice of Econometrics*, 2nd ed. New York: John Wiley.

Katz, D. A. 1982. *Econometric Theory and Applications*. Englewood Cliffs, N.J.: Prentice Hall.

Kelejian, H. A., and W. E. Oates. 1981. *Introduction to Econometrics: Principles and Applications*, 2nd ed. New York: Harper & Row.

Kennedy, P. 1992. *A Guide to Econometrics*, 3rd ed. Cambridge, Mass.: MIT Press.

Kmenta, J. 1986. *Elements of Econometrics*, 2nd ed. New York: Macmillan.

Krugman, Paul. 1995. *Development, Geography, and Economic Theory*. Cambridge, Mass.: MIT Press.

Krugman, Paul. 1996. *The Self Organizing Economy*. Cambridge, Mass.: Blackwell.

Lucas, R. E. 1976. 'Econometric Policy Analysis: A Critique,' in Karl L. Bronner (ed.), *The Phillips Curve and Labor Markets* (supplement to the *Journal of Monetary Economics*), pp. 19–46.

Maddala, G. S. 1992. *Introduction to Econometrics*, 2nd ed. New York: John Wiley.

Mills, T. C. 1990. *Time Series Techniques for Economists*. Cambridge: Cambridge University Press.

Nazara, Suahasil. 1997. *Total Factor Productivity in Indonesia Agriculture: An Analysis of Provincial Panel Data, 1983-1993*. Unpublished Master's Thesis. Ithaca, N.Y.: Cornell University.

Neter, J., W. Wasserman, and M. Kutner. 1990. *Applied Linear Statistical Models: Regression, Analysis of Variance and Experimental Designs*, 3rd ed. Boston: Irwin.

Perloff, H. S., E. S. Dunn, E. E. Lampard, and R. F. Muth. 1960. *Regions, Resources and Economic Growth*. Baltimore: The Johns Hopkins Press.

Pindyck, R. S., and D. L. Rubinfeld. 1991. *Econometric Models and Econometric Forecasts*, 3rd ed. New York: McGraw-Hill.

Rey, S. J. 1997. 'Integrating Regional Econometric and Input-Output Models: An Evaluation of Embedding Strategies,' *Environment and Planning A*, 29, 1057–1072.

Rey, S. J. 1998. 'The Performance of Alternative Integration Strategies for Combining Regional Econometric and Input-Output Models,' *International Regional Science Review*, 21, 1–35.

Sargent, T., and R. Lucas (ed.). 1981. *Rational Expectations and Econometric Practice*. Minneapolis: University of Minnesota Press.

Wonnacott, R. J., and T. H. Wonnacott. 1979. *Econometrics*, 2nd ed. New York: John Wiley.

Wonnacott, R. J., and T. H. Wonnacott. 1990. *Introductory Statistics for Business and Economics*, 4th ed. New York: John Wiley.

5. Programming and industrial and urban complex analysis

Walter Isard

5.0 Introduction

In the previous chapters we have discussed methods to examine basic problems in regional development: location of industry and services trade; market estimation and ways economic activities are interconnected from a technical production standpoint; impact of change in one sector upon others; and statistical estimation of basic structural relations and the testing of hypotheses concerning the dependence of key micro and macro variables (prices, wages, gross regional product, migration) upon diverse factors. However, hardly any attention has thus far been given to another exceedingly important question in regional development, namely, how best to utilize a region's or system's scarce resources — a problem that every region, whether rich or poor, confronts. This is a problem that is frequently best addressed by programming methods.[1]

To be more specific, a region may have limited water available for industrial development. How best employ that water in terms of a predetermined goal? Or a region may be short on both capital and skilled labor, as is true of many underdeveloped regions. How exploit these resources most efficiently to attain certain income, employment, or other objectives? Or a metropolitan area may confront a land shortage. Given the limited land available, how plan an industrial expansion program to maximize revenue or to achieve any other goal, subject to certain capital budget restrictions?

Like interregional input-output, interregional programming emphasizes general interdependence. Unlike interregional input-output, it is an optimizing technique, even when restricted to a system of linear relations (equations). And compared to other techniques such as industrial complex, to be discussed shortly, it can treat a much broader framework in the analysis of an interindustry system.

To be more specific consider the linear form of programming where for a given problem of a region the objective is to maximize or minimize some linear function, subject to certain linear inequalities. In such a situation it purports to answer this kind of question: given a set of limited resources (which may include plant capacities, transportation, and urban facilities, as well as mineral, labor, and other natural and human endowments), given a technology in the form of a set of constant production coefficients, given a set of prices (except on the factors in limited supply, for which shadow prices will emerge), how program diverse activities in order to maximize profits, social gains, total income, per capita income, employment, gross social product, or some other magnitude? Or how program diverse production activities in order to minimize transportation volumes, man-hours of work, or some other magnitude, subject to the achievement of certain levels of output and consumption? In an interregional setting the question can be still broader. For each of the several regions of a system, there is given a set of limited resources, a technology (which may be the same from region to region but which may lead to different production practices among regions because of different resource endowments), a set of prices on factors and commodities not in limited supply (where prices in the region are interrelated with prices in other regions through the existence or possibility of trade). How program the diverse production and shipping activities of any given region in order to maximize income, employment, or some other magnitude relating to the region? Or, more broadly, how program the diverse production and shipping activities of the several regions in order to maximize income, employment, or some other magnitude of the interregional system (or nation, if the several regions do comprise a nation)? Still more, when nonlinearities are allowed as when the objective function is nonlinear and subject to a set of linear and nonlinear (at the extreme just nonlinear) constraints, interregional programming may in time be able to provide insights and recommendations on policy for a system of regions, a subject to be examined in chapters 8 and 9.

In the following section, we illustrate the potential of programming with a highly simplified example employing the linear form of programming. Once the way the method operates is presented and generalized, we can leave the highly restricted world of linear programming and examine how nonlinear programming can be effectively employed for regional development, particularly within an interregional system. In section 5.2 we discuss basic aspects of nonlinear programming indicating its potential for a broad range of problems.

Section 5.3 presents an application, how in effect this programming underlies industrial complex analyses. In section 5.4 we suggest how nonlinear programming has potential for urban complex analyses, although it has scarcely been applied to the examination of the various spatial factors and relationships which need to be covered.

5.1 A simple linear programming problem: a graphic solution

To demonstrate the power of interregional programming, we start with a highly simplified problem requiring only a linear form of programming and proceed step-by-step to more complex problems which come to involve nonlinear relations.

Consider a hypothetical isolated region desiring to realize a maximum of new income from productive activities but having available for such purposes only a limited quantity of each of four resources: water, land, labor, and capital, the last being free for investment. Two economic activities have been identified as 'profitable.' To generate one dollar of new income, each activity requires a set of inputs of each resource as listed in Table 5-1. (In linear programming we must generally assume, as we do in this problem, constant production coefficients and fixed prices on all commodities but resources in limited supply.)

Table 5-1 Resource requirements per dollar new income

	Activities	
Required Units of:	1	2
Water	0.5	0.6
Land	0.2	0.15
Labor	0.4	0.2
Capital	3.0	2.0

If we define the unit level of operation of each activity as that level which generates one dollar of new income, the data of Table 5-1 refer to unit levels of operations. We now desire to find the most desirable combination of levels (i.e., multiples of these unit levels) at which to operate these activities. Since these levels are unknowns, they may be designated X_1 and X_2, respectively. To work with, the region has only 6 MM (million) units of water, 1.8 MM units of land, 3 MM units of labor, and 24 MM units of capital.

The problem can be solved rather easily with the use of a graph. Along the vertical axis of Figure 5.1, we measure level of activity 1; along the horizontal axis, that of activity 2. Next we construct resource limitation lines. The water limitation line NU indicates the various combinations of levels of activities 1 and 2 whose water requirements just use up the 6 MM units available for consumption. At one extreme (given by point N), operation of activity 1 at a level of 12 MM units could be achieved provided activity 2 were carried on at zero level. At the other extreme (given by point U) operation of activity 2 at a level of 10 MM units could be achieved provided activity 1 were carried on at zero level. Along the line and in between points N and U are the various combinations of levels of the two activities which just exhaust the available 6 MM units of water. Below and to the left of line NU are an infinite number of points, each of which, however, represents combinations of levels which require less than 6 MM units of water. Since for any given point below and to the left of NU there can always be found a point on line NU which corresponds to greater levels of both activities, all points in the positive quadrant bounded by NU (but not including NU) may be said to represent *inefficient* combinations *so far as the water limitation is pertinent.*

However, if we move up along the vertical axis (corresponding to zero level of activity 2), we find that well before the water limitation on the level of activity 1 takes effect, the limitations on labor, capital, and land have become effective. At point R, for example, the labor limitation becomes operative. At this extreme point, given only 3 MM units of labor and the requirement of 0.4 units of labor at unit level, the maximum level at which activity 1 can be operated is 7.5 MM units. Thus it becomes necessary to consider other resource limitations. To do so we have constructed the labor limitation line RP, the capital limitation line QW, and the land limitation line LW. These lines are constructed on the same basis as the water limitation line. For example, point P at an extreme of the labor limitation line indicates that activity 2 can be carried on at a maximum level of 15 MM units, provided activity 1 is pursued at zero level. And points along line RP indicate all combinations of levels of the two activities whose requirements of labor just equal the available 3 MM units. Points below and to the left of the labor limitation line RP are inefficient, *so far as the labor limitation is pertinent.*

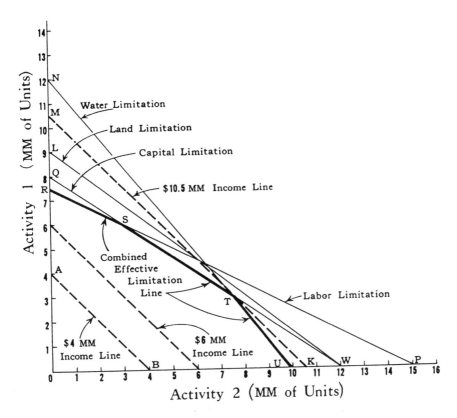

Figure 5.1   Graphic solution to a simple linear program

In this problem, where negative values for activities are precluded, consider the implications of *all* resource limitations. Any combination of levels represented by a point in the area above the stretch RS (e.g., the combination of 7.7 MM units of activity 1 and 0.1 MM units of activity 2) is unattainable. Although such a combination may consume amounts of capital, land, and water which do not exceed the available quantities of these resources, it does require labor in excess of available supply. Hence the labor limitation line, in particular stretch RS, is binding in this area of the positive quadrant. Passing to the right of point S — or more strictly to the right of a line drawn from the origin through S — another resource limitation line, namely that representing capital, becomes binding. In this area, any point representing a combination of activity levels that is feasible from the standpoint of available capital is also feasible from the standpoint of other available resources. On the other hand, any point representing a combination that is feasible from the standpoint of these other resources is not necessarily feasible from the standpoint of capital. For example, combinations represented by points directly above the stretch ST require a capital supply in excess of that available, although these combinations do not exceed other resource limitations. Hence, the capital limitation line, in particular stretch ST, is effective in this area.

Going still further to the right beyond T — more strictly to the area to the right of the ray from the origin through T — another resource limitation becomes binding, namely water. Water is the first resource whose available supply is fully utilized by combinations of levels of activities 1 and 2 which can be represented by points in this area. In particular, the stretch TU of the water limitation line becomes effective.

In brief, then, the segmented line RSTU, along with stretches OR and OU on the axes, delineates a closed set of points in the positive quadrant which represent all combinations of activity levels feasible from the standpoint of each and every resource limitation. These are attainable points. Combinations represented by points in the positive quadrant outside this closed set require at least one resource in excess of available supply. These combinations are not feasible; the corresponding points are *unattainable*. Further, since it can be shown that any point in this closed area not on RSTU is inferior to some point on the line, in that the latter point corresponds to greater achievable levels for both activities, we can state that all *efficient* points of the feasible set of points lie on the segmented line RSTU.[2]

Having eliminated 'inefficient' combinations of activity levels, we now seek to determine what efficient combination will maximize new income, that is, the optimal combination. To do this is relatively simple since for each activity we have already defined the unit level as the level that generates $1.00 of new income. Following standard procedures in economic analysis, we may construct 'iso-income' lines. For example, point A in Figure 5.1 represents a combination of a 4 MM-unit level of activity 1 and a zero-unit level of activity 2; therefore, it corresponds to $4 MM of new income. Point B represents a combination of a zero-unit level of activity 1 and a 4 MM-unit level of activity 2; it also corresponds to $4 MM of new income. Likewise combinations of levels represented by all points lying along a straight line from A to B yield $4 MM of income. Thus we have a $4 MM-income line (dashed in Figure 5.1). Similarly, we can obtain a $6 MM-income line (dashed in Figure 5.1) and other lines, each representing a locus of points which represent combinations yielding the same total income, and each with a slope of −1 when the scales along the vertical and horizontal axes are identical. Since the 'iso-income' lines increase in value as we move farther and farther from the origin, we wish to identify the highest 'iso-income' line on which any of our 'efficient' points (i.e., points on RSTU) lie. Such a line is the $10.5 MM-income line upon which point T lies. Thus point T represents the combination of activity levels (namely, 3 MM units for 1 and 7.5 MM units for 2) which maximizes new income. It is the optimal solution, which is therefore the solution to our simple problem.

This type of graphic solution is simple and effective when only two activities are considered. Unfortunately, the graphic solution becomes complex when a third activity is introduced into the problem. Three dimensions must then be used, the level of the third activity being measured along the third dimension. And when we introduce a fourth activity, a fifth, a sixth, ..., and finally an nth activity into the problem, a direct graphic solution is not possible. It is at this point that other types of solutions must be sought to the linear programming problem. It also becomes desirable at this point to state the problem in more formal, mathematical terms.

To begin, suppose $n = 3$, that is, that there are three activities to be considered. Associated with each activity is a set of data indicating inputs of each resource required in order for that activity to operate at unit level and thus generate one dollar of new income. We represent these data by a set of coefficients as follows:

$$\begin{bmatrix} -a_{11} & -a_{12} & -a_{13} \\ -a_{21} & -a_{22} & -a_{23} \\ -a_{31} & -a_{32} & -a_{33} \\ -a_{41} & -a_{42} & -a_{43} \end{bmatrix}$$

Note that each a_{ij} $(i, j = 1, 2, 3, 4)$ is preceded by a minus sign. This is because in a programming model each input is considered to be a negative quantity, and each output a positive quantity. (For example, we would need to follow this procedure when a production activity yields more than one output, say a unit of the main product, but a greater or smaller amount of a second by-product which needs to be counted.)

If the data of Table 5-1 are still relevant for the first two activities, then $-a_{21}$ which represents the requirement of *resource 2* (namely land) per unit level of *activity 1* is 0.2; $-a_{12}$ which represents the requirement of *resource 1* (namely water) per unit level of *activity 2* is 0.6; $-a_{32}$ which represents the requirement of *resource 3* (namely labor) per unit level of *activity 2* is 0.2; etc. Letting X_1, X_2, and X_3 represent the levels of activities 1, 2, and 3, respectively, which are to be determined and which are restricted to nonnegative values, we wish to maximize income which is equal to $1.00 × Z where

$$Z = X_1 + X_2 + X_3 \qquad (5\text{-}1)$$

or more specifically, to maximize Z (i.e., the number of dollar-generating units) subject to the condition that the sum of the requirement of any one resource by all activities not exceed the supply of that resource. If we denote R_1, R_2, R_3, and R_4 as the available supplies of water, land, labor, and capital, respectively (which in our problem are 6 MM, 1.8 MM, 3 MM, and 24 MM units, respectively), and if we note, for example, that $-a_{12}X_2$ represents the requirement of the first resource by the second activity [since this involves multiplying the requirements of resource 1 per unit level of activity 2 (i.e., $-a_{12}$) by the level of activity 2 (i.e., X_2)], the conditions can be written

$$\begin{aligned}
-a_{11}X_1 - a_{12}X_2 - a_{13}X_3 &\le R_1 \\
-a_{21}X_1 - a_{22}X_2 - a_{23}X_3 &\le R_2 \\
-a_{31}X_1 - a_{32}X_2 - a_{33}X_3 &\le R_3 \\
-a_{41}X_1 - a_{42}X_2 - a_{43}X_3 &\le R_4
\end{aligned} \qquad (5\text{-}2)$$

The first of these inequalities, for example, states that the requirement of resource 1 by activity 1 *plus* the requirement of resource 1 by activity 2 *plus* the requirement of resource 1 by activity 3 is less than or equal to the available supply of resource 1.

Note that our problem conforms to the general framework of linear programming. We are maximizing Z, which is a *linear* function of nonnegative variables (X_1, X_2, and X_3), subject to four restraints, each one of which is a *linear* inequality.

We can now generalize and consider many activities, $j = 1,...,n$, and many resource and other constraints, $i = 1,...,m$. Where c_j is the price of the good produced by activity j, the problem for a single region is:

Max: $Y = c_1X_1 + ... + c_nX_n$

subject to:

$$\begin{aligned}
-a_{11}X_1 - a_{12}X_2 - ... -a_{1n}X_n &\le R_1 \\
-a_{21}X_1 - a_{22}X_2 - ... -a_{2n}X_n &\le R_2 \\
... \quad ... \quad ... \quad ... \quad ... \quad ... \quad ... \quad ... \quad ... & \\
-a_{m1}X_1 - a_{m2}X_2 - ... -a_{mn}X_n &\le R_m
\end{aligned} \qquad (5\text{-}3)$$

$$X_1 \ge 0;\ X_2 \ge 0;\ ...;\ X_n \ge 0$$

or in compact form

Max: $\sum_{j=1}^{n} c_j X_j$ (5-4)

subject to:

$\sum_{j=1}^{n} -a_{ij}X_j \leq R_i$ $\qquad i = 1,...,m$

and

$X_j \geq 0$ $\qquad j = 1,...,n$

or in matrix form

Max $\mathbf{c}'\mathbf{X}$ (5-5)

subject to:

$\mathbf{AX} \leq \mathbf{R}$

and

$\mathbf{X} \geq 0$

where $\mathbf{c}'$ is a row vector of prices, $\mathbf{X}$ a vector of outputs, $\mathbf{A}$ a matrix of production coefficients and $\mathbf{R}$ a column vector of resource and other constraints.

For an interregional system of U regions, $L = A,B,...,U$, the problem becomes

Max $Z = \sum_{L=A}^{U} \sum_{j=1}^{v} c_j^L X_j^L$ $\qquad$ for nonnegative X_j^L (5-6)

subject to:

$\sum a_{kj}^L X_j^L + \sum_{\substack{J \\ J \neq L}} \sum a_{kj}^{J \to L} X_j^J \leq R_k^L$ $\qquad \begin{array}{l} k = 1,...,s \\ L = A,...,U \end{array}$

where activities $j = 1,...,v$ covers production activities, dummy activities and shipping (transport) activities and where $k = 1,...,s$ covers (1) constraints on use of resources, immobile or mobile, (2) constraints on intermediate use of commodities and (3) availability constraints on finished products. We do not develop the framework for an interregional system in this chapter since its statement is involved and rather technical, and since it will be demonstrated in chapter 8 below that an interregional programming model can often be viewed as an applied general interregional model (AGIE). The full-discussion of an interregional linear programming system is contained in Isard et al., 1960, chapter 10.

Once the problem for an *n*-activity linear program has been constructed for a region (or interregional system), the task of obtaining a solution arises. From the graphic presentation in Figure 5.1 it is clear that all that is required of a computer program is for it to identify the corners for the non-negative values of the activities and find that corner for which the value of the linear objective function is highest. At times, degenerate solutions may occur as when a stretch of the linear objective function coincides with an edge of the efficiency frontier, thereby yielding many possible optimal solutions to a problem. (See Miller, 1999, for treatment of this problem.)

However, it is obvious that *n*-activity linear programming today is relatively unimportant as a general regional science method. This is so since in most of our studies we now can introduce as a result of the computer revolution some nonlinearity. For a similar reason we shall not refer in this chapter to specific applications of linear programming. (See Isard et al., 1960 for presentation of some applications.) In general, we can now say that studies involving strict linear programming, interregional or not, are of limited interest. But as providing steps for the understanding of nonlinear programming, analysis of a linear programming model as thus far covered is extremely valuable.

It should be noted that for every linear program which has been designated the *primal program*, there exists a *dual*, often extremely difficult to attribute meaning to in the real world. The significance of the dual is that solving it, which yields the same solution as the primal, can at times reduce computer use and cost in reaching at the optimal solution.

5.2 Basic aspects of nonlinear programming

Thus far we have treated situations where all relationships are linear. But, to repeat, with the recent computer revolution we can now handle situations with nonlinearities. For example, if we have a nonlinear objective function which is convex such as a standard utility function (whether theoretical or inferred from interviews with representative consumers of a region) and which is as depicted in Figure 5.2a, point Q would be an optimal solution. If the objective function is concave as in Figure 5.2b, the end corner U would be the optimal solution. If one of the constraints contributes a concave stretch (edge) to the efficiency frontier (as the edge LM) while the objective function is linear, as in Figure 5.2c, the optimal solution would be Q'. Finally, if both a stretch of the efficiency

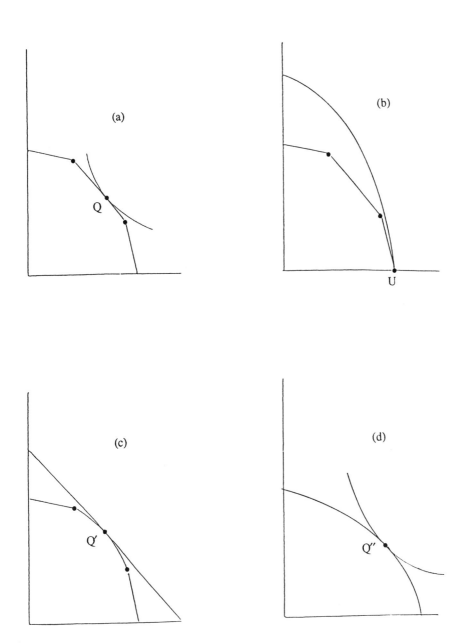

Figure 5.2   Nonlinear programming situations

frontier (or the entire frontier) is concave and the objective function convex, as in Figure 5.2d, the optimal solution would be Q''.

At this point the different kinds of nonlinear situations need not concern us. See Miller, 1998, for relevant discussion of types of situations. What we now wish to do, and what will be useful later for understanding both the methods and suggested research studies discussed in the last two chapters of this book, is to examine nonlinear programming when two or more different kinds of constraints are present.

5.2.1 Introduction of multiple types of constraints

Start from a highly simplified case of linear programming. There are two resources, capital and labor (resources #1 and #2), whose respective stocks are 0.8 and 2.0. There are two production activities whose unknown outputs are X_1 and X_2, and whose unit input requirements of capital and labor are k_1 (= 0.317) and ℓ_1 (= 1.467), and k_2 (= 0.805) and ℓ_2 (=1.242). Given final product prices P_1 (= 2.587) and P_2 (= 3.334), the problem is

Max: $P_1 X_1 + P_2 X_2$
(defined as Gross Regional Product, GRP)

subject to

$$k_1 X_1 + k_2 X_2 \leq 0.8$$
$$\ell_1 X_1 + \ell_2 X_2 \leq 2.0 \tag{5-7}$$
$$X_1 \geq 0; X_2 \geq 0$$

Figure 5.3 depicts the problem and the optimal solution for which $X_1 = 0.800$, $X_2 = 0.672$ and GRP = 4.311. In this example, we use numbers and relationships drawn from the presentation of the two-region, two-commodity, two-resource model of section 8.2 to facilitate the synthesis of nonlinear programming of this chapter with applied general equilibrium models of chapter 8.

Now consider a case where there is a local market at which consumers purchase goods #1 and #2, and where surplus production is sold on the world market. Assume that all resources are owned by consumers and that there has been set a fixed rent r (= 1.542) on capital and a fixed wage w (= 1) on labor. Thus the earnings are 2.0 from wages and 0.8 x 1.542 (= 1.234) from rent. Next assume that consumers maximize their utility, and that the utility function of the representative consumer, taken to represent the aggregate, is given by the Cobb Douglas

$$U = C_1^{0.5} C_2^{0.5} \tag{5-8}$$

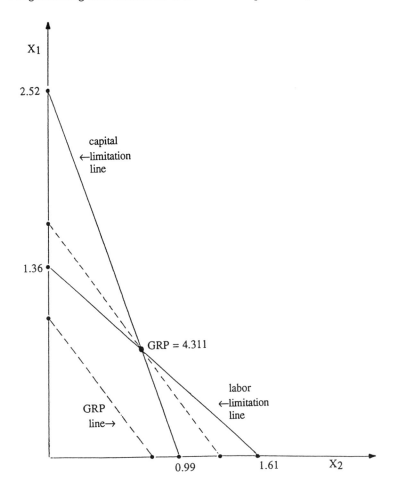

Figure 5.3   Optimal solution for a simple two-resource, two-commodity problem

With their total income of 3.234 as a budget constraint and assuming no saving, consumers will maximize their utility by buying $C_1 = Y/2P_1 = 0.625$ of good #1 and $C_2 = Y/2P_2 = 0.484$ of good #2.[3]

If there is a political leader whose objective is to maximize GRP for prestige or other reasons, so that Q' would still represent a solution to the programming problem, the amount of goods #1 and #2 available for sale on the world market would be $0.800 - 0.625 = 0.175$ and $0.672 - 0.484 = 0.188$, respectively. But if the political leader desires to maximize earnings of foreign exchange, subject to the constraint that his/her constituents be free to buy goods as they desire at the purely competitive local market (that is to maximize their utility), then a new programming problem arises. This problem is how best to utilize the capital and labor remaining, namely 0.212 and 0.482,[4] respectively, after the use of capital and labor to produce the amounts of utility-maximizing consumption just noted. When the foreign market and local market prices are the same, the new problem would then yield output of approximately 0.204 and 1.82 for goods #1 and #2, respectively, for sale in the world market (more of good #1 and slightly less of good #2). A larger amount of foreign exchange would be obtainable.

We can easily introduce another constraint into the maximizing problem. Set the wage of labor at unity ($w = 1$) and let the price of capital be determined at the market under conditions of pure competition (many producers of each commodity). Let the production functions be the Cobb-Douglas

$$X_1 = K_1^{0.25} L_1^{0.75} \tag{5-9}$$

and

$$X_2 = K_2^{0.5} L_2^{0.5}$$

Under profit maximization by firms and pure competition there results a price of capital (r) equal to 1.542, and unit capital and labor requirements:[5]

$$\begin{array}{ll} k_1 = (w/3r)^{0.75} = 0.317 & \ell_1 = (3r/w)^{0.25} = 1.467 \\ k_2 = (w/r)^{0.5} = 0.805 & \ell_2 = (r/w)^{0.5} = 1.242 \end{array} \tag{5-10}$$

Also, given these coefficients and the levels of output X_1 and X_2, total demands for capital and labor come to equal the exogenously given supplies.

Lastly, let there be, under conditions of pure competition (many consumers together with many producers), markets at which the prices of goods #1 and #2 and the rent of capital are to be determined. Also, let the production of goods #1 and #2 require as intermediate inputs both goods where the input and output coefficients are $-a_{11} = 0.05$; $-a_{12} = 0.2$; $-a_{21} = 0.15$ and $-a_{22} = 0.10$. Then we can set up a programming problem to maximize utility given as *constraints:* (1) the coefficients of intermediate inputs just noted; (2) the consumption function (5-8) and the two production functions (5-9); (3) conditions of pure competition (negligible influence of consumers upon commodity prices and producers upon resource and commodity prices); (4) the stocks of capital (0.8) and labor (2.0); (5) the wage of labor as a numeraire ($w = 1$); and (6) demand = supply on the capital market and both commodity markets. The outcome would be: outputs ($X_1 = 0.8$ and $X_2 = 0.672$); rent of capital ($r = 1.542$);

unit inputs of capital and labor (k_1 = 0.317, k_2 = 0.805, ℓ_1 = 1.467 and ℓ_2 = 1.242); prices of goods (P_1 = 2.585, P_2 = 3.334); income (Y = 3.234); and consumption levels (C_1 = 0.625, and C_2 = 0.487).

In brief, the purpose of this section is to provide some of the basic aspects of nonlinear programming, but more important to illustrate its potential for handling complex problems. When we move on to chapters 8 and 10 where we discuss applied general interregional equilibrium (AGIE) models we shall indicate how they might be construed as interregional programming problems for the real economy wherein distance and space must be treated explicitly. At the minimum this knowledge will facilitate understanding of complicated AGIE models and their solution procedures.

5.3 Industrial complex analysis as interregional programming

The presentations in the previous sections have not embodied any application. We have not done so in section 5.1 since, to repeat, linear programming, even of an interregional nature, is no longer of general relevance for regional science since nonlinearities can now be so easily introduced. With regard to nonlinear programming, we now wish to illustrate an application with an industrial complex study.[6] This study also indicates how nonlinear programming can be fused with comparative cost analysis of chapter 2, input-output of chapter 3 and econometric studies of chapter 4, and thus suggests how nonlinear programming can be at the heart of a 'complex analysis' study.

In an early study (Isard et al., 1960), an industrial complex was defined as 'a set of activities occurring at a given location and belonging to a group (subsystem) of activities which are subject to important production, marketing or other interrelations,' p. 377. In later years, the requirement in that definition that all activities in that set occur at a given location has been relaxed. However, to realize the externalities involved it is usually the case that at least some of the activities are spatially juxtaposed.

This early study was concerned with the development of an oil refinery-petrochemicals-synthetic fiber complex in Puerto Rico. It was essentially a nonlinear interregional programming problem involving two regions, the Gulf Coast and Puerto Rico, competing for the fertilizer market in Puerto Rico (which was being served by Gulf Coast producers), and the oil and synthetic fiber markets in the Rest of the United States (the Rest of the World for these two regions). The market for oil was the East Coast of United States centering around New York City while the market for synthetic fibers was in the South of the United States; selected petrochemicals were to be produced to serve as intermediate inputs into fertilizer and fiber production. Nonlinearity was involved primarily (1) in the scale economies in the use of the two resources, labor and capital, in each of the activities and (2) consequently in the spatial juxtaposition economies obtainable from capturing and using the gas streams from oil refining as raw material inputs into petrochemicals; these streams were frequently burned off in the operation of oil refineries.

This interregional nonlinear programming problem represented a fusion of two of the several methods already discussed (the comparative cost procedure, chapter 2, and input-output analysis, chapter 3 and could have embodied a third (econometrics, chapter 4) had data been available. It started with a comparative cost procedure. Recall that in that procedure one needs to compare the advantages of a potential location being studied with the most efficient existing location (or location pattern) or other locations or patterns that might be developed. In the complex study to be reported upon, Puerto Rico was the site being studied as a potential location for an oil refinery-petrochemicals-synthetic fiber complex. The most efficient location or location pattern that could exist in competition with Puerto Rico was a split location one, with synthetic fiber production in the South of the U.S. and the rest of the complex's activities at the Gulf Coast.

In this study three types of basic locational cost differentials were involved:

(1) the labor cost differentials, Puerto Rico's advantage as a cheap source of textile-type labor relative to the Gulf Coast being established at $0.92 per man hour,[7] its disadvantage on skilled chemical-petroleum labor arbitrarily taken at $1.00 per man hour.[8]

(2) the transport cost differentials, namely (a) a disadvantage of Puerto Rico at 14.3¢ per barrel on oil (largely a transport cost to be incurred on Venezuelan oil[9]) and (b) an advantage of 7.3¢ per barrel on gasoline products since Puerto Rico is closer to the major New York market.[10]

(3) agglomeration economies from varying the magnitudes of the aggregate of all production in a complex that is spatially juxtaposed.

The second method of analysis that was employed was input-output as discussed in chapter 3. First, the set of relevant production activities and processes needed to be identified. In the Puerto Rican study intensive interviewing of oil refinery and petrochemical operating and construction companies was undertaken; 73 processes were identified, as relevant, selected ones being listed at the head of the columns of Table 5-2. Also, 76 commodities were found to be relevant as outputs (+) and inputs (−), selected ones being listed along the rows of that table.[11] (Existing as well as new processes and commodities needed to be considered. In the Puerto Rico study the potential for the inclusion of a new commodity (perlon) was examined since its production was judged by some to come to be highly profitable.) From interviews, published literature, patents and through trading of information, data on inputs and outputs for each of the 73 relevant processes were obtained. From these data, the inputs for a unit level of any given process were best estimated to be constant production coefficients, except for labor and capital. This was in accord with the consensus of those knowledgeable with the relevant processes. Thus, once there was established the unit level of each activity that was convenient to use for computations, the set of constant production coefficients for each of the relevant 73 processes could be calculated and recorded in the complete 76 x 73 input-output type table corresponding to Table 5-2. With regard to labor and capital requirements, scale economies were significant. In the 1950s, expert judgment and the practice in the highly competitive and efficient set of production activities considered the use of a fractional power law to establish labor (L) and capital (K) requirements for the planned output (O) of a new plant. In particular, there was general use of the following formulae:

$$L = L_{ex}(O/O_{ex})^{0.22} \qquad K = K_{ex}(O/O_{ex})^{0.7}$$

where L_{ex}, K_{ex}, and O_{ex} refer to levels of an existing efficient plant.

With the input-output structure for the 73 relevant processes and 76 relevant commodities involved as inputs, outputs, or both, we next needed to set up meaningful complexes. First realistic constraints had to be set on the output of any synthetic fiber considered, dacron, dynel, orlon, nylon and perlon being the ones explored. From interviews and discussions with marketing personnel, it was deemed infeasible from an investment standpoint to consider an operation at a scale greater than that characteristic of recently constructed synthetic fiber operations, namely 36.5 million (MM) pounds annually. For fertilizer production a realistic scale was taken to be that amount of ammonium nitrate and urea that would meet the projected Puerto Rican annual local consumption of fertilizer estimated at 80 MM lbs. of nitrogen content.

From the constraints on both fiber and fertilizer output, estimated requirements of intermediate inputs and imports were calculated, finally arriving at an oil refinery operation consistent with reasonable scale economies having an annual input of 9.428 MM barrels of crude oil. Figure 5.4 illustrates the production flow chart (the interactivity structure)

Table 5-2 Annual inputs and outputs for selected oil refinery,

	Oil Refinery, Prototype 1 (1)		Oil Refinery, Prototype 4 (4)		Ethylene Separation Prototype 4 (10)		Ethylene Glycol (oxidation) (22)		Ammonia from Hydrogen (31)	Ammonia from Methane (32)
1. Crude Oil MM bbl.	−9.428	⋯	−9.428	⋯		⋯		⋯		
2. Gasoline, straight-run MM bbl.	+2.074		+1.300							
3. Gasoline, cracked MM bbl.	+1.484		+2.226							
4. Gasoline, reformed MM bbl.			+1.486							
5. Gasoline, polymerized MM bbl.	+0.219		+0.415		+0.029					
6. Naphtha, MM bbl.	+0.660									
7. Kerosene, MM bbl.	+0.943		+0.707							
8. Diesel oil MM bbl.	+1.414		+0.896							
9. Gas oil MM bbl.										
10. Cycle oil MM bbl.	+1.320		+1.980							
11. Heavy residual MM bbl.	+0.943									
12. Coke and carbon 10XMM lb.			+4.033							
13. L.P.G. 10XMM lb.	+6.860		+15.050		+0.508					
14. Hydrogen MM lb.	+0.950		+8.900						−2.000	
15. Methane MM lb.	+12.780		+34.860							−5.500
16. Ethylene (mixed) MM lb.	+6.510		+17.410		−16.100					
17. Ethane (mixed) MM lb.	+9.930		+32.250		−30.190					
18. Propylene MM lb.	+3.630		+7.580		−7.580					
19. Propane MM lb.	+2.150		+5.080		−5.080					
20. Butylenes MM lb.										
21. Butanes MM lb.										
22. Pure ethylene MM lb.					+16.100		−8.300			
23. Pure ethane MM lb.					+30.190					
24. Steam MMM lb.	−0.801		−1.402		−0.148		−0.103			−0.023
25. Power MM kw. hr.	−2.511		−3.999		−0.194		−0.800		−4.640	−5.600
26. Fuel 10XMMM Btu.	−139.000		−242.000				−2.010			−0.450
34. Nitrogen MM lb.							+68.000			
35. Ethylene Glycol MM lb.							+10.000			
39. Ammonia MM lb.									+10.000	+10.000
40. HCN MM lb.										
41. Acrylonitrile MM lb.										
42. Methanol MM lb.										
43. Sulphur MM lb.										
44. Sulphuric acid MM lb.										
45. Nitric acid MM lb.										
46. Paraxylene MM lb.										
47. Dimethyl terephthalate MM lb.										
48. Dacron polymer MMlb.										
49. Dacron Staple MM lb.										
59. Ammonium nitrate MM lb.										
60. Urea MM lb.										
61. Carbon dioxide MM lb.										
74. Nylon salt MM lb.										
76. Nylon filament MM lb.										

petrochemical, and synthetic fiber activities

Ammonia from Ethylene (33)	Ammonia from Ethane (34)	...	Nitric Acid from Ammonia (43)	Dimethyl Terephthalate (air oxidation) (44)	...	Dacron Polymer (46)	Dacron Staple (47)	...	Ammonium Nitrate from Ammonia (55)	Urea from Ammonia (56)	...	Nylon Filament (73)
− 6.290												
	− 5.780											
− 0.023	− 0.023			− 0.030		− 0.060	− 0.500		− 0.007	− 0.028		− 0.555
− 5.600	− 5.600		− 1.200	− 5.200		− 2.500	− 12.000		− 0.170	− 0.340		− 16.000
− 0.450	− 0.450			− 2.800		− 1.000				− 2.250		
												− 2.200
				− 3.230								
+ 10.000	+ 10.000		− 2.860						− 2.380	− 5.800		
				− 4.000		+ 3.350						
			+ 10.000						− 7.630			
				− 6.800								
				+ 10.000		− 10.100						
						+ 10.000	− 10.000					
							+ 10.000					
									+ 10.000			
										+ 10.000		
										− 7.500		
												− 10.000
												+ 10.000

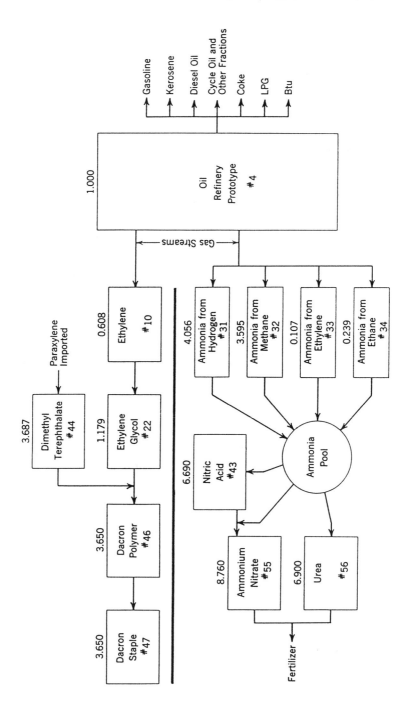

Figure 5.4   Dacron A program

for the Dacron A program (based on an oil refinery of prototype 4). Each box in the figure contains the name and number of an activity in Table 5-2 required in that program. The number atop each box is the multiple of the unit level at which that activity in Table 5-2 must be operated to meet the requirements of the program. Multiplying down the column by that number yields the outputs and required inputs of that activity. A vector covering each final output and the total of each required input (except for labor and capital) over all activities of that complex can then be formed. When each quantity in that vector is multiplied by the relevant cost advantage or disadvantage in the relevant vector of cost advantages or disadvantages by commodity (which can be developed), and the resulting products summed, there is obtained a scalar giving with respect to the linear part of the computation the total advantage or disadvantage of locating the Dacron A complex in Puerto Rico. (This assumes that the Gulf Coast/South location operates each of its activities at the same level as Puerto Rico.) To this scalar must be added the locational advantage or disadvantage on labor costs. (There would be no locational advantage or disadvantage at this stage on capital, since all capital is assumed to be obtained at the New York financial market or at the going New York interest rate.) The results (as good approximations) are recorded in the Dacron A row of Table 5-3, columns (1), (2) and (3). (They were obtained by iteration with the use of the best computers then available, namely a slide-rule and a hand desk computer.) When the items in the first three columns for Dacron A are added, they yield an annual advantage of $2,369,000 for Puerto Rico when compared to a Full complex when located at the Gulf Coast. When the items in columns (1), (4), (5) and (6) for Dacron A are added, they yield an annual advantage of $311,000 for Puerto Rico when compared to the split Gulf Coast/South complex.

Note that if we were to display graphically the net profits obtainable by this type of computation for different levels of output of the Dacron A complex, we would obtain a curve for the Puerto Rico location such as the one noted in Figure 5.5. An important point to observe is that when scale economies in labor and capital are of a significant size while other inputs are constant production coefficients, a concave net revenue curve is generated (where net revenue might be positive or negative). In essence for any given level short of the maximum that is acceptable for investment by the business community (that is the 36.5 MM lbs. of fiber), this maximum serves as a binding constraint and a boundpoint (i.e., a point at which a constraint becomes binding) emerges as a possible solution in the appropriate multidimensional mapping of this problem. In like manner,

Table 5-3 Overall net advantage (disadvantage) of a Puerto Rico location in dollars per year by complex[a]

(data rounded to nearest thousand)

Complex	Transport Cost Disadvantage (1)	Relative to Full Complex at Gulf Coast		Relative to Split Complex at Gulf Coast and Textile South			
		Advantage on Textile Labor (2)	Disadvantage on Chemical-Petroleum Labor (3)	Advantage on Textile Labor (4)	Disadvantage on Chemical-Petroleum Labor (5)	Scale (Moderate)[a] and/or Process Disadvantage (6)	Final Net Over-all Advantages (+) or Disadvantages (−) [(1) + (4) + (5) + (6)] (7)
Dacron A	− 263,000	+ 4,861,000	− 2,229,000	+ 3,963,000	− 2,229,000	− 1,160,000	+ 311,000
Dacron C	− 339,000	+ 4,860,000	− 2,226,000	+ 3,962,000	− 2,226,000	− 1,909,000	− 512,000
Orlon B	− 608,000	+ 4,890,000	− 2,329,000	+ 3,986,000	− 2,329,000	− 2,017,000	− 968,000
Orlon J	− 565,000	+ 4,858,000	− 2,217,000	+ 3,960,000	− 2,217,000	− 708,000	+ 470,000
Dynel A	− 760,000	+ 4,963,000	− 2,590,000	+ 4,046,000	− 2,590,000	− 2,916,000	− 2,220,000
Dynel F	− 437,000	+ 4,907,000	− 2,390,000	+ 4,000,000	− 2,390,000	− 1,445,000	− 272,000
Nylon A	− 457,000	+ 4,974,000	− 2,624,000	+ 4,055,000	− 2,624,000	− 2,543,000	− 1,569,000
Nylon G	− 772,000	+ 4,875,000	− 2,275,000	+ 3,974,000	− 2,275,000	− 335,000	+ 592,000

[a]Based on the operation of all Mainland activities except refinery and fiber production at scales moderately larger than in Puerto Rico.

each of the many other Dacron programs examined yield a boundpoint as a possible solution.

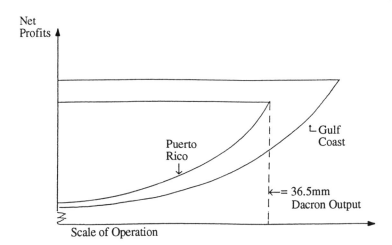

Figure 5.5 Hypothetical variation in net profits for different scales of a Dacron A complex

Similarly, many complexes for each of the other fibers — dynel, orlon and nylon — were carefully examined, each also producing regular refinery products and fertilizers. On the average, 40 to 50 complexes were investigated for every one of them, each complex being constructed to be a boundpoint in the appropriate multidimensional mapping of the problem. The results for two of the best for each fiber are displayed in Table 5-3.

Where the scales of activities are the same at Puerto Rico and the Gulf Coast/South, the iteration required is one which currently a nonlinear programming algorithm can easily perform. The objective function of a relevant problem would be

$$\underset{s\in S}{\text{Max }} \mathbf{P'X}_s \tag{5-11}$$

where:

s is a complex within the set S of complexes examined (approximately 200 in the case of Puerto Rico);

$\mathbf{P'}$ is a row vector of profitability differentials (negative when a disadvantage for Puerto Rico, positive when an advantage), one for each net input or output; and

$\mathbf{X}_s$ is a vector of required net inputs and outputs of complex s (as
would be determined by (1) the levels at which each activity in s
would be run, (2) the constant production coefficient of Table 5-2,
and (3) the labor inputs calculated using the fractional power law
for labor).

The objective function would be subject to many scale constraints such as
$X_{46} \leq 36.5$ MM lbs. in the case of Dacron A production in Puerto Rico
which in turn would reduce the complexity of computation. A
programming procedure could then start with some feasible basis, next
compare its solution with some boundpoint solution (there would be a
boundpoint for each complex of each fiber), and proceed boundpoint by
boundpoint, reaching that boundpoint as a best solution which has not been
eliminated as inferior by another boundpoint.

However, to be realistic the profitability of a Puerto Rico location must
be compared with that of a Gulf Coast/South location whose scales of
annual operations can well exceed those of Puerto Rico and thus where
scale and other agglomeration economies can be much larger. As roughly
indicated in Figure 5.5, for all levels below the Puerto Rico binding
constraint (scale) of 36.5 MM lbs. annually, the superiority of the Puerto
Rico location for a Dacron A complex exists. However, scales of activities
in a Gulf Coast/South location would reach much higher magnitudes before
they become constraints (for example, the maximum level of ethylene
glycol production might be 10.0 MM instead of the level of 1.179 MM as
indicated in Figure 5.4 and that of dimethyl terephthalate 10.0 instead of
3.687). Hence, in accord with the fractional power law, the Gulf
Coast/South location would need less labor and less capital per unit level of
output of each activity, and thus incur less labor and capital costs than
Puerto Rico. As a consequence, (1) the positive profitability differentials of
Puerto Rico for textile-type labor would diminish for some activities and
become negative for others, (2) Puerto Rico's disadvantage on chemical
and related labor would mount, and (3) a major disadvantage would come
to exist with respect to capital for most all activities. Full details on all
calculations of scale and other agglomeration economies are contained in
Isard, Schooler and Vietorisz (1959).[12] Thus, as indicated in Figure 5.5,
the advantage of Puerto Rico for Dacron A would diminish when
compared with increasing scales of the Gulf Coast/South operations and
become negative when the latter approach their maximum. What in effect
occurs is, when scales are allowed to vary, the column vector of outputs
and inputs must be expanded to include capital and the two types of labor,
and the row vector of profitability differentials must also be extended to

contain three more profitability differentials, each a function of the 73 scale differences, one for each activity. The computer program for this extended nonlinear programming problem would need to be revised. The objective function would still be a multidimensional linear surface but there would be many more boundpoints to consider. The results of some rough calculations employed, adequate however for the conclusions of the study, are presented in Table 5-3. Dacron A still retains some positive profitability for Puerto Rico when mainland scales are moderate, but Nylon G has the largest. When maximum mainland scales are taken into account, none of the complexes has a positive profitability differential for Puerto Rico; Nylon G has the least negative profitability differential.[13]

There were many other interesting aspects of the Puerto Rico study, which the reader may find in Isard et al., 1960, and Isard, Schooler and Vietorisz, 1959. The two major aspects this study embodied are (1) scale economies in each activity and consequently in the agglomeration and spatial juxtaposition of activities, and (2) an iterative computation procedure, which today with our tremendously increased computer capability can be replaced with a nonlinear programming procedure. In addition, through combining the use of comparative cost and input-output methods it opens up, as will be elaborated upon in chapters 8 and 10, many possible interregional studies which go well beyond the simple model (presented in this section) — namely, one of two regions interacting in trade and competing for markets in a third region.

There was, however, one crucial question which we were not able to probe; namely, to what extent the advantage of Puerto Rico in textile-type labor cost would disappear with its development. Unfortunately, there was not adequate data available on industrial development in other cheap labor areas of the world competing with developed regions to enable us to conduct an econometric-type study.

5.4 Urban and other complexes

Inability to analyze adequately agglomeration and spatial juxtaposition economies has always plagued economists and regional scientists concerned with urban analysis. The major obstacle has always been the extensive nonlinear character of the relationships involved. Now, however, with the potential for nonlinear programming made possible by the recent computer revolution, we can attack urban agglomeration analysis much more effectively. Already, we have suggested how the laborious (highly labor-intensive) effort in studying industrial complexes is no longer necessary.

As early as the 1950's when the field of regional science was established, there was much discussion of what can be designated *urban complex analysis*. This discussion was embedded in the question of what constitutes the optimum size of a city, of the central city of a metropolitan area, of satellite (suburban) towns and villages. And if one were planning a hierarchy of central places, what should be the sizes of the places at the different levels, and what functions should they serve?

In the 1960 Methods book we essentially stated that as in industrial complex analysis, it is first recognized that in addition to scale economies many activities within towns, cities and other urban areas tend to be bound by strong technical (production), marketing, and other interrelations. Oftentimes these are so pronounced and exert such an integrating effect that an adequate locational or other economic analysis must consider the activities together as an urban complex rather than separately.

We then noted that an obvious first step might be to identify general groups of urban-metropolitan activities, where the activities within each group have strong links affecting their costs and revenues. One such group might comprise: the several retail activities of major department stores, women's ready-to-wear shops, specialty stores of all types, drugstores, variety stores, etc.; services of restaurants, theaters, hotels, lawyers, doctors, dentists; diverse repair shops; and in fact the whole host of activities characteristic of a thriving full-blown central business district. At the other extreme, another group might consist of retail services of a local corner grocery store plus the services of one or a few other highly local establishments such as a shoe repair shop or a drugstore. Between these two extremes might be a group consisting of branch department stores, supermarkets, women's ready-to-wear shops, drugstores, variety stores, music shops, sporting goods stores, etc., as well as services of restaurants, bowling alleys, filling stations, partly specialized professional personnel, and other activities characteristic of regional shopping centers. And still other groups might be defined, existing or not.

In the delineation of groups such as those of the preceding paragraph, a considerable amount of subjective decision making would be involved. Many activities can be and are involved in several of these groups. Yet there are those that preliminary analysis excludes from some — such as funeral parlors in central business districts and in regional shopping centers, or auto repair shops in central business districts, or high-grade specialty stores in local neighborhoods, or hotels in smaller community shopping centers.

Once general groups of activities are identified in a systematic manner, a set of basic questions must be faced. It is immediately evident that an overall pattern of commercial establishments for a metropolitan area which consists of urban complexes of two orders only — say the order corresponding to central business districts and the order corresponding to local neighborhoods — is economically unwarranted, given the travel desires and shopping habits of consumers of a modern urban-industrial society. It is also evident that a pattern which excludes either of these two orders of urban complexes is also unrealistic. But exactly how many orders of urban complexes should there be? How dominant should be the central business district? What shares of total metropolitan activity should be allocated to the several other orders of urban complexes? How should the centers of each order be spatially distributed, and what should be their number and size? All these questions are interdependent. To a major extent, answers can only be found simultaneously.

However, a thorough and all out study of say a central place system (the set of urban areas) within a metropolitan region was at that time too difficult a task to attempt. Such also is the case today. More advisable would seem to be an urban complex study of a small city or regional shopping center to get a handle on treating in a single model a number of activities, each of which may be subject to scale economies together with agglomeration (urbanization) economies from spatial juxtaposition.

All that seems possible now (1997) is a beginning that would parallel the industrial complex analysis. The set of constant production coefficients per unit level of activity would be recorded in a table with each activity of the complex listed at the head of a column and with commodities (goods and services) listed along rows. Then, with regard to other inputs, as with labor and capital in the industrial complex study, fractional power laws or other functions might be employed to capture scale economies. Agglomeration (spatial juxtaposition) economies might be indicated by a fractional power law or other function of aggregate consumption, or of some other meaningful aggregate.

In this problem there would be the one or more binding constraints, for example fixed amounts of land area, or of capital available for investment in the case of a new town, etc. The feasibility of different consumption patterns would be examined, each consumption pattern playing the role of a specific complex. A utility function (perhaps a Cobb Douglas) with two or more representative goods, one a luxury item, another such as food or shelter, might constitute the objective function.

In the above manner, a nonlinear programming problem might be set up, utilizing some of the facilitating aspects of the industrial complex analysis and also capable of incorporating some of the fruitful (facilitating) aspects of the applied general interregional equilibrium model to be presented in conceptual fashion in chapter 8. Once the analysis of the isolated city as an urban complex has been successfully performed, the next step would be to attack a problem consisting of two cities of different size with specialization among them. This study could be followed by one for three cities, and so forth, until one for a complete metropolitan region can be undertaken.

In like manner, a number of other kinds of complexes can be researched. A single isolated hospital, as a hospital complex, can be examined. Then a system of two hospitals, three hospitals until a medical complex containing several hospitals and associated facilities can be investigated. Likewise for recreational complexes, for example, a system of parks of different size and specialization, and for still others such as a business services complex, a system of libraries and educational facilities, and a complex of department stores.

5.5 Concluding remarks

We now have indicated the greatly increased potential of nonlinear programming that has resulted from the computer revolution. Its potential for regional and interregional analysis lies in its ability to handle scale, localization and urbanization economies for a number of situations when a basic constraint exists. Such a constraint may be on (1) investment set by an investment community; (2) level of port development set by a government (national, regional or local); (3) scale of highway, airport or rail development set by a transport authority, or the World Bank when providing the required financial support; (4) the magnitude of a regional shopping center encompassing several department stores that generate major scale and localization economies leading to agglomeration economies for many smaller co-locating activities; (5) the scale of a comprehensive hospital complex providing a complete set of services; or (6) any of many other situations in which a clearly dominating scale economy is present. This potential for interregional analysis and study of a space-economy in general will become still more clear when we demonstrate ways to fuse nonlinear programming with regional science methods other than comparative cost, input-output and econometrics in chapters to follow.

Endnotes

1   The materials in sections 5.0 and 5.1 draw heavily upon Isard et al. (1960). Some general references on programming are Baumol (1977), Bazaraa, Sherili and Shetty (1993), Dorfman, Samuelson and Solow (1958), Gass (1985), Hadley (1964), Isard et al. (1960, ch. 10), Luenberger (1984), Miller (1998), Stevens (1958), Vanderbei (1996).

2   In linear programming parlance, the segmented line RSTU is designated the *efficiency frontier.*

3   See endnote 3 in chapter 8 for a comparable derivation.

4   These numbers are obtained by using the unit capital and labor requirements specified in the text.

5   See endnote 4, chapter 8 for a comparable derivation of these.

6   Space limitations allow us to cover only some of the basic aspects of this study. The full presentation is contained in Isard, Schooler and Vietorisz (1959) with supplementation in Isard et al. (1960).

7   However, relative to synthetic fiber production, where comparison is made with operations in the South of U.S., Puerto Rico's advantage was set at $0.75 per man hour.

8   See Isard et al., 1960, chapter 9 and Isard, Schooler and Vietorisz, 1969, for full discussion of all these and the following locational cost differentials. With regard to skilled chemical-petroleum type labor, it should be noted that little data existed for projecting its differential. It was therefore considered appropriate for any client using the results of the study to set his/her own estimated differential, the results of the study being presented in a form that would allow the client to do so easily.

9   This figure includes an f.o.b. price of oil at Venezuela that is 1.14¢ higher than at the Gulf Coast. This difference reflects the fact that Venezuela is closer to the major East Coast refineries than the Gulf.

10 Power, stream and fuel cost differentials were translated into transport cost on fuel oil of equivalent Btu value. A capital cost differential was taken to be negligible since it was assumed that a major industrial company, whether investing in Puerto Rico, the Gulf Coast or the South, would obtain its capital at the ongoing interest rate at the New York financial market. Tax differentials, although important, were considered to be largely a matter of political policy in Puerto Rico and considered to be unpredictable. Water and other cost differentials were considered to be of negligible importance.

11 These processes include import activities to acquire a necessary input, such as dimethyl terephthalate, since this item could not be effectively produced in Puerto Rico.

12 The calculations for the Gulf Coast also took into account gains from factor substitution, process substitutions and product mixes different from those most economic for Puerto Rico.

13 It should be noted that this study had practical application. Although the specific form that oil refining and petrochemical operations took in Puerto Rico differed in a number of ways from what was investigated, partly because of the system of tax rebates and subsidies that was provided, vigorous development occurred. Unfortunately, owing to exceedingly poor management of the oil refinery, the development was brought to an abrupt halt during the OPEC oil crisis when the oil refinery had failed to obtain assured sources of crude for the long run and had to pay at the spot market prices as high as $60 per barrel.

References

Baumol, William J. 1977. *Economic Theory and Operations Analysis.* Englewood Cliffs, N.J.: Prentice Hall.
Bazaraa, M. S., H. D. Sherili, and C. M. Shetty. 1993. *Nonlinear Programming Theory and Algorithms.* New York: Wiley.
Dorfman, Robert, Paul A. Samuelson, and Robert Solow. 1958. *Linear Programming and Economic Analysis.* New York: McGraw-Hill.
Gass, Saul I. 1985. *Linear Programming: Methods and Applications.* New York: McGraw Hill.
Hadley, George. 1964. *Nonlinear and Dynamic Programming.* Reading, Mass.: Addison-Wesley.

Isard, Walter, et al. 1960. *Methods of Regional Analysis.* Cambridge, Mass.: MIT Press.

Isard, Walter, Eugene W. Schooler, and Thomas Vietorisz. 1959. *Industrial Complex Analysis and Regional Development.* Cambridge, Mass.: MIT Press.

Luenberger, David G. 1984. *Linear and Nonlinear Programming.* Reading, Mass.: Addison-Wesley.

Miller, Ronald E. 1999. *Mathematics for Optimization: Linear and Nonlinear Models* (in preparation).

Stevens, Benjamin H. 1958. 'An Interregional Linear Programming Model,' *Journal of Regional Science*, 1, Summer.

Vanderbei, Robert J. 1996. *Linear Programming: Foundations and Extensions.* Boston: Kluwer Academic Publishers.

6. Gravity and spatial interaction models

Walter Isard

6.0 Introduction

A system of regions has an intricate structure. Only some of the major strands which interconnect people, households, firms, social groups, governmental agencies, and a variety of other operating and decision-making units have been isolated and subjected to analysis in the preceding chapters. The balanced scholar will therefore be uncomfortable, especially as he/she observes, perhaps at some distance in space, the geographic pattern in which human beings and their physical structures are massed in metropolises — metropolises which vary widely in size, configuration, and intensity of activity, such intensity tending to diminish in most all directions from the core. True, the fine-stranded generalized interdependence schemes as crystallized in interregional input-output and programming are powerful analytical tools. True, we have shown how urban complex analysis can be embodied in nonlinear programming and thereby capture some of the spatial juxtaposition (or agglomeration) economies and diseconomies. However, as yet, have they even in a small way, been able to cope with these economies? As already indicated, urban complex analysis has a very long way to go before it can fruitfully attack the complexities of metropolitan areas and the surrounding system of central places. An observer, impressed by the phenomena of human massing within any system of industrialized regions and the intricate spatial structures they possess, might ask: Is not society more than a matrix of finely detailed connections among units? Is not the structure of a system of regions more than the sum of the interactions of sets and patterns of units or sectors as conceived by interregional input-output and programming? Are there not other over-all forces pertaining to masses which pervade society and confine the multitude of possible interactions among its innumerable units? These questions motivate the analyst to explore fresh approaches, even quite different ones. One such approach is that of the gravity model and the diverse spatial interaction frameworks that have evolved or been associated with it.[1]

In the gravity, potential, and spatial interaction models — which for short we shall term gravity models whenever we speak generally of these models — the region is conceived as a mass. The mass is structured according to certain principles. These principles govern in an over-all fashion the range of behavior of the individual particles, both constraining and initiating their action. Interregional relations may be thought of as interactions among masses. Again, general principles may be said to govern the frequency and intensity of such interactions; and by so doing they influence the behavior of individual units (particles) within each mass. This approach is a macro one that resembles an approach frequently used by physical scientists. For example, Boyle's classic studies of the effects of pressure and temperature on the volume of gases were essentially investigations into the behavior of masses of molecules; the movement of any individual molecule was not a matter of inquiry.

6.1 A simple probability point of view

To develop the basic concepts underlying gravity models it is useful to start with a rather *simple and loose* probability point of view.[2] (A rigorous probability statement will be discussed in section 6.4.) Suppose there is a metropolitan region with population P. Let the region be divided into many subareas. Let there also be known the total number of internal trips taken by the inhabitants of this metropolitan region. We represent this number by the constant T. Further, let there be no significant differences among subareas in the tastes, incomes, age distributions, occupational structures, etc. of their populations and individuals within their populations.

Now, suppose we wish to determine the number of trips which originate in, let us say, subarea i, and terminate in, let us say, subarea j. Assume, for the moment, that no costs and no time are involved in undertaking a trip from one area to another, that is, that the friction of distance is zero. For this hypothetical situation we may expect that for a representative individual in subarea i the per cent of his journeys terminating in subarea j will be equal to the ratio P_j/P, the population of subarea j divided by the total population of the region, *ceteris paribus* — assuming that interaction opportunities are proportional to population size. That is, if the total population of the metropolitan region is 1,000,000 and that of subarea *j* 100,000, we may expect the individual to make 10 per cent of his/her trips to *j*. Additionally, since a representative individual in subarea *i* is by our homogeneity assumptions identical with a representative individual in any other subarea, and since his/her transport time cost is zero, we may estimate the number of trips he/she undertakes as the average number of trips per capita for the entire metropolitan region. This average is equal to T/P. Designating this average by the letter *k*, we find that the absolute number of trips which a representative individual in subarea *i* makes to subarea *j* is $k(P_j/P)$. That is, if 10 percent of the total population resides in subarea *j*, the individual in subarea *i* will tend to make 10 percent of his trips to subarea *j*; if the average number of trips per individual is 20, the individual will make, on the average, two trips to *j*.

This reasoning applies to one representative individual in *i*. But there are P_i individuals residing in subarea *i*. Therefore, the number of trips to subarea *j* which these P_i individuals will make will be P_i times the number of trips to subarea *j* which the representative individual in *i* makes. That is,

$$T_{ij} = k(P_iP_j/P) \qquad (6\text{-}1)$$

where T_{ij} designates the total number of trips taken by individuals in *i* (i.e., originating in *i*) which terminate in *j*. In this manner we can estimate the expected total number of trips for every possible combination of originating subarea and terminating subarea. Thus we obtain for the metropolitan region a set of expected or hypothetical trip volumes (total number of trips) between subareas.

Our next step is to determine the possible effect of the actual distance separating a pair of subareas on the number of trips occurring between them. First, for a typical metropolitan region we obtain actual data on the number of trips between every pair of its subareas. We let I_{ij} represent the actual trip volume between any originating subarea *i* and any terminal subarea *j*. We divide this actual number by the expected or hypothetical trip volume T_{ij} to derive the ratio of actual to expected trip volume, that is, I_{ij}/T_{ij}. We also note the distance d_{ij} which separates *i* and *j*. Finally, we plot on a graph with a logarithmic scale along each axis both the ratio I_{ij}/T_{ij} and distance d_{ij} for this particular pair of subareas. For example, in Figure 6.1 where the vertical axis measures the ratio of actual to expected trips and where the horizontal axis measures distance, we may note point L. Point L refers to a pair of subareas approximately 3.6 miles apart for which the ratio of actual to expected trips is approximately 0.4.

In similar manner, for every other combination of originating subarea and terminating subarea we plot the set of data on the ratio of actual to expected trips and intervening distance. Suppose our data are as indicated in Figure 6.1. They suggest a simple relationship between the log of the

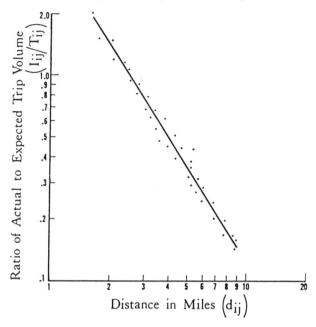

Figure 6.1   Relation between distance and the ratio of actual to expected person trips (hypothetical data)

ratio of actual to expected trip volume on the one hand and log of distance on the other hand. A straight line may be fitted to the plotted data by least squares or by other methods. Since our variables are the log of the ratio of actual to expected trip volume (the dependent variable) and the log of distance (the independent variable), the equation of the line is

$$\ln(I_{ij}/T_{ij}) = a - b \ln d_{ij} \qquad (6\text{-}2)$$

In this equation a is a constant which is the intercept of the straight line with the Y axis, and b is a constant defined by the slope of the line.[3] Removing logs from equation (6-3) and letting c equal the antilog of a, we have

$$I_{ij}/T_{ij} = c/d_{ij}^{b}$$

or

$$I_{ij} = cT_{ij}/d_{ij}^b \qquad (6\text{-}3)$$

Substituting in equation (6-3) the value of T_{ij} as given in equation (6-1), and letting the constant $G = ck/P$, where c, k, and P are constants as defined earlier, we obtain

$$I_{ij} = G(P_iP_j/d_{ij}^b) \qquad (6\text{-}4)$$

This simple relationship may then be taken to describe roughly the actual pattern of trip volumes within the metropolitan region, *ceteris paribus*. That is, it depicts the interaction of people within the metropolitan region as a function of the populations of subareas and the distance variable when this interaction is reflected in trips.

Suppose we study the relationship of actual to expected magnitude on the one hand, and distance on the other hand, for a number of other phenomena reflecting the interactions of people within the metropolitan mass and *among* metropolitan masses. We might examine telephone calls, telegraph messages, express shipments, money flows, migration, commuting and shopping patterns, etc. Suppose that for all these phenomena we find, as in Figure 6.1, a close linear association between the log of the ratio of actual to expected volume and the log of distance.[4] We might then conclude that the relationship in equation (6-4) reflects a basic principle underlying the structure of metropolitan areas and systems of metropolitan areas — namely that, all else being equal, the interaction between any two populations can be expected to be related directly to their size and inversely to distance. This relationship derived from a probability point of view is essentially the gravity model of physics where P_i and P_j stand for masses M_i and M_j, the exponent b takes the value of 2, and I_{ij} represents the gravitational force F.

Additionally, it is to be noted that equation (6-4) can be converted into another useful form. Suppose we are interested in the interaction between a single subarea i and all other subareas. We would therefore derive the interaction of i with the first subarea (i.e., I_{i1}) plus the interaction of i with the second subarea (i.e., I_{i2}) plus the interaction of i with the third subarea (i.e., I_{i3}) plus . . ., and finally plus the interaction of i with the nth subarea (i.e., I_{in}). From equation (6-4) we find values for each of the interactions, $I_{i1}, I_{i2}, I_{i3}, . . ., I_{in}$. By addition we obtain

$$I_{i1} + I_{i2} + I_{i3} + . . . + I_{in} = G(P_iP_1/d_{i1}^b) + G(P_iP_2/d_{i2}^b)$$
$$+ G(P_iP_3/d_{i3}^b) + . . . + G(P_iP_n/d_{in}^b) \qquad (6\text{-}5)$$

or

$$\sum_{j=1}^{n} I_{ij} = G(\sum_{j=1}^{n} P_i P_j / d_{ij}^b) \tag{6-6}$$

Since P_i may be factored from the right-hand side of the equation (6-3), we derive, after dividing both sides by P_i

$$\sum_{j=1}^{n} I_{ij}/P_i = G(\sum_{j=1}^{n} P_j / d_{ij}^b) \tag{6-7}$$

Note that the numerator of the left-hand side of equation (6-7) is the total interaction of i with all areas including itself,[5] which when divided by the population of i, namely P_i yields interaction with all areas *on a per capita basis* or more strictly *on a per unit of mass basis*. Interaction on such a basis has been designated *potential* at i, for which we employ the symbol $_iV$. By definition, then,

$$_iV = \sum_{j=1}^{n} I_{ij}/P_i \tag{6-8}$$

and, from equation (6-7) we have

$$_iV = G(\sum_{j=1}^{n} P_j / d_{ij}^b) \tag{6-9}$$

It is to be noted that this equation can be derived directly from a simple probability approach as was equation (6-4). Equation (6-9) is the basis of *potential* models and as developed is a variation of equation (6-4), the basic gravity model. It is effectively employed in spatial choice models, for example, in the choice of that one region among many to which an individual might migrate (or firm relocate) or of that shopping center or medical complex an individual might patronize.

Extensive literature exists on the history and development of the use of gravity models and related concepts by social scientists. (See Isard et al. (1960), Fotheringham and O'Kelly (1989), Sen and Smith (1995) and others cited therein.) For purposes of this chapter, we start with the most advanced framework reached in year 1960. At that time much thought was given to the possibility that weights, w_i and w_j, should be applied to the respective masses M_i and M_j. For example, should population be weighted by its per capita income to help explain the level of airline trips between the populations (masses) of metropolitan regions i and j? Moreover, because of different agglomeration (deglomeration) economies and externalities that might be associated with the masses, should exponents α and β be applied to the masses M_i and M_j, respectively.

With regard to distance, should physical, economic (transport cost), or travel-time distance be employed? Furthermore, should the exponent *b* (the distance sensitivity factor) be 2 (as in gravitational force) or unity (as in the mutual energy concept of physics) or some other, particularly to reflect the different intensities of the 'falling-off' effects that are observed with different kinds of trips (for example, to grammar schools in contrast to higher educational institutions).

Thus there evolved the more general formulation (where P_i and P_j of equation (6-4) are replaced, respectively, with M_i and M_j):

$$I_{ij} = G[w_i(M_i^{\alpha})w_j(M_j^{\beta})]/d_{ij}^{b} \tag{6-10}$$

where at times G_{ij} was suggested as a replacement for G to reflect complementarity of resources and other attributes of M_i and M_j and where at times other functional forms were employed in which distance (*d*) entered into the denominator in a different way than simply as a variable raised to some power.

Since 1960, a very large array of gravity and spatial interaction models has evolved. They relate to many different kinds of interactions, some purely theoretical but much more frequently interactions concerned with everyday problems and planning for which useful applications have been sought. Among others, these kinds of interactions have pertained to railway and airline trips; mail and telephone calls; large volume commodity movements; railway express shipments between urban areas; journey-to-work trips; trips to shopping centers, museums, libraries, recreational areas, hospitals, schools, universities and other cultural and educational sites; trade among nations; migration among regions; and in other fields of study such as magnitude of church attendance; social visits and marriages among neighborhood populations; and extent of gang warfare, conflicts among nations and competition among teams. These models are used to understand current and past interactions. However, they have also been fruitfully employed in many studies to forecast (project) the impacts of various changes in variables and policies that affect these variables — such as the impacts upon traffic of a new industrial area, a major residential development, a major shopping center construction, a new superhighway, the reorganization of the transportation system, and so forth. But such projection has been of a comparative statics type in which in most studies there is a shift from one stationary or equilibrium state to another, and wherein no significant structural change has taken place. Even in some studies, where state transitions have been permitted, the spatial interaction patterns that have been derived are stationary or equilibrium patterns, and do not involve a dynamical process that is in general pertinent to a gravity model.

Because there are so many types of applications and theoretical analyses that are capable of being embraced, or said to be embraced, by gravity and spatial interaction models, one cannot establish any particular models best for general use. Hence, in what follows, we shall discuss: (1) the various ways each variable can be defined and measured; (2) alternative distance measures and spatial separation and related functions that can be used; and (3) alternative hypotheses and theories that can be set forth as background for analysis. We leave to the researcher the problem of designing a specific model for the particular situation he/she is interested in, although we will have occasion to present a limited number of interesting formulations and applications of particular frameworks.

6.2 Definition and measurement of mass

What is a relevant mass? As in the above example, it can be population in an area taking trips to destinations whose masses are other population. But the mass of a destination area can be: number of jobs; square footage of retail space in a shopping center adjusted for the quality and diversity of its stores; number of hospital beds; amount of marina facilities; size of university; size of a region's economy (Gross Regional Product); its labor force; its income level; its total wholesale and retail sales; its level of consumption; its economic opportunities in general; its value added in manufacture; its investment in infrastructure; its newspaper circulation; its car registrations and a host of other of its magnitudes.

In the literature, population is often associated with a set of actors at one or more areas (points) of origination who are behaving in a conscious manner. In making decisions to undertake (produce) movement (travel, trips, migration), they are reacting to or being propelled to exploit opportunities, attractive attributes, and/or drawing forces elsewhere, in particular destination areas. However, these opportunities, attributes, and forces can be many in real life. So can the attributes of actors or elements of the originating mass which generate interaction. Hence, there can be innumerable pairs of a combination of actor attributes and a combination of destination attributes. But taking into account the specific attributes in a pairing in the modelling of the interaction within that pairing would diminish the effect of spatial separation and assign much more weight to the particularities of the attributes of the originating and destination elements and their complementarities. This would run counter to what is conceived in physics as gravitational interaction, namely the spatial interaction of the aggregate activity of the innumerable molecules comprising each mass. And *in general* it has been found in regional science and other social studies that the gravity model is most applicable when it pertains to the spatial interaction of large masses (aggregates), less applicable to that of their subaggregates, still less to that of the parts of these subaggregates, and even highly questionable to that of small groups and individuals. In brief, gravitational interactions are found to be much more pertinent on the *macro* level of analysis, where the effect of any specific attribute in the many diverse pairings of attributes averages out, than at the micro where there is no averaging.

To be specific, consider migration. Among others, significant attributes of destination areas may be number of unfilled jobs, wage levels, intensity of the drug problem, the crime rate, the level of interracial conflict, congestion, pollution, presence of cultural facilities, climate, probability of earthquakes, and other natural disasters. Significant attributes of originating areas may be unemployment rates, quality of the educational system, lack of social welfare programs, the conservativeness of a political regime, information level about opportunities, and a host of others including many, if not all, of those noted for destination areas. For a given individual or subclass of migrants some of these attributes may be pertinent in the decision to migrate to a new location and much more important than mere spatial separation. For others, different sets of attributes may dominate. However when the total of the migrations of all subclasses and individuals of a large national population is investigated, it will often turn out that spatial separation is one of the leading, if not dominant factor, that accounts for the aggregate pattern of migration. Obviously the extent to which there exists homogeneity of migrants and of destination areas, the more clearcut will be the spatial separation effect, and the smaller a sample of migrations will be required to establish the particular nature of the spatial separation effect.

Nonetheless, as we shall note below, modifications of the simple gravity model of equation (6-10) and its simpler forms have been found to be useful in particular situations where these modifications combine the gravitational interaction with the particular attribute complementarities of less aggregated masses — where subaggregates are designed (stratified) as much as possible to minimize the within-class variance with regard to each subaggregate's relevant elements.

In brief, all this is saying in another way that the gravitational interaction is more clearly discerned the fewer the differences among the elements of each mass and the larger the masses involved.

Up to now we have treated aggregates of behaving units (actors) as constituting the masses designated as origins. However, behaving units can comprise the masses of destinations, and elements like jobs and qualities of an urban region as origin attributes can set in motion interaction. For example, the impact of the development of a large industrial complex in a new district may be examined in terms of the area in which its labor force may come to take up residence. In brief, what is designated as origins and destinations depends on the objectives and other aspects of a particular study. Too, destinations and origins can often be viewed as interchangeable.[6]

Moreover, in some interaction, for example marriages among separated populations, there may exist mutual (bilateral) attractions (or opportunities) like mutual energy in physics. Similarly, in social correspondence, contract agreements and communications among firms, discussions among nations to reduce conflict, and so forth.

One way to handle the problem of heterogeneity among masses may be to employ weights. For example, take the effect of spatial separation upon first-class airline traffic among urban areas. It is reasonable to expect that, *ceteris paribus,* an area with high per capita income will generate a larger volume of such travel than an area of equal population but lower per capita income. One way to handle this particular heterogeneity is to multiply the population of each generating subarea i by its average per capita income — that is by applying the weight w_i noted in equation (6-10). Weights, w_j, might also be applied to destination areas to recognize the different quality of say recreational facilities when such air traffic is recreationally oriented.

Additionally, the investigator may wish to employ more than one type of weight to adjust for heterogeneity within and between masses, perhaps to take into account differences among behaving units in educational level, age-sex composition and other factors. Then each weight w_i might be a composite weight constructed and applied in an appropriate manner.

Processes internal to masses of an agglomerative, cross-catalytic nature, which affect the forces emanating from them, may be considered relevant, and may be captured in the exponents α and β in equation (6-10). In one sense when we set $\alpha = \beta = 1$ we assume a zero net effect on that basis. The α and β become parameters to be estimated in the log linear statement of equation (6-10) and in a sense provoke interpretation when in calibrations (in statistical estimation) they turn out to be other than unity.

To sum up, within each mass, M_i, $i = 1,...,n$, whether an origin or destination, many elements may be incorporated. From here on we shall designate the mass of an area as O_i when it plays the role of an originating area and as D_j when it plays the role of a destination area. O_i and D_j may be scalars, as when they represent the number of individuals, P_i and P_j, respectively, or when they constitute weight functions modified by agglomerative (cross-catalytic) effects of attributes captured in the α and β exponents of equation (6-10).

6.3 Definitions and measures of distance

In the literature, distance has on a number of occasions been defined physically along a straight line connecting two masses in terms of miles or other standard unit. However, if a metropolitan traffic study is being conducted, distance measured in terms of travel time may be considered more appropriate, or at times some combination of miles and travel time when both peak and off-peak travel are to be considered. In other studies, other measures of distance may be employed, for example: economic distance as measured by transport or travel cost, or the number of links in a transport route or communication channel. In these cases the symbol d_{ij} for distance is often replaced with the symbol c_{ij} to represent an economic (cost) distance. Also, when good estimates of social distance, political distance, ideological distance, psychological distance, or other distance (perhaps a cognitive-type) exist, they may be employed. Usually, however, such distances are inferred and estimated when for a given situation the number of interactions and size of the masses involved are known.[7]

6.4 Functional forms for spatial separation

While deterministic theories of the gravity model have been set forth, none have found wide acceptance and of practical significance. Theories that would view a mass as a composite of micro units each maximizing utility subject to a budget constraint to yield for each unit a demand function for 'interaction with spatial opportunities,' or which would associate disutility with transport and travel costs (travel time), have confronted difficulties. Proponents have not been able to conduct effective testing of relevant hypotheses. And while subjective notions such as spatial discounting may have some appeal (see Isard, 1975), rigorous probabilistic theories to explain spatial interaction phenomena noted above have found substantial acceptance; their hypotheses have been extensively tested and widely applied.

Among probabilistic theories, two forms, each with different desirable properties, have found extensive use. Each generally takes weights w_i and w_j, and exponents α and β as statistical parameters to be estimated. They differ with respect to the deterrence, attenuation or falling-off effect of distance. One views the deterrence function $F(d_{ij})$ as $(d_{ij})^{-b}$, namely as a *power* deterrence function, as in equation (6-4). The other views it as $\exp(-bd_{ij})$, namely as an *exponential* deterrence function, where b is a positive distance sensitivity parameter. The latter view yields the simple model form

$$I_{ij} = M_i M_j \exp(-bd_{ij}) \tag{6-11}$$

The power deterrence function is the one that derives directly from and takes the same form as the gravity model of physics. It has a framework that is suited for application across many studies, especially those involving forecasts. Specifically, it possesses a homogeneity property where estimated parameters are independent of the scale of a system and the units in which distance (cost) is measured. For example, if in a journey to work study, the number of opportunities at destination areas were to be doubled, then relative attraction would remain the same, that is for any two destinations, $j = r,s$, from equation (6-4) where M replaces P, we have

$$\frac{(2M_r)^\beta}{(2M_s)^\beta} = \frac{2^\beta M_r^\beta}{2^\beta M_s^\beta} = \frac{M_r^\beta}{M_s^\beta} \tag{6-12}$$

Similarly, if distance were to be measured in kilometers instead of miles. According to Fotheringham and O'Kelly (1989), this property, in contrast, is not possessed by an exponential deterrence model. As they note in discussing the situations for which a power or exponential function is most suited, 'a model with an exponential cost function calibrated with traffic flows from a major city could not be used to forecast traffic flows in a medium or small urban area' (p. 11).

However, this invariance property of power deterrence functions under similarity transformations is very questionable for very small distances or cost values, that is when d_{ij} or $c_{ij} \rightarrow 0$. Under these circumstances, the predicted (expected) spatial interaction would take on exceedingly large values — values that are not observed. However, this problem is easily exaggerated, being more theoretical than actual. For in a real situation, no two individuals can occupy the same space, and, in a significantly large aggregation d_{ij} or c_{ij} cannot approach zero. (After all black holes are not present in society.) A non-negligible average distance (and cost of spatial interaction) can be claimed to separate them. Alternatively, one can posit the existence of some ε to reflect a start-up, information gathering, or some terminal cost, especially given the fact that individuals are not truly homogeneous. Accordingly, d_{ij} would need to be replaced by

$$(\varepsilon + d_{ij})^{-b} \text{ or } [\varepsilon + d_{ij}{}^b]^{-1}$$

or some other expression. In contrast, this problem of overestimating low cost, short distance movements of an unmodified power deterrence function does not exist with an exponential deterrence function.

Another issue in evaluating the relative desirability of these two types of deterrence functions concerns treatment of expected cost increases. As discussed by Fotheringham and O'Kelly (1989, p. 11),

> Suppose in an analysis of passenger flows on public transit within a major city, costs are to be increased along certain routes. Two possible consequences of this action can result: the selective increase in costs will alter the whole trip matrix; or the trip matrix will remain stable. Also, two types of cost increase are possible; each fare can be increased by a constant multiple or a constant amount. This produces four scenarios under each of which one of the two spatial separation functions is appropriate and the other is inappropriate. For instance, if a multiplicative cost increase is to be applied and this is expected to alter the trip matrix, an exponential cost function should be employed. Conversely, if the cost increase is to be additive, a power function is more appropriate.[8]

The exponential deterrence function is not one that derives from the gravity model of physics. It developed from the early pioneering work of Wilson, 1970, 1974, who initially linked it to entropy analysis and statistical mechanics. This function also derives from the rigorous, independent work of Sen and Smith (1985) — namely a behavioral interpretation when probabilistic variations in interactions at the individual (micro) level are assumed to depend only on average interaction costs and activity levels and when individual interactions are assumed to be statistically independent.

Other issues exist. Fotheringham and O'Kelly conclude based on the kinds of interaction models they have studied and those with which they are familiar, there exists 'a reasonably widespread consensus that the exponential function is more appropriate for analyzing short distance interactions such as those that take place within an urban area. The power function, conversely, is generally held to be more appropriate for analyzing longer distance interaction such as migration flows' (pp. 12–13).[9]

Before concluding this section, we should make explicit the independence assumptions when an advanced formal behavioral interpretation of the gravity model is adopted, as in Sen and Smith, 1995. As they emphasize, each flow T_{ij} between every origin i and every destination j is to be considered a random variable. Thus these random variables can be converted into a set of random variables which are the estimators or estimates. These estimates, augmented by additional variables, yield other random variables which are the forecasts. Hence, the resulting mean (average) frequencies of spatial interactions of behaving units with respect to various origin-destination pairings imply an assumption of *locational independence*. That is, within any given interaction pattern involving a significant number of interactions the likelihood of any given interaction is assumed to be uninfluenced by the properties of the other realized interactions. It is posited for example that there are no congestion effects, such as would be realized and affect that likelihood if more individuals would want to shop at a store with insufficient capacity to serve them. It also is posited that there are no contagion or bandwagon effects, as when friends, shopping together, leads to identical interaction choices. A second assumption implied is that of *frequency independence*. That is, the realized value of each interaction frequency is assumed to be unaffected by the realized value of any other interaction frequency.

Practical application of probabilistic interpreted models must relax these independence assumptions. Their use requires that the masses at i and j are sufficiently large so as to minimize (1) the influence of an interaction associated with any individual behaving unit (or opportunity) on the likelihood of any other unit's interaction (or upon the effect of any other opportunity) and (2) the many types of frequency dependencies among the interaction types existing at the micro level. (See Sen and Smith, 1995 for further discussion.)

It should be noted that other advanced research with gravity models allows for the possibility of multiple measures of separation. If these models are power deterrence ones, the interaction would be a function of a set of positive cost (or distance cost) profiles, each raised to its own power. If these models are exponential deterrence ones, the logarithmic form of them would be linear combinations of the several separation cost measures, each with its own cost sensitivity parameter.

Another direction for advanced research concerns *threshold* models in which there is a genuine possibility that any given interaction (a migration, shopping trip, social visit) considered by an individual will not in fact be taken. Basically, individual behavior is postulated to involve in these models an implicit two-stage process in which a variety of potential interaction situations arise and are either acted upon or not, depending on the individual's current attitudes toward spatial interaction. In these models it is hypothesized that a given interaction will occur if and only if the anticipated travel costs (time, effort, stress) do not exceed the individual's current tolerance levels, designated as his interaction *threshold levels.*

Still another set of advanced gravity models motivated by the need (first forcefully stressed by Stouffer, 1940) to recognize the effect of 'intervening opportunities' on spatial interaction between locations. This has led to significant research on search processes and spatial choice behavior. In these models, each of a set of actors originating at one of a set of locations and attracted by opportunities distributed among a set of destinations, searches among these opportunities until (when there is no stopping rule) he/she identifies one meeting his/her needs (or none at all). These models need to specify for each origin a *search scheme*, namely the order in which spatially identified opportunities are evaluated by each of the relatively homogeneous actors at that origin. The search is concluded once a satisfactory opportunity is identified, all opportunities at a given destination being explored before a new destination is considered. (See Sen and Smith, 1995, for additional discussion.) Further research in the broad subject of spatial choice behavior, as it reflects spatial interaction, is presented in Fotheringham and O'Kelly (1989).

Gravity-type models can also be used to treat (1) interaction behavior of an hierarchical nature when first a relevant opportunity cluster is identified by a behaving unit and then a specific destination within the cluster is chosen,[10] (2) cases where prominence of a particular attribute, as perceived by actors, exists, (3) situations where actors possess limited information, and so forth.

6.5 Constrained gravity (spatial interaction) models

As already noted, the early development of exponential deterrence models was stimulated by the pioneering work of Wilson (1970, 1974) and his associates (see Fotheringham and O'Kelly, 1989). These models have often been designated maximum entropy and/or information-minimization models. The presentation of the basis for these designations is beyond the scope of this chapter as is their behavioralistic axiomatic formulation by

Sen and Smith (1995). From these models there has emerged a number of practical applications, particularly for situations where constraints on interaction exist or are provided exogenously. Where the constraints in a model specify the number of flows emanating from (or outflows produced at) each originating mass O_i (as defined above) (for example, the journey to work trips of residents at each i), the model has been designated *production-constrained*. Where these constraints specify the number of flows terminating at (or inflows attracted to) each destination mass D_j (for example, the number of jobs at each industrial area j), then the model has been termed *attraction-constrained*.

Where both types of constraints are specified the model has been termed *doubly-constrained* — in contrast to the two types of models just noted, which are often termed *singly-constrained*. At this point it is instructive to see how constraints affect the outcomes of a model. To do so, we use the example of a doubly-constrained model developed by Masser (1972) and reported upon in Haynes and Fotheringham (1984, pp. 24-29).[11]

Given O_i and D_j ($i,j = 1,2,3$), the task is to derive the T_{ij} for the cells in the O-D matrix below.

	D_1	D_2	D_3
O_1	T_{11}	T_{12}	T_{13}
O_2	T_{21}	T_{22}	T_{23}
O_3	T_{31}	T_{32}	T_{33}

Let the model we use be a most simple one, namely

$$T_{ij} = G(O_iD_j/d_{ij}) \qquad (6\text{-}13)$$

where T_{ij} represents journey-to-work trips from origin i to destination j and where we set α, β, b and all weights as unity. What is first desired is an initial estimate of the outflows (residents taking journey-to-work trips) from the three origins, O_1, O_2, and O_3 whose number of residents are, respectively, 160, 450, and 180. This number for each origin is indicated in the total outflows column (col. 4) of Table 6-1 below.

The destinations are three, D_1, D_2, and D_3, whose inflows (workers to perform the jobs to be done at each) are 200, 370 and 220, respectively. The total inflow at each destination is indicated in the total inflows row at the bottom of Table 6-1. Let the distances (in miles) between these origins and destinations be as indicated in Table 6-2.

Table 6-1 Origin and destination masses and first round estimates of interaction (trips) (figures rounded)

	D_1	D_2	D_3	Total Out-flows	Total Estimated Outflows	Ratio: col. 4/col. 5
	(1)	(2)	(3)	(4)	(5)	(6)
O_1	16,000	3,947	7,040	160	26,987	$0.005929 = \bar{A}_1$
O_2	6,000	83,250	9,900	450	99,150	$0.004539 = \bar{A}_2$
O_3	7,200	6,660	19,800	180	33,660	$0.005348 = \bar{A}_3$
Total Inflows	200	370	220			

Table 6-2 Distances between origins and destinations (in miles or other appropriate spatial separation measure)

	D_1	D_2	D_3
O_1	2	15	5
O_2	15	2	10
O_3	5	10	2

What needs to be computed are G, a gravitational-type constant, and the T_{ij}, $i = 1,2,3$ and $j=1,2,3$. The steps are:

(1) Calculate as follows a first extremely crude estimate of each outflow from each origin to each destination, to be designated $\bar{T}_{ij}$ using equation (6-13). For example: for $\bar{T}_{11}$ we multiply the total outflows for O_1 by the total inflow of D_1 and divide by 2 (namely d_{11} of Table 6-2) to obtain 16,000; for $\bar{T}_{12}$ we multiply the total outflow for O_1 by the total inflow for D_2 and divide by 15 to obtain 3,947; and so forth for each of the other seven $\bar{T}_{ij}$ to be calculated for the cells of Table 6-1.

(2) For each row, sum the items in it to obtain a first crude estimate of total outflows, designated $\hat{T}_i = \sum_j \hat{T}_{ij}$. For example, the total for the first row is 26,987.

(3) For each origin, calculate the ratio of the given total outflow constraint (160 for O_1) to the total of the first round estimate of outflows (26,987 for O_1). This ratio for O_1 is 0.005929 as given in column 6 of Table 6-1 and is designated $\bar{A}_1$. The corresponding ratios for the other two rows are 0.004539 and 0.005348. They are designated $\bar{A}_2$ and $\bar{A}_3$, respectively.

(4) Multiply the elements in each row by the corresponding ratio in column 6 to obtain the first round of rowwise adjusted trips as recorded in Table 6-3.

Table 6-3 Adjusted first round estimates of outflows and resulting first round estimates of destination inflows (figures rounded)

		D_1	D_2	D_3	Total Adjusted First Round Outflow Estimates
(1)	O_1	94.86	23.40	41.74	160.00
(2)	O_2	27.23	377.84	44.93	450.00
(3)	O_3	38.50	35.62	105.88	180.00
(4)	Total Estimated Inflow	160.60	436.85	192.55	
(5)	Total Inflows Constraints	200	370	220	
(6)	Ratio of row (5) to row (4)	1.2453 $= \bar{B}_1$	0.8470 $= \bar{B}_2$	1.1426 $= \bar{B}_3$	

(5) Sum the items in each column to obtain for each destination the first-round estimated total of inflows from all origins as recorded in row 4 of Table 6-3.

(6) Record the total inflow constraint for each destination in row 5 of Table 6-3.

(7) For each destination take the ratio of total inflow constraint (row 5) to total estimated inflow (row 4) and record the ratio in row 6. These ratios are designated $\bar{B}_1$, $\bar{B}_2$ and $\bar{B}_3$.

(8) Multiply the elements in each column by the ratio for that column in row 6 to obtain second round estimates of inflows $\bar{\bar{T}}_{ij}$ as recorded in Table 6-4.

(9) Sum the items across each row in Table 6-4 to obtain the total adjusted second-round outflow estimates for each origin, as recorded in column 4 of Table 6-4.

Table 6-4 Second round estimates of inflows and outflows (figures rounded)

	D_1	D_2	D_3	Total Adjusted Second Round Outflow Estimates	Constraint on Total Outflows	Ratio of col. 5 to col. 4
	(1)	(2)	(3)	(4)	(5)	(6)
O_1	118.14	19.82	47.69	185.65	160	0.8618 $= \bar{\bar{A}}_1$
O_2	33.91	320.02	51.34	405.27	450	1.1104 $= \bar{\bar{A}}_2$
O_3	47.95	30.16	120.97	199.08	180	0.9042 $= \bar{\bar{A}}_3$
Total Estimated Inflows	200.00	370.00	220.00			
Constraint on Total Inflows	200.00	370.00	220.00			

(10) List the constraints on total outflows in column 5 of Table 6-4. If for any origin the total adjusted second round outflows estimate differs from its respective constraint on total outflows, take the ratio of the latter (col. 5) to the former (col. 4) to derive a new set of adjustment factors $\bar{\bar{A}}_i$.

(11) Multiply the elements in each row of Table 6-4 by the corresponding ratio in column 6.

(12) Continue to repeat steps 7 to 11 until the ratios in column 6 and row 6 in the resulting tables approximate unity.

When the computation comes to an end, the T_{ij} will be as in Table 6-5. In the process, each row i will have been multiplied in succession by one or more ratio values $\bar{A}_i, \bar{\bar{A}}_i, \bar{\bar{\bar{A}}}_i,...$ and each column by one or more values $\bar{B}_j, \bar{\bar{B}}_j, \bar{\bar{\bar{B}}}_j,....$ The equation (6-13) will have been modified to be

$$T_{ij} = (A_iB_jM_iM_j)/d_{ij} \qquad (6-14)$$

where

$A_i = \bar{A}_i \times \bar{\bar{A}}_i \times \bar{\bar{\bar{A}}}_i...$ is taken to designate that for each element a_i of A_i,

$$a_i = \bar{a}_i \times \bar{\bar{a}}_i \times \bar{\bar{\bar{a}}}_i....$$

and

$$B_j = \bar{B}_j \times \bar{\bar{B}}_j \times \bar{\bar{\bar{B}}}_j... \text{ is taken to designate that for each element } b_j \text{ of } B_j,$$

$$b_j = \bar{b}_j \times \bar{\bar{b}}_j \times \bar{\bar{\bar{b}}}_j....$$

Table 6-5 Projected trips with a doubly constrained gravity model

	D_1	D_2	D_3	Total Outflows
O_1	107	13	40	160
O_2	47	334	69	450
O_3	46	23	111	180
Total Inflows	200	370	320	790

In equation (6-14) A_iB_j may be viewed as a derived gravitational constant G_{ij} reflecting the complementarity of the resources and other attributes of the two masses.

The above represents one practical way trip patterns can be estimated given values of α, β and b, assumed or obtained from previous calibration studies. For practical applications regarding constrained models, see Haynes and Fotheringham (1984) and Fotheringham and O'Kelly (1989).

From this example of flow estimation for a doubly constrained gravity model, where only totals (sometimes called marginals) of outflows and inflows are given, we can immediately see how the flows of singly constrained models are derived. If the constraints are on outflows only, that is are the 160, 450, and 180 for O_1, O_2, and O_3 in Table 6-1, then the resulting inflows after steps 1 to 5 are taken are those in row 4 of Table 6-3. These total inflows for D_1, D_2, and D_3 are, after crude rounding, 161, 437, 192 which total to 790, the total of trips. If the constraints are on total inflows, that is the 200, 370 and 220 of D_1, D_2, and D_3 respectively, then the derived total inflows that are produced when the equivalent of Steps 2 to 5 are done, first with respect to the columns rather than the rows of Table 6-1,[12] the resulting total inflows for O_1, O_2, and O_3 would be the resulting row totals of the estimated T_{ij}.[13]

This process for obtaining consistent numbers for cells of a matrix when only the totals of rows and columns are given and when the row and column totals need to add up to the same overall total is designated the RAS procedure. It is one that is often used in input-output studies for updating production coefficients, or for deriving a set of consistent production coefficients given some relevant other set. See chapter 3, pp. 89–92.

At this point consider the case where a researcher finds it more desirable to specify the masses at O_i and D_j ($i = 1,...,m; j = 1,...,n$) in terms of a single attribute (college population, or professional jobs) rather than in terms of a more appropriate measure of the masses that reflects say relevant weights modified by agglomerative (deglomerative) effects and externalities of attributes captured in the α and β exponents of equation (6-10). He/she may then accompany the single attribute measures of masses at O_i and D_j with two matrices. One would be the composite v_{ij} of factors pushing out units at O_i to destinations in general. See the (3x3) v matrix below. The second would be the composite w_{ij} of attracting factors pulling in units at D_j from origins in general. See the (3x3) w matrix below.

The v Matrix					The w Matrix		
O_1	v_{11}	v_{12}	v_{13}	O_1	w_{11}	w_{12}	w_{13}
O_2	v_{21}	v_{22}	v_{23}	O_2	w_{21}	w_{22}	w_{23}
O_3	v_{31}	v_{32}	v_{33}	O_3	w_{31}	w_{32}	w_{33}
	D_1	D_2	D_3		D_1	D_2	D_3

Also, he/she may set up a matrix G_{ij} of factors indicating the complementarity of attributes for each pair of origins and destinations, to take into account, for example, how the skill composition of workers at a given origin i matches the skill requirement of jobs at a given destination j.

6.6 Calibration, tests and applications of spatial interaction models

The calibration — the derivation of the parameters of a gravity model from a set of interaction data — has several valuable uses. First of all, we in regional science, geography and related fields may want not only to test for the influence of distance in many different sets of socio-economic-political interaction data but also to know the intensity of that influence. Further, there is the interesting question: does a satisfactory calibration suggest that the concept of mutual energy as defined by physics is more appropriate than that of gravitational force for the study of interactions of interest to social scientists. Moreover, if a statistically significant influence

Methods of Interregional and Regional Analysis

is not found in calibration, is such an outcome an indication of: an inadequate definition or measurement of mass, specification of weights, definition or measurement of distance; or the use of an improper functional form; or some combination of these inadequacies? These are indeed meaningful questions for one concerned with the identification of commonalities among physical, biological and social (cultural) interactions.

Aside from greater understanding and more insights resulting from calibration, the derived parameters may be extremely valuable for observing and gaining further knowledge of changes in a system. This is possible, for example, when calibration is performed for comparable sets of interaction data for different points of time to identify changes in migration patterns, shopping behavior, international trade (commodity movements) and so forth. However, as already indicated in previous sections, the most extensive use of a set of the derived parameters has been as a set of base period data for forward forecasting — for example, the impact of new investments in roads, transportation pricing, rehabilitation of central city districts, etc. On occasion, a base period set of data has been used for forecasting a situation in the past (backward forecasting).

Calibration involves the use of statistical procedures such as those discussed in chapter 4 on regional econometrics, the ones having been found most helpful by gravity modelers are Least Squares including Ordinary Least Squares (OLS) (see section 4.2.2) and Maximum Likelihood (see section 4.2.4). The particular use of these procedures and their variations in gravity modelling is well discussed in Fotheringham and O'Kelly (1989) and Smith and Sen (1995) to which the reader is referred since discussion of them is beyond the scope of this chapter. However, we do wish to present a sketch of each of two interesting calibrations.

6.6.1 The use of OLS (ordinary least squares) to test the effect of distance, cooperation and hostility upon trade of nations

While theoretically the potential usefulness of the gravity model in helping to understand trade among nations was pointed to decades ago (Isard and Peck, 1954), empirical work to calibrate a model to test the influence of the distance variable has only taken place in recent years.

A small scale study largely designed to calibrate one pertinent model of trade among nations was undertaken with regard to the spatial interaction of Turkey with selected OECD (Organization for Economic Cooperation and Development) nations. The basic model employed was that of equation (6-4) to which were added two political variables:

$$T_{ij} = g[(GNP_i \times GNP_j)/d_{ij}^b] \, (C_{ij}/H_{ij}) \qquad (6\text{-}15)$$

where

    T_{ij} = trade between originating country i and terminating country j

    g = a gravitational-type constant

  GNP_i = economic mass of originating country i (a measure of potential supply of commodities)[14]

  GNP_j = economic mass of terminating country j (a measure of potential demand for commodities)[15]

    d_{ij} = effective economic distance (in terms of equivalent nautical miles) between i and j

    H_{ij} = level of hostility between i and j

    C_{ij} = level of cooperation between i and j

    b = an exponent to which the economic distance variable is to be raised

The data for GNP for the diverse countries were obtained from standard sources; they were converted to US$ and adjusted to the exchange rates and price levels of 1985. Use of airline distances between capital cities, frequently employed in studies, was highly inadequate for this investigation. Instead, for each pair of nations, the weighted average of distances between their major economic centers was used, following the practice generally considered best of treating each land mile as equivalent to two nautical models.[16] Levels of hostility and cooperation between each pair of nations were COPDAB (Conflict and Peace Data Bank) data, or data developed by Yaman (1994) using the standard COPDAB procedures which have found wide acceptance among quantitative international relations scholars.[17] The data on trade were developed by taking the 1985 OECD data (converted to US dollars) on current exports from and imports to Turkey as a base. To them were applied other OECD data for each year on annual growth rate of total real exports from and imports to Turkey backward and forward from 1985, while at the same time maintaining the inter-temporal differences of the trade shares of each country.[18]

For testing (calibration) purposes, several equations were specified for (exports) EX_{ij} and for imports IM_{ij} (rather than a single equation for net trade) in order to determine whether the explanatory variables have differential impacts on imports and exports. For estimation purposes in a first model, the two basic equations were (in log form):

Model 1

$$\ln(EX_{ij}) = G + \beta_1 \ln(GDP_i) + \beta_2 \ln(GDP_j) + \beta_3 \ln(DIS_{ij})$$
$$+ \beta_4 \ln(COP_{ij}) + \beta_5 \ln(HOS_j) + U_{ij} \qquad (6\text{-}16)$$

and

$$\ln(IM_{ji}) = A + \alpha_1\ln(GDP_i) + \alpha_2\ln(GDP_j) + \alpha_3\ln(DIS_{ij})$$
$$+ \alpha_4\ln(COP_{ij}) + \alpha_5\ln(HOS_j) + \varepsilon_{ij} \qquad (6\text{-}17)$$

where $G = \ln\beta_0$, $A = \ln\alpha_0$, $U_{ij} = \ln u_{ij}$, $\varepsilon_{ij} = \ln e_{ij}$ and u_{ij} and e_{ij} are random disturbances; and where subscript i represents Turkey in each equation.

For comparative purposes, and to estimate the effect of the distance variable alone, a second model was constructed whose equations were

Model 2

$$\ln(EX_{ij}) = G + \beta_1\ln(GDP_i) + \beta_2\ln(GDP_j) + \beta_3\ln(DIS_{ij}) + U_{ij} \qquad (6\text{-}18)$$

and

$$\ln(IM_{ji}) = A + \alpha_1\ln(GDP_i) + \alpha_2\ln(GDP_j) + \alpha_3\ln(DIS_{ij}) + \varepsilon_{ij}. \qquad (6\text{-}19)$$

The data set consisted of pooled time series and cross-sectional data for Turkey and its OECD trading partners for the eleven-year period from 1980 to the end of 1990. There are at least three reasons for using a pooled data set in this study rather than separate time series or cross-sectional data sets. First, the pooled data set provides significantly more degrees of freedom than do either of the alternatives. Second, using only cross-sectional data would produce separate parameter estimates for each year, but within each year there would be no variation in the explanatory variable measuring Turkey's GDP. Third, although it would be possible using time series data to estimate import and export equations for Turkey and each trading partner individually, there would be no variation in the distance variable in each equation. Thus it would not be possible fully to test each equation's underlying hypotheses with either of the two alternative data sets. Ordinary least squares (OLS) then was used to estimate the parameters (which, in this case also represent the appropriate elasticities) of the two models.

Parameter estimates for the two models are presented in Table 6-6. The estimates for exports are followed by those for imports. M1 and M2 indicate, respectively, the model with cooperation and hostility variables included, and the model without the cooperative and hostility variables.

In both models, the GDP variables for Turkey and its trading partners have the expected sign (+) and are highly statistically significant. Similarly, for the distance (DIS) variable (but with an expected negative coefficient) in each model.

The results, however, are less sanguine when considering the cooperation and hostility variables. Although estimates of the coefficients

Table 6-6 Estimation results

			Constant	$LnGDP_i$	$LnGDP_j$	$LnDIS_{ij}$	$LnCOP_{ij}$	$LnHOS_{ij}$	R^2	Ad. R^2	F–Ratio
Exports 1980–90 (N=198)	M1	Coeff.	9.395	3.534	0.927	−2.184	0.097	0.008	0.862	0.858	239.0
		t-ratio	6.68	12	18.7	19.3	2.67	0.271			
		p-value	≤0.0001	≤0.0001	≤0.0001	≤0.0001	0.0082	0.7867			
	M2	Coeff.	9.275	3.754	1.011	−2.295	—	—	0.856	0.854	384.0
		t-ratio	6.62	13.1	26.1	−22.6	—	—			
		p-value	≤0.0001	≤0.0001	≤0.0001	≤0.0001	—	—			
Imports 1980–90 (N−198)	M1	Coeff.	5.565	2.771	0.935	−1.245	0.092	−0.029	0.854	0.851	225.0
		t-ratio	4.53	10.8	21.6	−12.6	2.9	−1.15			
		p-value	≤0.0001	≤0.0001	≤0.0001	≤0.0001	0.0042	0.2534			
	M2	Coeff.	5.165	2.945	0.991	−1.290	—	—	0.848	0.846	360.0
		t-ratio	4.21	11.7	29.2	−14.5	—	—			
		p-value	≤0.0001	≤0.0001	≤0.0001	≤0.0001	—	—			

for the cooperative (COP) variable have the correct sign (+) and are statistically significant in both the export and import equations, the same cannot be said for the hostility (HOS) index. In the import equation (M1), the coefficient of the hostility index has a negative sign as expected, but the evidence indicates that the null hypothesis (that is, where the coefficient is equal to zero) cannot be rejected at the usual confidence levels. In the export equation in model M1, the sign is positive, but again the evidence indicates that the coefficient is not statistically significantly different from zero.

In both the export and import equations in the M2 model, the coefficient estimates of both GDPs and distance are similar to their respective M1 model in terms of magnitude, sign and statistical significance. In addition, both R-squared measures are similar. The calculated elasticities estimate the relative impacts of each of the explanatory variables on both imports and exports, and in additon provide useful quantitative estimates for policy purposes. For example, Turkey's GDP has the greatest relative impact of any of these explanatory variables on Turkish exports, indicating an increase of 3.5 to 3.8 percent in Turkish exports for each percent increase in its GDP. The distance variable provides the next largest impacts (from −2.2 to −2.3) followed by the trading partner's GDP (from 0.9 to 1.0), and the political variables (from 0.008 to 0.097). A similar hierarchy of results was obtained with the import models.

Finally, there are differential impacts of the explanatory variables on both exports and imports, although these differences are, in some cases, quite small (see Table 6-6). Nevertheless, there is sufficient evidence to justify the use of separate models for exports and imports.

In this study, we have reported the results of an exploratory statistical analysis of two different models to explain separately the behaviour of imports and exports between Turkey and its more important trading partners in the OECD. The results of these preliminary analyses indicate that the traditional gravity model variables (economic mass and distance) are the most important in explaining the behaviour of both imports and exports. Although the cooperation variable is also statistically significant and of the expected sign in its model, the same cannot be said for the hostility variable. However, standardized coefficient analysis indicates that these political variables have only a relatively small impact on both the import-and export-dependent variables when compared to the impacts of the more traditional gravity model explanatory variables (economic mass and distance).[19]

6.6.2 *The use of maximum likelihood in a policy oriented application with particular attention to characteristics of origins, destinations and types of distance (separation) measures*

In a relatively advanced study, Lowe and Sen (1996) use a gravity model to analyze a hospital patient flow system within an urban area for the purpose of forecasting the impact of policies involving health care financing reform and hospital closure. Their model, involving an exponential deterrence relation, is of the general form

$$T_{ij} = M_i M_j F_{ij} \qquad (6\text{-}20)$$

where

$$F_{ij} = \exp\left[\sum_{k=1}^{K} c_{ij}^{(k)} \theta^k\right] \qquad (6\text{-}21)$$

and where

T_{ij} = hospital trips (disaggregated by type)[20]

M_i = characteristics of origins (disaggregatable by type of patients)

M_j = characteristics of hospitals (disaggregatable by type of function (or complex of functions) and

c_{ij} = is a vector of separation measures $c_{ij}^{(1)},...,c_{ij}^{(k)}$

and θ^k are parameters to be estimated.

However, they convert the model to the potential form which can either (a) emphasize access of an individual (patient) at i to all relevant hospitals as in

$$_iV = \sum_j T_{ij}/M_i = \sum_j M_j F_{ij} \qquad (6\text{-}22)$$

which is designated *patient access*, or (b) emphasize the access of a particular hospital j to all the individuals at relevant origins

$$_jV = \sum_i T_{ij}/M_j = \sum_i M_i F_{ij} \qquad (6\text{-}23)$$

which is designated *hospital success* in the market. In their forecasting they estimate M_j and F_{ij} from base period data on T_{ij} [which is the number of trips from each subarea (zip code district) i to each hospital j]. They then use these M_j and F_{ij} in their model to forecast T_{ij}.

Recognizing that the problem of evaluating policy impact requires the disaggregation of hospitals by characteristics (e.g., Medical School Hospitals, Major Teaching Hospitals, Community Hospitals, etc.), they treat flows to each type and examine hospital success by type. Thus, their study illustrates the need, frequently encountered, to attend to characteristics of origins and destinations in the application of the gravity model, especially when addressing spatial choice behavior. Because the authors had access to extensive data, they were able to conduct useful disaggregations, that is examine spatial interactions with respect to different types of hospitals, while still meeting the large sample size requirement.

Of particular interest is their examination of several different forms of spatial separation and definitions of pertinent distance. They first distinguish between the appropriateness of physical distance and travel time as a measure of the first spatial component ($c_{ij}^{(1)}$) in equation (6-21) by running their model (based on equation 6-20) using (1) distance (physical), (2) log of distance, (3) the square root of distance, (4) travel time, (5) log of time and (6) the square root of time. They obtain the results of Table 6-7. They conclude that travel time (models 4, 5, and 6) provide better fits than distance (models 1, 2, and 3). They also consider the square root of time to be the best of the time measures suggesting that one longer hospital trip is proportionately less burdensome than more than one shorter trips. That is, a model with a falling-off effect with increase in time is to be preferred to one with the more extreme falling-off effect realized with the use of the log of time measure.

Next, they consider a second type of separation measure (the ($c_{ij}^{(2)}$), a social-economic type of separation). They recognize that the poorer patients without hospital insurance or funds from government sources are discouraged from using certain identifiable hospitals, which insured patients from wealthier zip code areas can use. Accordingly, they develop a measure which reflects affordability and the admitting practices of hospitals with regard to sources of payments. A payer compatibility index is constructed, ranging from 0 (no match) to 1 (perfect match) of a zip code i with a hospital j that comprises the second component ($c_{ij}^{(2)}$) of equation (6-21).

Further, to recognize the geographically dispersed markets of medical-school affiliated hospitals, they create an indicator (a dummy variable) γ_{ij} which they set at unity for all i if hospital j is a medical school, or zero otherwise. Thus, they obtain $c_{ij}^{(3)} = \gamma_{ij} c_{ij}^{(1)}$.

Finally, to account for the relatively concentrated local markets characterizing all hospitals they set $c_{ij}^{(4)} = \delta_{ij} c_{ij}^{(1)}$ where $\delta_{ij} = 1$ when zip code i is adjacent to hospital j, otherwise $\delta_{ij} = 0$. The results are recorded in Table 6-8. The standard errors are quite small when additional separation measures are added to the measure given by the square root of travel time while the chi-square ratio is significantly reduced. Hence the authors conclude that the 'payer match, medical school and adjacent trip

Table 6-7 Parameter estimates for different distance and travel time separation measures, 1987 data[a]

Measure	Model 1	Model 2	Model 3	Model 4	Model 5	Model 6
Distance[b]	-0.00054 (0.0000)					
Log Distance		-1.92852 (0.0020)				
Square Root Distance			-0.07429 (0.0001)			
Travel Time[c]				-0.13526 (0.0002)		
Log Time					-3.18650 (0.0031)	
Square Root Time						-1.37392 (0.0015)
Chi-Square Ratio	9591.66	23.24	18.28	148.27	15.66	15.66

[a]Standard errors in parentheses.
[b]Units — UIC Geography coordinate system.
[c]Travel time in minutes from UIC Geography and Urban Planning.

Table 6-8 Parameter estimates and standard errors for gravity models 6 through 9, all trips 1987 data[a]

Separation Measure	Model 6	Model 7	Model 8	Model 9
Travel Time[b]	-1.37392 (0.0015)	-1.28388 (0.0016)	-1.21444 (0.0019)	-1.16160 (0.0019)
Payer Match		4.85569 (0.0315)		3.87926 (0.0313)
Medical School			0.33386 (0.0033)	0.29462 (0.0033)
Adjacent Zip			0.18678 (0.0011)	0.16275 (0.0011)
Chi-Square Ratio	15.66	13.07	10.99	9.64

[a]Standard errors in parentheses.
[b]Square root of travel time.

code measures provide additional explanation of hospital trip behavior,' p. 450.

In many other ways the authors fruitfully conduct a careful and advanced analysis of an application of gravity models for policy purposes. For example, using estimated parameters of origin and destination characteristics and spatial separation, they forecast what the impact of a universal health measure would be if it were appropriate to set the payer match from model 9 to zero.

6.7 Conclusion

In this chapter we have treated the gravity and gravity-type models, still not widely recognized by social scientists, as reflecting basic spatial behavior of society. We have looked at several of these models, and have cited literature on many others. The possibilities for fruitful applications are numerous.

An excellent source book on many of these applications is Fotheringham and O'Kelly (1989). These authors extensively develop the rationales of spatial choice models, emphasizing the discrete choice (trade-off decision) problem of an individual behaving unit and taking into account both spatial awareness and spatial information processing. They also examine interregional and interurban migration studies, examining hierarchical information processing use and interesting variations of the strict gravity model. With regard to retailing, they go beyond single-stop trip modelling and extend the analysis of and cover applications to situations where multi-stop multipurpose trips are involved. Finally, they examine applications of location-allocation models wherein an optimization framework is employed to identify both (1) the optimal site for a single facility (hub) and (2) the best set of sites for a network of facilities (hubs) wherein forces for clustering and decentralization are examined.

Still there are innumerable other potentially fruitful applications stemming from the commonality of the gravitational effect, not only in the diverse social and natural sciences, but also in non-scientific fields. And for the regional scientist, the applications will certainly be many following the development of the synthesis of the gravity models (models much more capable of treating space and spatial interactions) with others such as input-output, social accounting, econometric, programming and applied general equilibrium discussed in this book. These models just mentioned deal by and large with regions as points of concentrated activities connected at best by a discrete number of transport and communication lines.

Endnotes

1 Development and applications of gravity models may be found in, among others, the references cited at the end of this chapter, especially Carrothers (1956). In order to facilitate the understanding of the mathematical terms used in this chapter, we have followed traditional notation on gravity models and have refrained from using a strange (and to some extent more complicated) notation which would be consistent with that of the preceding chapters and with any mathematical formulation of the fused frameworks of the chapters to follow. Sections 6.1 and 6.2 draw heavily upon Isard et al., 1960.

2 This point of view is still effective in applications.

3 In Figure 6.1, $a = 3.9$ and $b = 1.5$.

4 Studies depicting such close association will be cited at later points in this chapter.

5 For the moment we ignore a discussion of the interaction of subarea i with itself. This point is taken up later in section 6.5.

6 We do not discuss here problems connected with the use of existing data on originating and destination areas, or in the choice of them. Carrothers (1956) has investigated the degree to which a potential calibration of a gravity model actually represents what it purports to represent when different sizes and shapes of areas are involved as well as different internal distributions of relevant masses. He concludes that the best set of general-purpose areas tends to satisfy as closely as possible, among others, the following criteria: (1) absence of concentrations of mass on the peripheries of the area; (2) existence within each area of a definite nodal center of gravity of mass; (3) coincidence of the center of gravity of a relevant mass with the center of gravity of the physical area; and (4) regular geometric shapes for the physical area of each region.

7 Theoretically an *effective distance* d_{ij} between actor categories (places) i and j may be conceived as the dot product:

$$d_{ij} = \mathbf{x}_{ij} \cdot \mathbf{w}_{ij}$$

where $\mathbf{x}_{ij}$ is a vector in n-dimensional space, each component of which measures one type of distance just noted, and where $\mathbf{w}_{ij}$ is an n-dimensional vector indicating the respective weights to be applied to the several components.

8   In another trip matrix study, Choukroun (1975) has noted that the exponential function is appropriate when all trip makers are relatively identical. When they are not and where the distance-decay parameters for the individuals are distributed according to a gamma distribution, the power deterrence function is to be preferred.

9   A spatial separation model may be generalized as: $I_{ij} = GM_i(\cdot)M_j(\cdot)F(d_{ij})$ where (1) $M_i(\cdot)$ and $M_j(\cdot)$ are unspecified origin and destination functions corresponding to the O_i and D_j variables when they are weight functions incorporating cross-catalytic effects of their attributes, (2) $F(d_{ij})$ is a distance deterrence function, simple or generalized, and (3) G is the *universal* gravitational constant. For other possible generalizations, see Sen and Smith (1995), chapter 2.

   A related general model, a theory of movement, considers a closed system of groups each composed of units wherein units move from one group to another, each group being both a possible origin and destination. (See Alonso, 1976, summarized in Anselin and Isard, 1979 and Fotheringham and O'Kelly, 1989.) Push-out factors of any group which induce units to leave are repulsive characteristics of the group (such as widespread poverty and high crime rates). Pull-in characteristics (low unemployment rates, low crime rates, etc.) are intrinsic attractions. The pull-in factors of groups, however, are attenuated by (1) the friction of distance in the broadest sense covering all forms of distance, inclusive of the affinity of a group i to any other group; and (2) the 'ease of entry' into any targeted group. The ease of entry may be related to congestion when many units attempt to enter existing groups, or to repugnance toward inmovers exhibited by existing members of an attracting group, etc. The push-out factors are also subject to attenuation. Aside from the friction of distance (again viewed in the most general sense), low responsiveness of dissatisfied units to attractions elsewhere, distrust of information disseminated by groups at potential destinations, and other elements may diminish the 'ease of exit' factor. Alonso's theory does yield as movement M_{ij} between group i and j the relation: $M_{ij} = k\,\bar{v}_i\,\bar{w}_j d_{ij}$ where $\bar{v}_i$ is the weighted sum of repulsive factors at group i adjusted for 'ease of exit,'

$\overline{w}_j$ is the weighted sum of attractive factors at group j adjusted for 'ease of entry' and k is a factor of proportionality.

10 Choice models of this sort involving the behavior of one or more individuals may be more appropriately designated 'competing destination' models. See, for example, Fotheringham (1991). See also Fotheringham and Pitts (1995) on the direction of distance variables.

11 We cite this example since the procedure for derivation of the outcome is somewhat different than the one adopted here. The reader is referred to the former procedure for further understanding.

12 Where the O_i are constrained,

$$A_i = (\sum_j B_j D_j / d_{ij})^{-1}$$

Where the D_j are constrained,

$$B_j = (\sum_i A_i O_i / d_{ij})^{-1}$$

13 For diverse uses of constrained models, see Fotheringham and O'Kelly (1989). From their experience these authors find that while the doubly-constrained model provides the highest quality of information, the singly-constrained model provides a larger amount of information though of lesser quality. The unconstrained model provides the most information, but this information is lowest in quality and consequently not generally considered to be acceptable.

These authors also discuss quasi-constrained interaction models, designated *relaxed spatial interaction models*. Such models have been developed to treat situations where because of limited information one or more of the marginal totals of the predicted interaction matrix is constrained to lie within a specified range of values. In addition, they discuss Tobler models that replace the traditional multiplicative framework with an additive one for achieving balance among the estimated T_{ij}.

14 Excluded were Iceland, New Zealand, Portugal and Greece. For reasons, see Yaman (1995), p. 4.

15 Admittedly, GNP is not as good a measure of mass of an exporting country (an originating area) as of mass of an importing country (a

destination area). Yet GNP is as least as good a general measure of productivity and export supply potential as any other.

16 See Yaman (1994) for details.

17 See Yaman (1994) for development of the levels of hostility and cooperation.

18 This procedure was designed to eliminate the effect on dollar data due to variation among the sample countries in their exchange rates and price indices. See Isard, Saltzman and Yaman (1997) and Yaman (1994) for further discussion.

19 Although the results of these preliminary experiments indicate that the theory behind the use of political variables to explain international trade finds little support in these data, it may be the case that these variables are, nevertheless, significant. For example, the data used to measure hostility and cooperation may not be wholly representative of the political phenomena which affect bilateral trade between nations. In addition, the defined hostility variable may not be a significant measure among a group of nations that are dedicated to cooperative efforts as are the members of the OECD. Clearly, more research remains to be done with these models in order to establish the importance of the political variables for explaining international trade.

The use of covariance models and/or error components models could help to sharpen our results by relaxing some of the assumptions inherent in the OLS models tested in this exploratory phase of the research. Also, more sophisticated model structures, such as those using simultaneous equations, could help to test and/or develop new theories about how economic, political and regional science variables interplay in bilateral trade.

20 Strictly speaking, for forecasting purposes T_{ij} is the expected number of trips, viewed as a Poisson random variable in a system where the locational and frequency independencies requirements are assumed by the authors to be approximately met — an assumption that some scholars may question with regard to the Chicago market which was the source of data.

References

Anderson, James E. 1979. 'A Theoretical Foundation for the Gravity Equation,' *American Economic Review*, 69, 106–16.

Beckmann, M. J., and T. F. Golob. 1972. 'A Critique of Entropy and Gravity in Travel,' in G. F. Newell (ed.), *Traffic Flow and Transportation*. New York: American Elsevier.

Bergstrand, J. H. 1985. 'The Gravity Equation in International Trade: Some Microeconomic Foundations and Empirical Evidence,' *Review of Economics and Statistics*, 67, 474–81.

Bergstrand, J. H. 1989. 'The Generalized Gravity Equation, Monopolistic Competition, and the Factor Proportions Theory in International Trade,' *Review of Economics and Statistics*, 71, 143–53.

Carrothers, G. A. P. 1956. 'An Historical Review of the Gravity and Potential Concepts of Human Interaction,' *Journal of the American Institute of Planners*, 22, 94–102.

Choukroun, J. M. 1975. 'A General Framework for the Development of Gravity-type Trip Distribution Models,' *Regional Science and Urban Economics*, 5, 177–202.

Fotheringham, A. S. 1991. 'Migration and Spatial Structure: The Development of the Competing Destination Model,' in J. Stillwell and P. Congdon (eds.), *Migration Models: Macro and Micro Approaches*. London: Bellhaven.

Fotheringham, A. S., and M. E. O'Kelly. 1988. *Spatial Interaction Models: Formulations and Applications*. Dordrecht, Netherlands: Kluwer Academic Publishers.

Fotheringham, A. S., and T. C. Pitts. 1995. 'Directional Variation in Distance-Decay,' *Environment and Planning A*, 27, 715–29.

Gasiorowski, M. J. 1986. 'Economic Interdependence and International Conflict,' *International Studies Quarterly*, 30, 23–38.

Gasiorowski, M., and S. W. Polachek. 1982. 'Conflict and Interdependence: East-West Trade and Linkages in the Era of Détente,' *Journal of Conflict Resolution*, 26, 709–29.

Haynes, Kingsley E., and A. Stewart Fotheringham. 1984. *Gravity and Spatial Interaction Models*. California: Sage Publications.

Hua Chang-i and F. Porell. 1979. 'A Critical Review of the Development of the Gravity Model,' *International Regional Science Review*, 4, 97–126.

Isard, W. 1975. 'A Simple Rationale for Gravity Model Type Behavior,' *Papers of the Regional Science Association*, 35, 25–30.

Isard, W., D. F. Bramhall, G. A. P. Carrothers, J. H. Cumberland, L. N. Moses, D. O. Price, and E. W. Schooler. 1960. *Methods of Regional Analysis: An Introduction to Regional Science.* Cambridge, Mass.: MIT Press.

Isard, W., and W. Dean. 1987. 'The Projection of World (Multiregional) Trade Matrices,' *Environment and Planning A,* 19, 1059–66.

Isard, W., and M. Peck. 1954. 'Location Theory and Trade Theory: Short-Run Analysis,' *Quarterly Journal of Economics,* 68, 305–20.

Isard, W., S. Saltzman, and A. Yaman. 1997. 'Trade and Conflict: A Gravity Model Reformulation,' in M. Chatterji and Kaizhong Yang (eds.), *Regional Science in Developing Countries.* London: Macmillan.

Linnemann, H. 1966. *An Econometric Study of International Trade Flows.* Amsterdam: North Holland.

Lowe, J. M., and A. Sen. 1996. 'Gravity Model Applications in Health Planning: Analyses of an Urban Hospital Market,' *Journal of Regional Science,* 36, 437–62.

Niedercorn, J. H., and B. V. Bechdolt. 1972. 'An Economic Derivation of the Gravity Law of Spatial Interaction: A Further Reply and a Formulation,' *Journal of Regional Science,* 12, 127–36.

Niedercorn, J. H., and J. D. Moorehead. 1974. 'The Commodity Flow Gravity Model: A Theoretical Reassessment,' *Regional and Urban Economics,* 4, 69–75.

OECD (Organization for Economic Co-operation and Development). 1987. *OECD Economic Surveys Turkey: 1985–86.* Paris: OECD.

OECD (Organization for Economic Co-operation and Development). 1991. *OECD Economic Surveys Turkey: 1989–90.* Paris, OECD.

OECD (Organization for Economic Co-operation and Development). 1994. *OECD National Accounts 1960–1992.* Paris: OECD.

OECD (Organization for Economic Co-operation and Development) (various years). *OECD Trade by Commodities Series C.* Paris: OECD.

Polachek, S. W. 1992. 'Conflict and Trade: An Economics Approach to Political International Interactions,' in W. Isard and C. H. Anderton (eds.), *Economics of Arms Reduction and Peace Process.* New York: Elsevier.

Pollins, B. M. 1989a. 'Does Trade Still Follow the Flag?,' *American Political Science Review,* 83, 465–80.

Pollins, B. M. 1989b. 'Conflict, Cooperation and Commerce: the Effect of International Political Interactions on Bilateral Trade Flows,' *American Journal of Political Science,* 33, 737–61.

Sayrs, L. W. 1989. 'Trade and Conflict Revisited: Do Politics Matter?,' *International Interactions*, 15, 155–75.

Sen, A., and T. E. Smith. 1995. *Gravity Models of Spatial Interaction Behavior*. New York: Springer-Verlag.

Sheppard, Eric C. 1984. 'The Distance-Decay Gravity Model Debate,' in G. L. Gaile and C. J. Wilmott (eds.), *Spatial Statistics and Models*. Dordrecht, Netherlands: Kluwer Academic Publishers.

Smith, T. E. 1976. 'Spatial Discounting and the Gravity Hypothesis, *Regional Science and Urban Economics*, 6, 331–56.

Smith, T. E. 1983. 'A Cost Efficiency Approach to the Analysis of Congested Spatial Interaction Behavior,' *Environment and Planning A*, 15, 435–64.

Stewart, J. Q. 1948. 'Demographic Gravitation: Evidence and Applications,' *Sociometry*, 11.

Stouffer, A. 1960. 'Intervening Opportunities and Competing Migrants,' *Journal of Regional Science*, 1, 1–20.

Summary, R. M. 1989. 'A Political-Economic Model of US Bilateral Trade,' *Review of Economics and Statistics*, 71, 179–82.

Van Bergeijk, Peter A. G. 1989. *Trade and Diplomacy: An Extension of the Gravity Model in International Trade Theory*, Research Memorandum No. 320, Institute of Economic Research, University of Groningen, Groningen, Netherlands.

Wilson, A. G. 1970. *Entropy in Urban and Regional Planning*. London: Pion Limited.

Wilson, A. G. 1974. *Urban and Regional Models in Geography and Planning*. London: Wiley.

Yaman, A. 1994. 'An Economic and Political Model of Turkish Bilateral Trade with the OECD Countries, 1970–1990: A Gravity Model Approach,' unpublished thesis, Ithaca, New York: Cornell University.

7. Social accounting matrices and social accounting analysis

Erik Thorbecke

7.0 Introduction

In the preceding chapters, attention has been devoted to the details of industrial structure and resource availability with little attention to people, specific social groups, specific government policies and programs, and details of capital structure. Moreover, concern has been concentrated on economic welfare, and not social welfare. It is with regard to incorporating these relatively neglected areas within a much more comprehensive regional and interregional framework that social accounting matrices and social accounting analysis make major contributions.

The genesis of the Social Accounting Matrix (SAM) goes back to Richard Stone's pioneering work on social accounts. Subsequently Pyatt and Thorbecke (1976) further formalized the SAM and showed how it could be used as a conceptual and modular framework for policy and planning purposes. The SAM is a comprehensive, disaggregated, consistent and complete data system that captures the interdependence that exists within a socioeconomic system. Thus, depending on the classification scheme used to record transactions and the extent of disaggregation, the SAM can provide useful information about such key issues as intersectoral linkages (such as between agriculture and industry); interregional flows within an economy; the determination of the income distribution by socioeconomic groups given the structure and technology of production and the resource endowments of these groups; and the relationship between a given regional economy and other regional economies within a nation, and with the rest of the world. Concomitantly, much more effective policy can be developed with respect to the provision of educational, medical and other facilities among poor and rich regions.

Alternatively the SAM can be used as a conceptual framework to explore the impact of exogenous changes in such variables as exports, certain categories of government expenditures, and investment on the whole interdependent socioeconomic system, e.g., the resulting structure of production, factorial and household income distributions. As such the SAM becomes the basis for simple multiplier analysis and the building and calibration of a variety of applied general equilibrium models. The SAM as a data system and as a conceptual framework is discussed in section 7.1, first for an isolated region, then for regions within a nation and lastly with the rest of the world.

Section 7.2 is devoted to a crucial issue in building and using a SAM, i.e. that of the appropriate classification and disaggregation scheme applying to the various accounts. The chosen taxonomy and the level of disaggregation depend critically on the questions that the SAM methodologies are expected to answer. If the SAM is to be used to explore issues related to income distribution then the household account is to be broken down into a number of relatively homogeneous household groups reflecting the socioeconomic characteristics of the country or region under consideration. Alternatively, if the purpose of the SAM is to analyze intersectoral linkages, then a relatively detailed sectoral disaggregation of production activities using such criteria as characteristics of the good or service produced and type of technology employed in production is called for. In section 7.2, criteria relevant to building appropriate taxonomies for each of the major SAM accounts (i.e., production activities cum commodities, households, factors, government, capital, and rest of the world) are discussed.

Section 7.3 is devoted to a discussion of the different data sources needed to construct a SAM and the processes through which inconsistencies among these data sources (e.g., regional and national income accounts data, input-output information, household income and expenditure surveys, agricultural and industrial censuses) can be reconciled. The SAM is almost an ideal instrument within which consistency checks among different data sources can be undertaken, inconsistencies reconciled and data gaps identified. Often these data gaps can be remedied through new surveys and other types of data collection and errors corrected — particularly when the preparation of the SAM is institutionalized within a Central Statistical Bureau, as is presently the case in Indonesia.

In section 7.4 the SAM-based multiplier methodology is presented. In particular the impact of exogenous shocks such as exports, government programs and investment on the structure of production, the factorial and the income distributions is analyzed. Depending on the extent of output responsiveness (excess capacity) in different production sectors, unconstrained and constrained multipliers are discussed. In a more general sense, starting from a given exogenous shock, the complete network of paths through which influence is transmitted within a socioeconomic system represented by a SAM is derived through structural path analysis. Finally, in the same section, it is shown how the SAM framework can be used to provide the initial conditions and help calibrate an applied general equilibrium model.

The final section is devoted to different applications of, and studies relying on the SAM. Since their inception in the 1970s SAMs have been built for a large number of developing and developed countries. Because of its emphasis on intersectoral linkages (particularly between agriculture and nonagriculture) and income distribution most of the early applications of the SAM were in the Third World. More recently this framework has been extensively used in developed countries. The geographical domain covered by existing SAMs extends over a wide range from nations to regions and even villages. Likewise, the range of policy issues in the innumerable applications is widespread. The few examples reviewed in this section help provide a feel for this diversity.

7.1 The overall conceptual framework

The Social Accounting Matrix (SAM) is both a data system and a conceptual framework useful for policy analysis.[1] As a data system, the SAM is 1) comprehensive and disaggregated, as it includes estimates of transactions among sectors, institutions and economic agents; 2) consistent in the sense that for every income there should be an equivalent outlay or expenditure; and, 3) complete in that both the receiver and the sender of every transaction must be identified. The SAM is a snapshot of the socioeconomic system during a given year. It provides a classification and organizational scheme for the data useful to analysts and policymakers alike. It is also a very useful diagnostic tool in understanding the anatomy and physiology of an interdependent socioeconomic system. It incorporates explicitly various crucial relationships among variables such as the mapping of the factorial income distribution from the structure of production and the mapping of the household income distribution from the factorial income distribution.

To appreciate the much more comprehensive framework of SAM we present a simplified Figure 7.1 for an isolated region. There, the production activities circle embody all those activities covered by an input-output matrix. The process depicted by the arrow designated valued added by sectors and components, leading down to the factor payments circle is also generally covered in the value-added rows of input-output. However, the process depicted by the arrow designated Income Distribution by Institutions (including Socio-Economic Household groups, companies and government) circle is not covered by input/output. Nor is the process depicted by the arrow designated Consumption Expenditure Patterns of Socio-Economic groups leading up to Production Activities, these patterns typically being aggregated to form one household column and one government column in the final demand sectors of input-output.

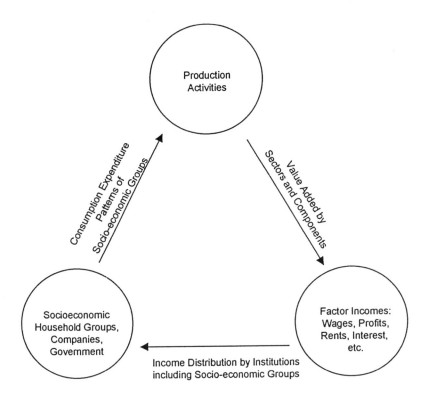

Figure 7.1 Simplified relationship among principal SAM accounts (productive activities, factors and institutions): an isolated region

A more detailed presentation is contained in Figure 7.2 for a given region (Region A) which is part of an interregional system within a nation. There we have separated government (depicted by the circle in the center of the figure) from households by type (socio-economic groups). We have added arrows depicting: (1) the flow of indirect taxes on production, (2) direct and corporate taxes of households and institutions (which include companies), (3) transfers and subsidies from government and interest payments. Further, we have depicted savings and investment flows associated with households, companies and government from other regions and the rest of the world.

Finally, we have indicated inflows representing (money) receipts from exports to other regions of the nation, as well as to the rest of the world, and outflows representing payments for inputs coming from other regions and the rest of the world. By distinguishing the rest of the nation (account 6a) from the rest of the world (6b) both the interregional trade pattern and the international trade patterns can appear in the SAM, especially when data are or become available so that account 6a can be regionally disaggregated and account 6b disaggregated by groups of countries.

Table 7-1 presents all the above flows in a basic SAM. A SAM is a square matrix in which each transactor or account has its own row and column. The payments (expenditures) are listed in columns and the receipts are recorded in rows. As the sum of all expenditures by a given account (or subaccount) must equal the total sum of receipts or income for the corresponding account, row sums must equal the column sums of the corresponding account. For example, the total income of a given institution (say a specific socioeconomic household group) must equal exactly the total expenditures of that same institution. This is the economic analog of the physicists' law of conservation of energy. Hence, analysts interested in understanding how the structure of production influences the income distribution can obtain useful insights by studying the SAM.

In the basic SAM of Table 7-1, six accounts are distinguished. Production activities produce different sectoral goods and services (e.g. textile products) by buying raw materials and intermediate goods and services (from the region under consideration, other regions within the nation and from abroad). In addition these accounts pay indirect taxes to the government and the remainder is, by definition, value added that is distributed to the factors of production (see column 1). Production activities receipts (row 1) derive from sales to households, exports and the government. In the present formulation of the SAM no distinction is made between production activities and commodities. For the sake of simplicity,

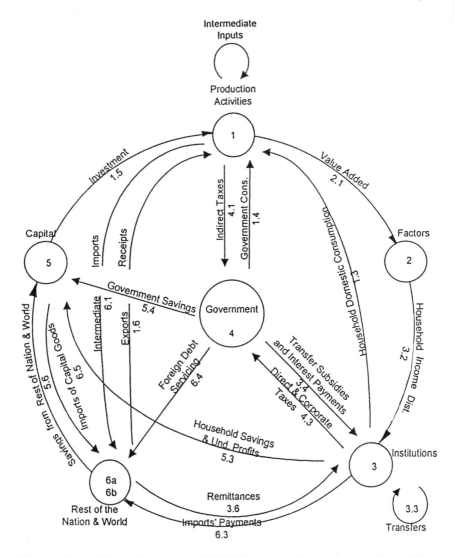

Figure 7.2 Flow diagram of SAM transactions for region A[a]

[a]The flow diagram reflects exactly the transactions and transformations in the SAM on Table 7-1. Note that transactions are numbered in a way consistent with the numbering of the Accounts in Table 7-1. For example, the allocation of value added is a receipt for the Factor Account (#2) and a payment by the Production Activities Account (#1); hence, the corresponding transformation (matrix) is denoted by 2.1.

Source: Based on Thorbecke (1988) but numbering has been modified.

Table 7-1 A basic social accounting matrix (SAM) for Region A

		1 Production Activities	2 Factors of Production	3a Households	3b Companies	4 Government	5 Combined capital account	6a Rest of the nation combined account with Regions B,C....	6b Rest of the world combined account	Totals
1	Production activities	Raw material purchases of goods within region		Household consumption expenditure on goods		Government current expenditure	Investment expenditures on region's goods	Exports	Exports	Aggregate demand – gross outputs
2	Factors of production	Value added payments to factors						Net factor income from B, C, ...	Net factor income from abroad	Incomes of the region's factors of production
3a	House-holds		Allocation of income to household	Current transfers between households	Profits distributed to region's households	Current transfers to region's households		Net non-factor incomes received from B, C....	Net non-factor incomes from abroad	Incomes of the region's institutions after transfers
3b	Comp.		Allocation of operating surplus to companies			Current transfers to region's companies				
4	Gov't	Indirect taxes on inputs		Direct taxes on income and indirect taxes on current expenditures	Direct taxes on companies plus operating surplus of state enterprises		Indirect taxes on capital goods			
5	Combined capital acct			Household savings	Undistributed profits after tax	Gov't current account surplus		Net capital from nation	Net capital from abroad	Aggregate savings
6a	Rest of the Nation combined account with Regions B, C....	Imports of goods and raw materials		Household consumption on imported goods			Imports of capital goods			Total imports from rest of nation
6b	Rest of the world combined account	Imports of raw materials		Household consumption expend. on imp. goods			Imports of capital goods			Total foreign imports
	Totals	Total costs	Incomes of the domestic factors of production	Total outlay of households	Total outlay of companies	Total outlay of government	Aggregate investment	Total receipts from rest of nation	Total foreign exchange receipt	

EXPENDITURES — Institutions (Current accounts: 3a Households, 3b Companies); Current Accounts / Institutions it is assumed that a production activity is equivalent to a corresponding commodity. In some instances, the SAM format distinguishes between production activities and commodity accounts. This would be the case when a given production activity produced different commodities, for example, so that these two sets of accounts would require different sectoral breakdowns. For this reason, many SAMs include both production activities and commodities accounts. When commodity accounts appear in a SAM they can best be seen as representing a region's or nation's product markets.[2]

Factors of production accounts typically include labor and capital subaccounts. They receive income (recorded in row 2) from the sale of their services to production activities in the form of wages, rent and net factor income received from abroad or from other regions (corresponding to the value added generated by the production activities). In turn, these revenues are distributed (col. 2) to households as labor incomes and to companies as distributed profits.

Institutions include households (typically further broken down by socioeconomic groups), companies (i.e. firms) and the government. From row 3a, it can be seen that households receive factor income (wages and other labor income, rent, interest and profits) as well as transfers from government and from the rest of the nation and world (e.g. remittances). Households' expenditures (in column 3a) consist of consumption on goods from the region, from other regions and from abroad, and income taxes with residual savings transferred to the capital account. Companies (3b) receive profits and transfers and spend on taxes and transfers with their residual savings channeled into their capital account.

The government account (4) is distinct from administrative public activities included in the production activities' account. These public services (such as education) buy intermediate goods, pay wages and deliver public and administrative services. The government account per se allocates its current expenditures on buying the services provided by the production activities account. Other government expenditures (col. 4) are transfers and subsidies to households and companies and the remaining savings are transferred to the capital account. On the income side, the government receives tax revenues from a variety of sources and current transfers from abroad (row 4). Although rarely done, in principle, the government account can be subdivided by level from federal to county.[3]

The fifth account is the combined capital account. On the income side (row 5) it collects savings from households, companies, the government as well as foreign and other regions' savings and, in turn, channels these aggregate savings into investment (col. 5).

Finally, transactions between domestic residents, residents of other regions and foreign residents, respectively, are recorded in the rest of the nation and world accounts (6a and 6b). These transactions include, on the receipt side, households' consumption expenditures on goods from other regions and imported final goods as well as imports of capital goods and raw materials (row 6). The economy receives income from the rest of the nation and world (col. 6) from exports and factor and nonfactor income earned. The difference between total foreign exchange receipts and imports is by definition net capital received from abroad or the rest of the nation and extraregional and foreign savings.

The SAM framework can also be used as a conceptual framework and as a basis for modelling. In this case the generating mechanisms influencing the flows appearing in Figure 7.2 have to be spelled out explicitly and quantitatively. Whereas the SAM in Table 7-1 is a snapshot of the economy, Figure 7.2 which reproduces all of the transformations appearing in Table 7-1, can be interpreted more broadly as representing flows (over a period of one year) which, in turn, have to be explained by structural or behavioral relationships.

The first question to address when using the SAM as a conceptual framework is which accounts should be considered exogenous and which endogenous. It has been customary to consider the government, the rest of the world and the capital accounts as exogenous and the factors, other institutions, (households and companies) and production activities' accounts as endogenous. To illustrate how the SAM approach lends itself to deriving the ultimate income distribution and expenditure pattern by socioeconomic group following, say, a change in the structure of production resulting from government actions or a change in exports, distinguishing between the determination of primary and secondary income distribution is useful. Thus a distinction is drawn between primary claims on resources which arise directly out of the productive process of work and accumulation, and secondary claims that result from the transfer of primary claims. The former results from prevailing patterns of 1) production and 2) resource endowment in terms of human capital, physical capital and land among households. In other words, the primary income distribution is determined through the triangular interrelationship linking production activities, factors and institutions — i.e. the various socioeconomic groups of households in Figure 7.2 which is reproduced in truncated form in Figure 7.3.[4] The secondary income distribution may work through the family,

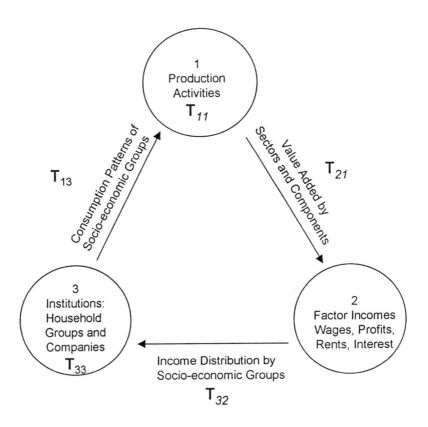

**Figure 7.3 Interrelationships among endogenous SAM accounts
(production activities, factors and institutions)[a]**

[a]**T** stands for the corresponding matrix and flow in the SAM which appears
in Table 7-1 and Figure 7.2. Thus, T_{21} refers to the matrix which appears
at the intersection of row 2 (account 2), i.e., 'factors of production' and
column 1 (account 1), i.e., 'production activities' in Table 7-1; T_{32} refers
to the matrix which appears at the intersection of row 3 (account 3), i.e.,
'households' and column 2 (account 2), i.e., 'factors of production'; and
T_{13} refers to the matrix which appears at the intersection of row 1 (account
1), i.e., 'production activities' and columns 3a and 3b (accounts 3a and 3b),
i.e., 'institutions.'

village or more importantly through the state in the form of transfers and subsidies (flow 3.4 in Figure 7.2) and taxes (4.3).

If we are to understand and explain, in an operational way, the mechanisms through which these transformations occur, great care must be exercised in designing appropriate classification schemes for each of the three endogenous accounts (production activities, factors and institutions). (This issue is discussed in more detail in section 7.2.) The triangular interrelationships among these accounts are shown explicitly in Figure 3. These transformations incorporate the mechanisms that translate the generation of value added by production into the incomes of different types of households and other institutions. The link is provided by factors of production. The level and structure of output by the different activities generate the aggregate demand for labor of different types, natural resources and capital services. Hence, employment enters into the analysis. The stream of value added, from the production side, rewards the factors of production, with wages going to different types of labor, rent going to land and other resources, and profits to capital. In this way a picture is obtained of the factorial distribution of income which is captured in Table 7-1 by the interface between column 1 and row 2 and, analogously, by matrix T_{21} in Figure 7.3.

With regard to production activities, four criteria suggest themselves in deriving an appropriate classification: 1) the nature of the item produced be it a good, service or commodity; 2) the type of technology used, in terms of labor and capital intensity, 3) the form of organization underlying the production process (i.e. farm or firm relying on family labor and self employment, as opposed to an incorporated, or even a state enterprise); and, 4) whether the commodities are tradable or nontradable.

In turn, the classification of factors and households should be consistent with our interest in income, employment and equity issues. With the qualification that any ultimate taxonomy should be country or region specific, the following breakdown of factors may be suggested: 1) labor broken down by skill or educational level; 2) capital distinguishing between land and other forms of capital.

Translation from factorial distribution to the distribution of incomes across institutions, and particularly across different household groups, depends on which institutions own which factors. Thus, for example, wage payments to unskilled labor go to the households that provide this type of labor; imputed labor income is received by small farmers from the services performed by self-employed family labor on their own farms, while rent income (whether imputed or not) accrues to the owners of land and other natural resources, and finally, profits accrue to owners of capital. This second transformation is shown in Table 7-1 by the interface between column 2 and row 3, as well as by matrix T_{32} in Figure 7.3. Three main criteria appear important in classifying households: a) location; b) resource endowment and wealth; and c) occupation of the head of the household. Location, particularly between rural and urban areas, is a crucial criterion largely on the grounds that policy often has a locational element and often an urban bias. Resource endowment is important at several levels. Access to land is a critical consideration in rural areas and the landless can be affected quite differently from the smallholder, or large farmers, by development policy. Likewise, the better educated in both the urban and rural areas are able to land jobs in formal and organized activities, whereas the uneducated are limited to employment opportunities largely in traditional agriculture and informal urban activities in developing countries and manual jobs in developed countries. The endowment of land and human capital is a crucial determinant of the ultimate income distribution and standards of living of the various socioeconomic household groups.

A third transformation in Figure 7.3 yields the consumption patterns of the different socioeconomic groups (interface between column 3a and row 1 in Table 7-1 and matrix T_{13} in Figure 7.3). It reveals the values of the commodities (assumed here to be equivalent to production activities) consumed by these groups. This transformation provides crucial information on the living standards of the various groups and the extent to which they are able to satisfy their basic needs. Two final endogenous transformations appear in Figure 7.3 reflecting transfers occurring within, respectively, the production activities' account and the institutions account. T_{11} represents the matrix of intermediate demand by production activities and is nothing else than the conventional input-output table. T_{33} captures transfers among institutions and, in particular, transfers from some relatively better off socioeconomic groups to other poorer groups.

At this stage, one qualification needs to be made. Whereas the SAM approach explains the determination of total incomes accruing to the various socioeconomic groups, it does not generate the intra-group income distributions. To the extent that poverty tends to be concentrated in a few groups, such as the landless and small farmers in rural areas and the informal sector workers in urban areas, between-group variance is likely to explain a reasonably high proportion of total income variance in society. If one wants to approximate more exactly the impact on poverty of measures affecting the structure of production, knowledge of the income distributions within socioeconomic groups is necessary because poor households (those with incomes below a given normative poverty line) are likely to be found even in socioeconomic groups enjoying average income levels significantly higher than the poverty line.

7.2 Classification and disaggregation of accounts

Classification matters in a fundamental sense whether the SAM is used as a diagnostic tool to understand better the underlying interdependent socioeconomic structure of an economy, or as a conceptual framework and basis for modelling. Economic concepts and variables must be represented in a SAM by appropriately corresponding classes and categories. To each conceptual framework, there must be a corresponding taxonomic and data system.

What are some of the key issues in deciding on a SAM classification scheme? First, the level and extent of disaggregation deserve consideration. In many instances given the policy issues a SAM is supposed to address, fairly aggregative SAMs broken down in relatively few categories will do. However, since it is always possible to consolidate and aggregate subaccounts — but not the other way around — it may be better to start at a level of disaggregation which is as detailed as data reliability allows. Secondly, the degree of homogeneity is crucial in the design of classifications. For example, in a classification of household groups, one would like to identify groups that are relatively homogeneous in terms of income sources and levels and expenditure patterns.

It has been argued that every classification should meet certain requirements if it is to be used in a SAM. A SAM taxonomy should a) correctly reproduce the socioeconomic and structural (production) stratification within the society and economy; b) distinguish relatively homogeneous groups and categories; c) be composed of socioeconomic groups that are recognizable for policy purposes and useful for socioeconomic analysis (i.e., specific target groups should be identified); d) be based on comparatively stable characteristics that can be measured relatively easily and reliably; and e) be derivable from (a combination of) existing data sources (Alarcon Rivero et al., 1986).

Applying these criteria to household groups, it is noteworthy that a household classification based on income or expenditure brackets does not satisfy any of these requirements — except perhaps the first one. Since the poorest segment of society (say the bottom decile of the income pyramid) may include very different household heads such as a landless agricultural worker and an urban informal sector worker, policies aimed at improving conditions in the two cases are likely to be very different.

There is no unique (standard) classification scheme or way of disaggregating and organizing the data in a SAM. The taxonomy used in any given SAM depends on the prevailing country or region specific characteristics and the objectives of the studies underlying the building of the SAM. In a SAM that emphasizes intersectoral linkages, the level of disaggregation of production activities needed to capture the structure of production is likely to be much smaller in poor developing countries than in an industrialized one. A SAM that is supposed to be used as a basis for exploring income distribution issues needs a finer disaggregation of socioeconomic household groups than one not highlighting income distribution.

Each account appearing in Table 7-1 can be disaggregated. A common approach is to start with selecting the most robust and appropriate classification criteria and then breaking the latter down further into subcriteria and subsubcriteria following a hierarchical top-down tree structure. In what follows major criteria and subcriteria typically used in the classification and disaggregation of the different accounts are mentioned briefly:

7.2.1 Production activities cum commodities

a) Production activities — two digit or three digit International Standard Industrial Classification (ISIC); further broken down according to technology level (e.g., distinguishing between formal and informal technologies for the same type of product; size of firms in terms of number of employees; domestic vs. foreign owned; location; tradable vs. nontradable);

b) Commodities — nature of the good or service fulfilling similar needs; tradable vs. nontradable; local vs. imported.

7.2.2 Institutions

a) Households — location (e.g., rural vs. urban); asset ownership (particularly land ownership in the rural areas and human capital in urban areas); characteristics of the head or main earner, distinguishing by main employment status, main occupation, main branch of industry and educational attainment, sex, main language, race (tribal) kinship; (see Figure 7.4);

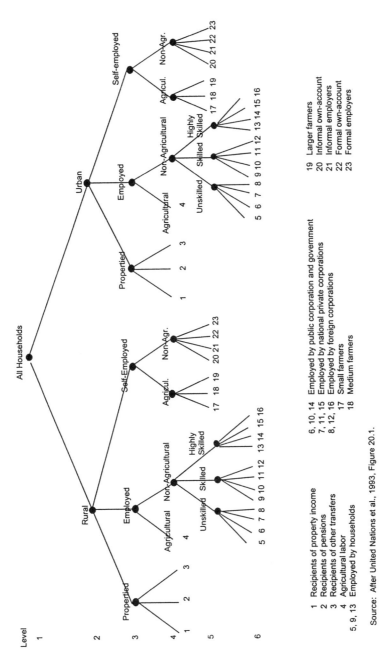

Level

1

2

3

4

5

6

All Households

Rural
  Propertied — 1 2 3
  Employed
    Agricultural — 4
    Non-Agricultural
      Unskilled — 5 6 7 8
      Skilled — 9 10 11 12
      Highly Skilled — 13 14 15 16
  Self-Employed
    Agricul. — 17 18 19
    Non-Agr. — 20 21 22 23

Urban
  Propertied — 1 2 3
  Employed
    Agricultural — 4
    Non-Agricultural
      Unskilled — 5 6 7 8 9 10 11 12 13 14 15 16
      Skilled — 11 12 13 14 15 16
      Highly Skilled — 17 18 19
  Self-employed
    Agricul. — 17 18 19
    Non-Agr. — 20 21 22 23

1 Recipients of property income
2 Recipients of pensions
3 Recipients of other transfers
4 Agricultural labor
5, 9, 13 Employed by households

6, 10, 14 Employed by public corporation and government
7, 11, 15 Employed by national private corporations
8, 12, 16 Employed by foreign corporations
17 Small farmers
18 Medium farmers

19 Larger farmers
20 Informal own-account
21 Informal employers
22 Formal own-account
23 Formal employers

Source: After United Nations et al., 1993, Figure 20.1.

Figure 7.4   Top-down approach to the classification of households: 6-level tree

b) Companies — ownership (distinguishing between national and foreign, and private and public status, respectively); legal status (incorporated vs. unincorporated and some family enterprises);

c) Government — central vs. local and breakdown by capital and current expenditure categories.

7.2.3 Factors of production

a) Labor — occupation (distinguishing by skill level and occupational category); wage employment vs. self-employment; location; education; sex; age; type and size of firm;

b) Land and other natural resources — land type and fertility; size of the holding; location; and

c) Capital — domestic vs. foreign, private vs. public and type or vintage of capital good.

A great strength of the SAM is that it explicitly breaks down households into relatively homogeneous socioeconomic categories that are recognizable for policy purposes and exhibit relatively stable characteristics. This type of disaggregation allows the SAM to be used to analyze the effects of government policies on income distribution (see specific examples in section 7.5). Although any classification is essentially arbitrary, there are many instances of effective classification such as the Standard Industrial Classification and the Standard Occupational Classification designed and used by Central Statistical Bureaux. Recently the community of statisticians designed and recommended the adoption of a hierarchical classification of households which shows a top down tree structure at different levels. This proposed taxonomy is reproduced in Figure 7.4. (For an interesting discussion of the importance of an appropriate households taxonomies, see Duchin, 1996.)

A final key issue that goes to the heart of defining and deciding on the domain of the SAM and that transcends across accounts is that of regionalization.[5] While most SAM studies have been undertaken with national objectives in mind, yet it has been realized that distinguishing regions within a country SAM can enhance both its realism and its usefulness. If the economy displays significant regional differences in the types of goods produced, structure of production and technology, these differences could affect the standards of living of different household groups. Another important advantage of the explicit inclusion of the regional dimension into a SAM conceptual framework is that a large number of policy means tend to be location-specific. These may include investment projects, current government expenditures on services, such as health and education, and price policies with respect to commodities and inputs at least to the extent that the production of specific commodities is regionally concentrated.

Whereas in principle there are compelling reasons for adding a regional dimension to the SAM, in practice there continue to be serious difficulties on the data side. Clearly, in the absence of a set of interregional social accounts, which are not available on a systematic basis in too many countries, production activities and interregional trade have not been able to be expressed in the form of an integrated set of interregional input-output tables.[6]

Given the data limitations, there are three alternative procedures which suggest themselves — short of a full-fledge multiregional SAM — and which appear to be feasible within the context of many countries, especially developing ones. The first procedure would be to divide the economy into a very small number of regions and divide production activities into those that are typically national and those that are more regional in character. A second more modest and perhaps more realistic procedure for capturing some of the regional effects of production consists of breaking down the factor and household accounts along regional lines without using a regional classification of production activities. Hence the mapping from production activities to factors of production would allocate the value added generated by the various national production activities to factors where at least some of the factors were defined on a regional basis. A specific example might be the allocation of value added generated by agricultural production activities directly to regional groups of smallholders. This type of information can be quite valuable in those instances where there exist marked interregional income differences which can be accounted for by differences in the pattern of interregional production. A third which has yet to be adequately explored is to tailor the extent of disaggregation and aggregation to the data that are available, so that the structure of one region in an interregional SAM may be very fine and in others crude.

Very few integrated interregional SAMs have been built so far. One example is that of a two-region SAM for Indonesia distinguishing between the Center (Java) and the Outer Islands that is discussed in section 7.5.3.

When the empirical and analytical focus is on a particular region or village, it makes sense to build corresponding regional or village SAMs. In those instances the 'rest of the world' account needs to be further broken down between transactions with the 'rest of the nation' and transactions with the 'rest of the world' outside the country in consideration. Again, an example of village SAMs is given in the final section of this paper (see section 7.5.4).

7.3 Data requirements in the construction of a SAM

A variety of data sources are required to build a SAM. Because the methods used in collecting and generating statistics differ significantly from one source to another (such as national income accounts, input-output, census information, surveys, etc.) the process of building a SAM provides a natural check on the mutual consistency of these sources and identifies possible data gaps and errors. In this sense the process of reconciliation that is endemic in generating a SAM has social value in its own right.[7] There are different techniques for reconciling and forcing consistency within a SAM that does not balance — the most naïve and mechanical one being the RAS technique (see the discussion on pp. 89–92 and pp. 258–263). Generally, it is far more preferable to use sound judgment than mechanical approaches in insuring that a SAM is consistent and balanced.

Given the degree of country or regional specificity and the numerous different objectives which construction of the SAM may have, it is not possible to identify a unique and general set of required data. The more disaggregated a SAM is intended to be, the more extensive are the data requirements. Some scholars maintain that 'in all cases, the starting point should be the building of a highly aggregated SAM based on the country's national accounts statistics' (Sadoulet and de Janvry, 1995, p. 280). Others would contend that a more accurate and sensible approach for regional and interregional analyses and even national is to construct a SAM region by region with interregional flows increasingly disaggregated.

There is no optimal sequence in which to proceed with the construction of a SAM. A good starting point is with the production activities' account since the SAM can be seen as a major expansion on, and extension of an I-O matrix. This would be particularly true when building a SAM for a region as opposed to a country. A recent I-O table can provide the basis for matrix T_{11} appearing in the basic SAM on Table 7-1, previously discussed. In particular, the I-O table will provide the needed information to fill in the appropriate production activities' row sums in representing the vector of aggregate demands and the corresponding vector of column sums (column 1) yielding the vector of aggregate supplies (sectoral outputs).

A second step might consist of breaking down value added (matrix T_{21} in Table 7-1) into income accruing to different labor categories and profits and rent going to one or more capital categories with the help of employment surveys and agricultural and industrial synthesis.

A third step could yield the incomes of the various socioeconomic groups relying on household income and expenditure surveys. Particularly crucial, in this context, is the mapping of the household income distribution from the factorial income distribution (T_{32}). On the household expenditure side, again consumption surveys together with information on taxes available from the government budget should provide the main spring for filling out column 3a of Table 7-1. With regard to companies, most SAMs aggregate all firms into one category and the information needed to fill in column and row 3b in Table 7-1 is normally available from national accounts data. The government budget and additional public finance information relating to the sources of government revenues and the composition of government expenditure should yield the required figures for the government account (row 4 and col. 4). Finally, a detailed balance of payments supplemented by disaggregated trade statistics should make it possible to record transactions with the rest of the world.

When all the cells (submatrices) of the SAM are filled in based on the above type of primary information for all accounts except for one account (say the capital account), the income row and expenditure column of this last account appears as by magic (a conceptual requirement under Walras' Law). The recorded entries in the SAM for the capital account can then be checked against whatever primary information is available relating to any specific receipt or outlay of that account.

A final data and formatting issue is that the great majority of the existing SAMs contain only a rudimentary breakdown of financial transactions. When one of the objectives of the SAM is to highlight the flow of funds among various financial institutions, households and firms and the portfolios of different financial assets of these institutions, a financial SAM needs to be built. An example of such a SAM is presented in section 7.5.2.b.

7.4 SAM multiplier analysis and extensions

7.4.1 Unconstrained multipliers

If a certain number of conditions are met — in particular, the existence of excess capacity and unemployed or underemployed labor resources — the SAM framework can be used to estimate the effects of exogenous changes and injections, such as an increase in the demand for a given production activity, government expenditures or exports on the whole system. As long as excess capacity and a labor slack prevail, any exogenous change in demand can be satisfied through a corresponding increase in output without having any effect on prices. Thus, for any given injection anywhere in the SAM, influence (e.g., an increase in the export demand for textile products, a government investment or private project leading to an increase in the production of food crops, or a subsidy or transfer accruing to a specific socioeconomic household group) is transmitted through the interdependent SAM system. The total, direct and indirect, effects of the injection on the endogenous accounts, i.e., the total outputs of the different production activities and the incomes of the various factors and socioeconomic groups are estimated through the multiplier process. For example, a public works program resulting in the construction of a new rural farm to market road would require, among others, a significant amount of unskilled labor that is typically provided by the landless and small farmers' household categories. In turn, a significant part of the incremental incomes earned by these two socioeconomic groups from their work on the road project is spent on food demand. The subsequent increase in food production to satisfy that demand leads to still further employment and income increments for these groups, and so on, until the multiplier process dampens.

To derive and illustrate the underlying logic of this methodology, let us at the outset assume, following the previous discussion in section 7.1, that the only three accounts which are endogenously determined are production activities, factors, and institutions (households and companies), while all other accounts are exogenous (government, capital, and the rest of the world). The resulting simplified SAM is presented in Table 7-2 and the corresponding endogenous flows in Figure 7.3. Thus the above simplified and truncated SAM consolidates all exogenous transactions and corresponding leakages and focuses exclusively on the endogenous transactions and transformations. Five endogenous transformations appear in Table 7-2. Note that the three exogenous accounts have been combined

Table 7-2 Simplified schematic social accounting matrix

			EXPENDITURES				
			Endogenous Accounts			Exog	
			Production Activities	Factors	Institutions, i.e. Households and Companies		
			1	2	3	4	5
RECEIPTS	Endogenous Accounts	Production Activities	1	T_{11}	O	T_{13}	f_1	y_1
		Factors	2	T_{21}	O	O	f_2	y_2
		Institutions, i.e. Households and Companies	3	O	T_{32}	T_{33}	f_3	y_3
	Exog.	Sum of Other Accounts	4	$\ell_1{}'$	$\ell_2{}'$	$\ell_3{}'$	ℓ	y_x
		Totals	5	$y_1{}'$	$y_2{}'$	$y_3{}'$	$y_x{}'$	

together in Table 7-2 and the sum of the exogenous injections from government expenditures, investment and exports, respectively, has been consolidated into three vectors f_1, f_2, f_3. (Note that the conventional SAM notation for an exogenous injection is x rather than f. We use the notation f, here, to be consistent with the earlier input-output chapter.) The first vector ($\mathbf{f}_1$) represents the total exogenous demand for the production activities (commodities) resulting from government consumption, investment and export demand. Similarly $\mathbf{f}_2$ and $\mathbf{f}_3$ represent respectively the total exogenous demand for factors (and hence income injection to reward factors) and total exogenous income accruing to the different socioeconomic household groups and companies from, say, government subsidies, and remittances from abroad. Likewise, ℓ_i represent the corresponding leakages, from savings, imports and taxation.

The logic underlying the scheme in Table 7-2 and Figure 7.3, as will be seen shortly, is that exogenous changes (the $\mathbf{f}_i$'s) in Table 7-2 determine, through their interaction within the SAM matrix, the incomes of the endogenous accounts, i.e., i) the production activities (vector $\mathbf{y}_1$); ii) the factor incomes ($\mathbf{y}_2$); and iii) the household and companies incomes ($\mathbf{y}_3$).

For analytical purposes, the endogenous part of the transaction matrix is converted into the corresponding matrix of average expenditure propensities or coefficients. These can be simply obtained as in Chapter 3 on input-output by dividing a particular element in any of the endogenous accounts by the total income for the column account in which the element occurs.[8] From Table 7-2 it can be seen that $\mathbf{A}_n$ is partitioned as follows (i.e. $\mathbf{A}_n$ is composed of different subsets of coefficients)

$$\mathbf{A}_n = \begin{bmatrix} \mathbf{A}_{11} & 0 & \mathbf{A}_{13} \\ \mathbf{A}_{21} & 0 & 0 \\ 0 & \mathbf{A}_{32} & \mathbf{A}_{33} \end{bmatrix} \qquad (7\text{-}1)$$

The subset $\mathbf{A}_{11}$ is the set of input output coefficients reflecting the cents worth of non-primary inputs per dollar of each production activity's output. The subset $\mathbf{A}_{21}$ is the set of cents worth of primary inputs per dollar of output of each production activity and corresponds to the set of coefficients in the values added rows of input output. The coefficients of the subset $\mathbf{A}_{13}$ show, on average, the cents worth of each commodity (production activity) that each (socioeconomic) household group purchases with each of its dollar of total expenditures. The coefficients of the subset $\mathbf{A}_{33}$ shows, on average, the cents worth of income transfers to other household groups per dollar of income. Finally, $\mathbf{A}_{32}$ shows the cents worth of each dollar earned by each type of resource (primary input) that is allocated to each of the household groups.

From the definition of $\mathbf{A}_n$, it follows that in the transaction matrix, each endogenous total income ($\mathbf{y}_n$) is given as

$$\mathbf{y}_n = \mathbf{A}_n \, \mathbf{y}_n + \mathbf{f} \qquad (7\text{-}2)$$

which states that row sums of the endogenous accounts can be obtained by multiplying the average expenditure propensities for each row by the corresponding column sum and adding exogenous income **f**.

Equation (7-2) can be rewritten as

$$\mathbf{y}_n = (\mathbf{I} - \mathbf{A}_n)^{-1} \mathbf{f}$$

$$= \mathbf{M}_a \mathbf{f} \qquad (7\text{-}3)$$

Thus, from (7-3), endogenous incomes $\mathbf{y}_n$ (i.e. production activity incomes, $\mathbf{y}_1$; factor incomes, $\mathbf{y}_2$; and institution incomes, $\mathbf{y}_3$ as shown in Table 7-2) can be derived by premultiplying injection **f** by a multiplier matrix $\mathbf{M}_a$. This matrix has been referred to as the *accounting multiplier matrix* because it explains the results obtained in a SAM and not the process by which they are generated. The latter would require the specification of a dynamic model including the different SAM accounts and variables.

One limitation of the accounting multiplier matrix $\mathbf{M}_a$, as derived in equation (7-3), is that it implies unitary expenditure elasticities (the prevailing average expenditure propensities in $\mathbf{A}_n$ are assumed to apply to any incremental injection). While this assumption may be defensible for all other elements of $\mathbf{A}_n$, it is certainly unrealistic for the expenditure pattern of the household groups ($\mathbf{A}_{13}$). A more realistic alternative is to specify a matrix of marginal expenditure propensities (the $\mathbf{C}_n$ below) corresponding to the observed income and expenditure elasticities of the different agents, under the assumption that prices remain fixed.[9] In this case, $\mathbf{C}_n$ formally differs from $\mathbf{A}_n$ in the following way: $\mathbf{C}_{11} = \mathbf{A}_{11}$, $\mathbf{C}_{33} = \mathbf{A}_{33}$, $\mathbf{C}_{21} = \mathbf{A}_{21}$, $\mathbf{C}_{32} = \mathbf{A}_{32}$, but $\mathbf{C}_{13} \neq \mathbf{A}_{13}$. Expressing the changes in incomes ($d\mathbf{y}_n$) resulting from changes in injections (df), one obtains

$$d\mathbf{y}_n = \mathbf{C}_n d\mathbf{y}_n + df$$

$$= (\mathbf{I} - \mathbf{C}_n)^{-1} df = \mathbf{M}_c df. \qquad (7\text{-}4)$$

(In what follows we prefer to use the differential $d\mathbf{y}_n$ notation rather than the $\Delta \mathbf{y}_n$.)

$\mathbf{M}_c$ has been coined a *fixed price multiplier matrix* and its advantage is that it allows any nonnegative income and expenditure elasticities to be reflected in $\mathbf{M}_c$.[10]

At this stage, it is important to spell out explicitly the multiplier mechanism which results from (7-3).[11] Equation (7-2) can be written out in explicit form as

$$
\begin{aligned}
y_1 &= A_{11}y_1 & & + A_{13}y_3 & & + f_1 \\
y_2 &= A_{21}y_1 & & & & + f_2 \\
y_3 &= & A_{32}y_2 & + A_{33}y_3 & & + f_3
\end{aligned} \tag{7-2a}
$$

which yields

$$
\begin{aligned}
y_1 &= & & (I - A_{11})^{-1}A_{13}y_3 & & + (I - A_{11})^{-1}f_1 \\
y_2 &= A_{21}y_1 & & & & + f_2 \\
y_3 &= & (I - A_{33})^{-1}A_{32}y_2 & & & + (I - A_{33})^{-1}f_3
\end{aligned} \tag{7-2b}
$$

This last set of relationships can be represented graphically (and superimposed on Figure 7.3) to yield Figure 7.5 which shows clearly and explicitly the mechanisms through which the multiplier process operates. Thus starting with an exogenous increase (injection) of export, government, or investment demand f_1, for example, this generates a rise in the output of the corresponding production activity of $(I - A_{11})^{-1}f_1$. In turn, the additional factors of production which have to be employed to create the additional output generate a stream of value added $A_{21}y_1$ which constitutes factor income in addition to any exogenous factor income received from other regions or from abroad and from the government, namely f_2. Thus, $y_2 = A_{21}y_1 + f_2$.

In the next link, households (and companies) receive income $(I - A_{33})^{-1}A_{32}y_2$ based on their resource endowment (A_{32}) and transfers system (A_{33}) as well as income $[(I - A_{33})^{-1}f_3]$ based on exogenous government subsidies and transfer payments and remittances from other regions and abroad. Thus,

$$
y_3 = (I - A_{33})^{-1}A_{32}y_2 + (I - A_{33})^{-1}f_3
$$

Finally, the triangle is closed through the pattern of household (and companies) expenditures on commodities which translates into new production and a corresponding additional flow of income accruing to production activities equal to,

$$
y_1 = (I - A_{11})^{-1} (A_{13}y_3 + f_3) \tag{7-2c}
$$

This formulation generalizes the Leontief model by including as one of the elements of final demand the effects of income distribution (y_3) on the consumption of the various socioeconomic groups (through A_{13}) which reflects the consumption pattern of each group of households. In contrast the open Leontief model with households in the final demand vector can be expressed as follows using the same notation

$$
y_1 = (I - A_{11})^{-1}f \tag{7-2d}
$$

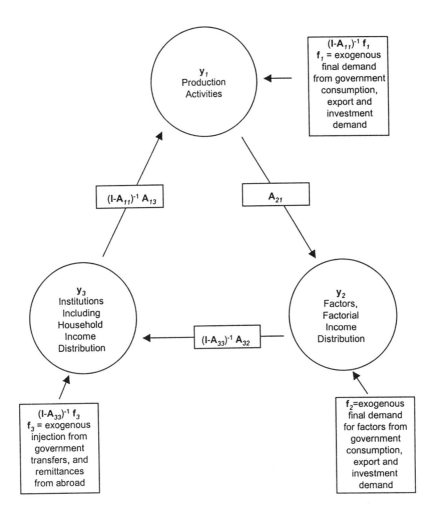

Figure 7.5 Multiplier process among endogenous SAM accounts[a]

[a]The different mechanisms through which an exogenous injection affects the three endogenous accounts (incomes of factors, incomes of socioeconomic groups and outputs of production activities) are made explicit in this diagram. It is based on the decomposition appearing in equation (7-2b).

where A_{11} is the input-output coefficient matrix and f is exogenous total final demand. It is obvious that the SAM formulation 7-2c contains more information and a higher degree of endogeneity since it captures the endogenously derived effects of income distribution on consumption which the Leontief national model does not. The SAM formulation also provides a more detailed and complete depiction of diffusion effects than the regional input-output models when the household sector is included as simply a column in the structural matrix.

In order to ascertain the extent to which the SAM multipliers, i.e. $[I - A_n]^{-1} = M_a$ differ from the Leontief multipliers $((I - A_{11})^{-1})$ on the national level the two sets were computed for Indonesia by Thorbecke (1989). The generalized SAM inverse which incorporates the induced changes in factor incomes and in income levels and, ultimately, the resulting expenditure pattern on commodities generates much higher multiplier values than the more limited Leontief multipliers.

7.4.2 Constrained multipliers

The assumption that supply is perfectly elastic in all sectors and that an increase in (exogenous) demand is sufficient to stimulate corresponding rises in output and incomes may not be too unrealistic in some settings, while quite unrealistic in others. In particular, many analysts believe that the assumption of excess capacity and unused resources is unrealistic when applied to the agricultural sector of many regions of developing countries. In such instances, it is posited that demand increases alone are inadequate in bringing forth more than a marginal agricultural output response. Likewise, some industrial sectors might be operating close to capacity. The accounting and fixed price multipliers described above will provide output and income multiplier estimates that are unrealistically high — owing to overly optimistic expectations regarding supply response. To address such concerns, a modified SAM multiplier methodology has been developed that allows for limited or even no supply response in output-constrained sectors while maintaining the assumption of excess capacity in all other non-supply constraint sectors. This has led to the formulation of constrained, or mixed, SAM multipliers and their application to regional, district and village settings (see Subramanian and Sadoulet, 1990; Lewis and Thorbecke, 1992 and Parikh and Thorbecke, 1996).

The logic underlying constrained, or mixed, SAM multipliers is as follows. If some excess capacity is available in a constrained sector, the fixed price multiplier, M_c, holds until the full capacity of such a sector is reached. Once the capacity is reached, the mixed multiplier, $\mathbf{M}_m$, can be used for the remaining demand (the definition and formal derivation of $\mathbf{M}_m$ are given in Lewis and Thorbecke 1992). Thus the final multiplier would be $\mathbf{M}_c + \mathbf{M}_m$. The following example illustrates this point. Say, the incremental capacity of agriculture is Rs. 150,000. Then corresponding to an exogenous increase in demand of Rs. 200,000, two different multipliers will have to be calculated, a fixed price multiplier, $\mathbf{M}_c$, up to Rs. 150,000 and a mixed multiplier, $\mathbf{M}_m$ for the remaining demand of Rs. 50,000. This final multiplier $\mathbf{M}_c + \mathbf{M}_m$ can be used for all the exogenous injections which require more goods than can be supplied by the constrained sector, while taking care of the limited excess capacity available in the constrained sector.

The above method can be easily extended to include more than one constrained sector.[12] Say there are two supply constrained sectors, x and y, with different capacity constraints. Then three multipliers have to be calculated. The first one, the fixed price multiplier, $\mathbf{M}_c$, holds as long as some excess capacity prevails in both the sectors. Once full capacity of one of these sectors, (say x), is reached, x will become an exogenous sector as per the methodology of mixed multipliers. The second multiplier, which is a mixed multiplier, $\mathbf{M}_{m1}$, with x as an exogenous sector, becomes operative while y still remains an endogenous sector since it has some additional capacity left. Finally, when the exogenous demand exceeds the supply capacity of y, a third multiplier, $\mathbf{M}_{m2}$ can be calculated, which treats both y and x as exogenous sectors. Thus the final total multiplier becomes $\mathbf{M}_c + \mathbf{M}_{m1} + \mathbf{M}_{m2}$.

In reality, many constrained sectors are likely to possess some excess capacity. Therefore, the actual multipliers are likely to lie somewhere between the unconstrained fixed price and mixed multipliers. Hence, a methodological novelty that was introduced in the Parikh and Thorbecke (1996) study was to relax the assumption of completely inelastic supply for some sectors and derive multipliers that allow a limited degree of supply response.[13]

Of course, the magnitude of constrained multipliers is always less than the corresponding unconstrained fixed price multipliers. At the limit, all sectors are supply constrained and the multiplier values collapse to zero. Thus, it can be argued that fixed price multipliers represent the upper bound estimates of the likely impact of an exogenous increase in demand on the outputs and incomes of the endogenous accounts in the SAM (outputs of production activities and incomes of factors and household groups).

7.4.3 Structural path analysis and transmission of economic influence within the SAM framework

The SAM framework represents an important addition to, and generalization of the input-output model since it captures the circular interdependence characteristic of any economic system among a) production activities, b) the factorial income distribution, and c) the income distribution among institutions (particularly among different socioeconomic household groups), which, in turn, determines the expenditure pattern of institutions. The global (direct and indirect) effects of injections from exogenous variables on the endogenous variables are captured, under certain conditions, by the fixed price and constrained multipliers. However, these multipliers do not clarify the 'black box', i.e. the structural and behavioral mechanism responsible for these global effects. From a policy standpoint, knowledge of the magnitude of multipliers is important but becomes of even greater operational usefulness if it is complemented by structural path analysis that identifies the various paths along which a given injection travels. In particular, structural path analysis reveals, in contrast to multipliers per se which are scalar numbers, the specific individual sectors (activities, factors and household groups) through which influence is transmitted in a socioeconomic system represented by the SAM. Structural path analysis provides a detailed way of decomposing multipliers, and of identifying the whole network of paths through which influence is transmitted from one sector of origin to its ultimate destination thereby opening the black box (see Defourny and Thorbecke, 1984, and Thorbecke and collaborators, 1992).

An example can be given to illustrate this concept before presenting it more formally. Assume that we are interested in explaining the main paths through which a new textile factory in a rural site affects directly and indirectly the incomes of small farmers. The increase in textile output will require unskilled labor that is to be provided by two different household groups, i.e., small farmers and the landless. Because these two groups are likely to be poor, a significant part of the incremental incomes accruing to them from earnings from work in the factory will be spent on food crops. The subsequent increase in food crop production, in turn, requires unskilled family labor from small farm households, thus, further raising their incomes. In this example, the following paths spanning textiles output, as the pole of origin, and incomes of small farmers, as the pole of destination can be identified: 1) a relatively direct path from larger textiles production to demand for unskilled labor supplied by small farmers, to incomes accruing to small farmers' households; and, 2) a more indirect path from increased output in the textiles sector, to increased demand for unskilled labor (as a factor of production), to increased expenditures on food, to increased demand for labor supplied by small farmers, to increased incomes accruing to small farmers' households. The multiplier value, which is a scalar measure of global influence between a given pole of origin and destination, can be decomposed into the sum of total influence travelling along the different paths spanning these two poles.

In conducting structural path analysis the starting point is to equate the notion of expenditure to that of 'influence.'[14] Graphically this means that each average expenditure propensity a_{ji} (or, alternatively, marginal expenditure propensity c_{ji}) of an 'arc' (i,j) linking two poles of the structure and oriented in the direction of the expenditure is to be interpreted as the magnitude of the influence transmitted from pole i to pole j.

The marginal expenditure propensity (c_{ji}) reflects the 'intensity of arc (i,j).' Fixed price multipliers derived from the matrix of marginal expenditure propensities, $\mathbf{C}_n$, assume that the intensity of the influence between any two poles is captured by the corresponding value of the marginal expenditure propensities. Since the empirical analysis which follows is based on fixed price multipliers, the analysis proceeds by equating influence with marginal expenditure propensity.[15] A path which does not pass more than one time through the same pole is called an 'elementary path.' Finally, a 'circuit' is a path for which the first pole (pole of origin) coincides with the last one (pole of destination). In Figure 7.6.a the path (i,x,y,j) is an elementary path, while in Figure 7.6.b the path (x,y,z,x) is a circuit.

The concept of influence can be given three different quantitative interpretations, namely, (1) direct influence, (2) total influence, and (3) global influence which are discussed below.

a. Direct influence The direct influence of i on j transmitted through an elementary path is the change in income (or production) of j induced by a unitary change in i, the income (or the production) of all other poles except those along the selected elementary path remaining constant. The direct influence can be measured, respectively, along an arc or an elementary path as follows,

Case of direct influence of i on j along arc (i,j)

$$I^D_{(i \to j)} = c_{ji} \tag{7-5}$$

where I represents the magnitude (intensity) of influence and the superscript D indicates that the influence is direct, c_{ji} being the (j,i)th element of the matrix of marginal expenditure propensities $\mathbf{C}_n$. Matrix $\mathbf{C}_n$ can therefore be called the matrix of direct influences — it being understood that the direct influence is measured along arc (i,j).

Case of direct influence along an elementary path (i,...,j) The direct influence transmitted from a pole i to a pole j along a given elementary path is equal to the product of the intensities of the arcs constituting the path. Thus,

$$I^D_{(i...j)} = c_{jn}...c_{mi} \tag{7-6}$$

For example, Figure 7.6.a below represents a given elementary path, $p = (i,x,y,j)$.[16]

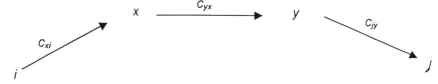

Figure 7.6.a   Elementary path

whose intensity of influence is

$$I^D_{(i...j)p} \equiv I^D_{(i,x,y,j)} = c_{xi}c_{yx}c_{jy} \tag{7-7}$$

b. Total influence In most structures, there exists a multitude of interactions among poles. In particular, poles along any elementary path are likely to be linked to other poles and other paths forming circuits which amplify in a complex way the direct influence of that same elementary path. To capture these indirect effects, the concept of total influence was introduced. Given an elementary path $p = (i,...,j)$ with origin i and destination j, the total influence is the influence transmitted from i to j along the elementary path p including all indirect effects within the structure imputable to that path. Thus, total influence cumulates, for a given elementary path p, the direct influence transmitted along the latter and the indirect effects induced by the circuits adjacent to that same path (i.e. these circuits which have one or more poles in common with path p). Figure 7.6.b reproduces the same elementary path $p = (i,x,y,j)$ appearing in Figure 7.6.a and in addition incorporates explicitly all circuits adjacent to it.

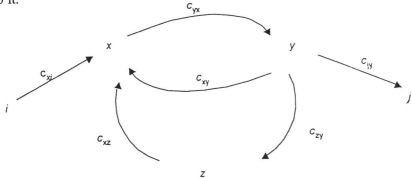

Figure 7.6.b   Elementary path including adjacent circuits

It can readily be seen that between poles i and y the direct influence is $c_{xi}c_{yx}$ which is then transmitted back from y to x via the two loops, the first loop generating an influence $c_{xi}c_{yx}c_{xy}$ and the second generating an influence $c_{xi}c_{yx}c_{zy}c_{zx}$. Together the feedback from these two loops yields an effect $(c_{xi}c_{yx})(c_{xy} + c_{zy}c_{xz})$. This effect in turn has to be transmitted back from x to y. This process yields a series (a sequence of rounds) of dampened impulses between x and y

$$c_{xi}c_{yx} \langle 1 + c_{yx}(c_{xy} + c_{zy}c_{xz}) + [c_{yx}(c_{xy} + c_{zy}c_{xz})]^2 + [c_{yx}(c_{xy} + c_{zy}c_{xz})]^3$$
$$+ \dots = c_{xi}c_{yx}[1 - c_{yx}(c_{yx} + c_{zy}c_{xz})]^{-1} \qquad (7\text{-}8)$$

(The terms on the left hand side of equation 7-8 is a geometric series with c_{ix}, c_{yx}, c_{xy}, c_{zy}, $c_{xz} < 1$. From high-school algebra, its magnitude is then given by the expression on the right hand side.)

To complete the transmission of influence along the above elementary path p the above effects have to travel along the last arc (y,j) so that the above effects have to be multiplied by c_{jy} to obtain the total influence along this path,

$$I^T_{(i \to j)p} = c_{xi}c_{yx}c_{jy}[1 - c_{yx}(c_{xy} + c_{zy}c_{xz})]^{-1} \qquad (7\text{-}9)$$

It can readily be seen that the first part of the expression on the right hand side, namely $c_{xi}c_{yx}c_{jy}$ represents the previously defined direct influence, $I^D_{(i \to j)p}$ and the other part is the path multiplier M_p, i.e.

$$I^T_{(i \to j)p} = I^D_{(i \to j)p}M_p \qquad (7\text{-}10)$$

M_p (a scalar) captures the extent to which the direct influence along path p is amplified through the effects of adjacent feedback circuits.[17]

c. Global influence Global influence, in contrast with direct and total influences, does not refer to topology, namely, the specific paths followed in the transmission of influence. Global influence from pole i to pole j simply measures the total effects on income or output of pole j consequent to an injection of one unit of output or income in pole i.

The global influence is captured by the reduced form of the SAM model derived previously in (7-4)

$$dy_n = (\mathbf{I} - \mathbf{C}_n)^{-1}df = \mathbf{M}_c df \qquad (7\text{-}11) = (7\text{-}4)$$

Let m_{cji} be the (j,i)th element of the matrix of fixed price multipliers $\mathbf{M}_c$ then, as was seen previously, it captures the full effects of an exogenous injection df_i on the endogenous variable j. Hence

$$I^G_{(i \to j)} = m_{cji}$$

and matrix $\mathbf{M}_c = (\mathbf{I} - \mathbf{C}_n)^{-1}$ can be called the matrix of global influences.[18]

It is important to understand clearly the distinction between global influence and direct influence. The latter is linked to a particular elementary path which is entirely isolated from the rest of the structure *ceteris paribus*. It captures what could be called the immediate effect of an impulse following this particular path. Global influence, in contrast, differs from direct influence for two fundamental reasons:

(i) It captures the direct influence transmitted by all elementary paths linking (spanning) the two poles under consideration. Indeed, given two poles i and j, the effects of an injection affecting the output or income of i on the output or income of j manifest themselves through the intermediary of all paths with origin i and destination j. The direct influence, transmitted by pole i to pole j along different elementary paths with the same origin and destination, is equal to the sum of the direct influences transmitted along each elementary path.

(ii) In addition, these paths are not considered in isolation but as an integral part of the structure from which they were separated to calculate the direct influence. Hence, global influence cumulates all induced and feedback effects resulting from the existence of circuits in the graph and is equal to the sum of the total influences of all elementary paths spanning pole i and pole j [see (7-13)].

An example should clarify this point. Figure 7.6.c reproduces the elementary path and adjacent circuits explored in Figure 7.6.b and adds two other elementary paths with the same origin i and destination j, i.e. (i,s,j) and (i,v,j).

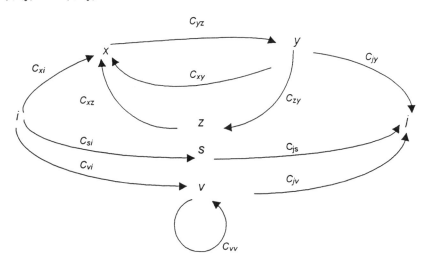

Figure 7.6.c Network of elementary paths and adjacent circuits linking poles i and j

In the above example, it is clear that path (i,s,j) is an elementary path without any adjacent circuit while path (i,v,j) contains one loop centered on v. For simplicity, we can refer to these last two paths as 2 and 3, respectively — the initial path being referred to as 1.

$$
\begin{aligned}
I^G_{(i \to j)} = m_{cji} &= I^T_{(i,x,y,j)} + I^T_{(i,s,j)} + I^T_{(i,v,j)} \\
&= I^T_{(i \to j)1} + I^T_{(i \to j)2} + I^T_{(i \to j)3} \\
&= I^D_{(i \to j)1} \, M_1 + c_{si}c_{sj} + (c_{vi}c_{jv})(\mathbf{I} - c_{vv})^{-1} \\
&= I^D_{(i \to j)1} \, M_1 + I^D_{(i \to j)2} + I^D_{(i \to j)3} \, M_3
\end{aligned}
\tag{7-12}
$$

Note that in the case of the second path, the multiplier is one since the path has no adjacent circuits. Thus, in general, the global influence linking any two poles of a structure can be decomposed into a series of total influences transmitted along each and all elementary paths spanning i and j, i.e.

$$
I^G_{(i \to j)} = m_{cji} = \sum_{p=1}^{n} I^T_{(i \to j)p} = \sum_{p=1}^{n} I^D_{(i \to j)p} M_p
\tag{7-13}
$$

where *p* stands for elementary paths *1,2,...,n*.

In 7.5.2a an application of the SAM multiplier methodology to estimate the impact on budget retrenchment on income distribution in Indonesia during the adjustment period (1982–1987) is presented. By using structural path analysis, the various direct and indirect paths can be identified through which given budget retrenchment policy scenarios — described in that subsection — ultimately influence the incomes of different socioeconomic groups. Clearly, the mechanisms through which a public works program in agriculture affects the income of the different households groups is likely to be very different from that of a reduction in, say, government current expenditures on education or the wages of public servants. An attempt is made in Figure 7.7 to identify the various paths through which alternative selective government current expenditure programs ultimately affected the incomes of a specific socioeconomic group. The respective marginal expenditure propensities (the *c*'s) are shown along each arc of the elementary paths linking a given pole of origin of the policy injection (different types of government expenditures) and a given pole of destination (in this instance, a given socioeconomic group). Thus, for example, in Figure 7.7, Case 1, 27% of the total output of the activity 'education and health' is used to pay the wages and salaries of the labor category 'professional paid urban.' In turn, 82% of the total income of this category is received by the 'urban high income' socioeconomic group. The product of these two marginal expenditure propensities amounts to .22 and is shown to the right of the second arc of this elementary path. In addition, the urban high income group receives some income from the 'clerical paid urban' labor category. Consequently the total income received by this group along the two elementary paths shown in case 1 of Figure 7.7 amount to .26 of the initial government expenditure on education and health which is the direct influence along these paths (given in column 5 of Figure 7.7). Finally, the global influence (i.e. the value of the multiplier from government expenditure on education and health on the income of the urban high income group) is shown in column 6 and the percentage of direct influence to global influence in column 7.

The main observations that are suggested by Figure 7.7 are, first, that government current expenditures on education and health benefit the urban high income group significantly more than the urban low income group (the corresponding multipliers being 0.37 and 0.28) and, likewise, government expenditures on 'other wages and salaries' (cases 3 and 4 in Figure 7.7) have the same relative impact. Secondly, government transfers to households tend to have a direct and very large impact on the incomes of

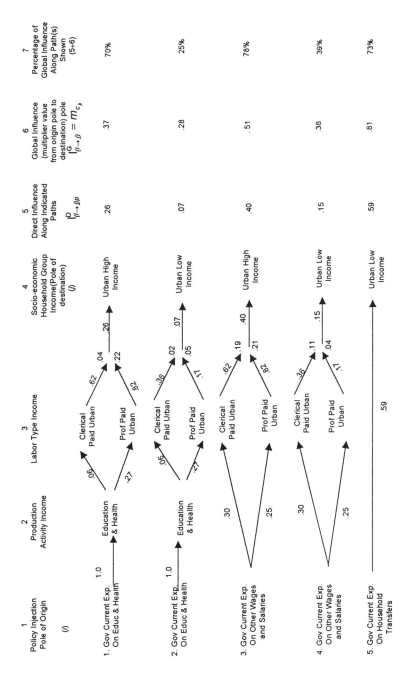

Figure 7.7 Structural path analysis of impact of government expenditure programs on income of socio-economic groups

the urban low income group (a multiplier value of 0.81). This suggests that reductions in food subsidies, for example, have a very strong negative effect on the incomes of the urban poor.

7.4.4 SAM as the foundation of computable general equilibrium models

A limitation of SAM-type multipliers is the underlying assumption of excess capacity and unused resources. This assumption allows one to ignore the effects of sectoral capacity and factorial bottlenecks on prices. Even constrained multipliers assume that prices remain fixed. The comparative static nature of the SAM multiplier analysis, as such, precludes capturing and estimating dynamic effects. For example, whereas investment demand, (i.e. the intermediate inputs, labor and capital required in the construction phase of a project) is explicitly incorporated in the SAM, the future effects of investment on productivity are ruled out by the fact that the SAM is only a one year snapshot of the economy. This limitation should be kept in mind when interpreting the SAM multiplier analysis reported in the various case studies in section 7.5. In order to incorporate different degrees of capacity and supply responsiveness in a socioeconomic system, the natural extension of the SAM framework is a computable general equilibrium (CGE) model. Such a model is built upon and takes as its initial conditions a base-year SAM but, in contrast with the simple SAM multiplier framework, includes a number of behavioral and structural relationships to describe the behavior of the various actors over time. In such models most prices are endogenously determined. CGE models are particularly useful in simulating the impact of policies and policy packages on the whole socioeconomic system. CGE and macroeconometric models can provide useful results concerning the trade-off between higher private and government consumption today (at the expense of relatively lower investment) and higher output, income and consumption growth tomorrow that would have resulted from lower consumption and more investment today. Section 7.5.2b presents an example of a general equilibrium model based on a corresponding SAM. Furthermore, chapter 8 in this volume is devoted to CGE models.

7.5 Studies and applications based on the SAM

7.5.1 General overview

The SAM methodology has been extensively used to analyze a variety of different questions at different levels of geographical aggregation. First, in developing countries, at the national level it has been used to explore such issues as, for example, 1) the impact of a variety of government expenditure patterns and commodity compositions of exports on income distribution in Indonesia, e.g. Keuning and Thorbecke, (1989) that is discussed further in subsection 7.5.2) a changing structure of production and alternative technologies on employment (e.g., the dualistic SAM built by Khan and Thorbecke, 1989, to compare the employment impact of traditional and modern technologies in Indonesia); 3) the impact of environmental policies on output, household incomes and health (Resosudarmo and Thorbecke, 1996); 4) intersectoral linkages (e.g., a SAM of Mexico to explore the intersectoral impacts of alternative adjustment strategies by Adelman and Taylor, 1990; and the impact of intersectoral linkages on rural poverty alleviation: Thorbecke, 1995); and 4) food consumption (e.g., Hay, 1978, work on a Food Accounting Matrix).

In industrialized countries, at the national level the SAM methodology has been used to analyze, and has been applied to such issues as the effects of different taxation and subsidy schemes on income distribution (e.g. a detailed SAM for the U.S. built by Reinert and Roland-Holst, 1992); the impact of alternative tariff structures on the pattern and composition of imports and exports as well as the resulting structure of output and employment (e.g., Reinert and Roland-Holst, 1989, who built a U.S. SAM for trade policy analysis); and a whole set of intersectoral, interregional and environmental questions.

At the regional level, SAMs have been built for a number of U.S. States to study most of the above issues, but at a lower level of geographical aggregation (e.g., a SAM for Oregon by Waters and Holland, 1996). Another example of a State SAM is that built by Kilkenny and Failde (1996) for Iowa to explore in a very comprehensive and disaggregated way the impact of federal, state and local taxes and spending on counties and other regional entities within Iowa. Kilkenny and Failde (1996) call their SAM a multi-regional, multi-jurisdiction fiscal SAM.

Similar efforts in Third World countries, mainly at the provincial or district level, highlighted intersectoral linkages particularly between agricultural and nonagricultural activities and interregional linkages with the rest of the country and the rest of the world (e.g., Lewis and Thorbecke, 1992 work on the Kutus district of Kenya).

Finally, at the village level, most if not all applications so far have been to settings of developing countries (see recent book by Taylor and Adelman, 1996). Village SAMs have analyzed such diverse issues as the impact of remittances from Mexican workers abroad or in urban centers to their families on the standards of living of various socioeconomic groups in those villages (Adelman, Taylor and Vogel, 1989); and the impact of a factory on the outskirt of a village on employment, incomes and the modernization trend within the village (discussed in section 7.5.4).

Space limitations preclude more than a very few examples of SAM-based studies from being presented in this chapter. The examples that follow attempt to provide a reasonably representative sample of those studies at different levels of disaggregation and addressing a variety of policy issues.

7.5.2 National applications

a. The SAM as a framework to estimate the impact of budget retrenchment on income distribution in Indonesia during the adjustment period (1982-1987): SAM multiplier analysis and simulation The Indonesian economy grew at a rapid annual growth rate of 7.2% in the 1970's largely because of rising oil prices. Earnings from crude oil and petroleum products accounted for two-thirds of all export earnings, one-fourth of total GNP, and almost three-fourths of government domestic revenue in 1982. Oil prices peaked in 1982, and then began to fall rapidly. With dwindling oil revenues, economic growth slowed to half its previous level. The government responded by introducing a stabilization program to reduce the economy's vulnerability to external shocks. One of the key instruments among the package of policy measures adopted was a selective budget retrenchment program to bring expenditures in line with dwindling government revenues from oil. Given this background Keuning and Thorbecke (1989) proceeded to estimate the impact on income distribution of alternative patterns of government expenditures, i.e., varying the composition of total public expenditures among different categories of current and capital expenditures.

A highly disaggregated SAM for 1980 (including 106 sectors) produced by the Indonesian Central Bureau of Statistics (CBS) provided the starting point. It was modified by incorporating a very detailed breakdown of government expenditures by categories and aggregating some sectors. This

SAM built by Keuning and Thorbecke (1989) consists of a total of 75 accounts, 70 endogenous and 5 exogenous. The 70 endogenous accounts are broken down into the following sets:

1 *factors of production*

a) sixteen labor categories (SAM 1–16) distinguished according to type of ocupation, rural as opposed to urban, and paid (i.e., employees) as opposed to unpaid (i.e., self-employed) status; and

b) seven types of capital (17–23), with four kinds of unincorporated capital and three types of corporate capital;

2 *institutions*

a) eight socio-economic household groups (24–31), i.e. agricultural employees (typically the landless), small farmers (farm operators cultivating less than half a ha), medium farmers (operating between 0.5 and 1 ha), large farmers (operating more than one ha), rural non-agricultural low, rural non-agricultural high, urban low, and finally, urban high; and

b) companies (32);

3 *government expenditures*

a) four programs of current government expenditures (33–36), on education and health, other wages and salaries, other goods and services, and household transfers; and

b) nine government investment programs (37–45) covering agriculture, industry and mining, energy, transport and tourism, education, health, housing and water works, general services, and other activities;

4 *production activities-cum-commodities*

disaggregated into twenty-four categories (46–69), including four public works categories (59–62): agriculture, transportation, utilities and communications, and other activities; and

5 *indirect taxes* (70)

Finally, the five exogenous accounts are: subsidies (71), total government current expenditures (72), total government capital expenditures (73), private capital (74), and the rest of the world (75).

The distinction between exogenous and endogenous accounts in a SAM is a crucial one. It is assumed that the socio-economic system represented by the SAM is affected by exogenous changes and injections, namely budgetary measures under the control of the government — i.e., subsidies, total government current and total government capital expenditures and their composition, changes originating in the rest of the world which influence exports, and the size and pattern of private investment. The impact of these exogenous shocks is transmitted through the interdependent SAM system; and their total, direct and indirect, effects on the endogenous accounts, i.e., the incomes of the various factors and socio-economic groups and the total output of the different production activities, is estimated through the multiplier process.

The treatment of public finance in this SAM deserves particular attention. The level and distribution of government current and capital expenditures among the four current expenditure categories and nine investment programs are specified exogenously. In turn, these thirteen programs are endogenous in the sense that once they receive given injections from the public sector, they spend them according to fixed proportions. Thus, for example, government current expenditure on education and health is assumed to be spent on the activity 'education and health' (68); government expenditures on 'other wages and salaries' are spent according to the distribution of civil servants' wages by labor type, i.e., mainly to the benefit of urban and rural paid professional and clerical labor. Likewise, the nine government investment programs allocate their exogenous injections to different categories of public works (i.e., in agriculture, transportation, utilities and communication, and other activities), to the building and construction sector, and to other activities such as metal products manufacturing.

By endogenizing the expenditure pattern of these thirteen government programs, one can capture their differential impact on the socio-economic system. The direct effects operate through such variables as wages of civil servants, commodities on which government consumption is expended; and on public works, building and construction, and other production activities embedded into public investment. The indirect effects generated by these direct effects are captured by the multiplier analysis.

For analytical purposes, the transaction matrix is converted into a corresponding matrix of average expenditure propensities (A_n as in (7-3)) and marginal expenditure propensities (C_n as in (7-4) above). From (7-4), $dy_n = (I - C_n)^{-1} df = M_c df$, the corresponding fixed price multiplier matrix (M_c) is derived.

Varying the matrix of exogenous demand — i.e. the expenditures of the exogenous accounts, namely subsidies, government current expenditures, government capital expenditures, private capital and the rest of the world — and pre-multiplying these injections by M_c, yields the corresponding total incomes of the 70 endogenous variables appearing in the SAM. Both direct and indirect effects are generated by injections circulating throughout the economy and these total effects are, in principle, captured by the multiplier matrix if a certain number of conditions are met. In particular, it is assumed that excess capacity exists — allowing prices to remain constant. Since most simulated policy experiments entail budget retrenchment or cuts, these policy scenarios are consistent with the assumption of excess capacity. A curtailment of different categories of government expenditures, *ceteris paribus*, reduces the degree of capacity utilization and should not per se invalidate the presumption that prices will remain fixed. The key assumption made throughout the analysis is that C_n and M_c accurately capture and reflect the structural and behavioral features of the Indonesian economy throughout the 1980s.

The major exogenous injections are referred to as F. This matrix consists of five columns representing the exogenous injections i.e. subsidies, total government current expenditures, total government capital expenditures, private capital investment and rest of the world (columns 71–75) and 70 rows which are the 70 endogenous accounts. F is thus a 70×5 matrix. The subscript 0 is used to refer to the base year (1980) values so that F_0 is the actual 1980 exogenous injection matrix. The following relationship can be obtained

$$M_c F_0 = Y_0 \qquad (7\text{-}14)$$

where M_c (70×70) is a fixed price multiplier for 1980. In turn, Y_0 would be a 70×5 matrix of endogenous receipts generated by the injection matrix F_0. Y_0 can be given the following interpretation. It yields the endogenous receipts for each of the 70 endogenous categories of the SAM generated directly and indirectly by each of the five endogenous injections. Thus, for example, one can break down what part of the total income of a given socioeconomic group (say small farmers) would be ascribed to the multiplier process to, respectively, subsidies, government capital or current expenditures, private capital and rest of the world (e.g., exports). By summing along the rows of Y_0 one obtains the resulting total incomes of each of the 70 endogenous categories, i.e.

$$Y_0 e = y_0 \qquad (7\text{-}15)$$

where e is the vector of units (5×1) and y_0 is the vector (70×1) of the total incomes accruing to the endogenous categories of the SAM.

By varying the pattern of exogenous demand, and more particularly the pattern of government expenditures, the impact on the whole socioeconomic system (and particularly on income distribution) can be estimated. In addition to the base year scenario which was used as a reference scenario, six alternative experiments were simulated. These experiments included different combinations of patterns of government expenditures among the thirteen expenditure categories. In the present context, this amounted to reflecting the counterfactual public expenditure scenarios postulating different alternative $\mathbf{F}_i$ matrices and measuring their effects on endogenous incomes, i.e., the $\mathbf{y}_i$ vector:

$$\mathbf{M}_c\mathbf{F}_i = \mathbf{Y}_i \qquad\qquad i = 0, 1, 2....6 \qquad\qquad (7\text{-}14b)$$

$$\mathbf{Y}_i\mathbf{e} = \mathbf{y}_i \qquad\qquad\qquad (7\text{-}15b)$$

The main conclusion suggested by the results of the counterfactual policy scenarios was that the Indonesian government, when faced with unexpected deteriorating external conditions (in the present context, the two oil shocks), opted for a policy which mitigated the short term income losses for the population at large and, in particular, for the politically important civil servants and small farmers in the rural areas. It was found that the actual pattern of expenditures cut was quite selective and shielded, in a relative sense, current expenditures on education and health. The government adjustment program also cut expenditures on large capital intensive projects significantly more than on labor intensive regional projects in areas such as rural infrastructure and irrigation, marketing and storage facilities and rural electrification. These regionally decentralized projects relied on unskilled labor largely supplied by the rural non-agricultural households, the agricultural employees' households and small farmers. These groups provide the bulk of the unskilled and manual labor required in the construction phase of investment projects, and they later enjoy the fruits of increased productivity.

b. General equilibrium model of Indonesia A general equilibrium model is a natural extension of the SAM in converting a static framework into a dynamic one and endogenizing prices. The SAM discussed in the preceding subsection (7.5.2a) became the basis for the calibration of a general equilibrium model of the Indonesian economy that was used to simulate alternative packages of adjustment policies on economic growth and equity (Thorbecke, 1992, ch. 4). The Indonesian model integrates a real and a financial sector. Building a general equilibrium model that integrates real and financial transactions requires the specification of a financial SAM in addition to a real SAM to capture the initial conditions prevailing at the outset of the adjustment period and the institutional structure and behavior of economic agents.

The financial SAM contains the same classification of households and production activities as the real SAM. It also includes five other institutions: firms, commercial banks, the Central Bank, government, and the rest of the world.

The complete model consists of 86 equations which, when disaggregated by sector, types of institutions, and factors, yield more than 600 equations. The model was used to simulate six alternative policy scenarios (combinations of different government expenditure patterns, currency devaluation, and monetary policy). A comparison of the results of the simulation of the alternative policy scenarios suggested that the policy package actually adopted and implemented by the government helped restore internal and external equilibrium without worsening the distribution of income. Whether by accident or by design (the latter is more probable), the package of adjustment measures actually implemented appeared almost optimal under the socioeconomic constraints faced by the government.

7.5.3 A regional-interregional application: the two-region Indonesian SAM for 1980

A two-region SAM for Indonesia (1980) was built by Hidayat (1992). This is an interregional SAM that divides Indonesia into the economically strong Center region (essentially Java) and the Outer Islands. The contrast between the two regions is dramatic. In 1987, some 61% of the population resided in the Center region that comprises only about 7% of Indonesia's land area, creating a considerable population density contrast between the two regions, 775 vs. 37 persons per square kilometer. The two-region SAM was used to examine the structure of interdependence among the two regions and to demonstrate the implications on the total economy, including the income distribution, of increasing production and particularly the exports of different sectors in the periphery as opposed to the Center region.

This interregional SAM consists of 45 sectors, five of which are exogenous. Thus, the endogenous part of the SAM is a 40 x 40 matrix and the multiplier matrix includes the 20 x 20 intraregional transactions, within the Center and Outer Islands, respectively, and the 20 x 20 interregional flows originating respectively in the Center region to the Outer region and in the Outer region to the Center region.

The multipliers generated by this interregional SAM are given in Table 7-3. Some interesting findings are suggested by Table 7-3. Comparing, first, the intra-regional multipliers of the Center vs. the Outer regions, it turns out that the intra-regional multipliers in the Center region are consistently larger than the corresponding ones in the Outer region. This means that an injection of investment (for instance a large project)

Table 7-3 Selected fixed price multipliers from the two region Indonesian SAM

Region			1	2	3	4	5	6	7	8	9	10	11	32	33	34	35	36	37	38	39	40
CENTER REGION	1	Agriculture Labor	1.214	0.169	0.174	0.196	0.069	0.178	0.268	0.254	0.250	0.187	0.232	0.113	0.090	0.134	0.098	0.025	0.145	0.071	0.068	0.100
	2	Manual & Manufacturing Labor	0.061	1.104	0.084	0.099	0.029	0.068	0.076	0.083	0.090	0.078	0.095	0.052	0.044	0.068	0.050	0.012	0.030	0.043	0.030	0.069
	3	Clerical Labor	0.063	0.079	1.092	0.106	0.029	0.053	0.065	0.072	0.081	0.074	0.092	0.061	0.044	0.072	0.063	0.013	0.028	0.037	0.024	0.076
	4	Professional Labor	0.024	0.028	0.028	1.023	0.009	0.022	0.019	0.018	0.019	0.025	0.021	0.031	0.047	0.039	0.038	0.008	0.017	0.025	0.021	0.091
	5	Other Factors	0.351	0.384	0.394	0.428	1.156	0.356	0.413	0.413	0.433	0.391	0.438	0.300	0.303	0.357	0.290	0.070	0.300	0.666	0.302	0.362
	6	Agricultural Workers	0.264	0.043	0.044	0.048	0.023	1.045	0.063	0.059	0.059	0.045	0.066	0.027	0.022	0.033	0.024	0.006	0.034	0.020	0.017	0.025
	7	Small Farmers	0.391	0.081	0.081	0.091	0.084	0.081	1.127	0.105	0.111	0.086	0.107	0.053	0.046	0.070	0.048	0.012	0.062	0.059	0.038	0.053
	8	Medium Farmers	0.083	0.027	0.025	0.023	0.028	0.025	0.029	1.028	0.029	0.027	0.031	0.023	0.026	0.026	0.022	0.005	0.039	0.028	0.022	0.028
	9	Large Farmers	0.113	0.045	0.042	0.034	0.031	0.042	0.048	0.038	1.042	0.045	0.043	0.045	0.069	0.062	0.046	0.011	0.088	0.069	0.063	0.062
	10	Rural Low Group	0.049	0.418	0.284	0.089	0.048	0.051	0.062	0.062	0.071	1.066	0.078	0.040	0.035	0.057	0.040	0.010	0.027	0.042	0.025	0.064
	11	Non Labor Force Rural Group	0.024	0.019	0.018	0.017	0.032	0.017	0.021	0.019	0.020	0.019	1.054	0.014	0.016	0.020	0.014	0.008	0.018	0.023	0.014	0.020
	12	Rural High Group	0.032	0.051	0.106	0.314	0.039	0.029	0.028	0.027	0.030	0.033	0.031	0.316	0.045	0.041	0.038	0.025	0.027	0.040	0.027	0.074
	13	Urban Low Group	0.078	0.581	0.567	0.136	0.091	0.081	0.096	0.099	0.110	0.098	0.120	0.067	0.060	0.090	0.066	0.016	0.045	0.075	0.043	0.090
	14	Non Labor Force Urban Group	0.023	0.028	0.026	0.021	0.041	0.021	0.024	0.024	0.023	0.024	0.026	0.020	0.026	0.403	0.022	0.019	0.020	0.032	0.019	0.034
	15	Urban High Group	0.053	0.094	0.237	0.751	0.070	0.052	0.052	0.061	0.068	0.059	0.060	0.068	0.075	0.073	0.260	0.038	0.043	0.068	0.044	0.128
	16	Companies	0.212	0.231	0.238	0.258	0.696	0.215	0.249	0.249	0.261	0.235	0.264	0.181	0.183	0.215	0.175	0.042	0.180	0.401	0.182	0.218
	17	Agriculture	0.400	0.372	0.383	0.435	0.152	0.391	0.594	0.564	0.556	0.412	0.516	0.243	0.186	0.289	0.209	0.064	0.283	0.155	0.141	0.214
	18	Mining	0.048	0.045	0.041	0.028	0.013	0.041	0.033	0.027	0.029	0.043	0.029	0.057	0.081	0.068	0.069	0.013	0.040	0.520	0.134	0.072
	19	Manufacturing	0.535	0.588	0.621	0.735	0.228	0.663	0.715	0.765	0.806	0.640	0.792	0.359	0.235	0.437	0.302	0.078	0.220	0.234	0.185	0.325
	20	Other Sectors	0.290	0.451	0.498	0.624	0.166	0.291	0.366	0.415	0.469	0.421	0.538	0.278	0.216	0.398	0.280	0.068	0.149	0.191	0.123	0.360
OUTER REGION	21	Agriculture Labor	0.595	0.119	0.114	0.106	0.042	0.123	0.150	0.130	0.129	0.125	0.121	0.114	0.134	0.121	0.109	0.026	0.325	0.058	0.100	0.102
	22	Manual & Manufacturing Labor	0.032	0.184	0.032	0.024	0.010	0.030	0.024	0.021	0.022	0.032	0.023	0.042	0.064	0.049	0.050	0.011	0.027	0.038	0.043	0.110
	23	Clerical Labor	0.050	0.055	0.143	0.029	0.015	0.047	0.030	0.024	0.026	0.047	0.028	0.076	0.126	0.091	0.097	0.020	0.042	0.052	0.047	0.255
	24	Professional Labor	0.028	0.029	0.026	0.012	0.007	0.025	0.015	0.011	0.011	0.025	0.012	0.043	0.074	0.051	0.056	0.012	0.024	0.034	0.031	0.147
	25	Other Factors	0.239	0.210	0.184	0.104	0.129	0.194	0.142	0.101	0.106	0.194	0.107	0.289	0.439	0.302	0.317	0.070	0.558	0.506	0.428	0.481
	26	Agricultural Workers	0.084	0.028	0.021	0.017	0.009	0.314	0.022	0.020	0.021	0.018	0.020	0.015	0.018	0.020	0.016	0.004	0.016	0.013	0.011	0.026
	27	Small Farmers	0.245	0.087	0.067	0.052	0.028	0.062	0.167	0.060	0.061	0.063	0.058	0.063	0.081	0.070	0.065	0.015	0.133	0.048	0.068	0.092
	28	Medium Farmers	0.142	0.050	0.042	0.031	0.019	0.042	0.043	0.036	0.036	0.042	0.034	0.048	0.065	0.061	0.050	0.011	0.108	0.060	0.064	0.067
	29	Large Farmers	0.235	0.092	0.082	0.067	0.044	0.085	0.080	0.064	0.065	0.085	0.063	0.106	0.150	0.112	0.112	0.025	0.231	0.140	0.134	0.155
	30	Rural Low Group	0.041	0.125	0.087	0.031	0.017	0.024	0.026	0.024	0.027	0.303	0.028	0.023	0.028	0.031	0.024	0.006	0.029	0.023	0.019	0.034
	31	Non Labor Force Rural Group	0.035	0.020	0.016	0.009	0.007	0.013	0.012	0.010	0.010	0.014	0.010	0.016	0.024	0.020	0.018	0.019	0.029	0.017	0.017	0.029
	32	Rural High Group	0.042	0.065	0.052	0.020	0.016	0.030	0.023	0.019	0.020	0.031	0.020	1.044	0.070	0.061	0.063	0.069	0.043	0.044	0.040	0.118
	33	Urban Low Group	0.039	0.175	0.169	0.044	0.031	0.034	0.035	0.034	0.037	0.040	0.040	0.035	1.048	0.053	0.039	0.009	0.036	0.041	0.030	0.056
	34	Non Labor Force Urban Group	0.021	0.033	0.026	0.011	0.010	0.017	0.013	0.010	0.011	0.018	0.011	0.025	0.041	1.061	0.030	0.044	0.026	0.026	0.023	0.057
	35	Urban High Group	0.048	0.076	0.084	0.028	0.026	0.042	0.031	0.025	0.026	0.043	0.027	0.063	0.100	0.074	1.078	0.136	0.060	0.066	0.057	0.170
	36	Companies	0.088	0.083	0.077	0.059	0.119	0.077	0.067	0.057	0.060	0.079	0.060	0.097	0.137	0.105	0.104	1.060	0.168	0.181	0.134	0.152
	37	Agriculture	0.315	0.233	0.196	0.096	0.062	0.234	0.165	0.098	0.101	0.219	0.101	0.332	0.491	0.324	0.340	0.077	1.359	0.138	0.365	0.300
	38	Mining	0.078	0.069	0.059	0.027	0.018	0.060	0.041	0.027	0.028	0.064	0.028	0.105	0.160	0.103	0.111	0.025	0.074	1.083	0.273	0.137
	39	Manufacturing	0.354	0.304	0.259	0.119	0.077	0.261	0.185	0.117	0.122	0.286	0.122	0.465	0.692	0.441	0.471	0.106	0.337	0.196	1.346	0.450
	40	Other Sectors	0.213	0.231	0.205	0.095	0.068	0.203	0.115	0.085	0.090	0.194	0.093	0.337	0.598	0.415	0.455	0.094	0.172	0.161	0.137	1.288

undertaken in the Center region would have greater direct and indirect total output effects within the Center region than a similar project would have had within the Outer region. The Outer region, on the other hand, shows stronger interregional multipliers than does the Center region. The implication of this is that a project undertaken in the Outer region would trigger greater output and employment effects in the Center region than vice versa. (In Table 7-3 the respective interregional multipliers from the Outer region to the Center are given in the quadrant cols. 21–40 and rows 1–20 and from the Center to the Outer region in cols. 1–20 and rows 21–40.) A pairwise comparison of these interregional multipliers indicate that the Outer region has greater interregional multipliers in 289 of 400 possible cases.

Another important finding is that the total multipliers (intra plus interregional multipliers) tend to be greater when the origin is in the Outer region than when it is in the Center region (again a pairwise comparison of the 400 possible total multipliers reveals that 260 are larger in the Outer region). This means that an injection of investment in the Outer region transmits greater total impact on the whole economy of Indonesia than a corresponding injection in the Center region.

The policy implications of these observations are potentially very important, particularly if these findings can be confirmed on the basis of more sectoral and micro evidence. It suggests that a process of regional decentralization with a somewhat greater concentration on the development of the Outer Islands could be rationalized not only on equity grounds but also in terms of its impact on total output and economic growth for the country as a whole. A comparable exercise based on a two-region SAM of Italy yielded fairly similar findings, i.e., that the most effective regional development policies are those that aim at increasing the production capacity of the economically weaker South (see D'Antonio et al., 1988).

7.5.4 A village application: impact of rural industrialization on village life and economy: a comparison of two Indian village SAMs

In a recent study (Parikh and Thorbecke, 1996) two relatively similar Indian villages, one close to a factory (Boriya) and another located in a remote area (Aurepalle) were compared to provide insights on the socioeconomic effects of industrial decentralization. To capture the socioeconomic interdependence and structure of the two villages, corresponding village-level SAMs were constructed on the basis of a variety of data sources including field surveys.

The two village SAMs used identical taxonomies that included ten production activities, seven commodities, four factors of production, five institutions (i.e., landless', small farmers', medium farmers', large farmers' households; and village government); and four exogenous accounts (maintenance, stock, capital, and rest of India). SAM multipliers were derived for each of these villages. These multipliers reflect the strength of the linkages among the different sectors of a village economy. Linkages are shown in the form of an increase or decrease in the incomes of different accounts as one rupee is injected into an account. These multipliers are used to compare the effects of factory salaries vis à vis other village production activities on the poor. By building SAMs of these villages and comparing them, some important structural and socioeconomic differences are highlighted. The results of this study show that rural decentralization of industries has, in fact, contributed considerably to rural development and poverty alleviation in Boriya. Households in the latter have become more aware of the advantages of education, investment in agriculture has increased, the exploitation of labor has been significantly reduced, and the factory salaries have raised standards of living and lowered income inequality among the different socioeconomic household categories.

Endnotes

1   Sections 7.1 and 7.2 are based on Pyatt and Thorbecke (1976), Thorbecke (1995) and Thorbecke (1988).

2   See, for example, the Schematic SAM given in Figure 3.1 of Devarajan, Lewis and Robinson (1994) and related discussion.

3   An interesting application using a multilevel government account(s) in exploring public finance issues in Iowa is that of Kilkenny and Faide (1997).

4   Note that Figure 7.3 is analogous to Figure 7.1 except that the endogenous institutions (the different household groups and companies) exclude the government account considered now as exogenous. Also, the transaction matrices linking the three endogenous accounts are shown explicitly.

5   This subsection on regionalization draws on Thorbecke (1985).

6 For a more technical discussion of how a multiregional SAM can be built, see Hewings and Madden (1995).

7 In this connection, it is relevant to note that when a team of resident experts attached to the CBS in Jakarta was trying to build the first SAM for Indonesia in the late 70s, the local Indonesian statisticians only became interested in, and supportive of this exercise when they realized that the SAM provided an ideal framework within which to check data consistency and help reconcile inconsistencies. Soon thereafter the process of building SAMs was institutionalized within the CBS and so far four large scale, highly disaggregated SAMs have been prepared and published by the CBS (for 1975, 1980, 1985 and 1990, respectively).

8 In fact, to be exact, the matrix of average expenditure propensities consists of two parts; A_n, which is the square matrix of average expenditure propensities for the endogenous accounts, while the second part, A_l consists of the so-called leakages i.e. the proportions of each endogenous variable which leak out (as expenditure) from any one of the three endogenous accounts into the exogenous accounts. While the transaction matrix is expressed in money flows, the A_n and A_l matrices are expressed as coefficients with each column adding up to exactly unity.

9 Since the expenditure (income) elasticity for household group h and commodity i namely: εy_{hi} is equal to the ratio of the marginal expenditure propensity (MEP$_{hi}$) to the average expenditure propensity (AEP$_{hi}$), it follows that the matrix of marginal expenditure propensities, C_{13}, can be readily obtained once the expenditure elasticities and average expenditure propensities (i.e., A_{13}) are known, i.e., since $\varepsilon y_{hi} = $ MEP$_{hi}$ / AEP$_{hi}$, it follows that MEP$_{hi} = \varepsilon y_{hi}AEP_{hi}$.

10 Note that the consumption function implicit in the above formulation has total household income as its argument. So the expenditure elasticities have to be estimated as a function of total income rather than as a function of disposable income or total consumption. Furthermore, price effects are ignored by definition. Notwithstanding the clear superiority of fixed price multipliers compared to accounting multipliers in reflecting actual consumption behavior, the latter continue to be used in much applied work because they can easily be derived from limited data.

11 The decomposition of the multiplier mechanisms that follows applies to the accounting multiplier $\mathbf{M}_a$. Exactly the same decomposition procedure can be used with respect to the fixed price multiplier $\mathbf{M}_c$.

12 The example that follows is based on Parikh and Thorbecke (1996).

13 In this sense this approach is more general than the approaches developed by Subramanian and Sadoulet (1990) and by Lewis and Thorbecke (1992). The latter becomes special cases of the methodology developed here.

14 The brief review of structural path analysis which follows draws heavily on Defourny and Thorbecke (1984).

15 A totally similar analysis would obtain if accounting multipliers had been used (where the notion of influence is equated to average expenditure propensity) rather than fixed price multipliers.

16 A concrete example of elementary paths linking the impact of budget retrenchment (through cuts in different categories of government current expenditures) on the incomes of different socioeconomic groups in Indonesia is shown at the end of this subsection (see Figure 7.7).

17 For a formal derivation of M_p, see Appendix in Defourny-Thorbecke (1984).

18 For a formal proof see Appendix in Defourny-Thorbecke (1984).

References

Adelman, I., and J. E. Taylor. 1990. 'A Structural Adjustment with a Human Face Possible? The Case of Mexico,' *Journal of Development Studies*, 26(3).

Adelman, I., Taylor, J. E., and S. Vogel. 1987. 'Life in a Mexican Village: A SAM Perspective,' paper prepared for the International Symposium on the Social Accounting Matrix Methods and Application, Naples, Italy.

Alarcon Rivero, J. V., J. van Heemst, S. Keuning, W. de Ruijter, and R. Vos. 1986. 'The Social Accounting Framework for Development,

Concepts, Construction and Applications,' draft, Institute of Social Studies, The Hague, April.

Cohen, S. I. 1989. 'Analysis of Social Accounting Multipliers Over Time: The Case of the Netherlands,' *Social Economic Planning Science*, 23(5).

D'Antonio, M., R. Colaizzo, and G. Leonello. 1988. 'Mezzojiorno/Centre-North: A Two Region Model for the Italian Economy,' *Journal of Policy Modelling*, 10(3).

Defourny, J., and E. Thorbecke. 1984. 'Structural Path Analysis and Multiplier Decomposition within a Social Accounting Matrix Framework,' *The Economic Journal*, 94.

Devarajan, S., J. D. Lewis, and S. Robinson. 1994. 'Getting the Model Right: The General Equilibrium Approach to Adjustment Policy,' (mimeo).

Duchin, F. 1996. *Household Lifestyles: The Social Dimension of Structural Economics*. Manuscript submitted to the United Nations University, August.

Hay, R. W. 1978. 'The Statistics of Hunger,' *Food Policy*.

Hewings, G. J. D., and M. Madden (eds.). 1995. *Social and Demographic Accounting*. Cambridge University Press.

Hidayat, T. 1991. *The Construction of a Two-Region Social Accounting Matrix for Indonesia and Its Application to Some Equity Issues*. PhD thesis, Department of Economics, Cornell University.

Keuning, S., and E. Thorbecke. 1989. *The Impact of Budget Retrenchment on Income Distribution in Indonesia: A Social Accounting Matrix Application*, Technical Paper No. 3, OECD Development Center, Paris.

Khan, H. A., and E. Thorbecke. 1989. 'Macroeconomic Effects of Technology Choice: Multiplier and Structural Path Analysis within a SAM Framework,' *Journal of Policy Modelling*, 11(1).

Kilkenny, M., and A. Failde. 1997. 'Fiscal SAMs and Fiscal Federalism,' Department of Economics, Iowa State University, draft.

Lewis, B. D., and E. Thorbecke. 1992. 'District-Level Economic Linkages in Kenya: Evidence Based on a Small Regional Social Accounting Matrix,' *World Development*, 20(6).

Parikh, A., and E. Thorbecke. 1996. 'Impact of Rural Industrialization on Village Life and Economy: A Social Accounting Matrix Approach,' *Economic Development and Cultural Change*, 44(2): 351–77.

Pyatt, G., and E. Thorbecke. 1976. *Planning Techniques for a Better Future*. Geneva, Switzerland: International Labour Office.

Ralston, K. 1996. 'Household Nutrition and Economic Linkages: A Village Social Accounting Matrix for West Java, Indonesia,' in J. E. Taylor and I. Adelman (eds.), *Village Economies.* Cambridge University Press.

Reinert, K. A., and D. W. Roland-Holst. 1989. 'Social Accounting Matrices for US Trade Policy Analysis,' U.S. International Trade Commission, Washington, D.C. (mimeo).

Resosudarmo, B., and E. Thorbecke. 1996. 'The Impact of Environmental Policies on Household Incomes for Different Socioeconomic Classes: The Case of Air Pollutants in Indonesia,' *Ecological Economics,* 17.

Roland-Holst, D. W. 1990. 'Interindustry Analysis with Social Accounting Methods,' *Economic Systems Research,* 2 (2).

Sadoulet, E., and A. de Janvry. 1995. *Quantitative Development Policy Analysis.* Johns Hopkins University Press.

Subramanian, S., and E. Sadoulet. 1990. 'The Transmission of Production Fluctuations and Technical Change in a Village Economy: A Social Accounting Matrix Approach,' *Economic Development and Cultural Change,* 39(1).

Taylor, J., and I. Adelman (eds.). 1996. *Village Economies.* Cambridge University Press.

Thorbecke, E. 1985. 'The Social Accounting Matrix and Consistency-Type Planning Models,' Chapter 10 in G. Pyatt and J. I. Round (eds.), *Social Accounting Matrices, A Basis for Planning.* Washington, D.C.: World Bank Symposium.

Thorbecke, E. 1988. 'The Impact of Stabilization and Structural Adjustment Measures and Reforms on Agriculture and Equity,' in E. Berg (ed.), *Policy Reform and Equity: Extending the Benefits of Development.* San Francisco: Institute for Contemporary Studies.

Thorbecke, E. 1989. 'The Social Accounting Matrix Framework to Capture the Interdependence between Domestic and Foreign Variables,' paper prepared for the conference on Large-scale Social Science Models, National Center for Super Computing Applications, University of Illinois, September.

Thorbecke, E. 1995. *Intersectoral Linkages and Their Impact on Rural Poverty Alleviation: A Social Accounting Matrix Approach.* UNIDO.

Thorbecke, E., and collaborators. 1992. *Adjustment and Equity in Indonesia.* Paris: Development Centre of the OECD.

Thorbecke, E., and H. S. Jung. 1996. 'A Multiplier Decomposition Method to Analyze Poverty Alleviation,' *Journal of Development Economics,* 48.

Waters, C., and D. W. Holland. 1996. 'What Is Oregon's Economic Base: Implications from an Oregon Social Accounting Matrix,' Washington State University, Department of Agricultural Economics.

8. Applied general interregional equilibrium

Walter Isard and Iwan J. Azis

8.0 Introduction

As noted in chapter 3, national, regional and interregional models have
stemmed from the pioneering work of Wassily Leontief. Leontief's
thinking in turn was greatly influenced by the purely conceptual Walrasian
general equilibrium system.[1] In order to obtain a very desirable
operational character for the portrayal of this system, which Leontief
termed an input-output model, he introduced, among others, assumptions
of constant production, consumption and trade coefficients. These
assumptions, however, have meant that market prices do not affect
production, consumption and trade; and that in the systems his models
portray, supply always adjusts to demand — falling if demand drops and
increasing if demand grows. These assumptions then imply that
unemployment of labor and capital have no effect on these systems, and in
fact are not present. Equally significant, they imply no resource
constraints; always, it is implicitly assumed that there exist unused facilities
and resources for the expansion of an economy.

In chapter 4 dealing with regional, interregional and spatial
econometrics, the existence of markets for factors of production and
commodities along with prices was introduced into our analytical
framework. But in doing so the very desirable requirement of supply and
demand equality (market equilibrium) was by and large ignored; and to a
significant degree in the past, extensive sets of data were employed for
identification of relevant structural relationships.

In chapter 5 on programming and industrial and urban complex
analysis, resource constraints were introduced as major factors affecting
development. However, the play of prices and the market were only

touched upon. Fixed final product prices were by and large assumed, the effect of unemployment of resources upon resource prices scarcely discussed, an excess supply often taken to imply a zero price. (There was, however, at the end of section 5.2, an indication of how nonlinear programming can be extended to cover price formation at the market.)

In the discussion of gravity and spatial interaction models of chapter 6, little attention was given to the formation of prices and the role of the market. In large part this results from the fact that gravity models pertain to masses and mass behavior. They average out the effects in reality of the numerous microelements — the behavior of individual units. For some spatial phenomena, the individual effects can be ignored; but they cannot be ignored for many other extremely significant phenomena, especially those associated with markets and monetary systems.

Like input-output, the SAM analysis of chapter 7, taken to embrace input-output, also assumes constant production and consumption coefficients. In effect it fails to capture the impact of changing markets and prices as major elements in a study, for example when policies of government are formulated and evaluated.

We now come to a chapter in which market equilibrium is a basic element, where prices are free to vary at least relatively and where they fully impact production, consumption, trade, and spatial interaction in general. Both linear and nonlinear functions will be involved. To reiterate, we now can obtain solutions to models extensively employing linear and nonlinear functions to characterize situations of reality, which until recently has not been possible — a result of the tremendous increase in computer capability. However, the reader is warned that this advance in analytical capability is achieved at a cost. Generally speaking, the magnitudes to be yielded by the models envisaged are not to be viewed as precise values. Rather these magnitudes have basic use only in indicating direction of change as change in exogenous inputs, such as policies, tastes and technology, are introduced. This is the result of the fact that the inputs of data that are currently employed to approximate parameters of a number of nonlinear functions is of lesser quality than the data in the models presented in the previous chapters. Moreover, most of these magnitudes will be cranked out by rather complex programs designed for high speed computers, and we will not be able fully, and often even partially, to follow how the play of the variables generated these magnitudes.

In the materials to follow we proceed step-by-step to develop the basic scaffolding for applied general interregional equilibrium (AGIE) models.

As far as the author is aware at the time of writing, there has not yet been developed in regional science such a model generally applicable for a space-economy although important forward steps have been taken. (These steps will be noted in section 8.5.) Distance, transport inputs and transport costs have been at best most inadequately treated. While, as a consequence, it would seem inappropriate to discuss in an introductory text for graduate and advanced undergraduate students a comprehensive method where no successful demonstration of its applicability can be pointed to, we do so for at least two reasons. First the method to be presented is highly likely soon to experience very rapid development and subsequently a fruitful application. Second, in the subsequent chapter major new research directions will be sketched which will involve the fruitful use of applied general interregional equilibrium, especially one involving a deeper probe with one or more methods of regional science — directions which graduate students may wish and are encouraged to pursue in dissertation work.

In section 8.1 we introduce some basic relationships of a relevant applied general interregional equilibrium analysis. We employ a highly simplified model. The model treats a two commodity, two resource, two region system with an external source of a raw material, a model intended to highlight distance and transport inputs to overcome the resistance of distance to movement. The next section considers trade and location within a two country world, each country comprising a single region. We do so in order to obtain a meaningful presentation of the impact of varying distance on specialization of production and the export/import pattern of a country. By so doing it avoids the pitfalls of the 'wonderland-of-no-dimensions' trade models so characteristic of many computable and applied general equilibrium analyses by economists. It also brings into consideration variables significant for treating a region engaged in trade outside its own nation.

Section 8.3 further approaches reality by considering a two country/three region world. One country comprises two regions, each of which possesses two resources. The aim of this section is to develop the scaffolding of a social accounting matrix to serve as a core for applied general interregional equilibrium analysis (AGIE) in which there is consumption, production, transport, government, investment and possibly financial activity in a market system — all in a many commodity, many country, many region world.

In section 8.4 we examine the problems and questionable character of the basic assumptions of standard applied general equilibrium (AGE) models, partly to be aware of them should we carry them over to interregional (AGIE) analysis and partly to make clear the need to reformulate some and discard others for effective AGIE analysis.

Section 8.5 notes some of the seminal contributions that regional scientists have already made for the yet-to-be realized effective AGIE model, and section 8.6 contains some concluding remarks.

8.1 A highly simplified model introducing distance and transport inputs as basic variables

We begin with a highly simplified interregional model covering production, consumption and trade using both nonlinear and linear functions with space explicitly included. Such inclusion implies that distance, transport inputs (in say ton miles) and transport costs must be able to be treated as *endogenous* variables.[2]

Accordingly, consider (for pedagogical purposes only) a model of the following *hypothetical* situation. There are two regions A and B and a location Z of a raw material, say coal. At A an agricultural commodity is produced by sector #1. At B a manufactured commodity is produced by sector #2, the production of which requires as input the raw material coal. In each region, consumption is an aggregate concentrated along with production at a single point. Region A possesses a fixed stock of the resource capital, 100 percent mobile, all the capital used in production in the two regions being owned by the set of consumers in A. Region B has a fixed amount of the resource labor completely mobile, i.e., the costs of commuting from region A to B are zero. All the labor required in production in the two regions is provided by the set of consumers in region B. Also, the supply of coal at Z is unlimited and available at its location at zero cost.

To obtain an equilibrium solution to this highly simplified situation, we need to specify the stocks of resources (as exogenous elements) that are available for production of the goods — which serve as both intermediate inputs into production and final products for household consumption. Let K be the fixed stock of capital, and L, the fixed stock of labor. Also let r represent the price of capital, and w, the price of labor.

Since a Walrasian-type general equilibrium framework can determine only relative prices, we are free to set the price of one commodity or resource as unity. We do so for the price of labor, which then serves as a numeraire for this particular exercise. Within a programming framework, a price of labor equal to unity would be a constraint.

8.1.1 The consumption subsystem

Under the assumption of pure competition among producers in each sector, profits are taken to be zero, Accordingly, the respective incomes for regions A and B will be the earnings from only their resources. Thus

$$Y^A = rK \text{ and } Y^B = wL \tag{8-1}$$

We take the consumption of each region to be given by the linear homogeneous Cobb Douglas function

$$U = (C_1^i)^{0.5} (C_2^i)^{0.5} \qquad i = A,B \tag{8-2}$$

If consumers (as an aggregate in each region) are taken to maximize utility, it follows that[3]

$$C_1^A = \frac{Y^A}{2P_1^A} \text{ and } C_2^A = \frac{Y^A}{2P_2^A} \qquad \text{consumption of commodities \#1 and \#2, respectively in region } A \tag{8-3}$$

$$C_1^B = \frac{Y^B}{2P_1^B} \text{ and } C_2^B = \frac{Y^B}{2P_2^B} \qquad \text{consumption of commodities \#1 and \#2, respectively in region } B \tag{8-4}$$

where P_1^A, P_2^A, P_1^B and P_2^B are prices of commodities \#1 and \#2 in regions A and B, respectively.

Note that here and later, both in the text and endnotes, we assume that functions to be optimized satisfy second-order conditions for equilibrium. For example, we assume utility functions are concave or quasi-concave at all points.

8.1.2 The production subsystem

Production of each commodity is restricted by known technology. For sectors \#1 and \#2 we assume the respective linear homogeneous Cobb-Douglas production functions

$$X_1^A = K_1^{0.25} L_1^{0.75} \tag{8-5}$$

and

$$X_2^B = K_2^{0.5} L_2^{0.5} \tag{8-6}$$

Given these two functions, maximization of profits leads to the following relations[4]

$k_1 = (w/3r)^{0.75}$, the capital input per unit of good #1 $\qquad$ (8-7)

$\ell_1 = (3r/w)^{0.25}$, the labor input per unit of good #1 $\qquad$ (8-8)

$k_2 = (w/r)^{0.5}$, the capital input per unit of good #2 $\qquad$ (8-9)

$\ell_2 = (r/w)^{0.5}$, the labor input per unit of good #2 $\qquad$ (8-10)

The intermediate inputs required are to be calculated from the exogenously specified input-output coefficients, a_{11}, a_{12}, a_{21}, and a_{22}, the respective requirements of good #1 per unit output of sectors #1 and of #2, and of good #2 per unit output of sectors #1 and #2. Thus we obtain the familiar demand-driven supply equal demand equations of input-output:

$$X_1 = a_{11}X_1 + a_{12}X_2 + C_1^A + C_1^B \qquad (8\text{-}11)$$

and

$$X_2 = a_{21}X_1 + a_{22}X_2 + C_2^A + C_2^B \qquad (8\text{-}12)$$

whose solutions, after rearranging terms using the familiar inverse **A**, are given by

$$X_1 = [(1 - a_{22})(C_1^A + C_1^B) + a_{12}(C_2^A + C_2^B)]/\mathbf{A} \qquad (8\text{-}13)$$

and

$$X_2 = [(1 - a_{11})(C_2^A + C_2^B) + a_{21}(C_1^A + C_1^B)]/\mathbf{A} \qquad (8\text{-}14)$$

The input of coal per unit output of good #2, namely a_{02}, must also be exogenously specified.

8.1.3 The transport subsystem

The basic activity of the transport subsystem is the production of transport inputs required for the shipment of goods. In the movement of a unit of a commodity, a transport input, is defined as the product of the *weight* of that unit and the *distance* over which it is to be moved. Thus a unit transport input can be defined as a shipment of one ton over one mile, that is a shipment of one ton-mile, which is of course equivalent to the movement of 100 lbs. of a commodity 20 miles, or 200 lbs. over 10 miles, etc. Use of other definitions is possible such as one kilogram-kilometer; in this book, however, we employ the term ton-mile.

In this highly simplified model, a Leontief production function is taken to characterize each of three transport activities: (1) shipment of coal from location Z to production sector #2 in region B (taken to be the activity of sector #3 in B); (2) shipment of commodity #1 produced in region A to meet final demand consumption in B as well as provide intermediate inputs of good #1 for the production of good #2 in B (designated the activity of sector #4 in A); and (3) shipment of commodity #2 produced in region B to meet final demand consumption in A as well as provide intermediate inputs of good #2 for production of #1 in A (designated the activity of sector #5 in B). Thus there are for sectors #3, #4, and #5 the respective constant production coefficients (capital and labor inputs per unit output)

$$k_3^B, \ell_3^B, k_4^A, \ell_4^A, k_5^B, \ell_5^B$$

where a unit output of each sector is a transport input. These coefficients need to be exogenously specified.

Where we let α_{32} represent the ton-miles (transport inputs) provided by the transport sector #3 in B to ship one unit of coal from Z to sector #2 in B, α_{41} represent the ton-miles (transport inputs) provided by transport sector #4 in A to ship one unit of good #1 to B, and α_{52} represent the ton-miles (transport inputs) provided by transport sector #5 in B to ship one unit of good #2 to A, the outputs of the transport sectors are:

$$X_3^B = \alpha_{32}\, a_{02}\, X_2^B \tag{8-15}$$

$$X_4^A = \alpha_{41}\, a_{12}\, X_2^B + \alpha_{41}\, C_1^B \tag{8-16}$$

$$X_5^A = \alpha_{52}\, a_{21}\, X_1^A + \alpha_{52}\, C_2^A \tag{8-17}$$

where α_{02} is the requirement of coal per unit output of sector #2 in B.

8.1.4 The market subsystem

Under the assumption of pure competition in each sector, the price of a good will come to be equal to its unit costs. Therefore, for sectors #3, #4, and #5 (in whose production only labor and capital are required as inputs), prices of a unit of output are:

$$P_3^B = r k_3^B + w \ell_3^B \tag{8-18}$$

$$P_4^A = r k_4^A + w \ell_4^A \tag{8-19}$$

and

$$P_5^B = r k_5^B + w k_5^B \tag{8-20}$$

Also, two prices are realized as delivered costs, namely

$$P_2^A = P_2^B + \alpha_{52} P_5^B \tag{8-21}$$

and

$$P_1^B = P_1^A + \alpha_{41}P_4^A \tag{8-22}$$

Once, prices P_1^A and P_2^B are determined, P_2^A and P_1^B can be directly calculated since P_4^A and P_5^B are given by equations (8-19) and (8-20) and α_{41} and α_{52} are determinable once the distances and weights are specified. However, P_1^A and P_2^B are not directly obtainable because intermediate inputs are required in the production of goods #1 and #2. Since pure competition insures zero profits for producers in sectors #1 and #2, we can obtain from this condition the relations

$$P_1^A = rk_1 + w\ell_1 + a_{11}P_1^A + a_{21}P_2^B + a_{21}\alpha_{52}P_5^B \tag{8-23}$$

and

$$P_2^B = rk_2 + w\ell_2 + a_{02}\alpha_{32}P_3^B + a_{22}P_2^B + a_{12}P_1^A + a_{12}\alpha_{41}P_4^A \tag{8-24}$$

Here equation 8-23 states that the price of good #1 in A equals the unit cost of capital *plus* the unit cost of labor *plus* the cost of using good #1 as an intermediate good *plus* the cost of using good #2 as an intermediate good. The last cost is indicated by two terms: the first is the cost at the site of production in region B of the intermediate input of good #2 $(a_{21}P_2^B)$; the second is the transport cost on that amount of intermediate input (a_{21}) from region B to A. That transport cost is equal to the a_{21} units of good #2 times the transport cost of shipping one unit of good #2 over the distance from B to A, namely $\alpha_{52}P_5^B$, where α_{52} is the transport input involved per unit of good #2 (namely the weight of a unit of good #2 times the distance $d^{B\to A}$) and P_5^B is the cost (the price) of a unit of that transport input. In other words, a_{21} units of good #2 need to be shipped; thus $\alpha_{52}a_{21}$ is the total transport inputs for the required shipment. Multiplying this total by the price P_5^B of a required transport input yields $a_{21}\alpha_{52}P_5^B$, the transport cost for delivering the intermediate input of good #2 per unit output of good #1.

In a similar manner equation 8-24 states that the price P_2^B of good #2 in region B is equal to the sum of (1) the unit cost of capital, (2) the unit cost of labor, (3) the transport cost of the coal input which is $a_{02}\alpha_{32}P_3^B$, namely the amount of coal, a_{02}, required per unit of output of good #2 times α_{32} (the weight of a unit of coal times the distance $d^{Z\to B}$ to be overcome) times the price P_3^B of a transport input, (4) the cost of using good #2 as an intermediate input, (5) the cost of using good #1 as an intermediate input (namely the amount used times the price of #1 in region A), and (6) the transport cost in shipping the amount of good #1 used as an intermediate input, α_{41}, being the weight of good #1, and $d^{A\to B}$, the distance that good needs to be moved.

Using equations (8-18), (8-19) and (8-20) to eliminate P_3^B, P_4^A and P_5^B, we obtain P_1^A and P_2^B in terms of r, w, the given values of the exogenous input-output coefficients and the α's.[5]

The market system also requires that supply and demand are equated for each factor. Thus

$$\bar{K} = \sum_i K_i \text{ where } K_i = k_i X_i \qquad i = 1,...,5 \qquad (8\text{-}25)$$

and

$$\bar{L} = \sum_i L_i \text{ where } L_i = \ell_i X_i \qquad i = 1,...,5 \qquad (8\text{-}26)$$

where $\bar{K}$ and $\bar{L}$ are the exogenously determined supply of capital and labor, respectively. In this highly simplified model we have 34 unknowns: r, w, Y^A, Y^B, C_1^A, C_2^A, C_1^B, C_2^B, X_1, X_2, k_1, k_2, ℓ_1, ℓ_2, X_3, X_4, X_5, P_1^A, P_2^A, P_1^B, P_2^B, P_3^B, P_4^A, P_5^B, K_1, K_2, K_3, K_4, K_5, L_1, L_2, L_3, L_4, and L_5. One of these, w, we take as numeraire and set at unity (recall, a Walrasian general equilibrium can determine only relative prices). Also, we have 34 equations,[6] of which only 33 are independent (if all but one market equation are independent, one becomes redundant). Thus we can solve our model, when we specify the values of all the exogenous variables, Setting these values as follows: $\bar{K} = 0.8$, $\bar{L} = 2.0$, $a_{11} = 0.05$, $a_{12} = 0.2$, $a_{21} = 0.15$, $a_{22} = 0.10$, $\alpha_{32} = 0.12$, $\alpha_{41} = 0.10$, $\alpha_{52} = 0.10$, $\ell_3 = 0.4$, $\ell_4 = 0.3$, $\ell_5 = 0.2$, $k_3 = 0.3$, $k_4 = 0.2$, and $k_5 = 0.5$, we present selected outcomes in row 6 of Table 8.1.

As noted in chapter 5, the solution to this problem can be obtained by programming where the nonlinear utility function is to be maximized subject to constraints. One of the constraints is that profits from production be nonpositive (which the assumption of pure competition requires). A second constraint is that profits be nonnegative (to insure that goods will be produced to satisfy consumption demands). Viewing the data of row 6 of Table 8-1 as the solution to a programming problem may be helpful to the reader in understanding the nature of general equilibrium analysis.

In order to make explicit the effect of distance, transport cost, and in general space upon the functioning of the economy depicted by our highly simplified model, we now let distances take different values. The results are recorded in Table 8-1.[7]

To see the impact of distance, we record in the first row the hypothetical case where the regions and Z (the coal site) as points all coincide — where in effect distances are zero — the economist's wonderland of no dimension. In this case, a 'delivered cost' price such as P_2^A is identical to the f.o.b. price P_2^B. In the second row, we show the results

Table 8-1   Impacts of the distance and transport input variables (weights of units of grain, textiles, and coal are 20 lbs.)

	distances (miles) A→B B→A	Z→B	$\alpha_{41};\alpha_{52}$ Transport inputs on (1) grain (2) textiles in ton-miles	α_{32} Transport inputs on coal in ton-miles	C_1^A	C_2^A	C_1^B	C_2^B	P_1^A	P_2^A	P_1^B	P_2^B	X_1^A	X_2^B	r	w	K	L
1	0	0	0	0	0.239	0.185	0.387	0.300	2.58	3.32	2.58	3.32	0.800	0.672	1.542	1.0	0.80	2.0
2	10	0	0.1	0	0.238	0.182	0.377	0.299	2.59	3.38	2.65	3.35	0.787	0.666	1.540	1.0	0.80	2.0
3	100	0	1.	0	0.229	0.159	0.308	0.289	2.65	3.81	3.25	3.46	0.693	0.613	1.513	1.0	0.80	2.0
4	300	0	3.	0	0.209	0.123	0.220	0.272	2.77	4.71	4.54	3.68	0.564	0.532	1.445	1.0	0.80	2.0
5	0	12	0	0.12	0.238	0.179	0.384	0.289	2.61	3.46	2.61	3.46	0.791	0.652	1.55	1.0	0.80	2.0
6	10	12	0.10	0.12	0.237	0.177	0.374	0.288	2.61	3.51	2.68	3.48	0.779	0.646	1.55	1.0	0.80	2.0
7	300	36	3.0	0.36	0.200	0.166	0.216	0.245	2.85	5.13	4.64	4.08	0.551	0.498	1.49	1.0	0.80	2.0
8	300	300	3.0	3.0	0.210	0.086	0.182	0.135	3.50	8.56	5.51	7.41	0.481	0.326	1.84	1.0	0.80	2.0

when 10 miles is taken to separate regions A and B, but where the coal site Z still coincides with B. When the results are compared with those in the first row, outputs decline (since the transport requirement eats up capital and labor resources) and consumption of each good in each region declines, while prices rise. When we increase the distance between A and B to 100 miles and then to 300, there are, as to be expected, significant decreases in outputs and consumption, and large increases in prices. For example, comparison of results of rows 2 and 4 show that output of good #1 (X_1^A) falls from 0.787 to 0.564, consumption of good #1 in region B (C_1^B) falls from 0.377 to 0.220 and its delivered price (P_1^B) rises from 2.65 to 4.54.

Rows 5-8 of Table 8-1 inject changes in the distance variable $Z \to B$. When this distance is 12 miles and A and B coincide, we see, when comparison is made with row 1, small decreases in outputs and consumption and small increases in prices. When we further introduce a distance of 10 miles between A and B, these changes tend to be somewhat larger. When we consider the distance magnitudes of row 7 $(Z \to B = 36$ miles, with $A \to B$ and $B \to A = 300$ miles) changes are much more pronounced; and when all distances are set at 300 miles the changes are enormous. In the latter case, for example, when compared with the wonderland case of row 1, output of good #1 falls from 0.800 to 0.481; of good #2 from 0.672 to 0.326; and except for good #1 in A, final consumption of goods is more than halved.

8.2 Transport inputs, location and trade in a two-country world

In the previous section we have considered the impact of the distance and transport input variables on consumption, production, prices and trade between two regions in a single nation. In regional science we also need to consider the impact of the distance and transport input variables upon trade (and location) among countries (political regions), especially since much of the exports of a given region within a country may go to another country or its regions. Again to do this, we have recourse to another highly simplified model to allow us to develop certain basic relations to be embodied in a core framework for a relevant applied general interregional equilibrium model.

To begin consider a simple two country model, each country having the same two production sectors but being endowed with different amounts of two resources. We choose to follow the framework embodied in the Heckscher-Ohlin model of trade between two differently endowed countries — a model which has been extensively discussed in the economic literature. Its important conclusion which has played a significant role in trade policy discussion for many years has been that a country's exports use intensively the country's abundant factor. For example, in a two-country situation involving the two scarce factors of capital and labor, the country having the greater stock of capital relative to labor will produce and export commodities that are capital intensive in production, and the country having the greater stock of labor relative to capital will produce and export commodities that are labor intensive in production. More significant for its effect on economic thought was the result that in the two countries factor prices will be the same when expressed in terms of the currency of either country. Hence, there will be no economic incentive or need for any factor migration. While in recent decades, many qualifications to the findings of the Heckscher-Ohlin model have been made from relaxing their assumptions in order to introduce more of reality into their analysis, the assumption of zero or negligible transport cost in trade has by and large not been relaxed. As a consequence, the development of applied general equilibrium (AGE) models which also have been concerned with trade, by and large have retained that transport cost assumption. This has led, as we will see, to serious shortcomings in the findings of these models, and also to inadequate analyses of the location problem for countries and regions of these countries.

Among others, the assumptions of Heckscher-Ohlin model are: (1) identical production functions in the two countries; (2) constant returns to scale in production and diminishing returns in the use of any given factor; (3) identical consumption patterns in the two countries at each relevant commodity price-ratio; (4) non-reversibility of factor intensities such that a given commodity is factor intensive in the use of labor (or capital) at all relevant factor price-ratios; and (5) zero or negligible transport costs in trade.[8] We now proceed to introduce the reality of transport inputs and transport costs into a simple Heckscher-Ohlin model.

Let two countries, *A* and *B*, have stocks of the two resources, labor and capital, *A* being labor abundant, and *B* capital abundant, relatively speaking. The factors are internationally immobile. Although different constant returns-to-scale production functions are taken to exist for the two goods #1 and #2, for any one good they are identical for the two countries.

8.2.1 The consumption subsystem

With pure competition in each sector, profits are zero. Therefore, *incomes* in the two countries will be

$$Y^i = r^i K^i + w^i L^i \qquad\qquad i = A,B \qquad (8\text{-}27)$$

and, as in the previous section, their *consumption* of goods upon utility maximization will be

$$C_1^i = Y^i/2P_1^i; \quad C_2^i = Y^i/2P_2^i \qquad\qquad i = A,B \qquad (8\text{-}28)$$

8.2.2 The production system

The production functions are

$$X_1^i = (K_1^i)^{0.25} (L_1^i)^{0.75} \qquad\qquad i = A,B \qquad (8\text{-}29)$$

and

$$X_2^i = (K_2^i)^{0.5} (L_2^i)^{0.5} \qquad\qquad i = A,B \qquad (8\text{-}30)$$

Thus, maximization of profits leads, as in the previous section, to

$$k_1^i = (w^i/3r^i)^{0.75} \qquad \ell_1^i = (3r^i/w^i)^{0.25}$$
$$\qquad\qquad\qquad\qquad\qquad\qquad i = A,B \qquad (8\text{-}31)$$
$$k_2^i = (w^i/r^i)^{0.5} \qquad \ell_2^i = (r^i/w^i)^{0.5}$$

Note that the first production function is labor intensive, and the second, capital intensive. We therefore start off by assuming that the labor abundant nation *A* will tend to export commodity #1 to *B*, and that the capital abundant nation *B* will tend to export commodity #2 to *A*. Under conditions of pure competition, maximization of profits will lead, as noted in the previous section, to

$$P_1^A = r^A k_1^A + w^A \ell_1^A \qquad\qquad (8\text{-}32)$$

and

$$P_2^B = r^B k_2^B + w^B \ell_2^B \qquad\qquad (8\text{-}33)$$

(Prices P_2^A and P_1^B are to be specified below.)
Since no intermediate inputs are required in our Heckscher-Ohlin type model, we have

$$X_1^A = C_1^A + Ex_1^{A \to B} \qquad\qquad X_2^A = C_2^A - Ex_2^{B \to A} \qquad (8\text{-}34)$$

$$X_1^B = C_1^B - Ex_1^{A \to B} \qquad\qquad X_2^B = C_2^B + Ex_2^{B \to A} \qquad (8\text{-}35)$$

where $\text{Ex}_1^{A \to B}$, $\text{Ex}_2^{B \to A}$ represent exports (and imports), where for example $\text{Ex}_1^{A \to B}$ represents exports of good #1 from A to B (also imports of good #1 of B from A).

8.2.3 *The transport subsystem*

Assuming A will export the labor intensive good #1 and B the capital intensive good #2, we have two *transport* activities. One is activity #4 in A which produces the transport inputs to ship good #1 from A to B, α_{41} being the amount of transport inputs required per unit of export of #1. The other is activity #5 in B which produces the transport inputs to ship good #2 from B to A, α_{52} being the amount of transport inputs required per unit of export of #2. Hence, we have

$$X_4^A = \alpha_{41} \text{Ex}_1^{A \to B} \tag{8-36}$$

and

$$X_5^B = \alpha_{52} \text{Ex}_2^{B \to A} \tag{8-37}$$

Both X_4^A and X_5^B are taken to be Leontief production functions whose only inputs (exogenously specified) are k_4^A and ℓ_4^A, and k_5^B and ℓ_5^B, respectively. Also under conditions of price competition

$$P_4^A = r^A k_4^A + w^A \ell_4^A \tag{8-38}$$

$$P_5^B = r^B k_5^B + w^B \ell_5^B \tag{8-39}$$

8.2.4 *The market subsystem*

Wages (w^A and w^B) and rents (r^A and r^B) are determined, respectively, by the supply = demand equations for labor and capital. In endnote 9, sixteen equations on capital and labor requirements by each of the six production activities and their four subtotals are presented. They result in the four total resource demands K^A, K^B, L^A and L^B that enter the four market clearing equations

$$
\begin{array}{ll}
K^A = \bar{K}^A & \qquad L^A = \bar{L}^A \\
K^B = \bar{K}^B & \qquad L^B = \bar{L}^B
\end{array}
\tag{8-40}
$$

where $\bar{K}^A$, $\bar{L}^A$, $\bar{K}^B$ and $\bar{L}^B$ are the exogenous (given) supplies.

In addition, pure competition among traders (brokers)[10] leads to

$$P_2^A = \text{fe}(P_2^B + \alpha_{52} P_5^B) \tag{8-41}$$

$$P_1^B = (1/\text{fe})(P_1^A + \alpha_{41}P_4^A) \tag{8-42}$$

where P_2^A and P_1^B are in effect 'delivered cost' prices and equivalent to world prices and fe is the foreign exchange rate converting B's currency into A's.

Finally, the exchange rate variable is determined by the condition that the value of B's imports at delivered cost prices (equal to the value of A's exports) is equal to A's imports at delivered cost prices (equal to the value of B's exports). That is, where M represents imports, where for example superscript $A \rightarrow B$ stands for an import of B from A,

$$(1/\text{fe})(P_1^A + \alpha_{41}P_4^A)M_1^{A\rightarrow B} - \text{fe}(P_2^B + \alpha_{52}P_5^B)M_2^{B\rightarrow A} = 0 \tag{8-43}$$

Altogether in this model, there are 49 unknowns and 49 equations to determine them. Recall that in a general equilibrium system, as is involved in this model, we can solve only for relative prices. However, we are free to set one price at unity to serve as numeraire. We thus set fe = 1, thereby insuring that the absolute prices in each country will be the same whether expressed in one currency (say dollars) or the other (say pounds). When we do set one price at unity, one of the equations can be taken to be redundant.[11] The prices are still relative to the magnitude set for the numeraire.

Taking initial resources to be $\bar{K}^A = 0.8$, $\bar{L}^A = 2.0$, $\bar{K}^B = 1.6$ and $\bar{L}^B = 1.8$ and setting as exogenous the values $\ell_4^A = \ell_5^B = 0.2$; $k_4^A = k_5^B = 0.25$; $d^{A\rightarrow B} = d^{B\rightarrow A} = 0$; and thus setting $\alpha_{41} = \alpha_{52} = 0$ (the dimensionless world of no transport costs and no space), we obtain with fe = 1 a solution where, in the first column (designated H/O) of Table 8-2, we list outcomes for selected variables. Since distance between A and B is set at zero, this column in effect yields Heckscher-Ohlin results given the above exogenous values. We particularly note that rents and wages in A and B are equalized.

We now introduce distance between A and B, for example 100 miles which for units of goods #1 and #2, each of which weighs 20 lbs., yield α_{41}, $\alpha_{52} = 1$ (one ton-mile). In column 2 (headed I/AI) of Table 8-2 we record the changed magnitudes that result. Changes in other magnitudes not noted in Table 8-2 are presented in an endnote.[12] First note that the output of two transport activities X_4^A and X_5^B now become relevant, and are of course, positive. And likewise the respective prices, P_4^A and P_5^B, for their unit outputs (one ton-mile of transport service). Because the production of transport inputs requires resources, the total of the regional outputs of each of the two goods has decreased [from 1.755 (1.432 + 0.323) to 1.744 (1.285 + 0.459) for #1, and from 1.560 (0.144 + 1.416) to 1.539 (0.260 + 1.279) for good #2]. Likewise, the total consumption of the two regions for

Table 8-2   Impact of distance on trade among nations and the location problem

	H-O	I/A1	I/A2	I/A3
K^A	0.8	0.800	0.6	0.783
L^A	2.0	2.000	1.8	1.982
K^B	1.6	1.594	1.584	1.419
L^B	1.8	1.795	1.812	1.603
X_1^A	1.432	1.285	1.711	1.285
X_2^A	0.144	0.260	0.155	0.243
X_4^A	—	0.485	0.485	0.485
X_1^B	0.323	0.459	0.489	0.404
X_2^B	1.416	1.279	1.256	1.151
X_5^B	—	0.428	0.412	0.401
C_1^A	0.797	0.800	0.686	0.800
C_2^A	0.708	0.688	0.567	0.644
C_1^B	0.958	0.944	0.974	0.889
C_2^B	0.852	0.851	0.845	0.751

	H-O	I/A1	I/A2	I/A3
Y^A	4.689	13.816	11.466	13.816
Y^B	5.640	16.719	16.719	15.754
P_1^A	2.943	8.635	8.357	8.635
P_2^A	3.312	10.045	10.118	10.728
P_4^A	—	0.224	0.223	0.224
P_1^B	2.943	8.859	8.580	8.859
P_2^B	3.312	9.823	9.896	10.491
P_5^B	—	0.222	0.222	0.237
r^A	1.614	5.162	5.46	5.162
w^A	1.699	4.843	4.55	4.843
r^B	1.614	4.585	4.585	4.9
w^B	1.699	5.213	5.213	5.48
Ex_2^{B-A}	0.564	0.428	0.411	0.401
Ex_1^{A-B}	0.635	0.485	0.485	0.485
fe	1.0	1.0	1.0	1.0

each good. However, notice that each region has become less specialized, producing less of the good in which it has comparative advantage and more of the good in which it has comparative disadvantage. Most important, no longer does trade equalize wages and rents over the two regions, the major conclusion of the Heckscher-Ohlin model extensively employed by trade analysts. As can be expected, rent in region *A* has increased *relative* to rent in *B* because indirectly through trade *A* has now diminished access (greater resistance or cost) to the relatively abundant supply of capital in region *B*. (Recall that the Heckscher-Ohlin model and our adaptation of it only solves for relative rents, wages and prices, so that no direct comparison of these items in the two models is possible.) And the wage in region *B* has increased *relative* to that in region *A* because indirectly through trade *B* has now diminished access (greater resistance or cost) to the relatively abundant supply of labor in region *A*.

Correspondingly, prices for each good in the two regions are no longer the same as they are in the Heckscher-Ohlin model. Under conditions of pure competition among producers and traders, prevailing prices are delivered costs which include the transport cost of a unit.

Having demonstrated the impact of the introduction of distance and transport inputs for one set of positive distances, we can proceed to do the same for other sets of distances, each of which would show the misleading results of a Heckscher-Ohlin model for the space-economy of reality.

8.2.5 The location problem in an applied general interregional equilibrium framework

Before leaving the above modified Heckscher-Ohlin framework we wish to use it to introduce the general location problem in an applied general equilibrium setting. More specifically we wish to go beyond the partial classical comparative cost approach.[13]

Suppose a private multinational enterprise seeks to construct a new facility, and on the basis of cost alone to determine the better location, whether in *A* or *B*. Suppose also that it anticipates that 50% of its output will be marketed or aimed to service users in each country. Further, it is well aware of the fact that future fluctuations of the exchange rate are random phenomena; however, it assumes that the current rate (which we have set at unity in our model) is the best one to use. It anticipates that the f.o.b. price of the item to be produced will be the same for all consumers, whether the facility will be located in *A* or *B*. Moreover, it assumes that whether located in *A* or *B* the transport costs will be the same whether borne by it or users. It estimates that for the scale of operations it has in mind its input requirements (inclusive of those for transportation) will be 0.2 units of both capital and labor.

Using the classical comparative cost approach, the multinational looks at current prices as recorded in the second column of Table 8-2, and might conclude that B is the better location given that its total costs (0.2 [4.585 (rent) + 5.213 (wage)]) are 1.960, whereas in A they would be 2.001, relatively speaking. However, knowing from experience that a location of a major facility in any area tends to raise factor prices there, the enterprise wishes to estimate what costs will be when the facility has been constructed and has been in operation, subject to desirable constraints.[14] It therefore conducts an applied general interregional equilibrium model to do so. Were it to use the model of the second column of Table 8-2, it would conduct two runs. In the first, it would reduce the stock of each resource in A by 0.2 and thereby obtain the results of column 3 (I/A2). In the second run, it would leave unchanged the stock of A's resources 0.8 (capital) and 2.0 (labor) and reduce the stock of each resource in B by 0.2. Thereby it would obtain the results of column 4 (I/A3). Based on the figures in the third column, the costs of a location in A would be 0.2 (5.46 + 4.55) = 1.001. Based on the figures in the fourth column, the costs of a location in B would be 0.2 (4.9 + 5.48) = 1.038. The unit might therefore choose to locate in A rather than in B, B being the classical location that comparative cost analysis would suggest. And as a consequence, the trade, production and consumption patterns in each of the two regions would be affected by the decision, as the data in the several columns indicate.

This simple exercise, of course, omits many diverse factors affecting location. But it clearly points up that a suitable applied general interregional equilibrium framework can provide a more probing locational analysis. This framework can serve as an extension, if not replacement, of the old-fashioned, classical partial equilibrium comparative cost approach in the consideration of the location of major facilities.

Parenthetically it should be observed that there disappears in thin air the relatively ancient controversy over whether a general trade theory incorporates location theory, or whether a general location theory incorporates trade theory. In reality there is only one general theory, a general theory of trade and location.

8.2.6 Some concluding remarks

We conclude this section with the observation that recognition of distance as a basic variable and of the need for transport inputs for trade between two countries invalidate the Heckscher-Ohlin model for any but extreme situations where transport costs are zero or negligible. Obviously this conclusion holds for a many-country world. Also, for a many-country world, the location problem can be probed more deeply with an applied general interregional framework.

8.3 The scaffolding of a core social accounting matrix for an applied general interregional equilibrium (AGIE) model

8.3.1 Trade in a two country/three region world: the scaffolding of an interregional (international) input-output core

Having shown that the injection of transport cost into the original Heckscher-Ohlin model invalidates its conclusions and those of many variants of that model developed over the last decades, we now wish to undertake the construction of a hypothetical model which, in as simple a manner as possible, captures the basic variables of a general interregional equilibrium framework for application — a framework that leaves the spaceless (dimensionless) world of the typical abstract economist.

We consider two nations, Q and Z, each of spatial extent, engaged in trade. Nation Q comprises two regions A and B. To avoid unnecessary complication, nation Z is taken to be a single region, having a different currency than Q. In both A and B the two final consumption commodities #1 and #2 are produced. However, in Z only a single commodity #3, say coal, is produced which serves as an intermediate input in the production of #1 and #2. While Z does not produce commodities #1 and #2, with income earned from coal production it imports #1 and #2 from A and B for final consumption. We assume that (1) the labor intensive region A producing the labor intensive commodity #1 ships it to region B (the capital intensive region) as well as to Z; and (2) the capital intensive region B producing the capital intensive commodity #2 ships it to region A as well as to Z. (Under certain configurations of distances and resource stocks, shipment of #2 from A to Z and of #1 from B to Z may also occur; however to keep the presentation simple, we confine the analysis to the more likely situation where A and B each ship to Z only one commodity, namely the one in which each has comparative advantage given their stocks of resources and existing technology.) Thus A engages in two transport activities, shipment of #1 to B (activity #4) and shipment of #1 to Z (activity #8). B also engages in two transport activities, shipment of #2 to A (activity #5) and shipment of #2 to Z (activity #9). Z in turn engages in two shipment activities, one of good #3 to A (activity #6), and the other of good #3 to B (activity #7). See Figure 8.1 which depicts the transport system.

We further simplify the model by allowing the use of the intermediate input coal (commodity #3) in the production of only good #1 in A (say a hot region requiring air conditioning in the plant manufacturing good #1) and in the production of only good #2 in B (say a cold region requiring heat for the production process of good #2). (We assume that the production process of #1 in B does not require heat and the production process #2 in A does not require air conditioning.) Again, see Figure 8.1. These simplifications do not interfere with the presentation of the basic interactions and interdependencies when more intermediate inputs and more possible transport activities are allowed.

When this highly simplified model is embodied in an applied general interregional equilibrium framework where labor and capital resources are taken to be immobile, ninety-one variables and corresponding equations become involved. To put all these variables and equations into the text would take an excessive amount of space, and is not necessary if the reader has digested the materials of the preceding sections. The equations and variables are placed in Appendix 8.1 of this chapter.

The equilibrium solution that results from the operation of this model using a GAMS program is presented in Tables 8-3 and 8-4. Table 8-3 records physical flows in the system; and above the body of the table are listed the equilibrium rents, wages, and prices. Table 8-4 records the corresponding money flows. Once again, a companion programming problem can be set up with consumers maximizing a nonlinear utility function under appropriate constraints that ensure equilibrium at commodity and resource markets. Its solution would yield the results of Tables 8-3 and 8-4.

Introduction of a third region (country Z) adds two final consumption variables C_1^Z and C_2^Z to the four for A and B. The six final consumption levels, in both physical and monetary terms, are presented, respectively, in the last columns of Tables 8-3 and 8-4, these levels having resulted from maximization of utility subject to income constraints. The three adjacent columns relate to: (1) production outputs; (2) exports ($-$) and imports ($+$) between the two regions A and B of country Q; and (3) exports and

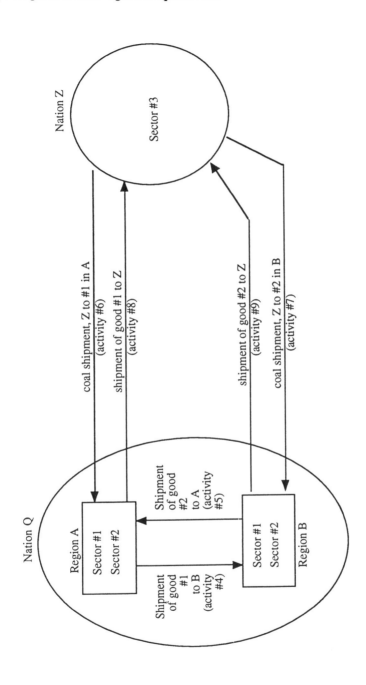

Figure 8.1 **The transport system in a two country/three region model**

Table 8-3 Physical magnitudes (inputs, outputs and flows) and prices

$r^A = 0.592$ $w^A = 0.512$ $P_1^A = 0.943$ $P_4^A = 0.025$ $P_2^B = 1.078$ $P_9^B = 0.035$ $P_3^Z = 0.148$

$r^B = 0.478$ $w^B = 0.579$ $P_2^A = 1.102$ $P_8^A = 1.102$ $P_3^B = 0.036$ $P_3^B = 0.222$ $P_1^Z = 0.979$ $P_6^Z = 0.074$

$r^Z = 4.536$ $w^Z = 0.290$ $P_3^A = 0.290$ $P_1^B = 0.222$ $P_1^B = 0.968$ $P_5^B = 0.024$ $P_2^Z = 1.112$ $P_7^Z = 0.074$

| | | Region A | | | | Region B | | | | Country Z | | | Out-put | Exports (−) Imports (+) | | Con-sumption |
		sec1	sec2	tr4	tr8	sec1	sec2	tr5r	tr9	sec3	tr6	tr7		A→B B→A	Z→A,B A,B→Z	C
A	sec1	0	0	0	0	0	0	0	0	0	0	0	1.180	−0.363	−0.023	0.794
	sec2	0	0	0	0	0	0	0	0	0	0	0	0.353	0.327	0	0.678
	tr4	0	0	0	0	0	0	0	0	0	0	0	0.363	−0.363	0	0
	tr8	0	0	0	0	0	0	0	0	0	0	0	0.023	0	−0.023	0
B	sec1	0	0	0	0	0	0	0	0	0	0	0	0.570	0.363	0	0.933
	sec2	0	0	0	0	0	0	0	0	0	0	0	1.185	−0.327	−0.020	0.838
	tr5	0	0	0	0	0	0	0	0	0	0	0	0.327	−0.327	0	0
	tr9	0	0	0	0	0	0	0	0	0	0	0	0.020	0	−0.020	0
Z	sec1	0	0	0	0	0	0	0	0	0	0	0	0	0	0.023	0.023
	sec2	0	0	0	0	0	0	0	0	0	0	0	0	0	0.020	0.020
	sec3	0.059	0	0	0	0	0.141	0	0	0	0	0	0.200	0	0	0
	tr6	0.059	0	0	0	0	0	0	0	0	0	0	0.059	0	0	0
	tr7	0	0	0	0	0	0.141	0	0	0	0	0	0.141	0	0	0
	L	1.611	0.380	0.009	0.001	0.715	1.077	0.008	0.001	0.008	0.001	0.003				
	K	0.464	0.328	0.007	0.001	0.289	1.304	0.007	0.001	0.006	0.001	0.002				

Note: Discrepancies arise from rounding of numbers.

Table 8-4   Money values (inputs, outputs and flows)

		Region A				Region B				Country Z			Output	Exports (−) Imports (+) A−B / B−A	Exports (−) Imports (+) Z−A,B / A,B−Z	Consumption C
		sec1	sec2	tr4	tr8	sec1	sec2	tr5	tr9	sec3	tr6	tr7				
A	sec1	0	0	0	0	0	0	0	0	0	0	0	1.113	−0.342	−0.021	0.750
	sec2	0	0	0	0	0	0	0	0	0	0	0	0.389	0.360	0	−0.750
	tr4	0	0	0	0	0	0	0	0	0	0	0	0.009	−0.009	0	0
	tr8	0	0	0	0	0	0	0	0	0	0	0	0.001	0	−0.001	0
B	sec1	0	0	0	0	0	0	0	0	0	0	0	0.551	0.351	0	0.903
	sec2	0	0	0	0	0	0	0	0	0	0	0	1.277	−0.353	−0.021	0.903
	tr5	0	0	0	0	0	0	0	0	0	0	0	0.008	−0.008	0	0
	tr9	0	0	0	0	0	0	0	0	0	0	0	0.001	0	−0.001	0
Z	sec1	0	0	0	0	0	0	0	0	0	0	0	0	0	0.022	0.022
	sec2	0	0	0	0	0	0	0	0	0	0	0	0	0	0.022	0.022
	sec3	0.009	0	0	0	0	0.021	0	0	0	0	0	0.030	0	0	0
	tr6	0.004	0	0	0	0	0	0	0	0	0	0	0.004	0	0	0
	tr7	0	0	0	0	0	0.010	0	0	0	0	0	0.010	0	0	0
L		0.825	0.194	0.005	0.000	0.414	0.623	0.005	0.004	0.002	0.002	0.001				
K		0.275	0.194	0.004	0.000	0.138	0.623	0.003	0.000	0.028	0.004	0.010				
Total Cost		1.113	0.389	0.009	0.001	0.551	1.277	0.008	0.001	0.030	0.004	0.010				

Note: Discrepancies arise from rounding of numbers.

imports between country Z and regions A and B. (Since two countries are involved, exports across countries must be distinguished from exports among regions of a given country.) Necessarily, for each production activity in each region and country the physical volume and money value of output must equal, respectively, the sum of the volumes and money values of net exports and consumption. Thus, for example, for activity #1 in A its volume of production, namely 1.180 (as noted in the first row of Table 8-3) equals its export to B, namely 0.363, plus its exports to Z, namely 0.023, plus its final goods consumption, namely 0.794. (If the commodity #1 in A were used as an intermediate input, the amount of that use would be indicated in the body of the table and would need to be added to the items just noted.) To take another example, for activity #2 in B the money value [in some standard currency of its output, namely 1.277 (see row 6 of Table 8-4)] equals the value of its exports to A, namely 0.353, plus its exports to Z, namely 0.021, plus its final goods consumption, namely 0.903. Also, for each good imported into a country, the physical volume and money value of the sum of the country's production and net imports of that good (less the use of that good as an intermediate in production activities of that country) must equal its consumption. For example, in row 2 of Table 8-3 the production output of sector 2 in A, namely 0.353, plus its imports, namely 0.327, equals its consumption, namely 0.680.

In the case of transport activities, the direct demands for final consumption are zero, but there are the indirect demands for their services from the need to export final consumption goods. In this connection these transport services represent exports for final consumption. When transport services are required to export intermediate inputs (such as coal), they also represent services exported as intermediate inputs.

In our simplified model the use of coal as an intermediate input into production activities #1 in A and #2 in B is specified, respectively, by the constant coefficients a_{31} (= 0.05) and a_{32} (= 0.119). As an intermediate input, coal like any other export item is a subtraction from output.

In the production subsystem the six transport activities, tr4, tr5, tr6, tr7, tr8, and tr9, whose respective levels of production are X_4^A, X_5^B, X_6^Z, X_7^Z, X_8^A and X_9^B, are listed in the rows and columns of the appropriate regions. While the unit labor and capital inputs for the production of commodities #1 and #2 in both regions are derived from maximization of profits subject to the production function constraints, the unit labor and capital inputs for the six transport activities are taken to be exogenously given as constant Leontief production coefficients. These constants are ℓ_4, ℓ_5, ℓ_6, ℓ_7, ℓ_8 and ℓ_9, and k_4, k_5, k_6, k_7, k_8 and k_9. Note, that here as previously, we treat the provision of transport services as production activity comparable to the treatment of the provision of other services — e.g., legal, health, educational and business. This is absolutely necessary in order to capture in full the reality of space and its implications for all socio-economic-political activity.

The addition of new production activities and their unit factor input requirements make new demands for the use of the stocks of resources. These unit factor inputs when multiplied by the aforementioned levels of output of the respective activities lead to the demands, by activity, for labor and capital, as recorded along the labor and capital rows at the bottom of Table 8-3. These rows cover A's and B's demands for resources as well as Z's, namely L^Z and K^Z. For each region, the resource requirements of each of its activities when summed are equal to its exogenously given immobile stocks of labor and capital.

The counterpart to Table 8-3 on physical magnitudes is Table 8-4 on monetary magnitudes (dollar values). There, money flows are derived by multiplying the physical flows by appropriate rents, wages and prices, as listed above the body of Table 8-3. In the fully interdependent framework of general equilibrium analysis, these prices are associated with balance (market clearing) equations. As already mentioned, demands in each region for each of its immobile resources must be equal to the exogenously given stock of the resource, which by up and down variation of rents and wages determines their equilibrium levels, namely w^A, w^B, w^Z, r^A, r^B, and r^Z. Except where imported, the prices of various goods in each region are determined by their unit production costs, the sum of the costs of the required factors (resources) and intermediate inputs. In the case of a finished consumption good that is imported in a region its price is the f.o.b. price in the country of export plus the cost of the required transport inputs. This relationship results from the assumption of pure competition among traders and producers. For example, if the price of a good produced in A based on unit factor (and intermediate input) costs were lower than the delivered cost price from B, then traders in B would find shipment of goods from B to A unprofitable and there would be no export from B. If the former price were higher than the latter, then there would be a positive gain (surplus) from export of the good but competition among traders would eliminate that gain.

Once we multiply the physical flows by the appropriate prices, we obtain the values recorded in Table 8-4. We observe that the value of output of each activity (listed in its row in the output column at the right of that table) is equal to its total production costs (factor plus intermediate input costs) listed at the bottom of its column below its labor and capital costs.

Next observe for each region the sum of payments by its activities for their labor and capital inputs in Table 8-4, alternatively viewed as a sum of value added by (or resource receipts from) its activities. We have defined this sum as regional income. For each region this sum also equals the sum of the values of the products made available for purchase as final consumption goods in each region, alternatively viewed as consumption expenditures. These purchases are listed in the final column of Table 8-4.

Further, if we now take for each region the sum of the value of outputs by its industries and subtract from it the region's *net* import (total imports from, less total exports to other regions), we have what we may define as its Gross Regional Product. Since in our highly simplified model we have not taken into account capital consumption and have implicitly set it at zero, this Gross Regional Product, from which capital consumption should be deducted to derive regional income, comes to equal regional income.

Since we are treating an international system involving two counties, Z and Q where Q comprises regions A and B, our equilibrium condition that the Balance of Payments among countries be zero requires that the value of imports of each country equals the value of its exports, namely that

$$P_3^A M_3^{Z \to A} + P_3^B M_3^{Z \to B} - \text{fe}(P_1^Z \text{Ex}_1^{A \to Z} + P_2^Z \text{Ex}_2^{B \to Z}) = 0 \qquad (8\text{-}44)$$

where P_3^A, P_3^B, $\text{fe}P_1^Z$ and $\text{fe}P_2^Z$ are delivered cost prices in the currency of Q, which in our two nation model some analysts may wish to view as world prices PW_3, PW_1, and PW_2, respectively. However, generally speaking, when there are more than two countries engaged in trade in a number of commodities, the use of the concept of world prices can be highly misleading. Because there exist at least several sources of supply and at least several different markets there is no world price of coal, or steel or many other goods since the delivered costs to these markets can be significantly different. Additionally, the transfer of assets or equities from A to B may be calculated as the imports of A from B and Z less the exports of A to both B and Z that is:

$$\Delta \text{Assets}^A = P_1^B \text{Ex}_1^{A \to B} - P_2^A M_2^{B \to A} + \text{fe}(P_1^Z \text{Ex}_1^{A \to Z} - P_3^A \text{Ex}_3^{Z \to A}) \qquad (8\text{-}45)$$

When the last term is zero (that is when the value of A's exports to Z equals the value of its imports from Z), then given the international balance of payments equation 8-44, A's change in assets depends only on the difference between A's exports to B and A's imports from B. However, if A's exports to Z are more than its imports from Z, then it follows from the international balance of payments equation 8-44, that B's imports from Z are greater than its exports to Z. Therefore, the change in A's assets is greater than from trade with B alone, and B's change in assets is smaller than that trade.

We now have presented the basic scaffolding of a core interregional input-output transactions table for use in developing a core interregional SAM. One can easily add: (1) more production sectors in each region; (2) explicitly consider more resources and many more intermediate inputs; (3) add government, investment and other final demand sectors (as we will do in the next section). Then he/she would have a detailed interregional input-output table similar to the interregional tables discussed in Chapter 3. To present such a table here, however, would make it much more difficult for the reader to see how the various magnitudes are derived, and nothing important for understanding the basic analytical process would have been gained. One point to note, however, is that Table 8-4 requires that there exist a foreign exchange market (endogenous or exogenous) to establish the foreign exchange rate(s) when all regions are not in the same country.

8.3.2 *Extensions to obtain the scaffolding of a core social accounting frame: a top-down approach*

The discussion of Social Accounting in Chapter 7 has made clear the need to introduce household groups into an applied general interregional equilibrium framework. We do so by deleting the last columns on consumption in Table 8-4 and adding two columns and two rows (representing urban and rural households) to both A's and B's block of transactors. To Z's block we add only one row and column for its city population, assuming the rural sector conducts subsistence agriculture. See Table 8-5 which represents monetary magnitudes (outputs, inputs and flows). We could also add columns and rows to the body of Table 8-3 on physical magnitudes, and such would indeed be useful for certain purposes. However, as indicated in chapter 7, social accounting matrices and analyses have primarily focused on monetary magnitudes, as we shall do from here on.[15]

Once columns are added for household groups in each region, it becomes necessary to add two columns, one for each of the two factors, in order to record the income received by each household group whereby the expenditures in its column can be realized.[16] Parenthetically, in moving from Table 8-4 to Table 8-5 we assumed (1) that each type of household had the same utility function, namely that of equation 8-3, although in

Table 8-5
Social accounting matrix

Column legend (top headers):

REGION A
- Production/Transport: 1 Textile, 2 Food, 3 Tr: A-B, 4 Tr: A-Z
- Factors: 5 Labor, 6 Capital, 7 Land
- Institutions: 8 Urban Hds, 9 Rural Hds, 10 Companies, 11 Government
- 12 Combined Capital

REGION B
- Production/Transport: 13 Textile, 14 Food, 15 Tr: B-A, 16 Tr: B-Z
- Factors: 17 Labor, 18 Capital, 19 Land

#	Account	1	2	3	4	5	6	7	8	9	10	11	12	13	14	15	16	17	18	19
	REGION A																			
1	Textile	0.11129												0.05514						
2	Food		0.03886																	
3	Tr: A-B																			
4	Tr: A-Z																			
5	Labor	0.82485	0.19432	0.00465	0.00040									0.41352	0.62279	0.00474	0.00041			
6	Capital	0.27495	0.19432	0.00430	0.00040									0.13784	0.62279	0.00312	0.00029			
7	Land																			
8	Urban Hds					0.20484	0.42657											0.31244	0.58449	
9	Rural Hds					0.81938	0.04740											0.72902	0.10315	
10	Companies								0.01137	0.0156										
11	Government																			
12	Combined Capital								0.06314	0.08668										
	REGION B																			
13	Textile								0.13107	0.17993		0.00633	0.03526		0.12768					
14	Food																			
15	Tr: B-A																			
16	Tr: B-Z								0.00292	0.00401		0.00014	0.00079							
17	Labor																			
18	Capital																			
19	Land																			
20	Urban Hds																			
21	Rural Hds																			
22	Companies																			
23	Government																		0.0764	
24	Combined Capital																			
	COUNTRY Z																			
25	Coal	0.00871													0.02082					
26	Tr: Z-A	0.00436													0.01041					
27	Tr: Z-B																			
28	Labor																			
29	Capital																			
30	Land																			
31	Urban Hds																			
32	Rural Hds																			
33	Companies																			
34	Government																			
35	Combined Capital																			
36	ROW																			
37	Total	1.22416	0.42750	0.00895	0.00080	1.02422	0.47397	0	0.63141	0.86678	0	0.02697	0.14982	0.60651	1.40450	0.00786	0.00070	1.04146	0.76404	0

Table 8-5 con't.

		REGION B (continued)					COUNTRY - Z												
		Institutions				Combined Capital	Production/Transport			Factors			Institutions				Combined Capital	ROW	Total
		Urban Hds	Rural Hds	Companies	Govern-ment		Coal	Tr: Z-A	Tr: Z-B	Labor	Capital	Land	Urban Hds	Rural Hds	Companies	Govern-ment			
		20	21	22	23	24	25	26	27	28	29	30	31	32	33	34	35	36	37
REGION A — Production/Transport	Textile 1	0.1633	0.15783		0.01449	0.00681							0.01921			0.00213			1.22416
	Food 2																		0.42749
	Tr: A-B 3	0.00427	0.00412		0.00038	0.00018													0.00895
	Tr: A-Z 4																		0.00080
REGION A — Factors	Labor 5																		1.02422
	Capital 6												0.00072			0.00008			0.47397
	Land 7																		0
REGION A — Institutions	Urban Hds 8																		0.63141
	Rural Hds 9																		0.86678
	Companies 10																		0
	Government 11																		0.02697
REGION A — Combined Capital	Combined Capital 12																		0.14982
REGION B — Production/Transport	Textile 13	0.26294	0.25413		0.02333	0.01096							0.01931			0.00215			0.60649
	Food 14	0.43053	0.41609		0.0382	0.01794													1.40450
	Tr: B-Z 15												0.00063			0.00007			0.00786
	Tr: B-Z 16																		0.00070
REGION B — Factors	Labor 17																		1.04146
	Capital 18																		0.76404
	Land 19																		0
REGION B — Institutions	Urban Hds 20																		0.89693
	Rural Hds 21																		0.83217
	Companies 22																		0
	Government 23																		0.07640
REGION B — Combined Capital	Combined Capital 24	0.03589																	0.03589
COUNTRY Z — Production/Transport	Coal 25																		0.02953
	Tr: Z-A 26																		0.00436
	Tr: Z-B 27																		0.01041
COUNTRY Z — Factors	Labor 28						0.00232	0.00034	0.00083										0.00349
	Capital 29						0.02721	0.00402	0.00958										0.04081
	Land 30																		0
COUNTRY Z — Institutions	Urban Hds 31									0.00314	0.03673								0.03987
	Rural Hds 32																		0
	Companies 33																		0
	Government 34									0.00035	0.00408								0.00443
COUNTRY Z — Combined Capital	Combined Capital 35																		0
	ROW 36																		0
	Total 37	0.89693	0.83217	0	0.07640	0.03589	0.02953	0.00436	0.01041	0.00349	0.04081	0	0.03987	0	0	0.00443	0	0	0

reality the utility functions would be different, and (2) that each shared its region's imports in proportion to its share of its region's income. These assumptions were made to facilitate the checking of magnitudes if the reader chooses to do so.[17]

Another basic extension in a core social accounting framework would involve the incorporation of the government sector.[18] This sector can produce commodities, such as postal services or services of railroads and diverse public utilities. In doing so, it would function much like a firm. It may confront a production function, purchase inputs for its operation, charge prices for its outputs and otherwise seek to maximize its profits, or minimize costs when a subsidy is provided from taxation or other revenue sources. When it does so, it can be treated much like any other production activity introduced into the model, whose level of operations would be derived from the operation of an AGIE model.

On the other hand, the government may function outside the market system to provide necessary services and goods to households and enterprises. In this type of functioning the government would need to make a decision on how much of each good and service to produce and distribute to consumers. Thus, where the level of these goods and services to be distributed to households in region A is represented by G^A, the typical household utility function becomes

$$U^A = ((C_1^A)^{0.5}(C_2^A)^{0.5}; G^A), \qquad (8\text{-}46)$$

G^A being an exogenous variable.

In its production, the government in A will typically need to enter the factor markets to purchase capital and labor inputs, namely L_g^A and K_g^A, which also are to be treated as exogenous variables. Thus, each of the balance equations for the respective factor markets will include an additional term. For example, the equation for the labor market in A will be

$$L_1^A + L_2^A + L_4^A + L_8^A + L_g^A = \bar{L}^A. \qquad (8\text{-}47)$$

In A there will be government expenditures H_g^A for factors and other goods. When no intermediate inputs and transport inputs are required we would have:

$$H_g^A = w^A L_g^A + r^A K_g^A \qquad (8\text{-}48)$$

These expenditures would need to be met by government revenues or income Y_g^A. If the government in A is not permitted to spend more than its income or to accumulate a surplus of funds, then we have an additional balance equation

$$Y_g^A - H_g^A = 0 \tag{8-49}$$

Revenues come from taxation. Typically, at least four sources are available: a tax (t_x) on production, a tax (t_c) on consumption, a tax (t_y) on factor earnings, and a tax (t_m) on tariff or imports. For example, if only the last three taxes are imposed in A, we would have

$$Y_g^A = t_c(C_1^A + C_2^A) + t_y(r^A K^A + w^A L^A) + t_m(M_2^{B \to A} + M_3^{Z \to A}) \tag{8-50}$$

The effective income equation of consumers in A would change to be

$$Y^A = w^A L^A + r^A K^A - Y_g^A \tag{8-51}$$

However, A's gross regional income (output) would be $Y^A + Y_g^A$. Also, the final goods price equations would change; for example, for commodity #1 in A we would have:

$$P_1^A = w_1^A \ell_1^A + r_1^A k_1^A + t_c \tag{8-52}$$

Thus, if for A only the income tax were to be endogenously determined, the above introduces five exogenous variables G^A, L_g^A, K_g^A, t_c, and t_m. There then exist for region A only three new endogenous variables, namely H_g^A, Y_g^A and the income tax rate t_y. These are matched by the three new equations (8-48, 8-49 and 8-50) to be added to arrive at a solution for the system if a government sector is introduced in region A only. (If government sectors are introduced in other regions, then similar new variables and equations come to exist for each.) In effect, the appropriate level t_y of the income tax in A insures revenues adequate to meet the expenditures of government programs designed to provide diverse services deemed essential for its constituents, the final consumers. Much more sophisticated treatments of the government sector have been developed in the dimensionless AGE literature. It is left for the regional science researcher to effect the modifications of these sophisticated treatments for the reality of a space economy.

To keep at a minimum the number of rows and columns in the scaffolding of a core social accounting matrix we have added, in going from Table 8-4 to Table 8-5, only one row and one column for the government sector in each region. Along the row the various sources of revenues of a government are recorded. Along the column, the various expenditures of a government are listed. In the case of region Z, we assume the government obtains its revenue from a 10% tax on factor (labor and capital) earnings so that the incomes of urban households in Z, as listed at the bottom of its column, is only 90% of total payments for labor and capital in Z, all these payments going to the urban households in say a mining town. [Note that country Z may be taken to have a rural household sector, but at the present time in most regions data on such a sector (in terms of equivalent money earnings and expenditures) are not available.[19]] In the case of region A, it is assumed that the government obtains its revenue from a personal (household) sales tax of 2 percent, imposed on the after-savings income of all households. To that extent, total household incomes available for expenditure are reduced. In the case of region B, it is posited that the government obtains its revenue from a 10% tax on the earnings of capital, no tax being levied on earnings from labor.

One more set of magnitudes to be entered into a core SAM framework are those on savings and investment. Savings might come from household income, unexpended revenue of government, undistributed profits of companies, foreign sources, etc. In a table for AGIE use there might be one row representing savings as a combined capital account or more than one row when specific types of savings need to be made explicit. Similarly, there could be one or more columns to represent investment. To illustrate these processes consider savings from household income only. Let there be an exogenously specified savings rate s (say 0.1 or 10 percent) of income. Then each of the consumption equations would change; for example for good #1 in A it would be

$$C_1^A = (1 - s)Y^A/2P_1^A \tag{8-53}$$

where total savings S^A in region A would be

$$S^A = sY^A \tag{8-54}$$

On the assumption that all savings would be absorbed by investment I^A in A when no credit is extended by banks, there would be the equation

$$I^A = S^A. \tag{8-55}$$

Finally, if the investment requires inputs of only labor and capital, namely L_I^A and K_I^A (assumed to be exogenously determined), there would be the equation

$$I^A = w^A L_I^A + r^A K_I^A. \tag{8-56}$$

Accordingly, the resource balance equations for A change; for example, for labor it becomes

$$L^A = L_1^A + L_2^A + L_G^A + L_I^A. \tag{8-57}$$

Thus we have three new exogenous variables, s, L_I^A, K_I^A, and two new endogenous variables, S^A and I^A, with the two additional equations 8-54 and 8-55 to determine them.

In a more realistic setting, we may have an interest rate (a price of savings) as another new variable to be involved in the determination of the level of savings by consumers, where also the interest rate is related to the level of profits (another new variable) of the companies engaged in production and investment whose inputs of labor and capital would be derived from maximization. Additional and extended equations related to conditions of maximization and market clearing would be involved.

Again, to keep the rows and column of Table 8-5 to a minimum we add to the blocks for regions *A* and *B* in Table 8-4 one row for savings (combined capital account) and one column for investment. In *A* we assume that before expending income on commodities and thus before incurring the consumption tax, all households save 10 percent of their money income and that this saving is available for investment. In *B*, we assume that only urban households save, and at the rate of 4 percent of their income. In nation *Z*, we assume that there is no saving and investment.

Once disposable income is obtained for each household group, we assume that the pattern of expenditure remains unchanged from that in Tables 8-3 and 8-4, only its size has been reduced from savings and/or taxation. To make it easy for the reader who desires to check out the figures in the SAM Table 8-5, we have assumed that government and investors expend their moneys over the same goods and in the same proportion as households. Hence the reader can easily work out the passage from an input-output table (whether in money or physical terms) to a SAM matrix.[20]

Finally in Table 8-5 we can easily introduce a second intermediate input, namely the use in each sector of its own product. We can do this without changing the price system and the reader-friendly production function that is assumed. To sectors 1 and 2 in both *A* and *B* we posit that this intermediate input can be represented by the constant production coefficient 0.1, that is amounts to 10 percent of each unit produced). Accordingly, output of each of these sectors is taken to expand by 10 percent. However, to keep prices unchanged, in effect to keep total demands and supplies at the commodity and factor markets the same, the capital, labor and coal input coefficients of sectors 1 and 2 in *A* and *B* are appropriately reduced, namely by dividing each by a factor of 1.1.[21]

8.3.3 Extensions and generalizations to a multi-region, multi-country world

We now have covered, admittedly in a highly simplified manner, the basic scaffolding of a SAM core of an AGIE model wherein countries (political regions) as well as regions within a country are considered. We now extend the SAM framework to cover many production sectors, many commodities, many resources, many consuming household groups, many governments and government programs, many investment sectors, many regions, and many countries. Doing so in equation form or in a single table such as Table 8-5 would consume much space, way beyond the space allotted to a chapter in a regional science text. Consequently, we can only mention and briefly discuss some of the procedures involved in effecting these extensions.

First, consider the inclusion of more production sectors, $j = 1,..., n$ and more commodities, $h = 1,..., h'$. Each sector might produce one or more of these commodities, and each commodity might be produced by more than one sector. The framework for handling this type of situation is already discussed in the input-output chapter, pp. 98–101. To avoid complication, we shall continue to assume that only one commodity is produced in any given sector and that pure competition among many producers prevails in each sector. Hence, in a table like Table 8-5 there would be added a column for each new sector containing inputs consistent with maximization of profits given the production technology of that sector. It would be done just as an additional column was added for each region A and B when we moved from the case of only one sector in each region (section 8.1) to the case where each region had two sectors (section 8.2). In effect, the extended framework could incorporate many if not all the sectors of an input-output structural matrix when consistent production coefficients can be taken to characterize production in each of the sectors incorporated.

Moreover, in any sector the use, as intermediate inputs, of the products of other sectors would be common, intermediate inputs being recognized in a manner similar to that in standard input-output analysis. These inputs would be treated just as coal, transport inputs and a sector's own product were in the previous section.

The existence of many new sectors to represent more adequately a realistic space economy would in turn require recognition of more than just two resources. Land as a resource would need to be introduced as well as mineral deposits and other items. Equally important, each of the broad categories of resources would need to be disaggregated — for example, labor by type, land by quality, and minerals by composition. Hence, there would be many more rows than two for resources. The extended set of resources would be denoted by $g = 1,..., g'$. Generally speaking, for each new resource, the stocks by region would need to be exogenously specified.

Another highly desirable extension would involve a much finer disaggregation of the household sector. Such would recognize for each region its several ethnic, economic, and other groups of families, each with different incomes, tastes and other characteristics. The utility functions of these groups might differ significantly as well as their stocks of resources, thus leading to different consumption patterns under maximization of utility. Each group and its pattern would be represented by a separate column. See the discussion in the previous chapter on how this might be done and incorporated into a framework for AGIE use.

Another major extension would involve the disaggregation of government. This sector might be split up into major subsectors (civilian and military); in turn each of these major subsectors can be extensively disaggregated. For most of the resulting categories, the disaggregation would relate to specific government programs, but in others to general activity such as the judicial. In most cases, a category's level and required inputs would need to be specified exogenously. In some cases, however, the output of a government program can be a commodity such as the postal service, and that program can be operated much like production of a firm. The investment sector can also be disaggregated in ways similar to that for the government and household sectors. Infrastructure investment by type (transportation, recreational, medical, etc.) may be distinguished from R and D investment, investment to preserve the environment, and normal industry investment in plant and equipment.

More regions can be added, each in a way that another region was added to the two nation modified Heckscher-Ohlin model, to yield a more comprehensive interregional/international framework. For example, see the study by Whalley and Trela (1989). The establishment of relevant delivered cost prices to determine relevant balance of payments among nations, and also regions, becomes more complex, and is a significant area for research by regional scientists. Also, the general concept of world prices for commodities would need to be dropped.

8.3.4 Extensions with a bottoms-up approach to AGIE models

As already noted, the previous discussion pertains primarily to a top-down approach in the development of a core interregional social accounting matrix appropriate for an AGIE. This reflects the fact that the construction of SAMs for individual countries has dominated past research activity in this field. But for many regional scientists including the authors, the most relevant approach to multi-region or more generally interregional analysis views the region as an active body in a multi-region system. It is subject to political and economic constraints imposed by an aggregate political unit — the nation. On the one hand, the region is not a replica of the national economy (or system). On the other, the magnitudes of the several relevant regions of a country (such as regions A and B in country Q) must add up to the national totals — totals that serve as constraints. Or, in the more general case which recognizes feedbacks from the regions that alter the constraints imposed by the nation, there must be consistency in that regional totals must add up to the changed national magnitudes (for example on employment).

With this perspective a scholar might design a new set of categories to handle transactions with units beyond a region's boundaries. This set would still keep explicit as a category each region such as A, B, C, ... However, when certain kinds of transactions are to be considered, it might often be necessary to introduce as meaningful units groups of regions (such as the first tier of regions surrounding each region, or each region's census region). For example, a scholar studying an urban region fully contained within a state would need to consider the state as an active unit for taxation purposes. This is so even though the scholar is primarily concerned with the interactions of that urban region's economy with the economies of other urban regions. Moreover, that urban region, as well as every other kind of region (for example the state itself), must also consider the nation as an aggregate unit (that affects say housing policy), and perhaps also an aggregate comprising a unit often designated the Rest of the Nation when concerned with the export market. Even more, the Rest of the World that is beyond the confines of a region's nation must be considered when again one is concerned with a region's export market. However, that Rest of the World might need to be disaggregated into meaningful categories (such as the European market, the Latin American market and the Asian market; this disaggregation can be extremely relevant for example when studying a Western U.S. region's export transactions). Even further, when foreign exchange transactions and thus the interest rate become key elements in a region's situation, it is not the Rest of the World, but the entire World which might be the relevant category. It should be noted that Rounds (1988, 1995) has taken a significant step in this direction with his notion of *supranational* units.

In short, the type of hand-me-down procedures for constructing regional SAMs coming from past SAM studies (biased by the perspective of national-oriented economists) may not be the most appropriate for AIGE models. Rather, the regional and interregional SAMs designed to serve as cores of AGIE models, must at the start be based upon an appropriate structure of active behaving units. It could be an hierarchical (nested) one, regular or irregular and overlapping — one that would replace the simple Rest of the Nation (regions *B*, *C*, ...) and Rest of the World categories noted in Figure 7.1. Admittedly, practical considerations stemming from data inadequacies and limited research resources may preclude the use of a framework that is ideal for constructing a SAM for an AGIE study. But it does not follow that the less-than-ideal structure of the SAM should be a standard one such as indicated in Figure 7.1. The required reduction in the scope of the SAM might be better achieved by eliminating and/or aggregating input-output and household categories than by reducing the number of categories of spatial and regional units of different orders and size. Or perhaps a reduction in both directions might be best.

8.3.5 The exploration of a Financial SAM and its fusion with a Real SAM

In recent years much exploration has been conducted at the national level on developing a *Financial SAM*. At times, the objective is to fuse in an AGE model such a SAM covering financial accounts with a type of SAM we have been discussing. The latter type has been designated a *Real SAM* since its monetary magnitudes are based on physical magnitudes and relative prices, and not on physical magnitudes and nominal prices. (For example, see Thorbecke, 1992, ch. 4; Lewis, 1994; and Azis, 1996.) One typical set of financial accounts and items covered are recorded in Figure 8.2. To fuse these accounts with those in a Real SAM, additional equations are required as well as the disaggregation of (1) each combined capital account in the rows of Table 8-5 by sources of savings, and (2) each combined capital account column by type of investment. For example, following Fargeix and Sadoulet (1994), consider one possible set of equations that can be employed to determine for a nation interest rates charged to loans and paid to depositors. (To simplify, we assume these rates to be approximately the same.) The basic equation relates the demand for (BD) and supply of loanable funds. It is given by

$$BD = \sum_h TD + DD - RR + AS_b \qquad (8\text{-}58)$$

where, for given year *t*,

Firms

Assets	*Liabilities*
Currency	Domestic borrowing
Demand deposits	Foreign borrowing
Stocks	Accumulated savings
Capital stock	Equity

Households

Assets	*Liabilities*
Currency	Accumulated savings
Demand deposits	(i.e., wealth)
Time deposits	
Foreign currency	
Equity	

Central Bank

Assets	*Liabilities*
Central Bank credit	Currency
to government	Required reserves
Foreign currency reserves	Accumulated savings
Direct credit to private sector	

Commercial Banks

Assets	*Liabilities*
Subsidized loans	Demand deposits
Unsubsidized loans	Time deposits
Required reserves	Accumulated savings

Government

Assets	*Liabilities*
Equity held	Central Bank credit
Capital stock	to government
Other stock	Domestic borrowing
	Foreign borrowing
	Accumulated savings

Rest of the World

Assets	*Liabilities*
Foreign loans	Foreign currency
	Accumulated savings

Figure 8.2   Balance sheet for a Financial SAM

$\sum_h TD$ = the total of time deposits supplied by households

DD = demand deposits (of households, firms, governments and ROW)

RR = required reserves of commercial banks

AS_b = the accumulated savings (undistributed profits) of banks.

In turn, AS_b is given by

$$AS_b = AS_b^{t-1} + S_b \tag{8-59}$$

namely, the accumulated savings of the previous time period $(t-1)$ plus savings S_b from operations during the current year. S_b is then given by

$$S_b = (1 - \tau_b - dr_b)Y_b \tag{8-60}$$

where

Y_b = income of banks

τ_b = tax rate on income of banks

dr_b = the fraction of income that is distributed

Income of banks Y_b is given by

$$Y_b = r^{t-1}(\sum_{i,g} BD^{t-1}) - r^{t-1}(\sum TD_h^{t-1}) \tag{8-61}$$

where

r^{t-1} = the nominal interest rate set by commercial banks in the previous time period $t-1$

$\sum_{i,g} BD^{t-1}$ = outstanding domestic loans to firms $(i = 1,2...)$ and government $(g = 1,2,...)$ at $t-1$

$\sum_h TD_h^{t-1}$ = outstanding time deposits of households at $t-1$

All these variables come to affect and be affected by the numerous other variables in the real and financial systems as well as by changes in the exogenous (policy) magnitudes.

In addition to determining the interest rate set by a region's commercial banks, the financial accounts can be used to determine other variables that may be considered relevant, for example the interest rate a Central Bank charges on loans to commercial banks; and many of the equations in the Real SAM can be considered for revision to capture the effect of changes in relevant financial accounts.

It is to be noted that the recent exploration with the construction and use of a Financial SAM has not led to widespread acceptance of this analytical construct and to the formation of a standard classification of and tabular framework for the accounts covered. However, see Azis (1996) for one interesting and useful classification for fusing a *national* Financial SAM with a *national* Real SAM.

Moreover, the framework of a national Financial SAM is inappropriate for interregional analysis. Compared to the current inadequacies of much of *national* social accounting for use in *interregional analysis,* the inadequacies of current national Financial SAM frameworks for use in interregional analysis are much more serious. A more satisfactory framework (perhaps too disaggregated) for interregional analysis is suggested in the 1960 Methods book in the table on *An Interregional Flow of Funds Matrix* and in the background discussion relating to financial flows (Isard et al., pp. 100–115, 144–173 and 610–621).[22]

A number of serious problems have arisen in constructing a national Financial SAM to be fused with a Real SAM. One arises from the fact that such a Financial SAM has been basically expressed in terms of *stocks at a point in time*, whereas the Real SAM pertains to flows over a time period, usually a year. Thus a fusion of a Financial SAM and a Real SAM requires the estimation of financial flows to connect up with real flows. To do this in this approach, one needs to estimate stocks at two successive time-points (for example, of current assets of commercial banks), the difference being a financial flow (savings). Thus more data are required and furthermore the data on stocks (wealth of households and assets and liabilities of institutions) are often very scarce. (See the commendable attack by Thorbecke et al., 1992, ch. 4 on this problem.)

However, additional difficulties arise from the introduction of a much more extensive set of intangible factors such as expectations and speculation. As we have already mentioned in simulating the impact of any exogenous change on a nominal basis and even a real one, the models on foreign exchange rates and the parameters that are used are only adequate for the situations covered in the sample time period employed for estimating the parameters. When one considers a new situation, as generated by an exogenous change, the prediction of such a model is found to be no better than a random walk. The same can be said for interest rates and generally speaking for all phenomena affected by the random gyrations of currency, stock and other financial markets. As a consequence, there remains considerable skepticism about the possibility of effectively fusing Financial and Real SAMs in applied research. See Mercenier and Srinivasan, 1994, pp. 5–7; and Lora, 1994.

It should be noted, however, that while in the judgment of the authors much more research is required before an applicable AGIE model can be constructed, the problem in integrating appropriate Financial and Real SAMS for an interregional system confined to a single country is less formidable than for a multi-nation system. First, the play of the foreign exchange rate is typically of lesser importance than in multi-country studies, and likewise for the interest rate. Further, the role of transport inputs and transport cost based on real meaningful space and other types of available data on regions is generally useful in adding anchorage to a model of the real world.

8.4 Problems and questionable character of the basic assumptions of standard applied general equilibrium models

We have now presented a simplified social accounting framework for an applied general interregional equilibrium model. We have set down the equations and a consistent set of hypothetical data for that model and discussed how that framework and model can be conceptually extended to embrace a many region structure in physical space. In each region there can be many commodities, many consumers, many production sectors with many firms in each, many traders, a number of governments and other institutions, savings and investments of many types, and many markets at which demand for and supply of each of the many resources, commodities and money itself (in the form of more than one currency) determine the many prices. We have also considered some extensions that are necessitated for a bottoms-up approach rather than a top-down one, and seriously questioned whether the top-down is appropriate. Nonetheless, there are advantages, at least until appropriate procedures for a bottoms-up approach are developed, in pursuing a top-down approach. This is so since a top-down approach begins with a country's structure and procedures for modeling which may have already been extensively researched. However, the models of a country's structure have been predicated upon many strong and questionable assumptions. We now examine these assumptions in order to be better aware of the relevance and applicability of the country type of framework and model for regional and interregional study.

8.4.1 Problems in representing the consumption subsystem

Underlying the conceived consumption system is the tenet that each consumer is motivated to maximize his/her utility, satisfaction or some equivalent notion. For an economist seeking quantitative measures of the desirability of policies within a market system, the relevant magnitudes are quantities of commodities and other elements when measurable and theoretically treatable. There are many ways in which utility for a behaving unit (a representative individual, or set of individuals, or household group in a given region) can be defined and has been. A most general way is:

$$U = U(C_1, C_2, C_3,...; Z_k) \tag{8-62}$$

where Z_k represents quantitatively measurable characteristics of the given behaving unit. This general function, over many commodities and characteristics, is beyond specification, and stands in extreme contrast to the highly operational Cobb-Douglas function employed in the previous sections, namely

$$U = (C_1)^{\alpha_1}(C_2)^{\alpha_2} \qquad\qquad \Sigma\alpha_i = 1; i = 1,2 \tag{8-63}$$

and where specifically $\alpha_1 = \alpha_2 = 0.5$. The widespread use of a Cobb-Douglas stems from the fact that it is conveniently embodied in and treated by an elaborate nonlinear model wherein commodity prices are allowed to vary. When this function covers two or more commodities, maximization of utility under budget constraint yields constant expenditure shares $\frac{\alpha_i Y}{P_i}$ with variation in income where $\Sigma\alpha_i = 1$, $i = 1, 2, 3, ...$[23] However, the resulting consumption pattern violates reality. Engle-type and many other consumption studies suggest other effects. For example, with increase in household income, they find positive but decreasing consumption of normal goods, positive and increasing consumption of luxury goods, and declining consumption of inferior goods.

Another widely used consumption framework, namely that of the unadjusted Leontief input-output model, directly assumes, as noted in Chapter 3, that per dollar of income, no matter what the level of income, the cents' worth of household expenditure on any commodity is constant — similar to the constant shares expenditure framework of the above Cobb-Douglas once equilibrium prices are given. An improvement on the Cobb-Douglas and Leontief frameworks is the Linear Expenditure System (LES). It derives from the Stone-Geary utility function where under utility maximization a household first spends its income on minimum subsistence goods, and then the remainder in fixed proportions on the commodities once subsistence is ensured. Hence we have

$$U = (C_1 - S_1)^{\alpha_1}(C_2 - S_2)^{\alpha_2}(C_3 - S_3)^{\alpha_3}, ...\Sigma\alpha_i = 1; i = 1, 2, 3, ... \tag{8-64}$$

where S_i ($i = 1, 2, 3, ...$) is the amount of good i required for the subsistence of the behaving unit (that is of the individual, or individuals contained in the behaving unit).[24]

Another type of consumption function which does allow, under budget constraint, substitution among commodities, is the constant elasticity of substitution (CES) function. The mathematical statement of the function is rather complicated but it yields the fairly simple outcome, namely that for each commodity i, the elasticity σ of the substitution in preferences between any pair of goods i,j is such that $\Sigma\alpha_i^{1/\sigma} = 1$. However, the use of the same elasticity σ of substitution regardless of the commodity j is another result which substantially violates reality as we know it. This CES notion can be also combined with the LES function to yield a utility level above survival when $(C_i - S_i)$ replaces C_i in the customary general utility function.

To facilitate calibration, that is the estimate of parameters for an applied model from existing data (often limited), a hierarchical (or nested) set of functions has been employed. The procedure is to construct at the top level of a hierarchy two or a few main (aggregate) categories of commodities, say normal (non-luxury goods) and luxuries, as in Figure 8.3, with an estimation of an appropriate elasticity σ_a of substitution between the categories. At the next (a lower) level, non-luxuries might be disaggregated into food and housing with another appropriately estimated elasticity σ_b. At a still lower level, food might be disaggregated into another set of commodities, again with still another appropriately estimated σ_c elasticity of substitution between them. Obviously, a more extensive and elaborate hierarchical structure might be employed.

There are a number of other procedures for deriving (estimating) consumption magnitudes such as the AIDS (Almost Ideal Demand System), GAIDS (Generalized Almost Ideal Demand System) which combine the LES and AIDS models, and so on. Clearly, from the standpoint of regional and interregional work, especially interregional, there is considerable advantage to retaining a Leontief structure when Engle-type findings are not available and when an interregional input-output table is available, even when such a table needs to be redeveloped for a less disaggregated set of household groups. Also when subsistence inputs are obtainable, this set of inputs augmented by an LES set of coefficients can replace the Leontief consumption coefficients.

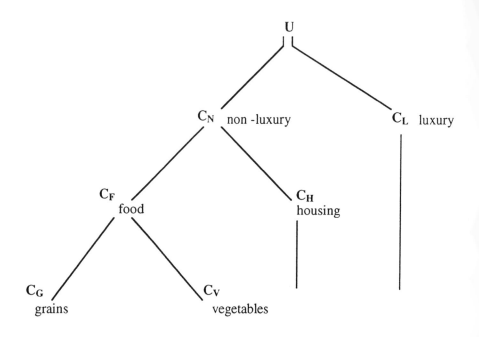

Figure 8.3   A CES hierarchy re: consumer demands

8.4.2 Questionable character of the production subsystem

With regard to the production subsystem, major problems need to be addressed for the construction of an AGIE model. Cobb-Douglas constant share production functions, such as 8-5 and 8-6, are widely employed in AGE studies. But clearly the fixed coefficients of labor and capital, which the use of such a function is often designed to yield for a set of factor prices endogenously determined, is not particularly helpful for considering realistic situations where substitution between these two basic primary factors occurs. Moreover, the use of Leontief-type constant coefficients for intermediate inputs that often accompanies the use of a Cobb-Douglas constant share function (as is done in the previous sections of this chapter), and which thus leads to constant unit cost of production, is also of questionable value in a general model. The employment of a CES production function which many analysts consider more desirable, also has its limitations. This is so even when one employs nesting operations like that depicted in Figure 8.3 to capture more substitutability among inputs in a mathematically tractable manner — for example: (1) between manufacturing and energy production, then between oil production and coal production as components of energy production, and so on; or (2) between a Value Added aggregate as a production element and intermediate goods as a second aggregate, and then on the one hand between capital and labor that comprise the Value Added aggregate and on the other hand an input-output breakdown of the intermediate aggregate by commodity input. Other production functions such as the generalized Leontief, the transcendental logarithmic, the generalized Cobb-Douglas, the generalized square root quadratic, etc. have their advantages but at the same time specific limitations, often failing to reflect market imperfections to be discussed below.

While at this time, one cannot state that there exists a satisfactory solution to the problem of representing adequately the production subsystem, the best approach may turn out to be the simultaneous employment of several different production functions for a regional economy, each function representing a set of a few basic activities. For example, one such set might comprise each of a number of oil refining and petrochemical production activities. As already indicated on p. 227, a careful survey and study of these activities found that based on the experiences of petrochemical and other chemical construction and operating companies, major economies of scale in the employment of both labor and capital could be reliably projected using the respective formulae

$$L = L_{ex}(O/O_{ex})^{0.22} \tag{8-65}$$

and

$$K = K_{ex}(O/O_{ex})^{0.7} \tag{8-66}$$

where L and K are labor and capital requirements, respectively, for a new plant with planned output O and where K_{ex}, L_{ex} and O_{ex} are magnitudes for an existing efficient plant.[25]

Other sets of activities, for example in steel and steel fabrication, or in food product manufacturing may also be found to be reliably projected by other formulae. In this way, a model might attain greater applicability.

8.4.3 Problems regarding scale economies in the transport and production
   subsystems, externalities, and market imperfections

Economies of scale and increasing returns to production are ruled out by classical general equilibrium theory which generally requires convexity of production functions, let alone absence of externalities, for the existence of an equilibrium. Such economies and returns, however, are omnipresent in the transport subsystem and elsewhere. In fact, in modern life, economies of scale has practically always characterized and dominated transport systems, a result of the large fixed investments that are required. Hence, even when transport inputs and costs have been introduced into AGE models, let alone recognized and properly estimated, they have not been adequately incorporated. And of course, the constant cost function for the production of transport inputs employed in the discussion of the above sections in this chapter is indeed most inappropriate, it being introduced solely for explicit recognition of the reality of space and the distance variable. However, given that extensive data are available on transport activities, a more reliable transport services production function by each mode ought to be developed to replace the constant cost one.

Additionally, the use of a constant elasticity of transformation function (CET) for the allocation of production of a tradable commodity to export markets on the one hand and to the domestic on the other has serious shortcomings. It fails to reflect adequately the interplay of delivered cost pricing and market imperfections at the different levels and circumstances under which a system functions and often embodies the shortcomings in the use of a single world price instead of a set of delivered cost prices.

There have been attempts in AGE modeling to handle increasing returns to scale in production in general and treat diverse imperfections in the market when conditions of oligopoly and monopoly prevail. The use of markups to bring convexity into production functions (see Gunning and Keyzer, 1995), or the use of tariffs on imports, export subsidies, or a combination of them (see deMelo and Roland-Holst, 1994) leave much to be desired. So also does the assumption of monopolistic competition (see Krugman, 1993 and Bröcker, 1994) where in a free entry system: (1) each of a large group of producers puts out a differentiated product and is assumed to ignore the income effect of his/her choices on his/her perceived product demand and (2) the utility to the consumer of each product brand is independent of utility derived from consumption of other brands, his/her utility being a simple aggregate of utilities.

Also, there arises a technical question of whether the introduction of a device to handle one or more market imperfections leaves untouched the independence of the choice of a numeraire and thus the framework of relative prices (see Ginsburgh, 1994).

Then, when oligopoly and monopoly are permitted in 'imperfect' AGE models by various presumptions, there is the serious question regarding the nature of the behavior of oligopolies and monopolies, their interaction and games they play, and externalities in general. The results of such models can be highly sensitive to the different assumptions about the situational environment in which the behavior and interaction occurs.

8.4.4 Questionable character of intertemporal analysis

Since AGE models are frequently employed to study the impact of alternative government policies or a possible change in policy, they typically need to be forward-looking and to have a dynamic aspect. Even a do-nothing policy requires recognition of on-going changes in economic structure and thus magnitudes of relevance. Included in such recognition would be the existing and likely changes in expectations of agents as they reach decisions on consumption, savings and investments. Typically, when parameters of savings, investment and other functions are estimated, they are oriented to current and past data and experience. They rarely, if ever, are, or can be, based on the future. Yet the desire and need to project the impact of changes and to project the future is central to the use of models, as we well know in regional science.

In previous chapters we have seen how comparative cost, input-output, econometric, gravity, programming, industrial complex and SAM-based studies have each conducted impact analysis to throw light upon the future, and have confronted similar problems. But these models have been much less complex than AGE ones and have involved fewer variables; and research associated with their use typically has needed to be less bold than that with AGE. They have also not been required to make, implicitly or explicitly, as many assumptions about expectations of behaving units. In some AGE models expectations are assumed to be consistent with the model's projections, when expectations are excluded as an endogenous variable. These models imply that each of the many behaving units possess an unrestricted information set in making their intertemporal decisions — that is 'take into account the complete sequence of signals they expect to face in the future, and that the expectations they form on endogenous variables will be self-fulfilling for a given exogenous environment'

(Mercenier and Srinivasan, 1994, p. 10). Other models, in contrast, pay little or no attention to forward-looking expectations. Some pursue policy impact analysis positing that current period outcomes (for example, on prices, profits, sales) fully govern future decisions on investment and other activities.

Still others posit imperfect foresight of agents with restricted information sets which then lead to a sequence of temporary (static) equilibria (see Benjamin, 1994, Shoven and Whalley, 1992). Problems then arise regarding the choice of a numeraire, calibration of the base period and the several temporary equilibria (if they can be considered to be equilibria), and so forth. But which of the many possible sets of assumptions on forward-looking expectations can be taken to characterize the hypothesized present and derived temporary equilibria? In any case, the recognition and use of forward-looking expectations, it must be admitted, leads to fragile projections which become even more fragile when technological advance in the real world and the uncertainty with respect to it and many other to-be-realized phenomena and behavior are considered.

8.4.5 Problems of capturing behavior of governments, the Rest of the World and feedback sequences

One of the major actors in the typical AGE study is the Government. Its behavior, however, is not as well captured as that of economic sectors. For example, the government, national, regional or state, may take an action, say to reduce its expenditures as a result of insufficient income from taxation. Its plan, perhaps based on a preliminary AGE study, may have in mind reductions in each of a set of programs and activities. Some of these programs involve infrastructure investments, such as education and construction of transportation facilities, whose benefits accrue over a fairly long period of time; the identification of these is currently beyond AGE capability. The evaluation of government plans involving such programs cannot be made with two-period counterfactual studies. Equally, and perhaps more important, whatever the plan, the government at least in a democratic or semi-democratic society involves negotiations and gaming among political actors and interest groups. The realized set of outcomes at the political market place is different from what might be the initial plan or expectation. On both these accounts, the behavior of government as a long-run investor and as an arena for the play of competitors seeking power and political influence, needs to be extensively researched.

An equally important need is research on feedbacks. While AGE models clearly distinguish between endogenous and exogenous sectors and take a policy or other exogenous event or action as given, *consistency with a general equilibrium philosophy* requires feedback of the endogenous world upon the exogenous and the subsequent rounds of action and reaction of both worlds. This is particularly important when both the exogenous sector ROW (Rest of the World) is considered and government is taken as an exogenous sector.[26] And it will be true for the RON (Rest of the Nation) when such a sector is introduced into an AGIE model and certainly whenever a Financial SAM is added.

Thus we must conclude that presently there remain serious questions about the relevance of any policy recommendations that may be put forth from the findings of AGE models although valuable insights about the coplay of factors may be obtained by the policy modellers themselves.

8.4.6 Non-economic factors and other structural shortcomings

It is maintained by the structuralist school of AGE modellers that the functioning of the real world is not that of the neoclassical economist, and this contention may be extended to cover many regional scientists and spatial equilibrium theorists, even when their findings are qualified to take into account non-economic and other factors. The structuralists claim that some of the real-world elements are so significant that they must be explicitly considered at the very start.

According to Taylor (1983), a leading exponent of this school, there are five key features of a structuralist's approach. First, given the available data and resources for data collection, they identify, as in a thorough SAM study, the relevant set of households and institutions in terms of income flows and possession of wealth. Among household groups there would be:

rentiers who receive distributed profits, interest, and other financial incomes, suffer capital losses and gains on their (often considerable) assets, and save more than they invest; workers who get income from wages nominally fixed in the short run, don't save very much, and battle with firms about how wage increases will respond to unemployment and price inflation; agriculturalists whose savings rates are often high but whose income fluctuates sharply, following flexible price movements; and urban and rural 'marginals' who pick up residual income flows, suffer from deprivation of basic needs, and save at low, often negative rates. The state in its fiscal, public investment, and central banking roles, the commercial banks, and foreigners also enter as partially independent and powerful actors. The degrees of freedom available to any actor depend on the institutions and history of the economy at hand incorporating them in convincing fashion is part of the model-building art (p. 4).

Second, structuralists eschew models in real terms with only relative prices. Rather they stick to the actuality of nominal prices and income in money terms. Third, they recognize that different prices are under varying degrees of control by distinct groups in the economy. For example, firms apply a fixed mark-up or rate to variable production costs, often reflecting an oligopolistic or monopolistic position in an industry. Unions and companies negotiate over wages. And so forth. In many markets the neoclassical pure competition is a myth.

Fourth, there needs to be considered in a situation to be modelled the amount of economic rationality and price-mediated substitution to be incorporated, whether one considers consumption behavior of households, production behavior of firms, trading behavior of brokers and asset holders, and so forth. Price responsiveness and optimizing behavior may need to be replaced by rules of thumb and other practices.

Fifth, and perhaps most important to the structuralist approach, is the need to capture in a model the key causal linkages. As Taylor (1983) notes:

> There are many ways in which the economy can adjust when it is perturbed — output levels or the income distribution across classes may change, interest rates may vary, positions of wealth may expand or erode. A model builder has to select *which* of these adjustment mechanisms to build into his or her equations — the qualitative nature of the solutions will depend upon the choice. In the jargon, a model's 'closure' has to be chosen and justified on the basis of empirical and institutional analysis of the economy at hand. Setting closure is impossible unless class structures and economic power relationships have already been defined. Searching for sites of power and macro causal links is the key to the structuralist approach (pp. 6–7).

In short, a structuralist would not begin with a neoclassical approach as we have done in this chapter, and then reevaluate behavior and other processes after a first framework is constructed or qualify a first set of results. He/she would start off with key imperfections of the market, e.g. an exogenous mark-up policy of firms, or key firms optimizing on market share, or an institutional rule of thumb governing investment behavior, or a cultural practice in household consumption, and so forth. Then with the embodiment of such elements firmly incorporated bring into play, as of secondary importance, estimation and use of elasticities and substitution operations in the several submarkets.

While the structuralist's position cannot be ignored and must be given considerable weight, the exact approach to be employed, whether neoclassical, structuralist or hybrid, is the decision of a researcher. In this chapter we have chosen the neoclassical approach primarily for ease of exposition and to point up the potential of this approach without claiming that it is the best in general.

8.5 Some seminal contributions by regional scientists to the development of an applied general interregional (AGIE) model for a pure space economy

From the previous discussion, it should not be inferred that regional scientists have not been involved in significant thinking on an applied general interregional equilibrium model. They have and have made seminal contributions. A first one to note is that of Bröcker (1995) in his conceptual article on spatial CGE modeling of a Chamberlinean type. He attempts to develop a multiregional, multisectoral computable general equilibrium model by bringing together different strands of theoretical reasoning — input-output analysis, gravity modeling, the theory of intraindustry trade and the theory of general equilibrium under conditions of monopolistic competition. However, as most others who conduct a regional or multiregional (interregional) study, he employs the questionable CES functions to define composite goods as inputs or products that households consume and uses other standard aspects of AGE models. His exploitation of the use of a monopolistic competition framework to recognize diversity (different brands) of a commodity, thus introducing an element of market imperfection into the model, is a significant step in the right direction. But clearly regional science research must come to build upon this step, to treat more generally scale economies which is such a major factor governing the behavior of firms, particularly transport ones. To mention a second forward step, among other commendable ones, he proposes to use, in calibration when relevant data are lacking, a doubly constrained gravity model to estimate an effective distance function.

However, he employs a Samuelson device for treating the transport factor by assuming a certain percentage of every transported commodity to be used up during transportation. He thus avoids the complexity that would be involved were the production of transport inputs directly to use resources as inputs. This Samuelson device is unacceptable. As stated at the beginning of this chapter, the production of transportation services as a resource-using activity, whether to provide intermediate inputs or furnish final consumption goods, must be introduced at the very start in treating a regional or interregional space economy.

With regard to empirical implementation, another bold attempt at an interregional AGE is that of Jones and Whalley (1989) and Walley and Trela (1989). They attempt to trace the impact of diverse governmental policies upon the six basic Canadian regions functioning as an interregionally interactive economy.

In this research, they do embody a transportation industry, they do set up transport margins (fixed transport input coefficients) for shipping a unit of good between each pair of regions, they do attempt to capture scale economies on an industry basis (but fail to embody major scale economies that each company in the highly oligopolistic transport industry does experience), and in other ways provide a rich set of ideas for the development of an applicable interregional space economy that remains to be constructed by regional scientists. However, they do use questionable CES production functions and other relationships inherited from dimensionless international trade studies. And in particular when it comes to labor migration, they set up a very strange model, starting with f.o.b. prices on goods that are the same in the six regions and ending up with an extremely odd set of utility functions while failing to exploit the many fertile ideas covered in interregional migration studies. While clearly the authors' work represents the best that could have been done to answer the pressing political questions that motivated their research, and does make very important contributions, in no way can their model be claimed to provide findings that capture or approximate the real operations of the Canadian interregional system as a space economy.

One study that presents an excellent coverage of transport costs, spatial equilibrium pricing and the role of transportation in a space economy is that of Elbers (1992). Unfortunately, his model was oriented to the task of developing an applied model for the small economy of Nepal, one for which there was a dearth of data. As a consequence he developed a useful *network general equilibrium model* wherein trade pools play a major role. [Within a given trade pool, trade flows between one region (country) and a central node, say a national (world) market, is taken to be independent of other regions' (countries') trade.] The introduction of the trade pool concept (which considerably lessens data requirements and computational needs) to be combined with standard spatial equilibrium analysis resulted, however, in a highly complicated model, albeit useful for a unique situation such as Nepal's, but not generally applicable as a framework for general use in interregional analysis.

Among other numerous studies that represent one or more forward steps for the development of a useful applied general interregional model are those of Ando and Shibata (1997), and Ando (1996). These authors ambitiously attempt to construct a multiregion AGE model for China. They recognize from the start the significance of transportation for the development of the several regions and the role of transport costs in determining prices in these regions. Employing a doubly constrained gravity model based on time distances, they estimate regional exports and imports against a background of existing and implied regional imbalances. With national production coefficients serving as regional coefficients, they then go on to determine net final demand, value added and other magnitudes typically computed in an AGE model. While their efforts are plagued by serious deficiencies in regional data, they nonetheless conduct important exploratory work on unearthing the play of space within huge areas composed of highly diverse regions.

Another initially valuable work is that by Harrigan and McGregor (1988, 1989) employing the Malaysian two-region SAM. They carefully construct a standard AGE model for East Malaysia, West Malaysia and the Rest of the World (ROW). They are motivated to demonstrate how different macroeconomic visions of regional systems may be captured and yield different findings. They interestingly do so utilizing a model which may be viewed as a beginning at an applied general interregional equilibrium model — a model which because of the sophisticated way in which it is constructed and its results interpreted has much of value for those who wish to design interregional models, especially with respect to migration phenomena. However, since the production and demand in the third region (ROW) is taken as exogenous, only the two Malaysian regions are involved in basic interactions and feedback. Further, while they do not introduce transport costs into the model, they state that transport margins (presumably consistent ones) can be easily introduced in their essentially two-region system. This indeed is the case, but such margins would not capture the variation from interaction and feedback within a system of more than two regions, nor reflect major scale economies in transportation which must be incorporated in a truly spatial AGIE.

An insightful examination of the potentials for interregional AGE, but one which again is largely influenced by standard dimensionless studies, is that of Spencer (1988). However, it is one that does recognize the importance of transport costs.

One more insightful and extremely useful study is that of Kilkenney (1995) who develops a rural-urban AGE using a bi-regional SAM, but one which 'due to the nature of the regional delineation ... accounts for market segmentation but not distance' (p. 165). Skillfully employing questionable CES and CET functions in nested structures and other standard AGE concepts and carefully constructing an appropriate bi-region SAM, she paves the way for advanced rural-urban analysis of a more general nature and able to cover more than two interacting regional markets. The structure of her analysis is such that distance and transport costs can be explicitly introduced and can come to impact interregional trade and prices.

Among still other valuable studies, which space limitations preclude discussing, are Harris (1984), Harrison, Rutherford and Wooton (1995), Li and Rose (1995), Peter, Han, Meagher and Naqvi (1996),[27] Haddad (1998)[28] and ongoing research at the University of Strathclyde.

8.6 Concluding remarks

Applied general equilibrium analysis is a relatively new approach in economics and regional science which has only become available as a result of the recent computer revolution. There thus remain many important questions to attack in this approach. And this is especially so in its use for problems addressed in regional science since, to reiterate, this approach has been developed by policy-oriented economists who for the most part have dwelt in a world of no dimensions. For interregional study, insufficient general advances have been made by them and by regional scientists who have followed in their path.

Accordingly, in this chapter we have not been able to present a demonstration of an effective AGIE study that has general applicability in terms of the basic relationships covered and usefulness of findings. A number of seminal contributions that are of great value as steps for the attainment of such a demonstration have been made by regional scientists and others (only some of whom have been mentioned in the previous section because of space limitations); and these scholars are to be applauded. Because of these valuable steps that have been taken, that demonstration should be forthcoming in the near future.

The promise of an effective AGIE model is, to repeat, a much more comprehensive coverage of forces interacting within a space economy. We have indicated how an AGIE can effectively attack the location problem, embrace input-output, industrial complex and social accounting (SAM) analyses, extend the realm of optimization and scope of programming analysis by capturing the process of price formation at the market, and embody spatial equilibrium pricing when distance, transport costs and transport inputs are effectively incorporated at the start. Yet at the same time on a number of occasions, a comprehensive AGIE model may not be the best approach in regional and interregional studies given limited availability of research resources and relevant data. A less comprehensive AGIE involving the synthesis of a smaller combination of regional science methods discussed in previous chapters with perhaps an intensive use of one or more methods may constitute a more fruitful way to attack a problem. Or a non-general equilibrium framework involving another synthesis of methods may be more useful. In chapter 10, we examine the possibilities of such syntheses.

Appendix 8.1 The basic functions, exogenous magnitudes, variables and equations of the two nation/three region model

Basic functions

1. $X_1 = K_1^{0.25} L_1^{0.75}$ technology in producing commodity #1 in both A and B

2. $X_2 = K_2^{0.5} L_2^{0.5}$ technology in producing commodity #2 in both A and B

3. $U = C_1^{0.5} C_2^{0.5}$ utility in consumption, the same for all household groups

4. Constant input-output coefficient functions for producing commodity #3 and each type of transport service (transport input).

Exogenous magnitudes

1. $\bar{K}^A = 0.8$ $\bar{K}^B = 1.6$ $\bar{K}^Z = 0.009$ (capital stocks)

2. $\bar{L}^A = 2.0$ $\bar{L}^B = 1.8$ $\bar{L}^Z = 0.012$ (labor endowments)

3. weight of a unit of each commodity = 20 lbs

4. distances $A{\to}B, B{\to}A, Z{\to}A, Z{\to}B, A{\to}Z, B{\to}Z = 100$ miles

5. $\alpha_{41}, \alpha_{52}, \alpha_{63}, \alpha_{73}, \alpha_{81}, \alpha_{92} = 1$ ton mile

6. $k_4^A, k_5^B = 0.02$; $k_6^Z, k_7^Z = 0.015$; $k_8^A, k_9^B = 0.03$ (unit capital requirements in transport activities)

7. $\ell_4^A, \ell_5^B = 0.025$; $\ell_6^Z, \ell_7^Z = 0.020$; $\ell_8^A, \ell_9^A = 0.035$ (unit labor requirements in transport activities)

8. $k_3^Z = 0.03$; $\ell_3^Z = 0.04$ (unit factor requirements in producing coal)

9. $a_{31} = 0.05$; $a_{32} = 0.119$ (respective coal inputs per unit of output of #1 and #2)

Variables

1. $C_1^A, C_2^A, C_1^B, C_2^B, C_1^Z, C_2^Z$ consumption of final goods

2. $X_1^A, X_2^A, X_1^B, X_2^B, X_3^Z$ outputs of commodities (excluding transport services)

3. $X_4^A, X_8^A, X_5^B, X_9^B, X_6^Z, X_7^Z$ outputs of transport inputs (transport services)

4. $P_1^A, P_2^A, P_3^A, P_1^B, P_2^B, P_3^B, P_1^Z, P_2^Z, P_3^Z$ prices of commodities

5. $P_4^A, P_8^A, P_5^B, P_9^B, P_6^Z, P_7^Z$ rates (prices) per ton mile of transport services (units of transport inputs)

6. $r^A, r^B, r^Z, w^A, w^B, w^Z$ rents and wages

7. $k_1^A, k_2^A, k_1^B, k_2^B$ unit capital requirements in production

8. $\ell_1^A, \ell_2^A, \ell_1^B, \ell_2^B$ unit labor requirements in production

9. $K_1^A, K_2^A, K_4^A, K_8^A$ capital demands of A's activities

10. $K_1^B, K_2^B, K_5^B, K_9^B$ capital demands of B's activities

11. K_3^Z, K_6^Z, K_7^Z capital demands of Z's activities

12. $L_1^A, L_2^A, L_4^A, L_8^A$ labor demands of A's activities

13. $L_1^B, L_2^B, L_5^B, L_9^B$ labor demands of B's activities

14. L_3^Z, L_6^Z, L_7^Z labor demands of Z's activities

15. K^A, K^B, K^Z total regional demands of capital

16. L^A, L^B, L^Z total regional demands of labor

17. Y^A, Y^B, Y^Z regional incomes

18. $M_2^{B \to A}$, $M_3^{Z \to A}$, $M_5^{B \to A}$, $M_6^{Z \to A}$, $M_1^{A \to B}$, $M_4^{A \to B}$, $M_3^{Z \to B}$, $M_7^{Z \to B}$, $M_1^{A \to Z}$, $M_8^{A \to Z}$, $M_2^{B \to Z}$, $M_9^{B \to Z}$ imports by commodity (including transport services)

19. fe   foreign exchange rate (the number of units of Z's currency for one of Q's)

20. $\Delta Assets^A$ balance of payments between A and B (change in assets of A)

Equations

1. $C_h^i = Y^i/2P_h$ $i = A, B, Z;\ h = 1, 2$

2. $X_1^A = C_1^A + Ex_1^{A \to B} + Ex_1^{A \to Z}$; $X_2^A = C_2^A - Ex_2^{B \to A}$

3. $X_1^B = C_1^B - Ex_1^{A \to B}$; $X_2^B = C_2^B + Ex_2^{B \to A} + Ex_2^{B \to Z}$

4. $X_3^Z = Ex_3^{Z \to A} + Ex_3^{Z \to B}$; $X_4^A = \alpha_{41}Ex_4^{A \to B}$; $X_5^A = \alpha_{52}Ex_5^{B \to A}$

5. $X_6^Z = \alpha_{63}Ex_6^{Z \to A}$; $X_7^Z = \alpha_{73}Ex_7^{Z \to B}$; $X_8^A = \alpha_{81}Ex_8^{A \to Z}$; $X_9^B = \alpha_{92}Ex_9^{B \to Z}$

6. $k_1^i = (w^i/3r^i)^{0.75}$ $i = A, B$ $k_2^i = (w^i/r^i)^{0.5}$ $i = A, B$

7. $\ell_1^i = (3r^i/w^i)^{0.25}$ $i = A, B$ $\ell_2^i = (r^i/w^i)^{0.5}$ $i = A, B$

8. $K_g^A = k_g^A X_g^A$ $g = 1, 2, 4, 8$ $K_g^B = k_g^B X_g^B$ $g = 1, 2, 5, 9$

9. $K_g^Z = k_g^Z X_g^Z$ $g = 3, 6, 7$

10. $L_g^A = \ell_g^A X_g^A$ $g = 1, 2, 4, 8$ $L_g^B = \ell_g^B X_g^B$ $g = 1, 2, 5, 9$

11. $L_g^Z = \ell_g^Z X_g^Z$ $g = 3, 6, 7$

12. $K^A = \Sigma K_g^A$ $g = 1, 2, 4, 8$ $K^B = \Sigma K_g^B$ $g = 1, 2, 5, 9$

13. $K^Z = \Sigma K_g^Z$ $g = 3, 6, 7$

14. $L^A = \Sigma L_g^A$ $g = 1, 2, 4, 8$ $L^B = \Sigma L_g^B$ $g = 1, 2, 5, 9$

15. $L^Z = \Sigma L_g^Z$ $g = 3, 6, 7$

16. $K^A = \bar{K}^A$ $K^B = \bar{K}^B$ $K^Z = \bar{K}^Z$ $L^A = \bar{L}^A$ $L^B = \bar{L}^B$ $L^Z = \bar{L}^Z$

17. $P_1^A = r^A k_1^A + w^A \ell_1^A + a_{31} P_3^A$ $P_2^B = r^B k_2^B + w^B \ell_2^B + a_{32} P_3^B$

18. $r^A k_2^A + w^A \ell_2^A = P_2^B + \alpha_{52} P_5^B \equiv P_2^A$

19. $r^B k_1^B + w^B \ell_1^B = P_1^A + \alpha_{41} P_4^A \equiv P_1^B$

20. $P_3^A = fe(P_3^Z + \alpha_{63} P_6^Z)$; $P_3^B = fe(P_3^Z + \alpha_{73} P_7^Z)$

21. $P_1^Z = (1/fe)(P_1^A + \alpha_{81} P_8^A)$; $P_2^Z = (1/fe)(P_2^B + \alpha_{92} P_9^B)$

22. $P_3^Z = r^Z k_3^Z + w^Z \ell_3^Z$; $P_4^A = r^A k_4^A + w^A \ell_4^A$

23. $P_5^B = r^B k_5^B + w^B \ell_5^B;$ $\qquad$ $P_6^Z = r^Z k_6^Z + w^Z \ell_6^Z$

24. $P_7^Z = r^Z k_7^Z + w^Z \ell_7^Z;$ $\qquad$ $P_8^A = r^A k_8^A + w^A \ell_8^A$

25. $P_9^B = r^B k_9^B + w^B \ell_9^B$

26. $Y^i = r^i K^i + w^i L^i$ $\qquad$ $i = A, B, Z$

27. $P_1^A Ex_1^{A \to Z} + \alpha_{81} P_8^A Ex_8^{A \to Z} + P_2^B Ex_2^{B \to Z} + \alpha_{92} P_9^B Ex_9^{B \to Z}$

$\qquad = \text{fe}(P_3^Z Ex_3^{Z \to A} + \alpha_{63} P_6^Z Ex_6^{Z \to A} + P_3^Z Ex_3^{Z \to B} + \alpha_{73} P_7^Z Ex_7^{Z \to B}$

28. $\Delta \text{Assets}^A = P_1^B Ex_1^{A \to B} - P_2^A M_2^{B \to A} + \text{fe}(P_1^Z Ex_1^{A \to Z} - P_3^A M_3^{Z \to A})$

29. $M_1^{A \to B} = Ex_1^{A \to B}$ $\qquad M_1^{A \to Z} = Ex_1^{A \to Z}$ $\qquad M_2^{B \to A} = Ex_2^{B \to A}$

$\quad M_2^{B \to Z} = Ex_2^{B \to Z}$ $\qquad M_3^{Z \to A} = Ex_3^{Z \to A}$ $\qquad M_3^{Z \to B} = Ex_3^{Z \to B}$

$\quad M_4^{A \to B} = Ex_4^{A \to B}$ $\qquad M_5^{B \to A} = Ex_5^{B \to A}$ $\qquad M_6^{Z \to A} = Ex_6^{Z \to A}$

$\quad M_7^{Z \to B} = Ex_7^{Z \to B}$ $\qquad M_8^{A \to Z} = Ex_8^{A \to Z}$ $\qquad M_9^{A \to Z} = Ex_9^{A \to Z}$

These equations together with four production functions less two redundant price (or import equal export) equations are 93 in number.

Endnotes

1   An interregional general equilibrium system under conditions of pure competition generally involves U regions ($J, N = A,..., U$) and ℓ commodities ($h = 1,..., \ell$) with prices P_h^J in each region J. In each region J there are also

1. m consumers ($i = 1,..., m$), each of whom buys $b_{h,i}^J$ amount (in reality often zero) of each good h;

2. n producers ($j = 1,..., n$), each of whom is involved with $y_{h,i}^J$ amount (in reality often zero) of each good h, this amount being negative when h is an input and positive when h is an output; and

3. $\bar{f}$ exporters ($f = 1,..., \bar{f}$), each of whom ships $s_{h,f}^{J \to N}$ amount (in reality often zero) of good h to each region N ($N \neq J$).

The unknowns are

1.   the $Um\ell$ purchases $b_{h,i}^J$,

2.   the $Un\ell$ inputs and outputs $y_{h,j}^J$,

3.   The $U(U-1)\bar{f}L$ unknown shipments $s_{h,f}^{J \to N}$,

4.   the $U\ell - 1$ prices P_h^J, and

5.   the $U - 1$ balance-of-trade positions of regions.

To determine these unknowns there are:

1. $Um\ell$ budget balance and utility-maximizing conditions for consumers;
2. $Un\ell$ transformation constraints and profit-maximizing conditions for producers;
3. $U(U-1)\overline{f}\ell$ 'no profit from trade' conditions associated with traders trying to maximize gains from trade;
4. $U\ell - 1$ demand-equals-supply conditions; and
5. $U - 1$ balance-of-trade relations.

For detailed discussion, see Isard et al. (1969, chapter 11).

2   At the time of writing most computable general equilibrium models have bypassed such treatment of space. Many of the models developed by economists have treated a dimensionless world. And models by regional scientists and others that may have been designated as interregional have been anemic. Either they have treated each region as a point, with transport cost fixed or ignored entirely; or if they have introduced transport cost as a variable they have presented a structure too highly restricted in coverage or insufficiently comprehensive.

3   For example, to derive the first part of equation 8-3, we specify the budget constraint

$$Y^A = P_1^A C_1^A + P_2^A C_2^A \tag{8-3a}$$

that consumer A is taken to face. We then construct the Lagrangian

$$\mathscr{L} = (C_1^A)^{0.5}(C_2^A)^{0.5} + \lambda(P_1^A C_1^A + P_2^A C_2^A - Y^A). \tag{8-3b}$$

To maximize utility we set

$$\partial\mathscr{L}/\partial C_1^A = 0.5(C_1^A)^{-0.5}(C_2^A)^{0.5} + \lambda P_1^A = 0 \tag{8-3c}$$

$$\partial\mathscr{L}/\partial C_2^A = 0.5(C_1^A)^{0.5}(C_2^A)^{-0.5} + \lambda P_2^A = 0 \tag{8-3d}$$

$$\partial\mathscr{L}/\partial\lambda = P_1^A C_1^A + P_2^A C_2^A - Y = 0 \tag{8-3e}$$

Eliminating λ in 8-3c and 8-3d yields

$$P_2^A = P_1^A[0.5(C_1^A)^{0.5}(C_2^A)^{-0.5})/0.5(C_1^A)^{-0.5}(C_2^A)^{0.5}]$$
$$= P_1^A C_1^A/C_2^A \tag{8-3f}$$

Replacing P_2^A in 8-3a with its expression in 8-3f we obtain

$$C_1^A = \frac{Y^A}{2P_1^A} \qquad (8\text{-}3g)$$

4   For example, given the linear homogeneous Cobb-Douglas production
    function (equation 8-5, wherein exponents of K_1 and L_1 add to unity),
    constant returns to scale obtains. It follows that total costs (TC) of
    production can be stated as

$$TC = rK_1 + wL_1 \qquad (8\text{-}5a)$$

After multiplying the expression of equation 8-5 by 4/3, we obtain

$$L_1 = (X_1^A)^{4/3}/(K_1)^{1/3}. \qquad (8\text{-}5b)$$

Substituting the expression for L_1 into equation 8-5a, we have as one
condition for total cost minimization (which under pure competition
implies profit maximization)

$$\partial TC/\partial K_1 = 0 = r - (1/3)w(X_1/K_1)^{4/3} = r - (1/3)w/(k_1)^{4/3} \qquad (8\text{-}5c)$$

or

$$k_1 = (w/3r)^{3/4} \qquad (8\text{-}5d) \equiv (8\text{-}7)$$

In similar fashion, the expressions for ℓ_1, k_2, and ℓ_2 are derived.

5   Rearranging terms in equations 8-23 and 8-24 and using equations
    8-18, 8-19 and 8-20, we obtain

$$(1 - a_{11})P_1^A - a_{21}P_2^B = EC \qquad (8\text{-}24a)$$

where $EC = rk_1 + w\ell_1 + a_{21}\alpha_{52}P_5^B$, and

$$-a_{12}P_1^A + (1 - a_{22})P_2^B = ED \qquad (8\text{-}24b)$$

where $ED = rk_2^B + w\ell_2^B + a_{02}\alpha_{32}P_3^B + a_{12}\alpha_{41}P_4^A$.
We can use the input-output inverse **A** to obtain

$$P_1^A[(1 - a_{22})EC + a_{21}(ED)]/A \qquad (8\text{-}24c)$$

and

$$P_2^B[(1 - a_{11})ED + a_{12}(EC)]/A \qquad (8\text{-}24d)$$

where $\mathbf{A} = (1 - a_{11})(1 - a_{22}) - a_{12}a_{21}$

6   The 34 equations are 8-1 (two income equations), 8-3 and 8-4 (four consumption equations), 8-7 to 8-10 (four unit factor input equations), 8-13 to 8-17 (five output equations), 8-18 to 8-24 (seven price equations), 8-25 (constituting six equations, namely the capital market equation, instrumental in determining the price of capital and five capital requirements equations, $i = 1, 2, 3, 4, 5$), and 8-26 (constituting six equations, namely the total labor market equation, instrumental in determining the price of labor and five labor requirements equations, $i = 1, 2, 3, 4, 5$).

7   The data of Table 8-1 were obtained by an iterative process and the use of a spreadsheet; therefore they are only approximations. More advanced computation programs, such as GAMS (and its likely successors), can yield more precise results, but unfortunately results more difficult to check for the presence of errors.

8   See Takayama and Judge (1976), Bhagwati (1983), chapters 59–61.

9   The sixteen equations determing the total demands for each of the four factors are:

$$K^A = K_1^A + K_2^A + K_4^A \qquad\qquad L^A = L_1^A + L_2^A + L_4^A$$

$$\text{(8-40a)}$$

$$K^B = K_1^B + K_2^B + K_5^B \qquad\qquad L^B = L_1^B + L_2^B + L_5^B$$

where

$$K_h^A = k_h^A X_h^A \qquad\qquad L_h^A = \ell_h^A X_h^A \qquad\qquad h = 1, 2, 4$$

$$K_g^B = k_g^B X_g^B \qquad\qquad L_g^B = \ell_g^B X_g^B \qquad\qquad g = 1, 2, 5$$

10 Unlike the conceptual framework depicted in endnote 1, we do not explicitly treat traders in this model in order to avoid excessive notation. They are, however, implied and operate at zero gains from trade.

11 The unknowns are: Y^A, Y^B, C_1^A, C_2^A, C_1^B, C_2^B, X_1^A, X_2^A, X_1^B, X_2^B, k_1^A, ℓ_1^A, k_2^A, ℓ_2^A, k_1^B, k_2^B, ℓ_1^B, ℓ_2^B, P_1^A, P_2^B, P_2^A, P_1^B, $\text{Exp}_1^{A \to B}$, $\text{Exp}_2^{B \to A}$, X_4^A, X_5^B, P_4^A, P_5^B, r^A, r^B, w^A, w^B, K_1^A, K_2^A, K_4^A, L_1^A, L_2^A, L_4^A, K_1^B, K_2^B, K_5^B, L_1^B, L_2^B, L_5^B, K^A, L^A, K^B, L^B and fe. Necessarily, in this two country model, exports of A correspond to imports of B ($M_1^{A \to B}$) and exports of B correspond

to imports of A ($M_2^{B \to A}$). For more than two country (region) models, there will not be this correspondence.

The corresponding equations are 8.27 (2 income equations), 8.28 (four consumption equations), 8.29 and 8.30 (four production functions), 8.31 (eight unit factor input equations), 8.32 and 8.33 (two price equations), 8.34 and 8.35 (four commodity supply = demand equations, instrumental in determining market prices and exports), 8.36 and 8.37 (two transport production equations), 8.38 and 8.39 (two transport input price equations), 8.40-8.43 (four factor supply = demand equations, instrumental in determining factor prices), 8.40a (sixteen factor requirements equations, see endnote 9), and 8.43 (the equation instrumental in determining the foreign exchange rate).

Also note that the Balance of Payments of each nation is zero, namely

$$P_2^A M_2^{B \to A} - fe P_1^B Ex_1^{A \to B} = 0 \tag{8-43a}$$

and

$$P_1^B M_1^{A \to B} - (1/fe) P_2^A Ex_2^{B \to A} = 0 \tag{8-43b}$$

where $P_2^A M_2^{B \to A}$ and $P_1^B M_1^{A \to B}$ are the value of imports (at delivered prices) of A and B, respectively, and $P_1^B Ex_1^{A \to B}$ and $P_2^A Ex_2^{B \to A}$ are the value of exports (at delivered prices) of A and B, respectively.

12 The changes in magnitudes are for: K_1^A, from 0.653 to 0.537; K_2^A, from 0.147 to 0.252; K_1^B, from 0.147 to 0.222; K_2^B, from 1.453 to 1.364; L_1^A, from 1.860 to 1.718; L_2^A, from 0.140 to 0.268; L_1^B, from 0.420 to 0.585; L_2^B, from 1.380 to 1.199; k_1^A, from 0.456 to 0.418; k_2^A, from 1.026 to 0.969; k_1^B, from 0.456 to 0.483; k_2^B, from 1.026 to 1.066; ℓ_1^A from 1.299 to 1.337; ℓ_2^A from 0.975 to 1.032; ℓ_1^B from 1.299 to 1.275; and ℓ_2^B from 0.975 to 0.938. New magnitudes are: $K_4^A = 0.010$, $K_5^B = 0.009$; $L_4^A = 0.012$ and $L_5^B = 0.011$.

13 See pp. 8–21 and Isard et al. (1960), pp. 233–245 for discussion of this approach.

14 Here, for example, we impose the constraint that the exports of an essential good, namely #1 from A, remain unchanged.

15 Of course for a central planning system which might correspond to that of the Soviet Union before its collapse, an enlarged table on physical magnitudes would be the one that would be most relevant.

16 In an enlarged table on physical magnitudes, the consumption of different goods by each type of household would need to be determined outside the market subsystem.

In the case of region *A*, we allocated: (1) 80 percent of its labor income to rural households and 20 percent to urban; and (2) 10 percent of its rent income to rural households and 90 percent to urban. For region *B*, the corresponding figures are 70, 30, 15, and 85. For *Z*, where the rural households are taken to be 100 percent self-subsistent, all income goes to urban households.

17 In terms of variables, this specification of household group in each region requires that the six consumption variables whose magnitudes are listed in the last column of Table 8-4 be replaced by twelve new consumption variables, the three utility functions 8-2 be replaced by five new ones, the three regional income equations by five new household income equations and the six consumption level equations by 12 new ones. See Appendix 8.1.

18 See Isard and Liossatos (1979), pp. 93–105, for one approach to a comprehensive treatment of the government sector. Also see Isard et al. (1970).

19 Only in rare instances has such a sector been included in SAM tables, although logically they should be, especially when these tables are employed to study the impact of government policies on redistribution in real terms, directly or indirectly.

20 Implicit in these statements and the continued use of the utility function 8-2, whose maximization yields the consumption levels of Tables 8-3 and 8-4, is that the provision of government services (outputs such as security) and outcomes from investment (for example, higher quality goods) be such that at all possible consumption patterns the utility derived would be increased by the same amount as the utility foregone from the corresponding reductions in consumption levels resulting from savings and taxation.

21 Note that if we were to add to each sector inputs from other sectors, production functions would need to be respecified and prices reestimated.

22 In this connection it is useful to refer back to the extensive thinking and insights of regional economists in the 1950s and their considerable research on interregional financial flows and social accounts. See Isard et al. (1960), chapters 4, 5, and pp. 611–621.

23 See Shoven and Whalley (1992) for a bird's eye presentation of this and other functions discussed here.

24 See the discussion in Li and Rose (1995), who in their one-region Pennsylvania study reject the use of Cobb-Douglas, CES and Leontief functions because of their undesirable properties, such as pre-determinate restrictions on substitution elasticities.

25 See Isard, Schooler, and Vietorisz (1959) for details.

26 While a government as an exogenous sector may tax exports and impose a tariff on imports, for many studies it cannot be considered to have a negligible impact on the ROW. There is very likely to be retaliation which then can lead to sequences of action and reactions among the sectors and nations in a true general equilibrium framework. When the sequence of feedbacks is ignored, the model should be more truthfully designated ATGE, applied truncated general equilibrium.

27 A draft of a study which to some scholars may seem to be an AGIE type, but clearly is not, is by Peter, Han, Meagher and Naqvi (1996) entitled *MONASH–MRF: A Multiregional Model of the Australian Economy.* It is indeed an excellent study in terms of the ingenious ways the authors exploit many of the devices employed by regional scientists in input-output and related studies when the dearth of regional data requires the use of national and other sources of data. For example, they split the columns and rows of a national input-output table to obtain after a series of steps estimates of interregional flows. However, this study essentially ignores space as a variable and its changing configuration as reflected in transport costs and effective distance. For interregional analysis, two unacceptable and basic procedures that are used are: (1) the Armington constant-elasticity-of-substitution mechanism for projecting change in interregional trade (a hand-me-

down from the dimensionless world of the typical international trade economist) and (2) the use of margins as a composite of transportation and communications on an aggregate basis, which in no way captures the basic transport cost variable. Nonetheless, the study remains extremely valuable for overcoming regional data deficiencies.

28 As this book goes to press, a study just completed by Haddad (1998) represents a major step forward. In his three region model of Brazil, which follows closely the multiregional structure of the MONASH–MRF study, Haddad does introduce transport cost as a basic variable affecting commodity trade among regions. However, he still retains the Armington constant-elasticity-of-substitution concept in depicting the structure of trade among regions and other traditional CGE procedures, for example expressing effects in terms of percentage changes. His work, which presents a good summary of the literature, still does not start with a proper scaffolding.

References

Ando, Asao, and Takanori Shibata. 1997. 'A Multi-Regional Model for China Based on Price and Quantity Equilibrium,' in Manas Chatterji (ed.), *Regional Science Perspectives for the Future*. London: MacMillan, pp. 326–344.

Azis, Iwan J. 1997. 'The Relevance of Price-Endogenous Models,' *Regional Science Review*, 19.

Azis, Iwan J. 1997. 'Impacts of Economic Reform on Rural-Urban Welfare: A General Equilibrium Framework,' *Review of Urban and Regional Development Studies*, 9, 1–19.

Bhagwati, Jagdish. 1983. *Essays in International Economic Theory. Vol. 2: International Factor Mobility.* Cambridge, Mass.: MIT Press.

Bröcker, Johannes. 1995. 'Chamberlinean Spatial Computable General Equilibrium Modelling: A Theoretical Framework,' *Economic Systems Research*, 7, 137–149.

de Melo, Jaime, and David Roland-Holst. 1994. 'Tariffs and Export Subsidies When Domestic Markets Are Oligopolistic,' in Mercenier and Srinivasan, *op. cit.*, ch. 5.

Dervis, Kemal, Jaime de Melo, and Sherman Robinson. 1982. *General Equilibrium Models for Development.* Cambridge: Cambridge University Press.

Dinwiddy, C. L., and F. J. Teal. 1988. *The Two-Sector General Equilibrium Model.* New York: St. Martin's Press.

Elbers, Chris. 1992. *Spatial Disaggregation in General Equilibrium Models with Application to the Nepalese Economy.* Amsterdam: VU University Press.

Fargeix, André, and Elisabeth Sadoulet. 1994. 'A Financial Computable General Equilibrium Model for the Analysis of Stabilization Programs,' in Mercenier and Srinivasan, *op. cit.*, ch. 4.

Ginsburgh, Victor. 1994. 'In the Cournot-Walras General Equilibrium Model, There May Be "More to Gain" by Changing the Numéraire Than by Eliminating Imperfections,' in Mercenier and Srinivasan, *op. cit.*, ch. 6.

Gunning, Willem Jan, and Michiel A. Keyzer. 1995. 'Applied General Equilibrium Models for Policy Analysis,' in J. Behrman and T. N. Srinivasan (eds.), *Handbook of Development Economics* III. Amsterdam: Elsevier Science, pp. 2025–2107.

Haddad, Eduardo A. 1988. *Regional Inequality and Structural Chances in the Brazilian Economy.* Dissertation, University of Illinois at Urbana.

Harrigan, Frank, and Peter G. McGregor. 1988. 'Price and Quantity Interactions in Regional Economic Models: The Importance of "Openness" and "Closures,"' *London Papers in Regional Science*, 19, 179–205.

Harrigan, Frank, and Peter G. McGregor. 1989. 'Neoclassical and Keynesian Perspectives on the Regional Macro-economy: A Computable General Equilibrium Approach,' *Journal of Regional Science*, 29, 555–573.

Harris, Richard. 1984. 'Applied General Equilibrium Analysis of Small Open Economies with Scale Economies and Imperfect Competition,' *American Economic Review*, 74, 1016–1032.

Harrison, Glenn W., Thomas F. Rutherford, and Ian Wooton. 1995. 'Liberalizing Agriculture in the European Union,' *Journal of Policy Modeling*, 17, 223–255.

Hewings, Geoffrey J. D., and Moss Madden (eds.). 1995. *Social and Demographic Accounting.* Cambridge: Cambridge University Press.

Isard, Walter et al. 1960. *Methods of Regional Analysis.* Cambridge, Mass.: MIT Press.

Isard, Walter et al. 1969. *General Theory: Social, Political, Economic and Regional.* Cambridge, Mass.: MIT Press.

Isard, Walter, and Panagis Liossatos. 1979. *Spatial Dynamics and Optimal Space-Time Development.* New York: North Holland.

Isard, Walter, Eugene W. Schooler, and Thomas Vietorisz. 1959. *Industrial Complex Analysis and Regional Development.* Cambridge, Mass.: MIT Press.

Jones, Rich, and John Whalley. 1984. 'A Canadian Regional General Equilibrium Model and Some Applications,' *Journal of Urban Economics*, 25, 368–404.

Kilkenny, Maureen. 1995. 'Operationalizing a Rural-Urban General Equilibrium Model using a Bi-Regional SAM,' in Hewings and Madden, *op. cit.*, ch. 9.

Kilkenny, Maureen, and Adam Rose. 1995. 'Interregional SAMs and Capital Accounts,' in Hewings and Madden, *op. cit.*, ch. 3.

Krugman, Paul. 1993. 'On the Number and Location of Cities,' *European Economic Review*, 7, 293–298.

Lewis, Jeffrey D. 1994. 'Macroeconomic Stabilization and Adjustment Policies in a General Equilibrium Model with Financial Markets: Turkey,' in Mercenier and Srinivasan, *op. cit.*, ch. 3.

Li, Ping-Cheng, and Adam Rose. 1995. 'Global Warming Policy and the Pennsylvania Economy,' *Economic Systems Research*, 7(2): 151–171.

Lora, Edwardo. 1994. 'Comment,' in Jean Mercenier and T. N. Srinivasan (eds.) *op. cit.*, pp. 137–144.

Mercenier, Jean, and T. N. Srinivasan (eds.). 1994. *Applied General Equilibrium and Economic Development.* Ann Arbor: University of Michigan Press.

Peter, M. W., S. H. Han, G. A. Meagher, and F. Naqvi. 1996. *MONASH–MRF: A Multiregional Model of the Australian Economy*, draft. Monash University, Australia.

Rounds, Jeffrey I. 1988. 'Incorporating the International, Regional and Spatial Dimension into SAM: Some Methods and Applications,' in H. J. Harrigan, J. W. McGilvray and I. H. McNicoll (eds.), *Environment and Planning*, A, 12, 927–936.

Rounds, Jeffrey I. 1995. 'A SAM for Europe: Social Accounts at the Regional Level Revisited,' in Geoffrey J. D. Hewings and Moss Madden (eds), *Social and Demographic Accounting*. New York: Cambridge University Press, pp. 15–40.

Sadoulet, Elisabeth, and Allain de Janvry. 1995. *Quantitative Development Policy Analysis.* Baltimore: Johns Hopkins University Press.

Shoven, John B., and John Whalley. 1992. *Applying General Equilibrium.* New York: Cambridge University Press.

Spencer, J. E. 1988. 'Computable General Equilibrium, Trade, Factor Mobility, and the Regions,' in *Recent Advances in Regional Modelling*. London: Pion.

Takayama, Takahashi, and George G. Judge. 1976. *Spatial and Temporal Price and Allocation Models*. Amsterdam: North Holland.

Taylor, Lance. 1983. *Structuralist Macroeconomics: Applicable Models for the Third World*. New York: Basic Books.

Whalley, John, and Irene Trela. 1989. *Regional Aspects of Confederation*. Toronto: University of Toronto Press.

9. Interregional and spatial microsimulation

Walter Isard

9.0 Introduction

In the preceding chapter, we developed the framework for an applied general interregional equilibrium (AGIE) model. It is an outgrowth of the purely conceptual general equilibrium system of Walras that is provided with interregional framework (Isard et al., 1969). As noted in endnote 1 of that chapter, this general interregional equilibrium framework embraces many regions in each of which there are many individual consumers, many firms each producing many commodities, many traders each shipping the many goods to each of the other U-1 regions, and many markets. Admittedly, any AGIE model that creative regional scientists will be able to construct and effectively apply in the foreseeable future will fall far short of this ideal micro framework. Realistically speaking, an applicable AGIE model at best will handle only a small number of variables and functions that limited data sets and computational costs will permit. Therefore, it is important to be aware of, and employ when appropriate, other micro approaches for analyzing and attacking problems of a space-economy. One approach, of relatively recent origin, is microsimulation. It was pioneered by Guy Orcutt (1957), and Orcutt et al. (1961, 1976). With its use of probabilities, simulation and application of relevant constraints (and excitations when appropriate), it has been demonstrated to be effective in attacking a number of urban and regional problems and promises to be an effective research tool for a number of others. In this chapter we wish to examine briefly the rapidly developing potential of this research method. Since much more extension and experience with this method is required to evaluate its overall promise as a *truly* general method for attacking problems of interest to regional scientists, we leave for later a more extensive discussion of it and its subsequent applications.

9.1 Basic features of microsimulation

In his early work at the Urban Institute in the United States designed to depict more appropriately and precisely the impact of national welfare policy upon relevant populations, Orcutt wrote (1976, p. 90):

In microanalytic models of an economy the components represent recognizable entities met in everyday experience. The type of component occupying center stage is called a *decision unit.* Decision units include individuals, nuclear families, households, manufacturing firms, retailers, banks, insurance companies, labor unions, and local, state, and federal government units. Individuals are imbedded within more extensive family or household units. Firms are imbedded within industry units.

The decision units in microanalytic models interact with each other either directly or indirectly through a second major type of component called a *market.* The markets in a model represent markets in the economy, and it is through them that the third type of component flows from decision unit to decision unit. For brevity, components of this last type will be referred to as *goods.* But it must be noted that such components include not only goods which may be provided, held, sold, bought, or consumed by decision units, but also instruments used to represent wealth — such as money, bonds, shares of stock, deeds, and mortgages.

A description of any decision unit would include a listing of its own input, status, and output variables along with those relationships which are used in updating status variables and in generating output variables.

For example, for a given entity, say the head of a household, its (1) inputs, (2) status and (3) output variables might be respectively: (1) age, sex and years of education; (2) type of employment, wealth, and ethnicity; and (3) marriage, relocation, and job promotion. *Behavioral relationships, or operating characteristics* take inputs and via probability data and relevant constraints generate updated status variables and output results. The operating characteristics may include new influences on a behaving unit.[1]

In each run of a simulation, the solution is a specific set of time paths of endogenous variables for each actor in the system (the number of actors may run up to the hundred thousands). The operating characteristics do not produce events, but state the probabilities of them. For example, an operating characteristic may state the probability that a head of a household with specified attributes (such as a particular age and wealth status) may die, or marry and so forth. A Monte Carlo decision rule determines if the event is to occur. In this way, the operating characteristics will determine the number of heads of like attributes who will die or marry. In general, while an entire population is represented and the number of units may run into millions, only a random sample of a population properly drawn from an available and appropriate data base is required to produce probability data.[2] As computer capabilities increase, entire populations (rather than samples) may be simulated.

For example, when a set of processes or operating characteristics of a demographic-type simulation of an entire population say of the United States is performed, imputations of: (1) births, deaths and immigration change the size and composition of the population; (2) marriage and divorce associated with those remaining and leaving home change the number and composition of families; (3) interregional migration changes the distribution of individuals and families over regions as areas to reside in; (4) work, wage rates, government transfer payments, tax rates, and credit conditions change family income, savings, housing ownership, other capital stocks from investments, and consumption expenditures.

Like other regional science methods, microsimulation is concerned with conditional and unconditional projection. In microsimulation, projection is a natural phenomenon. A microanalytic simulation advances in time, say over a year, a sample representation of a real population of behaving units. Thus, future states of that population are obtainable from a sequence of successive microsimulations, each operating on the state resulting from the previous microsimulation. As a result, micro unit histories become possible. Moreover when Census data and other public use data are available, the reliability of projections over a series of time periods, say years, can often be enhanced when the microsimulation results for a census year (or key year for other published data) are aligned to the data of that year. As a result, time series can be constructed for magnitudes otherwise unobtainable. Additionally, the employment of cross-sectional data when available can produce extremely useful information on a regional or other areal basis.

Microsimulation scholars have emphasized the usefulness of microsimulation in conducting experiments to help analyze the impact of public policies. Through changing the parameters of a given policy, one can conduct useful sensitivity studies to help identify the 'best' structure of that policy. Such experimentation which has been conducted extensively with reference to the welfare of the different constituent groups of a population points up one of the major advantages of microsimulation. Unlike standard input-output which treats households as one or a relatively few sectors, and unlike social accounting which deals with averages for given household groups, microsimulation provides data (input, status and output) for individuals, families and other relevant behavioral units (at least to the extent that relevant base year data are available from random sampling and other sources). Thus when the impact of a welfare policy or in general of any exogenous change is of concern, the distributional pattern of outputs (impacts) can be obtained to almost any level of detail required given an adequate data source, and the results can be much more valuable for a meaningfully disaggregated population. This advantage has greatly stimulated the growth and development of microsimulation as a research method.

Speaking more generally, distribution is a basic (core) aspect of any space economy, and any method that can in general anticipate distributional changes on a much finer (more disaggregated) basis can be invaluable for many spatio-regional studies. This feature is particularly desirable for urban and regional planners and government officials, especially when they are involved in taxation, transfer payments and complex institutional regulations. At the same time, the microsimulation outputs can very often be aggregated to whatever level desired to provide aggregate data by whatever category, variable, or other element that is desirable for: (1) research efforts utilizing other methods of analysis and (2) decision making by institutions, organizations, firms, government units which require aggregate data as inputs, whether or not such decision making is based on models.

At this point it is important to distinguish clearly between several types of microsimulation. In one type, a single cross-section of many micro units is involved and the pattern of effects upon their behavior (consumption, travel, labor force participation, housing demand, etc.) of several different policies (say regarding low income housing, child care provision, urban transit, industry subsidy) or of each of several variants of some given policy are examined. In this type of microsimulation the set of micro units essentially remains the same; only the distribution within a single year of the diverse changes in their behavior pattern for each policy or variant of a given policy is forecasted. Useful comparisons of the outcomes for the different policies or variants of a given policy can then be made.

A more dynamic type of microsimulation involves ongoing 'aging' processes. For example, each micro unit is aged for each time period by appropriate information on death probabilities, drop-out probabilities in schooling, marriage probabilities, etc. and their characteristics. As a result, the number of units in a cross section changes from time period to time period in a way that mimics the evolution of a real population. For example, the number of students age 15 attending high school as sophomores in a given year may be different from the number of students age 16 attending high school as juniors one year later, which in turn is different from those students attending high school as seniors one more year later.

A still more dynamic approach in microsimulation involves the construction of what some have designated synthetic micro units. Here it is recognized that the occurrence of events, for example, a job loss, illness or natural hazard which compels a relocation of a unit can and frequently does alter the behavioral pattern of it. In effect, the interaction of a microunit with the set of situations (events), both constraining and propelling (exciting), that it encounters in its life-time governs the time path of that unit's behavior. Thus, in addition to standard life-cycle analysis (the study of the regular stages in life that a microunit passes through,which has been found to provide one useful direction for studying time paths), analysis can and should be extended to include as much as possible 'predictable' situations or events (see discussions in Birkin et al., 1996, Hooimeijer, 1996, and Clarke, 1996). This then requires the coupling of this more dynamic type of microsimulation with other research methods that throw light on possible predictable events and constraints, economic, social, political and environmental. See the discussion of some possible couplings in the following chapter.

9.2 Likely extensions, costs, and other limiting factors in microsimulation

Since the first development by Orcutt, the appreciation of the potential of microsimulation as a research approach has mounted. Its scope has been redefined and greatly extended. Currently, there is widespread agreement that one highly desirable feature of microsimulation should be spatial disaggregation (the listing of *location* as an attribute of all actors). As Caldwell (1986, p. 61) notes

National or single-region (i.e., nonspatial) models lack policy relevance to all but one group of decision-makers (i.e., national or regional decision-makers). Gains in policy relevance tend to depend in a nonlinear way on the degree of spatial detail. In the case of the U.S., if spatial disaggregation reaches only to the level of census region (four or nine) classification, the policy analysis payoff turns out to be relatively limited, since the American political system generally is not organized for decision-making at this level. Policy analysis payoffs become more substantial when spatial disaggregation reaches the state level in American models. But the gains accumulate exponentially when the level of spatial disaggregation becomes even finer than the state level.

Moreover, microsimulation researchers have come to emphasize increasingly that corporate actors [firms (local, national, multinational), institutions (financial, political, social, etc.), governments (local, state, and national) must be more extensively embraced. These actors, too, are born, grow, make significant decisions, and have a time path. They interact with individuals, households and other micro units, influencing them and in turn are influenced by them. Also, like individuals and other units, they, too, are affected by settings, and in turn their decisions have impacts upon settings, which then have consequences for the time paths of individuals and all other microunits.

In essence, the proposed developments of microsimulation come to embrace a framework, increasingly extended to cover: (1) more types of actors, and thus more actors; (2) more attributes of actors and more kinds of attributes; (3) more explicit treatment of events, constraints and other elements of settings; (4) more requirements of data; (5) more processing of data and with the increased number of actor attributes covered, more alignment of the data with this increased number; and (6) more sources of data and data processing and thus increased computation requirements and costs.

In the past it can be claimed that computational power and costs have severely limited the growth of microsimulation research. And while some microsimulation scholars are optimistic about future advances in computation capability, it does not appear that these advances will enable them to achieve as much progress as they envisage as desirable. For example, the addition of an explicit spatial dimension, as has been urged by Caldwell (1986) and which would be of great value, will alone necessitate immense increases in computation requirements and data processing costs. Thus, while major achievements will undoubtedly be scored in the use of microsimulation, spatial and non-spatial, they will be bounded as is and will be the case with AGIE and other regional science methods. In particular, behavioral relations that involve more than one round of feedback effects and decision making by units such as governments, multinationals, and other large institutions will not be able to be covered, as will be evident from the discussion of the next section on specific applications. Hence in no way will microsimulation be able to encompass the many types of behavioral relations that highly optimistic members of the microsimulation community imagine possible — relations [including interactions with the setting (environment)] which seem to cover even more areas of study than that encompassed by, and more appropriately dealt with in general interregional equilibrium analysis fused with other regional science frameworks.

Moreover, microsimulation scholars need to devote much time and effort now to improve the quality of their forecasts and validate results (see Hoschka, 1986), and undoubtedly will need to do so increasingly in the future as the nature of the problems they attack grow in complexity.

9.3 Applications

We now wish to throw additional light on the potentials of microsimulation with discussion of two excellent studies.

9.3.1 Wealth in the United States: family stock ownership and accumulation, 1960–1995

Motivated by the need to have for policy impact analysis better information on wealth distribution in the United States over the historical period 1960–1995 and to have better forecasts (however conditional these forecasts must be) of wealth distribution over the future period 1995–2030, Caldwell and Keister (1996) undertake a most impressive microsimulation study. In this study, they employ a dynamic PC-based (personal computer) microsimulation model designated CORSIM. This model

> incorporates about 50 economic, demographic, and social processes by means of approximately 900 stochastic equations and rule-based algorithms, constructed with the use of over 17 different national microdata files. The CORSIM wealth module incorporates 14 different types of family wealth (11 assets and 3 debts). For simulations involving wealth, CORSIM uses relatively large samples (1/1000 of the US population; that is 250,000 persons in 1990) in order to have sufficient

observations representing top wealth-holding families. The project integrates major data files on family wealth: estate tax data files dating from 1962–1992; an ongoing study of economic differentials in mortality in one million Americans; panel data from the Surveys of Consumer Finances (SCF) conducted by the Federal Reserve Board since 1983; cross-sectional survey data on family wealth collected between 1960 and 1992; and national flow of funds data from 1960-1992 on national household wealth totals by type of wealth. (Caldwell and Keister, 1996, p. 89)

Here, we report on only one of the fourteen types of wealth, namely family stock ownership and value, the other types of wealth being: six other financial assets (checking and savings accounts, money market accounts, etc.), ownership and accumulation of four real assets (the primary residence, business assets, etc.), three debts (mortgages, etc.). Two microdynamic equations for each type of wealth were estimated using national panel 1983–86 survey data — data based on interviews and reinterviews of a sample of 2,791 households. (The random sample had to be augmented to select additional high-income households since they own most of the wealth of U.S. households; and families whose head was 24 years or less had to be excluded because of possible significant marriage status change.) A first equation (a logistic) for each type of wealth was one in which the dependent variable is set at unity if the family owned that type and zero otherwise. The second equation (an ordinary least squares type) for each kind of wealth related the family's holding (the dependent variable) to the demographic characteristics of the family, namely the variables: (1) NOT WHITE (1 = family is black, Hispanic, native American, or Asian, otherwise zero); (2) AGE (of the household head in years); (3) AGE SQUARED; (4) indication of level of EDUCATION using a set of four dummy variables; and (5) household INCOME; where several types of relevant adjustments had to be made.

Once the regression equation was obtained, its coefficients were used to produce the initial (prealignment) updates of each family's wealth and for every update that followed. Thus, as indicated in Figure 9.1, for 1960, the start of the period, the microunits of the 1960 adjusted Census sample were assigned initial wealth values for 1962 which were aligned with historical data — for example available estate tax data for top wealth holders, and survey data for non-top wealth holders. Then, as depicted in Figure 9.1, the sample was updated to 1965, alignment with diverse data repeated, and so on for every three years up to 1995. Throughout this operation, processes such as birth, death, immigration, family formation and income generation were taken into account, and thus had an effect on the ownership of each type of wealth.

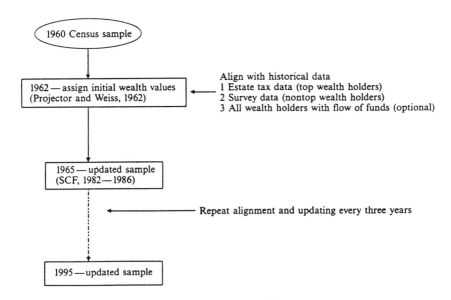

Figure 9.1 Steps in the CORSIM Wealth Module

It is not necessary to enter here into the fine details of the study, and the careful way in which alignment with the several sources of relevant historical data was conducted. To examine the results of the simulation a number of figures were presented. Figure 9.2, for example, charts by three year intervals from 1962 to 1992 the proportion of top wealth holders who owned stock. Three separate estimates are presented. The lowest line in the figure records the microsimulation estimates unaligned. The top line displays the historical estate tax estimates. The third line represents the aligned microsimulation estimates. This figure indicates that the proportion of top wealth families owning stocks lies in the range from approximately 65 percent to approximately 85 percent.[3] This figure and others that present estimates by married couple households and for different age groups lead the authors to conclude that after alignment is conducted, the microsimulated estimates of the proportion of top wealth families owning stocks closely approximates the historical data.

To indicate the potential of their approach for policy analysis, the authors point to useful types of experiments, especially counterfactual ones. Such can involve changes in the specification of the microdynamic

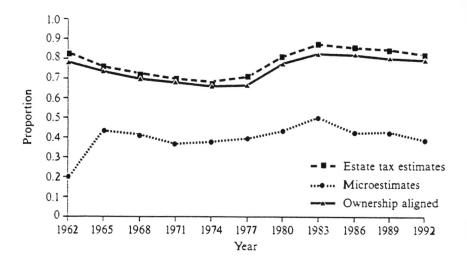

Figure 9.2   Proportion of top wealth holders owning stock, by three-year intervals

equations, which then would result in changes in the coefficients derived. To illustrate, they omitted the family's race from the specification used in the microsimulation reported above. Differences between the results of the unchanged and changed specifications were then presented. The authors found that a substantial change resulted from the closing of the race difference, but also that considerable difference remained, suggesting among other 'causal' factors racial differences in wealth ownership at the starting point in 1960.

While this application pertained only to the nation as a whole, the authors point out that the CORSIM data bank contains information about the state in which families live as well as data about state-to-state migration and thus that wealth can be examined within a spatial context.

9.3.2   The potential of microsimulation for urban models

A second application that demonstrates the significant potential of spatial microsimulation is the study by Wegener and Spiekermann (1996) of the housing market of the city of Dortmund. However, to provide a proper perspective for their study, the authors first note some of the new challenges to the urban-modelling community.

The new generation of travel models, such as activity-based travel demand models, requires more detailed information on household demographics and employment characteristics. New neighborhood-scale transport planning policies to promote the use of public transport, walking, and cycling require more detailed information on the precise location of activities. In addition models need to be able to predict not only economic but also environmental impacts of land-use transport policies, and this requires small-area forecasts of emissions from stationary and mobile sources as well as of immissions in terms of affected population. (p. 149)

The authors go on to note that most existing urban models are too aggregate, that their zone-based data fail to capture the reality of socioeconomic activities and their environmental impacts which are continuous in space. They then proceed to outline a major microanalytic study of the Dortmund region. In this study, aimed ultimately at developing a comprehensive microsimulation *urban land-use transport model*, they decompose urban development into a series of subprocesses. Within each they intend to examine choices, transitions and policies.

The first submodel which has been completed is strictly not a pure microsimulation. It combines both sampling and aggregation. However, its emphasis is on the use of microsimulation processes to obtain much more detailed information for urban study. This submodel effectively employs a combination of microsimulation and econometrics where the econometrics involves the use of a logit choice model. It is a type of fusion of microsimulation with one or more other methods that will occur frequently in the future if only to avoid the problem of excessive data requirements and costs which plague many desirable pure microsimulation studies. Such fusion, however, can capture the strengths of more than one analytic method and thereby lead to more effective urban analysis.

The first submodel relates to the residential land use and the urban housing market. In it, households make intraregional migration decisions viewed as search processes for more desirable dwellings, an unsuccessful search being tantamount to no migration. They start out, using population and housing census data for:

(1) Households, as a distribution classified by:
  nationality (native, foreign),
  age of head (16–29, 30–59, 60+),
  income or skill (low, medium, high, very high),

size (1, 2, 3, 4, 5+ persons).
and
  (2) Dwellings, as a distribution, classified by
        type of building (single-family, multifamily),
        tenure (owner-occupied, rented, social housing),
        quality (low, medium, high, very high),
        size (1, 2, 3, 4, 5+ rooms).

Collapsing the population and housing distributions into thirty more aggregate household and dwelling types allows the authors to construct an *occupancy matrix* for each zone where along rows are listed 30 household types and along columns 30 dwelling types. One cell of such a matrix might represent the number of three-person households of medium age and medium income occupying an owner-occupied, four-room medium quality dwelling. Against this background framework of aggregate data for each zone, a Monte Carlo microsimulation study of the Dortmund urban housing market is pursued. Based on a sufficiently large sample of *housing-market transactions*, this study simulates intraregional migration. Unlike *aging* processes, which are appropriately incorporated in the model, each decision is a *search* process of an *actor* resulting in a move or no move, that is the choice of a new dwelling type or not, the migration to another zone or not. If the actor chooses not to move, it enters into another search. For the end of each time period, the new set of aggregates (entries into each zone's occupancy matrix) is calculated. This aggregation phase embodies all changes of households and dwellings resulting from the set of transactions when multiplied by the sampling factor.

To derive the probabilities for the *sampling phase* (for example, the probability that of all households of type *h* living in zone *i*, a household occupying a dwelling of type *k* will be sampled),[4] a multinomial logit choice function is employed (see pp. 186–87 for a brief discussion of this function).

Also, a multinomial logit choice function is used to derive for the *search phase* the probability that the selected household searches in zone *i´* for a new dwelling, and that it looks over a dwelling of type *k´* there before making a choice.[5]

In the *choice phase* that is in making a decision to move or not to move, the household behaves as a satisficer rather than a utility maximizer. It considers two different kinds of utility measures, one expressing the attractiveness of a dwelling, the other the attractiveness of a zone. The utility measures are weighted aggregates of attributes, which are held constant throughout the entire time period. The household chooses to move if such will improve its housing situation by a considerable margin.[6] Otherwise, it continues to search, but after a number of unsuccessful attempts it abandons the idea of a move. The amount of improvement necessary to make a household move is assumed to depend on its prior search experience, that is, to go up with each successful search and down with each unsuccessful search. In other words, households are assumed to adapt their aspiration levels to supply conditions on the market.

The above discussion presents the basic elements of the microsimulation study of the Dortmund housing market. For a much more detailed, thorough and precise presentation, see Wegener (1985) and Wegener and Spiekermann (1996). Also for some early tests of calibration of the equations and validation of the results, see Wegener (1985).

While the Dortmund study represented a state-of-the-art Monte Carlo simulation in the early 1980s and is concisely discussed in the 1996 article by Wegener and Spiekermann, the significance of this study lies in the authors' conception of a comprehensive urban land-use transport model involving an overall integrated microsimulation, one that involves simulation within each of several submodels. One essential step for the development of this model is a microsimulation of a transport submodel in order to capture the interrelated effects of the diverse forms of travel behavior (e.g. car pooling) as well as provide travel data on a spatially disaggregated basis. Such data is depicted in Figure 9.3c. Depicted along with this data, are the spatially disaggregated data on residences (Figure 9.3a) and workplaces (Figure 9.3b). [Figure 9.3 is obtained by disaggregating zonal land-use density data into pixel (raster) form, a pixel being one of the small discrete elements that constitutes an image, as for example on a television screen.] Moreover, the spatially disaggregated data depicted by Figure 9.3 would also be invaluable for microsimulations within other submodels, for example, that of air pollution (dependent as well upon spatially disaggregated data from sources of pollution emissions other than travel) and that of noise pollution. In turn, the microsimulations on air and noise pollution would provide data (in a feedback manner) on significant attributes that may be added to the set of attributes considered in the housing and transport submodels.

Among other processes that might also be investigated with microsimulations in an integrated land-use transport model are residential construction and demolition, job creation and dissolution, water use and diverse infrastructure investments.

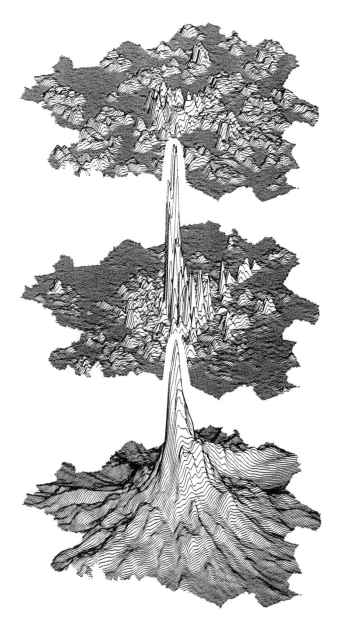

Figure 9.3 Three-dimensional synthetic depiction of residences, workplaces (center), and work types (bottom) in Dortmund

Source: Wegener and Spiekermann, 1996, *European Research in Regional Science*, 10, Pion Limited London, p. 160.

9.4 Concluding remarks

While microsimulation is in a relatively early development stage, largely because of high costs of operation and the limited data available, and likely to evolve only slowly for the same reasons, it has great potential for many types of analysis. As: (1) more and more spatially disaggregated data are collected; (2) as more and more synthetic data are produced from microsimulations leading to the development of more and more synthetic time series for more and more spatially disaggregated regions; and (3) as computer capabilities become more and more advanced, spatial microsimulation will come to be employed more and more extensively by regional scientists. The two applications presented, both of clear value, are examples of others that are being and likely to be realized.

Endnotes

1   Other non-behavioral relationships (operating characteristics) may need, of course, to be recognized and taken into account (such as obsolescence of physical capital, an item of wealth), but these relations are usually not of central importance.

2   As Orcutt et al. (1976), p. 13 note:
    Any current or updated population may be represented by a random sample drawn from it. Means, variance, covariance, and other functions of the sample will be estimates of the corresponding functions of the population sampled. The properties of samples and of sample statistics in relation to populations and population statistics have been extensively investigated and are readily available. Clearly, for many purposes the United States population may be satisfactorily represented by a sample of a few thousand persons and larger samples can be used when the use justifies the added expense.

3   Note, in Figure 9.2 the initial estimate yielded by the microdynamic equations is well below the historical estimate. Of the several possible explanations for this shortfall Caldwell and Keister (1996) point to the fact that it was necessary in their study to 'assume that the relationship between demographic characteristics of families and the probability of wealth ownership and the value of family wealth holdings was time

invariant' pp. 100–101. They were not able to estimate time-specific
microdynamic equations since data from panel and other sources were
not available or of sufficient quality, particularly during the 1960s and
1970s.

4   This probability $p_{k|hi}$ is given by

$$p_{k|hi} = R_{hki} \exp[-\alpha_h^h u_{hki}^h(t)]/\sum_k R_{hki} \exp[-\alpha_h^h u_{hki}^h(t)] \qquad (9\text{-}1)$$

$$h = 1, 2, 3,... \qquad k = 1, 2, 3,... \qquad i = 1, 2, 3,...$$

where R_{hki} = the number of households of type h living in a
                     dwelling of type k in zone i

u_{hki}^h = the attractiveness for household type h of dwelling
                     type k in zone i

$-\alpha_h^h$ = the negative of a coefficient to yield 'a higher
                     proportion of dissatisfied households entering the
                     housing market than would result from *pro rata*
                     sampling' (Wegener, 1985, p. 166)

In turn, u_{hki}^h is given by

$$u_{hki}^h = (u_{hi}^h)^{w_k^{hi}} (u_{hk}^h)^{w_h^{hk}} (u_{hki}^{hr})^{w_h^{hr}} \qquad (9\text{-}2)$$

$$h = 1, 2, 3,... \qquad k = 1, 2, 3,... \qquad i = 1, 2, 3,...$$

where u_{hi}^h = the attraction of zone i as a location for household
                      type h

u_{hk}^h = the attraction of housing type k for household h

u_{hki}^{hr} = the attraction of the rent r of the dwelling k in
                      relation to h's housing budget

The w_k^{hi}, w_h^{hk} and w_h^{hr} are importance weights adding to unity. Functions
for determining u_{hi}^h and u_{hk}^h map attributes to utility, while u_{hki}^{hr} is
based on rent and income.

5   This probability $p_{i'|hki}$ is given by

$$p_{i'|hki} = \sum_{k'} D_{k'i'} \exp[\beta_h^m u_{hii'}^m(t)] / \sum_{i'} \sum_{k'} D_{k'i'} \exp[\beta_h^m u_{hii'}^m(t)] \qquad (9\text{-}3)$$

$$k' = 1, 2, 3,... \qquad i' = 1, 2, 3,...$$

where $D_{k'i'}$ = the number of vacant dwellings of type k' in zone i'

β_h^m = a coefficient

$u_{hii'}^m$ = a measure of the attractiveness of zone i' as a new location for household of type h currently in dwelling k in zone i (a migration utility)

See Wegener (1985) and Wegener and Spiekermann (1996) for further discussion of the functions that are involved.

6   A measure $u_{hii'}^m$ of the attractiveness of zone i' as a new location for household of type h currently located in zone i (which may be designated *migration utility*) is involved. So also is the prior determination of the probablility $p_{i'|hki}$ that the household searches in zone i' for new housing, and the probability $p_{i'|hkii'}$ that h inspects housing of type k' before making a choice. See Wegener (1985) and Wegener and Spiekermann (1996) for the presentation of the social functions involved.

References

Birkin, M., G. P. Clarke, and M. Clarke. 1996. 'Urban and Regional Modelling at the Microscale,' in Clarke, G. P. (ed.) *op. cit.*, 10–27.

Birkin M., and M. Clarke. 1988. 'SYNTHESIS—a Synthetic Spatial Information System for Urban and Regional Analysis: Methods and Examples,' *Environment and Planning A*, 20: 1645–1671.

Caldwell, S. B. 1986. 'Broadening Policy Models: Alternative Strategies,' in Orcutt et al., *op. cit.*, 59–77.

Caldwell, S. B., and L. A. Keister. 1996. 'Wealth in America: Family Stock Ownership and Accumulation, 1960–1995,' in G. P. Clarke (ed.) *op. cit.*, 64–87.

Clarke, G. P. (ed.) 1996. *Microsimulation for Urban and Regional Policy Analysis*. London: Pion Limited.

Clarke, M. 1986. 'Demographic Processes and Household Dynamics: A Microsimulation Approach,' in R. Woods and P. H. Rees (eds.), *Population Structures and Models: Developments in Spatial Demography*. London: Allen and Unwin, 245–272.

Clarke, M. 1995. 'A Micro-approach to Demographic and Social Accounting,' in P. Hewings Hooimeijer, 1996. 'A Life-course Approach to Urban Dynamics: State of the Art and Research Design for the Netherlands,' in G. P. Clarke (ed.) *op. cit.*, 28–63.

Isard, W. et al. 1969. *General Theory: Social, Political, Economic and Regional.* Cambridge, MA: MIT Press.

Krupp, H. J. 1986. 'Potential and Limitations of Micro Simulation Models,' in Orcutt et al., *op. cit.*, 3–41.

Merz, J. 1991. 'Microsimulation—A Survey of Principles, Developments and Applications,' *International Journal of Forecasting*, 7: 77–104.

Orcutt, G. 1957. 'A New Type of Socio-Economic Systems,' *The Review of Economics and Statistics*, 58, 773–797.

Orcutt, G., S. Caldwell, and R. Wertheimer II. 1976. *Policy Exploration through Microanalytic Simulation.* Washington, D.C.: The Urban Institute.

Orcutt, G., M. Greenberger, J. Korbel, and A. Rivlin. 1961. *Microanalysis of Socioeconomic Systems: A Simulation Study.* New York: Harper & Row.

Orcutt, G., J. Merz, and H. Quinke (eds.). 1986. *Microanalytic Simulation Models to Support Social and Financial Policy.* Amsterdam: North-Holland.

Wegener, M. 1985. 'The Dortmund Housing Market Model: a Monte Carlo Simulation of a Regional Housing Market,' in J. K. Stahl (ed.), *Microeconomic Models of Housing Markets. Lecture Notes in Economics and Mathematical Systems.* Berlin: Springer, pp. 144–191.

Wegener, M. 1986. 'Integrated Forecasting Models of Urban and Regional Systems,' in P. W. J. Batey and M. Madden (eds.), *Integrated Analysis of Regional Systems.* London: Pion, pp. 9–24.

Wegener, M. 1994. 'Operational Urban Models: State of the Art,' *Journal of the American Planning Assocation*, 60: 17–29.

Wegener, M., and K. Spiekermann, 1996. 'The Potential of Microsimulation for Urban Models,' in G. P. Clarke, *op. cit.*, 149–163.

10. New channels of synthesis: the fusion of regional science methods

Walter Isard

10.0 Introduction

We now come to the last chapter of this book. In this chapter we will discuss possible new channels of synthesis of regional science methods. We do so in the same spirit as was done in the chapter on *Channels of Synthesis* in the 1960 Methods book (Isard et al., 1960). In each of the previous chapters we deal with a specific tool, technique or group of tools or techniques which relates to a particular subsystem of a region, the region as a whole, the interregional system or to several of these as entities. And in these chapters, a number of the syntheses suggested in 1960 have been realized, as evident in brief reports and references to past and current research studies. Still there is much ground to be covered.

In this chapter on *New Channels of Synthesis* we shall attempt to move further along the path toward the attainment of an ideal comprehensive synthesis. Within the confines of this chapter we cannot develop a full-blown empirical study which achieves that synthesis. Such would be well beyond our resources and time. However, it is possible to set down in a systematic manner possible new, more comprehensive syntheses than those already achieved. We shall explicitly differentiate between those that are both conceptual and operational and those that, in the light of available data, know-how, theory, and experience, can only be conceptual. Once more we shall supplement our discussion with diagrammatic sketches of main channels that can be investigated. In doing so we shall repeat some of the discussion in the 1960 chapter on Channels of Synthesis. By and large, however, we shall concentrate on fruitful channels which are new, and as far as the author is aware, have not yet been realized in the literature. However, we recommend to the incoming graduate student and research worker that he/she peruse the 1960 chapter, which is much more extensive than this one, to gain a fuller awareness of significant aspects of the field of regional science. Needless to say, we do not have an adequate set of completed empirical studies of the relatively recent developments such as microsimulation to evaluate the more advanced syntheses proposed.

10.1 Location analysis for industry and service trades and its fusion with input-output, econometrics and programming

We begin by explicitly recognizing some of the many assumptions lying behind the conduct of location analysis in and of itself. We do so since the fusion of location analysis with other regional science methods is aimed at relaxing some of the strong assumptions underlying location analysis when pursued in isolation. However, in doing so we must bear in mind that the fusion process with other methods often involves the introduction of new assumptions, hopefully on net weaker than the ones relaxed. In effect, a benefit-cost calculation should be involved in examining the desirability of a fusion.

We start with Figure 10.1 for the New Channel I. This channel begins with comparative cost analysis for the location of industry and service trades. In addition to information on several cost differentials relevant for such analysis (such as those on transport, labor, energy, land, capital, and environmental matters), a number of basic assumptions are required. One of these pertains to markets. As indicated at the close of chapter 2, in making a decision to locate a production or service activity at a specific site we need to assume that there exists in the relevant system (regional, interregional or national) *markets* which over a relevant time-period can absorb the planned output of the activity and allow anticipated scale economies to be realized. But for the assumption of a large enough market there needs to be others such as those listed at the extreme left of Figure 10.1. These pertain to outputs of industries (requiring as inputs the goods to be produced) and *Gross System Income* (available for purchase of the goods. In turn, Gross System Income depends on *Gross System Product* and implicitly on a viable system of prices by which to weight the set of sector outputs that the system produces. Alternatively, Gross System Product may be viewed more loosely as the result of an existing *labor force* multiplied by its *average productivity*. The existing labor force may be estimated from assumptions regarding rates of participation by the several age groups of each sex in the system's *population*. Average productivity (output

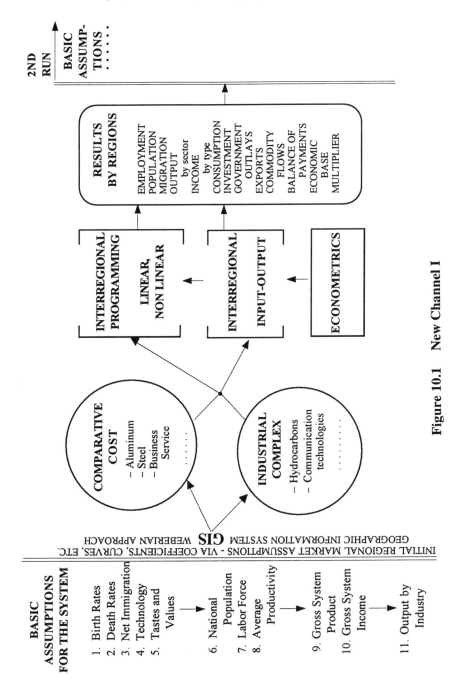

Figure 10.1   New Channel I

per man hour) derives from assumptions on the state of *technology*, anticipated work week and the industry and services composition of the system's economy. System population in turn is governed by assumed *birth and death rates* and *net immigration*.

In addition to these basic assumptions, there will very often be the need for an appropriate GIS system to provide spatial disaggregation of relevant macromagnitudes — of population, labor force by type skill, Gross System Product and Income — and, most important, the spatial distribution of assumed markets, at the minimum to derive improved estimates of transport costs. The GIS system may often embody location quotients, coefficients of localization and the like to help develop spatial disaggregation when primary sources of data are unavailable.

However, greatly improved analysis may often be realizable when the combined GIS-comparative cost analysis can be fused with a regional or more desirably an interregional input-output table. Such a table would provide good estimates of the existing market for the product of the activity whose location is being considered. Further, an input-output study of the possible impact of that industry upon the several production sectors would provide even better market estimates. Moreover, if by chance projections based on any of the regional (or interregional) input-output tables have been made, they could provide useful information on future markets.

Thus, the fusion in Channel I of input-output tables with GIS and comparative cost analysis provides very useful information for market estimation and for other purposes. Already, at the end of chapter 3, we recorded how fruitful fusion had already been early achieved in the Greater New York–Philadelphia Region steel study (Isard and Kuenne, 1953). Since in the 1960 Methods book, there is much discussion of different ways that this fusion can be fruitful, we need not repeat that discussion here nor mention other useful studies already conducted. However, as indicated by the box (lower center) in Figure 10.1, such fusion should be conducted within an interregional framework. The impact of a new industry to be located in a given region should be investigated in terms of effects upon not only the given region (as in the Greater New York–Philadelphia Region steel study) but also other regions (for example, the Greater Pittsburgh region) which might provide not only significant inputs in the construction and operation of a new steel plant in the given region but also be subject to the relocation of some of their own industry (for example, steel fabricators) to that region.

But this type of fusion has already been or can easily be achieved in a number of studies, and we wish to move on. We have already mentioned in section 4.7 the fruitfulness of the fusion of input-output and econometrics. This fusion has not been extended, as far as the author is aware, to a study of a combined interregional input-output/econometric analysis to obtain a deeper investigation of interactions within a system of regions, where within each region an appropriate econometric model is employed. Moreover, as far as the author is aware, there has been no impact study involving a fused GIS comparative cost/input-output/econometric framework — one involving a full blown comparative cost study of the feasibility of a new basic industry or business services center and its impact directly upon a region and indirectly through an already fused input-output/econometrics framework. Initially in this type of study, the feedback upon the comparative cost evaluation might be deferred as well as the impact upon other regions. Subsequently, however, the feedback effects should be at least partially captured as well as effects on other regions in the interregional system — ideally where in each region there is employed an appropriate econometric model.

The New Channel I also depicts how *Industrial Complex analysis* can be connected to a fused input-output/econometric framework. It simply takes the place of comparative cost analysis, since in one sense it may be viewed as comparative cost analysis extended to cover a set of connected activities (linked spatially or otherwise). For example, it might be fruitful to study how the closing of a major naval base with all its ancillary activities such as the Philadelphia Navy Yard impacted the Philadelphia economy or how the demise of the Lackawanna steel-steel fabricating complex affected the greater Buffalo region. Or conversely, how the new *shipping activities complex* at the site of the old Philadelphia Naval Yard may impact the Greater Philadelphia Region economy, and even more desirably this economy and the economies of the neighboring regions. Similar studies might be performed to evaluate the desirability of Special Economic Zones such as the Free Trade Zone in North Korea, or the establishment of growth pole centers.

Another possible low-order fusion suggested in Figure 10.1 would involve that of comparative cost or industrial complex directly with nonlinear programming. We have already noted in chapter 5 that the Puerto Rico oil refinery-petrochemical-synthetic fiber complex was, in spirit, such a fusion. However, at the time of its study, methods for programming were not available for use by the authors and the computations had to be performed with a slide rule and a primitive desk computer. As a result, sensitivity studies and the attainment of more precise results was not possible. Today, much more sophisticated analysis is possible with advanced computer technology. Given the constraint on the maximum size of a fiber plant or other key element of a proposed complex that may be set by the investment community, by political and other factors or by simply environmental ones, the impact of an industrial complex where its analysis is combined with nonlinear programming can easily be investigated on a comprehensive basis. One could conduct significant sensitivity analysis and easily probe the trade-off between net revenue or employment and air pollution or other environmental variables where relevant data exist.

Moreover, when resources permit, an input-output matrix can be introduced so that impacts on many more sectors of a region can be investigated, and a deeper probe into environmental effects can be obtained with the introduction of pollution coefficients, by type pollutant, by sector and by Final Demand category.

Going even further, a combined input-output/econometric module may be added so that the full involvement of the regional science tools of the New Channel I would be achieved. To reiterate, this involvement is easily conducted where (1) input-output tables are available, (2) where one of the several input-output/econometric modules is employed and (3) where there has been placed an upper limit on the scale of a basic industry, industrial complex, or an industrial development or district. In many other situations, such can occur when financing considerations set an upper limit on capital that can be raised, or when political or other bodies specify constraints on port development, railroad construction, modernization of airport facilities or other extensive transport project incurring major scale economies that would dominate other economies.

Finally, many useful sensitivity analyses can lead to sets of trade-offs from changing constraints, when trade-offs can be quantitatively estimated as in the case of air pollution from industrial output — and even where they cannot as when change in the subjective factor of an investment community's risk is involved and can only be stated in terms of more or less, or the equivalent.

It should be noted that in the New Channel I, where we do not cover the full array of market prices to equate supply and demand by commodity and by resource, we retain the concept of rerun used in the 1960 Methods book. Clearly, a first run of the model can yield results inconsistent with the initial basic assumptions. There will be discrepancies. For example, consider the outputs by industry (and by region) assumed initially, say to gauge the market for steel in order to evaluate the feasibility of an integrated iron and steel works. If it turns out that the construction of such a works is justified, the resulting projection of sector outputs may differ significantly from the initially assumed outputs. Thus the latter must be replaced by the new set (or some still more appropriate set). But this in turn can lead to another set of outputs significantly different from that new set. And so on. In short, reruns must take place in order to remove any major discrepancies. For more detailed discussion of possible discrepancies and the rerun procedure, the reader is referred to the 1960 Methods book, pp. 593–600. It should be kept in mind that this rerun procedure is not equivalent to the more appropriate notion of feedback effects, instantaneous or within a short period of time, when market prices are determined in a fused framework.

10.2 Channel II. Social accounting analysis and its fusion with applied general interregional equilibrium analysis and other methods

We now proceed to the New Channel II, in Figure 10.2, a channel that introduces interregional SAM and *Applied General Interregional Equilibrium (AGIE)* into our analytic framework. Unlike Channel I this channel requires significant new effort at model development — in particular models using both of these techniques. As is evident from the discussion of chapter 7, most of the research on SAM has been oriented to the problems of national systems, and accordingly constructed in terms of concepts and data collection and processing useful for the study of such systems. Although the relevance of SAM as a *regional* technique was presented in the 1960 Methods book, little research has been devoted to its development *per se,* especially in terms of its usefulness for interregional analysis. To function as a general regional science tool, SAM must go beyond the presentation of data for a single region, or for a set of regions, each unconnected with others. In general, in the uses of Channel II and for projection into the future, an interregional SAM is requisite. Its detail should expose the interregional connections of each account of each region. This should be so not only for production activities such as captured by an interregional input-output table to be embraced in an interregional SAM, but also for factors of production, households, companies, government, combined capital account and the Rest of the World. Admittedly, there will be data problems, which in the past have precluded the incorporation of the

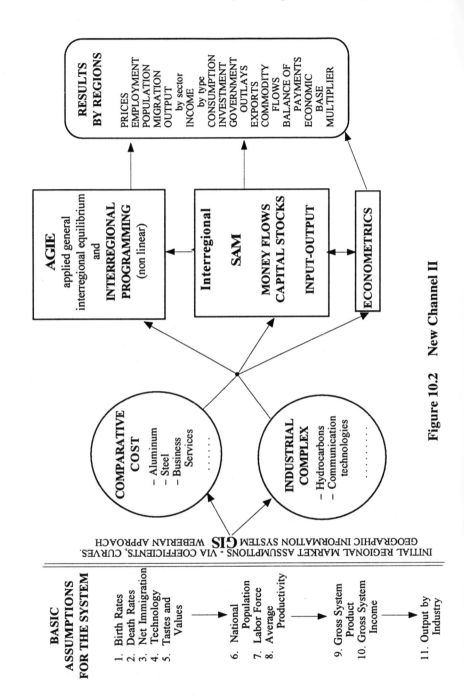

Figure 10.2   New Channel II

interregional frame in practically all regional SAM studies; however, the further development of GIS should help remove such problems.

Figure 10.2 on the New Channel II explicitly presents this important future link of GIS to SAM. Specifically, more extensive data should become available on the flow of factor payments among regions, the distribution of household expenditures among regions, interregional receipts and outlays of various institutions, and so forth. With such development, it will then be possible to involve an interregional SAM in a much more analytical manner within impact studies — an involvement that is common place with interregional input-output analysis. Such would be along the lines already taken by Hewings, Sonis, Lee and Jahan (1995) in their interregional structural path and decomposition analysis for the four regions, Dhaka, Chittagong, Rajshahi, and Khulna of Bangladesh.

Additionally, in accordance with the recent development of *Financial SAMs* noted in chapters 7 and 8, the combined capital account of the *Real SAM* should be disaggregated by key elements of a *Financial SAM,* each element to be presented on an interregional basis. When appropriately organized, such can yield an interregional flow of funds table. Thus, as can be noted in Figure 10.2, we have listed money flows under SAM to indicate this extension. Necessarily, as observed in chapter 8, an interregional flow of funds study would need to go hand in hand with an accounting of changes in capital stocks (wealth, or assets and liabilities) of economic agents (households, companies, government and other institutions). Accordingly, we have listed *capital stocks* under money flows in Figure 10.2. It should be noted that the 1960 Methods book, pp. 611–21, presented a conception of an interregional flow of funds with some attention paid to changes in assets and liabilities of economic agents. This conception has still not been empirically implemented. However, recently Kilkenny and Rose (1995) have presented, again on a conceptual basis only, a compact and comprehensive framework which significantly extends the 1960 one and whose empirical implementation is being undertaken. The Kilkenny and Rose study is focussed on a developed country (the United States). Their conceptual framework needs to be significantly modified for studies of developing countries.

In a narrow, restricted sense the SAM of Channel II may be viewed as designating a *matrix* wherein there is included (1) an interregional input-output (interindustry) transactions table plus a Final Demand sector by region, (2) the additional accounts by region corresponding to factor payments, households, companies, government and other institutions, and the Rest of the World; and (3) a money flows submatrix with an accompanying set of changes in capital stock (assets and liabilities) accounts. In this sense it is a grand statistical snapshot of an economy with overlaps with parts of the rest of society. However, in Channel II the interregional SAM needs to be viewed much more broadly. In the same way that an interregional input-output table is viewed as the empirical base for interregional input-output analysis, the SAM matrix in the future must be viewed as the empirical base for conducting *Social Accounting Analysis* (SAA). Structural path analysis, as described in chapter 7, which parallels and which can be extended to incorporate some of the more advanced structural industrial decomposition analysis in input-output analysis (see Rose and Caster, 1996), is one such element of SAA. However it should be of an interregional character. Other SAA analyses should be developed, particularly in connection with interregional impact study.

As noted in chapter 8, an interregional system is not simply a nation decomposed into regions which trade with each other within the given structure of the nation. Rather, the nation and its regions constitute a system wherein there are constant *up* and *down* direct effects and feedback — a recognition which has by now been well established in regional and interregional input-output analysis. That is, while it is accepted doctrine that change in a nation's structure causes changes in each region and that a change in a given region may also lead to change in every other region, it is also so that changes in any one region affect the nation (as an aggregate of regions, economically, physically and in other respects). The relation of a region's economic structure with that of a nation has on a number of occasions not been fully recognized in regional SAMs. Moreover, aside from a nation, there are other supraregional aggregates to which a region's accounts within an interregional SAM need to be connected. Along with the supraregional accounts of the national government there must be recorded all the accounts of (1) supraregional units such as metropolitan, local and other governments, (2) multi-region authorities such as a Port Authority and other intergovernmental units involving several states or their parts, and (3) blocks of nations such as NAFTA and any future European monetary union. See Rounds (1995) for a partial recognition of this need. At times such an organization of an interregional SAM may take on a hierarchical character. Again, reliance on an extended GIS will be necessary.

With an interregional SAM, fully enlarged and analytically extended as a regional science technique, we now consider its linkage with other regional science methods. First, we note its possible fusion with Econometrics. This can be easily perceived, since as noted in the new

Channel I, the synthesis of econometrics with input-output analysis (a key component of SAM) has already been achieved in several studies. However, in the context of an interregional SAM, there should be involved, as in Channel I, an appropriate econometric model for each of the regions covered, particularly for estimation of the magnitudes of Final Demand categories.

An even more advanced fusion would add a comparative cost component to the fused framework. This would be relevant when there arises the question of the location of a major industry, the development of an industrial complex, the establishment of an industrial district or Special Trade Zone, or the construction of a major business services center. At least, two key interrelated questions need to be examined. One concerns the feasibility of any such development in terms of whether an adequate market would exist. Such would require estimates of not only direct demand, but also indirect demand based on the series of indirect (round-by-round) effects generated by the SAM framework, especially its input-output and household expenditure components. The second question would relate to the total impact of the development — impact upon employment, income, environmental disturbance, and other elements. Further, if environmental impact were to be investigated, the SAM framework, at least its interindustry component, would need to be extended to cover the environmental inputs and outputs of each production, household, government, institutional and other sector which has a direct connection with the environmental subsystem. At this point, still greater reliance upon a GIS framework would be called for.

Alternatively, the study of the feasibility of such a development and its impact could, on a less advanced basis, proceed without the econometric components — in particular, when insufficient resources and time are available for inclusion of this technique in the fused model. It could also be the case that inadequate resources and time would not allow the inclusion of the interregional money flow and associated 'change in capital stock' components in the interregional SAM to be employed — and perhaps necessitate a less disaggregated SAM than in other studies that might be undertaken. However, when adequate resources are available, the interregional SAM should be consistent with the scaffolding developed in chapter 8. There should of course be in each region of a multi-region system much more disaggregation of the household sector than in the scaffolding presented, many more production activities and commodities and many more companies, governments and institutions. Furthermore the transport activities of the transport subsystem of each region must be explicitly covered to embody all interregional shipments of commodities and movements of household members. Ideally the complete set of interregional money flows and capital stock changes by agent and by region should be contained.

The second major analytical method added to the New Channel II is Applied General Interregional Equilibrium (AGIE). As indicated in chapter 8, this method is still in a stage of infancy and needs extensive nurturing. It has great potential for advancement of regional science. Its basic contribution lies in the determination of prices in diverse markets via the equation of demand and supply — that is in the introduction of equilibrium analysis.

Already in section 8.2.5 we have indicated the fruitful fusion of this approach with comparative cost for a more advanced location analysis. Typically a comparative cost analysis looks at existing costs and revenues at several possible locations for an economic activity — an industry, service trade or other economic enterprise. However, it is well recognized that the very location of an activity at a potential site may alter the existing set of costs and revenues at that site. Hence, it is the altered (the future) set of costs and revenues that is relevant for determining an optimal location of an activity.

In section 8.2.5 we specified the potential effects of the location of a new major enterprise upon the demand and supply for factors (albeit via simple demand and supply functions) in each of two regions considered as possible sites. Via the equation of supply and demand we generated what the altered set of factor prices (capital and labor) would be for each region were the enterprise located in it, and the better (the optimal) location for that enterprise could be discerned. Thus, the equilibrium analysis (the basic tool of AGIE) provided a better framework for an evaluation of that location problem. In general, in this way the fusion of comparative cost and AGIE (however simple its framework) can easily lead to improvement of many types of location decisions.

Additionally, for impact analysis an interregional input-output procedure can be easily brought into the fused framework. The resulting framework would not only provide additional information on markets (by specifying demand for the output of the enterprise by each economic sector), but also permit a more accurate determination of the impact of a basic location decision than would be achieved were only a combination of comparative cost and interregional input-output employed. For example, the fusion of comparative cost and input-output in the Greater New York– Philadelphia Region steel study (reported on in section 3.5), would have profited from an AGIE approach (were it then available) to determine the effect of the location of that facility upon labor costs in the region. This would have permitted a better estimate by the authors of how the change in these costs would impact the operations of each of the 42 sectors covered in that study — an estimate required for the round-by-round procedure pursued.

In similar manner the fusion of industrial complex (already a partial fusion of comparative cost and input-output) with AGIE analysis can be easily achieved. We have already indicated in chapter 5 how the Puerto Rico industrial complex study can be perceived as involving nonlinear programming. Since in this study and many others AGIE may be viewed as equivalent to nonlinear programming, the possibility of fusion of AGIE and industrial complex is immediately grasped. The Puerto Rico study would have profited from an AGIE look (however simplified) at the labor market, and pressure for changes in wages therein. Better estimates of wages that would come to prevail might have resulted. They could have replaced the speculative estimates that were employed.

Also, for evaluating development policy for cheap labor regions based on a combination of cheap labor and agglomeration economies a simplified AGIE type model for estimating the effects of that policy on labor costs (and in general upon all costs and revenues) could be useful to replace speculative judgments.

A more complex problem is encountered when one considers the fusion of AGIE with a comparative cost/input-output/econometric framework where the econometric component is employed to estimate the magnitudes of final demand sectors. This is partly so because of the different orientation of econometrics and AGIE. On the whole, the econometric approach is based on statistical inference from relevant structural data of the past which can involve situations subject to some, if not considerable, disequilibrium within a number of commodity and other markets. This orientation stands in sharp contrast to the equilibrium requirement of AGIE.

Nonetheless, for cases where the level of demand or supply or both can only be speculations for macromagnitudes, such as on investment and government expenditures, and where a market does not exist (and thus where AGIE procedure is non-operative), econometric estimates can be useful. They can, for example, establish totals for one or more final demand sectors to serve as exogenous constraints for AGIE analysis.

The most ambitious undertaking suggested in the new Channel II would involve the fusion of all the regional science methods mentioned — of

AGIE with interregional SAM where SAM incorporates an interregional input-output framework integrated with econometrics, interregional money flows and the associated changes in capital stocks of economic agents, and with comparative cost or industrial complex. As indicated at top of the central box of Channel II, this fusion could also in many situations be viewed as equivalent to a nonlinear interregional programming operation employing all the other regional science methods.

The discussion in chapter 8 on AGIE emphasized the need for an *interregional* SAM when a multi-region system is being examined and when the regions are not completely isolated — as might be the case where two regions are separated by an impassable mountain barrier and no means other than land transport exists. Since no operational AGIE model has as yet been conducted, and since at least in a limited manner such a model is achievable, highly desirable, and can be extremely useful for evaluating a development policy or situation where a dominant scale-economy possibility exists, we prescribed in that chapter a scaffolding covering the essential accounts and agents for such a SAM. It is hoped that the scaffolding presented will serve as a challenge to young research scholars and graduate students to develop an applicable AGIE model.

However, the reader is to be reminded that there are major problems in the attainment of such an applicable model based on an interregional SAM with interregional money flows and associated changes in capital stocks (holdings of wealth). First, many of the problems encountered in national-type AGE will be confronted — problems such as: (1) the identification of appropriate production functions for the several types of firms and consumption functions for the different household sectors; (2) the presentation of the different revenue and expenditure relations for the diverse central government programs and administrative, judicial and other categories of activities; (3) the specification of the several sources of savings and relevant investment categories; and (4) the coverage of the diverse money flows among accounts inclusive of changes in assets and liabilities of different agents and institutions.

Next, there are the additional problems of establishing appropriate sets of accounts for the regions within an interregional system and for the supraregional sectors (aside from the central government) — the urban and metropolitan governments, multi-region behaving units and other authorities, and even blocks of nations already mentioned.

Just presenting a list of accounts for each of these supraregional units, however, is not enough. It is necessary to establish the relationships that govern their behavior and their interconnections (backward and forward feedbacks) with the sectors and accounts of each region, the central government and among themselves. The backward and forward feedbacks can be up and down interactions in an hierarchical structure, perhaps where the accounts and agents at the local region, the lowest level of the hierarchy, generate the grassroots activity.

Furthermore, when interregional money flows and changes in assets and liabilities of different agents and institutions are added to the SAM structure, there are problems of identifying relationships, such as those that determine the interest rates charged by the commercial banks in the different regions, and the discount rate the central bank sets for loans to commercial banks.

In brief, there are many problems to overcome in developing a comprehensive AGIE study based on a detailed interregional SAM — room for many important contributions. Most likely such a study will evolve in a step-by-step fashion where initially highly simplified frameworks are employed, involving at first fusion of two or three of the regional science methods, but which in time become more elaborate and embody more regional science techniques until ultimately all the regional science methods are embraced.

It should also be borne in mind that where scale economies can be present in many activities and when none are dominant, an optimal solution may not be able to be identified. However, when there is a dominant (overriding) scale economy in a major activity, an AGIE as a nonlinear programming problem with an appropriate objective function (to be discussed in Channel IV) may yield a solution when a boundary constraint is set on the activity. The sensitivity of the solution to changes in the constraint may also be a fruitful research activity.

10.3 Channel III. Methods for analyzing urban and metropolitan processes

Channel III is designed to employ regional science methods to further our understanding of urban/metropolitan processes and to evaluate better possibilities for urban development. See Figure 10.3. First, note that social scientists in general have been able to unravel at best only a modest (though significant) part of the phenomena of city growth and decline. Where we social scientists have been most successful is in examining *impacts* of exogenous shocks (outside events). Impacts take place in time, usually after a shock, but on occasion before the shock (through anticipation) and rarely instantaneously. The very involvement of time introduces dynamic elements into the phenomena, complicating them in ways which, admittedly, we fail to unearth in any but a small way. Nonetheless, with our regional science methods we can conduct useful urban/metropolitan impact studies without addressing adequately the dynamic aspects.

Early on, in chapter 3, we addressed impact analysis, projecting with use of input-output analysis: (1) how changes in the operations of Boeing, a major industrial enterprise in Washington state, comes to impinge on that state's economy; and (2) how the location of a Trenton integrated iron and steel works comes to affect the Greater New York–Philadelphia Region. However, all this was done with hardly any consideration of effects upon the spatial, urban land use configuration. In chapter 4 we presented in econometric fashion how economic growth in Europe contributed to change in the producer services sector of the New York–New Jersey region and in New York City's tax revenues, etc., but stated nothing about the impact on New York City's spatial structure. On the other hand, when we discussed discrete spatial choice models in section 4.4.2 and spatial econometrics in section 4.5, we did have some reference to elements of the spatial structure of an urban area.

It was in chapter 5 that we introduced in a major way the need to examine in depth urban structure and its spatial configuration. One suggested way was through *urban complex analysis*. But we did not conduct such analysis. In chapter 6 we did explore at considerable depth the use of gravity and spatial interaction models for studying urban configuration. Except for the integration of these models with econometric methods, they were not fused with other regional science methods. In the remaining chapters, little reference was had to the gravity model and urban complex analysis. Finally, in section 9.3.2 we reported briefly upon how microsimulation, as a regional science method of great potential, can be very effectively employed in the analysis of urban structure; however its fusion with gravity models was at best only implicitly involved.

10.3.1 Fusion centering around gravity and gravity-type models

We now proceed to examine the fruitful fusion of regional science methods to enhance our understanding of urban processes and their associated spatial configurations. As with Channels I and II we start with Basic Assumptions and proceed to GIS and comparative cost analysis. From there we go immediately to fusion of methods with gravity models. For an urban area for which comparative cost analysis justifies the location there of a

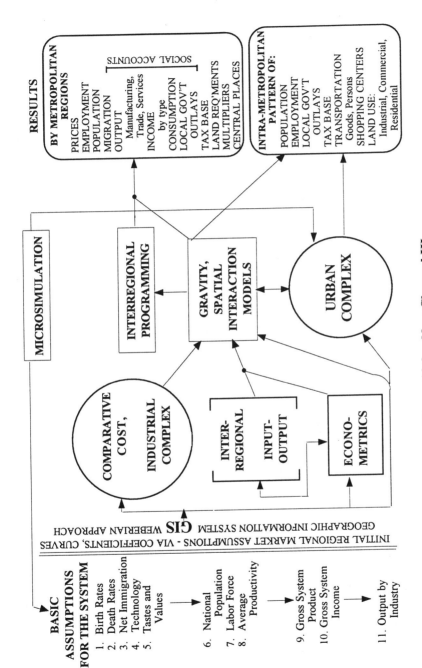

Figure 10.3   New Channel III

major industrial operation, such fusion yields the implications for changes in migration to and the journey-to-work pattern within that area. This type of fusion was accomplished early on by Lowry (1966) and others who followed. This type also has application when the location of economic activity in an urban area is based upon industrial complex analysis or when other cost-type of analysis justifies the development of an industrial district, a business services center, or a Special Trade (Economic) Zone to serve as a growth pole, or when political factors intervene to establish a major army base or other government facility in or close by an urban area.

This fusion of methods is easily extended to include input-output analysis which when pursued with comparative cost analysis yields as in the Greater New York–Philadelphia Region steel study the implications for change in employment by economic sector in the given urban area. Then via the gravity model implications for the journey-to-work pattern within that urban area can be projected. Also, with the use of the gravity model the effects upon shopping, hospital and other trip patterns can be investigated. More extended fusion can include the use of an econometric model to establish relevant changes in the Final Demand sectors of the input-output table for that urban area. All this would result in a set of even more relevant changes in employment by sector, and consequently in journey-to-work and other trip patterns.

Additionally, the gravity model can be employed to help judge whether an urban area (together with the neighboring outlying areas) provides a large enough market to justify the location in it of a major development: a business services center, industrial district, or regional shopping center. For example, take the case of a proposed regional shopping center. Is its potential market large enough to justify its development? The answer to this question would rest, among other factors, upon the total number of trips that on average each family in the area to be served is expected to take to the center and the estimate of that family's expenditure per trip. That number and expenditure would be dependent on the dollar or time cost of travel (that is, the effective distance to the shopping center). These findings, together with other factors that can be taken into account, would yield an estimate of the potential volume of sales or revenues. On the supply side, the cost of providing the goods and services demanded would need to be estimated. If under an appropriate pricing scheme the projected revenue were to equal or exceed projected costs, the regional shopping center would be economically justifiable. Or in another situation, this type of threshold-attainment use of a gravity model may be employed to determine whether projected sales to the population of the area to be served would be sufficient to justify a department store complex that is to achieve the scale economies necessary for that complex to function as the driving force behind a regional shopping center. In either case, the employment generated by such a center alone, or along with growth in the urban area (à la input-output or input-output fused with an econometric analysis) would with further use of the gravity model yield changes in the urban area's journey-to-work and other trip patterns.

Or the use of a relative income potential model (as extensively discussed in the 1960 Methods book, chapters 11 and 12) may be considered. (Relative income potential is defined as the ratio of the income potential of a given year (time period) to that of the previous one, where income as the relevant mass replaces population in equation 6-9). With the use of this concept or another appropriate variant of the gravity model, the urban area may be projected to experience expansion in its economic activities from growth in export trade with other regions within or outside its nation. The new employment generated whether from export trade growth alone, or export trade growth plus growth in the associated sectors in the urban area (à la input-output, or à la input-output fused with an econometric analysis) would with the use of a gravity model generate changes in the journey-to-work and other trip patterns.

Still another use of a regional income potential model or an appropriate variant of the gravity model in a fused framework would be to project migration from declining (surplus labor) or rural regions to growing (deficit labor) or urban regions. From such projection adjusted to yield changes in total employment, changes in the journey-to-work and other trip patterns can be estimated from fused frameworks in the manner already discussed.

Another fruitful extension of the above fused framework would include nonlinear programming. For example, consider the threshold-attainment use of the gravity model already mentioned to project the potential sales to the population of an urban region or subarea to determine whether a department store complex can be justified, that is, can achieve the required scale economies. With the inclusion of nonlinear programming, more useful analysis could be obtained. For different levels of department store scale economies [based upon different estimates of potential sales in turn dependent upon different estimates of the numbers of population and its composition (per capita income, family size, age distribution, educational level, ethnic character, etc.) which might reside within the urban region or subarea], different magnitudes for the optimum size (and composition) of a regional shopping center could be obtained. The best of these in terms of an *appropriate* objective function — for example to maximize net revenues or taxable base — may then be identified. In general, an extension that embraces nonlinear programming may be fruitful in a number of other ways — for example in: (a) the projection of a time-path of growth of a selected regional shopping center (if one is developed) that might be associated with a time-path of growth and change in composition of the supporting population, and (b) conducting general sensitivity analysis related to different levels of the binding constraints.

10.3.2 Fusion centering around urban complex analysis

We now move on to consider urban complex analysis as an integral part of the new Channel III. As far as the author is aware, no full-scale urban complex analysis has been conducted, in particular for a system of cities (or a central place system). However, we may speculate on one way of proceeding.

Say a regional shopping center is to be constructed with a department store component (to be well defined) as its core, capable of attaining major scale economies. From past experience a well-defined set of retail and related services can be expected to develop around this core. To start, assume that each of these activities operates under constant unit cost conditions to obtain a first set of resulting magnitudes of employment, income generated, space requirements and so forth for the center. Then relax the constant unit cost assumption and allow each retail or other related activity to have small scale economies in the use of labor and capital — assuming such has negligible effect on department store activity and its realizable scale economies. Allow the latter economies still to dominate the scale economy picture. As with industrial complex analysis, a nonlinear programming format may be employed to determine an optimal array and set of levels of activities.

Next introduce, except for department store activity, conditions of monopolistic competition for a number of relevant activities. One path might draw upon the work of Bröcker (1995). In developing a theoretical framework of a Chamberlinian spatial computable general equilibrium model, he has: (a) a large number of different brands of a commodity being produced by each sector; (b) a diversity of productive factors being used by firms as inputs; and (c) a heterogeneous bundle of brands of commodities being consumed by households — brands which are more or less close substitutes. Each firm produces a unique brand or set of brands of a commodity and thus has some monopoly power and limited ability to set prices. Within such a conception of an urban complex structure, scale economies can be introduced for these economic firms. With additional creative research to achieve consistency, an optimal structure should be obtainable with the use of a nonlinear programming framework with an appropriate objective function. With still later research it should be possible to add on to the resulting fused framework additional elements of input-output with or without an econometric component, and even with additional basic elements of SAM.

While the above procedures have been suggested for an investigation of a particular question, namely the feasibility of a regional shopping center, they are applicable to the examination of the feasibility of other developments. For instance, it might be a new town development around a major industry, medical/hospital center, government facility or recreational district where the feasibility of the development and the spatial configuration of the entire new town would be related to a dominant scale economy, perhaps associated with one of the developments noted. To this fused framework already extended a gravity model component can be added. This might provide not only helpful information on the magnitude of the new transportation investment required but also information on new or expanded transport links necessitated by changes in and emergence of new trip patterns — shopping, journey-to-work, hospital, recreational and/or others. Such would be generated by not only the existing population but also new population that comes to reside in the general area surrounding the development.

The above approach for the analysis of a proposed development, say the regional shopping center, can also be extended to cover analysis of the entire urban area of a small town. More difficult would be an extension to an urban area having more than one regional shopping center competing with each other, or a central city core and an outlying suburban core. The difficulty of analysis would mount considerably for an urban area with more than two cores, and even more so for a metropolitan area. For such analysis, it may also be necessary to recognize that the major scale economies realized in transportation systems need to be treated jointly with at least the major scale economies of the department store or other core component.

The research problem would involve still more complexity for competing multi-core urban areas and for a system of cities (central places) — a problem whose definition the author leaves for others to define.

A final additional component of Channel III is the relatively new regional science method of *microsimulation*. In the preceding chapter we presented elements of a microsimulation conducted for the city of Dortmund (Wegener and Spiekermann, 1996). It was crystal clear how based on data of housing-market transactions, relevant probabilities were obtained to provide a first cut at estimates of future intraregional migration of each specified household type h from zone i to zone i' and from dwelling type k to dwelling type k'. While accessibility to facilities and job location enter into the analysis via a transport submodel affecting utilities that a household perceives in a decision to migrate, the disaggregation by type household, by type housing and other significant attributes allowed other factors to enter into the probabilities obtained from the detailed data on the existing pattern of intraregional migration.

When the study is combined in an effective way with other research, using the finely disaggregated data on residences, workplace and work trips depicted in Figure 9.3, an integrated transport land-use microsimulation model can be constructed. In this way microsimulation can be added to the fused frameworks of Channel III already discussed. In the less complicated fused frameworks of this channel, microsimulation can clearly complement in a significant way a number of the uses of a gravity and the urban complex approach oriented to economic activity.

In other ways, microsimulation can add to the analytical strength of Channel III (and previous channels) through capturing the effects of the aging and other processes upon macromagnitudes by type and aggregate — labor force, its aggregate and by type; investment, its aggregate and by type; and other interconnected macromagnitudes such as GRP and GNP. This effect, which a microsimulation study can have, such as the one on wealth ownership that is being conducted on a spatially disaggregated basis, is indicated by the arrow from the microsimulation box to the Basic Assumption column. Microsimulation can also effectively enhance the rerun procedures or the introduction of feedback mechanisms that may be desirable in operating Channel III and other channels. The value of this effect need not be detailed.

It should be noted that the use of a gravity model together with disaggregated urban complex analysis and microsimulation need not generate inconsistencies because of their different approaches. They can effectively complement each other just as econometrics and input-output do (as indicated in section 4.7) even though the rationales for the use of econometrics and input-output differ greatly. To reiterate, the gravity model performs best when masses of behaving units are involved or when their behavior and when origins and destinations of a non-behavioral nature are viewed in their aggregate as masses. When this takes place, the different significance of each particular attribute or factor in influencing the behavior of the diverse units tends to cancel or average out, leaving the common pervasive effect of distance and accessibility to stand out. This is so when we estimate or project journey-to-work, shopping and other trips. On the other hand, whenever we disaggregate behaving units, origins and destinations by attributes or characteristics (for example, income level, type of retail store, or industry), the gravity model in general becomes less applicable. In contrast, urban complex analysis becomes more applicable the more masses are disaggregated by type. For example, analyses could be upgraded when there are employed different consumption functions for different types of households and different production functions for different firms that produce different outputs or brands of a given good. And with microsimulation, disaggregation by type unit is even still more applicable. However, such contrast among models with regard to different levels of aggregation need not introduce serious obstacles to joint use.

For example, we can employ a gravity model when the question is whether the sales of a proposed cluster of department stores would be large enough to justify its establishment as the core of a regional shopping center. The gravity model might be based on the spatial distribution of population and its income in a well-defined subarea. If the proposed cluster is justified, urban complex analysis could then be pursued to determine the scale and composition of shops by type that might flourish at the center, and microsimulation might be used to yield a much more detailed pattern of new transport links to be constructed.

In brief, a combined gravity model/urban complex analysis/micro-simulation framework can be appropriately developed for application without significant inconsistency, and to this framework there can be added nonlinear programming with its diverse connections to input-output, econometrics and comparative cost analysis. Application on an interregional (interareal) scale is much more complex, but should in time be realizable.

10.4 Channel IV. On comprehensive syntheses and conflict management

We now come to the final channel of this chapter. It covers the ground covered by Channels IV and V in the 1960 Methods book. It represents a far-reaching attempt to extend the task of regional science and its conceptual framework beyond the arena of operation covered by the three channels already discussed. It brings into consideration objectives and policy analysis that go beyond the attainment of efficiency and/or system equilibrium with maximization of utility, profits, revenues, etc., or minimization of costs, unemployment or other magnitudes. It examines a setting where *implicitly* or *explicitly* different utility functions exist among behaving units — more particularly, differences among individuals, groups, regions and cultures as to specific objectives a system should have and the weights that are either objectively or subjectively assigned to them. This is so even when an objective function is specified in a well-constructed linear or nonlinear programming model since such a model has binding constraints whose magnitudes, if meaningful in a setting of conflicting objectives, have been set with regard to a resolution (implicit or explicit) of the conflict. For example, if an industrial policy specifies minimization of unemployment as an objective, such can be meaningful only if a relevant constraint or set of constraints is established, such as on expenditure for training of labor, for subsidizing industry and others.

Thus, processes of interaction among both behaving units and regions in conflict need to be examined and procedures to manage conflicts become an essential area of study for regional scientists. It is to be observed that regional scientists have explored this area — among the works of other scholars see those of Paelinck (1997), Nijkamp (1979, 1984), T. Smith (1969), and C. Smith (1988). But little of this work has been incorporated in the central body of regional science.

In Channel IV the extension of the scope of regional science to cover conflict analysis and management is examined. This extension is particularly relevant for regional science since as a relatively new science it is much less bogged down by traditional and embedded forms of analysis than other social sciences such as economics, sociology, psychology, anthropology, geography and political science.

We present the comprehensive Channel IV in Figure 10.4. Ignore for the moment, the new ovals on the top of the figure relating to Values, Goals: System and Subsystem, and CMPs, conflict management procedures. The remaining boxes, matrices, circles, rectangles and ovals have all appeared in one of the previous channels. They relate to concepts and methods already discussed, and represent the bringing together of all these methods into one framework. Most of the interconnections of these methods have been dealt with, and ways in which these interconnections can be captured have been examined. One interconnection not already discussed relates to connections between urban complex analysis and interregional SAM (inclusive of Money Flows and Capital Stocks). But clearly the output

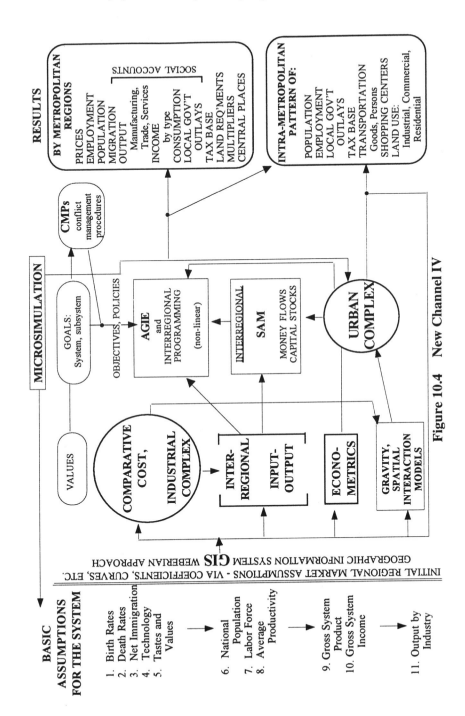

Figure 10.4   New Channel IV

of urban complex analysis (and also whatever microsimulation research is fused with it) are data pertaining to such variables as production of goods and services, factor inputs, wages, rents, profits, and so forth, all of which are aggregatable by production sector, companies, broad classes of consumption expenditures and other categories meaningful for a SAM matrix to be constructed and structural path analysis to be pursued. This is so even when within a given urban complex study only one urban area is investigated and needs to be consolidated with data on non-urban areas. And this is so even when the urban complex analysis is fused with interregional programming and other regional science methods noted in Channel III. Likewise, the interconnections between the gravity model and SAM are clear, for example in anticipating migration or new exports and imports as changes in the structure of SAM for SAA analysis. In turn, an interregional SAM framework can provide basic information for operation of gravity models and urban complex analysis.

Therefore, it is not necessary to discuss any further the fusion of the regional science methods already examined. What we now wish to do is to move on to investigate how Values, Goals: System and Subsystem, and Conflict Management Procedures (CMPs) can be introduced, when appropriate and/or necessary, into a regional science study.

First, note that in Channel IV of the 1960 Methods book the roles of Values and Goals: System and Subsystem were fully discussed. That channel was presented as a conceptual one only. Possible application of it was not considered. Here we wish to explore application. We wish to investigate how the use of CMPs can be fused into regional science studies — as represented by the arrow from the CMPs conflict management procedures oval to the objectives and policies that enter AGIE and interregional programming in Channel IV of this current book.

Since 1960 there has been considerable concern for, and notable progress in, the development of effective CMPs from experience and research on dispute resolution and negotiation processes and in the field of Peace Science. Such allows us to consider the embodiment within regional science of procedures to help resolve the many major conflicts over objectives among parties within a region or interregional system.

At this point it would be premature to specify particular CMPs that regional scientists might consider useful for any one or more given situations. This is so partly because the work on CMPs for use by regional scientists is still in a beginning and exploratory stage. However, it is possible to set down some basic information on needed concepts and fruitful guidelines for their use. A first basic consideration centers around how participants to a conflict can state their preferences concerning joint actions, policies or proposed solutions. Among other ways, three relevant ones that need to be considered are:

(a) participants can only rank their preferences for joint actions, policies or proposed solutions (they may have ordinal utility functions);

(b) participants can assign only relative values to these elements (they may have relative utility functions);

(c) participants can assign precise values to these elements (they may have cardinal utility functions).

A second basic element concerns the number of options that can be considered in a given situation, whether *small* or *many* (a continuous set). A third consideration is whether the participants are at a (0,0) point where their *improvement* is at stake, or an infeasible (1,1) point representing each participant's most preferred joint action, from which concessions need to be made. A fourth one to note is whether participants can be persuaded to concentrate on *actions* only (in demanding improvement or accepting concessions) or cannot be diverted from considering *outcomes*.[1]

Since regional scientists have just touched upon the use of conflict management procedures in resolving conflicts, there exists no systematic and comprehensive statement of available CMPs for regional science. One such statement, however, has been drawn up in the field of Peace Science (Isard and C. Smith, 1982, ch. 12 and Table 12.2) which may be of use for regional science. The list of CMPs in this statement is presented in Table 10-1 in compact form. Based on this statement twenty-four tables have been constructed, one for each combination of the four basic considerations noted above. To illustrate we present as Table 10-2 that table (with minor changes) which identifies some procedures for situations in which there exists a *small* number of options and where participants can focus on *outcomes* and can *rank* them in order of preference and where they need to focus on *improvements*. (Along the left-hand side of Table 10-2 is the number of each technique as listed in Isard and C. Smith, 1982, Table 12.2.)

Focus on one of these procedures, namely *method of determining group priorities* which was pioneered by and extensively developed by Saaty (1996), and designated by him as an *Analytic Hierarchy Process*. (Also, this procedure has been used to forecast the most likely choice among a set of options or outcomes.) We now wish to present the main features of this CMP to illustrate the kind of regional research that at times can be fruitfully conducted with the use of a CMP. In doing so we shall modify extensively Saaty's description of a possible transportation problem (Saaty, 1980, pp. 113–20) of a type often confronted in regional science. Saaty's

Table 10-1 A partial list of quantitative conflict management procedures*

1. Compromise over proposed actions (outcomes)
   — in one step *or* a sequence of steps

2. *Min. total of:* ranks (highest rank = 1), rank concessions, percentage concessions, percentage goal shortfalls, absolute concessions, *or* absolute goal shortfalls

3. *Max. total of:* rank improvements, percentage improvements, percentage goal achievements, absolute improvements, absolute goal achievements, *or* utility

4. *Min. the difference in:* ranks, rank improvements (concessions), percentage improvements (concessions), percentage goal achievements, absolute improvements (concessions) *or* absolute goal achievements

5. *Max. the min. in:* rank improvements, percentage improvements, *or* absolute improvements

6. *Min. the max. in:* rank concessions, percentage concessions, *or* absolute concessions

7. *Max. equal:* rank improvements, percentage improvements, absolute improvements, *or* goal achievements

8. *Min. equal:* rank concessions, percentage concessions, absolute concessions, *or* goal shortfalls

9. Changing actions to 'if ... then ... ' policies

10. Achievement of minimum requirements (satisficing)

11. Median efficient joint action

12. Concession along efficiency frontier

13. Split the difference in action space *or* outcome space
    — one step *or* a sequence of steps

14. Weighted average in action space *or* outcome space
    — one step *or* a sequence of steps

15. Alternating leader-follower
    — in action space *or* outcome space

16. Leadership principle
    — in action space *or* outcome space

17. Aggressive follower principle
    — in action space *or* outcome space

18. GRIT (reciprocated tension-reducing actions, a sequence of)
    — in action space *or* outcome space

19. Incremax (maximizing in each of a series of small improvement steps) in action space
    — with split the difference
    — with weighted average
    — with alternating leader-follower
    — with GRIT
    — with minimum information

Table 10-1 cont'd

20. Incremax in outcome space
— with split the difference
— with weighted average
— with alternating leader-follower
— with GRIT

21. Decremax (maximizing in each of a series of small concession steps) in action space
— with split the difference
— with weighted average
— with alternating leader-follower
— with GRIT

22. Decremax in outcome space
— with split the difference
— with weighted average
— with alternating leader-follower
— with GRIT

23. Equidistant movement in action space
— regarding improvement
— regarding concession

24. Last offer arbitration (with incentive to think of others)

25. Hierarchical programming (relaxed or not)

26. Zeuthen concession (least to lose goes first)

27. Method of determining group priorities (Saaty)

*Procedures 2–8 may or may not involve weights to be assigned to the relevant item of each participant.

Table 10-2 A *small* number of options, participants can *rank* outcomes in order of preference, need to focus on *improvements*, can focus on *outcomes*[a]

5. min. total of ranks (highest rank = 1) (weighted or unweighted)

6. min. difference in ranks (weighted or unweighted)

7. max. total of rank improvements (weighted or unweighted)

9. max. the min. in rank improvements

11. min. difference in rank improvement (weighted or unweighted)

12. max. equal rank improvement (weighted or unweighted)

15. changing actions to 'if ... then ... ' policies

16. max. good-cause payment

17. use of apportionment principles (criteria)

20. achievement of minimum requirements (satisficing)

41. last-offer arbitration (with incentive to think of others)

75. method of determining group priorities (Saaty)

[a]The numbers record the position of the CMP in the complete list of CMPs in Isard and Smith (1972), Table 12.2.

description of this problem involves three conflicting proposals regarding the crossing of a river, over which there is heated disagreement among political leaders or other interest groups. They are: build a bridge, construct a tunnel, and stay with the existing ferry operations. Suppose the governor of the state in which this river is located appoints a committee of three, each political or interest group being represented by one and only one committee member. Also, assume that one of the members is a regional scientist familiar with accepted methods designed to estimate impacts of developments. Each of the three is highly regarded and considered to be a fair and trustworthy individual. Recognizing that some factors to be considered can be quantified (such as employment and capital costs) and others cannot (such as disruption of the ecological system and lifestyles), the committee decides to employ a *priority determining procedure* (à la Saaty) to resolve the conflict. This procedure requires pairwise comparisons, that is statement of how much more important one factor is compared to another in a pair. The committee members are aware (at least the regional scientist could inform them) that many scales of importance can be employed.[2] They agree to use the scale that Saaty tends to favor, which is reproduced as Table 10-3).

Next, they recognize that there are three general classes of factors that are involved, namely economic, social and environmental. Also, since they have been asked by the Governor to examine both the specific benefits and specific costs of each proposal, they break down each of the above three classes into eleven specific benefits and nine specific costs. The eleven benefits as noted in Figure 10.5 are: *time* (time saved in using a new bridge or tunnel), *income* (toll revenue from outside the area), *commerce, across* (new commerce generated by the new traffic from outside the area), *commerce, near* (from increased sales of gas stations, restaurants, etc.), *construction jobs*, greater *safety and reliability*, more *communications* (more trips among families, to museums, etc.), increased *community pride*, greater *comfort*, increased *accessibility* of the natural environment, and improved *aesthetic* features.

The nine costs, as noted in Figure 10.6 are: *capital costs, operating and maintenance costs, disruption of ferry business, disruption of life styles, disruption of people* in their activities associated with traffic congestion, *dislocation of people, increased auto emissions, water pollution from bridge*, and *disruption of ecology*. The eleven benefits and nine costs perceived by Saaty to be relevant for a particular transportation problem will of course vary in number and relevance for other transportation problems of this general type.

Table 10-3 The Saaty Scale and its description

Intensity of importance	Definition	Explanation
1[a]	Equal importance	Two policies contribute equally to the objective
3	Weak importance of one over another	Experience and judgment slightly favor one activity over another
5	Essential or strong importance	Experience and judgment strongly favor one policy over another
7	Demonstrated importance	A policy is strongly favored and its dominance is demonstrated in practice
9	Absolute importance	The evidence favoring one policy over another is of the highest possible order of affirmation
2, 4, 6, 8	Intermediate values between the two adjacent judgments	When compromise is needed
Reciprocals of above nonzero numbers	If policy i has one of the above nonzero numbers assigned to it when compared with policy j, then j has the reciprocal value when compared with i	
Rationals	Ratios arising from the scale	If consistency were to be forced by obtaining n numerical values to span the matrix

[a]On occasion in 2 by 2 problems, Saaty has used $1 + \varepsilon$, $0 < \varepsilon < 1/2$ to indicate very slight dominance between two nearly equal activities.

Source: adapted from Saaty and Khouja (1976:34).

Start the pairwise comparisons with benefits. Each committee member makes pairwise comparisons of the relative importance of the three classes of benefits: economic, social and environmental. The comparisons on which they agree and which are consistent are recorded in Table 10-4 in which the benefit classes are listed in the same order by row and column. In going across the first row, the number in the second cell indicates that the three participants judge economic benefits to be three times as important as social benefits, and the number in the third cell indicates that

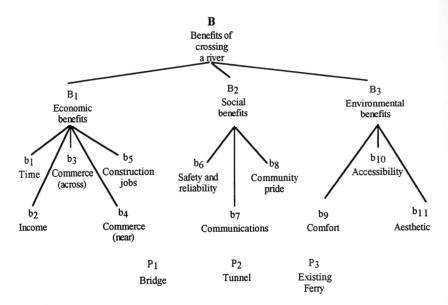

Figure 10.5 A hierarchy of benefits in a transportation problem

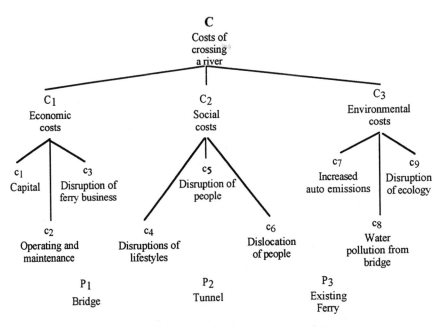

Figure 10.6 A hierarchy of costs in a transportation problem

Table 10-4 Pairwise comparisons of benefit classes

B (Benefits)	B_1: Econ. Benefits	B_2: Social Benefits	B_3: Env. Benefits	Weights
B_1: Econ. Benefits	1	3	6	0.67
B_2: Social Benefits	1/3	1	2	0.22
B_3: Env. Benefits	1/6	1/2	1	0.11

the members judge economic benefits to be six times as important as environmental benefits. Necessarily, the number in the first cell in the first row is one (unity) indicating that economic benefits are equally important as themselves.

Going along the second row the first cell indicates that the members judge social benefits to be one third as important as economic benefits, equally important to themselves, and twice as important as environmental benefits. Note that if the relative judgments are consistent, the numbers in the cells of the second and third rows are implied. For example, if economic benefits are three times as important as social benefits, then for consistency social benefits can only be one-third as important as economic benefits (as recorded in the first cell of the second row); and if economic benefits are also six times as important as environmental benefits, then social benefits must be 6/3 times or twice as important as the environmental benefits (as recorded in the third cell of the second row). In the discussion that follows we do not allow there to be any inconsistency in the committee's judgments since a regional scientist is one of the members and can point out inconsistency when it exists and help eliminate it.[3]

From the pairwise comparisons in the first three columns of Table 10-4 the weights of the three classes of benefits can be obtained through standard normalization of their relative importances.[4] These weights are listed in the last column of the table.

The next step is to calculate weights to be assigned to each of the specific benefits. First pairwise comparisons need to be made: (1) between each specific economic benefit and every other economic benefit to obtain their relative importance as economic benefits; (2) between each specific social benefit and every other specific social benefit to obtain their relative importance as social benefits; and (3) between each specific environmental benefit and every other specific environmental benefit to obtain their relative importance as environmental benefits. In Table 10-5 pairwise comparisons are recorded between the five specific economic benefits. The first row of that table, for example, states that the committee judges that b_1

(time saved) is equally important to itself, one-third as important as b_2 (income), one-seventh as important as b_3 (commerce across), one-fifth as important as b_4 (commerce near), and one-sixth as important as b_5 (construction jobs). From the pairwise comparisons in the first five columns of Table 10-5, the relative weights of the five specific economic benefits are derived via normalization and recorded in the last column of that table.

Table 10-5 Pairwise comparisons of specific economic benefits

B_1: Economic Benefits	b_1 Time	b_2 Income	b_3 Commerce (across)	b_4 Commerce (near)	b_5 Construction jobs	Weights
b_1: Time	1	1/3	1/7	1/5	1/6	0.05
b_2: Income	3	1	3/7	3/5	1/2	0.14
b_3: Commerce (across)	7	7/3	1	7/5	7/6	0.32
b_4: Commerce (near)	5	5/3	5/7	1	5/6	0.22
b_5: Construction jobs	6	2	6/7	6/5	1	0.27

Given these five relative weights, what do they signify? The answer is that these weights indicate how the total weight of the economic benefits as a class, namely 0.67, is to be allocated among the five specific economic benefits. Thus, the importance of specific economic benefit b_1 (time saved) in the total benefits picture is given by the product of the class weight 0.67 and b_1's relative weight 0.05, namely 0.67 x 0.05 = 0.0335. This figure, when rounded, is put in the first cell of column (4) of Table 10-6 and viewed as an *adjusted* weight. We also have put in column (1) of the table the relative weights of the three benefit classes from Table 10-4, and in column (3) the relative weights of the five specific economic benefits.

Likewise, the importance of the specific economic benefit b_2 (income) is the product of the class weight (0.67) and its relative importance (0.14), namely 0.094. This figure, as an adjusted weight, is entered into the second cell of column (4) of Table 10-6. In a similar manner, the importance of the remaining three specific economic benefits are derived and entered into column (4) of the same table as adjusted weights. The data on the pairwise comparisons made by the committee members are presented in Table 10A-1 in the appendix to this chapter.

Table 10-6 The calculation of total benefits for each proposal

(1)	Specific Economic benefits (2)	(3)	Adjusted Weight (4)	Bridge (5)	Tunnel (6)	Ferry (7)	Comparative Importance Bridge (8)	Tunnel (9)	Ferry (10)
Economic benefits 0.67	time	0.05	0.034	0.609	0.304	0.087	0.021	0.010	0.003
	income	0.14	0.094	0.320	0.640	0.040	0.030	0.060	0.004
	commerce (across)	0.32	0.214	0.727	0.182	0.091	0.156	0.039	0.019
	commerce (near)	0.22	0.147	0.462	0.462	0.076	0.068	0.068	0.011
Social benefits 0.22	constr. jobs	0.27	0.181	0.195	0.783	0.022	0.035	0.142	0.004
	safety	0.78	0.172	0.718	0.180	0.102	0.123	0.031	0.018
	communications	0.13	0.029	0.455	0.455	0.090	0.013	0.013	0.003
	commun. pride	0.09	0.019	0.652	0.131	0.217	0.012	0.003	0.004
Environmental benefits 0.11	comfort	0.19	0.021	0.755	0.151	0.094	0.016	0.003	0.002
	access	0.78	0.086	0.677	0.226	0.097	0.059	0.019	0.008
	aesthetic	0.03	0.003	0.162	0.027	0.811	~0	~0	0.003
Total			1.000				0.533	0.388	0.079

In the same way, a pairwise comparison table is constructed for the three specific social benefits, their relative weights determined (as recorded in column (3) of Table 10-6) and then multiplied by the weight of the social benefits class (namely 0.22) to derive their importance as adjusted weights, which are entered in column (4). Likewise, for deriving the importance (adjusted weights) of the three specific environmental benefits, recorded in column (4). The pairwise comparison data are in the appendix Table 10A-1.

Finally, the three proposals (Bridge, Tunnel, Ferry) are subject to pairwise comparisons to determine their possible contribution to the *realization of each* specific economic benefit. Thus, for realizing the first economic benefit b_1 (time saved), the relative weights of the three proposals, as calculated from the pairwise comparisons in the subtable b_1 of the appendix Table 10A-1 are 0.609, 0.304, and 0.087, respectively. Thus multiplying the importance (0.034) of the b_1 benefit-factor (time saved) by the weights 0.609, 0.304, and 0.087 yields 0.021, 0.010 and 0.003 which are recorded, respectively, in columns (5), (6) and (7) in Table 10-6. These last figures indicate respective benefits that the three proposals (bridge, tunnel and ferry) each yield via contributing to the realization of the specific time benefit, *which is just one of the eleven specific benefits to which these proposals contribute.* In the same manner, pairwise comparisons among the three proposals are made to obtain their relative weights in the realization of each one of the ten other specific benefits; and the three relative weights derived with regard to any one given specific benefit are multiplied by the importance of that benefit to derive the contribution via that specific benefit that each proposal makes to the total benefits that each proposal will realize. The products are recorded in the appropriate cells in columns (5), (6), and (7) of Table 10-6. Finally, the totals of the figures in each of the three columns (5), (6) and (7) can then be taken to represent the overall benefits (comparatively speaking) of the corresponding proposals. They are 0.533, 0.388 and 0.079 for the bridge, tunnel and ferry proposals, respectively.

In exactly the same manner via pairwise comparisons the relative importance (weights) of the three classes of costs (economic, social and environment) are derived and recorded in column (1) of Table 10-7. Then the relative weights of the three specific economic costs, the three specific social costs and the three specific environmental costs are each derived and recorded in column (3) of that table. Next, after multiplying their relative weights by the relative importance of their respective cost class, the importance of each of these nine cost factors are derived and recorded as adjusted weights in column (4) in Table 10-7. Finally, pairwise comparisons are made for each of the proposals (bridge, tunnel and ferry) to determine their relative weights in contributing to each of the nine specific cost factors, which then when multiplied by the importance of any one given cost factor result in the figures of columns (5), (6), and (7) of Table 10-7 in the row corresponding to that specific cost factor. Each of these figures represent a contribution to the total costs of one of the proposals via one specific cost factor. Lastly, summing the items in each of the columns (5), (6) and (7) yields the respective total cost of each of the three proposals.

From the totals in columns (5), (6), and (7) of Tables 10-6 and 10-7, Table 10-8, a benefit/cost table, can be constructed where for each proposal the total benefits, the total costs and the benefit/cost ratios are presented respectively in columns (2), (3), and (4). These figures suggest that staying with existing ferry operations, the proposal having the highest benefit/cost ratio, should be given the highest priority.

Table 10-7 The calculation of total costs for each proposal

(1)	Specific Economic costs (2)	(3)	Adjusted Weight (4)	Bridge (5)	Tunnel (6)	Ferry (7)	Comparative Importance Bridge (8)	Tunnel (9)	Ferry (10)
Economic costs 0.745	capital	0.797	0.594	0.243	0.727	0.030	0.144	0.432	0.018
	operating	0.114	0.085	0.243	0.727	0.030	0.021	0.062	0.002
	ferry disruption	0.089	0.066	0.474	0.474	0.052	0.031	0.031	0.004
Social costs 0.149	lifestyle disruption	0.111	0.016	0.735	0.184	0.081	0.012	0.003	0.001
	people disruption	0.333	0.050	0.474	0.474	0.052	0.024	0.024	0.002
	people dislocation	0.556	0.083	0.474	0.474	0.052	0.039	0.039	0.005
Environmental costs 0.106	increased auto emissions	0.632	0.067	0.686	0.228	0.086	0.046	0.015	0.006
	water pollution	0.210	0.022	0.677	0.226	0.097	0.015	0.005	0.002
	ecologic disruption	0.158	0.017	0.140	0.840	0.020	0.002	0.014	0.001
Total			1.000				0.334	0.625	0.041

Table 10-8 The proposals' benefit/cost ratios

	Total Benefits	Total Costs	Benefit/ Cost Ratio
Bridge	0.533	0.334	1.60
Tunnel	0.338	0.625	0.62
Ferry	0.079	0.041	1.93

This particular example is sufficient to point up the potentialities of the priority-determining (AHP) procedure for use in many conflict situations met by regional scientists (and clearly regional planners) in their applied research.[5] This hypothetical example can of course be extended to involve another level in the hierarchy, for example when the national, state and local governments are involved in financing bridge or tunnel construction and therefore have influence on the priority-determining process. Alternatively, feedback processes of various kinds can be introduced, as they are often in reality, and the use of the supermatrix approach of Saaty might be relevant. In one example Saaty uses a network approach to capture feedback in the task of predicting for college-educated individuals job growth in five regions of the United States: Northwest, Southwest, Midwest, Northeast and Southeast. Taking into account twenty-two specific attributes of relevance he develops six clusters of them: Quality of Life, Infrastructure, Housing, Education, Cost of Living, and Quality of Residents. In his study, the Southwest is predicted to have the highest percent job gowth (Saaty 1996, pp. 250–55). When the network approach is employed in combination with other regional science methods it has promise of being useful in conducting different kinds of sensitivity analyses.

In the preceding discussion we have illustrated how a conflict management procedure may be usefully applied to a conflict problem in which a regional scientist may be intensively involved. This involvement is legitimate, in view of his/her competence at impact analysis. Currently, such analysis requires the use of several interconnected models, and this will be increasingly so in the future as more advanced methods and fused frameworks are employed. Especially, in future analysis of envronmental problems where conflict is almost omnipresent and where regional science with its use of (1) comparative cost analysis (to make explicit environmental cost as a relatively new major location factor), (2) input-output (to embody output coefficients by type pollutant and abatement processes), (3) programming (to incorporate scale and nonlinear relations), (4) AGIE (to capture trade-offs among producing units with regard to emission allowances) and (5) microsimulation (in connection with both gravity models and urban complex analysis in identifying the mutual interrelations of the behavior of urban residents and pollution emission levels) — all these regional science methods to help attack comprehensively environmental conflicts make it almost incumbent on the regional scientist with competence in the use of these methods to embody CMPs in his/her tool kit.

10.5 Conclusion

In this chapter only some of the innumerable possibilities for fusing regional science methods have been discussed. We have presented at least eight distinct methods — comparative cost, input-output, econometrics, programming, gravity and spatial interaction, social accounting, AGIE, and microsimulation. Each could be a first method to start with and to which there can be added one or more other methods in any number of different ways. Moreover, some of these eight methods can be subdivided into major components — for example, programming may be split into linear and non-linear and into industrial complex, urban complex, and other complexes[6] — each component able to serve as a starting point to which one or more other methods or techniques can be added in different sequences. It is therefore up to the researcher to determine which way of combining techniques best suits his particular research task.

Moreover, if a regional scientist confronts a conflict problem in his/her research task and has chosen a CMP which he/she wishes to employ,[7] he/she still confronts the problem of selecting among the many combinations or sequences of methods or techniques to yield the kind of data he requires to implement that CMP.

It should be noted that the depiction by Figures 10.1–10.4 of channels of synthesis is just one way of viewing fusion, synthesis or integration of methods and models. Elsewhere the author has presented diagrams involving sets of interconnected modules, each based on a particular method. See Isard and Anselin (1982), Isard and C. Smith (1983) and Isard (1990). For example the interconnected modular structure with numerous feedbacks presented in Isard and C. Smith (1983) contains the following modules: (1) A National Econometric, (2) A Regional Econometric, (3) A Comparative Cost, Industrial Complex, Input-Output, Programming, (4) A Network, Commodity Flow, Transport Cost, (5) A Factor Demand and Investment Supply, (6) A Demographic (7) A Conflict Management–Multipolicy Formation, and (8) A Multiregional Policy Analysis. Potentially of great relevance and interest to regional scientists will be the inclusion in the above set of interconnected modules those involving both inputs and outputs of relevant environmental modules with rounds of feedbacks to and from other modules. See Isard (1990). The environmental modules will necessarily need to consider spatial processes explicitly.

Lastly, note that this book has given relatively little attention to intertemporal and dynamic analysis. This is so since the social sciences have relatively little to say about structural change. However, see the noteworthy attempt and insightful works of Harris (1988) in conceptualizing a spatial and dynamic operational multiregion model.[8] We can handle aging processes in the way that microsimulation does. We can examine impacts of new industry and other developments, but only on the assumption of no (or negligible) structural change and other assumptions typically underlying the use of a comparative statics approach. We can make reasonable projections about change in labor productivity, GRP and other variables based on historical trends and the like. With mathematics and historical perspective, we can imagine reasonable time paths and development stages of spatial structures [see, for example, Isard and Liossatos, 1979, chaps. 7–9 (written with Y. Kanemoto) on the application of a continuous frame to location and land-use problems]. We can use 'dynamical systems' analysis specifying time rates of change of variables based on pure theory or physical models (see, for example, Isard and Liossatos, 1979, chaps. 4–6). However, as Mercenier and Srinivasan (1994) conclude, after summarily evaluating in their introduction the many shortcoming of efforts and difficulties in capturing intertemporal effects in AGE models, 'there is plenty of work ahead' p. 17. So too, and even more, with the AGIE models that will evolve, where regional scientists will want to and should exploit equilibrium analysis intertemporally and/or dynamically. But also, of equal moment should be their want and attempts to exploit other regional science methods intertemporally or dynamically.

Appendix: Tables of pairwise comparison and relative weights

In the set of minitables presented in Table 10A-1, the first column of numbers in each refers to the relevant pairwise comparisons. Since we assume consistent judgments, only the first column of numbers needs to be specified to determine the relative weights of the specific items, which weights are recorded in the last column. In the set presented, the first one derives weights for the three specific social benefits, the second for each of the three specific environmental benefits; and the next eleven derive the relative weights of the three proposals for realization of each of the eleven specific benefits, the specific benefit being recorded in the upper left cell.

The next thirteen minitables refer to costs. The first derives relative weights of the three classes of costs, the second of the three specific economic costs, the third of the three specific social costs, and the fourth of the three specific environmental costs. The next nine derive the relative weights of the three proposals for realization of each of the nine specific costs, the specific cost being recorded in the upper left cell.

Table 10A-1 Pairwise comparisons and relative weights tables

B_2	b_6 ... wgts.	B_3	b_9 ... wgts.	b_1	P_1 ... wgts.	b_2	P_2 ... wgts.
b_6	1 ...0.78	b_9	1 ...0.19	P_1	1 ...0.609	P_1	1 ...0.32
b_7	1/6...0.13	b_{10}	4 ...0.78	P_2	1/2...0.304	P_2	1/2...0.64
b_8	1/7...0.09	b_{11}	1/6...0.03	P_3	1/7...0.087	P_3	1/8...0.04

b_3	P_1 ... wgts.	b_4	P_1 ... wgts.	b_5	P_1 ... wgts.	b_6	P_1 ... wgts.
P_1	1 ...0.727	P_1	1 ...0.462	P_1	1 ...0.195	P_1	1 ...0.718
P_2	1/4...0.182	P_2	1 ...0.462	P_2	4 ...0.783	P_2	1/4...0.180
P_3	1/8...0.091	P_3	1/6...0.076	P_3	1/9...0.022	P_3	1/7...0.102

b_7	P_1 ... wgts.	b_8	P_1 ... wgts.	b_9	P_1 ... wgts.	b_{10}	P_1 ... wgts.
P_1	1 ...0.455	P_1	1 ...0.652	P_1	1 ...0.755	P_1	1 ...0.677
P_2	1 ...0.455	P_2	1/5...0.131	P_2	1/5...0.151	P_2	1/3...0.226
P_3	1/5...0.090	P_3	1/3...0.217	P_3	1/8...0.094	P_3	1/7...0.097

b_{11}	P_1 ... wgts.	C	C_1 ... wgts.	C_1	C_1 ... wgts
P_1	1 ...0.162	C_1	1 ...0.745	c_1	1 ...0.797
P_2	1/6...0.027	C_2	1/5...0.149	c_2	1/7...0.114
P_3	5 ...0.811	C_3	1/7...0.106	c_3	1/9...0.089

C_2	c_1 ... wgts.	C_3	c_1 ... wgts.	c_1	P_1 ... wgts.	c_2	P_1 ... wgts.
c_1	1 ...0.111	c_1	1 ...0.632	P_1	1 ...0.243	P_1	1 ...0.243
c_2	3 ...0.333	c_2	1/3...0.210	P_2	3 ...0.727	P_2	3 ...0.727
c_3	5 ...0.556	c_3	1/4...0.158	P_3	1/8...0.030	P_3	1/8...0.030

c_3	P_1 ... wgts.	c_4	P_1 ... wgts.	c_5	P_1 ... wgts.	c_6	P_1 ... wgts.
P_1	1 ...0.474	P_1	1 ...0.735	P_1	1 ...0.474	P_1	1 ...0.474
P_2	1 ...0.474	P_2	1/4...0.184	P_2	1 ...0.474	P_2	1 ...0.474
P_3	1/9...0.052	P_3	1/9...0.081	P_3	1/9...0.052	P_3	1/9...0.052

c_7	P_1 ... wgts.	c_8	P_1 ... wgts.	c_9	P_1 ... wgts.
P_1	1 ...0.686	P_1	1 ...0.677	P_1	1 ...0.140
P_2	1/3...0.228	P_2	1/3...0.226	P_2	6 ...0.840
P_3	1/8...0.086	P_3	1/7...0.097	P_3	1/7...0.020

Endnotes

1   Still other considerations in identifying whether a CMP may be
    relevant for use in a conflict situation are: does it have a predetermined
    outcome? does it require of a participant little or no information about
    other participants' preferences? does it incur high cost? does it require
    side payments? is it efficient? if not, does it require constraints to be
    efficient? does it guarantee improvement over each step if many are
    required? if not, does it require constraints to do so? can it be
    constrained to involve limited commitment? does it have a unique
    solution? is it trust building? does it eliminate bluffing? does it give
    one or more participants a veto power? and so forth.

2   In this approach the choice of a scale should be one that fits the
    perspectives and knowledge base of the individuals who will be making
    the pairwise comparisons.

3   There are procedures to eliminate inconsistencies in situations where
    inconsistencies do exist and members of a committee do not wish to be
    bothered by the problem of achieving 100% consistency in a situation
    where so much subjectivity is present. One approximate method is to
    (1) sum the values in each column of pairwise comparisons, (2) divide
    the number in each cell by the total of this column, (3) sum the
    resulting numbers in the cells of each row, and (4) divide the row total
    by the number of columns of pairwise comparisons. Using this
    procedure, the relative weights in the weights column of a table such as
    Table 10-4 are obtained.

    Technically speaking the relative weights in the weights column
    should be derived as an eigenvector. Also an index of inconsistency can
    be constructed. See Saaty (1996) and Saaty and Vargas (1991) for
    discussion of inconsistency, its elimination and index.

4   One can easily normalize the relative values, when consistency exists,
    by taking the sum of the numbers in any column and dividing the
    number in each cell by the total.

5   As is indicated by these possibilities for further development, we have
    not covered all the potentialities of AHP. In stating its general
    advantages, all of which have not been exploited in our example, Saaty
    states: (1) it can serve as a model for a wide range of unstructured
    problems; (2) it can enable people to refine their definition of a

problem and to improve their judgment and understanding through repetition; (3) it does not insist on consensus but synthesizes a representative outcome from diverse judgments; (4) it takes into consideration the relative priorities of factors in a system and enables people to select the best alternative based on their goals; (5) it leads to an overall estimate of the desirability of each alternative; (6) it tracks the logical consistency of judgments used in determining priorities; (7) it integrates deductive and systems approaches in solving complex problems; (8) it can deal with the interdependence of elements in a system and does not insist on linear thinking; (9) it reflects the natural tendency of the mind to sort elements of a system into different levels and to group like elements in each level; and (10) it provides a scale for measuring intangibles and a method for establishing priorities.

6   Target programming, whether linear or nonlinear, may be considered to be another major type of programming. Here over a number of years (or other time periods) a development path is envisaged where at the terminal year (the target year) targets are to be reached — where targets are specified in both the objective function and binding constraints. See Isard et al. (1960), pp. 715-18, and Isard, Smith et al. (1969), pp. 989-90. Here, of course, CMPs may be useful in resolving conflict not only among the initial targets (and their weights) that may be set, but also among changes in targets when the initial set of targets either cannot be reached or are exceeded. Target programming can be fused with other regional science methods just as nonlinear programming, in general, can be.

7   Note that the choice of a CMP may also involve the choice of an agenda, the choice of weights and other parameters to be employed, the choice of constraints and binding magnitudes, the choice of a fairness or optimizing principle and the choice of a stabilizing principle in addition to the determination of the participants' preference structures. For example, see the *Conflict Management — Multipolicy Formation* module in Isard and C. Smith, 1983, p. 8.

8   This model is based on his general spatial equilibrium theory designed along the lines of Arrow and Debreu (1954) and Debreu (1959). It is aimed at *long-term* forecasting and analysis. It is indeed a comprehensive one and provides many useful ways of coping with difficulties arising from the dearth of regional data, but also it is subject to inability to predict technological change and change in

consumer tastes, to handle expectations, to treat government except in a highly restricted fashion, and to confront diverse methodological and other problems. Nonetheless, it is a significant step in the right direction.

References

Bröcker, J. 1995. 'Chamberlinian Spatial Computable General Equilibrium Modelling: A Theoretical Framework,' *Economic Systems Research*, 7, 137–149.

Harris, C. C. 1988. 'From General Spatial Equilibrium to Multiregional Operational Models' in *London Papers in Regional Science*, 19, 153–77.

Hewings, G. J. D., M. Sonis, Lee, and Jahan. 1995. 'Alternative Decomposition of Interregional Social Accounting,' in M. Madden and G. J. D. Hewings, *Social and Demographic Accounting.* New York: Cambridge University Press.

Isard, W. 1990. 'Progress in Global Modeling for World Policy on Arms Control and Environmental Management,' *Conflict Management and Peace Science*, 11, 57–94.

Isard, W. et al. 1960. *Methods of Regional Analysis.* Cambridge, MA: M.I.T. Press.

Isard, W. et al. 1969. *General Theory, Social, Political, Economic and Regional.* Cambridge, MA: M.I.T. Press.

Isard, W., and L. Anselin. 1982. 'Integration of Multiregional Models for Policy Analysis,' *Environment and Planning A*, 14, 359–76.

Isard W., and C. Smith. 1983. 'Linked Integrated Multiregional Models at the International Level,' *Papers of the Regional Science Association*, 51, 3–19.

Lowry, Ira. S. 1966. *Migration and Metropolitan Growth: Two Analytical Models.* San Francisco: Chandler.

Mercenier, J., and T. N. Srinivasan (eds.). 1994. *Applied General Equilibrium and Economic Development.* Ann Arbor: University of Michigan Press.

Nijkamp, P. 1979. *Multidimensional Spatial Data and Decision Analysis.* London: Wiley.

Nijkamp, P. 1984. 'A Multidimensional Analysis of Regional Infrastructure and Economic Development,' in A. E. Andersson, W. Isard, and T. Puu (eds.) *Regional and Industrial Development Theories, Models and Empirical Evidence.* Amsterdam, North Holland, 267–93.

Paelinck, H. P. 1997. *Hypergraph Conflict Resolution Revisited*, mimeographed.

Saaty, T. 1982. *Decision Making for Leaders*. London: Wadsworth.

Saaty, T. L. 1996. *The Analytic Network Process*. Pittsburgh: RWS Publications.

Saaty, T., and J. M. Alexander. 1989. *Conflict Resolution: The Analytic Hierarchy Approach*. New York: Praeger Publishers.

Saaty, Thomas L., and L. G. Vargas. 1991. *Prediction, Projection, and Forecasting*. Boston: Kluwer Academic Publishers.

Smith, C. 1988. *Integration of Multiregional Models for Policy Analysis: An Australian Perspective*. Amsterdam: North Holland.

Smith, T., with W. Isard et al. 1979. *General Theory: Social, Political, Economic and Regional*. Cambridge, MA: M.I.T. Press, chapters 5–9.

Index

Methods of Interregional and Regional Analysis

companies, in SAM taxonomy 296
comparative cost analysis 8, 35, 203, 238
    fusion with regional science methods
        422–25
    GIS potentialities for 31
    and industry location principles 8–21
    input-output fusion with 95–97
    nonlinear programming fused with
        225, 226, 235
competition, among traders 346
'complex analysis' study, and nonlinear
    programming 225
composite goods 383
computable general equilibrium models,
    SAM as foundation of 316
computer manufacturing 43
computer revolution 3
    and applied general equilibrium
        analysis 386
    effect on linear programming 220
    and microsimulation 406, 413
    and nonlinear programming 236, 238
concave net revenue curve 233
concave objective functions 221
conceptual framework, SAM used as
    282, 283–93
confirmation, and GIS 31
conflict management procedures 440–56
    basic elements in 444–45
    in Peace Science 444
    in transport conflict problems 445–55
    tables of 446–47
    use for regional conflict problems
        442, 456
    use with regional science methods
        442, 456
connected regional input-output model 71
consistency, and social accounting
    matrices (SAMs) 282, 298
consistent estimators 146–47
constant cost function 378
constant elasticity of substitution function
    (CES) 375, 376
constant elasticity of transformation
    function (CET) 378
constant production coefficients 212,
    213, 231, 237
constrained models 275n
constrained multipliers 283, 306–8, 316

constraints 233
    and microsimulation 401, 405
    multiple types of 221–25
construction industry 42
consumer price index 138
consumption 333
    equations 393n, 394n
    expenditures 358
    functions 374, 375
    magnitudes 375
    patterns 238, 292
    and prices 334
    subsystem of AGIE model 337, 373–
        75
convergence hypothesis 163
convex hull 239n
convex objective functions 220
Conway, Richard S. 201, 202, 203
cooperative (COP) variable 268
COPDAB (Conflict and Peace Data Bank)
    data 265
corners 220, 233
correlated error terms 173–80
CORSIM model, wealth module within
    407–10
cost sensitivity parameter 256
costs
    increases and deterrence functions
        255
    and industrial complex 225–26
    and industry location 8–21
    minimization of 35
covariance model 189, 276n
credibility, of econometric analysis 200–
    201
cross-section error component 189
cross-section models 136, 137, 187–91
cross-sectional data, for Turkey and its
    OECD partners 266
crossing a river problem, see transport
    conflict problem
currency devaluation 323

dacron 227, 233
Dacron A production, in Puerto Rico
    233, 234, 235
D'Antonio, M. 325
data gathering, in commodity-by-industry
    form 98